CONSISTENCY OF TRANSLATION
TECHNIQUES IN THE TABERNACLE
ACCOUNTS OF EXODUS
IN THE OLD GREEK

SOCIETY OF BIBLICAL LITERATURE
SEPTUAGINT AND COGNATE STUDIES SERIES

Series Editor
Melvin K. H. Peters

Editorial Advisory Committee
N. Fernández Marcos, Madrid
I. Soisalon-Soininen, Helsinki
E. Tov, Jerusalem

Number 49

Consistency of Translation
Techniques in the Tabernacle
Accounts of Exodus
in the Old Greek
by
Martha Lynn Wade

Consistency of Translation Techniques in the Tabernacle Accounts of Exodus in the Old Greek

Martha Lynn Wade

Society of Biblical Literature
Atlanta

CONSISTENCY OF TRANSLATION TECHNIQUES IN THE TABERNACLE
ACCOUNTS OF EXODUS IN THE OLD GREEK
Copyright © 2003
Society of Biblical Literature

No part of this work may be reproduced or transmitted in any form or by any means, electronic or mechanical, including photocopying and recording, or by means of any information storage or retrieval system, except as may be expressly permitted by the 1976 Copyright Act or in writing from the publisher. Requests for permission should be addressed in writing to the Rights and Permissions Office, Society of Biblical Literature, 825 Houston Mill Road, Atlanta, GA 30329 USA.

Library of Congress Cataloging-in-publication Data

Wade, Martha Lynn.
    Consistency of translation techniques in the tabernacle accounts of Exodus in the Old Greek / by Martha Lynn Wade.
        p. cm. — (Society of Biblical Literature septuagint and cognate studies ; no. 49)
    Includes bibliographical references and index.
    ISBN 1-58983-039-3 (pbk. : alk. paper)
    1. Bible. O.T. Exodus. Greek—Versions—Septuagint. 2. Bible. O.T. Exodus—Translating. 3. Tabernacle. I. Title. II. Septuagint and cognate studies series ; no. 49.
    BS1244.G7 W33 2002
    222'.12048—dc21

                                          2002011761

11 10 09 08 07 06 05 04 03 5 4 3 2 1

Contents

ACKNOWLEDGMENTS	xi
ABBREVIATIONS	xiii

CHAPTER ONE
INTRODUCTION 1
   I. Identifying the Problem 2
   II. Past Solutions to the Problem 4
   III. Methodology and Contribution 10
   IV. Contents 11

CHAPTER TWO
HEBREW *VORLAGE* 14
   I. Variants "Irrelevant" to the Old Greek Translation 15
      Grammatical Markers 16
         Changes in Grammatical Gender 16
         Other Nominal and Adjectival Changes 18
         Changes of Aspect and Stem 18
         Locative he 19
         Object Marker 20
      Waw Conjunction 21
      Article 23
      Summary 24
   II. Variants That Could Affect the Old Greek Translation .. 25
      Changes in Morphological Forms 25
         Pronominal Suffixes 25
         Verbs 27
      Changes in Order 29
         Word Order 30
         Verse Order 31
      Synonymous Variants 34
         Prepositions 34

Nouns, Adjectives, and Participles	35
Verbs	36
Phrases	37
Minuses	39
Pronominal Suffixes	39
Prepositions	40
Nouns, Adjectives, and Participles	41
Phrases	42
Pluses	42
Prepositions and Prepositional Phrases	43
Nouns, Pronouns, and Adjectives	44
Verbs	44
Clauses	45
Summary	46
III. Other Observations about the Tabernacle Accounts	47
Patterns of Adjustment in the 𝔐	49
Adjustments of First Account to Second	49
Adjustments to Both Accounts	49
Adjustments of Second Account to First	49
Orthography	51
Summary	54
IV. Conclusion	54

Chapter Three
LEXICAL CONSISTENCY

	56
I. Defining and Measuring Lexical Consistency	57
Survey of Past Methodologies	58
Methodology Used in This Study	62
Factors That Affect Lexical Consistency	62
Comparing the Degree of Lexical Consistency	67
II. Lexical Consistency within the Tabernacle Accounts	68
Comparison of Lexical Consistency in Four Sections of Exodus	69
Comparison of Lexical Consistency in Three Sets of Texts	71
Factors Affecting Choice of Lexical Equivalents	74
Identical Lexical Equivalents	74
Partially Shared Lexical Equivalents	76
Contrastive Lexical Equivalents	85
III. Lexical Equivalents That Affect Decisions about the Number of Translators	88
Technical Terminology	89
Poles	89
Curtains	90

Pillars and Related Items	92
Compass Points	98
IV. Other Observations Gained from Studying Lexical Equivalents	100
Clarifying Ambiguities	101
Identifying Interpretations of the Translators	103
V. Conclusions	105

CHAPTER FOUR
GRAMMATICAL CONSISTENCY 107
   I. Defining and Measuring Grammatical Consistency 107
      Survey of Past Methodologies 108
      Methodology Used in This Study 114
  II. Grammatical Consistency within the Tabernacle Accounts 114
      Preposition בְּ 114
      Simple Construct Chains 125
      Relative Clauses with אֲשֶׁר 131
      Summary 141
 III. Other Observations Gained from Studying
     the Translation of Grammatical Structures 142
      Clarifying or Reinterpreting Ambiguous Structures 142
      Grammatically Influenced Choices 144
      Summary 146
 IV. Conclusions 146

CHAPTER FIVE
ACCURACY 149
   I. Defining and Measuring Accuracy 150
      Survey of Past Methodologies 150
      Methodology Used in This Study 153
      Summary 158
  II. Accuracy in the Tabernacle Accounts 158
      Pluses 159
         That Reflect a Vorlage Similar to the 𝔐 159
         That Reflect a Difference in the Status of Meaning 163
         That Reflect a Difference in the Quantity of Meaning 167
      Minuses 176
         That Reflect a Vorlage Similar to the 𝔐 178
         That Reflect a Difference in the Status of Meaning 179
         That Reflect a Difference in the Quantity of Meaning 183
      Synonymous Variants 189
         That Reflect a Vorlage Similar to the 𝔐 190
         That Reflect a Difference in the Status of Meaning 194

That Reflect a Difference in the Meaning		197
Differences in Order		204
That Reflect a Vorlage Similar to the 𝔐		204
That Reflect a Difference in the Status of Meaning		205
That Reflect a Difference in the Meaning		207
Summary		212
III. Evaluating the Tabernacle Accounts in Light of Accuracy		212
Comparison of the Two Accounts		213
Sections That Are More Ambiguous in First Account		215
Construction of the Breastpiece		215
Construction of the Lampstand		217
Structurally Significant Pluses		222
𝔊 38:18-21		222
𝔊 39:11-12a		225
Summary		226
IV. Unanswerable Questions about Translation Techniques		227
Two Approaches to Translation in Antiquity		227
Faithfulness and Reordering		228
V. Conclusions		230

CHAPTER SIX
CONCLUSION   233
 I. Summary of Four Main Chapters   233
 II. Comparison with Previous Hypotheses   236
    Unity of the Core and Remainder of Second Account   236
    Unity of the First and Second Tabernacle Accounts   238
    Nature of the Translation   240
 III. One View of the Production of the Tabernacle Accounts   243

APPENDIX A
CLASSIFICATION OF MINUSES IN THE SECOND ACCOUNT   246

APPENDIX B
COMPARISON OF SOME PARALLEL PASSAGES   247

APPENDIX C
CONSTRUCTION AND ASSEMBLY OF THE BREASTPIECE   250

BIBLIOGRAPHY   251

INDEXES   261

Tables

Table 1.	"Reordering" of items in the 𝔐	33
Table 2.	Adjustments of first account to second	48
Table 3.	Adjustments to both accounts	50
Table 4.	Adjustments of second account to first	51
Table 5.	Lexical equivalents of nouns in four sections of Exodus	70
Table 6.	Lexical equivalents of verbs in four sections of Exodus	71
Table 7.	Identical, partially shared, and contrastive lexical equivalents of nouns	72
Table 8.	Identical, partially shared, and contrastive lexical equivalents of verbs	73
Table 9.	Translation of בְּ by ἐν	115
Table 10.	Translation equivalents of בְּ	117
Table 11.	Translation equivalents of simple construct chains	126
Table 12.	Translation equivalents of אֲשֶׁר in four sections of Exodus	132
Table 13.	Translation equivalents of כַּאֲשֶׁר in four sections of Exodus	133
Table 14.	Categories of meaning	156
Table 15.	Types of meaning in the pluses of 𝔊 Exodus	160
Table 16.	Types of meaning in the minuses of 𝔊 Exodus	177
Table 17.	Types of meaning in the synonymous variants of 𝔊 Exodus	191
Table 18.	Types of meaning in the differences in order of 𝔊 Exodus	205

Acknowledgments

The research for this book began when Dr. S. Dean McBride, Jr. suggested that the tabernacle accounts of Exodus in the Old Greek (25-31; 35-40) might be a productive area of study for my doctoral dissertation at Union-PSCE. His suggestion and introduction to some of the key literature in the study of this passage sparked an interest that continues to spur me on both in my study of Exodus and in my study of the translation techniques of the Old Greek. In addition to introducing me to the academic study of the Old Greek Scriptures, he also encouraged me to draw upon my training as a linguist and missionary Bible translator during the process of examining the Old Greek translation. This linguistic perspective influenced my choice of which aspects of the translation to examine, the methodology used in the study, and my evaluation of translation decisions. Throughout the study of the text, it was fascinating to realize that modern Bible translators in Papua New Guinea are still using many of the same translation techniques used by translators who lived over 2,000 years ago.

No book of this nature is produced without the support of a wide range of people who encouraged, offered comments on the manuscript, and provided financial support during the research. Southwest Christian Church and Pioneer Bible Translators have generously supported me and allowed me to complete this project while continuing my main task of Bible translation. In addition to the assistance of Dr. S. Dean McBride, I would like to acknowledge and thank Dr. William Brown and John W. Wade for their assistance in spotting errors of various types in early versions of the manuscript. Finally, I would like to thank Dr. Melvin K. H. Peters for his encouragement and patience in working with me to bring this book through the final stages of the publication process. His positive comments helped me to persevere when it seemed that there was no end in sight in the editing process. His patience in trying to communicate with an author who was often secluded in a small village in the jungles of Papua New Guinea taught me much about the characteristics of a good editor. In a work of this nature typographic errors are almost inevitable despite careful editing. All such errors are, of course, my responsibility, but it is my hope that none are serious enough to distract from the main purpose of the study. Throughout this book, all Biblical references refer to Exodus unless otherwise indicated.

This book is dedicated to my parents, John and Barbara Wade, who raised me in a strong Christian home and instilled in me a desire to serve God. Because of their encouragement and their willingness to entrust me to God's protection, I was able to become a Bible translator among a small people group in Papua New Guinea, who speak the Apal language. The Apal-speaking people accepted me into their lives and taught me to look at languages, the world, and God from a new perspective. That perspective, which is reflected in small ways throughout this book, is a culmination of the past twenty years of my life as a sojourner whose true home is heaven.

Abbreviations

𝕲	Old Greek (Within the tabernacle accounts, this symbol refers to the Göttingen edition of Exodus. Elsewhere it is used to refer to various electronic versions of Rahlfs' diplomatic edition. In quoted material, LXX and OG are frequently used to refer to various versions of the Old Greek translation.)
𝔐	Masoretic Text (In quoted material, MT and *BHS* are often used to refer to the Masoretic Text as seen in *Biblia Hebraica Stuttgartensia*.)
𝕼	Qumran
𝔚	Samaritan Pentateuch (In quoted material, SP is often used to refer to the Samaritan Pentateuch.)
Ant.	*Jewish Antiquities*
CEV	Contemporary English Version
DJD	Discoveries in the Judaean Desert
Gooding	Gooding, David W. *The Account of the Tabernacle: Translation and Textual Problems of the Greek Exodus.*
HOTTP	Hebrew Old Testament Text Project
Nelson	Nelson, Russell David. *Studies in the Development of the Text of the Tabernacle Account.*
NIV	New International Version
NJPS	*Tanakh: The Holy Scriptures: The New JPS Translation according to the Traditional Hebrew Text*
NRSV	New Revised Standard Version
P.Cair.Zen.	Zenon Papyri
RSV	Revised Standard Version
TEV	Today's English Version
Tok Pisin	*Buk Baibel (The Bible in Tok Pisin)*
WeversNotes	Wevers, John William. *Notes on the Greek Text of Exodus.*
WeversText	Wevers, John William. *Text History of the Greek Exodus.*

CHAPTER ONE

Introduction

The purpose of this study is to examine the translation techniques in the tabernacle accounts of Old Greek (𝔊) Exodus as a basis for evaluating the contradictory claims about the number of translators that produced these sections.[1] Specifically, the translation will be examined with respect to choice of lexical equivalents, translation of grammatical structures, and accuracy in communicating equivalent information. Before evaluating the translation techniques, however, textual variants in the Qumran scrolls (𝒬), the Samaritan Pentateuch (𝔐), and the Masoretic Text (𝔐) will be examined in order to identify Hebrew textual variants that might be a possible source of translation differences.[2]

Evidence from this multifaceted study of the tabernacle accounts of 𝔊 Exodus indicates that a second translator likely produced the second tabernacle account (35-40) of 𝔊 Exodus using the translation of the first tabernacle account

---

1. The critical text, John William Wevers, ed., *Exodus*, Septuaginta. Vetus Testamentum Graecum Auctoritate Academiae Scientiarum Gottingensis editum, vol. 2 (Göttingen: Vandenhoeck & Ruprecht, 1991), has been used for the sections of 𝔊 Exodus that are the focus of this study. Other references to the 𝔊, however, are based on various electronic versions of Alfred Rahlfs, ed., *Septuaginta* (Stuttgart: Deutsche Bibelgesellschaft, 1935).

2. For the tabernacle accounts, the main 𝒬 manuscripts are 4QpaleoGen-Exod^l, 4QpaleoExod^m, and 4QExod-Lev^f. In addition, a few small fragments are found in 4QExod^k, 2QExod^a, and 2QExod^b. References to these manuscripts are from DJD editions unless otherwise noted. See M. Baillet, J. T. Milik, and R. de Vaux, *Les 'Petites Grottes' de Qumrân: Exploration de la falaise, Les grottes 2Q, 3Q, 5Q, 6Q, 7Q à 10Q, Le rouleau de cuivre*, vol. 3, pt. 1, Discoveries in the Judaean Desert of Jordan (Oxford: Clarendon Press, 1962); Patrick W. Skehan and others, *Qumran Cave 4.IV Palaeo-Hebrew and Greek Biblical Manuscripts*, vol. 9, Discoveries in the Judaean Desert (Oxford: Clarendon Press, 1992); and Eugene Ulrich and others, *Qumran Cave 4.VII: Genesis to Numbers*, vol. 12, Discoveries in the Judaean Desert (Oxford: Clarendon Press, 1994).

The primary source for the 𝔐 used in this analysis was the database found in *Accordance* Ver. 3.0 (Altamonte Springs, Fla.: OakTree Software Specialists, Altamonte Springs, Fla.). This electronic version of the 𝔐 is based on the text published in Abraham Tal, *The Samaritan Pentateuch: Edited According to MS 6 (C) of the Shekhem Synagogue* (Tel Aviv: Tel Aviv University, 1994). At every point the computer version of the 𝔐 has been compared with the standard edition of the 𝔐 in August Freiherrn von Gall, *Der hebräische Pentateuch der Samaritaner* (Berlin: Alfred Töpelmann Verlag, 1966). Differences were noted and decisions were made based on the critical notes provided by von Gall.

The Masoretic Text used is that found in K. Elliger and W. Rudolph, eds., *Biblia Hebraica Stuttgartensia* (Stuttgart: Deutsche Bibelgesellschaft, 1977) = *BHS*.

(25-31) as a point of reference.³ This thesis is supported by the differences in patterns of choices of lexical equivalents between the two tabernacle sections. The translation of grammatical structures, in contrast, indicates that the same context-sensitive approach was used throughout both tabernacle accounts with only minor differences in interpretation seen between the two tabernacle accounts. While the second account is often described as being less accurate because of its abbreviated nature, a comparison of the translation of several parallel sections shows that the first tabernacle account tends to be more ambiguous than the second tabernacle account.⁴ This difference in accuracy provides further support for the hypothesis that a different translator produced the second tabernacle account. Thus, while both tabernacle accounts use a similar approach to the translation of grammatical structures, the evidence from the choice of lexical equivalents and the accuracy of the translation points to the probable involvement of a second translator.

In this chapter I will first identify the nature of the text critical problem in the tabernacle accounts of 𝔊 Exodus. Next, I will summarize past scholarly solutions to this problem. In the third section I will describe the methodology and contributions of this study. Finally, I will give a preview of the contents of this book.

I. Identifying the Problem

The 𝔊 translation of Exodus is generally considered to be an accurate, relatively free translation in good Koine Greek. The tabernacle accounts, however, are always included in lists of difficult text critical problems in the Pentateuch.⁵ In brief, the first tabernacle account (25-31) is considered to be a fairly accurate translation consistent with the style of the first part of Exodus. The second tabernacle account (35-40), which uses almost identical terminology in Hebrew, is so aberrant in the 𝔊 that even Origen, in the early third century A.D., commented on

---

3. Throughout this book, all Biblical references refer to Exodus unless otherwise indicated.

4. Ambiguity, as used in this book, refers to the unintentional lack of clarity that is present to some extent in all texts, both translated and natural. This type of ambiguity is generally clarified for the reader by the context. When the author/translator and reader do not share the same cultural knowledge and implicit information, however, the text will often remain ambiguous to the reader.

5. See Emanuel Tov, *The Text-Critical Use of the Septuagint in Biblical Research: Second Edition, Revised and Enlarged* (Jerusalem: Simor, 1997), 256 and Marguerite Harl, Gilles Dorival, and Olivier Munnich, *La Bible grecque des Septante: Du judaïsme hellénistique au christianisme ancien*, Initiations au christianisme ancien (Paris: Cerf, 1988), 173-74. Aejmelaeus refers to this as "One of the greatest textual problems in the Greek Pentateuch." See Anneli Aejmelaeus, "Septuagintal Translation Techniques—A Solution to the Problem of the Tabernacle Account," in *Septuagint, Scrolls and Cognate Writings: Papers Presented to the International Symposium on the Septuagint and Its Relations to the Dead Sea Scrolls and Other Writings, Manchester, 1990*, ed. George J. Brooke and Barnabas Lindars, Septuagint and Cognate Studies, no. 33 (Atlanta, Ga.: Scholars Press, 1992), 382.

the differences as follows: "What needs there speak of Exodus, where there is such diversity in what is said about the tabernacle and its court, and the ark, and the garments of the high priest and the priests, that sometimes the meaning even does not seem to be akin?"[6]

The major differences regularly noted in the second tabernacle account of the 𝕲 are the unique vocabulary, significant reordering of the material in the center portion of the account, the abbreviated nature of the text, and internal conflicts. Several major studies of the tabernacle accounts include lists of contrasting terms, many of which are considered to be technical terms.[7] In addition to lists of terms, most complete studies include a comparison of at least the order of the 𝔐 and 𝕲 of the second account and occasionally they also compare this with the order of the 𝔐 and 𝕲 in the first account.[8] The major difference in order in the second tabernacle account involves the location of the production of the priestly garments at the beginning of the constructed items in the 𝕲 (𝕲 36:8-38) instead of towards the end, as in the 𝔐 (𝔐 39:1-31). In addition, the construction of the courtyard (38:9-20 [𝕲 37:7-18]) is located before the construction of the furniture of the tabernacle in the 𝕲 (37:1-38:8 [𝕲 38:1-26]). These two differences in order have shifted the verse numbering of a sizable portion of the second tabernacle account, but with the exception of these two large differences, the remainder of the items maintains the same approximate relationship to one another in the 𝔐 and 𝕲.[9] Along with these differences in order, the construction of the tabernacle is

---

6. Origen, *Epistula ad Africanum* 4.

7. Both Finn and Gooding referred to the list of seventeen terms found in A. H. McNeile, *The Book of Exodus* (London: Methuen and Company, 1908), 226 and identified errors in his analysis. They also highlighted the incompleteness of the picture that he presented. Nelson examined the translation of over 140 words from the tabernacle accounts in comparison to other translations and Josephus in search of a means of objectively placing the words in a specific time period. In the discussion of each word he carefully noted the translations used in each account, many of which were identical, and then attempted to assign the unique terms to either the Old Greek or to a Palestinian revision. The complete list may be found in Nelson, 42-47. At the conclusion of Wevers' comparison of the two tabernacle accounts, he noted five words that were not found elsewhere in the LXX and five that were unique to the second tabernacle account. See WeversText, 144.

8. McNeile's table compared both accounts in the 𝔐 and 𝕲 according to sections or topics. (McNeile, *The Book of Exodus*, 224-25.) Nelson's table was similar, but instead of focusing on topics, he presented a verse-by-verse comparison. (Nelson, 21-27.) The most concise presentation of the differences in ordering between the 𝔐 and 𝕲 of the main part of the second tabernacle account (𝔐 36:8-39:31) is probably found in Henry Barclay Swete, *An Introduction to the Old Testament in Greek* (Peabody, Mass.: Hendrickson Publishers, 1989), 235. Studies without tables of this nature often included a verbal description of the differences, such as WeversText, 117-18.

9. Because of these differences in verse numbering between the 𝔐 and 𝕲, I have chosen to indicate the verse number of the 𝕲 in parentheses after the 𝔐 verse number when the 𝕲 differs from the 𝔐. To minimize the use of this double numbering of verses, I have chosen to use the verse numbering in Rahlfs, which generally follows the 𝔐, rather than the verse numbering of the critical edition of the text, which is often slightly different from that of the 𝔐. The text used is that of the critical edition of the text, but Rahlfs numbering of the verses makes for an easier comparison of the 𝔐 and 𝕲. Parallel

largely absent in the 𝔊 of the second tabernacle account, as are also other verses.¹⁰ Internal conflicts are the least mentioned of the difficulties in the second tabernacle account, but for Gooding they are the key factor that leads to his hypothesis that a later editor compiled 𝔊 38 and rearranged the Greek text from its original order, which was more like that of the 𝔐.¹¹

As noted above, these differences have been known since the time of Origen. Indeed, Origen himself or an earlier revisor of the 𝔊 text apparently despaired of finding any easy way of bringing the Greek into agreement with the Hebrew and instead produced a version of the Greek that more "accurately" reflected a text similar to the 𝔐. This revision may be found in all major editions of the 𝔊. The character of these revisions has been discussed by Wevers and analyzed in detail by Fraenkel, but will not be discussed in this book.¹² The fact that the Hexaplaric revision of the 𝔊 is so distinct from the 𝔊, however, is clear evidence that the differences between the Greek and Hebrew were recognized at an early stage and that the cultural definition of an acceptable translation had changed sufficiently enough (or the Hebrew text that the revisers used differed enough from the one used by the translator(s) of the 𝔊) that this part of the 𝔊 was outside of the limits of what they were willing to tolerate. Thus, the Hexaplaric evidence highlights the fact that the second tabernacle account of 𝔊 Exodus has been considered a major text critical problem since the beginning of serious text critical work.

II. Past Solutions to the Problem

Modern scholarly discussions of this problem began in the nineteenth century with Frankel's (1851) comments on the tabernacle accounts.¹³ Popper (1862),

---

verses in the two tabernacle accounts are indicated by placing an equal sign between the two references, e.g., 25:10=37:1 (𝔊 38:1).

10. The construction of the tabernacle discussed in 𝔐 36:10-33 is a minus in the 𝔊. Other verses that are minuses in the 𝔊 of the second account include the following: 35:8, 18; 37:12, 24-28; 38:2, 6; 39:39; 40:7, 11, 28. In addition, many parts of verses are minuses, as will be discussed in chapter five.

11. According to Gooding, 𝔊 38 contains many "mistakes and absurdities." See Gooding, 67. Gooding described these contradictions in detail in chapter six of his book.

12. John William Wevers, "PreOrigen Recensional Activity in the Greek Exodus," in *Studien zur Septuaginta—Robert Hanhart zu Ehren: Aus Anlass seines 65. Geburtstages*, ed. Detlef Fraenkel, Udo Quast, and John William Wevers, Mitteilungen des Septuaginta-Unternehmens, no. 20 (Göttingen: Vandenhoeck & Ruprecht, 1990), 121-39 and Detlef Fraenkel, "Die Quellen der asterisierten Zusätze im zweiten Tabernakelbericht Exod 35-40," in *Studien zur Septuaginta—Robert Hanhart zu Ehren: Aus Anlass seines 65. Geburtstages*, ed. Detlef Fraenkel, Udo Quast, and John William Wevers, Mitteilungen des Septuaginta-Unternehmens, no. 20 (Göttingen: Vandenhoeck & Ruprecht, 1990), 140-86.

13. Z. Frankel, *Über den Einfluss der palästinischen Exegese auf die alexandrinische Hermeneutik* (Leipzig: Joh. Ambr. Barth, 1851). See summary of Frankel's views in relationship to those of Popper and others in Cornelis Houtman, *Exodus*, vol. 3, *Chapters 20-40*, Historical Commentary on the Old

however, is the one who brought the issues into focus and presented a systematic study of both tabernacle accounts using quotations from Frankel as his starting point on some discussions.[14] Popper concluded that 36:8-38:20 was the latest part in the 𝔐 and that the 𝔊 of that section was produced by a different translator using a *Vorlage* that differed from the 𝔐.[15] His conclusions, when modified by Kuenen, fit well with the development of the text that had been suggested on other grounds by those of the historico-critical school.[16]

Popper's views were introduced to English speaking scholars mediated through the views of Kuenen, Smith, Swete, McNeile, and Driver.[17] In this mediated view, the entire second tabernacle account was generally viewed as having been produced by a second translator due to the contrasting vocabulary, but difference in arrangement was viewed either as the product of that translator or as

---

Testament, trans. Sierd Woudstra (Leuven: Peeters, 2000), 314-16. See also the survey of literature on this topic in Alain Le Boulluec and Pierre Sandevoir, *L'Exode*, vol. 2, La Bible D'Alexandrie, ed. Marguerite Harl (Paris: Cerf, 1989), 61-69.

14. For instance, Popper quoted approximately one and a half pages from Frankel on the contrasting vocabulary of the tabernacle accounts and then added his own list of translations to that of Frankel. See Julius Popper, *Der biblische Bericht über die Stiftshütte: Ein Beitrag zur Geschichte der Composition und Diaskeue des Pentateuch*. (Leipzig: Heinrich Hunger, 1862), 172-74. As Nelson noted, Popper did not agree with Frankel, but he did use his comments as a starting point. See Nelson, 32-33 n. 20.

15. Popper, *Der biblische Bericht über die Stiftshütte*. For a summary of Popper's study see Nelson, 3-8. Popper's views are also discussed throughout Gooding.

16. In historico-critical studies, 35-40 is generally viewed as a later stratum of the priestly source. (McNeile, *The Book of Exodus*, 226.) For the influence of Popper on Kuenen see Simon J. De Vries, "The Hexateuchal Criticism of Abraham Kuenen," *Journal of Biblical Literature* 82 (1963): 42-43. Kuenen's discussion of the tabernacle may be found in Abraham Kuenen, *An Historico-critical Inquiry into the Origin and Composition of the Hexateuch (Pentateuch and Book of Joshua)*, trans. Philip H. Wiksteed (London: Macmillan and Co., 1886), 76-80. Aejmelaeus, in particular, has been influenced by Kuenen and quotes his criticism of Popper, "Kuenen already saw in the divergencies of the Septuagintal version reason to 'suspect that the final redaction of these chapters was hardly completed — if indeed completed — when that translation was made, i.e., about 250 B.C.' . . . He rejected the theory of two successive translators which was put forward by his contemporary J. Popper . . . , because 'we have no right to place the original Greek translator between the composition of Ex. 39, 40 (+ Lev. 8) and the compilation of 36-38' . . . , an opinion still worth noting." See Aejmelaeus, "Septuagintal Translation Techniques," 399-400.

17. Kuenen modified Popper's views slightly by stating "that the differences between Ex. 25-31 and 35-40 in the Greek version indicate different translators." (Kuenen, *Historico-critical Inquiry*, 79.) Kuenen's views were then echoed in a slightly modified form in Smith, who used the tabernacle accounts in 𝔊 as evidence "either that the text of this section of the Pentateuch was not yet fixed in the third century before Christ, or that the translator did not feel himself bound to treat it with the same reverence as the rest of the Law. But indeed there are strong reasons for suspecting that the Greek version of these chapters is not by the same hand as the rest of the Book of Exodus, various Hebrew words being represented by other Greek equivalents than those used in the earlier chapters. And thus it seems possible that this whole section was lacking in the copy that lay before the first translator of the Law." See W. Robertson Smith, *The Old Testament in the Jewish Church: A Course of Lectures on Biblical Criticism*, 2d ed. (London: Adam and Charles Black, 1892), 125. Swete quoted from Smith con-

evidence of a *Vorlage* that differed from the order of the 𝔐.[18] In either case, the *Vorlage* was viewed as a later stratum of P than 25-29. Thus, partially due to the influence of the historico-critical approach in which 35-40 was generally viewed as a later addition to Exodus, Popper's emphasis on the distinct character of 36:8-38:20 was ignored and his emphasis on the difference in *Vorlage* was diminished in favor of the possibility that the change in order had been produced by the translator. This shift in perspective on the part of some scholars (especially Swete) may have been due to the growing recognition of the variety of translation techniques used in the 𝔊, as noted by Thackeray.[19]

Finn (1915) was the earliest proponent of the opposite approach to the differences between the tabernacle accounts. He concluded that these differences were the result of the translation techniques used and that only one translator was involved in the project.[20] Finn clearly identified the presuppositions that were the basis of his predecessor's conclusions about the tabernacle accounts and strove to illustrate the incorrectness of these presuppositions that led to the conclusion that each tabernacle account had been produced by a different translator.[21] Furthermore, he was often able to show that the evidence used in McNeile's study had been incomplete and thus did not give the correct picture of the translation techniques. Instead of noting the contrasts, Finn emphasized the variation found in each account, the passages in which the second account shows an obvious knowledge of the first account, the shared "careless mistakes," and the similar "tendency to omit or paraphrase perplexing passages, and occasionally to insert explanatory words or phrases." The strength of Finn's argument, however, was probably dismissed because of the fact that he tried to use the unity of the translation as "evi-

---

cerning the differences between the 𝔊 and 𝔐 of this passage and then noted two possible options for the source of the difference in ordering between the two accounts, i.e., the translator or the *Vorlage*. (Swete, *Introduction to the Old Testament in Greek*, 234-36.) In later works, however, it was often Swete rather than Smith who was quoted. McNeile emphasized both vocabulary differences and differences in order and then quoted Swete on the possible source of the difference in ordering. (McNeile, *The Book of Exodus*, 223-26.) In his commentary on Exodus, Driver referred to McNeile and again quoted Swete's conclusion. See S. R. Driver, *The Book of Exodus*, The Cambridge Bible for Schools and Colleges, ed. A. F. Kirkpatrick (Cambridge: Cambridge University Press, 1918), 378-79.

18. Swete, *Introduction to the Old Testament in Greek*, 234-36.

19. Henry St. John Thackeray, *A Grammar of the Old Testament in Greek According to the Septuagint*, vol. 1, *Introduction, Orthography and Accidence* (Cambridge: Cambridge University Press, 1909).

20. A. H. Finn, "The Tabernacle Chapters," *Journal of Theological Studies* 16 (1915): 449-82.

21. One presupposition he noted is that "the LXX translators were fairly consistent in their rendering of Hebrew words." Finn showed the error of this presupposition by listing translations of terms that varied within short stretches of text in Exodus and elsewhere in the Pentateuch. Finn also noted the contradictory nature of the claims made by those who critiqued the translator(s) for not being consistent and yet at the same time advocated that the translators of the second account had a Hebrew *Vorlage* unlike the 𝔐. As Finn rightly questioned, "But if the translators of Group II had before them a text different from that which we now possess, how can we be sure that they had the same words to translate?" Ibid., 450, 457.

dence that as far back as 250 B.C. the book of Exodus was substantially complete as we now have it."[22] Further, because Finn was arguing in support of the priority of the 𝔐 in its present form, he failed to recognize features that are characteristic of any translation and so he denigrated the 𝔊 in order to elevate the 𝔐.[23] A large section of Finn's article was spent arguing against the claims that 30-31 were a later addition to the first account and that the second account in the 𝔐 was a still later addition to the text. Thus, for Finn the key issue was the unity and priority of the 𝔐 of the tabernacle accounts and the discussion about the number of translators that produced the 𝔊 was simply an argument that could be used to support his larger concern.

Gooding (1959) likewise affirmed that most of both tabernacle accounts was produced by one translator using a consistently inconsistent translation technique. While this inconsistent translation technique could be used to account for most of the differences in the text, Gooding assumed that the translator would not have reordered the text in the drastic way that it was reordered in the second account. In addition, he identified what he considered to be blatant contradictions within the Greek text, especially in 𝔊 38, that must have been the work of another translator or editor. As a result, Gooding concluded that most of 𝔊 38 and the reordering in the second tabernacle account were the work of a later editor.[24] Gooding's thorough, if caustic, description of the translation techniques was generally well received in the academic community.[25] This was partially due to the fact that Gooding, unlike Finn, had separated the issue of the number of translators who produced the text from the discussion about the formation of the Hebrew text.

Nelson (1986), like Popper, viewed the 𝔊 of the second tabernacle account as clear evidence of a different Hebrew *Vorlage*. His emphasis on the evidence from the 𝔊 is probably due to his acceptance of Cross' local text theory, which sees the 𝔊 as evidence of the textual family that developed in Egypt.[26] Nelson's examination of the vocabulary of the tabernacle accounts, however, turned Popper's timetable around and as a result he concluded that the oldest part of both tabernacle accounts was 36:8-38:20, which was translated first, and that the rest of the translation was based on a revised version of the Hebrew text. The main criterion he

---

22. Ibid., 455-57.

23. For instance, Finn claimed, "*Where the order differs, the Hebrew is consistent and natural, the Greek confused and contradictory.*" (Ibid., 466.) After quoting a list of similar comments found in Finn's article, Wevers concluded by saying, "Such statements do not induce much confidence in a writer's objectivity." See WeversText, 119.

24. Gooding, 99-101.

25. See Raymond Thornhill, review of *The Account of the Tabernacle: Translation and Textual Problems of the Greek Exodus*, by David W. Gooding, *Journal of Theological Studies*, n.s. 11 (1960): 124-27 and George S. Glanzman, review of *The Account of the Tabernacle: Translation and Textual Problems of the Greek Exodus*, by David W. Gooding, *Theological Studies* 23 (1962): 106-8.

26. Nelson, 14.

used was a comparison of the vocabulary in Exodus with that of Josephus, the temple sections of the 𝔊 translation of 1 Kings and 2 Chronicles, and the *kaige* recension.[27] Nelson's study thus reunited the issues of the formation of the Hebrew text and the Greek translation, but in a way that was the exact opposite of Finn. Rather than advocating the unity and priority of the 𝔐, Nelson attempted to show that a text similar to the current 𝔐 of the tabernacle texts was one of the final stages in the development of the text. Nelson's study also differed from some of the earlier studies in the authority that he granted to the 𝔊 text as an indicator of the probable *Vorlage*.

In the past decade, three Septuagintal scholars have weighed in on this issue. Wevers (1992, 1993) claimed that because of several major translation issues, one of which was the translation of the compass points in relationship to the tabernacle, there had to have been two translators. The Hebrew text used by the translators, however, was basically the same as the 𝔐 that we use today. Unlike some scholars, Wevers was quite willing to assign the reordering of the second account to the translator. For Wevers, assigning differences between the 𝔊 and 𝔐 to a difference in *Vorlage* is considered to be a last resort that should only be used when no other explanation can be found for a difference.[28]

Aejmelaeus (1992), in contrast, claimed that the translator of Exodus must have been using a Hebrew text vastly different from the current text. According to Aejmelaeus, smaller differences were due to translation technique, but even in a free translation, like that of Exodus, there was no reason for the translator to reorder the text so drastically. Aejmelaeus used her discussion of the tabernacle accounts to illustrate her position that "it is possible to have both free translation and a different *Vorlage* in the same text," rather than having to assign differences to either translation technique or a difference in *Vorlage*.[29]

Bogaert (1996) would agree with Aejmelaeus in pointing to both differences due to translation technique and differences in the Hebrew text used by the translators. He claimed that the solution to some of the problems, especially in 35-40, could be found by examining the Old Latin text, which points to a different Greek translation and thus to a different Hebrew text than the one that we currently use.[30] In addition to a difference in *Vorlage*, however, Bogaert (1981) was the first to suggest a possible difference in translators due to the difference in orientation of the courtyard in the first and second accounts, a significant contribution that was recognized by Wevers.[31]

---

27. Ibid., 364-70.

28. John William Wevers, "The Building of the Tabernacle," *Journal of Northwest Semitic Languages* 19 (1993): 123-31 and WeversText, 144-46.

29. Aejmelaeus, "Septuagintal Translation Techniques," 398.

30. P. M. Bogaert, "L'importance de la Septante et du «Monacensis» de la Vetus Latina pour l'exégèse du livre de l'Exode (chap. 35-40)," in *Studies in the Book of Exodus: Redaction-Reception-Interpretation*, ed. Marc Vervenne (Leuven: Leuven University Press, 1996), 399-428.

31. P. M. Bogaert, "L'orientation du parvis du sanctuaire dans la version grecque de l'Exode

Several other articles in this past decade have also dealt with some of the problems in the 𝕲 tabernacle accounts by either comparing the tabernacle accounts with other texts or by discussing the differences in the tabernacle accounts as an aspect of the translation techniques in the 𝕲. Fraenkel (1995) accepted the theory of multiple translators and focused on the literary art of the translation in both of the tabernacle accounts.[32] Because of his emphasis on literary artistry, the possibility of differences in *Vorlage* was not often raised. Brooke (1990) noted similarities between the Temple Scroll and 35-40 and argued for the possibility of a different Hebrew text as the basis for the translation.[33] Whether or not one agrees with all of Brooke's conclusions, his emphasis on the existence in antiquity of different forms of similar material is an important one that should not be dismissed. Cook (1996), in contrast, noted the reordering of the text in Proverbs 31 and suggested that 𝕲 38 may be following a similar model of translation in which reordering was an acceptable option.[34] Thus, as can be seen by these more recent contributions on the topic, the diversity of solutions and arguments concerning the tabernacle accounts of 𝕲 Exodus has continued to grow throughout the last decade of the twentieth century.

As can be seen in this brief survey of conflicting theories, there is no consensus about either the development of the Hebrew text or the effect this has had on the 𝕲 translation that we currently use. Each scholarly contribution has identified issues that need to be resolved, but no theory has provided a convincing argument that will explain all the differences in the 𝕲. The issue-oriented nature of discussions in brief articles has probably contributed to this lack of a coherent solution to all of the problems. Lists of similarities or differences between the sections are found in most of the longer studies, but there has not been a comprehensive examination of the translation techniques within both tabernacle accounts. This book will contribute to the text critical study of the tabernacle accounts by providing a basis for further discussion of the development and translation of the text.

(*Ex.*, 27, 9-13 LXX)," *L'Antiquité classique* 50 (1981): 79-85. Bogaert's main contribution was that he identified the clear difference in orientation instead of following the normal path of reinterpreting the directional terms, as had been done in previous studies such as Popper's. Wevers succinctly describes Popper's rationalization of the compass points as "simply wrong." See WeversText, 123.

32. Detlef Fraenkel, "Übersetzungsnorm und literarische Gestaltung—Spuren individueller Übersetzungstechnik in Exodus 25ff. + 35ff.," in *VIII Congress of the International Organization for Septuagint and Cognate Studies, Paris, 1991*, ed. Leonard Greenspoon and Olivier Munnich, Septuagint and Cognate Studies, no. 41 (Atlanta, Ga.: Scholars Press, 1995), 73-87.

33. George J. Brooke, "The Temple Scroll and LXX Exodus 35-40," in *Septuagint, Scrolls and Cognate Writings: Papers Presented to the International Symposium on the Septuagint and Its Relations to the Dead Sea Scrolls and Other Writings, Manchester, 1990*, ed. George J. Brooke and Barnabas Lindars, Septuagint and Cognate Studies, no. 33 (Atlanta, Ga.: Scholars Press, 1990), 81-106.

34. Johann Cook, "Exodus 38 and Proverbs 31: A Case of Different Order of Verses and Chapters in the Septuagint," in *Studies in the Book of Exodus: Redaction-Reception-Interpretation*, ed. Marc Vervenne (Leuven: Leuven University Press, 1996), 537-49.

III. Methodology and Contribution

The major research methodology in this book will be an exhaustive examination of the translations of Hebrew words and grammatical structures in 25-31 and 35-40, with special attention to their semantic and grammatical contexts. In addition, 11-13 will be examined to provide a "control sample" of a similar genre from outside of the tabernacle accounts. After the data are examined, a comparison will be made of translation techniques throughout the tabernacle accounts to determine the nature and location of any distinctive translation techniques.

In addition to providing a basis for further discussion of the development and translation of the tabernacle accounts, as noted above, this study will also contribute to recent discussions about methodologies for examining and evaluating translation techniques in the ⅏. The ⅏ Scriptures contain a variety of translation styles from woodenly literal translations, such as Qoheleth, to very free translations, such as Isaiah. Early descriptions of the differences in these translation techniques tended to be anecdotal in nature. A scholar asserted that the translation was literal, gave a long list of items to "prove" his point and then noted that there were a few exceptions.[35] In the last few decades there has been a growing consensus that a more objective means of analysis is needed. One major approach that strives for objectivity uses a computerized, statistical model that attempts to eliminate the human factor in analysis. Studies from within this framework have focused on lexical consistency, consistency in word order, the degree to which all elements of the Hebrew text are represented in the Greek, and similar factors.[36] Another major approach involves exhaustive studies of one type of grammatical structure throughout a section of the ⅏. The results of these types of analyses are then compared with the usages of the same structures in non-translated Greek texts. Statistics are also used in this approach as a means of presenting the results.[37] Both of these approaches produce valid observations, but neither gives a holistic picture of the translation. In this study I intend to combine aspects of both of these approaches in an examination of the translation techniques of the tabernacle accounts in the ⅏ Exodus.

This study will contribute to the discussion about the proper methodology for evaluating a translation by illustrating the semantic and grammatical bases for

---

35. Tov, *Text-Critical Use of the Septuagint*, 25 n. 39.

36. Emanuel Tov and Benjamin G. Wright, "Computer-Assisted Study of the Criteria for Assessing the Literalness of Translation Units in the LXX," *Textus* 12 (1985): 149-87.

37. Ilmari Soisalon-Soininen, *Die Infinitive in der Septuaginta* (Helsinki: Suomalainen Tiedeakatemia, 1965); Raija Sollamo, *Rendering of Hebrew Semiprepositions in the Septuagint* (Helsinki: Suomalainen Tiedeakatemia, 1979); Anneli Aejmelaeus, *Parataxis in the Septuagint: A Study of the Renderings of the Hebrew Coordinate Clauses in the Greek Pentateuch*, Annales Academiae Scientiarum Fennicae: Dissertationes Humanarum Litterarum, no. 31 (Helsinki: Suomalainen Tiedeakatemia, 1982); and Raija Sollamo, *Repetition of the Possessive Pronouns in the Septuagint*, Septuagint and Cognate Studies, ed. Bernard A. Taylor, no. 40 (Atlanta, Ga.: Scholars Press, 1995).

many of the decisions made by the translator. Too often, the variations within Exodus, especially the choices of lexical equivalents, have been attributed either to the translator's desire for variety, the inconsistency of the translator's technique, or a difference in either the translator or the *Vorlage*. Most of the choices of lexical equivalents, as well as the choices of translation equivalents for grammatical structures, within the sections of Exodus used in this study, however, can be explained on the basis of a careful examination of the semantic and grammatical contexts.

The major resources used in this book are the Accordance computer program, which includes the MT/LXX aligned text file, in conjunction with the standard critical editions of the 𝔐, 𝔪, 𝔊, and published editions of pertinent 𝔔 manuscripts.[38] The linguistic framework used in this analysis is eclectic and focuses on semantic and grammatical factors that may affect choices of lexical equivalents and other types of adjustments commonly found in modern translations. Rather than using technical linguistic terminology, I will attempt to use grammatical terminology that is found in standard Greek and Hebrew reference grammars and to define carefully any terminology that is deemed to be outside the norm of Biblical scholarship.

IV. Contents

In chapter two I will address the issue of the Hebrew text used by the translator(s) of the tabernacle accounts. This will be accomplished through a detailed discussion of Hebrew textual variants in the 𝔔 manuscripts, 𝔪, and 𝔐. In past scholarly studies, variants have often been broadly divided into two groups—variants that are irrelevant to the 𝔊 translation and variants that could have affected the 𝔊 translation. These categories will be used in chapter two. In the tabernacle accounts, however, the "irrelevant" variants sometimes prove to be quite important for understanding the interpretation of the text that is reflected in the 𝔊 translation. In addition to discussing the variants found in the Hebrew texts of the tabernacle accounts, I will also discuss the consistent, secondary nature of the revision that is seen in the 𝔪 and the irrelevance of claims about the development of the Hebrew text that are based on spelling differences within the 𝔐. Finally, I will conclude by emphasizing the importance of examining all textual variants within their immediate and larger context before making any conclusions about the importance of the variants.

In chapter three I will focus on lexical consistency, which has been one of the major criteria used for claims about the number of translators and the nature of the translation techniques used. Lexical consistency has been defined and mea-

---

38. *Accordance* Ver. 3.0 (Altamonte Springs, Fla.: OakTree Software Specialists, Altamonte Springs, Fla.).

sured using a variety of methodologies. This chapter will begin by identifying some of these methodologies, which have ranged from strictly intuitive studies to computer-based statistical analyses. In contrast to past studies, the methodology that will be used in this study emphasizes factors in the semantic and grammatical contexts that have affected the choice of lexical equivalents for nouns and verbs in the tabernacle accounts and control sample of 𝔊 Exodus. After presenting an analysis of the choices of lexical equivalents within the tabernacle accounts, it will be shown that choices of lexical equivalents within the tabernacle accounts are mainly conditioned by the semantic and grammatical context of the word, rather than being the work of a Palestinian revisor, as suggested by Nelson, or simply synonyms, as often suggested by Wevers. The choices of lexical equivalents for some words, however, do point to the probability that a second translator produced the second tabernacle account. Evidence from the translation of technical terminology and the points of the compass will be discussed in the third section of this chapter and will provide further support for the two-translator hypothesis. In the fourth section of this chapter I will demonstrate that a careful examination of choices of lexical equivalents in the 𝔊 translation will often provide exegetical insights concerning the interpretation of the Hebrew text in the third century B.C.

Consistency in the translation of grammatical structures is only rarely used as a basis for claims about the number of translators that produced the tabernacle accounts of 𝔊 Exodus. In chapter four, I will survey grammatical studies of aspects of the 𝔊 Pentateuch as well as other statistical studies that have been used in discussions of differences of style in the Koine Greek. In contrast to some statistical studies, I have chosen to analyze the translation of grammatical structures by means of an emphasis on both the structures used as translation equivalents and the semantic functions that these translation equivalents convey. In the second section of this chapter I will use this approach in the analysis of three frequently occurring grammatical structures—the preposition בְּ, the simple construct chain, and the relative clause with אֲשֶׁר. As with choices of lexical equivalents, choices in the translation of grammatical structures in 𝔊 Exodus are generally context-sensitive in that they are controlled by the semantic and grammatical context in which they occur. In the third section of this chapter I will highlight differences in the interpretation and translation of grammatical structures that may indicate that the tabernacle accounts were produced by different translators. These differences, however, are rather minute and thus the main contribution of this study of the translation of grammatical structures is the fact that it indicates that both tabernacle accounts have been translated with a sensitivity to the semantic and the grammatical contexts, both of which can affect the choice of translation equivalents.

Ultimately, the resolution of the text critical problem of the tabernacle accounts revolves around the issue of accuracy. Since the *Vorlage* of the 𝔊 is unknown, accuracy, as used in this chapter, will refer to the degree to which the 𝔊 communicates the same meaning as the 𝔐. In the first section of this chapter I will review two text critical studies of Exodus and attempt to show the effect of one's presuppositions on the interpretation of the differences (pluses, minuses, synonymous variants, and differences in order) that exist between the 𝔊 and 𝔐. Rather than a traditional approach to textual variants in the 𝔊, I have chosen to analyze the differences using three categories of meaning (referential, organizational, and situational) that are used in analyzing modern translations. Within each category of meaning, differences may reflect either a quantitative change or a change of the status (implicit versus explicit) of the meaning. The combination of these factors results in six categories that will be used in the second section of this chapter to categorize over nine hundred textual variants that have been identified in the control sample and tabernacle accounts. This detailed analysis will show that textual variants in all of these sections have similar effects on the meaning. The major difference between the accounts is in the quantity or distribution of these variants rather than in the type of variants. The comparison of parallel sections and the analysis of the pluses in the second tabernacle account, however, provide evidence that would support the hypothesis that a second translator produced the second tabernacle account using the translation of the first tabernacle account as a point of reference. These will be discussed in the third section of the chapter. While this evidence contributes to the growing mountain of minutiae that would support a two-translator theory, the problem is ultimately unsolvable because of our lack of a complete knowledge of the translator's culture and the acceptable limits of modifications that could be introduced by a translator, as will be discussed in the fourth section. Because of this lack of knowledge, most conclusions ultimately are based on the scholar's presuppositions about what translators in antiquity would or would not have done.

Chapter six will begin with a summary of the four main chapters of this book. The results obtained from studying three aspects of the translation techniques of the tabernacle accounts will then be used to evaluate previous hypotheses with respect to the unity of the core and the remainder of the second tabernacle account, the unity of the first and second tabernacle accounts, and the nature of the translation. I will conclude by briefly sketching a hypothetical sociological setting that would account for the results produced by this examination of the tabernacle accounts of 𝔊 Exodus. In light of the results of this study, I will suggest that a second translator likely produced the second tabernacle account of the 𝔊 Exodus using the translation of the first tabernacle account as a point of reference. No theory about the translation of the tabernacle accounts is ultimately "provable," but the results of this study will show that some of the past claims about the tabernacle accounts were based on inaccurate statements about translation techniques in 𝔊 Exodus.

CHAPTER TWO

Hebrew Vorlage

The Old Greek translation of the tabernacle accounts of Exodus can only be effectively evaluated by comparing it with its Hebrew *Vorlage*. Unfortunately, the Hebrew *Vorlage* of the Old Greek (𝔊), like the often discussed *Urtext*, is not available for our examination. Instead, we are faced with a multiplicity of Hebrew textual variants from the Qumran scrolls (𝒬), the Samaritan Pentateuch (𝔐), and the Masoretic Text (𝔐),[1] any of which may represent the Hebrew *Vorlage* of the 𝔊.[2] In this chapter, I will discuss variants in the Hebrew texts and their relationship to the 𝔊. The standard text that will be used as the starting point for identifying variants will be the 𝔐 of *BHS*.[3] Most of the significant textual variants discussed in this chapter are from the 𝔐. Unique readings from the 𝒬 manuscripts will be noted where relevant.

Hebrew textual variants have been grouped into two categories. The first category contains variants that are supposedly "irrelevant" for translation into Greek. The second category contains variants that could have affected the 𝔊 translation. Within both of these categories I will discuss variants according to appropriate grammatical categories. I will conclude with a discussion of two secondary issues involving the Hebrew texts. These are the patterns of adjustments within the 𝔐 and spelling differences within the Hebrew texts. Orthographic differences

---

1. See note 2 in chapter one.
2. Retroversions from the 𝔊 are another possible source of Hebrew variants. See chapter three in Emanuel Tov, *The Text-Critical Use of the Septuagint in Biblical Research: Second Edition, Revised and Enlarged* (Jerusalem: Simor, 1997), especially pp. 66-67 for examples of retroversions from 𝔊 that are also found in the 𝒬 manuscripts. Retroverted variants will not, however, be used in this discussion of the Hebrew *Vorlage* of the 𝔊.
3. Flint's third step in collecting and organizing textual variants is to "Collate all Variant Readings against a Standard Text." See Peter W. Flint, "Methods for Determining Relationships between Manuscripts, with Special Reference to the Psalms Scrolls," in *Methods of Investigation of the Dead Sea Scrolls and the Khirbet Qumran Site: Present Realities and Future Prospects*, ed. Michael O. Wise, et al., vol. 722, Annals of the New York Academy of Science (New York: The New York Academy of Sciences, 1994), 201. The standard text that was used by Flint was the 𝔐 of *BHS*. He considers this to be a "*practical* or *working* standard" rather than an "*ideal* standard." Because of the accessibility of the *BHS*, it has been chosen as the starting point for all discussions in this chapter. The terms "pluses," "minuses," and "synonymous variants" are used simply to represent a text's relationship to this edition of the 𝔐 and not as an evaluation of the variant in relationship to the *Urtext*.

are probably the most frequent type of variant in the Hebrew texts of the tabernacle accounts, but these differences are the least likely to affect a translation and will only be briefly discussed.

From a detailed examination of the Hebrew variants, the following observations can be made. First, textual variants in the 𝔐 that are often discounted as "irrelevant" may point to an interpretation of the text that was shared by the translators of the 𝔊. Second, other "irrelevant" textual variants point to ambiguous passages that the 𝔐 has attempted to clarify by means of grammatical particles that are pluses. The 𝔊 has likewise identified and attempted to clarify these same passages, though not always in the same manner as in the 𝔐. Third, within the textual variants that are considered to be significant for translation, the 𝔊 and 𝔐 often seem to agree on smaller changes, but rarely on any major changes in the text. These apparent agreements may indicate that the Hebrew *Vorlage* of the 𝔊 was similar to the text from which the 𝔐 was derived, but this proto-Samaritan form of the text did not yet contain the major adjustments in order, such as the placement of 𝔐 30:1-10 after 26:35. Closer examinations of the apparent agreements, however, often show that the agreements may be due more to the fact that the 𝔊 and 𝔐 shared the same interpretive approach to the Hebrew text, rather than an actual shared text.

I. Variants "Irrelevant" to the Old Greek Translation

Many Hebrew variants are "irrelevant" for the evaluation of the 𝔊 translation, though they might be quite useful for the determining of the *Urtext*. In the tabernacle accounts of Exodus the "irrelevant" variants are grammatical morphemes that are not reflected in Greek due to language differences.[4] Many text critics would include in this category the large number of differences in articles and conjunctions.[5] Recently, however, some text critics have been placing more emphasis on these minute differences and have shown that differences in conjunctions may at times reflect significant differences in the interpretation of the text.[6] I have chosen to discuss articles and conjunctions in this section, but have noted a few of the changes that may not be irrelevant for translation.

---

4. John William Wevers, "The Use of Versions for Text Criticism: The Septuagint," in *La Septuaginta en la investigacion contemporanea: V Congreso de la IOSCS*, ed. Natalio Fernandez Marcos, Textos y Estudios «Cardenal Cisneros» de la Biblia Poliglota Matritense, no. 34 (Madrid: Instituto «Arias Montano» C.S.I.C., 1985), 15-24.

5. Tov, *Text-Critical Use of the Septuagint*, 154-62. See also Anneli Aejmelaeus, "What Can We Know about the Hebrew *Vorlage* of the Septuagint," *Zeitschrift für die alttestamentliche Wissenschaft* 99 (1987): 58-89.

6. Andrew E. Steinmann, "Jacob's Family Goes to Egypt: Varying Portraits of Unity and Disunity in the Textual Traditions of Exodus 1:1-5," *TC: A Journal of Biblical Textual Criticism* [http://purl.org/TC] 2 (1997): pars. 1-27.

Grammatical Markers

Many markers of grammatical functions are not directly translated from Hebrew to Greek in a relatively free translation such as Exodus.[7] Variants included in this category are changes in grammatical gender, other nominal and adjectival changes, changes in the aspect and stem of verbs, the presence or absence of the locative *he*, and the presence or absence of the so-called object marker, אֵת.[8] Some of these variations may be due to changes in the Hebrew language, but the Greek translation would probably have been the same whether its Hebrew *Vorlage* was similar to the variants in the 𝔐, the 𝔚, or one of the 𝔔 manuscripts.

Changes in Grammatical Gender. According to Wevers, "Gender in the source language [Hebrew] is almost entirely irrelevant and untranslatable."[9] The irrelevance of gender for the 𝔊 translation can be easily illustrated by noting that in 25:29, Greek uses a feminine possessive pronoun, which agrees with its referent τράπεζα, whereas Hebrew uses a masculine suffix, which agrees with שֻׁלְחָן, a masculine noun. This same verse, however, also contains an example of a common modification in the 𝔚, i.e., the reassigning of traditionally feminine nouns to the masculine gender.[10] The 𝔐 refers to the utensils, all of which are feminine plural nouns, by using the feminine plural suffix, בָּהֵן. The 𝔚, in contrast, uses בהם. Of twenty-seven changes in gender within the tabernacle accounts of the 𝔚, seventeen are changes from feminine in the 𝔐 to masculine in the 𝔚.[11] The ten remain-

---

7. "In the various translation-technical studies which describe the translators' way of handling typically Hebrew syntactical phenomena, Exodus has proved to be one of the most freely translated books in the LXX and one of those in which the requirements of Greek idiom have been best taken into account." See Anneli Aejmelaeus, "Septuagintal Translation Techniques—A Solution to the Problem of the Tabernacle Account," in *Septuagint, Scrolls and Cognate Writings: Papers Presented to the International Symposium on the Septuagint and Its Relations to the Dead Sea Scrolls and Other Writings, Manchester, 1990*, ed. George J. Brooke and Barnabas Lindars, Septuagint and Cognate Studies, no. 33 (Atlanta, Ga.: Scholars Press, 1992), 388. In contrast to the free translation style of Exodus, the translation of Qoheleth literally renders grammatical markers, such as its translation of the object marker by means of σύν plus the accusative. See Choon-Leong Seow, *Ecclesiastes: A New Translation with Introduction and Commentary*, vol. 18C, The Anchor Bible (New York: Doubleday, 1997), 7.

8. Waltke has thoroughly discussed the kinds of changes that are commonly found in the 𝔚. See Bruce K. Waltke, "The Samaritan Pentateuch and the Text of the Old Testament," in *New Perspectives on the Old Testament*, ed. J. B. Payne (Waco, Tex.: Word Books, 1970), 219-39. See also *The Anchor Bible Dictionary*, s.v. "Samaritan Pentateuch," 5:932-40.

9. Wevers, "Use of Versions for Text Criticism," 18.

10. E. Kautzsch, ed., *Gesenius' Hebrew Grammar*, Second English ed. (Oxford: Clarendon Press, 1910), § 135o, refers to the "weakening in the distinction of gender" in Hebrew. In linguistic terms, this represents a move from a more "marked" form to an "unmarked" form. See the brief discussion about this issue in Bruce K. Waltke and M. O'Connor, *An Introduction to Biblical Hebrew Syntax* (Winona Lake, Ind.: Eisenbrauns, 1990), 96.

11. Changes in grammatical gender from feminine to masculine that do not affect the interpretation include changes in pronominal suffixes (25:17 [2x]=37:6 [2x]; 25:29=37:16) and changes in the

ing changes are from a masculine form (at least in the *Kethiv* reading) to a feminine form and include all five examples of changes of gender of independent pronouns.[12] Several of these changes (25:29; 31:13) are also found in 4QpaleoExod^m, which gives further evidence that changes in grammatical gender were common in the Hebrew language of that period. Some of these changes may be due to the correcting of a perceived incongruity in gender that was present in the 𝔐.[13] A few cases, however, may be due to ambiguity of reference in that both feminine and masculine nouns are present in the context and could be the referent for the pronoun. Of these, two (27:5; 30:36) are noteworthy because the 𝔊 has in each case used a plural where the 𝔐 has a 3fs suffix and the 𝔰𝔪 has a 3ms suffix.[14] In 27:5, the 𝔊 seems to be referring to the rings (a masculine plural noun) rather than the "network" that is being referred to by the 3fs suffix in the 𝔐. The 𝔰𝔪 uses a feminine verb with "network" later in the same verse so it is probable that its use of the 3ms suffix rather than referring to the "network" refers to the "grating" as a whole, which is the only possible masculine referent.[15] Wevers notes that in the 𝔊 there is a substitution of the hearth (grating) for the network in 𝔊 27:4.[16] The 𝔰𝔪 and 𝔊, therefore, seem to share a common understanding of the text. This example shows that while Wevers' statement about grammatical gender is generally true, some changes in gender in Hebrew variants are important because they signal a change in the referent and changes in referent often affect a translation.

---

gender of a number (25:36=37:22; 38:24 [variant in 𝔰𝔪]). In addition, there are eight cases that may involve differences in the interpretation of the referent (27:5; 29:41 [2x]; 30:7, 35, 36 [2x]; 35:2).

12. Changes of grammatical gender from masculine to feminine include one change to a cognate noun of the feminine gender (30:21); four cases of the perpetual *Qere* הִוא being replaced by the 3fs pronoun (31:13, 14 [2x], 17); one example of the replacement of a 3ms pronoun with a 3fs pronoun in a non-verbal clause with a feminine noun (29:14); one case in which the choice of grammatical gender in the 𝔰𝔪 is also the more frequent usage in the 𝔐 (29:40); one change of gender to bring it into agreement with a plus in the 𝔰𝔪 (28:20); and two cases that may be due to a difference in referent (30:35; 39:40). In 4QExod-Lev^f 39:7 a feminine plural pronoun is used instead of a masculine, a difference that may reflect a change in reference.

13. See Waltke, "Samaritan Pentateuch and the Text," 218.

14. In 30:36, both the 3fs suffix in the 𝔐 and the 3p demonstrative pronoun in the 𝔊 are ambiguous. According to Wevers, the 3fs suffix in the 𝔐 refers to לְבֹנָה in 30:34 and the plural pronoun in the 𝔊 refers to ἡδύσματα, also in 30:34. See WeversNotes, 503. It could be just as easily argued, however, that the 3fs pronoun in the 𝔐 refers to קְטֹרֶת in 30:35 and that the 3p pronoun in the 𝔊 refers to the entire list of items in 30:34. The use of the 3ms pronoun in the 𝔰𝔪 may refer to מַעֲשֵׂה in 30:35, which would agree more with the usage in the 𝔊, if it is referring to the entire list. Due to other difficulties with grammatical gender and references in this passage, the most that can be said is that the presence of the 3ms suffix in the 𝔰𝔪 is an attempt to clarify a very ambiguous passage and that the 𝔊 attempts to solve the same problem, but in a slightly different manner.

15. The noun מַעֲשֵׂה, which is in apposition to מִכְבָּר, is likewise a masculine noun. Its referent, however, is the same as מִכְבָּר, i.e., the "grating."

16. WeversNotes, 433. Wevers says that the 𝔊 "having taken the 'network' to be the composition of the hearth, naturally has 'for the hearth.'"

Other Nominal and Adjectival Changes. Other "irrelevant" changes that are found in the 𝔐 include differences in the use of construct versus absolute forms and differences in the use of singular forms for collective terms. In 25:18, the 𝔐 has an absolute form of the number two, שְׁנַיִם, being used adjectivally with the following noun, but the 𝔐 has changed this to a construct form, שְׁנֵי, being used substantivally, which is the form more commonly found in Exodus. In 26:18, 19, and 20, the 𝔐 uses a commonly found combination of a plural number with a singular noun, עֶשְׂרִים קֶרֶשׁ. In the 𝔐 this is "corrected" so that the noun is also plural. These types of differences in forms of numbers and in the agreement between nouns and adjectives for plural terms are easily identified as problems that do not affect a translation. There are, however, eleven other nouns or adjectives that are plural in one form of the text and singular in the other. Both the 𝔐 and 𝔐 contain a mixture of plural and singular forms, though the 𝔐 definitely tends to use plural forms more frequently.[17] The 𝔊, in contrast to both the 𝔐 and 𝔐, simply translates according to context, which means that it uses plural for all forms except for the "stem" in 25:31. As a result, the 𝔊 "agrees" with the 𝔐 four times and with the 𝔐 three times.[18] These kinds of "agreements," however, are meaningless for determining textual affinities. The 𝔊 was using the forms natural in Greek, whereas the contrasting forms in the 𝔐 and the 𝔐 illustrate the variations allowable at certain stages of the Hebrew language and also the changes in language usage that occurred through the centuries.

Changes of Aspect and Stem. According to Waltke, "SP *sometimes replaces waw-consecutive ('conversive') and the perfect with the waw conjunctive and the normal tense.*"[19] In the tabernacle accounts, a change similar to this is seen in the use of an imperfect without a conjunction in the 𝔐 instead of the *waw*-consecutive used with the perfect (28:7; 29:33; 30:21).[20] Both of these Hebrew forms refer to future activities and would be translated by a future in the Greek. Therefore, the only difference that might be noticed in Greek is the lack of a conjunction, as is the case in these three examples. Other adjustments in aspect made by the 𝔐 also

---

17. There are three plural forms of the 𝔐 that are probably singular in the 𝔐 (28:3; 35:25; 39:21) and eight singular forms of the 𝔐 that are plural in the 𝔐 (25:31 [2x]=37:17 [2x]; 29:9; 31:18; 35:28; 36:8).

18. The 𝔊 "agrees" with the 𝔐 in contrast to the 𝔐 in the use of singular or plural nouns and adjectives four times (25:31; 28:3; 35:25; 39:21 [𝔊 36:28]) and agrees with the 𝔐 in contrast to the 𝔐 in the use of plural nouns and adjectives three times (25:31; 29:9; 35:28). In addition, the 𝔊 uses a plural adjective instead of a singular noun as in the 𝔐 (31:18) and is lacking a translation of the Hebrew text in verses that are either abbreviated or are minuses in the 𝔊 (36:8 [𝔊 37:1]; 37:17 [𝔊 38:13]).

19. Waltke, "Samaritan Pentateuch and the Text," 215.

20. The lack of a conjunction in the 𝔐 may have been due to orthographic confusion between ו and י, but due to the tendency noted by Waltke, I believe that this is a grammatical change rather than an orthographic error.

do not seem to affect the 𝔊 in that the 𝔊 uses Greek forms that are appropriate for the context.[21]

Waltke has noted the tendency of the 𝔐 to use the hiphil over other forms.[22] Some changes to the hiphil in the 𝔐 result in changes in meaning. These will be discussed in the next section. Often, however, the Hebrew forms seem to have approximately the same meanings in several different stems. In the tabernacle accounts, these "irrelevant" changes include changes from both the qal and piel to the hiphil and also one example of a change from a qal passive to a hophal.[23]

Locative he. Waltke notes the frequent omission of the locative *he* suffix and says that "its absence in the SP is best understood as a later modernization of the text of the SP."[24] He then gives several examples of omission and also notes that "sometimes the SP preserves the form where it is omitted in the MT."[25] Within the tabernacle accounts of the 𝔐 and the 𝔔 manuscripts, both of these processes are present, but they are not random processes. All pluses (or "preservations") of the locative *he* in the 𝔐 and 𝔔 manuscripts occur on the directional terms that refer to north, south, and west.[26] The 𝔐 has a locative *he* as a plus on each of the directional terms that was lacking the locative *he* in the 𝔐. The opposite pattern, however, is followed with the adverb שָׁם. All occurrences without the locative *he* in the 𝔐 are maintained in the 𝔐. All occurrences of the locative *he* with שָׁם, except for when it occurs with the verb יעד, are minuses in the 𝔐.[27] The evidence in the 𝔔

---

21. The *waw* conjunctive plus the imperfect of the 𝔐 is retained in the 𝔐 three times (25:2; 27:20; 28:28), but is changed to a *waw* consecutive plus perfect two times (26:24; 35:10). In 35:10, the 𝔊 has translated the conjoined verb forms by means of a participle plus a finite verb, which is a common translation technique noted by Aejmelaeus in "Hebrew *Vorlage* of the Septuagint," 75. For a fuller discussion of parataxis and its translation in the 𝔊, see Anneli Aejmelaeus, *Parataxis in the Septuagint: A Study of the Renderings of the Hebrew Coordinate Clauses in the Greek Pentateuch*, Annales Academiae Scientiarum Fennicae: Dissertationes Humanarum Litterarum, no. 31 (Helsinki: Suomalainen Tiedeakatemia, 1982). One *waw* consecutive plus imperfect used with a participle in the 𝔐 is also changed to a *waw* consecutive plus perfect in the 𝔐 (37:9). The 𝔊 here simply uses a present participial clause, which emphasizes the continuing nature of the activity and could be a translation of either the 𝔐 or 𝔐 forms. The change in aspect in 𝔐 36:29 is a bit more complicated, but the 𝔊 is missing for this verse.
22. Waltke, "Samaritan Pentateuch and the Text," 216.
23. In 27:21, the qal form יַעֲרֹךְ is changed to a hiphil יַעֲרִיךְ; in 35:3, the piel form תְבַעֲרוּ is changed to a hiphil תַבְעִירוּ; and in 30:32, the qal passive form יִיסָךְ is changed to a hophal יוּסַךְ. The 𝔊 translations of all three of these would probably be the same no matter which form was in its Hebrew *Vorlage*.
24. Waltke, "Samaritan Pentateuch and the Text," 217.
25. Ibid.
26. Pluses of the locative *he* in the 𝔐 occur with נֶגֶב (27:9=38:9; 36:23), צָפוֹן (26:20=36:25, 26:35, 27:11=38:11), and יָם (27:12=38:12).
27. The locative *he* with שָׁם is a minus with a variety of verbs (26:33; 30:18; 40:30). The verb יעד does occur once with שָׁם in the 𝔐 (25:22) and this occurrence without the locative *he* is maintained by the 𝔐. All other occurrences of the locative *he* on שָׁם following the verb יעד are either main-

manuscripts is mixed, indicating the probable state of transition that the language was experiencing at that time.[28] Wevers has stated that "grammatical elements are not per se translatable. That is to say translations should involve both decoding the message of a source language and then recoding it in the target language."[29] The locative *he* would seem to qualify as this type of grammatical element that is "not per se translatable." Both שָׁם and שָׁמָּה can be translated by either ἐκεῖ or ἐκεῖθεν in Exodus. An examination of the actual occurrences of ἐκεῖθεν, however, reveals a pattern that is similar to the usage of שָׁמָּה in the 𝔐. When the verb יעד is translated by γνωσθήσομαι, the adverb, whether שָׁם or שָׁמָּה, is translated by ἐκεῖθεν (25:22; 29:42; 30:6, 36).[30] The fact that a similar pattern was shared by the 𝔊 and the 𝔐 does not necessarily indicate that the 𝔊 was using a *Vorlage* similar to the 𝔐, but it may indicate that both the 𝔊 translation and the 𝔐 were sensitive to the manner in which God revealed himself.[31]

Object Marker. According to Waltke, the object marker, אֵת, has often been inserted in the 𝔐 "*to achieve greater clarity.*"[32] As with most grammatical particles, there is no simple rule to explain all the pluses. The three examples of minuses of the object marker, likewise, defy any easy explanation.[33] In a free translation, the

---

tained in the 𝔐 (29:42; 30:6 [located after 26:35 in the 𝔐], 36) or a different verb root is used in the 𝔐 and the locative *he* is a minus (29:43). This shift in the 𝔐 may indicate a change in language with reference to the usage of the locative *he* with certain verbs or it may be that special attention was being given to the concept of God meeting with humans. According to Lowy, the reason for the change of verb root in 𝔐 29:43 was that in the 𝔐 "'meeting God' could not apply to all the people of Israel," but was reserved as the "exclusive prerogative of Moses." See S. Lowy, *The Principles of Samaritan Bible Exegesis* (Leiden: E. J. Brill, 1977), 90.

28. Sanderson says that 4QpaleoExod^m belongs to the same "text-type or traditions" as the 𝔐. (Skehan and others, DJD 9, 66.) This may be true, but it contains three readings that lack the locative *he* and thus agrees with the reading in the 𝔐 as opposed to the 𝔐 (27:9, 11; 36:23). Ulrich says that 4QpaleoGen-Exod^l is a "conservative and careful text" that "lacks the typological expansions of the Exod^m𝔐 tradition, but which in smaller variants sometimes agrees with 𝔐, sometimes with 𝔐, sometimes with Exod^m, and sometimes preserves a unique reading." (Ibid., 23.) This "conservative and careful" text contains one reading with the locative *he* that agrees with the 𝔐 in 27:9, one without the locative *he* that agrees with the 𝔐 in 27:11, and one without the locative *he* in 26:33 that agrees with a variant in the 𝔐. A third manuscript, 4QExod-Lev^f, contains the only example of a minus (with respect to the 𝔐) of the locative *he* from a directional term, north, in 40:22.

29. Wevers, "Use of Versions for Text Criticism," 19.

30. These are the only occurrences of ἐκεῖθεν in Exodus. In several of these verses (29:42; 30:6), there is evidence of a later revision of the 𝔊 from ἐκεῖθεν to ἐκεῖ in order to make the translation more "consistent." Wevers notes that ἐκεῖθεν is connected with "the idiom 'I will be known to you there,'" but does not mention the similarity of this pattern to that of the 𝔐. See WeversText, 268.

31. Alternately, this could be a case of coincidental collocational similarities of verbs in two different languages, but given the theological importance of the event, I tend to doubt that possibility.

32. Waltke, "Samaritan Pentateuch and the Text," 221.

33. In the 𝔐, the object marker is used as a clarifying plus where there is a fronted object (26:35), at the beginning of a list that functions as the direct object (25:29), when there is a change in

Hebrew Vorlage

pluses and minuses of the object marker come close to being one of the "not . . . translatable" particles that Wevers described above. Here again, though, the presence or absence of the object marker has served to separate the interpretation of the 𝔐 from that of the 𝔐 and this does affect decisions about the *Vorlage* of the 𝔊. For instance, in 25:31 the pointing of the 𝔐 indicates a 3fs niphal imperfect verb, but in the 𝔐, the plus of the object marker probably indicates that תעשה was being read as a 2ms qal imperfect, as was also done in the 𝔊.

The 𝔊 translation of 29:22 fairly accurately renders every part of the 𝔐 version, except for the initial part of the list. The fact that this was a perplexing structure is signaled in the 𝔐 by the attempt to clarify the matter by adding an object marker and deleting a *waw* conjunction.[34] A comparison of modern translations likewise indicates the problems that this passage continues to cause.[35] Thus, the object markers, while technically unimportant for the evaluation of the 𝔊 of Exodus, often do either confirm the reading of the text in the 𝔐 or highlight the ambiguity of the passage when the 𝔐 was developing. Rather than being ignored in text critical studies, the plus of object markers in the 𝔐 should be especially noted as indicators of potential problems in interpretation.

Waw Conjunction

According to Waltke, Gesenius noted that "the prefix *waw* is added two hundred times and deleted one hundred times; the LXX, with very few exceptions, follows the SP exactly."[36] While noting that "Gesenius typically overstated the case," Waltke nevertheless agreed with his analysis that the 𝔐 and LXX had "identical secondary expansions," which included the article and conjunctions.[37] Secondary

---

the form of the verb (25:31; 29:21), with the plus of a verb (27:19), when there are changes in the structure of a noun phrase that is the direct object (39:17), and where the normal word order has been disturbed (28:9; 29:22). The object marker is a minus three times (along with an article in the first two examples—27:1; 36:35; 40:14).

34. 4QpaleoExod^m gives a conflated reading that includes both the object marker of the 𝔐 and the *waw* of the 𝔐 in 29:22. In 4QExod-Lev^f, two other pluses of object markers in potentially ambiguous clauses were noted. In 40:14 it was used to mark a direct object and in 40:17 it was used to mark the subject of a hophal verb, which according to Cross is a "not unexpected" usage of the object marker with "the subject of passives." See Ulrich and others, DJD 12, 142.

35. The major translation problem involves deciding whether the first term, חלב, is a generic term in apposition to the following list (NJPS "You shall take from the ram the fat parts—the broad tail, the fat that covers the entrails . . .") or a member of the list (NRSV "You shall also take the fat of the ram, the fat tail, the fat that covers the entrails . . ."). CEV "solves" the translation problem by deleting the generic term "fat" and leaving the members of the list, a tactic that is similar to the one used in the 𝔐, which has read the first "fat" as an adjective modifying the ram and then begins the list with the fat tail as the first item to be removed from the ram. The 𝔊 has "deleted" the "the fat tail" and according to Wevers is reading the fat as a generic term specified more clearly by the following phrase, i.e., "'its fat, even the fat which . . . .'" See WeversNotes, 475.

36. Waltke, "Samaritan Pentateuch and the Text," 230.

37. Ibid.

pluses of conjunctions in the 𝔐 are generally accepted as a "given" and ignored. Steinmann, however, closely examined the textual variants in 1:2-4 and concluded that some of the changes in usage of conjunctions indicate different views of the "unity or disunity that existed in Israel as it entered Egypt."[38] In the tabernacle accounts, one would be hard pressed to assert that major ideological differences are indicated by the changes in conjunctions, but the pluses and minuses are far from haphazard. Most pluses and minuses are due to the desire to clarify grammatical structures and differences in perceived groupings of items.[39] The consistency of the changes in the 𝔐 can be seen in the fact that identical changes were made in both tabernacle accounts.[40]

Contrary to Gesenius' findings, the 𝔊 did not follow the 𝔐 exactly "with very few exceptions."[41] In the pluses of conjunctions in the 𝔐, the 𝔊 tended to follow the 𝔐. In the minuses of conjunctions in the 𝔐, however, the 𝔊 tended to follow the 𝔐 and retain the conjunctions. Both the pluses and minuses in the 𝔊 might be better explained by the acknowledged differences in the Greek and Hebrew languages, especially in lists, which comprise most of the examples in this data. One might conclude that conjunctions that are pluses or minuses in the 𝔐 should just be ignored, but as with other "minor" particles, changes in the conjunctions often accompany other changes. For instance, in 40:31, a conjunction is missing between the names Moses and Aaron. In this same clause, the 3mp verb וְרָחֲצוּ in the 𝔐 has been changed to a 3ms verb וירחץ in the 𝔐. These two changes emphasize the prominence of Moses and "correct" this verse so that it fits better with the

---

38. Steinmann, "Jacob's Family," par. 2.

39. Clause level *waw* conjunctions are most frequently pluses in the 𝔐 that serve to separate two clauses and indicate the relationship between the clauses. In the tabernacle accounts all of these pluses occur when the 𝔐 juxtaposes a verbal clause with a fronted element directly after the preceding clause. These examples occur in what are now initial positions in verses (26:3, 35:24, 29) as well as before final clauses in verses (27:8, 30:32, 36:11). In addition, a conjunction is a plus at the beginning of 27:19, but this is part of a larger change that includes the plus of a verb. The 𝔐 often contains *waw* conjunctions that are pluses in lists. The 𝔐 tends to group items by the absence of *waw* conjunctions, but the 𝔐 tends to use conjunctions between all items in a list, thus eliminating the hierarchical or semantic groupings of the 𝔐. This may be seen in the plus of three *waw* conjunctions in 35:11. Groupings similar to the 𝔐, however, are sometimes maintained, possibly when they are viewed as being in apposition to the preceding element, such as in 35:16, where the stand and basin are the vessels that are being discussed. Other examples of pluses are found in lists (25:6 [2x], 7, 39; 35:17, 18, 19, 25, 31, 35; 39:36, 37, 39, 40, 41) or in juxtaposed nonverbal clauses (38:10).

Minuses of clause level conjunctions and conjunctions within the clause are more diverse in nature. Often these minuses occur before non-verbal clauses (27:10, 11, 14; 36:38); in conjunction with other changes involving the verb or a fronted element (25:19 [𝔐 25:18]; 28:7; 29:33; 30:21); in lists (28:20; 30:28; 31:7, 8 [3x], 9, 10, 11; 35:14, 22); with numbers (38:25, 28); or as indicators of different interpretations (28:4; 29:22; 40:31).

40. Identical minuses of *waw*'s are found in 25:3=35:5; 25:4=35:6; 25:31=37:17; 26:1=36:8 (and a similar phrase in 39:29); 26:16=36:21; and 26:24=36:29.

41. Waltke, "Samaritan Pentateuch and the Text," 230.

surrounding context. Prominence is given to Moses by the use of a 3ms verb with a compound subject.[42] In addition, the change to the *waw*-consecutive imperfect form of the verb in the 𝔐, which is similar to the verbs found in the surrounding context (40:30, 33), has remedied two inconsistencies in the 𝔐. First, it has made the agent, Moses, consistent throughout the passage (at least as far as always having a 3ms verb is concerned). Second, it has made all the activities sequential, rather than retaining the habitual activity of the 𝔐 in 40:31. Both the emphasis on the importance of Moses and the tendency to "correct" inconsistencies in the text are known tendencies of the Samaritans.[43] The 𝔊, in contrast to the 𝔐, follows a text that is similar to the 𝔐, though there has been some syntactical restructuring and reordering of the passage (located in 𝔊 38:27) that may reflect a different approach to "solving" the grammatical inconsistencies of 40:31-32 with respect to the difference in aspect. Thus, the absence of a conjunction, while normally "irrelevant," is one of several changes that mark a shift that has taken place in the text of the 𝔐.

Article

Waltke lists the article as one of the types of "identical secondary expansion" that unite the 𝔊 and the 𝔐.[44] Wevers, in contrast, notes that the "articulation patterns are quite different in the two languages. In fact, the presence or absence of the article in the target language is often irrelevant for the text critic."[45] Within the tabernacle account, the pluses and minuses of articles often are connected with other changes in the understanding of the relationship between two words and with the tendency toward consistency of expression in the 𝔐.[46] As with the *waw* conjunc-

---

42. According to Revell, "A singular component typically stands first in a compound nominal denoting humans which contains one or more such components. This initial component is the "principal" of the compound, it designates the leader or superior among those represented by the compound. . . . The choice of a singular verb recognizes the status of the singular component (already marked by the structure of the compound) as principal, as representing the most important actor in the context. . . ." See E. J. Revell, *The Designation of the Individual: Expressive Usage in Biblical Narrative* (Kampen, Netherlands: Kok Pharos, 1996), 230.

43. See Lowy, *Samaritan Bible Exegesis*, 86-94 for a discussion of the "glorification of Moses by the Samaritans," and pp. 83-85 for a discussion of "the belief in the indefectibility and perfection of the Law (and tradition), which cannot possibly tolerate any contradictions or discrepancies, whether in the text or in interpretation."

44. Waltke, "Samaritan Pentateuch and the Text," 230.

45. Wevers, "Use of Versions for Text Criticism," 19.

46. The reanalysis of a phrase is seen in the definite construct chain תּוֹלַעַת הַשָּׁנִי of the 𝔐 (28:5; 35:25; 39:3), which in the 𝔐 is a definite noun phrase התולעת השני. Most other pluses of articles come between a number and the following noun. The 𝔐 text will often have a definite construct chain with a number followed by an indefinite form of the same chain, as with "five curtains" in 26:3. In the 𝔐, however, the second occurrence of the construct chain also has an article. The pluses of articles after numbers is probably the most frequent type of plus (26:3=36:10; 26:8=36:15; 28:25=39:18; 38:27). Minuses are less frequent and cannot be easily categorized. Pluses and minuses are also found in the 𝔔

tions, the 𝔊 tends to agree with the pluses in the 𝔐, but very seldom does it follow the minuses. This is probably due to the different usages of articles in each language and the frequency with which articles are used in Greek. As with other "irrelevant" particles, however, ignoring the differences in articles can sometimes mean missing a more important point of difference between the 𝔐 and 𝔐. For instance, in the 𝔐 tabernacle accounts, a construct chain מִשְׁכַּן אֹהֶל מוֹעֵד is used to refer to the tabernacle (39:32; 40:2, 6, 29), i.e., tabernacle of (the) tent of meeting. In the 𝔐, however, an article is added to the word מִשְׁכָּן in all four occurrences of the phrase. Thus, the construct chain of the 𝔐 becomes a definite noun followed by a construct chain in apposition to it, המשכן אהל מועד, i.e., the tabernacle, that is, (the) tent of meeting. The 𝔊 translates this phrase with a phrase similar to σκηνὴν τοῦ μαρτυρίου.[47] If the Hebrew *Vorlage* used by the 𝔊 was similar to that of the 𝔐, then even more credence is given to the choice of collapsing the two ways of referring to the tabernacle into one phrase in the 𝔊.[48]

Summary

Most text critics agree that many grammatical categories are irrelevant for the purpose of evaluating the 𝔊 translation. Hebrew variants that fall into this category of "irrelevant" changes include changes in grammatical gender; some changes in state and number of nouns and adjectives; some changes in aspect and stem of verbs; and the presence or absence of the locative *he*, the object marker, the article, and the *waw* conjunction. The majority of these variants are probably correctly considered to be "irrelevant," but the text critic who takes the time to investigate these minutiae is often rewarded for the effort. Besides providing evidence of probable linguistic change in the Hebrew language, the "irrelevant" changes in the tabernacle accounts of the 𝔐 shed light on translations in the 𝔊 that have often been considered slightly deficient. Other "irrelevant" changes point towards interpretations shared by the 𝔐 and 𝔊 and a few changes point to interpretations that are only found in the 𝔐, such as the increased emphasis on Moses. Above all, these "irrelevant" changes in the 𝔐 often indicate the presence of an ambiguity in the text. Translators frequently have to resolve such ambiguities before a passage can be translated. Thus, these minute changes in the 𝔐 often indicate the places where translation decisions would have had to have been made and the resulting 𝔊 translation reflects those decisions.

manuscripts. When the 𝔐 and 𝔐 differ, the 𝔔 manuscripts sometimes agree with the 𝔐 (4QpaleoExod[m] 26:8; 4QpaleoGen-Exod[l] 27:7) and sometimes agree with the 𝔐 (4QExod-Lev[f] 39:17). Some pluses, however, are not found in either the 𝔐 or the 𝔐 (4QpaleoExod[m] 29:22; 4QExod-Lev[f] 40:14, 21). The presence of these variants in the 𝔔 manuscripts simply affirm that there were variations present in early times and that they are not simply corruptions unique to the 𝔐.

47. This form of the phrase is seen in 40:2, 6. In 39:32 (𝔊 39:9) and 40:29, this phrase is part of a larger phrase and is translated as τῆς σκηνῆς τοῦ μαρτυρίου.

48. In many modern functional equivalent translations, the phrases are assumed to be in apposition and one phrase is used instead of two (CEV, *Tok Pisin*).

between the 𝕞 and the 𝕲 in the choice of pronominal references is rather unusual because languages often differ greatly in the use of pronouns. This suggests that either the 𝕲 had a *Vorlage* similar to the 𝕞 or that these changes are a part of a larger set of changes that the 𝕲 has made in participant referencing. The ℚ manuscripts contain only a few examples of this type of change with only one clear example of a variant not found in the other traditions.[53]

Verbs. The 𝕞 and ℚ manuscripts generally agree with the 𝔐 in the area of person and number of verbs. Within the tabernacle accounts of the 𝕞, however, there are at least thirty-two changes in the person and number of verbs. Of these changes, the 𝕞 and 𝕲 agreed against the 𝔐 fourteen times, the 𝕲 agreed with the 𝔐 against the 𝕞 eight times, each tradition took a separate route eight times, and two times the 𝕲 was missing a verse in which there was a change in the 𝕞. On the surface level, the 𝕲 does appear to share more agreements with the 𝕞, but a closer examination of the data gives a slightly different picture. In 25-28, the 𝔐 fluctuates between 2ms, 2mp, and occasionally 3mp and 3ms in the instructions part of the tabernacle accounts. The 𝕞 tends to smooth out some of these differences and uses the 2ms form more consistently, a tactic that is also followed by the 𝕲.[54] In addition, the 𝕲 continues the same process of adjustment and has a 2s verb form in several places where the 𝕞 has a 3mp instead of the 3ms of the 𝔐.[55] In the actual construction part of the tabernacle accounts, 35-40, the 𝕞 and 𝔐 both switch back and forth between 3ms and 3mp with no consistent pattern in their differences.[56] When the 𝕞 differs from the 𝔐, the 𝕲 tends to use the 3p form of the

---

decision to follow B, which has no possessive pronoun, but did so because he failed to see any "particular pattern" in the possessive pronouns in the list. (WeversText, 188.) Thus, the one "exception" to the pattern of agreements of the 𝕲 with the 𝕞 in this type of pronominal usage is suspect, to say the least. For a further discussion of this "exception," see chapter three.

53. In 40:16, 4QExod-Lev^f has a 3mp suffix אותם rather than the 3ms אות that is in the 𝔐 and the 𝕞 and that is also reflected in the 𝕲 translation. Cross calls this a "*lapsus calami*," i.e., a slip of the pen, though he also discusses other possible reconstructions. (Ulrich and others, DJD 12, 142.) Both 4QpaleoGen-Exod^l and 4QpaleoExod^m seem to provide support for the reading וְיֵי הָעַמֻּדִים in 𝔐 27:11, but the phrase is not complete in either manuscript.

54. In 25-28, the 𝕞 and 𝕲 agree in this type of change to the 2s, as follows: 25:9, 10, 19, 37, 39 (moved to the end of 𝕲 25:38); 27:7.

55. In 25:29 and 26:31, the 𝔐 has 3s, the 𝕞 has 3p, and the 𝕲 has 2s. In addition to the commands, the 𝕞 differs from the 𝔐 in two descriptive clauses. In 25:28, the 3ms niphal of the 𝔐 has been changed to a 3mp qal, but the 𝕲 agrees with the 𝔐 and uses a 3ms passive form. In 25:37, the 𝔐 refers to the light shining by using a 3ms form (probably referring to the entire lampstand and lights as a unit), but the 𝕞 and the 𝕲 use a 3p form that probably refers to the multiplicity of lamps that are discussed in the immediate context.

56. The 𝕞 probably tends to use more 3mp forms, but because of the use of 3ms forms with collective noun phrases in the 𝕞, i.e., phrases with "all" (35:10 [2x], 22, 25) and coordinated noun phrases (36:6; 40:31), the total count of 3mp versus 3ms forms is about the same in both the 𝔐 and the 𝕞.

verb, which means that it alternately agrees with either the 𝔐 or the 𝔘 depending on which of these has the 3p form.⁵⁷ That the 𝔊 agrees with one versus the other is not significant, because the agreements are accidental to the apparent attempt at consistency in the 𝔊.⁵⁸ Changes in the 𝔘 form of 29-31 occur in material that is more descriptive or procedural in nature rather than being direct commands to Moses. The 𝔊 agrees with the changes made by the 𝔘 against the 𝔐 in three out of six times.⁵⁹ The pattern of agreements may, however, be more coincidental than real because the changes involve the handling of the choice of singular versus plural verbs with coordinate subjects and collective nouns. In both Greek and Hebrew, the author's choice of singular and plural is influenced by a variety of factors including the prominence of the subject(s).⁶⁰ The 𝔊 tends to "agree" with the 𝔘 in the treatment of collectives, but not with the consistent tendency of the 𝔘 to give prominence to Moses over Aaron and Aaron over his sons.⁶¹ When all examples of the phrase "Aaron and his sons" in the subject position within the tabernacle accounts are collected and compared, the uniqueness of the approach of the 𝔘 stands out clearly. All six occurrences of "Aaron and his sons" are used with singular verbs in the 𝔘, whereas in the 𝔐 and 𝔊 the examples are divided between 3s and 3p verbs with no clear pattern of agreement between the two traditions, i.e.,

---

57. This difference is especially noticeable in 39 (𝔊 36) in the translation of the verb עשׂה by ποιέω. In 39:2, 8, and 22, the 𝔐 has 3ms forms, the 𝔘 has 3mp forms and the 𝔊 has 3p forms (𝔊 36:9, 15, 29). In 39:4 and 39:9, however, the 𝔐 has 3mp forms, the 𝔘 has 3ms forms, and the 𝔊 has 3p forms (𝔊 36:11 [connected with the previous verse in the critical text] and 𝔊 36:16). In addition, there are three other examples of the 𝔊 sharing the 3p with the 𝔐 in contrast to 3ms of the 𝔘 (35:22; 36:6; 40:31 [𝔊 38:27]) and one additional example of 𝔊 sharing the 3p with the 𝔘 in contrast to the infinitive absolute of the 𝔐 (36:7).

58. In the eight other places where the 𝔘 differs from the 𝔐 in 35-40, the 𝔊 is either missing (36:31), has used an infinitive (35:25, 35), or has made other adjustments in the verb form. These include the probable reading of the 3fs niphal form of the 𝔐 as a 2ms form (35:2), the use of a passive in addition to other changes (39:3 [𝔊 36:10]), the use of a 3ms form that agrees with the 𝔐 (39:7 [𝔊 36:14]), and the use of a participle plus 3s verb, in agreement with the 𝔘, as a translation of two conjoined verbs with a collective subject (35:10).

59. In 30:4 and 30:14, the 𝔘 and 𝔊 have 3p forms in contrast to the 3ms form of the 𝔐, which is being used in a collective or distributive sense. In 30:19, both the 𝔊 and 𝔘 use a 3s form that gives prominence to Aaron in contrast to the 3mp form in the 𝔐.

60. For Greek, see Daniel B. Wallace, *Greek Grammar Beyond the Basics: An Exegetical Syntax of the New Testament* (Grand Rapids, Mich.: Zondervan, 1996), 400-402. For Hebrew, see Revell, *Designation of the Individual*, 221-41.

61. This tendency was discussed earlier in reference to 40:31, where the 𝔊 (𝔊 38:27) agrees with the 𝔐. In 𝔘 29:21, Moses is given prominence by changing a descriptive clause into a transitive clause with Moses as the subject, which also makes the clause more consistent with the surrounding material. In 𝔘 29:15, Aaron is given prominence over his sons through the use of the singular verb form, but the 𝔊 uses forms that are more in agreement with the 𝔐 both here and in 29:21. As noted above, however, the 𝔊 does "agree" with the 𝔘 in the prominence given to Aaron in 30:19.

the 𝔊 and 𝔐 follow the usage that is viewed as appropriate for that language in the specific context.[62]

In addition to changes in person and number, the 𝔐𝔐 four times has a hiphil form of בוא instead of the qal or hophal form as in the 𝔐. In two of these (35:21, 22) the 𝔊 appears to agree with the 𝔐𝔐 by its choice of φέρω as a translation equivalent, but in 36:4, the 𝔊 agrees with the 𝔐, as is shown by its choice of παραγίνομαι, a common translation equivalent in Exodus for the qal form of בוא. These apparent agreements between the 𝔐𝔐 and 𝔊, however, are not as clear cut as they would first appear because the 𝔐 has a hiphil form of בוא shortly after the qal form in both 35:21 and 35:22. The difference in context alone could have brought the 𝔊 into apparent agreement with the 𝔐𝔐. In 27:7, however, the 𝔊 clearly follows a Hebrew *Vorlage* similar to that of the 𝔐𝔐, והבאת, as indicated by both the usage of the 2s verbal ending and the choice of translation equivalent, i.e., εἰσάγω.

The ꝘQ manuscripts of the tabernacle accounts contribute very little to the discussion of the *Vorlage* of the 𝔊 in the area of morphological changes of verb forms. A 3ms verb form (28:11) and a 2mp verb form (28:41) are attested in 4QpaleoExod^m and the variants of an infinitive absolute (40:10) and a hiphil imperfect in conjunction with a change in order (40:12) are found in 4QExod-Lev^f. In all of these verses, the 𝔐, 𝔐𝔐, and 𝔊 are in agreement and differ from the readings in the ꝘQ manuscripts. This unified witness of the 𝔐, 𝔐𝔐, and 𝔊 shows that while variants did occasionally occur due to a variety of factors, they were not the accepted norms of the three main traditions. The changes that were accepted into these traditions were ones that led to increasing consistency.

Changes in Order

Changes in order that are not accompanied by other types of changes do not normally affect the referential meaning of the passage, but they often affect emphasis and in larger changes of order, the interpretation of a passage may also be affected by being in a new context. In the 𝔐𝔐 recension of the tabernacle accounts, changes of order are found both on the clause level and in the reordering of a verse or an entire passage. If the *Vorlage* of the 𝔊 had been similar to the 𝔐𝔐, then one would expect the larger changes of order to be present, but changes in the word order

---

62. The 𝔐 uses 3ms verbs four times (27:21; 29:10, 19, 32) and 3mp verbs two times (29:15; 30:19). The 𝔊, in contrast uses 3s verbs three times (27:21; 29:19; 30:19) and 3p verbs three times (29:10, 15, 32). Since the 𝔐𝔐 is consistent in this matter, the important facts are that the 𝔐 and 𝔊 only agree once on the choice of 3p verbs and that the 𝔊 has two unique usages of 3p verbs and the 𝔐 has one unique usage of a 3p verb. Thus, in the choice of 3p verbs with the compound subject "Aaron and his sons," each tradition has used a separate tactic that only coincidentally agrees at times due to the fact that only two options are available with each verb, i.e., 3s or 3p. In addition to these examples, there is a similar agreement of the 𝔐 and 𝔊 in 40:31 (𝔊 38:27), but this compound contains an additional agent, Moses, and so it has not been included here.

within a verse would be partially dependent on the translation techniques used. Greek word order is flexible and thus could reflect some of the changes seen in the 𝕸.

Word Order. In the 𝕸 there are at least ten changes of word order that occur within a verse. Of these, the 𝕲 follows an order like that of the 𝕸 in three verses.[63] One change of order found in the 𝕸 and followed by the 𝕲 is an inversion of noun and number (26:10). This change of order is also seen in 4QpaleoExod[m]. The only other change of this type in the 𝕼 manuscripts is a change of order from verb-subject to subject-verb in 4QExod-Lev[f] (40:12), a change that is not reflected in any other tradition. In the places where the 𝕲 does agree with the word order of the 𝕸, the resulting change either creates an exactly parallel structure in a verbal clause (40:38) or it creates a chiastic-like reversal of the order found in an identical noun phrase (26:10) or a parallel non-verbal clause (26:8). Thus, the changes in the 𝕲 that "agree" with the 𝕸 may be parallel stylistic changes rather than clear examples of agreement.

Other changes of order in the tabernacle accounts of the 𝕸 do not involve parallel structures and are not followed by the 𝕲. Sanderson dismissed these changes saying,

> The one moderate difference, 29.21, is easily explainable as parablepsis later corrected. Scarcely any of the others give evidence of anything other than scribal lapses. Once again we see how close these two traditions are.[64]

On the contrary, rather than being scribal lapses, some of these changes are examples of the known tendency of the 𝕸 to "correct" the text to make it more like the later portions of the Pentateuch. For instance, in 25:29, the 𝕸 order of jugs and bowls, וּקְשׂוֹתָיו וּמְנַקִּיֹּתָיו, is "corrected" to the order, וּמְנַקִיֹּתָיו וּקְשׂתָיו, which is found in the 𝕸 in 37:16 and Num 4:7.[65] Some changes of order (26:8, 10) are "corrections" to make the phrases like those found in the parallel 𝕸 text (36:15, 17). Likewise, the change in 29:18, in addition to making it parallel to the previous

---

63. The 𝕲 appears to agree with the 𝕸 against the 𝕸 word order three times (26:8, 10; 40:38). In the remaining examples the 𝕲 either seems to agree with the order of the 𝕸 (25:29; 29:18, 21; 30:13, 19; 36:1) or the use of an idiom prevents any direct comparison of word order (35:29). The agreement between 𝕸 and 𝕲 in 36:1, however, may be more apparent than real because the 𝕲 has used a passive verb instead of an active verb as in the 𝕸.

64. Judith E. Sanderson, *An Exodus Scroll from Qumran: 4QpaleoExod[m] and the Samaritan Tradition* (Atlanta, Ga.: Scholars Press, 1986), 235.

65. Each language has accepted orderings of word pairs. Changing the order of a word pair, for instance, "jelly and peanut butter" instead of "peanut butter and jelly," does not change the meaning in American English, but for the native speaker the second order is the "correct" order. These kinds of preferences in word order can change or become more established with the passage of time.

phrase in the verse, also makes it parallel to an identical phrase in Lev 8:21. Other changes in word order in the ⅏ result in changes of emphasis within the clause.⁶⁶

Verse Order. The placement of ⅏ 29:21 after 29:28 was initially explained by Sanderson as "parablepsis later corrected." In her later work, however, this change of verse ordering was more correctly analyzed as an adjustment that "agrees with the fulfillment of the command as recorded in ⅏ 𝔐 𝔊 of Lev 8:22-30."⁶⁷ The ⅏ recension corrects the order of the instructions in 29:21 so that it matches the order of the fulfillment in Lev 8:30, i.e., the anointing taking place after the giving of the offerings (29:27-28; Lev 8:29). In addition to the change in order of the verse itself, there is also a change in order of the blood and oil that makes it more nearly similar to Lev 8:30. The 𝔊 reflects neither of these changes in order.

The major change in order in the ⅏ tabernacle accounts and also 4Qpaleo-oExodᵐ, according to Sanderson, is the placement of 𝔐 30:1-10 after 𝔐 26:35.⁶⁸ Sanderson includes a lengthy discussion of the differences between the placement of this passage in the various traditions and notes that "in the account of the construction, ⅏ 𝔐 . . . place the incense altar in an order which seems logical: . . . ."⁶⁹ In the instructions part of the tabernacle accounts, however, she claims,

> Neither order seems obviously superior or inferior to the other judging from context, nor is it obvious that or why anyone would have deliberately transposed these ten verses from one of these positions to the other.⁷⁰

Sanderson concludes by saying, "Since neither order seems correct, neither can be chosen as preferable; it may well be that both reflect insertions of a secondary pericope."⁷¹

In response to Sanderson's evaluation of the text, it should be noted that she seems to be focusing on this text as being just a list of instructions for building the

---

66. The fronting of the prepositional phrase in ⅏ 30:19 may be a correction to make the verse more like the order found in 40:31, which in the ⅏ also contains a similar change in the form of the verb. This change in order may, however, be similar to the changes in 35:29 and 36:1, in which the "normal" Hebrew word order is changed, thus emphasizing the displaced item. See Christo H. J. van der Merwe, Jackie A. Naudé, and Jan H. Kroeze, *A Biblical Hebrew Reference Grammar* (Sheffield: Sheffield Academic Press, 1999), 336-50, for a discussion of word order and emphasis in Hebrew. The change of word order in 40:38 may result in a change of emphasis, but more likely it is a change to create parallelism, a change that the 𝔊 likewise made, as noted above.

67. Compare Sanderson, *Exodus Scroll from Qumran*, 235 and Skehan and others, DJD 9, 118.

68. Sanderson's arguments for the presence of this change of order in 4QpaleoExodᵐ are largely based on reconstructed order and estimations of the space that would have been available for the text rather than on a large amount of direct textual evidence, since only three words of the pericope are extant. See Sanderson, *Exodus Scroll from Qumran*, 111-15. See also Skehan and others, DJD 9, 113.

69. Sanderson, *Exodus Scroll from Qumran*, 113.

70. Ibid., 111.

71. Ibid., 115.

tabernacle and thus fails to grasp the main point of the passage. According to Longacre's analysis of the linguistic features of the passage,

> The Peak of the whole text can plausibly be considered to be 29:38-46. That this is clearly meant to be a major section—although consisting of only one paragraph—is seen by the use of a cleft sentence in its introduction (29:38).
>
> This is, in a sense, the "target" of the whole discourse: the institution of the daily worship.
>
> . . . .
>
> The consecration of the priests in prepeak and the construction and projected implementation of the incense altar in postpeak partake of some of the culminating tension that is expressed in the peak itself.[72]

When the reader grasps the main purpose of the passage, the "logic" of the 𝔐 order becomes more comprehensible.

Meyers, likewise, examined the 𝔐 order to discern the reason for the "odd" placement of the instructions for the construction of the incense altar. Her conclusion is worth quoting in totality.

> The connection of the golden incense altar with the three realms of sanctity of the tabernacle complex thus sets it apart from the golden appurtenances of the outer sanctum, or the middle zone, that were otherwise similar in conception and material. The text of Exodus 25-27 signifies an ordered sacred reality. As such, the text could not be disrupted by the presence of an object that functionally interrupted this order. The golden altar of incense is hardly misplaced in its present position. It appears outside the carefully graded sequence of the core of the prescriptive texts precisely because it crosses the realms of sanctity that the texts represent with such exquisite precision.[73]

It is to be noted that Meyers, approaching the text from a very different perspective, has, like Longacre, focused on the ritual acts, the worship, as being the key to understanding the placement of the incense altar in the text. Contra Sanderson, there is a reasonable explanation for the placement of the construction of the incense altar in the 𝔐 version of the text.

Sanderson's claim that there is no "obvious" reason for moving these ten verses is also incorrect. The change in placement of 30:1-10 fits well with the demonstrated practice of the 𝔐 to "correct" the text to make it more like parallel sections later in the Pentateuch. These corrections never involve major changes to the actual text, but as seen in the smaller examples above, reordering was an accepted method of "correcting" the Hebrew text. In the construction section of

---

72. Robert E. Longacre, "Building for the Worship of God: Exodus 25:1-30:10," in *Discourse Analysis of Biblical Literature: What It Is and What It Offers*, ed. Walter R. Bodine (Atlanta, Ga.: Scholars Press, 1995), 32-34.

73. Carol L. Meyers, "Realms of Sanctity: The Case of the "Misplaced" Incense Altar in the Tabernacle Texts of Exodus," in *Texts, Temples and Traditions: A Tribute to Menahem Haran*, ed. Michael V. Fox, et al. (Winona Lake, Ind.: Eisenbrauns, 1996), 46.

Table 1. "Reordering" of items in the 𝕄

Items discussed	Order in 𝕄 form of instructions	Order in construction account	Order in final list	Order in placement
lampstand	25:31-40	37:17-24	39:37	40:4b
tabernacle and placement of table and lampstand	26:1-35	—	—	—
golden altar	30:1-5	37:25-28	39:38a	40:5a
placement of golden altar and worship with incense	30:6-10	—	—	—
oil and incense	—	37:29	39:38b	—
screen at tent's entrance	26:36-37	—	39:38c	40:5b
bronze altar	27:1-8	38:1-7	39:39	40:6

the tabernacle account, the key passages that are the basis for understanding the placement of 30:1-10 in the 𝕄 are 39:38-39 and 40:4b-6. Both of these lists and the actual construction account in 37:17-38:7 place the three major items (lampstand, golden altar, and bronze altar) in the same order. In table 1 the order of these lists and the construction account are placed in comparison with the order of the 𝕄 (using the verse numbering of the 𝕞) in 25:31-27:8.

Since the 𝕄 seems to accept expansionary pluses, as will be seen later in this chapter, the presence of the extra sections about the tabernacle and worship was probably not viewed as a disruption of the order.[74] Earlier in this section I noted that the 𝕄 often "corrected" the order of minor items. It is my suggestion that the 𝕄 likewise corrected this problem in the order of a major item of the tabernacle, the golden altar. Therefore, the order in the 𝕄 is probably a secondary variant rather than a synonymous variant whose status cannot be determined, as claimed by Sanderson. The order of the 𝕲 has not been affected by this change of order in the 𝕄.

---

74. See Jeffrey H. Tigay, ed., *Empirical Models for Biblical Criticism* (Philadelphia: University of Pennsylvania Press, 1985), especially chap. 2, "Conflation as a Redactional Technique."

Synonymous Variants

Within the tabernacle accounts of the 𝔐, there are synonymous variants that involve the substitution of one phrase or word for an equivalent phrase or word. Many of these synonymous variants may be the result of changes in language usage or confusion due to phonological convergence, but only occasionally does a synonymous variant affect the meaning. Most synonymous variants do not have a clear affect on the 𝔊 because the 𝔊 has chosen a separate way of expressing the idea. There are, however, several prepositions, nouns, and participles in the 𝔐 that may reflect more accurately the *Vorlage* of the 𝔊.

Prepositions. Prepositions that are synonymous variants most frequently involve the exchange of עַל and אֶל. Cross says that this is due to the loss of contrast between the way the two words were pronounced, i.e., phonological convergence.[75] While this may indeed be true, many of the changes seem to have a semantic component or are affected by the attempt in the 𝔐 to make the text more consistent grammatically. For instance, 25:11 contains the only example of a gold molding being made "upon" עַל rather than the more common expression of being made "for" לְ. The 𝔐 has "corrected" 25:11 to the more common grammatical construction.[76] Other corrections are either a correction of the form in the first account to that of the second account or a "correction" of both accounts in the 𝔐.[77] The fact that it is not a sporadic change is also seen in the fact that the "corrections" can go in either direction, i.e., עַל to אֶל or אֶל to עַל, and usages with the same verbs are all changed even when they are not in parallel accounts.[78] The remaining synonymous variants that involve prepositions can probably best be explained by a growing differentiation between the functions of the two prepositions, with אֶל being increasingly used for directional motion and עַל being used more for a location in relationship to another item rather than including a directional component.[79] For instance, when נתן is used with the meaning of "put" in 28:30, the 𝔐 has used the locative preposition עַל rather than the directional preposition אֶל, as in the 𝔐. The 𝔊 also reflects this interpretation of נתן, which connects it with a locative meaning. As a result, it has translated the verb with ἐπι-

---

75. According to Cross, "The confusion of אֶל and עַל is frequent owing to the falling together of the two in pronunciation in the late period." See Ulrich and others, DJD 12, 142.

76. Similar phrases may be found in the 𝔐 25:24, 25; 30:3; 37:2, 11, 12, 26.

77. Corrections of the first account of the 𝔐 to that of the second are found in 28:7=39:4; 28:24=39:17. The phrases in both accounts of the 𝔐 have been changed in 28:26=39:19.

78. Nonparallel corrections can be seen in 26:12, 13.

79. This factor is probably involved in other changes of עַל and אֶל that are found in the 𝔐 (25:37; 26:24). Changes of other prepositions are also found in the 𝔐 (26:4=36:11; 26:25; 27:19; 35:30). There were, however, too few examples of these other prepositions in the tabernacle accounts to make any suggestions about the reason for these changes. Three examples of other changes of prepositions were noted in the 𝔔 manuscripts (4QpaleoExod^m 37:13; 4QExod-Lev^f 40:20, 22).

τίθημι and the preposition with ἐπί, which is the normal translation equivalent of עַל. In 30:16, however, the opposite direction has been taken. The 𝔐 has interpreted נתן with the meaning of "give" with a directional preposition אל being used to indicate that the "work" was the "recipient" of the silver that was given, rather than עַל as in the 𝔐. The 𝔊 again follows the same interpretation using δίδωμι to translate נתן and εἰς to translate the preposition. This "agreement" of the 𝔊 and 𝔐 does not necessarily mean that the *Vorlage* of the 𝔊 was similar to that of the 𝔐. Rather, the interpretive decisions of the 𝔊, as seen in the usage of different verbs to translate נתן, affected the choice of prepositions and created a surface level agreement in translation equivalents between the 𝔐 and 𝔊. The most that can be said is that the 𝔊 and 𝔐 shared the same interpretive heritage.[80]

Nouns, Adjectives, and Participles. Synonymous variants that involve nouns, adjectives, and participles in the 𝔐 include corrections of inconsistencies in the 𝔐 and the substitution of words that are almost synonymous.[81] These changes do not seem to be reflected in the 𝔊. In addition, there are several changes that are probably orthographic or due to inner Hebrew corruptions of the 𝔐.[82] Most of

---

80. This same "agreement" between the 𝔊 and 𝔐 is also seen in 28:7. In one example, the 𝔊 could be said to agree with the 𝔐 against the 𝔐 (26:13). A more tenuous "agreement" of the 𝔐 and 𝔊 may occur in 26:25, but in the remaining instances where the 𝔐 differs from the 𝔐, one would be hard pressed to say that the 𝔊 agrees specifically with either the 𝔐 or the 𝔐 against the other tradition.

81. Corrections of the text may be seen in 27:18 where the 𝔐 has substituted בַאמה for a difficult phrase, בַּחֲמִשִׁים, but the 𝔊 faithfully follows the tradition reflected in the 𝔐. In 26:35 the 𝔐 has substituted ירך for צֶלַע and in 27:15, פאה for כָּתֵף. Both of these pairs share translation equivalents in Greek. The choice of equivalents is controlled more by the context than by the Hebrew *Vorlage*. The change in 𝔐 27:15 does not seem to be for the purpose of consistency, but the change in 26:35 is probably due to the fact that יֶרֶךְ הַמִּשְׁכָּן is the phrase more commonly used in the 𝔐 with the preposition עַל. The phrase used in the 𝔐, צֶלַע הַמִּשְׁכָּן, is more commonly found in a phrase describing the boards (e.g., 26:26, 27), rather than as a location (40.22, 24). Thus, the context may have been the factor that influenced the 𝔐 to "correct" the text. Similarly, in 27:11, the 𝔐 has substituted בַאמה for אֹרֶךְ. This synonymous variant makes it more nearly parallel 38:11 and it also clears up a difficult phrase, אֹרֶךְ מֵאָה, that is especially difficult because the word "length" is already present in the clause. The 𝔊 likewise resolves the problem following an interpretation similar to the 𝔐, i.e., adding the implicit information that the "one hundred" was referring to cubits. In contrast to the 𝔐, however, the 𝔊 resolves the issue of the double occurrence of the word for length by deleting the first occurrence, rather than the second occurrence, as was done in the 𝔐. The 𝔊 parallel to this verse (𝔊 37:9) contains a different translation problem and the changes in 27:11 do not make the two more nearly parallel in the 𝔊. Thus, any move towards parallelism would have had to have been in the Hebrew *Vorlage* only. If the Hebrew *Vorlage* was like the 𝔐, then this change in the 𝔊 would simply illustrate the translator's tendency to make implicit information explicit.

82. Spelling differences or other variants within the 𝔐 tradition that do not seem to affect the 𝔊 may be seen in the following differences between the 𝔐 and the 𝔐: עֶבֶר (𝔐) and חבר (𝔐) (25:37; 28:26=39:19); יְדֹתָיו (𝔐) and יתדתיו (𝔐) (26:19 [2x]=36:24 [2x]); אוּרִי (𝔐) and חורי (𝔐) (31:2; 35:30; 38:22). The use of the synonymous variant מקטיר (𝔐) instead of מִקְטַר (𝔐) in 30:1 may be a difference in form or spelling, but it seemingly has no effect on the 𝔊 translation. The use of the synonymous variant הכפרת (𝔐) instead of הַפָּרֹכֶת (𝔐) in 40:3 may be due to a scribal error or the accidental

the differences in spelling will not be discussed as they rarely affect translation. The 𝔐 contains several examples, however, in which two very similar words are used for the same item, often within the same verse.[83] The 𝔐 "corrects" several of these discrepancies and the 𝔊 reflects a similar tradition. For instance, in 26:4 the 𝔐 uses both חֹבֶרֶת and מַחְבֶּרֶת. A surface level examination of the 𝔐 would suggest that the longer form of the word, מַחְבֶּרֶת, has been chosen and used in both places in an attempt to make the text consistent, but this hypothesis fails to explain all the differences. A comparison with the 𝔊, however, provides the needed insight for solving the problem. In the text of the 𝔐, a noun and a participle from the same root are used, whereas in the 𝔐 there are two nouns and a participle. When the 𝔐 has used the nominal form, מחברת, the 𝔊 has consistently used the term συμβολή.[84] When the 𝔐 has used a participle, חברת, the 𝔊 has used the participial forms of two different verb roots—συνέχω and συνάπτω.[85] This could, however, just be a coincidental agreement based on a similar interpretation that assumes that חברת with the preposition ב is a noun and that the same form with the article or with no prefix is a participle. Likewise, every form of מַחְבֶּרֶת is assumed to be a noun that is synonymous with חֹבֶרֶת. Because four verses containing these terms are minuses in the 𝔊, there are too few examples to allow a firm conclusion to be reached, but the 𝔊 definitely shared the same interpretation as the 𝔐, if not a similar text as its *Vorlage*.[86]

Verbs. Very few synonymous variants occur in finite verb forms in the tabernacle accounts of the 𝔐. Of these, most changes only occur once and thus I can only speculate about the reasons for the changes.[87] One change is part of the nor-

---

substitution of another item that is commonly placed on the ark. In either case, the change has not affected the 𝔊, which follows the tradition seen in the 𝔐.

83. The 𝔐 uses שַׁרְשְׁרֹת three times (28:14 [2x]; 39:15) and שַׁרְשֹׁת one time (28:22). The 𝔐 has eliminated this inconsistency and has written all occurrences as שרשרות. The 𝔊 follows its own strategy using κροσσωτός and κροσσός, as will be discussed in chapter five.

84. See 𝔐 26.4 (2x), 5, 10; 39:20 (𝔊 36:27).

85. The plural participle חברות is used in 𝔐 26:3 [2x] while the singular is found in 𝔐 26:10. There is an inner Greek variant, the participle of ἔχω, that is found as the translation equivalent of the first occurrence of חברות in 𝔐 26:3.

86. A similar phenomenon is also seen in 26:24 and its parallel in 36:29, which in the 𝔐 contain תֹּאֲמִים and תַּמִּים. In the 𝔐, however, תאמים occurs twice in both verses. Only 26:24 is found in the 𝔊 translation and ἴσος is seemingly used to translate both terms. This points to an interpretive tradition or text similar to that of the 𝔐. Elsewhere in Exodus, and even in the entire Pentateuch, this translation equivalent is not found for תַּמִּים.

87. The use of the synonymous variant דרש instead of יעד in 29:43 was part of a composite change mentioned in the discussion of the locative *he*. In 36:6, the 𝔐 has ויכל instead of וַיִּכָּלֵא. This may be a change in the root from כלא to כלה. A similar change is found in Gen 8:2, but the verb root only occurs once in 𝔐 Exodus, which limits what can be said. In addition there was one change from פרש to נתן in 4QExod-Lev^f (40:19) and a minor change in form that Sanderson considered to be an error in 4QpaleoExod^m (31:4). See Sanderson, *Exodus Scroll from Qumran*, 90.

mal pattern of "correcting" similar passages.⁸⁸ The only recurring change is the interchange of אמר and דבר, which has been thoroughly discussed by Sanderson. Her conclusion is that "These variations may indicate some degree of concern within the 𝕸 tradition to alternate the verbs in such cases for the sake of variety."⁸⁹ There are only three variants of this type in the tabernacle accounts of the 𝕸.⁹⁰ Of these, only one (31:12) is possibly reflected in the 𝕲 usage of ἐλάλησεν instead of the typical εἶπεν. Other factors, however, may have influenced this change in the 𝕸 towards the more frequent use of דבר. In Miller's discussion of speech in the Pentateuchal legislation, she notes that "more utterances introduced with דבר לאמר are attributed to YHWH than to any other participant in the narratives."⁹¹ Two of the verbs changed in the 𝕸 (30:34; 31:12) would fall into this category and make YHWH's "speeches" consistently introduced in the same way. If this "reported speech" is also functioning as "a narrative trope to structure and segment the narrative,"⁹² then the changes would also affect the narrative structure by highlighting the instructions for the incense (30:34-38) and the rules for the Sabbath (31:12-17). The other example in the tabernacle accounts in which the 𝕸 has substituted דבר for אמר is 36:5. According to Miller's analysis of speech in Biblical Hebrew narrative, 36:5 in the 𝕸 represents a usage of אמר לאמר for "choral speech," a function that is more frequently indicated by דבר לאמר, the form used in the 𝕸.⁹³ These changes in the 𝕸 may have been for the sake of "variety," but as the text was changed, it was intuitively changed to patterns that made the text more consistent and at the same time changed the text towards the forms used more frequently for certain functions in Hebrew narrative. The 𝕲 translation follows neither the 𝕸 nor the 𝕸 consistently on these three changes. Instead, the translator(s) seem to translate according to their perception of the context.⁹⁴

Phrases. Most phrases that are synonymous variants in the 𝕸, whether they involve substitution of a different grammatical structure or a different wording,

---

88. In 40:22 the 𝕸 substitutes the verb שׂים for נתן to make it like the usage in 26:35. The 𝕲 uses τίθημι, which can be used to translate either verb.

89. Sanderson, *Exodus Scroll from Qumran*, 228-230. This would be similar to the translation technique of "dissimilation," i.e., the use of two lexical equivalents for one term in contexts where the term's meaning seems to be the same. See Nechama Leitier, "Assimilation and Dissimilation Techniques in the LXX of the Book of Balaam," *Textus* 12 (1985): 79-95.

90. 30:34; 31:12; 36:5.

91. Cynthia L. Miller, *The Representation of Speech in Biblical Hebrew Narrative: A Linguistic Analysis*, Harvard Semitic Monographs, ed. Peter Machinist (Atlanta, Ga.: Scholars Press, 1996), 383-84.

92. Ibid., 384.

93. Ibid., 377 and 388 n. 126.

94. In 30:34 and 36:5, the choice would seem to reflect the 𝕸 root אמר, but in 31:12, the 𝕲 has copied the pattern of similar phrases that "structure and segment the narrative" in 25:1; 30:11, 17, 22; 31:1, 12. See Miller, *Speech in Biblical Hebrew Narrative*, 384.

do not change the basic meaning of the passage, but instead are indicators of the "correcting" of the parallel accounts in the 𝕸. In addition, these synonymous variants may indicate changes in language usage. Synonymous variants in 26:25 and 26:26 make both of these verses more like their parallels in 36:30 and 36:31.[95] Sanderson says that the use of the construct in the 𝕸 and the absolute in the 𝕽 of 26:26 are synonymous variants of equal status, i.e., no decision can be reached about the preferability of one over the other.[96] Her analysis of this difference is faulty on two accounts. First, while quoting Gesenius about the use of construct chains for materials from which items are constructed, she fails to recognize that the text in the 𝕽 is probably a double accusative, a common structure with the verb עשׂה that is also discussed by Gesenius.[97] Second, while noting that the use of a construct chain in the 𝕸 makes it like the parallel phrase in 36:31, she fails to recognize this as a part of the consistent pattern of "corrections" that the 𝕸 has made in the tabernacle account.[98] Thus, this variant in the 𝕸 is clearly secondary rather than a synonymous variant of equal status.

The phrases that are most consistently changed in the 𝕸, אִישׁ אֶל־אָחִיו and אִשָּׁה אֶל־אֲחֹתָהּ, have been thoroughly discussed by Sanderson.[99] Like Waltke, she sees the 𝕽 as being the original reading in 25:20, but differs with him on the reason for the change in the 𝕸. Waltke follows Geiger and classifies this change with those phrases where the "*SP replaces rare and lively expressions with customary and prosaic expressions.*"[100] Sanderson correctly points to "the motive of standardizing parallel passages" as a factor in the change.[101] She also notes that the 𝕸 does agree

---

95. In 𝕸 26:25 the phrase תַּחַת הַקֶּרֶשׁ הָאֶחָד is a minus. As a result, the 𝕸 contains the phrase שְׁנֵי אֲדָנִים שְׁנֵי אֲדָנִים, a phrase that is likewise found in the parallel verse (36:30). This could be a case of parablepsis, but the fact that the preposition was also changed to make it like a phrase in 26:17 seems to point to more than a simple scribal error. An additional reason for asserting the intentionality of this correction towards the second account is that similar repeated phrases are maintained when they are found in their parallel passages in the second tabernacle account (26:19=36:24). The 𝕲 follows the 𝕽 in that it does not delete the phrase "under the one board," but instead it has its own rather free translation of the phrase, which would almost appear to be a double translation. This identical phrase is also found in the 𝕲 in 26:19 (2x) and 26:21 (2x).

In 26:26, the change is less drastic in that it only involves the minus of one letter that changes the double accusative to a construct chain. This change makes the verse more nearly similar to its parallel in 36:31, which also contains a construct chain. The 𝕲 uses a prepositional phrase, a structure that is generally used to translate similar phrases that are clearly double accusatives (25:28). This type of prepositional phrase in 𝕲, however, can also be used to translate construct chains when the clause has added complexity (27:6).

96. Sanderson, *Exodus Scroll from Qumran*, 118.

97. E. Kautzsch, ed., *Gesenius' Hebrew Grammar*, Second English ed. (Oxford: Clarendon Press, 1910), § 117hh-ii.

98. The patterns of adjustments in the 𝕸 will be discussed fully in the third section of this chapter.

99. Sanderson, *Exodus Scroll from Qumran*, 94-95.

100. Waltke, "Samaritan Pentateuch and the Text," 220.

101. Sanderson, *Exodus Scroll from Qumran*, 94.

with the 𝔐 when this phrase is used for humans. In my opinion, standardization is the key factor for the changes, but Sanderson could have gone one step further in her analysis of the use of these phrases with animate beings (including humans) versus inanimate objects. In the 𝔐, male animate beings are only referred to by the phrase אִישׁ אֶל־אָחִיו, but inanimate objects can be referred to either by this phrase (or its feminine equivalent) or אַחַת אֶל־אֶחָת (or the masculine equivalent, though it does not occur in the 𝔐 form of the tabernacle accounts). The 𝔐 retains the use of the phrase אִישׁ אֶל אחיו for humans (all examples are masculine gender in Exodus), but uses the phrases אחת אל אחת or אחד אל אחד with all inanimate objects. The cherubim are viewed as a problem in Sanderson's analysis because the 𝔐 consistently reads אִישׁ אֶל־אָחִיו in contrast to the 𝔐, thus taking away the motive of standardizing 25:20 to match its parallel in 37:9. This difference, however, is probably due to a change in the "animacy" status of the cherubim. In the 𝔐 the cherubim were considered to be "alive" and thus were discussed using the same phrase as for male humans, אִישׁ אֶל־אָחִיו. In the 𝔐, however, the cherubim were just another inanimate object with which they consistently used the masculine phrase אחד אל אחד. The changes in this phrase in the 𝔐 are, therefore, the result of two processes. The major factor was the correcting of the first tabernacle account to match the second, i.e., standardization.[102] In addition, the changes in 25:20 and 37:9 were the result of a change in the "animacy" classification of the cherubim. The 𝔊 translation uses a variety of phrases in its translation of these Hebrew phrases and thus could be seen as a valid translation of either the 𝔐 or the 𝔐 forms of the phrases.

Minuses

Minuses are less frequent than pluses in the 𝔐 and generally do not affect the main content. Items that are minuses in the 𝔐 include pronouns, pronominal suffixes, prepositions, nouns, and a few phrases. In the first tabernacle account, the 𝔊 is a "fuller" translation and tends not to follow the 𝔐 in its minuses. In the second tabernacle account, however, the 𝔊 tends to abbreviate the information and in the process often coincidentally agrees with the minuses of the 𝔐. Minuses of pronominal suffixes and prepositions in the 𝔐, however, do not lend themselves to any firm conclusions about the *Vorlage* of the 𝔊.

Pronominal Suffixes. At least six pronominal suffixes have been deleted in the 𝔐 and an additional minus is also found in 4QpaleoGen-Exod[l].[103] In all cases, the

---

102. This factor accounts for the changes in 𝔐 26:3 (2x), 5, 6, 17.
103. In 26:30, 4QpaleoGen-Exod[l] is missing the pronominal suffix found at the end of the 𝔐 form כְּמִשְׁפָּטוֹ. The 𝔊 translation of this noun is a definite noun, which is a common equivalent in Exodus of a Hebrew possessed noun. Thus, the 𝔊 could have had a *Vorlage* similar to that of the 𝔐, even though there is no possessive pronoun per se.

pronoun is also missing in the 𝔊, but in two cases it is missing because of the abbreviated translation in the 𝔊.[104] In at least two of the other four instances, the 𝔊 could be said to follow the 𝔐.[105] Three of these minuses in the 𝔐 illustrate the tendency of the 𝔐 to strive for consistency in phrases. These three minuses are found in material that does not have a parallel, per se, in the second tabernacle account.[106] In each case, the phrase לְכַהֲנוֹ in the 𝔐 has been changed to לכהן in the 𝔐, which makes it identical to the six other examples of the infinitive construct of this verb in the tabernacle accounts.[107] Other than making the text more consistent, this minus also makes the text easier since subjective suffixes on infinitive constructs of transitive verbs are a relatively rare phenomenon. The 𝔊 translates each of these three phrases (28:1, 3, 4) in a slightly different way, so no firm conclusions can be reached about the *Vorlage* of the 𝔊 in these cases.

Prepositions. Most minuses of prepositions in the 𝔐 result in increased consistency in that the phrase becomes identical to a phrase either in the surrounding verses or in the parallel account.[108] While corrections towards parallel passages are fairly obvious, phrases that appear to be corrected towards phrases in surrounding verses tend to be more of a challenge because of the mixed evidence. For instance, in 29:13 there is no obvious reason for a scribal minus, עַל, from the phrase הַיֹּתֶרֶת עַל־הַכָּבֵד due to the immediate context, though the minus does make the phrase more nearly parallel to the phrase יֹתֶרֶת הַכָּבֵד in 29:22. On the surface level, the absence of ἐπί in the translation of the phrase in 𝔊 29:13 would also affirm the 𝔐 form, יותרת הכבד. The translation of this phrase in similar passages in Leviticus, however, gives mixed evidence.[109] In 29:13 and 29:22, this par-

---

104. 38:1 (𝔊 38:22) (2x).

105. In 28:1 and 28:4, the 𝔊 is clearly missing an explicit equivalent of the pronominal suffix on the infinitive constructs. In 28:3 the pronominal suffix on the infinitive construct could be said to be equivalent to the 3ms subject marker on the finite verb form used to translate the infinitive. The minus of the 3ms suffix on בַּדָּיו in 27:7 in the 𝔐 may be part of the restructuring that results in an active clause in the 𝔐 rather than the passive clause in the 𝔐. In addition, the 𝔐 contains the plus of an article on the word for poles. The 𝔊 reflects the grammatical structure of the 𝔐 and likewise lacks a possessive pronoun on the word for poles.

106. The same type of minus is found three times in the 𝔐 (28:1, 3, 4).

107. In the 𝔐, this form of the infinitive construct without the suffix is found in 29:1, 44; 30:30; 31:10; 35:19; and 39:41.

108. In 25:27, the preposition לְ is a minus in the 𝔐, which means that the phrase is more nearly similar to 37:14. The preposition בְּ is a minus in 𝔐 26:8, which makes it more nearly similar to its parallel in 36:15 and in 𝔐 38:12 the same preposition in a similar construction is a minus, which makes it more nearly similar to its parallel in 27:12. The fact that the same change is made in opposite parts of the tabernacle accounts may indicate that this is part of a change in the language away from describing something as "[number] in cubits" towards simply "[number] cubits," at least in certain contexts.

109. In Lev 8:16 an ἐπί is present in the translation despite the contrary evidence of both the 𝔐 and the 𝔐 forms of this verse and in Lev 3:15 the preposition ἐπί is missing despite the fact that both the 𝔐 and 𝔐 have the preposition עַל. The fact that this kind of variation occurs in Leviticus, which is

ticular phrase is translated identically by the Greek phrase τὸν λοβὸν τοῦ ἥπατος. The immediately preceding phrase in both verses, which is identical in both 𝕸 and 𝔐, however, is translated differently in each verse, illustrating one of the known tendencies of the 𝔊 translation of Exodus, i.e., the use of dissimilation as a translation technique. Thus, the arguments can become quite circular and one is tempted to go with Sanderson's classification of this change as a synonymous variant in which there is no preferable form, but the pervasiveness of the tendency of the 𝕸 to "correct" leads me to believe that the preposition was present in the *Urtext* and then was deleted in the 𝕸. Similar circular arguments can also be used for the minuses of other prepositions, but ultimately these changes affect the meaning only slightly and may have little or no impact on a relatively free translation such as the 𝔊 of Exodus.[110]

Nouns, Adjectives, and Participles. In most examples of minuses of nouns, adjectives, and participles in the 𝕸, the 𝔊 supports the 𝔐 reading. These minuses, contrary to other changes in the 𝕸, do not bring parallel passages into greater consistency. In fact, in a few places they make parallel passages less nearly parallel.[111] Many of these examples are similar in that the minuses involve words that occur at least twice in the verse and the evidence of the 𝔊 supports the 𝔐.[112] These minuses may be due to the perceived "redundancy" in the Hebrew or scribal errors. In 29:5 the minus הָאֵפֹד, which is a modifier of the robe, may have been due to the presence of the ephod itself as the next item in the list. Other minuses in the 𝕸, however, are either changes towards more frequently used grammatical structures or are nouns that are also minuses in the 𝔊.[113]

---

normally more literal than Exodus, raises further doubts about the possibility of reaching a firm conclusion.

110. In 𝕸 29:41, the preposition לְ is a minus. According to Wevers, the 𝕸 "represents Exod's [𝔊] parent text," and the preposition εἰς, which is found in some manuscripts, is a hexaplaric reading. (WeversNotes, 485.) One of the major factors in Wevers' argument is the naturalness of the Greek grammatical structure, an issue which will not be discussed here. (WeversText, 210.) The 𝔊, however, is consistent even when the Hebrew has different forms as in 29:18 and 29:25. Exodus 29:18 seems to be the most nearly parallel to the structure in 29:41, which would mean that this minus in the 𝕸 could also be part of the tendency towards making the text "consistent" and that the preposition would have been present in the *Urtext*. See also the minus לְ and other resulting changes in placement of the article in 𝕸 35:28, which results in a text that is similar to 35:14.

111. 28:17=39:10; 28:23=39:16.

112. In the 𝕸, these include the minus אֶבֶן (28:17); שְׁנֵי and שְׁתֵּי (28:23); מַחֲצִית (30:13); כָּל (35:24); כָּפוּל (39:9); חֲשׁוּקֵיהֶם (while leaving a related term מְחֻשָּׁקִים in 38:17). The 𝔊 translates both of these terms in 38:17 by a participle form of περιαργυρόω (𝔊 37:15). The 𝕸 makes the reference to the "robe" consistent in both 39:22 and 39:23 by means of a minus, הָאֵפֹד, in 39:22, but the 𝔊 agrees with the 𝔐 and contains a translation of ephod. The adverb סָבִיב is also probably missing in 4QpaleoGen-Exod[l] 25:11, but is found in the 𝔐, 𝕸, and 𝔊. Likewise, מִלְמַעְלָה appears to be a minus in 4QExod-Lev[f] 40:20. These are the only identified examples from the 𝔔 manuscripts that fit in this category.

113. In 35:22, the 𝕸 uses כל אשר instead of כָּל־אִישׁ אֲשֶׁר, as in the 𝔐. This minus represents a move to a more frequently used structure, though there are examples of both structures in the imme-

Phrases. Most of the minuses of phrases in the first tabernacle account of the 𝔐 are found in both the 𝔐 and 𝔊, but in the second tabernacle account the phrases deleted in the 𝔐 are often also missing in the 𝔊, though sometimes this is due to the abbreviated nature of the translation. Some of the minuses of phrases that only occur in the 𝔐 may be due to scribal errors with orthographically similar words, but that explanation cannot easily be used for other minuses.[114] Some phrases that are minuses in both the 𝔐 and 𝔊 are minuses of repeated phrases that are found either in the same verse or in an adjacent verse.[115] Out of a total of eight minuses of phrases, only three could be said to reflect a possible difference in *Vorlage* for the 𝔊.[116] All of these, however, are minuses of repetitions, a common translation technique in the 𝔊 Exodus. As a result, their value for discerning the *Vorlage* of the 𝔊 is negated.

Pluses

Pluses within the tabernacle accounts of the 𝔐 are relatively frequent, but few of these add any new information to the text. Most of these pluses are copies of material found in the immediate context and result in grammatically more symmetrical patterns. Occasionally, the pluses serve to clarify ambiguities in the grammatical structures. When new information is added, it is mostly information that would be known by anyone reading the entire book. Several of these pluses are also found in the 𝔊 or the plus in the 𝔐 clarifies a problem in the 𝔊 translation.

---

diate context. The 𝔊 translation of Exodus never includes "man" in its translation of this phrase, though it is found in Leviticus, which is more literal. The minus כֹל in the standard phrase כְּכֹל אֲשֶׁר צִוָּה יְהוָה, likewise, changes the form in the 𝔐 to the more frequently used expression כַּאֲשֶׁר צִוָּה יְהוָה. The Greek translation would seem to agree with the 𝔐 in the lack of the term "all" (39:32 [𝔊 39:10]), but this may only be a surface level agreement because in 39:42 (𝔊 39:22) "all" is again missing even though it is present in both the 𝔐 and 𝔐. The 𝔊 is even less likely than the 𝔐 to use the word "all" in this kind of expression. The minus נְחֹשֶׁת in 38:10 is unexplainable and the 𝔊 equivalent (𝔊 37:8) is an abbreviated translation that does not include this part of the verse, though one might speculate that the term was also missing in their *Vorlage*. This "minus," if it really is a minus, is the opposite of the trend to "add" נְחֹשֶׁת, which is seen in 𝔐 27:12, 14, 15, 16.

114. Orthographically similar words may have led to minuses in the 𝔐 in a few cases, as follows: אֲשֶׁר אֶתֵּן אֵלֶיךָ (25:21); לִפְנֵי יְהוָה (29:25); לִפְנֵי הַכַּפֹּרֶת אֲשֶׁר עַל־הָעֵדֻת (30:6—a minus in both 𝔐 and 𝔊); וְאֶת־נֵרֹתֶיהָ (35:14—this part of the verse is not found in 𝔊). Other cases, however, are doubtful, such as מְשֻׁחִים בַּשָּׁמֶן (29:2) and לוֹ (37:13). The minus in 37:13 does make it more like 38:5, but at the same time it disturbs the parallelism in 25:26=37:13. The source of this minus cannot be easily determined.

In addition, Sanderson suggests that fourteen words of 31:13-14 are part of a large minus in 4QpaleoExod^m. (Skehan and others, DJD 9, 123.) Cross likewise notes a minus, מֹשֶׁה אֶת־הַמִּשְׁכָּן וַיִּתֵּן, in 4QExod-Lev^f 40:18 that he attributes to haplography as well as other differences. (Ulrich and others, DJD 12, 142.) Neither of these minuses, however, is supported in the three major traditions (𝔊, 𝔐, and 𝔐).

115. In 38:25 (𝔊 39:2) בְּשֶׁקֶל הַקֹּדֶשׁ is a minus, which is also found in 38:24, 26 (𝔊 39:1, 3). In 39:25 (𝔊 36:32), the first occurrence of בְּתוֹךְ הָרִמֹּנִים is a minus.

116. 30:6; 38:25 (𝔊 39:2); 39:25 (𝔊 36:32).

Prepositions and Prepositional Phrases. There are at least nine prepositions or prepositional phrases that are pluses in the tabernacle accounts of the 𝕾. The 𝕲 translation of all but three of these passages either clearly supports the 𝕸 or the 𝕲 translation equivalent is one that is used in other verses for both the form of the phrase found in the 𝕾 and also the form found in the 𝕸. One exception is 37:5 (𝕲 38:4), in which the 𝕾 contains the plus בהם and the 𝕲 has a clear equivalent of this Hebrew phrase. Unfortunately, the clarity of this example loses its weight as support for an alternate reading when one notices that the 𝕲 also contains a translation of this phrase as a plus in 25:27, a passage in which both the 𝕸 and 𝕾 agree on its absence. Therefore, this passage becomes one more example of a trait shared by both the 𝕾 and 𝕲, i.e., the filling out a passage by means of pluses that contain information known from the general context. Other examples in this category are the plus בהר in 25:9 and the plus לצאתם ממצרים as a modifier of "second year" in 40:17. At first glance both of these would appear to be synonymous variants that could be viewed as preferable. In light of the occurrence of similar phrases in the 𝕸 and the tendency of the 𝕾 to make phrases more nearly similar, however, these examples should probably be considered secondary variants that are also reflected in the 𝕲.[117]

Other prepositions and prepositional phrases that are not reflected in the 𝕲 could be pluses that are due to scribal errors. For instance, the plus of מ to אשר in 29:26 could be a case of dittography since the preceding word ends in ם. Given the tendency of the 𝕾 towards "correcting" passages to make them more nearly similar to other passages, however, this plus is more likely to be a "correction" towards the identical phrase in the following verse.[118] An additional piece of evidence that may support this conclusion is the lack of ἀπό in the Greek, which is present in the translation of the almost identical phrase found in the following verse.[119] The only example that does not fit this pattern of "correcting" a passage towards a parallel is the plus ל in 38:17. This preposition is a plus that occurs with a phrase in apposition to the subject of a non-verbal clause in the 𝕸 and 𝕲. The phrase in the 𝕸 is difficult, to say the least, and there have been other modifications in the 𝕾 form of the verse, but the intent of this plus seems to be to clarify the relationship of the phrase to the rest of the clause. Clarifying difficulties in the 𝕸 has been pre-

---

117. Similar phrases with "on the mountain" are found in 25:40; 26:30; 27:8. A slightly variant phrase, "of their going out from the land of Egypt," is found in Num 1:1; 9:1. In 2QExod^a a similar type of plus is seen in 30:25, [לדורות]יכם, which is similar to phrases in 30:21, 31.

118. Other pluses of prepositions and prepositional phrases that make the passages similar are as follows: ב (27:19); בם (29:33); לפני יהוה (40:27); and לפני (40:29). A similar plus, לפניו, is also found in 4QExod-Lev^f 40:27.

119. The argument from Greek alone would not be sufficient, given the tendency towards dissimilation as a translation technique, but combined with the tendency towards "corrections" in the 𝕾 it becomes more persuasive. Compare, however, with the discussion of circular argumentation in the section on the minuses of prepositions.

viously discussed as a characteristic of some of the changes in the 𝕌 and is again seen in this category.[120]

Nouns, Pronouns, and Adjectives. In the 𝕌, nouns and adjectives often occur as pluses that make implicit information explicit and result in parallel phrases within the text.[121] Most of these pluses are not reflected in the 𝕲.[122] The pronouns that are pluses, but are not copies of other pronouns, serve to clarify the grammatical structures and may be reflected in the similar restructuring of a verse in the 𝕲.[123] The pluses of כל are interesting in that each one that was identified as a plus in the 𝕌 was also found in the 𝕲. This may indicate that some of these occurrences of כל were accidental minuses in the 𝔐 or it may indicate that both the 𝕌 and the 𝕲 were making the phrases parallel to other phrases.[124] Three pluses in the 𝕌, however, are new information that may represent the Hebrew *Vorlage* of the 𝕲. They also result in a text that is more nearly similar to other phrases in Exodus or elsewhere in the Pentateuch.[125]

Verbs. Pluses of finite verbs and other verbal forms often fill in ellipses in the 𝔐. The 𝕲 likewise fills in some of the same ellipses, but only about half of the ones that are handled in the 𝕌.[126] The most common verb that is a plus is עשה, which

---

120. See discussions above under the categories of the object marker, article, *waw* conjunction, and others.

121. The following pluses are copies of words in the same verse and function to make the phrases more nearly parallel other parts of the verse or an adjacent verse: האחד (26:16=36:21); יהוה פתח (29:10); אתם (29:25); איש (35:21); הקדש (30:13 [along with other changes]); צלע (36:32). Pluses of implicit information may be seen in the following pluses: טהור (26:37); אמה (27:15); נחשת (27:12, 14, 15, 16); האחת (36:17); זהב (39:26 [2x]). The noun phrase שתי משבצות זהב is a plus in 28:23 that results in this verse being more nearly similar to the parallel verse (39:16). In 39:24, ושש is a plus, which makes it parallel the many other occurrences of this phrase.

122. Of the examples listed in the preceding footnote, only the pluses of "one" in 26:16, "cubit" in 27:15, and one occurrence of "gold" in 39:26 (𝕲 36:33) are also found in the 𝕲. The 𝕲 is missing 𝔐 28:23, although 𝕲 28:29a contains most of the elements of the verse, including a reference to the "chains" in the 𝕌.

123. Pronouns are pluses in 28:12, which the 𝕲 translation reflects in the verb εἰσὶν, and also in 30:13, where it is connected with other modifications. This latter plus is not reflected in the 𝕲.

124. In the 𝕌, כל is a plus with three occurrences of כלי (30:27; 31:8; 35:14). In addition, כל is a plus with המלאכה in 40:33, which makes the phrase more nearly parallel 39:43. In other phrases with מלאכה, however, the 𝕌 seems to faithfully follow the 𝔐 in the presence or absence of כל.

125. The phrase שש משזר in 28:33 is a plus that is also found in the 𝕲. This plus makes the passage in the 𝕌 more nearly similar its parallel in 𝕌 39:24. The word עגיל is a plus in 𝕌 35:22 and is reflected in the 𝕲, which also lists five items, rather than the four items in the 𝔐. This word is also found in a list of golden jewelry in Num 31:50, but only three of five items are the same as in the list in 𝕌 35:22. The phrase עלת תמיד is a plus in 𝕌 29:38 and is also found in the 𝕲. This plus in the 𝕌 makes the verse more like Num 28:3, which also mentions the daily offering of two lambs.

126. The 𝕲 fills in a different set of ellipses in addition to these due to the differences in Greek and Hebrew grammar.

is understandable since the tabernacle accounts involve the "making" of things.¹²⁷ Other verbs that are pluses are generally copies of verbs found in the immediate context or in similar phrases.¹²⁸ Because of differences between the Greek and Hebrew languages and the fact that the 𝔊 does not attempt to make parallel passages identical, only two of these pluses in the 𝔐 are also found in the 𝔊.¹²⁹

Clauses. The tabernacle accounts of the 𝔐 contain several pluses that are entire clauses. The interesting aspect of these pluses is that they too strive to increase the parallelism and consistency of the text. In the 𝔐, there are no references to the making of the Urim and Thummim. The 𝔐 has corrected this "inconsistency" by adding a clause at the beginning of 28:30 giving directions to make the Urim and Thummim. Then at the end of 39:21 the 𝔐 contains a plus with the simple fulfillment of those instructions followed by a duplication of the preceding phrase that affirms that this was done "just as Yahweh commanded Moses." These pluses are not found in the 𝔊, but Cross notes that a similar phrase is found in 4QExod-Levᶠ 39:21. He considers it to be an original phrase that was "lost by parablepsis" from the other traditions.¹³⁰ Whether this was a plus of the type often seen in the 𝔐 or an original phrase lost by parablepsis, the presence of this variant in 4QExod-Levᶠ shows that some variants in the 𝔐 were known at an early period even though they were not present in the 𝔊.

In 29:5, the 𝔐 contains the plus אתו והלבשת אבנים אתו חגרת in the middle of the verse. This plus serves to "correct" a possible problem concerning the order of dressing the priests and also makes the verse more nearly similar to Lev 8:7, which gives a detailed account of the fulfillment of these instructions. The order of putting on the garments in Lev 8:7 is the same as that in the 𝔐 form of 29:5. The 𝔊 again does not agree with the 𝔐 in this plus.

In 27:19, the 𝔐 and possibly 4QpaleoExodᵐ add a clause instructing Moses to make garments of the various materials.¹³¹ The reason for this plus is a bit com-

---

127. The verb עשה is a plus in 25:33; 26:10, 20; 27:19; 36:8.

128. Copies from the immediate context are seen in the plus תהיין in 26:3 as well as most of the examples of עשה. In 30:34, the infinitive phrase לאמר is a plus that makes the verse more like the speech phrases that were discussed earlier in this chapter. The plus of the participle מוסבות in 28:20 makes the verse parallel to 39:13. In the process, however, the consonantal text of the following word in the 𝔐, מְשֻׁבָּצִים, has been "corrected" to the feminine gender and the word is probably being read as the noun מִשְׁבְּצוֹת, rather than the participle that is in the 𝔐.

129. Pluses of identical verbs in the 𝔊 are found in 26:3 and 26:10.

130. Ulrich and others, DJD 12, 139.

131. Sanderson describes 𝔐 27:19b as "a very strange expansion because it seems so unnecessary and because (in 𝔐 at least) it has been put in the wrong place." Sanderson does recognize its similarity to 39:1, but fails to grasp the importance of that similarity. As a result she concludes, "it is perhaps misleading to group it with the major expansions, since all the others reflect careful scribal deliberation. Possibly it should be classified rather as the result of a scribal lapse." (Sanderson, *Exodus Scroll from Qumran,* 209-11.) In this work Sanderson suggested other possible positions for this text in

plex, but understanding this plus may help explain a "problem" in the 𝔊 of 28:6. First, at no place does the 𝔐 specifically give directions for the type of material to be used in the constructing of the garments. The types of garments to be constructed are given in a list in 28:4. The next verse begins with an unidentified 3mp agent that is referred to by הֵם, one of the few usages of this pronoun as an agent in the entire tabernacle account.[132] The 𝔐, by its use of the *petuha* at the end of 28:5, has signaled that the verse is the end of a section and that the next verse is a new section. The use of the pronoun, however, may indicate that 28:5 is the beginning of a new section and should be read together with 28:6. If 28:5 is read as the gathering of the material for the making of the ephod, then the presence of the gold is explained and the text does not conflict with 39:1, in which the colored yarns or materials are listed for the making of the garments, but the gold is absent. Gold was reserved for the ephod and other additional items that were attached to the priest's garments. The 𝔐 seemingly read 28:5 as a list of the materials for the ephod and added a clause at the end of 27:19 that gave instructions for the making of the garments, thus preserving the cherished balance between instructions and fulfillment. The 𝔊, while not agreeing with this plus, seems to agree with the interpretation of 28:5. Using the translation technique of combining repeated material, the duplicate items in the list of materials in 28:6 were deleted. The "linen" was probably maintained in 28:6 because it was the major construction material and because the Hebrew text here has the phrase שֵׁשׁ מָשְׁזָר rather than just הַשֵּׁשׁ as in 28:5. When the 𝔊 is read with the understanding provided by the 𝔐, it can be seen that the 𝔊 accurately represented the Hebrew text rather than "limiting the materials for the ephod to ἐκ βύσσου κεκλωσμένης," as claimed by Wevers.[133]

Summary

In this section I have examined a variety of changes in morphological forms, changes in order, synonymous variants, minuses, and pluses found in the 𝔐 and the 𝕼 manuscripts. The tendency of the 𝔐 to correct inconsistencies and make phrases and passages more nearly parallel has been noted repeatedly as one of the main factors that influenced these changes. Most of these changes are not reflected directly in the translation of the 𝔊, but there are several significant agreements in interpretive approaches that have influenced the 𝔊 translation and caused a surface level agreement. These surface level agreements were seen in the choice of 2s subjects of verbs in the instruction part of the tabernacle accounts,

---

4QpaleoExod^m, but in her later analysis she affirms that 4QpaleoExod^m agrees with 𝔐 on the position of this plus. See Skehan and others, DJD 9, 114.

132. See discussion of personal pronouns used with finite verbs in Takamitsu Muraoka, *Emphatic Words and Structures in Biblical Hebrew* (Leiden: E. J. Brill, 1985), 47-59.

133. WeversNotes, 447.

the choice of prepositions when there has possibly been confusion between אֶל and עַל, parallel stylistic changes in order, and similar interpretations of "synonymous" Hebrew words that have been "corrected" in the 𝕸. Other agreements, however, such as some of the pronominal references, pluses of the word כֹּל, and a few of the added phrases, may indicate that the 𝕲 was following a Hebrew *Vorlage* similar to that of the 𝕸. These agreements, especially ones in which the 𝕲 consistently follows the 𝕸 in a particular type of change that is scattered throughout the text, are hard to explain by any other method except by an appeal to a similar shared text.

In addition to discussing changes that may indicate a different Hebrew *Vorlage* of the 𝕲, several changes in the 𝕸 were discussed in detail to determine if they were synonymous variants equal in status to the 𝔐 or scribal lapses, as often claimed by Sanderson, or if they were secondary variants characteristic of the 𝕸. On the basis of probable language change and the tendency of the 𝕸 to correct inconsistencies both in the text itself and especially in the order of items and events within the text, I argued that these were mostly secondary variants. Most of these secondary variants were not reflected in the 𝕲, but the secondary variants in the 𝕸 do provide the necessary insight to interpret correctly the 𝕲 translation of 28:6, which has often been viewed as slightly deficient. Thus, as with the "irrelevant" variants in the 𝕸, the more significant variants in the 𝕸 must be examined both within their immediate context and as representatives of patterns of changes in order to evaluate correctly whether or not they possibly reflect the Hebrew *Vorlage* of the 𝕲 or an interpretive approach shared by the 𝕸 and 𝕲.

III. Other Observations about the Tabernacle Accounts

Two other areas of interest remain to be commented on in this chapter. First, throughout this chapter, I have repeatedly referred to the tendency of the 𝕸 to "correct" a passage to make it more like a parallel passage. Most of these changes involve grammatical minutiae and rarely change the basic meaning, but when these changes are examined as a whole, they reveal the pervasiveness and intentionality of the changes that were being made in the text. The first part of this section will discuss the patterns of adjustments in the 𝕸. The largest quantity of variants in the Hebrew texts, however, is found in the area of orthography. While these variants do not normally affect the 𝕲 translation, they deserve at least a passing mention. In addition, variations in spelling within the 𝔐 have been the basis for some claims about the formation of both the Hebrew text and the 𝕲 translation. Because of this, it is necessary to discuss briefly the claims and counterclaims that have been made on the basis of orthographic differences in the tabernacle accounts.

Table 2. Adjustments of first account to second

First account	Second account	Type of change
25:6	35:8	added *waw* conjunction (2x)
25:7	35:9	added *waw* conjunction
25:11	37:2	changed preposition
25:27	37:14	deleted preposition
25:29	37:16	changed order of words
25:31	37:17	added object marker
25:33	37:19	deleted article
25:39	37:24	added *waw* conjunction
26:3	36:10	changed idiom (2x)
26:5	36:12	changed idiom
26:6	36:13	changed idiom
26:8	36:15	changed word order
26:8	36:15	deleted preposition
26:10	36:17	changed word order
26:10	36:17	added verb
26:10	36:17	changed word
26:17	36:22	changed idiom
26:18	36:23	changed noun to plural
26:19	36:24	changed noun to plural
26:20	36:25	added verb
26:20	36:25	changed noun to plural
26:24	36:29	changed preposition
26:24	36:29	changed aspect of verb (?)
26:25	36:30	deleted phrase
26:26	36:31	changed to construct chain
27:7	38:7	deleted suffix and added article
27:7	38:7	changed verb stem to hiphil
27:11	38:11	changed phrase
27:11	38:11	deleted *waw* conjunction
27:11	38:11	changed pronominal suffix
27:15	38:15	added noun
28:7	39:4	changed preposition
28:7	39:4	deleted *waw* conjunction
28:20	39:13	added verb
28:20	39:13	deleted *waw* conjunction
28:20	39:13	changed gender
28:23	39:16	added phrase
28:24	39:17	changed preposition
28:33	39:24	added word
29:5	Lev 8:7	added clauses
29:18	Lev 8:21	changed order of words
29:21	Lev 8:30	changed order of words

Patterns of Adjustment in the 𝕸

When the 𝕸 account is examined as a whole, three patterns of adjustments become evident.[134] The most frequent pattern is the adjustment of the first account to conform to the second account. The next most frequent pattern of adjustments is the "correcting" of both accounts. In addition, there is a limited number of examples in which the second account has been adjusted to conform to that of the first. In the following sections I will include tables of all the adjustments according to these categories and briefly mention the types of changes found in each category.

Adjustments of First Account to Second. The first pattern of adjustments involves changes made in 25-29 that result in verses becoming more like their parallels in 35-39 and parts of Leviticus. At least forty-four changes of this type are found in the first account. (See table 2.) Because of the minor nature of these changes, it would be tempting to say that they were just haphazard, accidental agreements of scribal "errors." The quantity of changes, the fact that they occur throughout the account, and the variety of types of changes that have been made, however, point to a concerted effort to make the accounts more nearly parallel without significantly changing the content of the first account.

Adjustments to Both Accounts. In addition to adjustments to make the first account more like the second, the 𝕸 also contains at least thirty-one adjustments that were made in each account, i.e., at least sixty-two changes altogether. (See table 3.) Many of these adjustments were probably due to language change and the desire to "correct" the grammar of the Hebrew text to make it more like the current practice of that time. This may be seen in both tabernacle accounts in the four changes of gender, four pluses of locative *he*'s, and the three pluses of articles to nouns that follow numbers.[135] It is highly unlikely that these kinds of changes were just scribal errors that happened to occur in parallel accounts.

Adjustments of Second Account to First. The final set of adjustments is much smaller. There are only thirteen changes of the second account that make it more like the first account. (See table 4.) Several of these changes were probably due to language change, such as the plus of a locative *he* (36:23) and the avoidance of the

---

134. In addition, there are some changes made in the 𝕸 that do not result in increased conformity to a parallel passage. These changes have been noted throughout this chapter, but are not the focus of this section.

135. These items are discussed in the first section of this chapter.

Table 3. Adjustments to both accounts

First account	Second account	Type of change
25:3	35:5	deleted *waw* conjunction
25:4	35:6	deleted *waw* conjunction
25:17	37:6	changed gender (2x)
25:20	37:9	changed idiom
25:29	37:16	changed gender
25:31	37:17	deleted *waw* conjunction
25:31	37:17	changed to plural (2x)
25:33	37:19	deleted article
25:36	37:22	changed gender
26:1	36:8	deleted *waw* conjunction
26:3	36:10	added article
26:4	36:11	changed preposition
26:8	36:15	added article
26:8	36:15	changed form of word
26:16	36:21	added word
26:16	36:21	deleted *waw* conjunction
26:19 (𝕸 variant)	36:24 (𝕸 variant)	changed noun (2x)
26:20	36:25	added locative *he*
26:24	36:29	deleted *waw* conjunction
26:24	36:29	changed word
27:9	38:9	added locative *he*
27:11	38:11	added locative *he*
27:12	38:12	added locative *he*
28:15	39:8	added article
28:25	39:18	added article
28:26	39:19	changed preposition
28:30	39:21	added clause
28:33	39:24	added word

niphal verb form (35:2), a known characteristic of the 𝕸.[136] It is possible that the wording in the first account of some of these examples was considered to be clearer or more explicit than the wording in the second account. This would explain the two pluses of זהב in 𝕸 39:26 and other examples.

---

136. Waltke, "Samaritan Pentateuch and the Text," 219. Waltke groups this under the classification, "SP *replaces passive constructions with active constructions*."

Table 4. Adjustments of second account to first

Second account	First account	Type of change
35:2	31:15	changed verb form
36:23	26:18	added locative *he*
36:32	26:27	added word
36:35	26:31	deleted object marker
36:35	26:31	deleted article
37:5	25:14	added phrase
37:9	25:20	changed verb aspect (?)
38:10	27:10	changed number of suffix
38:12	27:12	deleted preposition
39:17	28:24	added object marker
39:17	28:24	deleted article
39:26	28:34	added noun (2x)

Orthography

The 𝔐 is known for its consistently fuller orthography and this is quickly confirmed in the tabernacle accounts, though occasionally defective forms are found.[137] The 𝔔 manuscripts also contain a similar, fuller orthography, though sometimes at variance with both the 𝔐 and 𝔐.[138] The importance of the orthography of the 𝔐 and 𝔔 manuscripts, however, is due more to the fact that it provides a standard against which the 𝔐 can be compared. For Nelson, the comparison of the orthography of the 𝔐 with that of the 𝔐 provides evidence that the 𝔐 text developed as a revision of the original section, which was the Hebrew *Vorlage* of 𝔊 37-38 (𝔐 36:8-38:20). This comparison of orthographies also provides a tentative time-table for the development of the 𝔐. Nelson summarizes this evidence as follows:

> A final piece of evidence for revision was found in the orthography of the MT In one member of parallel verses an increased use of <u>matres lectionis</u> was found. The increased use of <u>waw</u> and <u>he</u> was similar to that found in 4QEx^f. The slightly fuller orthography of the SP and the Hasmonaean fragments sug-

---

137. In a quick count of the tabernacle accounts of the 𝔐, I found over 380 words that were spelled more fully in contrast to the more defective forms of the 𝔐. Most examples involved *plene waw*'s, though there were a few with *yod*'s and *he*'s. In addition, there were a few forms in the 𝔐 that were written more defectively than in the 𝔐, such as פקדי (38:25), וקשתיו (25:29), and רקח (30:35).

138. For instance, 4QpaleoExod^m contains spellings such as בבוקר (29:39), הקודש (30:13), אהרון (29:32), and אוהל (30:16). See the discussion of the spelling differences within 4QExod-Lev^f in David Noel Freedman, "The Massoretic Text and the Qumran Scrolls: A Study in Orthography," in *Qumran and the History of the Biblical Text*, ed. Frank Moore Cross and Shemaryahu Talmon (Cambridge, Mass.: Harvard University Press, 1975), 207-9.

gests that the Tabernacle Account was revised sometime in the fourth-third centuries B.C.E. Neither the MT nor the SP compare to the very full orthography of the Herodian fragments from Qumran.[139]

On the surface level, Nelson's comments appear to have some validity. In the tabernacle accounts of the 𝔐 there is on the average less than one word (.84) per verse that has been spelled more fully. In the section that Nelson considers to be "original," however, there is a slightly higher ratio of fully spelled words (about one per verse) because there are more defectively spelled words in the 𝔐 form of this section. Barr, in his study of spelling in the Hebrew Bible, also notes that there are more defectively spelled words in the second tabernacle account (35-40) than in the first (25-31).[140] Within the first account, however, he notes that there are sections that tend towards shorter spellings and sections that tend towards longer spellings.[141] Barr's conclusion from his detailed study of spelling is as follows:

> Neither of the two texts shows any sign of having been modified from the existing spelling of the other. The evidence is entirely compatible with the supposition that both Text I and Text II were derived from an earlier text that was dominantly short, and that both of them independently added a certain number of waws and yods, both of them inconsistently and haphazardly.[142]

Orthographic differences are only one piece of evidence used by Nelson to argue his case for the development of the tabernacle accounts. The fact that his arguments and evidence are flawed at this point does not destroy his case, but it definitely raises questions about the validity of other examples used in the dissertation.[143] More disturbing is his attempt to argue that the first tabernacle account is a later development with fuller spellings than the second tabernacle account and yet at the same time he attempts to explain away "discrepancies" in the second tabernacle account by claiming,

---

139. Nelson, 287-88.

140. James Barr, *The Variable Spellings of the Hebrew Bible: The Schweich Lectures of the British Academy 1986* (Oxford: Oxford University Press, 1989), 174-76.

141. According to Barr, 25:1-28:19 tends to have shorter spellings than the parallel text, 28:20-32 tends to have the longer spellings, and in 28:33-40 the texts vary back and forth. Beginning in 29:1, Barr notes that the first account has shorter spellings than its parallel in Leviticus. Ibid., 177.

142. Ibid.

143. For instance, in his list of examples of final *he*, נתתה = נתת, he lists the parallel references 28:24, 25, 27=39:17, 18, 20, but the 2ms form of the verb, נתת, is not found in these examples from 39. Nelson claims that "When there is variation of form in the Tabernacle Account, MTI alone reads a final *he*." The 2ms verb is, however, found in both long, נתתה (25:12; 26:32, 33; 27:5; 28:14, 24, 25, 27; 29:12, 20; 30:6, 36; 40:5, 6) and short form, נתת (25:16, 21, 26, 30; 26:34; 28:23, 30; 29:3, 6, 17; 30:16, 18 [2x], 40:7 [2x], 8), in both tabernacle accounts of the 𝔐 and does not occur in the core of the second account. Another example that he uses is a contrast of אתתה (26:3, 5, 6) and אחת (36:10, 12, 13), as examples with and without the final *he*, but these are different words so his example is irrelevant. (Nelson, 184.) These are probably just inadvertent errors that occur in all dissertations, but the frequency of such errors in this dissertation has led me to check personally any data that is being used to prove an important point.

Most MT II examples [of the use of *waw* to represent ō derived from ā] are found in chapter 39 or before 36:8, those sections found in the Greek to be a Palestinian revision. This may be an indication that these sections along with MT I were part of a revision in Hebrew by a Palestinian hand.[144]

Thus, Nelson is, on the one hand, claiming that the spelling of these sections of the second tabernacle account is due to the same revision as that of the first account and yet many of his examples "proving" that the first account has fuller spellings than the second account are from the same sections of the second account that were supposedly revised.

Finally, in an endnote, Nelson approvingly quotes from O'Connell who says,

> The scribe who composed it [𝔐 28:23-28] on the basis of MT Exod. 39:16-21, apparently used a fuller orthography in his own new composition, while he retained the more defective orthography when simply copying the older passage.[145]

If, as Nelson claims, this is "true throughout the Tabernacle Account," then one would expect that in all parts of the "new composition" the fuller orthography would be used.[146] That is not, in fact, the case. Since this is a minor point, I will give just one example to the contrary. As O'Connell noted, the *plene* form טַבְּעוֹת is used in 28:23 (2x), 26, 27. These verses are almost exact copies of the parallel passage in 39. In the rest of the first tabernacle account, however, the word is always spelled defectively, טַבְּעֹת or טַבְּעֹת.[147] In the second tabernacle account, it is likewise spelled defectively except for one *plene* spelling, טַבְּעוֹת, in 37:3, which is part of Nelson's "original" version of the text.[148] Examples of this type could be multiplied, but Barr's conclusion, as follows, seems to have some validity, "There is no correlation, then, between the spelling tendencies and the date of origin of the books."[149]

As a result of his study, Barr criticized both Cross' use of orthography in restoring the original text and his claim that as a part of the formation of the "official text, ... A single orthographic tradition, in part archaizing to pre- or non-Maccabaean spelling practices, was systematically imposed."[150] Even if one rejects

---

144. Ibid.

145. Kevin G. O'Connell, S. J., *The Theodotionic Revision of the Book of Exodus: A Contribution to the Study of the Early History of the Transmission of the Old Testament in Greek* (Cambridge, Mass.: Harvard University Press, 1972), 70.

146. Nelson, 295.

147. Defectively spelled forms of this word are found in the following verses in the first tabernacle account: 25:12 (3x), 14, 15, 26 (2x), 27; 26:29; 27:4, 7; 28:24, 28; 30:4.

148. Defectively spelled forms of this word are found in the following verses in the second tabernacle account: 36:34; 37:3 (2x), 5, 13 (2x), 14, 27; 38:5, 7; 39:16 (2x), 17, 19, 20, 21 (2x).

149. Barr, *Variable Spellings*, 201.

150. Frank Moore Cross, "The History of the Biblical Text in the Light of Discoveries in the Judaean Desert," in *Qumran and the History of the Biblical Text*, ed. Frank Moore Cross and Shemaryahu Talmon (Cambridge, Mass.: Harvard University Press, 1975), 185. See Barr's criticism of this statement in *Variable Spellings*, 187.

Barr's conclusion about variation in spelling, accepting Cross' claim could also lead one to the same rejection of spelling differences as evidence for the development of any stage of the text. If a spelling system, even one that Barr views as irregular, had been "systematically imposed" on the text, one would conclude that significant variations could no longer be assumed to be part of the "original" text. Therefore, Nelson's discussion of spelling variations is irrelevant and his case for the development of the text must be judged on other evidence that he presents. Spelling variations are also irrelevant for the evaluation of the 𝔊 translation of the tabernacle accounts, which is the focus of this study.

Summary

The 𝔐 and 𝔔 manuscripts do contain a consistently fuller spelling of words in the tabernacle accounts. Orthographic differences in the 𝔐 have been used by Nelson as supporting evidence for his theory about the development of the Hebrew text of the tabernacle accounts along with the 𝔊 translation of these accounts. This theory, however, cannot be proven on the basis of Hebrew orthography. Variations in spelling occur throughout both accounts and often in the same verses, which led Barr to claim that some of the *waw*'s and *yod*'s were added "inconsistently and haphazardly."[151]

In the first part of this section, over one hundred changes were noted that resulted in the two tabernacle accounts of the 𝔐 being more alike in form. These changes are not major and most of them do not significantly change the meaning of the text, but the sheer quantity of the changes points unavoidably to the purposeful revision of the text that was carried out in the 𝔐.[152] This revision also included the "correcting" or standardizing of the grammar rather than allowing the diversity of the 𝔐.[153] The 𝔊 reflects some of these changes, but due to the grammatical nature of many of the changes, they were only relevant for the Hebrew.

IV. Conclusion

Text critics have generally concentrated on tabulating agreements and disagreements among various textual traditions as the basis for making statements about

---

151. Ibid., 177.

152. Skehan has used a similar argument for the revisions he noted in the Isaiah Scroll. Patrick W. Skehan, "The Qumran Manuscripts and Textual Criticism," in *Qumran and the History of the Biblical Text*, ed. Frank Moore Cross and Shemaryahu Talmon (Cambridge, Mass.: Harvard University Press, 1975), 216.

153. This trend in the 𝔐 is another indicator of the lateness of this recension. Modern day translators working in previously unwritten languages have also noted (and in many cases encouraged) the standardization of written language. In the process much of the variation that is noted in spoken language is gradually eliminated and the written language becomes a "homogenized and pasteurized" form of the spoken language.

textual affinities. Most text critics acknowledge that it is not the simple total of the number of agreements, but also the types of agreements that are important. While this has been generally claimed by text critics, some text critical studies still tend to be tabulations of lists with discussions of only the types of major changes that are interesting to that text critic. Few text critics have combined an in-depth examination of both the changes within their contexts and the changes in comparison to other changes of a similar nature. Using this approach in the tabernacle accounts of Exodus has produced an emerging picture of the 𝔐 as a recension that cherished the balance between instructions and fulfillment. To increase the parallels between the two parts of the tabernacle account, the 𝔐 intentionally modified either one or both accounts through changes in morphology, changes in order, synonymous variants, minuses, and pluses. These changes did not, in most cases, change the basic meaning of the text. Rather, the text was simply made more consistent and some of the text was updated to suit the grammatical usages of the Hebrew language in their times.

In general, the 𝔊 did not follow the tendency of the 𝔐 towards consistency between parallel passages of the tabernacle accounts. Many of the grammatical changes in the 𝔐 were "irrelevant" for the 𝔊 because of differences in grammar between the Greek and Hebrew languages. The importance of the 𝔐 for understanding the 𝔊, however, was demonstrated repeatedly throughout this chapter. Minor changes in the 𝔐 often indicated an interpretation that was at variance with the 𝔐. Often, similar interpretations of an ambiguous Hebrew *Vorlage* could also be seen in the 𝔊. Pluses and other changes in the 𝔐 also provided the insight needed for understanding some of the 𝔊 translations that have in the past been viewed as slightly deficient. Other changes in the 𝔐 that were reflected in the 𝔊 can only be explained on the basis of a Hebrew *Vorlage* that was more like the text of the 𝔐. As a result of this evidence, text critics working in the Pentateuch would be wise to note carefully changes in the 𝔐, because these changes often indicate passages containing ambiguities that had to be resolved in the 𝔊.

CHAPTER THREE

Lexical Consistency

The tabernacle accounts of 𝔊 Exodus are characterized by a consistent pattern of using lexical equivalents that are grammatically, semantically, and exegetically appropriate for each context. Because of the variety of contexts in the tabernacle accounts of 𝔊 Exodus, the traditional methods that have been used for evaluating lexical consistency lead to the conclusion that the translation was produced by at least two translators. In contrast, those who claim that the translator of the tabernacle accounts of 𝔊 Exodus was consistently inconsistent are able to claim that the wide variety of lexical equivalents used for terms in the first tabernacle account effectively negates any claims made about differences in vocabulary between the two tabernacle accounts.[1] A closer inspection of the lexical equivalents in both accounts, however, demonstrates that the choices of lexical equivalents are context-sensitive rather than being inconsistent. When all words are examined in their contexts, only a small percentage of the contrasting lexical equivalents can be used to support a two-translator theory of the production of the 𝔊 tabernacle accounts. Rather than true contrasts, many of the choices of lexical equivalents for words that occur in both accounts demonstrate a pervasive shifting of the usages of the lexical equivalents as well as the maintaining of lexical cohesion by the use of lexical equivalents that appear in both tabernacle accounts.[2] It is this evidence of the shifting of usages of lexical equivalents, rather than actual contradictory lexical equivalents, that makes it doubtful that both tabernacle accounts were produced by the same translator.

---

1. A modified view of this position is held by Gooding, who claims that the lack of consistency means that one translator produced all but a small section of the second tabernacle account that contains internal contradictions. See Gooding.

2. In this study, lexical cohesion is used in a narrow sense to refer to the repetition of words. Lexical cohesion both defines the boundaries of a text or portion of a text and also holds a text together as a coherent unit. See Mildred L. Larson, *Meaning-Based Translation: A Guide to Cross-Language Equivalence*, 2d ed. (Lanham, Md.: University Press of America, 1998), 431-33, for a discussion of lexical cohesion used in a wider sense that includes "synonyms, antonyms, substitution of generic words for specific words, parallel expressions," and "expectancy chains," i.e., language or cultural specific events that can be expected to occur together in a set order in a text. For a broader introduction to cohesion see Kathleen Callow, *Discourse Considerations in Translating the Word of God* (Grand Rapids, Mich.: Zondervan, 1974), 29-48.

In this chapter I will begin with a discussion of various methods of measuring lexical consistency. This will include both a survey of past methodologies as well as a description of the means of measuring and comparing lexical consistency that will be used in this study. Next, I will present a survey of the types of lexical consistency seen in four sections of Exodus as well as presenting a comparison of various sets of sections. In the third section I will discuss the translation of some of the technical terminology of the tabernacle and also the translation of the compass points. In past studies, the translation of technical terminology and compass points has been the key evidence used to support one of the theories about the number of translators who produced the tabernacle accounts. In the fourth section, I will discuss other observations that can be gained from studying lexical equivalents in the 𝕲. Specifically, I will discuss choices of lexical equivalents that clarify ambiguous sections of the Hebrew text as well as choices of lexical equivalents that indicate the translator's interpretation of the text. Finally, I will conclude by summarizing some observations about lexical consistency and its effect on the discussion concerning the number of translators that produced the tabernacle accounts of 𝕲 Exodus.

I. Defining and Measuring Lexical Consistency

Historically, lexical consistency has been defined and measured based on the assumption that the 𝕲 translation was a literal translation. This assumption has been modified with time, but it is still an underlying part of most studies. It is true that the 𝕲 Exodus is literal in some aspects of its translation methodology, but the choice of lexical equivalents is not one of those aspects. Because of the context-sensitive nature of the choices of lexical equivalents, past methodologies, which were largely intuitive analyses of a handful of terms, failed to grasp the nature of the translation. Modern statistical methodologies likewise fail because computers are not yet able to examine semantic contexts and evaluate the effect of these contexts on choices of lexical equivalents. As a result, a different approach will be used in this study. Rather than calculating the percentage of the occurrences that use a stereotypical translation of a term, I will instead compare the percentage of nouns and verbs that are rendered by one lexical equivalent in contrast to those that are rendered by more than one lexical equivalent. This methodology highlights the context-sensitive nature of choices of lexical equivalents for nouns and especially for verbs. While this methodology will use statistics to summarize the results of the examination of the verbs and nouns in four sections of Exodus, the statistics are not considered to be the most important aspect of the methodology. Rather, the verbal description of the types of factors that have affected the choices of lexical equivalents in 𝕲 Exodus is the main method that will be used to highlight the true nature of the translation, i.e., that it is a context-sensitive translation with respect to the choice of lexical equivalents.

In this section I will first survey past studies of lexical consistency beginning with Thackeray and ending with computer-dependent models. Included in this survey will be brief descriptions of the use of lexical consistency within these studies. Following this survey, I will describe in more detail the methodology that will be used in this study and briefly illustrate some of the factors that affect choices of lexical equivalents in 𝕲 Exodus.

Survey of Past Methodologies

Lexical consistency or the lack thereof has long been used as one of the main criteria in evaluating the 𝕲 translation with regard to the degree of literalness of the translation, the number of translators, and the possibility of producing an accurate retroversion to the Hebrew *Vorlage*. The importance of lexical consistency is seen in the wide variety of ways that it has been used.

In Thackeray's examination of the entire corpus of 𝕲 Scriptures, he clearly explained his methodology and grouped the putative component translations according to the manner in which they translated certain terms or phrases. In choosing this approach, he noted that "Vocabulary affords the easiest criterion to begin with: the results which it yields can then be tested by grammatical phenomena."[3] His classification of the books of the 𝕲 Scriptures has generally been validated by more recent studies of other aspects of the 𝕲. For Thackeray, however, the changes in lexical equivalents also provided a basis for claims about the theology of the translators. For instance, noting the changes in the translation of the term "servant" he says,

> We cannot fail to note in the LXX renderings a growing tendency to emphasize the distance between God and man. Θεράπων "the confidential attendant" is replaced by οἰκέτης (which may include all members of the household and therefore implies close intimacy), then by the more colourless but still familiar παῖς, finally by δοῦλος the "bond-servant" without a will of his own.[4]

Some of these changes in the choice of lexical equivalents may, however, be the result of the translations being produced over a long span of time. Thus, the differences may reflect a shift in language usage, rather than a changing theology.[5]

---

3. Henry St. John Thackeray, *A Grammar of the Old Testament in Greek According to the Septuagint*, vol. 1, *Introduction, Orthography and Accidence* (Cambridge: Cambridge University Press, 1909), 7.

4. Ibid., 8.

5. Benjamin G. Wright, "Δοῦλος and Παῖς as Translations of עֶבֶד: Lexical Equivalences and Conceptual Transformations," in *IX Congress of the International Organization for Septuagint and Cognate Studies, Cambridge, 1995*, ed. Dirk Büchner and Bernard A. Taylor, Septuagint and Cognate Studies, no. 45 (Atlanta, Ga.: Scholars Press, 1997), 261-77. Wright points to changes in the use of terms for

Traditionally, lexical consistency or the lack thereof has been one of the criteria for determining whether a book was translated by one or more translators. Early studies by Thackeray, Baab, and others emphasized the different ways that terms were translated and on the basis of the distribution of these terms divided books, such as Genesis, Jeremiah, and Ezekiel, into two or more parts.[6] These studies generally made no claims about being complete studies of the vocabulary of the book, but rather emphasized lexical inconsistency between the parts of a book because they assumed that the 𝔊 translations were basically literal and that one translator would not suddenly switch vocabulary.

In Gooding's study of the tabernacle accounts of Exodus, however, lexical inconsistency was seen as one of the defining features of the translator's technique.[7] Because of the presence of lexical inconsistency throughout Exodus, Gooding claimed that the lexical differences between the two tabernacle accounts were primarily due to the translator's technique rather than the presence of two translators, as had been claimed by Smith, Swete, and others.[8]

Gooding's negative evaluation of lexical inconsistency has, in recent times, been countered by Leitier, who sees some examples of lexical inconsistency as a positive attribute of a translator's techniques.[9] These techniques are described as assimilation, in which different Hebrew terms are translated by the same Greek term, and dissimilation, in which the same Hebrew terms are translated by different Greek terms. Leitier found both of these techniques being used within very

---

servants and emphasizes the lack of contrast between some of the terms both in the 𝔊 Scriptures and later Greek literature. There are, however, several key factors that Wright has not included in his analysis of the contexts in which these terms are used. Wright fails to remember that usages in quotations may be different from those found in narrative texts. He also forgets that sociolinguistic factors are most likely to affect speech, e.g., when speaking to a superior, a person will often refer to himself by a "lower" term. This does not make the "lower" term synonymous with the "higher" term used in the surrounding narrative, as Wright would have us believe. An example of the effect of a different set of sociolinguistic factors may be seen in a comparison of 11:3 and 11:8. In 11:3, Pharaoh's officials are referred to in the narrative by the term θεράπων. In Moses' speech, however, these same officials are derogatorily referred to using the term παῖς (11:8).

6. Henry St. John Thackeray, "The Greek Translators of Jeremiah," *Journal of Theological Studies* 4 (1902-3): 245-66; idem, "The Bisection of Books in Primitive Septuagint MSS.," *Journal of Theological Studies* 9 (1907): 88-98; and Otto J. Baab, "A Theory of Two Translators for the Greek Genesis," *Journal of Biblical Literature* 52 (1933): 239-43.

7. Gooding, 28. Gooding describes the translator's style by pointing to "his disregard for technicalities, his inconsistencies, his inaccuracies" and "his positive errors." This emphasis on lexical inconsistency is also seen in an earlier study by A. H. Finn, "The Tabernacle Chapters," *Journal of Theological Studies* 16 (1915): 449-82.

8. Henry Barclay Swete, *An Introduction to the Old Testament in Greek* (Peabody, Mass.: Hendrickson Publishers, 1989), 236. See also the discussion and bibliography in Emanuel Tov, *The Text-Critical Use of the Septuagint in Biblical Research: Second Edition, Revised and Enlarged* (Jerusalem: Simor, 1997), 256-57.

9. Nechama Leitier, "Assimilation and Dissimilation Techniques in the LXX of the Book of Balaam," *Textus* 12 (1985): 79-95.

short sections of text in which there were no obvious semantic differences in the contexts. Gooding and Leitier, in contrast to some earlier scholars, agree that translators can sometimes be inconsistent. The difference between Gooding and Leitier is that Gooding referred to this as a sloppy translation technique and Leitier described it as a purposeful choice.

Tov, in his study of Jeremiah, did a more complete analysis of the vocabulary than that done by Thackeray.[10] As a result, Tov was able to show that while there was some lexical inconsistency in Jeremiah, Thackeray's study failed to recognize the importance of the consistency that existed in many areas of the vocabulary. On the basis of lexical consistency within both parts of Jeremiah, as well as other factors, Tov tried to show that the small amount of lexical inconsistency between the two parts of the book was due to a revision of the second part of the book. Tov also expressed his disagreement with Thackeray's attitude towards literal translations, as follows:

> Further, it seems to us that Thackeray's group of "literal or unintelligent versions" in which he includes Jer. β' is based on a wrong assumption: "literal" versions are not necessarily "unintelligent" and *vice versa*.[11]

Tov's more positive attitude towards literal translations is probably due to his interest in textual criticism as is seen in his statement about the value of the LXX, as follows: "For OT scholarship, the main importance of the LXX lies in its Hebrew *Vorlage*, which at times may be superior to MT."[12]

Barr's study on literalness pointed to lexical consistency as one of a set of criteria used in defining the degree of literalness of a translation.[13] His assumption was that all the ⅏ translations were literal and that they only varied in the degree of literalness. He also noted that translations could be more or less literal in various aspects of their work. Tov and Wright built on Barr's study and began to identify features of the translation that could be counted with the help of computer technology.[14] Because of Tov and Wright's interest in the Hebrew *Vorlage*, their main reason for producing the statistics was to have an objective measurement of the degree of literalness of a translation. The objective measurements could then

---

10. Emanuel Tov, *The Septuagint Translation of Jeremiah and Baruch: A Discussion of an Early Revision of the LXX of Jeremiah 29-52 and Baruch 1:1-3:8*, Harvard Semitic Monographs, no. 8 (Missoula, Mont.: Scholars Press, 1976).

11. Ibid., 159.

12. Ibid., 168. See also J. Gerald Janzen, *Studies in the Text of Jeremiah*, Harvard Semitic Monographs, no. 6 (Cambridge, Mass.: Harvard University Press, 1973).

13. James Barr, *The Typology of Literalism in Ancient Biblical Translations*, Mitteilungen des Septuaginta-Unternehmens, no. 15 (Göttingen: Vandenhoeck & Ruprecht, 1979), 279-325.

14. Emanuel Tov and Benjamin G. Wright, "Computer-Assisted Study of the Criteria for Assessing the Literalness of Translation Units in the LXX," *Textus* 12 (1985): 149-87.

be used as a basis for generalizations "about the character of the translation," which "is the only help in evaluating deviations of the LXX."[15]

Wright's statistical study was likewise focused on determining the degree to which one can confidently recover the Hebrew *Vorlage* by retroversion from the Greek.[16] A more literal translation would probably provide a sounder basis for retroversion, so Wright statistically analyzed several aspects of various translations to provide an objective basis for determining the degree of literalness of a translation. One criterion he used was lexical consistency. Since his study was based on Sirach, which is only partially extant in Hebrew, his statistical studies of lexical consistency used Greek as their starting point. In general, Wright's study supported Thackeray's earlier descriptions of the books of the 𝔊 Scriptures.

The problems involved in defining lexical consistency, along with the variety of terms that have been used to describe this concept, have been thoroughly discussed by Olofsson.[17] In an extremely literal translation, lexical consistency is manifested by a one-to-one correspondence of Hebrew to Greek terms. Aquila's revision of the 𝔊 is often described as a translation with this kind of lexical consistency that is sometimes called "stereotyping." Statistical studies that measure lexical consistency generally are trying to measure the degree to which a one-to-one correspondence is maintained either from Hebrew to Greek or vice versa. In a less literal translation of the Hebrew, on the other hand, lexical consistency is manifested by the degree to which the 𝔊 consistently represents the different meanings of the Hebrew terms by repeatedly using the same Greek terms for the same meanings. These two types of lexical consistency have sometimes been described as pseudo concordance (stereotyping) and real concordance (the consistent representation of semantic concepts).[18] A translation that consistently represents semantic concepts may at times appear to be a "stereotyping" translation if the terms in both languages generally refer to the same concept. Due to the nature of languages and the probability that the concepts referred to by nouns are more likely to coincide, Olofsson suggests that "the consistent rendering of a verb is as a rule a better sign of a literal translation than the stereotype translation of a noun."[19]

In summary, lexical consistency has long been recognized as a means of evaluating various aspects of the 𝔊 translations. The most frequent foci of these studies were the question of the number of translators and the retroversion to the

---

15. Ibid., 150-51.
16. Benjamin G. Wright, *No Small Difference: Sirach's Relationship to Its Hebrew Parent Text*, Septuagint and Cognate Studies, ed. Claude E. Cox, no. 26 (Atlanta, Ga.: Scholars Press, 1989).
17. Staffan Olofsson, "Consistency as a Translation Technique," *Scandinavian Journal of the Old Testament* 6 (1992): 14-30.
18. Larson, *Meaning-Based Translation*, 162-63.
19. Olofsson, "Consistency as a Translation Technique," 20.

Hebrew *Vorlage*. The methods used to study lexical consistency have generally been what Tov has called "intuitive description."[20] In the last two decades, however, computer technology has made it possible to analyze statistically large segments of the 𝔊. These statistical analyses reportedly provide an objective analysis of the lexical consistency of the 𝔊 translations.

Methodology Used in This Study

In a relatively free translation, such as Exodus, lexical consistency is best described by means of identifying the factors that affect the lexical choices and the degree to which these same factors are used throughout the translation rather than by means of a statistical study of the frequency with which stereotypical equivalents are used.[21] In this section I will first list and illustrate some of the factors that affect lexical choices for nouns and verbs in 𝔊 Exodus.[22] Following this, I will briefly describe the method that will be used in this study for comparing the degree of lexical consistency in four sections of Exodus.

Factors That Affect Lexical Consistency. Lexical consistency in 𝔊 Exodus is affected by a variety of semantic and grammatical factors. Because of the influence of these factors, 𝔊 Exodus appears on the surface to be relatively inconsistent in its choice of lexical equivalents. Some of the factors that affect the choice of lexical equivalents include the grammatical forms of the Hebrew verb, the nature of the object of the verb, and the contextual translation of nouns.

One of the more frequently cited factors that affect lexical equivalents in the 𝔊 is the grammatical forms of verbs. Included in the list of oft cited forms are verbs in the hiphil and infinitive absolutes.[23] Examples of the effect of these gram-

---

20. Tov, *Text-Critical Use of the Septuagint*, 25.

21. A statistical analysis of 11-13 using Wright's methodology indicated that it was a fairly literal translation, but an examination of the actual words in context showed that the translation choices were affected by a variety of semantic and grammatical factors. This kind of disparity between statistical results and the actual usage in the text is especially problematic in smaller books or portions of text. Because of this, I have chosen not to use a statistical approach in this study. See Martha L. Wade, "Evaluating Lexical Consistency in the Old Greek Bible," *Bulletin of the International Organization for Septuagint and Cognate Studies* 33 (2000): 53-75.

22. Within the category of nouns I have included adjectives, which may be analyzed as a subcategory of nouns. I have not, however, included demonstratives, numbers, pronouns, or proper nouns. For a Hebrew grammar that treats adjectives as a subcategory of nouns, see Christo H. J. van der Merwe, Jackie A. Naudé, and Jan H. Kroeze, *A Biblical Hebrew Reference Grammar* (Sheffield: Sheffield Academic Press, 1999), 57. In addition, idiomatic phrases are not included in the statistics.

23. Emanuel Tov, "The Representation of the Causative Aspects of the *Hiph'il* in the LXX: A Study in Translation Technique," *Biblica* 63 (1982): 417-24; Raija Sollamo, "The LXX Renderings of the Infinitive Absolute Used with a Paranymous Finite Verb in the Pentateuch," in *La Septuaginta en la Investigacion Contemporanea: V Congreso de la IOSCS*, ed. Natalio Fernandez Marcos, Textos Y Estudios «Cardenal Cisneros» de la Biblia Poliglota Matritense, no. 34 (Madrid: Instituto «Arias

matical forms may be found in both of the tabernacle accounts of Exodus and also the control sample (11-13). For instance, infinitive absolutes that immediately precede a finite form of the same verb are translated by cognate nouns rather than by a verb form.²⁴ Likewise, hiphil forms of many verbs are translated by different lexical equivalents than the qal forms. For instance, בוא in the qal is often translated by a form of ἔρχομαι whereas in the hiphil it is frequently translated by a form of φέρω.²⁵ The grammatical form alone, however, is not sufficient for explaining the variety of lexical choices found in 𝔊 Exodus.²⁶

Another major factor that affects the translation of the verb is the direct object. For instance, within the tabernacle accounts רחץ is translated by λούω, νίπτω, and πλύνω. The Hebrew term, as used in Exodus, is a generic term that can refer to various types of washing, but the Greek terms are specific terms that refer to the washing of particular objects.²⁷ Likewise, the translation of קטר by

---

Montano» C.S.I.C., 1985), 101-13; and Emanuel Tov, "Renderings of Combinations of the Infinitive Absolute and Finite Verbs in the LXX—Their Nature and Distribution," in *Studien zur Septuaginta—Robert Hanhart zu Ehren: Aus Anlass seines 65. Geburtstages*, ed. Detlef Fraenkel, Udo Quast, and John William Wevers, Mitteilungen des Septuaginta-Unternehmens, no. 20 (Göttingen: Vandenhoeck & Ruprecht, 1990), 64-73. See also Swete, *Introduction to the Old Testament in Greek*, 308 and Thackeray, *Grammar of the Old Testament in Greek*, 47-50.

24. Translations of this usage of the infinitive absolute are found three times in the control sample (ἐκβολῇ [11:1], ἐπισκοπῇ and ὅρκῳ [13:19]), but only once in the critical text of the tabernacle accounts (θανάτῳ [31:14]). The relative frequency of this structure in the control sample may be due to its action-oriented nature.

25. The following are a few of the contrasting translations of qal and hiphil forms of verbs that may be found in the tabernacle accounts and control sample: בוא—qal (εἰσέρχομαι [29:30] and εἰσπορεύομαι [28:30]) and hiphil (εἰσάγω [25:14], εἰσφέρω [26:33], and φέρω [36:3]); ראה—qal (ὁράω [12:13]) and hiphil (δείκνυμι [25:9] and παραδείκνυμι [27:8]); קרב—qal (προσέρχομαι [12:48] and προσπορεύομαι [36:2]) and hiphil (προσάγω [28:1] and προσφέρω [29:3]); יצא—qal (ἐξέρχομαι [11;8], εἰσπορεύομαι [11;4], ἐκπορεύομαι [13:4]) and hiphil (ἐκφέρω [12:39] and ἐξάγω [29:46]); and עלה— qal (ἀναβαίνω [13:18] and συναναβαίνω [12:38]) and hiphil (ἀναφέρω [30:9], ἐπιτίθημι [40:4], ἐξάπτω [30:8], and συναναφέρω [13:19]). Frequently, verbs that are intransitive in the qal are translated by a different lexical choice when they occur in the hiphil because of the change in transitivity, i.e., the addition of a "causer."

26. In addition to grammatical form, the choice of lexical equivalents for verbs of motion, such as יצא, is affected by prepositional clauses indicating the direction of motion (compare the translation of יצא in 11:4 and 11:8). Another even more pervasive factor is the animate versus inanimate nature of the item that is being caused to move in hiphil forms of verbs. If the direct object is an inanimate item that has to be carried (meat or dough), then it will be translated with a form of φέρω (12:39, 46). If the direct object is animate (people), then a form of the verb ἄγω will be used (29:46). The effect of the nature of the object of the verb may be seen in several of the lexical equivalents of the verbs mentioned above, but there are "exceptions," such as 25:14 where εἰσάγω is used for the insertion of the poles, which are inanimate objects. This "exception," however, may be due to the fact that בוא is referring to the guiding of the poles into the rings rather than to the carrying of the poles, a difference that is also seen when animate beings are caused to move.

27. If objects, such as pieces of a sacrificial ram (29:17), were being washed, the Greek translator used the term πλύνω. When a human was washing his hands or feet, the term νίπτω was used

ἀναφέρω and θυμιάω is dependent on the items being "turned into smoke" in a particular context. The term ἀναφέρω is the more generic term that can be used in a wider context, whereas θυμιάω is limited to the burning of incense alone. Gooding, however, used the translations of קטר as an example of "variety in the translation of technical terms."[28]

Finally, the translator's theology and hermeneutical approach will occasionally affect lexical choices for verbs. For instance, the translator's understanding of God has affected the translation of the term שכן. In the 𝔊 Exodus, God does not "dwell" among the Israelites. Instead, God is either "seen" or "called upon."[29] Likewise, the translator's understanding about service by women at the door of the tent of meeting has affected his translation of צבא in 38:8 (𝔊 38:26).[30] Rather than

---

(30:18, 19, 20, 21; 40:31 [𝔊 38:27a], 32 [𝔊 38:27b]). Finally, λούω was used for the bathing of the entire person (29:4; 40:12). These usages reflect the definitions of the words in Johannes P. Louw and Eugene A. Nida, eds., *Greek-English Lexicon of the New Testament: Based on Semantic Domains*, 2d ed. (New York: United Bible Societies, 1989), s.v. 47.8, 9, 12. See also the discussion of these terms in J. A. L. Lee, *A Lexical Study of the Septuagint Version of the Pentateuch*, Septuagint and Cognate Studies, no. 14 (Chico, Calif.: Scholars Press, 1983), 36-40.

28. Gooding, 19. In contrast to Gooding's conclusion, the translation of קטר is context sensitive. When the object of the verb קטר is either a meat product or a combination of meat and other products that are turned into smoke on the altar of burnt offering, then the verb ἀναφέρω is used to refer to the event (29:18, 25; 30:20). If the object of the verb קטר is incense only, then the verb θυμιάω is used to refer to the event (30:7, 8; 40:27). In Exodus, the only exception to this description of the lexical equivalents for קטר is 29:13, where the verb ἐπιτίθημι is used. Interestingly enough, this is also the one occurrence where Wevers discusses the variants in the targums that may reflect another interpretation. See WeversNotes, 471. Thus, what Gooding describes as variation for variation's sake is in actuality choices of lexical equivalents that either reflect the difference in the object being burned or point to a difference in either the interpretation or the Hebrew *Vorlage*.

29. In 25:8, the 𝔊 translates שָׁכַנְתִּי with ὀφθήσομαι when God is "seen" in a physical dwelling place. When שכן is used in the context of God's relationship with his people, however, the translator uses a term that focuses on their interaction, ἐπικαλέω (29:45, 46). This same lexical equivalent, ἐπικαλέω, is frequently used in Deuteronomy to translate a similar phrase that refers to the place of worship where God's name will "dwell" (Deut 12:11, 14:23; 16:2, 6, 11; 26:2). When the subject of שכן is the cloud, the translator appropriately used a term that described the physical relationship of the cloud over the tent, ἐπισκιάζω (40:35). There is no evidence that these differences should be attributed to the presence of a different *Vorlage*. Wevers simply notes that "Exod [𝔊] changes the notion of God's dwelling into a matter of self-revelation." (Wevers Notes, 395.) Fritsch contends that this change is theologically motivated by the translator's avoidance of "the idea of God's meeting with man, an idea which would not agree with the more spiritualized conception of God generally found in the Greek translation of the Old Testament." See Charles T. Fritsch, *The Anti-anthropomorphisms of the Greek Pentateuch* (Princeton: Princeton University Press, 1943), 32-33. Fritsch's study, however, overemphasizes the theological differences in the Greek. Many of the issues he discusses are language related differences that are found in relatively free translations. It cannot, however, be denied that a translator's theology can affect the translation, as will be seen below.

30. Gooding discusses the possibility that the translator's Hebrew text contained the verb צום instead of צבא (or that the translator misread the verb), but dismisses this option. If the original had read צום, there would have been no reason to change it to צבא, which is the more difficult reading. Gooding sees the use of the term for fasting as an example of midrash. According to Gooding, "It is the

using the generic term λειτουργέω, which is used to translate צָבָא in Num 4:23, the translator of Exodus used νηστεύω, a term that refers to a specific kind of service that was appropriate for women.[31]

Nouns, likewise, are affected by a variety of contextual factors. One of the major grammatical factors that affects nouns is their grammatical function in a phrase or clause. For instance, in Hebrew the three types of metals used in the tabernacle construction are referred to by nouns, but in Greek they are translated by either nouns or adjectives depending upon the grammatical structure in which they occur and the syntactical requirements of the verb.[32] In addition to materials

---

common habit of midrash, not to *confuse* Hebrew words, but to interpret a (difficult, or objectionable, or sometimes quite innocent) word by deliberately *substituting* another, quite different word, the only justification for which is that it faintly resembles the first word in sound." See David W. Gooding, "Two Possible Examples of Midrashic Interpretation in the Septuagint Exodus," in *Wort, Lied und Gottesspruch: Festschrift für Joseph Ziegler*, ed. Josef Schreiner (Echter Verlag: Katholisches Bibelwerk, 1972), 44-45.

In contrast to Gooding, I believe that this translation choice is the result of the translator's hermeneutical approach that views Scriptures as a unified, non-contradictory whole. Because there is no other reference to women performing cultic service in the Pentateuch, the translator chose to translate this single, ambiguous verse in the light of the remainder of the Pentateuch. This resulted in the use of a specific term for a kind of service that women could do, νηστεύω, rather than using the more generic term for service, λειτουργέω, that could have been misinterpreted. This same hermeneutical approach was also used by other translators of the 𝔊 and as a result the other reference to women "serving" at the door of the "tent of meeting" in 1 Sam 2:22 was deleted. This type of "sanitizing" of the text (if it was done by the translator instead of being caused by a difference in the Hebrew *Vorlage*) is not a phenomenon limited to ancient translators. In my translation work in Papua New Guinea, I have had many long "discussions" with national translators who did not want their Bible to contain passages such as Gen 38 or crude remarks such as that of Paul in Gal 5:12.

Tov, in contrast, views the phrase in 1 Sam 2:22 as an addition to the 𝔐 based on 38:8. His discussion has some merit, but fails to include a reason for the change in the 𝔊 translation of 38:8 (𝔊 38:26). Since Tov connects these two passages, I believe that an explanation for the changes should also include both passages. See Emanuel Tov, *Textual Criticism of the Hebrew Bible* (Minneapolis, Minn.: Fortress Press, 1992), 273-74.

31. Concerning this choice of lexical equivalents, Wevers says, "Exod [𝔊] rather ingeniously has . . . 'the women who fasted,' fasting being one kind of cultic practice which anyone could perform; the women were thus performing their service by fasting, hardly a translation, but it is an interpretation," in WeversNotes, 631. Wevers, however, fails to see that the use of a specific term instead of a generic term is a frequently used translation technique, as has been described above.

32. A few of the grammatical and semantic factors that affect the translation of grammatical structures such as construct chains will be more thoroughly discussed in chapter four, but a few examples of the translations of זָהָב will illustrate some of the conditioning factors. If זָהָב is an unmodified noun in the *nomen rectum* position of a construct chain, the adjective, χρυσοῦς, will be the normal translation choice (25:26; 37:3 [𝔊 38:3]; 40:26). If זָהָב is modified by an adjective, such as טָהוֹר, then the normal translation choice will be the nominal form χρυσίον (25:17; 37:2 [𝔊 38:2]; 39:15 [𝔊 36:22]), but there are two exceptions in the first account that cannot currently be explained (28:36 and 30:4, which is a plus in the 𝔊). In addition, the grammatical requirements of the verb may affect the translation choices for זָהָב. For instance, when זָהָב is a double accusative with the verb עשה, it is normally translated by an adjectival form (37:7 [𝔊 38:6]), but with צפה, it is generally translated by a

used in the manufacture of items, other concepts that are expressed by means of nouns in Hebrew may be translated by either nouns or adjectives in Greek depending on the context.³³

In Exodus, the lexical equivalents used for generic terms and terms with multiple meanings are determined by their contexts. For instance, יָרֵךְ is translated by καυλός when it refers to the stem of the lampstand (25:31; 37:17 [𝔊 38:13]), by μηρός when it refers to a person's thigh (28:42), and by κλίτος when it refers to the side of the tabernacle (40:22, 24).³⁴ Context also affects the translation of terms that can refer to the same item. For instance, אֹהֶל and מִשְׁכָּן rarely co-occur and thus both are translated by σκηνή unless the context forces the translator to distinguish between the two.³⁵ When the Hebrew text clearly uses the two terms to refer to distinct items, מִשְׁכָּן, which is the inner tent, is always translated by σκηνή and the outer tent is referred to by either generic terms for coverings or by specific terms for curtains.³⁶

---

nominal form (25:13). The contrast between these two verbs can best be seen in 26:29, which contains both verbs in parallel constructions using their contrasting choices of adjective versus noun for the translation of זָהָב. Many clauses with עשׂה, however, are ambiguous in that זָהָב could be interpreted either as a double accusative or as a *nomen rectum* of a construct chain, both of which would be translated by an adjective in 𝔊 Exodus (25:24; 39:16 [𝔊 36:23]). In contrast, most clauses with צפה have a pronoun that refers to the item being covered. The presence of this pronoun limits the translation choice for זָהָב to a nominal form in Greek (26:37; 37:15 [𝔊 38:11]). As can be seen by the above references, the factors that affect the translation choices for זָהָב and similar words are widely varied and can be found in all sections of the tabernacle account. Similar choices are found in the lexical equivalents for the following Hebrew words that refer to materials used in the building of the tabernacle: אֵבֶן, תְּכֵלֶת, שֵׁשׁ, עֵז, נְחֹשֶׁת, כֶּסֶף, and זָהָב.

33. For instance, בֹּקֶר is normally translated by πρωί (29:34), but as the *nomen rectum* of a construct chain it is translated by πρωινός (29:41). Likewise אֱלֹהִים is generally translated θεός, but when אֱלֹהִים is interpreted as an attribute in the *nomen rectum* of a construct chain, i.e., a godly spirit rather than the Spirit of God, it is translated by θεῖος (31:3). This contrasts with the more frequent part-whole interpretation of a construct chain in which θεός is the lexical equivalent used, e.g., "the finger of God" (31:18).

34. Another example of a similar nature is the translation of בָּשָׂר by κρέας when it refers to the flesh of animals (12:8, 46; 29:14, 31, 32, 34), by σάρξ when it is referring to the human body (30:32), and by χρώς when it refers to the skin (28:42), though the difference between σάρξ and χρώς is not clear from these limited contexts. The fact that κρέας would not be a meaningful replacement for σάρξ or χρώς, however, points to the fact that context affects the choice of lexical equivalents in 𝔊 Exodus.

35. This is an example of assimilation, i.e., two distinct Hebrew terms being translated by one Greek term.

36. In 26:7, σκέπη was used to designate the outer tent, but in 26:11 אֹהֶל is translated δέρρις when it refers to the curtains that were joined together to form the outer tent. In 35:11, the plural form of παράρρυμα was used as the translation of אֹהֶל in a list of items connected with the inner tent. In 40:19, the plural form of αὐλαία was the term used to refer to the item being spread over the inner tent. When אֹהֶל and מִשְׁכָּן co-occur in the phrase, מִשְׁכַּן אֹהֶל מוֹעֵד, they are treated as terms in apposition and are collapsed into a form of the Greek phrase σκηνὴ τοῦ μαρτυρίου (𝔊 39:9; 40:2, 6, 29). This is similar to the exegetical understanding seen in the 𝔐, which has המשכן אהל מועד (39:32; 40:2, 6, 29). See the discussion of this phrase in chapter two.

These examples illustrate the context-sensitive nature of choices of lexical equivalents in 𝕲 Exodus. A wide diversity of factors has been shown to affect these choices for both nouns and verbs in all sections of the tabernacle accounts. Below, I will describe the method that will be used to quantify the amount of variation in lexical equivalents and to compare the degree to which choices of lexical equivalents are affected in sections of 𝕲 Exodus.

Comparing the Degree of Lexical Consistency. As has been previously noted, lack of lexical consistency has been one of the main criteria used for assigning parts of the tabernacle account to different translators. These studies, however, have tended to focus on the few "obvious" differences without acknowledging the high degree of consistency in both accounts.[37] In order to gain a better perspective on the nature of the similarities and differences in the lexical choices within the tabernacle accounts, the methodology used in this study will include the presentation of a detailed comparison of the tabernacle accounts with respect to lexical choices for nouns and verbs. This comparison will include analyses of lexical consistency in four sections of Exodus—a control sample (11-13), the first tabernacle account (25-31), the "core" of the second tabernacle account (𝔐 36:8-38:20), and the remainder of the second tabernacle account (35:1-36:7; 38:21-40:38).[38] Before comparing the lexical equivalents in these sections, however, I will present an analysis of the degree to which single versus multiple lexical equivalents of nouns and verbs are used within each section. The lack of stereotypical translations of nouns and verbs in these sections will demonstrate that Exodus in not an excessively literal translation in the sense that it uses only stereotypical lexical choices, i.e., one Hebrew word being consistently translated by one Greek word. At the same time, however, a comparison of the degree to which multiple lexical equivalents are used points to the similarity of approach in all four sections of Exodus.

The first tabernacle account has generally been considered to have been produced by the same translator as the first part of Exodus.[39] Because of this, the first

---

37. In Tov's study of Jeremiah, the amount of shared unique renderings between the parts of Jeremiah was one of the factors that led Tov to conclude that the second part of Jeremiah was a revision rather than a separate translation. This examination of the shared features of the translation is one way in which Tov's study of Jeremiah differed from Thackeray's. See Tov, *Jeremiah and Baruch*.

38. In Nelson's analysis of the tabernacle accounts he concludes that "there were two hands at work in the Tabernacle Account. The earliest level was the Old Greek, maintained in the core of Greek II." See Nelson, 130. This "core" section for Nelson is the translation of the 𝔐 36:8b-38:20, which is found in 𝕲 37-38. Due to different divisions of 36:8 in other studies, for the purpose of this study I have included 𝔐 36:8-38:20 in the core. The difference of a half verse is not likely to have affected the statistical evidence presented in this chapter.

39. In an early study by Thackeray, he proposed that Exodus be divided in half, but the division was for the purpose of transcription and not translation. According to Thackeray, the two sections could be identified by the "use or disuse of the form ἐάν for ἄν with the relative pronoun ὅς (ὅστις, ὅσος) or with a conjunction (ἡνίκα)." In addition, he notes the difference in the use of ἐναντίον and

tabernacle account and the control sample, which is of a similar genre, will be compared and used as a basis for evaluating the similarities and differences in lexical consistency of other sections of the tabernacle accounts. The other sets that will be compared are the core section in relationship to the remainder of the second tabernacle account and the entire second account in relationship to the first account.[40] For each of these sets of sections, a comparison will be made of the lexical equivalents of Hebrew nouns and verbs that occur in both sections of a set. These comparisons will include the degree to which the two sections in a set have identical lexical equivalents, partially shared lexical equivalents, and contrastive lexical equivalents. This comprehensive comparison of each set will show that a large percentage of both nouns and verbs is translated with either identical or partially shared lexical equivalents in both sections of a set. This high degree of shared lexical equivalents contrasts with the relatively small percentage of completely contrastive lexical equivalents that have been the basis for many discussions about the number of translators that produced the tabernacle accounts.

II. Lexical Consistency
within the Tabernacle Accounts

In this section I will first present tables that will show that all sections of Exodus examined for this book contain examples of the contextual translation of nouns

---

ἔναντι. The two parts of Exodus identified on the basis of these factors were 1:1-23:19 and 23:20-40:38. (See Thackeray, "Bisection of Books," 88-98.) The scribal nature of these differences may be seen in Wevers' comments about the gradual shift in usage from ἄν in the third century B.C. to ἐάν in the second century A.D. Wevers concludes, "Accordingly one is fully justified to accept only ἄν in relative clauses for the Pentateuch regardless of the witness of the fourth and fifth century manuscripts B and A which often have ἐάν." See John William Wevers, "The Göttingen Pentateuch: Some Postpartem Reflections," in *VII Congress of the International Organization for Septuagint and Cognate Studies, Leuven, 1989*, ed. Claude E. Cox, Septuagint and Cognate Studies, no. 31 (Atlanta, Ga.: Scholars Press, 1991), 53.

40. There are, of course, some difficulties with any comparison of dissimilar material, but the similarities between the first set (control sample [11-13] and first tabernacle account [25-31]) and the second set (core of the second tabernacle account [36:8-38:20] and remainder of the second tabernacle account [35:1-36:7; 38:21-40:38]) are worth noting. First, while the number of verses in the first set represents an approximately 1 to 3 ratio (83 verses in the control sample and 243 verses in the first account), the second set on the surface appears to have a very different ratio, 1 to 1.6 (80 verses in the core and 134 in the remainder of the second account). This difference, however, is more apparent than real because the 𝔊 translation of the core section contains fewer than 47 verses. The remaining verses are part of the numerous "minuses" that will be discussed in chapter five. Thus the ratio of the verses in the second set is about the same as that in the first set. In addition, the second set, like the first set, does not contain identical material. This contrasts with the third set (first and second tabernacle accounts), which contains the translation of large sections of material that are almost identical in the 𝔐 of both accounts. One would expect a greater number of shared vocabulary items in the comparison of this final set.

and verbs by more than one lexical equivalent. Second, I will present tables that show the degree to which translation choices are identical, partially shared, or contrastive in the three sets of sections discussed above. Finally, a larger sampling of the choices of lexical equivalents contained in both tabernacle accounts will be examined to further identify the factors that have affected these choices. Included in this will be discussions of lexical equivalents that may have been caused by either a different *Vorlage*, a misreading of the Hebrew text, or different translators. Major differences in lexical consistency that have been cited as evidence either for or against a single-translator theory will be discussed in the third section of this chapter.

Comparison of Lexical Consistency in Four Sections of Exodus

In all sections of Exodus studied for this book, a large percentage of both nouns and verbs had two or more lexical equivalents. In general, the more frequently a word was used, the more likely there were to be two or more lexical equivalents. Thus, the largest sections (first tabernacle account and remainder of second tabernacle account) contained larger percentages of nouns with multiple lexical equivalents than the smaller sections (control sample and core of second tabernacle account). (See table 5.) In addition, nouns were more likely to have stereotypical lexical equivalents than verbs, i.e., nouns were more likely to have one fixed lexical equivalent than verbs. (Compare tables 5 and 6.)

The core of the second tabernacle account was noticeably deficient in verbs available for analysis. This is due to both the nature of the Hebrew text and the fact that the 𝔊 contains an even further reduction of the number of verbal clauses. Despite the scarcity of verbs, however, this section, like the other sections, translated verbs contextually.[41] The factors that affected these choices, however, were

---

41. The conditioning factors for these three verbs lie in the larger context of the text. For instance, עשׂה is normally translated by ποιέω in the core section, as can be seen in the verses surrounding the one exception (36:35, 37 [𝔊 37:3, 5]). In 36:36 (𝔊 37:4), however, עשׂה is translated by ἐπιτίθημι. The use of ἐπιτίθημι makes the second tabernacle account almost identical to the parallel verse in the first tabernacle account with only minor changes in the case of a noun phrase (changed from genitive to accusative), the tense of the verb (changed from the future to aorist), and a minor plus, ἐν, that is probably added in conjunction with the choice of καταχρυσόω instead of χρυσόω. This choice to make the verse parallel to the first account allows the translator to shift the focus from the construction of the wood and metal items in the 𝔐 to the focus on the placement of the curtain in the 𝔊. It also makes explicit the fulfillment of the command in the first account. Alternately, the *Vorlage* used by the translator could have been more like the parallel first account verse (26:32). In addition, the participle in the phrase בְּעֹשֵׂי הַמְּלָאכָה (36:8) is translated by a participial form of ἐργάζομαι and הַמְּלָאכָה is technically a minus. Thus, the use of a specific term, ἐργάζομαι, instead of a generic term, ποιέω, is appropriate for the context. Due to the large quantity of difficulties in this verse, however, little more can be said about this choice of lexical equivalents.

Table 5. Lexical equivalents of nouns in four sections of Exodus

	Control sample	First tabernacle account	Core of second tabernacle account	Remainder of second tabernacle account
Nouns with 1 lexical equivalent (2-4 occurrences)	42	65	25	40
Nouns with 1 lexical equivalent (5-9 occurrences)	10	22	5	17
Nouns with 1 lexical equivalent (10 or more occurences)	4	16	1	8
Nouns with 2 lexical equivalents	18	54	10	30
Nouns with 3 or more lexical equivalents	2	29	1	14
Total of nouns	76	186	42	109
Percentage of nouns with 2 or more lexical equivalents	26%	45%	26%	40%

The translation of רקם (36:37 [𝕲 37:5]) by ὑφάντος instead of ποικιλτής (38:18 [𝕲 37:16]) is connected with other changes of vocabulary that make the curtain of the entranceway of the tent (outer curtain) identical to the inner curtain. This change in lexical equivalents for רקם is one of a series of difficulties in the text that resulted in an ambiguous translation with respect to the two curtains of the tent. If this change was due to the translator, then it reflects his interpretation that the entire tent was of the same construction with cherub designs on the inner tent and both curtains, i.e., the curtain that separated the Holy of Holies from the Holy Place and the curtain at the entranceway of the tent (𝕲 26:1; 37:3, 5). In the 𝔐, in contrast, the inner tent and inner curtain were works made by חשׁב, whereas the curtain at the entranceway of the tent (outer curtain) and the curtain at the gate of the courtyard were made by רקם (𝔐 26:36; 27:16). See Menahem Haran, *Temples and Temple-Service in Ancient Israel: An Inquiry into Biblical Cult Phenomena and the Historical Setting of the Priestly School* (Winona Lake, Ind.: Eisenbrauns, 1985), 160-63, for a discussion of the three types of fabric used in the tabernacle accounts. Positing a different *Vorlage* because of this lexical equivalent, however, would not resolve the other interrelated differences in the text and thus it is likely that the lexical equivalent used was due to the translator's choice.

The final verb in the core of the second tabernacle account that used two lexical equivalents is יצק. Unlike the other lexical equivalents discussed above, the translation of יצק by ἐπιτίθημι instead

Lexical Consistency

Table 6. Lexical equivalents of verbs in four sections of Exodus

	Control sample	First tabernacle account	Core of second tabernacle account	Remainder of second tabernacle account
Verbs with 1 lexical equivalent	12	20	3	13
Verbs with 2 lexical equivalents	18	19	2	13
Verbs with 3 or more lexical equivalents	11	19	1	10
Total of verbs	41	58	6	36
Percentage of verbs with 2 or more lexical equivalents	71%	66%	50%	64%

often the larger context of the verse and the conforming of the second account to the first account. In any case, the lexical equivalents were not synonyms used simply for the sake of variation.

Comparison of Lexical Consistency in Three Sets of Texts

Tables 7 and 8 are comparisons of the lexical equivalents of shared vocabulary in three sets of sections. Within each set being compared, a Hebrew word either has

---

of χωνεύω seems to be due to difficulties in the Hebrew text. The combination of יצק plus בְּ is not found elsewhere in the tabernacle accounts. In 1 Kgs 7:46, however, the בְּ identifies the material (clay) used for the mold into which the metal is poured. Context and the parallel passage (27:4) would indicate that this is not the appropriate meaning for 38:5. The translator could have ignored the Hebrew preposition and made 38:5 (𝔊 38:24b) parallel to 37:3, 13 (𝔊 38:3, 10). This, however, would not have faithfully rendered the distinctiveness of the Hebrew text. Instead, the translator used a generic term, ἐπιτίθημι, which often occurs as the second step of the process of attaching the rings, as is seen in 25:12, 26; 39:19, 20 (𝔊 36:26, 27). In the 𝔐, the making of the rings in 38:5 is explicit, but the attaching of the rings is left implicit. In the 𝔊, the reverse is true. The making of the rings is left implicit and the attaching of the rings is made explicit. (In the CEV, the translators likewise chose to leave the making of the rings implicit and simply said, "Then he attached a bronze ring beneath the ledge at the four corners to put the poles through." Other modern translations [TEV, Tok Pisin] have made both the making and the attaching of the rings explicit.) This verse in Hebrew is also difficult because it appears to contradict the parallel verse in the first account. In the first account, the rings are "made" on the רֶשֶׁת, but in the second account they are "poured out" on/in the sides of the מִכְבָּר. It is possible that by choosing to translate the term as "put on" the translator was attempting to ease the apparent "contradiction" between the parallel accounts in the Hebrew.

Table 7. Identical, partially shared, and contrastive lexical equivalents of nouns

	Control sample and first tabernacle account	Core and remainder of second tabernacle account	First and second tabernacle accounts
Nouns with identical lexical equivalents (2-4 occurrences)	8	10	36
Nouns with identical lexical equivalents (5-9 occurrences)	7	7	19
Nouns with identical lexical equivalents (10-14 occurrences)	3	5	9
Nouns with identical lexical equivalents (15 or more occurrences)	3	3	14
Nouns with both lexical equivalents shared	1	1	10
Nouns with 1 of 2 lexical equivalents shared	8	13	29
Nouns with multiple lexical equivalents of which 1 or more are shared	9	6	31
Nouns with contrastive lexical equivalents	9	2	22
Total of nouns	48	47	170
Percentage of nouns with identical lexical equivalents	46%	55%	52%
Percentage of nouns with partially shared lexical equivalents	35%	41%	35%
Percentage of nouns with contrastive lexical equivalents	19%	4%	13%

Table 8. Identical, partially shared, and contrastive lexical equivalents of verbs

	Control sample and first tabernacle account	Core and remainder of second tabernacle account	First and second tabernacle accounts
Verbs with 1 identical lexical equivalent	3	1	9
Verbs with 1 or 2 lexical equivalents shared	6	0	8
Verbs with multiple lexical equivalents of which 1 or more are shared	13	3	23
Verbs with contrastive lexical equivalents	9	3	13
Total of verbs	31	7	53
Percentage of verbs with identical lexical equivalents	10%	14%	17%
Percentage of verbs with partially shared lexical equivalents	61%	43%	58%
Percentage of verbs with contrastive lexical equivalents	29%	43%	25%

one lexical equivalent that occurs in both sections (identical), multiple lexical equivalents with at least one lexical equivalent that occurs in both sections (partially shared), or multiple lexical equivalents that are contrastive, i.e., one lexical equivalent occurs in one section and the other(s) in the second section. Given that the choice of lexical equivalents is often controlled by the semantic and grammatical contexts, the presence of multiple lexical equivalents, either partially shared or contrastive, does not necessarily point to the presence of different translators. Rather, it may simply point to different contexts. The only significant differences are those that are found in identical contexts.

Tables 7 and 8 show that all three sets share a similarly large degree of identical and partially shared lexical equivalents. In all three sets the percentage of contrastive lexical equivalents is relatively small. Thus, those who point to contrasting vocabulary as the main criteria to support a two-translator theory are focusing on a very small set of the vocabulary, whereas the majority of the words share all or some lexical equivalents. Verbs, as expected, contain fewer examples of identical lexical equivalents and most of these are verbs that occur infrequently. Thus, the relatively low percentage of identical lexical equivalents for the verbs again confirms that Exodus is a relatively free translation that is not characterized by a high degree of stereotyping.

Factors Affecting Choice of Lexical Equivalents

Lexical equivalents for Hebrew nouns and verbs that occur in both tabernacle accounts may be broadly grouped into three categories—nouns and verbs with identical lexical equivalents in both accounts, nouns and verbs with one (or more) shared lexical equivalents, and nouns and verbs with contrastive lexical equivalents. In this section I will summarize some of the factors that affect the choice of lexical equivalents in each of these categories.

Identical Lexical Equivalents. Lexical equivalents that were identical in both tabernacle accounts included a few verbs and a large number of nouns. The verbs, in general, occurred infrequently and thus the use of identical lexical equivalents was largely due to the identical environments in which they occurred.[42] The nouns included both common vocabulary items and items that were more technical in nature. Many of these common nouns were translated with lexical equivalents that are found throughout the 𝔊 Scriptures.[43] Other items only occurred once in each tabernacle account and were translated in an identical manner.[44] The

---

42. Verbs that were translated with identical equivalents included a few common verbs with equivalents found elsewhere in the 𝔊 Scriptures (e.g., כתב—γράφω, לקח—λαμβάνω, שרת—λειτουργέω), as well as more specific verbs that occurred in similar contexts in both accounts (e.g., אדם—ἐρυθροδανόω, רבע—τετράγωνος, נסך—σπένδω, רום—ἀφαιρέω). Identical lexical equivalents of verbs were occasionally found in parallel verses, but often the unifying factor was the meaning rather than the parallel nature of the verses. In the wider context of the entire book of Exodus, these verbs were often found to have other contextually appropriate lexical equivalents.

43. A few of the common nouns found in 𝔊 Exodus that used a lexical equivalent found throughout the 𝔊 Scriptures were as follows: אַיִל—κριός, אֵשׁ—πῦρ, בֵּן—υἱός, דּוֹר—γενεά, יָם—θάλασσα, כֹּהֵן—ἱερεύς, כָּנָף—πτέρυξ, מַחֲנֶה—παρεμβολή, מַיִם—ὕδωρ, עַם—λαός, רֶגֶל—πούς, שֻׁלְחָן—τράπεζα, שֵׁם—ὄνομα.

44. This is especially true of the list of twelve precious stones that was translated identically in both accounts (28:17-20 and 39:10-13 [𝔊 36:17-20]). In the context of the list, twelve distinct lexical equivalents were used for the stones. Outside of the lists, however, the term שֹׁהַם was also translated by the terms σάρδιον and σμάραγδος, which were used in the lists for two of the other stones, אֹדֶם and בָּרֶקֶת. Wevers says that the source of this variety of terms was the "uncertain identity" of the stone.

technical nature of these items and their occurrence in lists, however, may mean that either these terms were the common lexical equivalents of that time or that the translator of one list had access to the other list and copied the lexical choices. In either case, the combination of common vocabulary items and the translation of infrequently used technical terms resulted in a large percentage of nouns that were translated identically in both tabernacle accounts.

In addition, there was a limited number of Hebrew nouns that had two identical lexical equivalents in both accounts. In most cases, these were grammatically determined combinations of nouns and adjectives that functioned as lexical equivalents of nouns, as was discussed earlier in this chapter.[45] Other cases of identical lexical equivalents are due to possible differences in the *Vorlage* that were either present in the parallel passages of both accounts or were copied from one account to the other.[46] Finally, a few words with shared equivalents are best analyzed as examples of dissimilation that are either true synonyms or are used to increase the lexical cohesiveness of larger sections of the text.[47]

(WeversNotes, 394.) The important point for the comparison of the two tabernacle accounts, however, is that the translations are identical in the parallel passages despite the conflicting patterns of assimilation (two terms translated by the same term) and dissimilation (one term translated by a variety of terms) that are found in the translation of the term שָׁהַם. This points with high probability to the dependence of one account on the other account. In addition, several pieces of equipment associated with the tabernacle are identically translated, but because of differences in the surrounding contexts and occasionally in the order of the items, there is less of an impression of a list just being copied into another account. These lexical equivalents include the following: מִזְלָג—κρεάγρα and מִזְרָק—φιάλη (27:3=38:3 [𝕲 38:23]); and מְנַקִּית—κύαθος, קְעָרָה—τρυβλίον, and קַשְׂוָה—σπονδεῖον (25:29=37:16 [𝕲 38:12]).

45. These included the following nouns that were translated by either a nominal or an adjectival form depending on context: זָהָב, נְחֹשֶׁת, שֵׁשׁ, and תְּכֵלֶת. In addition, one noun, כְּרוּב, had two lexical equivalents due to the transliteration of the singular form of the noun by χερουβ (25:19 [2x]; 37:8 [𝕲 38:7 (2x)]) and the plural form of the noun by χερουβιμ (25:18, 19, 20 [2x], 22; 26:1, 31; 36:35 [𝕲 37:3]; 37:7 [𝕲 38:6]). Rather than translating the terms that refer to cherubs, the translator treated these terms as proper names and transliterated them following the Hebrew form in the text.

46. Either a difference in *Vorlage* or the misreading of the text led to the translation of 𝔐 מֵאָה בָאַמָּה by ἑκατὸν ἐφ' ἑκατόν (27:18; 38:9 [𝕲 37:7], 38:11 [𝕲 37:9]). This resulted in a phrase that was parallel to the translation of חֲמִשִּׁים בַּחֲמִשִּׁים (27:18). The second tabernacle account in the 𝔐 does not contain the phrase חֲמִשִּׁים בַּחֲמִשִּׁים. Because of this, there would have been no reason in the immediate context to adjust the translation in the second account. Therefore, the source of the difference must be sought elsewhere. The most likely source for this difference in lexical equivalents is either a different *Vorlage* or the dependence of the second account on the translation of the first account.

47. For example, מִשְׁחָה is translated by χρῖσις (29:21; 30:31; 31:11; 35:28; 37:29 [𝕲 38:25]; 39:38 [𝕲 39:15]) and χρῖσμα (29:7; 30:25 [2x]; 35:15 [𝕲 35:12a]; 40:9). Both lexical equivalents are used in both accounts, but only one pair of verses is similar and these use different lexical equivalents (30:25=37:29 [𝕲 38:25]). These two terms appear to be either true synonyms or at least words with overlapping referential meaning. In either case, the difference in meaning cannot be determined from the present contexts in the 𝕲 Exodus.

The translation of עֵדוּת by μαρτύριον and διαθήκη is an example of a different type of dissimilation that uses two distinct Greek terms that can refer to the same item (the tablets or the ark that

Partially Shared Lexical Equivalents. Words with partially shared lexical equivalents fall into one of three patterns. In the first pattern, the first account has additional lexical equivalents that are not present in the second. In the second pattern, the second account has additional lexical equivalents that are not present in the first account. In the third pattern, each account has unique, additional lexical equivalents. Verbs with partially shared lexical equivalents were almost equally distributed among the three patterns with slightly fewer following the second pattern because the second account is slightly shorter and has fewer verbal clauses.[48] Nouns, however, were unevenly distributed with the preponderance of the nouns belonging to the first pattern. A slightly higher number of nouns would have been expected because of the larger number of contexts in the first account that would have allowed for more variety of word meaning. While the nouns in the second and third pattern were approximately equal in quantity, there were over two times as many nouns in the first pattern as in the other categories.[49] This difference may indicate that when the first account was translated, the lexical equivalents were not established and thus a greater variety of terms was used as the translator attempted to communicate the ideas in the first tabernacle account. When the second account was translated, the translator had access to a set of lexical equivalents and was able either to choose the best from those equivalents for use in the

---

contains them). In their more frequent usages, however, the meanings of these terms are distinct ("witness" versus "covenant"). The lexical equivalent עֵדוּת—μαρτύριον occurs most frequently in the tabernacle accounts (25:16, 21, 22; 26:33, 34; 30:6, 26, 36; 31:18; 38:21 [𝔊 37:19]; 40:3, 20, 21). The lexical equivalent עֵדוּת—διαθήκη, in contrast, only occurs three times in the tabernacle accounts. Twice it is used as part of the designation for the ark (31:7; 39:35 [𝔊 39:14]) and once it refers to the tablets and by extension the ark (27:21). The term διαθήκη is the most frequent lexical equivalent for בְּרִית in the 𝔊 Scriptures. In Joshua, the ark is repeatedly referred to as אֲרוֹן הַבְּרִית (e.g., Josh 3:6), but this terminology is not found in the Pentateuch. Thus, it is unlikely that the difference in 𝔊 Exodus is due to the *Vorlage*. Instead, the term עֵדוּת is used to refer to the two tablets as one type of witness or testimony to God's covenant with the people (e.g., 2:24; 6:4; 19:5). The term בְּרִית, in contrast, refers to the actual covenant, but can also be used to refer to the two tablets. The term בְּרִית is only used once in the tabernacle accounts (31:16), but it occurs frequently throughout other parts of Exodus to refer to God's covenant with the people. The reason for the use of two lexical equivalents for עֵדוּת is unknown, but the effect of this choice is to provide lexical cohesion between otherwise distinct parts of Exodus through the use of the term διαθήκη. The use of the lexical equivalent עֵדוּת—διαθήκη in the second account is only found in a list in 39:35 (𝔊 39:14). This list is the parallel of the list in 31:7 and functions to summarize the list of items that were constructed, just as the list in 31:7 is the final list in the instructions given by God. Because of the parallel nature of the lists, it is unlikely that the lexical equivalents in the two accounts were independently made decisions, though the lists are by no means identical. Rather, this lexical equivalent provides further evidence of the interrelationship of the translation of the two accounts, though the direction of the interrelationship cannot be determined by the lexical equivalents used for עֵדוּת.

48. In the lists compiled from the tabernacle accounts, ten verbs followed the first pattern, eight verbs followed the second pattern, and thirteen verbs followed the third pattern.

49. In the lists compiled from the tabernacle accounts, thirty-two nouns followed the first pattern, thirteen nouns followed the second pattern, and fifteen nouns followed the third pattern.

second tabernacle account or to choose to reject those options and use a lexical equivalent that was viewed as an improvement over the choices in the first account. This does not necessarily point to a second translator for the second account, but it would point to the priority of the first account, especially if choices in the second account are generally an "improvement" over those of the first account.⁵⁰

Despite the difference in the amount of variation in the first account in comparison to the second account, the choices of lexical equivalents have been influenced by many of the same factors that were discussed above. A few nouns are translated by either a noun or an adjective depending on the grammatical structure in which they occur.⁵¹ Many nouns are translated by contextually controlled variants in which the first tabernacle account has a wider variety of contexts. Some of these are words that have meanings in different semantic domains, such as the term כַּף, which is translated by χείρ when it refers to the human hand

---

50. This suggestion is based on the assumption that translation quality tends to "improve" rather than degenerate when past experiences are used as a basis for future work. "Improvement," however, is culturally defined. Cultures that value a literal translation would see increased lexical consistency as an improvement. Cultures that value a meaning-based translation would see increased clarity as an improvement. The difficulty with any speculation in this area is that our knowledge of their culture must be derived from the results of their labors. See Roger G. Omanson, "Translation as Communication," *The Bible Translator* 47 (1996): 407-13 for a brief discussion of contrasting views of Bible translation in the modern world. According to Omanson, James Barr, as a representative of the academic community, desires a more literal translation in contrast to the functional equivalent approach used by many Bible societies. For a contradictory view of the development of texts that expects the text to degenerate, see James R. Davila, "Text-Type and Terminology: Genesis and Exodus as Test Cases," *Revue de Qumran* 16 (1993): 15. Concerning the creation account, Davila argues "that the more consistent pattern of G [𝔊] is the more original and that the inconsistent readings of M [𝔐] in 1,7 and 20 are due simply to entropy." See also William P. Brown, *Structure, Role, and Ideology in the Hebrew and Greek Text of Genesis 1:1-2.3*, SBL Dissertation Series, no. 132 (Atlanta, Ga.: Scholars Press, 1993).

51. Some nouns are translated by either an adjective or a noun, but only one of the two grammatical contexts is found in both accounts and the other is found only in the first account. These include the following nouns, whose conditioning factors are similar to those discussed in the category of identical equivalents: אֶבֶן, אֱלֹהִים, בֹּקֶר, כֶּסֶף, עוֹלָם, and עֵז. Both the nominal and adjectival lexical equivalents of כֶּסֶף are found in both tabernacle accounts, but the first account has an additional nominal equivalent, ἄργυρος (27:11) that was later revised to a form of ἀργύριον in the majority (Byzantine) text. (WeversNotes, 437.) In similar phrases in the second tabernacle account, only the more frequent nominal equivalent, ἀργύριον, is used (38:17, 19 [𝔊 37:15, 17]). Thus, the second account is more consistent through the elimination of an "unnecessary" lexical equivalent.

Both tabernacle accounts contain the adjectival equivalent of אֱלֹהִים, which was discussed above. The fact that the nominal lexical equivalent, θεός, is only present in the first account, however, is due to its probable absence from the *Vorlage* and not due to a translation choice. The word θεός does, however, occur in 36:2 as the translation of יהוה in the 𝔐 or possibly as the indicator of the presence of אֱלֹהִים in the *Vorlage* used by the 𝔊 translators. Wevers, however, notes that "Exod [𝔊] did not always carefully distinguish between יהוה and אֱלֹהִים. . . ." See the brief discussion of this issue in WeversNotes, 206.

(29:24) and by θυίσκη when it refers to a censer or type of dish (25:29; 37:16 [𝔊 38:12]).⁵² For a few terms, the "extra" lexical equivalent in the first account is due not so much to a change in meaning, but rather to the introduction of a new item in a part of the discourse, such as the translation of כַּפֹּרֶת by ἱλαστήριον ἐπίθεμα when it first occurs (25:17).⁵³ These are just a few examples of the diversity of fac-

---

52. Another example of contextually controlled meaning is seen in the translation of אִישׁ. The distributive usage of אִישׁ is translated ἕκαστος, but when אִישׁ is used to refer to a male human it is translated by ἀνήρ. The distributive usage of אִישׁ is found in both accounts (28:21; 30:12; 35:21; 36:4; 39:14 [𝔊 36:21]). The usage of אִישׁ to refer to a male human, however, is only found in conjunction with אִשָּׁה in the second account (35:22a, 29; 36:6). This does not, however, give the complete picture. In addition, the word אִישׁ is translated as a part of an idiom (25:20) and the parallel to this verse is part of a "minus" in the second account (37:9 [𝔊 38:8]). Finally, when אִישׁ occurs as the head of a relative clause, it is generally not literally translated and could be analyzed as a minus (25:2; 30:33, 38; 35:22b, 23; 36:1, 2).

The word רוּחַ is another example of a word that is translated by an "extra" lexical equivalent in the second account due to the presence of another semantic context. In the first account, רוּחַ is described as something that "fills" a person and is translated by πνεῦμα. This same usage is found in 35:31, which is the parallel of 31:3, but in 35:21, the רוּחַ is described as the moving force behind a person and is translated by ψυχή. The word ψυχή in all other occurrences in Exodus is a translation of נֶפֶשׁ. One could suggest that the use of ψυχή represents a different *Vorlage*, but this ignores the fact that πνεῦμα does not co-occur with δοκέω in the 𝔊. Thus, co-occurrence restrictions may have affected the choice of lexical equivalents for רוּחַ in this clause. This also ignores the fact that the translation of רוּחַ is part of the literary artistry discussed in Detlef Fraenkel, "Übersetzungsnorm und literarische Gestaltung—Spuren individueller Übersetzungstechnik in Exodus 25ff. + 35ff.," in *VIII Congress of the International Organization for Septuagint and Cognate Studies, Paris, 1991*, ed. Leonard Greenspoon and Olivier Munnich, Septuagint and Cognate Studies, no. 41 (Atlanta, Ga.: Scholars Press, 1995), 83.

53. The word כַּפֹּרֶת is translated in both accounts by the term ἱλαστήριον. The first occurrence of this term in the first account (and also in the entire Pentateuch), however, is translated by ἱλαστήριον ἐπίθεμα. This is the only place in the 𝔊 that the term ἐπίθεμα is used as a part of the translation of כַּפֹּרֶת. Nelson correctly notes that the word ἐπίθεμα was the term used by Josephus (*Ant.* 3.135, 137) to refer to the mercy seat. (Nelson, 143 n. 136.) Josephus, however, was writing to an audience that was uninformed about both the Jewish religion and the tabernacle. Because of his audience, he used a very generic term that described the physical appearance of the mercy seat, i.e., ἐπίθεμα "cover." The other two usages in Josephus that are cited by Nelson affirm the generic nature of the term because Josephus is using them not for the mercy seat, but rather as part of his attempt to describe some of the plants that he envisioned as models for part of the high priest's headdress (*Ant.* 3.176, 177). Thus, contra Nelson, the term ἐπίθεμα cannot be called a "Palestinian gloss" rather than the Old Greek simply on the basis of its generic usage by Josephus. Indeed, according to Liddell and Scott, the term has been in regular use from the Iliad down to at least the second century A.D. See Henry George Liddell and Robert Scott, *A Greek-English Lexicon*, 9th rev. and augmented with Revised Supplement ed. (Oxford: Oxford University Press, 1996), s.v. "ἐπίθεμα."

Prior to Nelson's attempt to explain the usage of ἱλαστήριον ἐπίθεμα, Frankel, as quoted by Popper, and McNeile had listed the "contrasting" translations of כַּפֹּרֶת as evidence that supported the theory that two translators produced the two tabernacle accounts. See Julius Popper, *Der biblische Bericht über die Stiftshütte: Ein Beitrag zur Geschichte der Composition und Diaskeue des Pentateuch*. (Leipzig: Heinrich Hunger, 1862), 173 and A. H. McNeile, *The Book of Exodus* (London: Methuen and Company, 1908), 226. Gooding rightly critiqued their usage of this and other similar examples because they referred to singular occurrences in each account rather than examining all the terms that

Lexical Consistency 79

tors that have resulted in the presence of an "extra" lexical equivalent in either the first or second account. These extra lexical equivalents, however, are contextually

---

were used in each account. Gooding dismisses the translation of כַּפֹּרֶת by ἱλαστήριον ἐπίθεμα as just another example of the translator's use of "variety in the translation of technical terms." (Gooding, 32-37.) Le Boulluec and Sandevoir, in contrast, suggest that ἐπίθεμα is an etymologizing gloss based on כפר. See Alain Le Boulluec and Pierre Sandevoir, *L'Exode*, vol. 2, La Bible D'Alexandrie, ed. Marguerite Harl (Paris: Cerf, 1989), 256-57. Finn allows that ἐπίθεμα may be part of the text "due to a variant reading which has crept from the margin into the text," but he seems to prefer the possibility "that when the Mercy-seat is first mentioned the translators thought it advisable to define ἱλαστήριον more closely as a 'covering', and afterwards dropped the explanatory word." (Finn, "The Tabernacle Chapters," 451.) This same thought is also seen in WeversNotes, 398. Even if ἐπίθεμα were a gloss, one would still need to explain why it appears only with the first occurrence of the term ἱλαστήριον. Linguistically, this is the position in a discourse in which one would expect a fuller reference because of the fact that new information was being introduced to the reader. (Larson, *Meaning-Based Translation*, 482-84.) The "rules" for introducing new information, however, are very language specific and extra identification was evidently not needed in Hebrew. (In Hebrew, both the first usage [25:17] and the usage of כַּפֹּרֶת in the parallel verse [37:6] are indefinite and all other occurrences are definite. In Greek, however, the first occurrence is indefinite and all other occurrences are definite including the parallel verse in the second account.) In either case, whether gloss or translation technique, the use of ἐπίθεμα is appropriate for its position in the discourse and cannot be used as evidence in the discussion about the number of translators who produced the tabernacle accounts. For a more theological discussion of the translation of כַּפֹּרֶת see Klaus Koch, "Some Considerations on the Translation of kapporet in the Septuagint," in *Pomegranates and Golden Bells: Studies in Biblical, Jewish, and Near Eastern Ritual, Law, and Literature in Honor of Jacob Milgrom*, ed. David P. Wright, David Noel Freedman, and Avi Hurvitz (Winona Lake, Ind.: Eisenbrauns, 1995), 65-75.

Another example of a translation or gloss that is appropriate for its place in the discourse is the use of the appositional phrase ἔλαιον ἄλειμμα as a translation of the term שֶׁמֶן (30:31). In all other occurrences in both accounts, the term שֶׁמֶן is translated simply by ἔλαιον. In these other occurrences, however, the oil is always further defined by the context, so that the reader knows the function of the oil, e.g., oil for the light (27:20; 39:37 [𝔊 39:16]); oil that is used with bread and flour (29:2, 23, 40); oil of anointing that is poured, sprinkled, or "anointed" on an object (29:7, 21; 40:9); oil that is made by a perfumer (30:25); or oil that is in a list with spices (30:24; 31:11; 35:15 [𝔊 35:12a], 19 [a plus in the 𝔊], 28; 37:29 [𝔊 38:25]; 39:38 [𝔊 39:15]). In 30:31, however, שֶׁמֶן occurs in a simple stative clause in which the oil is the item being identified. In the following verses, the oil is described, but only in negative terms of what cannot be done with it or made like it. In addition, this reference is in a quotation that is within the larger quotation (the instructions from God). Within a new quotation, information is often treated as "new" information even if it has been discussed in the discourse prior to the quotation. Given that the usage of שֶׁמֶן in 30:31 is unique in that it is in a quotation and lacks a context that defines the oil's function, Le Boulluec and Sandevoir's suggestion that the addition of ἄλειμμα was for the purpose of defining the usage of the oil, i.e., as an ointment, seems appropriate. (Le Boulluec and Sandevoir, *L'Exode*, 311.) Thus, as with the addition of ἐπίθεμα, ἄλειμμα was added to clarify the identification of an item. Like ἐπίθεμα, it also cannot be proven whether it was an addition through a gloss that was incorporated into the text or part of the translation technique. The appropriateness of its location in the text argues against this addition being accidental, but unlike the addition of ἐπίθεμα, the addition of ἄλειμμα was not accepted by later scribes. (See discussion of textual variants in WeversNotes, 501.) This may be due to the fact that while ἐπίθεμα was viewed as a good explanation of the ἱλαστήριον, the שֶׁמֶן was viewed by the later scribes not as ἄλειμμα, but as a flowing oil that could be poured. Again, as with כַּפֹּרֶת, this additional lexical equivalent for שֶׁמֶן cannot be used as part of the evidence for a two-translator theory of the production of the 𝔊 tabernacle accounts.

determined and cannot be used as support for a two-translator theory of the production of the 𝔊 tabernacle accounts.

As mentioned above, the first account often appears to distinguish carefully the contexts in which Hebrew words occur and then to use a distinct Greek term for each significant context. The second account, however, tends to modify the usage of the terms in the first account while maintaining lexical cohesion through the use of some of the same terms, especially in parallel or similar verses. One example of this is תְּרוּמָה, which in the first account is translated by three terms from the same semantic domain—ἀπαρχή, ἀφαίρεμα, and εἰσφορά. In the second account, ἀπαρχή and ἀφαίρεμα continue to be used, but the "pluses" in the 𝔊, the careful placement of ἀπαρχή to form an inclusio around a list, and the literary effect of the use of ἀφαίρεμα to translate related Hebrew terms demonstrate the shift in usage of the lexical equivalents.[54] A similar shift in the usage of lexical

---

54. The lexical equivalents ἀπαρχή and ἀφαίρεμα are found in both tabernacle accounts, but εἰσφορά is only found in the first tabernacle account. As with other lexical equivalents, the context determines which lexical equivalent is used in each occurrence of the first account. The term ἀπαρχή is used to refer to the gifts brought for the building of the tabernacle (25:2 [2x], 3). The term ἀφαίρεμα is limited to the offerings/sacrifices made by the priests (29:27, 28 [3x]). The term εἰσφορά is used for the head tax of the census (30:13, 14, 15). In the second account, the term ἀπαρχή is used as the translation of תְּרוּמָה only at the beginning of the list of materials (35:5b) and at the conclusion when the people are prohibited from bringing any further contributions (36:6). The literary effect of these lexical choices is to form an inclusio that separates the list of materials in the introduction from the actual production of the tabernacle. It also creates lexical cohesion between the first and second tabernacle accounts. In the last part of the second tabernacle account, the translator has created further lexical cohesion by using ἀπαρχή as the translation of תְּנוּפָה at the beginning of the summary that lists the amounts of metal used in the construction of the tabernacle (38:24 [𝔊 39:1]). This context is parallel to that of 35:5b, which also begins its list of materials with gold. All other occurrences of תְּרוּמָה in the second tabernacle account are translated by ἀφαίρεμα (35:5a, 21, 24 [2x]; 36:3). The term ἀφαίρεμα is also used to translate תְּנוּפָה (35:22, 38:29 [𝔊 39:6]) and נְדָבָה (35:29). As a result of these lexical choices, the introduction of the second tabernacle account (35:1-36:7) uses ἀφαίρεμα to refer to all the contributions with the exception of the use of ἀπαρχή in the inclusio. Thus, ἀφαίρεμα in effect becomes the generic term that is used for all types of offerings in the second account. It is even included as a "plus" in the text of 38:25 (𝔊 39:2) so that all three metals—silver from the census (38:25 [𝔊 39:2]), bronze (38:29 [𝔊 39:6]), and the left-over gold (𝔊 39:11 [This entire verse is a "plus" in the 𝔊.])—are referred to by the term ἀφαίρεμα, as is also the case in 35:24 for the silver and bronze.

In the first tabernacle account, the terms ἀπαρχή and ἀφαίρεμα are used in two distinct contexts to refer to separate types of gifts or offerings. Both lexical equivalents are retained in the second account and used to refer to the same items, the gifts. In this sense, Wevers is correct in noting that the terms are "synonyms." (WeversNotes, 391.) This, however, fails to capture the shift in usage between the two accounts. Nelson's suggestion "that the Old Greek is ἀφαίρεμα and that in the introductory sections of Gk II ἀπαρχή has been used by a Palestinian revisor," would be hard to defend given the fact that both terms are used in both accounts. (Nelson, 96.) This is especially true since his "Old Greek" term, ἀφαίρεμα, is used in a section of the first account that discusses the offerings made by the priests, a section that has no parallel in the second account and thus could not have been copied from Nelson's "core" account or from anywhere in the second tabernacle account, which is an earlier translation according to Nelson. Instead of a shift in preferences from ἀφαίρεμα to ἀπαρχή over the passage of time, as Nelson claims, the usage of these two terms in the second tabernacle account repre-

equivalents between the two accounts may also be seen in an examination of the lexical equivalents of שֶׁקֶל and לֵב.⁵⁵ The translations of these terms show both

---

sents a change of usage with ἀφαίρεμα assuming the role of a more generic term that can refer to the same items referred to by ἀπαρχή. The term ἀπαρχή, in turn, is mainly used to accomplish a literary effect (inclusio) and to provide lexical cohesion between the first account and both the beginning and end of the second account.

55. In the first tabernacle account, the term שֶׁקֶל is transliterated, σίκλος, when it refers to a weight (30:24), but δίδραχμον is used when שֶׁקֶל refers to a monetary amount (30:13 [4x], 15). In the second tabernacle account, the word שֶׁקֶל is always transliterated. The fact that a שֶׁקֶל is the equivalent of a δίδραχμον is, however, also presupposed in the second tabernacle account, as can be seen by the translation of בֶּקַע "half of a shekel" by δραχμή (38:26 [𝔊 39:3]). Thus, the underlying meaning is identical in both accounts, but in the second account the translator chooses to use the same lexical equivalent, σίκλος, for every occurrence of שֶׁקֶל rather than using two lexical equivalents as is done in the first account.

In the first tabernacle account, the word לֵב is translated by στῆθος when it refers to the placement of the breastpiece on Aaron's chest (28:29, 30), a passage that has no parallel in the second tabernacle account. In both accounts, the term לֵב, when it refers to the mental and/or psychological center of a person, is translated either by καρδία or διάνοια. Fraenkel suggests that the variation between καρδία and διάνοια in 35:21-29 is part of a literary technique built around the use of repetition, chiastic structures, and other literary phenomena. (Fraenkel, "Übersetzungsnorm und literarische Gestaltung," 81-84.) While there is no doubt that the translator's literary skill has affected the choice of vocabulary in 35, this does not explain the choices in the other parts of the accounts nor does it explain why two seemingly synonymous lexical equivalents existed. After examining the lexical equivalents of לֵב, Nelson says, "The conclusion from this evidence is that the Old Greek is καρδία and the Palestinian form διάνοια. This is another indication that the introductory material has undergone Palestinian revision." (Nelson, 70-71.) His conclusion, however, fails to adequately explain the continued existence of both lexical equivalents in both accounts after supposedly undergoing such a revision. It also does not explain the continued usage of καρδία to represent this concept in both Intertestamental and NT literature. If Nelson's hypothesis about διάνοια being a part of a Palestinian revision is correct, then this revisionary tendency was a phenomenon of very limited scope that did not leave a lasting impression on language usage. In contrast to Nelson, Wevers says concerning a text critical decision between καρδία and διάνοια in 35:10 (35.9 in the Göttingen edition), "In view of the obvious preference which the translator of ch. 35 had for διανοίᾳ this would seem to be a wise choice for critical text in v. 9." See WeversText, 271. This may be true, but the translator's "obvious preference" does not explain the remaining three occurrences of καρδία in the second account.

The interrelatedness of the first and second accounts may be seen in the fact that the two sets of verses that would be considered to be either parallel (25:2=35:5) or at least similar (31:6 and 36:2) use the same lexical equivalent, καρδία. The presence of parallel or similar passages would, therefore, explain two occurrences of καρδία in the second account. In addition, the usage of πᾶσι τοῖς σοφοῖς τῇ διανοίᾳ in 28:3 is mirrored in the singular phrase πᾶς σοφὸς τῇ διανοίᾳ in 36:1, though the verses themselves are not similar. Thus, all the lexical choices in the first account that refer to the mental and/or psychological center of a person (whether καρδία or διάνοια) are replicated in the second account. This leaves "unexplained" only the use of καρδία in 35:21, which Fraenkel claims is part of the literary technique. The remainder of the occurrences of לֵב in the second account are all translated by διάνοια, which is the more "natural" Greek equivalent for the mind. Thus, the lexical choices in the second account are best explained using the first account as the point of reference. The fact that καρδία and διάνοια are used interchangeably for this meaning of לֵב is best viewed as a reflection of a sociolinguistic setting in which two linguistic systems (Greek and Hebrew) collided and became mixed. This same phenomenon is seen regularly when there is interaction between two language sys-

continuity and change in the choice of lexical equivalents in the second tabernacle account with respect to the first tabernacle account. The fact of the interdependence of the two accounts is clearly seen in these examples. In addition, the detailed discussions of these words in the notes below show that the shift in usage of lexical equivalents for at least תְּרוּמָה and לֵב is best explained when the first account is used as the point of reference for the choices in the second account.

Besides simply shifting the usage of the lexical equivalents in the process of translating the second account, in a few cases it appears that the translator of the second account chose to abandon the multiplicity of nouns used in the first account and bring a degree of consistency to the translation.[56] Other variations in lexical equivalents in the second account are due to the occurrences of Hebrew words in more grammatically complex structures in the second account than those found in the first account. Occasionally, however, even when the same structure occurs in parallel verses in both accounts, different translations are used. This does not necessarily indicate that the second account was produced by a different translator, but it does highlight the fact that the early translator(s) like their modern counterparts struggled with grammatical difficulties in the text and resolved the problems using a variety of approaches.[57]

---

tems and one system encroaches upon the other. In this type of sociolinguistic setting, the morphology of the language being used (Greek) is the least likely to be affected by the other language, whereas equivalent lexical items and concepts are often substituted or used "interchangeably" within even the first generation of bilingual speakers. This kind of "interchangeability" is never, however, either complete or random. Rather, it is controlled by the "audience" being addressed and other factors such as the speaker's background. In the multi-lingual sociolinguistic setting of Hellenistic times, the usage of both καρδία and διάνοια can best be understood when the audience that was being addressed and other sociolinguistic factors are considered. Examples of differing usages in Philo, Josephus, NT, and others may be seen in the *Theological Dictionary of the New Testament*, s.v. "καρδία," 3:605-14. For a more theoretical discussion of some of the factors that affect language change, see Carol Myers-Scotton, *Duelling Languages: Grammatical Structure in Codeswitching* (Oxford: Clarendon Press, 1993).

56. The "extra" lexical equivalents for מַעֲשֶׂה in the first account are mainly due to the use of more specific terms in phrases that elsewhere in the first account are translated with the more generic term ἔργον. For instance, מַעֲשֶׂה is translated by ἐργασία (26:1), ποικιλία (27:16), and τέχνη (30:25) in clauses where its grammatical role is also reinterpreted from being in apposition to another phrase in the 𝔐 to being in the dative case as a description of the manner in which the item was made in the 𝔊. The dative case can also be used with ἔργον (27:4), so the grammatical and contextual factors that led the translator to use a dative case are not sufficient in and of themselves to explain the variety of lexical equivalents used for מַעֲשֶׂה. In addition, when מַעֲשֶׂה is used as a point of comparison for the workmanship of another item, the translator of the first account again uses more specific terms. In 28:15, the term ῥυθμός is used after earlier using ποίησις for a similar concept (28:8), though admittedly in a more complex grammatical structure. This last usage, which is appropriate since a product rather than an activity is being discussed, is retained in the parallel verse in the second account (39:5 [𝔊 36:12]). The retention of this term provided some continuity between the accounts, since this parallel verse in the second account is modified in several other ways. All other occurrences of מַעֲשֶׂה in the second account are translated by ἔργον (36:35, 37 [𝔊 37:3, 5]; 37:29 [𝔊 38:25]; 38:4 [𝔊 38:24]; 38:18 [𝔊 37:16]; 39:3 [𝔊 36:10]).

57. The word מְלָאכָה is used in very limited contexts in the first account and thus is always translated by ἔργον (31:3, 5, 14, 15 [2x]). In the second account, the lexical equivalent ἔργον is used

Finally, the translation choices in the second tabernacle account often demonstrate a desire to express a concept using a more specific or accurate term. As a result of this, the second tabernacle account contains lexical equivalents that are not found in the first account. Two of these "extra" lexical equivalents in the second tabernacle account demonstrate the same translation technique of using a referentially correct, but definitely non-literal translation of a term.[58] In other

---

most frequently (35:2 [2x], 21, 24, 29, 33, 35 [2x], 36:1, 2, 3, 4 [2x], 5, 7; 38:24 [𝕲 39:1]; 39:43 [𝕲 39:23]; 40:33), but there are also a number of verses that have been adjusted due to the complexity of the grammatical context and its co-occurrence with other words. For instance, 31:3 and its parallel verse, 35:31, contain a phrase that is difficult to interpret due to the unequal nature of the four items that are conjoined, i.e., בְּחָכְמָה וּבִתְבוּנָה וּבְדַעַת וּבְכָל־מְלָאכָה. The first three items in this phrase are terms from the same semantic domain that are often found in parallel expressions. The fourth item, "all work," however, does not seem to "fit" with "wisdom, understanding, and knowledge." While some modern exegetes and translations have attempted to maintain the four categories represented by these terms (RSV; see also Durham, *Exodus*, 409-10, who maintains the four categories in his translation, but not as clearly in his comments.), others have interpreted the final phrase as being subordinate to the third term or one that modifies the previous three terms (NIV, NJPS, NRSV, TEV). This latter interpretation is the one chosen by the 𝕲, although the more literal translation in the first account, ἐν παντὶ ἔργῳ, is adjusted to πάντων in the second account with a "plus," κατὰ πάντα τὰ ἔργα, in the following verse that looks similar to a more literal translation of the phrase. Thus, the first and second accounts represent two attempts at translating a difficult phrase that still causes problems for translators and exegetes. These could represent two attempts by the same translator or separate attempts by two different translators.

In addition to ἔργον, מְלָאכָה is also translated by a variety of terms that are largely determined by the grammatical context and other terms in the context. For instance, in 36:6 the direct object מְלָאכָה has been incorporated into the translation of the verb, i.e., "to work" instead of "to do work." This simplifies the translation of the following grammatical structure. While this exact translation technique is not found elsewhere in Exodus (with the possible exception of a problematic verse [36:8]), the verb ἐργάζομαι is used elsewhere as a translation of עשה in both accounts (31:4, 5; 35:10; 36:4). In two cases, the word מְלָאכָה fills two different semantic functions in the same clause. The second occurrence of מְלָאכָה in each of these cases is translated by a distinct, but appropriate term, κατασκευή (36:7) and ἐργασία (38:24 [𝕲 39:1]). In 36:4 the word מְלָאכָה also occurs twice in the same clause, but here the second occurrence of the word is in a phrase that is in apposition to a phrase in the main clause. Because of this, it is semantically acceptable to use the same lexical equivalent, ἔργον, two times. Thus the "extra" lexical equivalents for מְלָאכָה in the second tabernacle account are primarily due to the grammatical complexities of the Hebrew text. Wevers fails to see the effect of semantic function on the choice of lexical equivalents and thus somewhat obtusely comments about (38:24 [𝕲 39:1]), "the translator thus distinguished between the cognates מלאכה and מלאכת by using cognate nouns as well." See WeversText, 139.

58. The term קֹדֶשׁ is translated by either ἅγιος or ἁγίασμα in both tabernacle accounts, depending on the context. In 38:27 (𝕲 39:4) the same term, קֹדֶשׁ, refers to the tabernacle and is used in the phrase אַדְנֵי הַקֹּדֶשׁ. Rather than being translated with its normal lexical equivalent, ἅγιος, however, it is translated by σκηνή. This usage of the term is referentially correct, but it is not a literal translation. It is possible that the translator's text contained a different *Vorlage* or that he somehow misread the text, but the translation, in any case, fits well with the following chapter in which the 3ms suffix on the term אֲדָנָיו refers back to the מִשְׁכָּן (40:18) or possibly to אֹהֶל (39:33 [𝕲 39:13]). In either case, the item to which the bases are related in the following chapters is translated by σκηνή in the 𝕲.

This same translation technique is also seen in the choice of a lexical equivalent for עֹלָה in 38:1 (𝕲 38:22). In the first tabernacle account, the frequently seen approach that uses unique terms for each

examples, the second account uses more specific terms instead of the generic terms used in the first account.[59] A few differences, such as the translation of מְכֻבָּר and related terms, may reflect a difference in interpretation as well as a difference in translation technique that will be discussed in section four of this chapter.

Verbs with partially shared lexical equivalents were more likely than nouns to include contextually controlled lexical equivalents. The choice of these lexical equivalents may be controlled by either semantic or grammatical factors in the context. Because of the differences in contexts, "extra" lexical equivalents may be found in either or both tabernacle accounts.[60]

---

unique context is probably the source of the four different lexical equivalents for the term עֹלָה—ὁλοκαύτωμα (29:18; 30:28), ὁλοκαύτωσις (29:25), θυσία (29:42), and κάρπωμα (30:9). In contrast, the second tabernacle account uses only κάρπωμα (40:6, 10, 29), except for 38:1 (𝔊 38:22), which refers to the altar as τὸ θυσιαστήριον τὸ χαλκοῦν rather than τὸ θυσιαστήριον τῶν καρπωμάτων. The choice of this lexical equivalent is probably due to the "plus" in the 𝔊 that identifies the source of the material used for the making of the bronze altar. This "plus" could have been present in the Vorlage used by the translator of the 𝔊, but it is more likely due to the translator's hermeneutical approach to the text, as will be discussed further in chapter five.

59. The word כָּתֵף, when it refers to the shoulder-pieces of the ephod, is translated by ἐπωμίς (in the plural) in both accounts (28:7=39:4 [𝔊 36:11]). Both accounts likewise translate כָּתֵף by ὦμος when it occurs in the phrase כִּתְפֹת הָאֵפֹד (28:12=39:7 [𝔊 36:14]; 39:18, 20 [𝔊 36:25, 27]). When כָּתֵף is used to refer to the parts of the courtyard curtains on either side of the gate of the courtyard, however, the first account uses the generic term κλίτος (27:14, 15), which has also been used for the longer sides of the courtyard (27:9, 11), whereas the second account uses the more accurate term νῶτον (38:14, 15 [𝔊 37:12, 13]). This same Greek term is also used for the parts of the walls on the sides of the gates in Ezekiel's vision of the temple (Ezek 40:41, 44; 46:19), which confirms the accuracy of this translation in the second tabernacle account.

A second example is seen in the translations of קָצָה. In parallel verses, in which קָצָה refers to part of the ephod, both accounts use the term μέρος (28:7=39:4 [𝔊 36:11]). When קָצָה is used to refer to the part of the mercy seat to which the cherubs are attached, the first account uses the generic term κλίτος (25:18-19), but the second account uses the more specific term ἄκρος (37:8 [𝔊 38:7]), which is used to refer to the extremities of various items in Exodus. Likewise, while the first account again uses κλίτος to refer to a part of the breastpiece (𝔊 28:29a), the second account, in contrast, translates קָצָה with the more specific term ἀρχή (39:16 [𝔊 36:23]). According to Louw and Nida, this term refers to "the corner of a two-dimensional object, such as a sheet of cloth." (Louw and Nida, Semantic Domains, s.v. 79.106.) The remaining occurrences of קָצָה in the first account's description of the breastpiece and ephod are a "minus" in the 𝔊, but in the translation of the parallel second account, the lexical equivalents συμβολή (39:18 [𝔊 36:25]) and πτερύγιον (39:19 [𝔊 36:26]) are used in an attempt to describe accurately the construction of this item.

60. For instance, the qal passive participle of כפל, which refers to the doubled over fabric of the ephod, is translated appropriately by the adjective διπλοῦς in both tabernacle accounts (28:16=39:9 [𝔊 36:16]). In the first account, however, a finite form of כפל is also used to refer to an event and is correctly translated ἐπιδιπλόω (26:9).

As with nouns, verbs are often translated with distinct terms for each context in the first account. The verb צפה is most frequently translated by καταχρυσόω in both tabernacle accounts (25:11a, 13, 28; 26:29 [2x]; 30:3, 5; 36:36, 38 [𝔊 37:4, 6]; 37:2 [𝔊 38:2]; 37:15 [𝔊 38:11]; 38:28 [𝔊 39:5]), but the first account also uses three other lexical equivalents that are probably determined by both the item being "covered" and the metal that is used to "cover" the item. For instance, bronze bars are cov-

Contrastive Lexical Equivalents. In addition to nouns and verbs that either have identical or partially shared lexical equivalents, there is a limited number of nouns and verbs that have contrastive lexical equivalents. These contrasting choices often represent differences in interpretation. The second interpretation may reflect either a new understanding by the same translator or the interpretation of a second translator.[61] These contrastive lexical equivalents are often found,

---

ered using the term περιχαλκόω (27:6), whereas the bronze horns on the altar are covered using the term καλύπτω (27:2). The only difficult term to explain is the use of χρυσόω. In 25:11, χρυσόω is used for the covering of the inside of the ark with gold. This verse includes a difference in the ordering of "inside" and "outside" between the 𝔊 and 𝔐 and the choice of lexical equivalents may be due to the collocational clash between "inside" and the verb καταχρυσόω. In the parallel passage of the second account these two clauses are combined into one clause in both the 𝔐 and 𝔊 and the verb καταχρυσόω is used (37:2 [𝔊 38:2]). Thus, there is not enough evidence available to reach any firm conclusions about the basis for the differences. The remaining two instances of χρυσόω in the first tabernacle account are used in reference to the pillars that support the inner and outer curtains of the tent (26:32, 37). In the second tabernacle account, in contrast, the term καταχρυσόω is used for all occurrences of צפה except for those in 36:34 (𝔊 38:18). This verse is difficult both because of its meaning and also because of its lack of a clear *Vorlage* in the 𝔐. (Most analyses treat 𝔊 38:18 as a plus, as will also be done in chapter five of this book.) The verb צפה appears to be translated by χρυσόω, when it is used to refer to covering the bars of the tabernacle with gold and by περιαργυρόω, which appears to be a mistranslation that is one of many differences between the 𝔐 and 𝔊. This verse will be discussed further in chapter five.

The translation of the verb מלא also involves contextually controlled lexical equivalents. Of the translated usages of מלא, the most frequent and most literal lexical equivalent used in both accounts is ἐμπίπλημι, which is used with reference to God filling people with wisdom, understanding, and knowledge (28:3; 31:3; 35:31, 35). In the initial occurrence of the idiom referring to the dedication of the priests ("fill the hands"), מלא is translated literally using ἐμπίπλημι (28:41), but in all occurrences after that the translator has used the term τελειόω (29:9, 29, 33, 35). When the glory of the Lord fills the tent in the second account, the 𝔊 uses the passive of the verb πίμπλημι (40:34, 35), which is more appropriate than ἐμπίπλημι. The one context in which the tabernacle accounts appear to differ is in the use of מלא to refer to the manner in which the precious stones are put on the breastpiece. In the first account, the translator uses καθυφαίνω (28:17), but in the second account the term συνυφαίνω is used (39:10 [𝔊 36:17]). Because of the limited occurrences of these two verbs I can only speculate that the difference between the lexical equivalents may be due to the translator's perception of how the precious stones are affixed to the breastpiece. In the second account, the translator has chosen to use συνυφαίνω, a term that is also used to translate other terms in the tabernacle accounts. These other occurrences are translations of generic verbs and are used to refer to the weaving of the band around the neck of the robe (28:32) and the interweaving of the gold with colored threads in the making of the ephod (39:3 [𝔊 36:10]). Thus, the translator has chosen to use a term that was elsewhere used to refer to woven works. This choice resulted in assimilation, i.e., the translation of three different Hebrew terms (היה, עשה, and מלא) by the same Greek term (συνυφαίνω). The translator of the first account, in contrast, followed his normal pattern of using distinct terms for each distinct context and has chosen to use the term καθυφαίνω to translate this usage of מלא. The term καθυφαίνω is also used in Jdt 10:21 in reference to precious stones, but that is the only other occurrence of this verb in the 𝔊. In addition, the difference in lexical equivalents may have been affected by the fact that καθυφανεῖς (28:17) is an active verb, whereas συνυφάνθη (39:10 [𝔊 36:17]) is a passive translation of an active Hebrew verb, which results in a shift of focus.

61. One clear contrast is the translation of מֶלְקָחַיִם by ἐπαρυστήρ in the first account (25:38) and by λαβίς in the second account (37:23 [𝔊 38:17]). The translation choice in the second account

however, in sections in which the first account appears to be less accurate in either the choice of vocabulary or in the completeness of the translation. Because of the ambiguity that was created in the translation, the parallel passage in the second account appears to diverge widely from the first account in 𝔊, and sometimes even from the Hebrew. Yet in a sense, the translation in the second account is more accurate. These changes will be discussed more thoroughly in chapter five.[62]

Like nouns, there are a few verbs that have contrastive lexical equivalents in the two tabernacle accounts. Most of these "contrasts" are due to the contrasting contexts of the accounts and thus are contextually controlled lexical equivalents that demonstrate the translator's understanding of the usage of the Hebrew verb.[63] Contrastive lexical equivalents of verbs can also illustrate the tendency of

---

could represent a difference in *Vorlage*, but given that it is in a passage that contains multiple differences, it may rather reflect part of the attempt to "improve" the translation by making it more accurate in comparison to the first account. Thus, the interpretation of מֶלְקָחַיִם as a funnel rather than as tongs was viewed by the translator of the second account as an inaccurate representation of the Hebrew text. In Gooding's discussion of this contrast, he calls the translation in the first account a "mistaken translation." See Gooding, 34-35.

The word צַד was translated in accordance with the normal practice of the first account, i.e., different lexical equivalents for each context—πλάγιος for both sides of the lampstand or tabernacle when treated as a unit (25:32, 26:13), κλίτος for each individual side of the lampstand (25:32), and πλευρόν for the two sides of the incense altar treated as a unit (30:4). In the second account, צַד is only translated in one verse where it refers to the sides of the lampstand. Instead of using one of the two terms used for the side of the lampstand in the first account, the translator of the second account chose to use a neutral term, μέρος (37:18 [𝔊 38:14]).

The lexical equivalents of מִקְשָׁה are a frequently cited difference between the two accounts and possibly reflect two contrasting understandings, though this would be hard to prove from the limited evidence in the tabernacle account. In the first account, מִקְשָׁה is translated τορευτός (25:18, 31, 36), which envisions the cherubim and parts of the lampstand as being things that are "worked in relief," whereas in the second account the lampstand is envisioned as something that is "solid" and מִקְשָׁה is translated by στερεός (37:17 [𝔊 38:13]).

62. The instructions for and construction of the breastpiece (28:13-29=39:8-21 [𝔊 36:15-28]) and the lampstand (25:31-39=37:17-24 [𝔊 38:13-17]) are two of the most divergent sections that are found in both accounts. In these sections, the 𝔊 of the first account contains either ambiguities or "minuses" in comparison to the 𝔐. The second account, in contrast, is a much clearer translation, but the lexical equivalents used are very different. In addition, the construction of the lampstand in the second account is much shorter in the 𝔊.

63. The verb כלה is translated by καταπαύω in the first account when it refers to the cessation of God's speaking to Moses (31:18), but it is translated by συντελέω in the second account when it refers to the completion of the work (40:33). (The occurrence of כלה in 39:32 is part of a "minus" in the 𝔊.) These contrastive lexical equivalents show that the translator correctly thought that the "completion" of speaking had a different result than the "completion" of work.

A similar case can be made for the translator's perception of the context being the controlling factor that affected the translation of the term נוף in the tabernacle accounts. In the first tabernacle account, נוף refers to activities that would be performed in the ordination of the priests and thus is translated ἀφορίζω (29:24, 26, 27). In the second tabernacle account, however, נוף refers to the bringing of gifts by the people for the construction of the tabernacle and is translated by a more generic term, φέρω, that could not be construed as having cultic significance (35:22).

the second account to attempt to "improve" on the translation of the first account. This is seen in examples such as יצא, which was translated literally by ἐκπορεύομαι in the first account's description of the lampstand (25:32, 33, 35), and by a more descriptive term, ἐξέχω, in the second account (37:19 [𝕲 38:15]).⁶⁴ Other verbs with contrastive lexical equivalents seem to be true contrasts that do not appear to improve the translation. For instance, in the first tabernacle account קום is translated by ἀνίστημι in reference to setting up the tent (26:30), whereas it is translated by ἵστημι in the second tabernacle account (40:2, 17, 18, 33).⁶⁵ These choices still may be affected by some unidentified factor in the context, but they are the best available examples of verbs with contrastive lexical equivalents in the tabernacle accounts. Thus, the few examples of verbs with contrastive lexical equivalents provide little evidence that can be used independently to support a two-translator theory for the tabernacle accounts, though some of them could be construed as supporting evidence for a two-translator theory of the production of the 𝕲 tabernacle accounts.

In this section I have demonstrated that all four sections of 𝕲 Exodus examined for this book contain the same type of context-sensitive lexical consistency.

---

64. Other lexical equivalents used for יצא have been discussed above and are contextually determined.

65. In the remainder of Exodus, קום is translated in the typical context-sensitive manner. When a person begins an activity (including the Hebrew usage of קום in which everyone first "rises up" before doing anything else), the lexical equivalent ἀνίστημι is used (1:8, 2:17; 12:30, 31; 24:13; 32:1, 6). When a person physically goes out from his house, however, the lexical equivalent ἐξανίστημι is used (10:23; 21:19). When the qal form of קום is used to refer to people that are standing in a fixed location (33:8, 10) or when the hiphil form of קום is used figuratively to refer to establishing a covenant (6:4), then the lexical equivalent ἵστημι is used. Finally, people who are opposing them are referred to using a qal participle form of קום in the Hebrew, but in the 𝕲 these people are referred to with the term ὑπεναντίος (32:25). Because all other usages appear to be determined by context, there may still be some unidentified reason for this difference in usage between the two tabernacle accounts. On the surface, however, the contexts appear similar enough that the same term could have been used and thus this difference may be due to a difference in translators.

A similar though less persuasive example may be seen in the lexical equivalents used for סכך. The second account contains one clear contextually controlled difference in translation in that the "covering" or "concealing" of the ark with the curtain is expressed by means of the term σκεπάζω (40:3, 21). (See Lee, *Lexical Study*, 50, for a discussion of the probable shift in meaning of this term from "cover" to "conceal.") This usage is distinct from the remaining two usages, which are in parallel passages that describe the "covering" or "overshadowing" of the ark with the wings of the cherubim (25:20=37:9 [𝕲 38:8]). In the first account סכך is translated by συσκιάζω, whereas in the second account it is translated by σκιάζω. On the surface this would appear to be an example that could be used in the support of a two-translator theory. If so, it would also be a counter example to Nelson's thesis in that the word used in the core section of the second account is also used in a similar context in the temple account of 1 Chr 28:18, which probably is a later translation. Alternately, the difference in terms could be due to the fact that in the first account the term ἐκτείνω is used in conjunction with συσκιάζω and so the translator chose to use a more specific term, whereas in the second account, the term פרש is a "minus" in the 𝕲 and thus a more generic term σκιάζω is used in the more generic context of the 𝕲 38:8.

Nouns, in general, were rendered with more consistency than verbs, but this is more due to the fact that nouns are more likely to be used for items that can be consistently referred to with a single term. Because of the context-sensitive nature of the translation of verbs in Exodus, only a few verbs could be used as evidence in the discussion of any theory of the number of translators for the tabernacle accounts of 𝕲 Exodus. The choice of lexical equivalents for most nouns was also more likely to be a context-sensitive choice rather than providing clear evidence of another translator. Nelson's attempts to explain these choices as the result of the work of a Palestinian revisor as well as Wevers' dismissal of differences as the simple use of synonyms, were generally found to be non-productive approaches to the text. There was, however, a small number of nouns for which the choice of lexical equivalents was best explained by the hypothesis that the second tabernacle account was produced by a second translator who used the translation of the first account as his point of reference.

III. Lexical Equivalents That Affect Decisions about the Number of Translators

The main evidence that has been used as a basis for deciding how many translators produced the tabernacle accounts has been the variation in the translation of technical terminology and/or the contrasting translation of the compass points in the tabernacle accounts. One of the key problems with this approach is the assumption that technical terminology should be translated consistently. Included in this is also the problem of determining which terms should be included in a list of technical terminology. In modern meaning-based translation theory, the focus is generally on communicating concepts rather than maintaining identical translations of a set list of terms.[66] Evidence from this analysis of 𝕲 Exodus has placed the 𝕲 Exodus more toward the side of a meaning-based translation rather than a literal one with respect to the choice of lexical equivalents. Because of this, it is likely that the use of consistent terminology was not the main focus in the translation, but even in light of this, some of the variation and apparent contradictions in the 𝕲 translation are difficult to explain apart from the hypothesis of either a second translator or a revisionary attempt by the first translator.

---

66. Meaning-based translations do, however, encourage the use of consistent representation of "key terms" that refer to the same concepts. Minimally these include such nouns as God, angel, king, priest, and prophet. Maximally, these "key terms" include a wide range of concepts that occur repeatedly in the Scriptures. Identification of "key terms" is based to a certain extent on cultural and/or theological considerations of the people group for whom the translation is being produced. See Katherine Barnwell, Paul Dancy, and Anthony G. Pope, *Key Biblical Terms in the New Testament: An Aid for Bible Translators* (Dallas, Tex.: Summer Institute of Linguistics, forthcoming).

In this section, I will first analyze a few of the technical terms for parts of the tabernacle structure that have been discussed in past studies of the tabernacle accounts. This list of terms will not be all-inclusive, but it will provide a sampling of some of the problems that are encountered when one tries to explain the choices of lexical equivalents in the tabernacle accounts. After this I will discuss in detail the translation of the compass points, an issue that has been cited in several recent studies as the key factor that makes the two-translator theory more necessary.

Technical Terminology

The translation of technical terminology has been the focus of several studies of the 𝔊 tabernacle accounts. Those who argue for a two-translator theory generally assume that translators would be consistent in their use of technical terminology, whereas those who argue for a one-translator theory emphasize the consistent inconsistency of the translator of the first tabernacle account. By doing this, they show that the differences in the second tabernacle account are a continuation of the same pattern of inconsistency that was seen in the first account. There have been a few exceptions, however, to this approach. For Nelson, the "inconsistencies" in technical terms represent opportunities for determining if the section contained the vocabulary of the 𝔊 or the vocabulary of a later Palestinian revisor. Each "variation" thus had to be assigned to a particular time period. Wevers gives a more sympathetic reading of each variation as he attempts to see the effect of the choice of terminology on the meaning of the translation. Thus, unlike Gooding, who lambastes the translation, Wevers generally gives it a positive review, but even he notes that the translator of the second tabernacle account avoids some of the terminology used in the first account. In this section, I will focus on the translation of a few of the technical terms in the tabernacle accounts. These include the poles, curtains, pillars, and several items connected with the pillars.

Poles. According to Nelson, one of the most frequently cited differences between the tabernacle accounts is the translation of the term בַּד.[67] Wevers also uses this term to illustrate his point that the translator of the second account "distances himself from" the choices made in the first account.[68] In brief, the term בַּד is translated by ἀναφορεύς, σκυτάλη, and φορεύς in the first tabernacle account and by ἀναφορεύς, διωστήρ, and μοχλός in the second tabernacle account. Nelson suggests that διωστήρ is the 𝔊 term and that the presence of ἀναφορεύς in the second account is due to the Palestinian revisor, who used two additional terms that were also used in the Palestinian sources analyzed by Nelson.

---

67. Nelson, 53.
68. WeversText, 144.

A closer examination of the translation of בַּד, however, shows that it too follows the characteristic patterns of choices of lexical equivalents that have been seen in the examination of other terms. In the first account, three terms are used to distinguish carefully the poles of the ark and table (ἀναφορεύς), the poles of the bronze altar (φορεύς), and the poles of the incense altar (σκυτάλη). [69] From the choices used in the first account, the second tabernacle account retains the use of ἀναφορεύς for the first occurrence of בַּד in the second tabernacle account (35:12). Aside from this first occurrence, which provides lexical cohesion between the two accounts, the translator of the second account, like the translator of the first tabernacle account, used one term for the poles of the ark and table and a separate term for the poles of the bronze altar, though the latter may be due to a misreading of the Hebrew *Vorlage*.[70] Thus, there is lexical cohesion between the two accounts in the shared usage of one lexical equivalent and the use of a similar type of consistency within each account. This pattern is similar to that of other terms discussed above.

Curtains. The terms for the curtains of the inner tent, outer tent, and courtyard have been discussed in several studies, but are not generally used as a starting point for the discussion of the differences between the two accounts because of the confusing pattern of both assimilation and dissimilation in lexical equivalents. The Hebrew text in both accounts uses one word, יְרִיעָה, to refer to the curtains of both the inner and outer tent; and a second term, קֶלַע, for the curtains of the courtyard. The first account in 𝕲, however, uses three terms to distinguish carefully the curtains of the three items (αὐλαία, δέρρις, and ἱστίον). The second account, in contrast, elevates one of the terms, αὐλαία, to a generic term that can be used to refer to all three types of curtains and then also uses another term from

---

69. Examples of these usages are as follows: ἀναφορεύς (25:13, 14, 15, 27, 28), φορεύς (27:6, 7), and σκυτάλη (30:4, 5).

70. Most of the occurrences of the term בַּד in the second tabernacle account are in verses that are part of the minuses in the 𝕲. In the remaining examples, the first occurrence (35:12) is in a fairly literally rendered verse and uses ἀναφορεύς. The text of the 𝕲 38 is greatly abbreviated in comparison to the 𝔐 37. In the abbreviated form of the 𝕲, the poles of both the ark and table are constructed after the construction of the table (𝕲 38:11). The lexical equivalent διωστήρ is used here for בַּד. Because of the abbreviated nature of the text, a literal translation was no longer possible for 37:5 (𝕲 38:4). In the 𝔐, the poles are described as being moved into the rings, but since the poles had not yet been constructed in the 𝕲 text order, the rings were simply described as being wide enough for the poles. This same translation was then used throughout the remainder of the second account using εὐρύς to describe the rings (37:14 [𝕲 38:10], 38:5 [𝕲 38:24]) and διωστήρ to refer to the poles (37:14, 15 [𝕲 38:10, 11]; 39:35 [𝕲 39:14]; 40:20). The one exception (38:5 [𝕲 38:24]), may be due to the misreading of בַּדִּים as a form of the word בְּרִיחַ, which was translated by its normal lexical equivalent μοχλός. (Gooding says that μοχλός was "mistakenly" used. See Gooding, 33.) The fact that this only occurred with the bronze altar, however, raises the question of whether this use of a separate lexical equivalent parallels the use of φορεύς for the bronze altar in the first account. It is also noteworthy that in the 𝕲 of the second account poles are never said to be constructed for the bronze altar. The naive reader might, therefore, think that the bars (μοχλός) of the tabernacle were used to carry the bronze altar.

the first account, ἱστίον, as a synonym for one of the usages of αὐλαία.⁷¹ The word δέρρις, even though it can be used in a more generic way to refer to a tent or curtain, is not used in the second account, possibly because it could be misinterpreted as referring to skins rather than curtains of goat hair.⁷²

The word יְרִיעָה is the least problematic of the terms. In the first account, the word יְרִיעָה is translated by αὐλαία when it refers to the inner tent and by δέρρις when it refers to the outer tent.⁷³ In the second account, the parallel verses referring to the outer tent are part of a "minus" in the 𝔊. Because of the limited contexts within the 𝔊 of the second account, the only lexical equivalent used for יְרִיעָה is αὐλαία, which is used to refer to the inner tent, as in the first account. On the basis of the translation of אֹהֶל by αὐλαία in 40:19, however, one suspects that the translator of the second account would have used the more generic term αὐλαία for the outer tent curtains if the material had not been part of a "minus" in the 𝔊.⁷⁴

While the difference in the translation of יְרִיעָה in the second tabernacle account can be explained on the basis of the difference in referential meaning, the lexical equivalents used for קֶלַע are much more difficult to explain. The word קֶלַע is translated only by ἱστίον in the first account, but by both ἱστίον and αὐλαία in the second account. In the second account, the terms αὐλαία and ἱστίον are used in contexts that refer to almost identical parts of the courtyard.⁷⁵

---

71. Nelson makes an unconvincing argument about the usage of the lexical equivalents of יְרִיעָה to illustrate his point that "While Greek I [first account] and Josephus use different words to translate the Hebrew terms, they agree on the basic understanding of the terms they translate. This leads to the conclusion that Greek I and Josephus present alternate Palestinian translations." He makes a similar comment on קֶלַע noting that "the distinction between the Old Greek and the Palestinian revision in Greek I is not in the differing words used to translate but in the differing use of those words. Greek I and Josephus make the same distinction between the curtains of the tent and those of the tabernacle, even though they use different words to translate. Greek II makes no distinction." (Nelson, 110-11 and 114.) Nelson is correct in noting differences in the usage of the terms in the two accounts, but there is no evidence that would necessitate that this difference be assigned to a later Palestinian revision. These two terms, like many other terms, exhibit a similar pattern of shared and distinctive lexical equivalents.

72. For a good discussion of this term, see WeversText, 124. For an example of a modern misunderstanding of the 𝔊 due to reading the word δέρρις without looking at the larger context, see Durham, *Exodus*, 367.

73. When יְרִיעָה refers to the curtains of the inner tent in the first account, it is translated by αὐλαία (26:1, 2 [3x], 3 [2x], 4 [2x], 5 [2x], 6). When יְרִיעָה refers to the goat hair curtains of the outer tent, it is translated by δέρρις (26:7 [2x], 8 [3x], 9 [3x], 10 [2x], 12 [2x], 13). In the second account, יְרִיעָה refers to the inner tent and is translated by αὐλαία (36:8, 9 [𝔊 37:1, 2 (2x)]).

74. When אֹהֶל refers to the outer tent, it is translated by δέρρις in the first account (26:11) and by αὐλαία in the second account (40:19). This shows that the same referential meaning was maintained for the two terms in their respective sections despite the fact that they were used to translate different terms. Understanding this difference also helps explain the variety of terms used in translating אֹהֶל in the tabernacle accounts.

75. The term קֶלַע is translated by ἱστίον in two parallel verses referring to parts of the courtyard: "southern" side—27:9=38:9 (𝔊 37:7) and first side of the gate—27:14=38:14 (𝔊 37:12). In two

Wevers uses this to affirm that the terms are synonymous. Nelson uses this to affirm his position that the examples of ἱστίον are due to the work of a Palestinian revisor. The pattern of usage, however, is similar to that seen with תְּרוּמָה in which two equally acceptable words are used, but the translator of the first account prefers to distinguish carefully each usage based on referential meaning. The translator of the second account, in contrast, uses the first account as a point of reference for his own translation, but then uses the terms with a slightly different pattern of distribution than was seen in the first account.

Pillars and Related Items. The next set of vocabulary items that have been widely discussed includes terms that refer to the upright pillars and related paraphernalia, i.e., capitals, bands, hooks, and bases. The term used for the pillars

---

additional parallel verses, the first account uses ἱστίον and the second account uses αὐλαία as follows: "western" side—27:12=38:12 (𝔊 37:10) and second side of the gate—27:15=38:15 (𝔊 37:13). The term קֶלַע is lacking in the description of the "north" side in the second account, but in the first account it is present and is translated by ἱστίον (27:11). In the general reference to the eastern side that precedes the description of its parts, the term קֶלַע is lacking in both accounts, but the first account has made this implicit referent explicit using the term, ἱστίον (𝔊 27:13). In addition, the first and last occurrences of קֶלַע in the second account are translated by ἱστίον (35:17 [𝔊 35:12a], 39:40 [𝔊 39:19]). Another occurrence of ἱστίον is in a verse that emphasizes that the dimensions of the curtain at the gate of the courtyard were the same as that of the ἱστίον of the courtyard (38:18 [𝔊 37:16]). The only other occurrence of קֶלַע is in a summary verse that states that all the αὐλαία of the courtyard were linen (38:16 [𝔊 37:14]). If, as Nelson claims, the word αὐλαία is the Old Greek and the occurrences of ἱστίον are due to the Palestinian revisor, then the occurrence of so many revisions in the sections that Nelson considers to be the core of the second account must be explained. The translations of this term in the second account, however, reflect an approach that is similar to the translations of תְּרוּמָה and לֵב. The initial occurrence of the term קֶלַע uses the term ἱστίον, the term used in the first account, in order to provide lexical cohesion between the two accounts. The use of ἱστίον in the two parallel verses is likewise to be expected. If αὐλαία was indeed the more natural Greek equivalent, as might be suggested from its occurrence in deuterocanonical literature (Jdt 14:14 and possibly 2 Macc 14:41), then the translator chose to introduce this term with the description of the western side where he retained the same lexical equivalent for the same compass point as in the first account. By doing this, he introduced a "new" usage of a term (αὐλαία) that was different from the first account on the side of the courtyard where most of the other information was "old" information, i.e., words that were identical with the first account. (See below for a discussion of the compass points.) The usage of the term αὐλαία on an opposing side of the gate would have been another opportunity for the two terms, one possibly less well known, to be equated. The summary verse (38:16 [𝔊 37:14]) only occurs in the second account and thus the more "natural" term αὐλαία is used. The usage of ἱστίον in 38:18 (𝔊 37:16) may have been a very deliberate choice to help the readers interpret the usage of ὕψος in the first account. This usage of the word ὕψος, which is a "plus" in the first account (27:14, 15, 16), has drawn much criticism from Gooding, 25-26. The use of ὕψος in the second account is, at least, based on a Hebrew text, even if it is very ambiguous. Thus, by using the term ἱστίον the translator was trying to correct possible misunderstandings in the first account. It would be possible to reverse this argument in favor of a revisionist's approach, such as Nelson's approach. The lack of later evidence for ἱστίον and the fact that the types of translation choices reflected here are similar to those of לֵב, where the natural Greek term, διάνοια, is known, however, leads me to conclude that the priority of the first account is a better basis for explaining the change in usages.

themselves has not been the source of a major problem, but the translation of אֶדֶן, which is found with both עַמּוּד and קֶרֶשׁ, is dependent on the translator's understanding of these terms. In the 𝕲, the translation of עַמּוּד and קֶרֶשׁ by the same Greek term, στῦλος, is an excellent example of assimilation.[76] The choice of στῦλος for the translation of קֶרֶשׁ is appropriate in light of the first occurrence of הַקְּרָשִׁים in which they are described as עֹמְדִים.[77] Thus, both עַמּוּד and קֶרֶשׁ refer to upright items from which curtains are hung, according to the Greek.

In the 𝔐, both עַמּוּד and קֶרֶשׁ are connected to one or more אֶדֶן. In the first account, the term אֶדֶן is consistently translated βάσις. In the second account, however, אֶדֶן is translated by both βάσις and κεφαλίς. As expected, this difference has been used as "proof" that the second account was the work of a second translator or that the translator was inconsistent or that the occurrence of κεφαλίς as the translation of אֶדֶן is evidence of a Palestinian revisor.[78] Obviously, all of these conclusions cannot be correct, but they do point to a major problem in the trans-

---

76. This is similar to the translation of אֹהֶל and מִשְׁכָּן by the term σκηνή, as discussed above, but unlike עַמּוּד and קֶרֶשׁ, the terms אֹהֶל and מִשְׁכָּן occur several times in a context that required a distinction to be made. The terms עַמּוּד and קֶרֶשׁ, in contrast, only co-occur in lists that are largely abbreviated in the 𝕲. In these lists, either the two terms were translated by one occurrence of στῦλος or the term קֶרֶשׁ is a "minus" in the 𝕲 due to the abbreviated nature of the text's Vorlage (35:11, 39:33 [𝕲 39:13]; 40:18). The only time קֶרֶשׁ is possibly translated in the second account is in 36:34 (𝕲 38:18), but even here the 𝕲 is ambiguous with respect to the 𝔐 because the word στῦλος occurs twice. Gooding views 𝕲 38:18-20 as "an incomplete compilation of details collected inefficiently from the Greek of the other chapters of Exodus," rather than as a translation of a particular Hebrew text. See Gooding, 47.

77. WeversNotes, 420-21. In addition, the 𝕲 noticeable leaves out the translation of the term אֶדֶן in 26:16. Wevers simply notes that the word has been replaced in the 𝕲 by the verb ποιήσεις. If, however, קֶרֶשׁ was viewed as a vertical pillar, then the presence of the term μῆκος would have created a confused translation, since length is normally attributed to horizontal items. All other occurrences of אֶדֶן in the first tabernacle account are translated by μῆκος except for the second occurrence of אֶדֶן in the 𝔐 27.11, which is a minus in the 𝔊 version of the verse. If the absence of μῆκος in 26:16 was an accidental minus, then it is interesting to note that it occurs in the one verse where μῆκος could have created a misunderstanding.

78. This difference is noted in a list of contrasts used by Popper, Der biblische Bericht über die Stiftshütte, 172. Gooding views the inconsistencies of the translation of this term as beyond even the normal practices of the translator of Exodus. Because of this, he contends that there was originally a mistranslation of אֶדֶן in 𝕲 39 that was later used in "a very carelessly compiled and incomplete list that has culled its information not directly from a Hebrew text, but indirectly and with obvious lack of understanding from the Greek of other chapters." This is the work of the editor that Gooding posits as the one who rearranged the material in the second tabernacle account. (Gooding, 50). Nelson appeals to the work of his Palestinian revisor for the translation of אֶדֶן by κεφαλίς, but he does this by merely asserting that this must be the case since it is near a section (38:24-31) that "shows signs of revision by a Palestinian hand." (Nelson, 48-49.) Wevers tries to let the translator off the hook by saying that the term κεφαλίς was being used in a generic sense of "extremity" since the translator viewed the frames of the tabernacle as having "bases" on both ends. Ultimately, even Wevers struggles with the translator's choice and says, "but one could wish that he had not been quite so clever about it and had used βάσεις throughout...." See WeversText, 136.

lation. The word κεφαλίς also occurs in 𝕲 38:20, a verse that is a "plus" in the 𝕲. Because of the lack of a *Vorlage*, this usage will be discussed with other "pluses" in chapter five instead of incorporating it into the discussion of the lexical equivalents of אֶדֶן.[79] In the two verses in which the probable Hebrew text אֶדֶן was translated by κεφαλίς, the word אֶדֶן is in phrases in which it is related to an item other than the pillars or frames. As has been demonstrated throughout this chapter, the translation of words in Exodus is context-sensitive. Therefore, it is possible that the translator of the second account thought that the אֶדֶן of the pillar or frame was distinct from the אֶדֶן of the הַקֹּדֶשׁ or הַפָּרֹכֶת and thus used the lexical equivalent κεφαλίς in the latter contexts (38:27 [𝕲 39:4]).[80] This understanding of the choice of lexical equivalents is affirmed by the translation of אֲדָנָיו by κεφαλίς in 40:18. In this phrase, the possessive pronoun refers back to הַמִּשְׁכָּן, the same item referred to by הַקֹּדֶשׁ in 38:27. The translation of אֶדֶן by βάσις in 39:33 (𝕲 39:13), however, is an apparent counter-example in that the possessive pronoun on אֲדָנָיו refers back to either the tent or tabernacle. The 𝔪 version of this verse, however, reads אַדְנֵיהֶם and the 3mp suffix refers back to the pillars. Given that the 𝕲 often reflects a *Vorlage* similar to the 𝔪, it is likely that this "exception" is actually a reflection of a *Vorlage* that is not like the 𝔐. Thus, the evidence from the examination of the translation of אֶדֶן suggests the translator of the second account translated contextually. The second account, however, contained contexts that were not found in the first account and thus the translator had to choose a lexical equivalent for these new contexts. Modern readers may disparage his choices of lexical equivalents, but he was consistent with his probable *Vorlage*, which may have been more like the 𝔪.[81]

---

79. Gooding used this verse to prove that a contradiction was created if κεφαλίς did not refer to "bases" and yet at the same time he showed that κεφαλίς was used throughout the 𝕲 with its more natural Greek meaning of "capital." (Gooding, 46-47.) Interestingly, even in this plus there is a sense of consistency in that the κεφαλίς of the tent is silver, as also is the case in 38:27 (𝕲 39:4).

80. The bases of pillars (עַמּוּד) (26:32, 37; 27:10, 11, 17, 18; 36:36, 38 [𝕲 37:4, 6]; 38:17 [𝕲 37:15]); the bases of frames (קֶרֶשׁ) (26:19, 21, 25); the bases of curtains (קֶלַע) (or more likely pillars (עַמּוּד) although it is ambiguous) (27:12, 14, 15, 16; 38:10, 11, 12, 14, 15 [𝕲 37:8, 9, 10, 12, 13]; 38:19 [𝕲 37:17]); the bases of the door of the tent of meeting (38:30 [𝕲 39:7]); the bases of the courtyard and the gate of the courtyard (38:31 [𝕲 39:8]) are all translated by the term βάσις. Other occurrences of אֶדֶן are minuses in the 𝕲 (35:11, 17; 36:24, 26, 30; 39:40 [𝕲 39:21]).

81. An additional factor that is not generally brought into the discussion of this translation choice is the fact that βάσις is also used in this same section of the second account to refer to the foundation of the bronze altar and the stand of the laver. The presence of βάσις being used for separate items would not require the use of a different translation choice for אֶדֶן, but it may have been a small factor that influenced the choice. In the first tabernacle account βάσις is used to translate יְסוֹד (29:12) and כֵּן (30:18, 28; 31:9), but none of these examples are found close to contexts in which the bases of the pillars are found. In the second account, however, βάσις is used to translate סִיר (38:3 [𝕲 38:23]) (though the translator may have had a different *Vorlage* in this instance) and כֵּן (38:8 [𝕲 38:26]) in a section that also contains bases of pillars.

The translation of וָו by κεφαλίς and κρίκος in the first account and by κεφαλίς, κρίκος, and ἀγκύλη in the second account is, as usual, interpreted in contradictory ways by analysts who have discussed this term. Explanations include the following: dismissing the translation as incompetent, saying that the translations of וָו are another example of the use of variety, and explaining the source of each of these lexical equivalents by pointing to either a different *Vorlage* or a Palestinian revision.[82] Nelson's suggestions about the reasons for the variety of terms used in the translation have some merit, but ultimately begin to unravel because he uses an unlikely understanding of the Hebrew grammar as the basis for his claim about the presence of a difference *Vorlage*.[83] A better explanation,

---

82. Gooding argues that the use of κεφαλίς as a translation of וָו is due to carelessness rather than to the presence of a different Hebrew *Vorlage*. See Gooding, 22-23. See also Finn, "The Tabernacle Chapters," 450, who cites the examples in the first account to show the use of variety in the same context. These views and that of Popper have been summarized by Nelson, 57-58.

83. Nelson argues that the presence of κεφαλίς in the 𝔊 of the first account indicates that its *Vorlage* contained ראש instead of וָו. Further, he asserts that the Old Greek term for וָו was ἀγκύλη, which was then replaced by κρίκος in the Palestinian revision. Nelson's explanation of the use of these three terms to translate וָו, however, depends on being able to "explain away" the usage of κεφαλίς through his suggestion that it represents a different *Vorlage*, ראש, thus leaving two terms, one of which is assigned to the Old Greek and the other is assigned to the Palestinian revisor.

Nelson correctly notes that the term ראש is not used with reference to the pillars in the first account, though it is used generically for the top (?) of the frames (26:24). This lack of ראש in the first account in combination with a supposed difference in the construction of the hooks in the two accounts is used by Nelson as a basis for his claim that the Hebrew text used by the 𝔊 contained the term ראש instead of וָו. Nelson says, "There is an important difference between the Hebrew of MT I and MT II. In MT II the 'hooks' (וויהם) are said to be made (עשה), while the 'capitals' (ראשיהם) are said to be overlaid (צפה). In MT I there are no capitals, but the hooks are said to be overlayed [sic]. The Gk I readings suggest that no hooks were mentioned in its Hebrew text, but that it is the capitals that were overlaid." (Nelson, 58.) This supposed difference is used by Nelson as the basis for his claim that the Hebrew *Vorlage* read ראש in the instances where וָו is translated by κεφαλίς. It is interesting to note that while Nelson suggests the presence of a different *Vorlage* for these occurrences of κεφαλίς, he does not make that same suggestion when κεφαλίς is used as a translation of the term אדן. The validity of Nelson's argument for a different *Vorlage* rests entirely on his claims about the differences in construction. These claims, however, are based on an inaccurate reading of the Hebrew text that is not reflected in the 𝔊 translation. In both tabernacle accounts, וָו, is translated by κεφαλίς when it occurs in a stative clause that identifies the material from which the hooks are made. This stative clause is juxtaposed after a verbal clause and is in each case directly followed by a statement concerning the bases and the material of which they are composed (26:32, 37; 27:17; 36:36 [𝔊 37:4]). Nelson's reading of these verses would involve ellipsis of the verb, a phenomenon that is more often seen in poetry than in prose. See M. O'Connor, *Hebrew Verse Structure* (Winona Lake, Ind.: Eisenbrauns, 1980), 122-29. This elliptical reading, however, was clearly not the one used by the 𝔊, which uses the nominative case for both κεφαλίς and the following adjective that describes the material used for this part of the posts. A better explanation for the lack of the term ראש in the first account is the possibility that in the 𝔐 ראש is being used generically to refer to a part of the posts rather than referring to a separate item that had to be constructed. Thus, in the second account of the 𝔐, which gives more details of a few parts of the construction, the tops of the pillars are described as being overlaid with various

however, is found when the first account is used as the beginning point. Except for one usage that creates an apparent contradiction (27:17), the first account translates וָו with two distinct terms whose usages are referential determined, i.e., each term refers to a distinct type of hook that was located on separate items. The translation choices in the second account, however, are affected by a variety of contextual factors that allow the translator to maintain lexical cohesion through the use of both of the terms used in the first account, while at the same time compensating for the apparent contradiction in the first account through the use of a third term.[84] In addition, the terms κρίκος and ἀγκύλη both occur in a large

---

metals, rather than the overlaying of a "capital." In the 𝔊, however, the ראש assumed a higher visibility due to the translation choices and may have been viewed as a discrete entity. According to Meyers, the ancient incense burners, which were pillar-like, had "bulging ring or rings, giving the appearance of a capital, at the point where the shaft narrows." See Carol L. Meyers, *The Tabernacle Menorah: A Synthetic Study of a Symbol from the Biblical Cult*, American Schools of Oriental Research Dissertation Series, ed. David Noel Freedman (Missoula, Mont.: Scholars Press, 1976), 64. It is possible that the bands on the posts, חִשּׁוּק, made the posts appear to have a separate capital, just as the ancient incense burners appeared to have capitals.

84. As has often been noted throughout this chapter, in the first account Hebrew terms are translated with distinct terms for each context. The translations of the first four occurrences of וָו appear to follow this pattern in that κεφαλίς is used when the וָו is a part of a pillar that supports a curtain at an entranceway, whether the curtain that separates the Holy of Holies from the Holy Place (26:32) or the curtain at the door of the tent (26:37). When וָו is a part of the pillars that support the curtains of the courtyard, however, it is translated by κρίκος and occurs in conjunction with ψαλίς, which translates חִשּׁוּק (27:10, 11). In 27:17, however, the translation of the courtyard section contains an apparent contradiction in that the וָו that is located on the pillars of the courtyard is translated by κεφαλίς. This translation choice may have been a mistake due to the combination of the similarity of this phrase with phrases used in the descriptions of the pillars for the door (26:37) and also the lack of ψαλίς, which normally is used in conjunction with κρίκος. Whatever the source of the apparent contradiction, this difficulty is just one of many in a section in which the translator had difficulties with the compass points, as will be discussed below. In addition to this apparent contradiction, the use of κρίκος to translate וָו is another example of assimilation, i.e., κρίκος was used in the first account to translate both וָו and קֶרֶס, the clasps that were used for joining together the curtains of the tent (26:6 [2x], 11).

In the second account, the translator begins by following the usage of the first account with κεφαλίς being used in conjunction with the curtain that separates the Holy of Holies from the Holy Place (36:36 [𝔊 37:4]). This usage creates lexical cohesion between the two tabernacle accounts and is a pattern that has been seen elsewhere, i.e., the first occurrence of the term in the second account is identical with the usage in the first account. As discussed above, the translation of 36:36 (𝔊 37:4) was also heavily modified so that the 𝔊 form of this verse is almost an exact parallel of 𝔊 26:32 despite the fact that the Hebrew texts are different. In the next occurrence of וָו (36:38 [𝔊 37:6]), however, κεφαλίς could not be used for the hooks on the pillars at the door of the tent because of the presence of ראש in the Hebrew text, which naturally was translated κεφαλίς. Because of the presence of ψαλίς, which translates חִשּׁוּק, the term κρίκος was used in this verse and the verse was also modified so that these hooks, וָו, are specifically described as being golden, a statement that is found in the parallel verse in the first account (26:37), but not in the 𝔐 form of the second account (36:38). Thus, despite the differences in the 𝔊 choice of terminology for translating וָו, the overall meaning of the passage is kept the same through modifications in the 𝔊 of the second account. In the remaining occurrences that are

"plus" found in the 𝕲. This "plus" will be discussed in chapter five, but it appears to bring together phrases from the first account both with their original lexical equivalents and with the substitution of the neutral term used in the second account, ἀγκύλη, in an attempt to defuse the apparent contradictions. The success of this endeavor may be disputed, but it reflects a similar approach seen with other terms and with other "pluses" in the same chapter.[85]

This brief discussion of some of the technical terms used in the tabernacle accounts reveals that contradictory usages of technical terms are present in the translation. The question that must be resolved, however, is whether this is due to a different *Vorlage*, the work of a second translator or an incompetent editor, or one of the problems that unavoidably appears in most translations. The presence of other problems that have created ambiguity in the translation would argue that the latter may be the source of at least some of the problems.[86] Fortunately, most of the choices of lexical equivalents for technical terms in the tabernacle accounts did not result in outright contradictions. Rather, many of the terms demonstrated the same type of shifting of meaning combined with the maintenance of lexical cohesion between the two accounts that has been described in other terms discussed in previous sections. The usages of the technical terms in the "pluses" of the 𝕲, however, will have to be examined in more depth in chapter five before any firm conclusions can be reached about the usage of technical terms in the tabernacle accounts.

---

translated in the second account, וָו refers either to the hooks for the courtyard curtains (38:17 [𝕲 37:15]), the hooks for the curtain at the gate of the courtyard (38:19 [𝕲 37:17]), or to unspecified hooks (38:28 [𝕲 39:5]). In all three verses it is found in conjunction with רֹאשׁ, which is translated κεφαλίς, but due to other translation choices (a verbal rather than a nominal translation of חִשַּׁק in 38:17 [𝕲 37:15] and 38:19 [𝕲 37:17-18]) ψαλίς is not in the 𝕲 text. Without ψαλίς in the verse, which would have encouraged the use of the normal word pair κρίκος and ψαλίς, the translator was free to use a more neutral term. Rather than using one of two terms that had been used in the first account with the result that an apparent contradiction had been created, the translator of the second account used ἀγκύλη in these three occurrences of the second account (38:17, 19 [𝕲 37:15, 17], 28 [𝕲 39:5]). The term ἀγκύλη is used in the first tabernacle account to translate לֻלָאֹת, the item that the קֶרֶס connected together to form the tabernacle and the outer tent. This Hebrew term, however, is not translated in the second account of the 𝕲 and thus no immediate problem would have occurred by using ἀγκύλη. Rather, this is another case of assimilation in which two items (לֻלָאֹת and קֶרֶס) used in connecting curtains to other curtains or to a pillar were translated by one term ἀγκύλη. This assimilation, however, occurs between accounts, rather than within one account.

85. This is similar to the mixing of the translation of לֵב by καρδία and διάνοια. On a larger scale, the "plus" of Korah's rebellion in 38, whether in the *Vorlage* or due to the translator's hermeneutical approach, illustrates the practice of placing two "contradictory" pieces of information together and thus attempting to dispel an apparent contradiction. This passage will be discussed further in chapter five.

86. I have argued elsewhere that the placement of the incense altar in the Holy of Holies in Heb 9:4 was partially due to the ambiguity of the 𝕲 Exodus. See Martha L. Wade, "Translation as Interpretation in the Old Greek Exodus" (paper presented at the Fellowship of Professors, Johnson Bible College, 1999).

Compass Points

The translation of compass points in the tabernacle accounts is considered by several scholars to be one of the major pieces of evidence in favor of a two-translator theory.[87] Within the first tabernacle account, the points of the compass are translated by two distinct sets of lexical equivalents. In 26, three of the points of the compass are used to designate the sides of the tabernacle and are translated using the expected terminology.[88] In the next chapter, however, the sides of the courtyard are described using a different set of lexical equivalents for the points of the compass.[89] A third set of slightly different lexical equivalents is used for the points of the compass in the parallel passage about the courtyard that is located in the second tabernacle account.[90] In addition, both tabernacle accounts use the common lexical equivalents for north and south to describe the placement of the table and lamp in relationship to the altar.[91] This contrasting usage of vocabulary for the points of the compass is considered by Gooding to be just another example of the translator's consistent inconsistency.[92] Bogaert, however, has argued that the terms used in 27 point to an Alexandrian orientation of the courtyard with the gate of the courtyard facing south. His argument has been accepted by Wevers, who says that one translator could not have produced two such "schizophrenic" translations.[93] While the difference between the two courtyard passages can be explained by positing the presence of two translators, this does not, however, solve the difficulty caused by the contrast of an eastern-facing tabernacle in 26:18-22 and a southern-facing courtyard in 27:9-13. Wevers tentatively suggests that this may be an ideological statement about the relationship of the diaspora to Jerusalem.[94] Fraenkel takes a more holistic view of the text and tries to explain

---

87. P. M. Bogaert, "L'orientation du parvis du sanctuaire dans la version grecque de l'Exode (*Ex.*, 27, 9-13 LXX)," *L'Antiquité classique* 50 (1981): 79-85 and WeversText, 146.

88. In 26, נֶגְבָּה תֵימָנָה is translated by νότος (26:18 [𝔊 26:20]), צָפוֹן by βορρᾶς (26:20 [𝔊 26:18]), and יָמָּה by θάλασσα (26:22). The parallel passage in 𝔐 36 is part of a large minus in the second tabernacle account of the 𝔊.

89. In 27, נֶגֶב־תֵּימָנָה is translated by λίψ (27:9), צָפוֹן by ἀπηλιώτης (27:11), יָם by θάλασσα (27:12), and קֵדְמָה מִזְרָחָה by νότος (27:13).

90. In 𝔐 38, נֶגֶב תֵּימָנָה is translated by λίψ (38:9 [𝔊 37:7]), צָפוֹן by βορρᾶς (38:11 [𝔊 37:9]), יָם by θάλασσα (38:12 [𝔊 37:10]), and קֵדְמָה מִזְרָחָה by ἀνατολή (38:13 [𝔊 37:11]).

91. The 𝔊 terms for north and south used here are identical to those in 26, i.e., צָפוֹן (26:35) and צָפֹנָה (40:22) are translated by βορρᾶς, while תֵּימָנָה (26:35) and נֶגְבָּה (40:24) are translated by νότος.

92. Gooding, 23-24.

93. Wevers says, "... I find it hard to believe that the translator who translated ch. 27 using an Alexandrian point of view could also in schizophrenic fashion have translated the B [second] account in the way in which it was done," in WeversText, 146.

94. Wevers says, "It is possible that the Alexandrian translators were subtly saying something about the relation of Jerusalem to the diaspora in placing a Jerusalem oriented σκηνή within an Alexandrian oriented αὐλή, but this should not be pressed," in WeversNotes, 435.

both the change in the orientation of the courtyard (27:9-13) as well as the reversal of north and south (𝔊 26:18, 20) as part of a literary technique that was used to form chiastic pairs of directional terms.[95]

Any explanation of the translation of the terms used for the points of the compass in the tabernacle accounts needs to be able to account for both the difference between 26:18-22 and 27:9-13 as well as the contrast between the two parallel accounts. Despite the differences in terminology, no one claims that 26:18-22 and 27:9-13 were produced by different translators. In both 26:22 and 27:12, the word יָם is translated literally by θάλασσα and is used for a compass point.[96] In 27:12, however, the translator has used the preposition κατά instead of πρός. Wevers says that κατά is being used to "draw attention to the fact that θάλασσαν was not taken in the usual Palestinian sense of 'west' but rather as 'north'; ...."[97] While the conclusion that "sea" is here being used to refer to "north" might be disputed, Wevers is correct that the translator is signaling a difference in usage of the word "sea." In both tabernacle accounts the translator has chosen a literal rendering of the term יָם rather than substituting one of the more natural Greek equivalents for "west"—λίψ, δύσις, or δυσμή. In 26:22 the translator uses the normal preposition for points of the compass and thus forces his readers to interpret it by the context in which it is seen as a point of the compass other than north or south, which are represented by the pair νότος and βορρᾶς. In 27:12, however, the translator used θάλασσα in a more literal sense and signaled this distinction through the use of κατά, i.e., "along the sea." In addition, the translator chose to use ἀπηλιώτης and λίψ, terms for east and west that were often used for winds, rather than the terms that are based on the rising and setting of the sun, ἀνατολή and δύσις. The pair of terms he chose, however, were ones that were commonly found in the literature from that location (Egypt) and time period (third century B.C.).[98] The normal term for south, νότος, was maintained even though this created a potential ambiguity with the presence of both λίψ and νότος, both of which were used for the south in the 𝔊. As a result, the translation in 27:9-13 was both ambiguous and inaccurate, if the translator was trying to represent the Hebrew text rather than adding a Alexandrian ideological twist to the translation.

As is the case with other ambiguous sections of the first tabernacle account, the translation of the parallel text in the second tabernacle is a definite improve-

---

95. Fraenkel, "Übersetzungsnorm und literarische Gestaltung," 77-81.

96. This usage of θάλασσα as a compass point is not found in the NT. In the 𝔊 Scriptures, however, it is used fairly frequently in this way, e.g., Gen 13:14; 28:14; Josh 17:10; Ezek 47:20.

97. WeversNotes, 437-38.

98. According to Moulton and Milligan, the term λίψ is found in third century B.C. Egypt with the meaning "west" and is used opposite ἀπηλιώτης, but in the 𝔊 Scriptures λίψ could also be used for "south" (e.g., Gen 13:14; 28:14; Num 35:5; Deut 3:27). See James Hope Moulton and George Milligan, *The Vocabulary of the Greek Testament: Illustrated from the Papyri and Other Non-Literary Sources* (London: Hodder and Stoughton, 1952), s.v. "λίψ."

ment in that it is less ambiguous and more accurate.[99] The translation in 𝕲 37:7-11 has returned to the usage of θάλασσα as a compass point, as signaled by the use of the preposition πρός. This term can then be properly interpreted in a context in which there are clear terms for north, βορρᾶς, and east, ἀνατολή. The choice of λίψ instead of νότος, however, remains problematic. Possibly the translator was seeking to reflect the difference between נֶגֶב and נֶגְבָּה.[100] All examples of נֶגֶב are translated by λίψ, whereas all examples of נֶגְבָּה are translated by νότος.[101] A more likely reason for the choice of λίψ, however, is that it maintains continuity with the first account. This is accomplished both by the use of λίψ and by the fact that the λίψ sides in both accounts were one hundred cubits in length. If the translator of the second account had chosen the term νότος, then a blatant contradiction would have been present in that the νότος side would have been fifty cubits in length in 27:13, whereas in the second account it would have been one hundred cubits in length. Thus, the translation of the parallel passage in the second account improves on the first account by restoring the proper orientation of the courtyard and yet maintains continuity by retaining the directional terms for two contiguous sides of the rectangle, θάλασσα and λίψ. The source of the different orientation of the courtyard in 27:9-13 could be either ideological or due to a series of errors on the part of the translator, but this is best evaluated in light of the overall accuracy of the tabernacle accounts, which is the topic of chapter five.

IV. Other Observations Gained from Studying Lexical Equivalents

In addition to providing evidence for the discussion about the number of translators that produced the tabernacle accounts, the examination of choices of lexical equivalents in the 𝕲 provides insights into the exegetical approach used by translator(s) in the third century B.C. As was seen in chapter two, the 𝕲 and the 𝔐 often shared the same exegetical understanding of the text, or at least both saw the same ambiguity in a text even though they often resolved the ambiguity in different manners.

In this section, I will begin by giving a few examples of ambiguities in the Hebrew text that have been clarified in the 𝕲. These ambiguities include a phrase

---

99. Other examples of ambiguous sections will be discussed in chapter five.

100. In the 𝔐 this difference was eliminated by the addition of a locative *he* where it was lacking in the 𝔐 (27:9; 36:23; 38:9). If the *Vorlage* of the 𝕲 was more like that of the 𝔐, then another reason for the difference must be sought, but it is possible that this change in the 𝔐 was part of a later change in language usage. See discussion of locative *he* in chapter two.

101. Examples of the translation of נֶגְבָּה by νότος may be found in 26:18 (𝕲 26:20) and 40:24. The translation of נֶגֶב by λίψ may be found in 27:9 and 38:9 (𝕲 37:7).

with disputed meaning as well as parallel passages in the tabernacle accounts that contain known textual variants as well as an apparent contradiction between the two Hebrew texts. Following a discussion of how the translator(s) resolved these ambiguities in the text, I will give a few examples of choices of lexical equivalents that in a sense add meaning to the text. Most of this "extra" layer of meaning is not contradictory to the Hebrew text, but it states the meaning of the Hebrew text in a manner that is more specific than the Hebrew text may have intended for it to be. Choices of this type reflect the exegetical understanding of the translator's time rather than any explicitly stated meaning in the Hebrew text.

Clarifying Ambiguities

The phrase בֵּין הָעַרְבָּיִם has been much discussed by both rabbinic and modern exegetes.[102] Identifying the time period that this phrase refers to is seen as important for the proper fulfillment of the commands concerning the Passover and other offerings. The translator of the first part of Exodus (including the control sample and first account), however, followed his normal procedure of interpreting the phrase in context rather than using one fixed lexical equivalent. The phrase בֵּין הָעַרְבָּיִם was translated by πρὸς ἑσπέραν when it referred to the slaughtering and eating of food (12:6; 16:12), i.e., the slaughtering was done "towards" evening rather than "at dusk" so that there was plenty of time to accomplish the task. When the phrase refers to the time period for the evening sacrifice, it is translated τὸ δειλινόν, a phrase that is found paired with morning, πρωινός, both in the first tabernacle account and in literature from third century B.C. Egypt.[103] In 30:8, the translator uses another term, ὀψέ, to refer to the time when the lamps would be lit and incense offered. The term ὀψέ would seem to refer to a slightly later period in the day than that referred to by πρὸς ἑσπέραν, as indicated both by the preposition with ἑσπέρα and the choice of lexical equivalents.[104] This choice fits with the probable cultural norm of the translator's time, i.e., lamps are not lit until they are needed, rather than being lit in the afternoon. Thus, whereas the Hebrew phrase is ambiguous at best and has been much discussed, the transla-

---

102. Nahum M. Sarna, *Exodus: The Traditional Hebrew Text with the New JPS Translation*, The JPS Torah Commentary (Philadelphia: The Jewish Publication Society, 1991), 55, 244-45 n. 16.

103. Lee, *Lexical Study*, 110. Lee cites P.Cair.Zen. 207.37 as an example of the third century B.C. usage of this term. This same combination of morning and afternoon is seen in 29:41 in which instructions are given for the second lamb to be sacrificed like the morning (πρωινός) sacrifice. In 29:39, τὸ πρωὶ is used to refer to the time period for offering the first sacrifice. The term τὸ πρωὶ also occurs in 16:12, but the similarity of the context (eating) to that of 12:6 probably influenced the translator to use πρὸς ἑσπέραν rather than τὸ δειλινόν.

104. According to Louw and Nida, ἑσπέρα refers to "a period from late in the afternoon until darkness," whereas ὀψέ refers to "the period after sunset and before darkness" in *Semantic Domains*, s.v. 67.191, 197.

tor of the 𝔊 made the meaning clear according to what was appropriate for the context.¹⁰⁵

In addition to phrases whose meaning may be disputed, the translator of the 𝔊 also had to interpret texts that were both grammatically complex as well as being complex because of the structural details that had to be communicated. The parallel passages about the construction of the bronze altar contain this kind of a combination of grammatical difficulties and technical terminology. In each account, a distinct approach was taken to the resolving of these difficulties. In the first account, the translation reflects the interpretation seen in the 𝔐, which treats the hearth (grating) as a unit composed of net-work rather than carefully distinguishing the network from the grating.¹⁰⁶ In addition, the translator either misread כַּרְכֹּב or his *Vorlage* read מִכְבָּר instead of כַּרְכֹּב and as a result, the translator of 27:4-5 was able to use ἐσχάρα to translate three distinct terms—כַּרְכֹּב, מִכְבָּר, and רֶשֶׁת.¹⁰⁷ The resulting translation is a coherent, but simplified version of the instructions for the construction of the bronze altar in the 𝔐. The translator of the second tabernacle account, in contrast, was faced with a different set of challenges. Because of the conflicting usage of ἐσχάρα in the first account, the term ἐσχάρα was not used in the second account. As a result, כַּרְכֹּב was translated by a separate term, πυρεῖον. In addition, the translator of the second account had to resolve an apparent discrepancy between the Hebrew texts of the first and second accounts, which was discussed above.¹⁰⁸ Thus, the translation of these parallel passages illustrates two distinct approaches to clarifying ambiguities through the choice of lexical equivalents. In the first account, the passage was clarified through simplification and the use of assimilation in lexical equivalents, i.e., three Hebrew terms were translated by one Greek term. In the second account, the translator clarified the passage by choosing distinct terms for each item in the passage and by eliminating the apparent contradictions in the 𝔐. In the process, the translator avoided the use of the term ἐσχάρα and thus there were no new contradictions created with respect to the translation in the first tabernacle account.

---

105. Interestingly, while the NIV consistently translates the phrase "at twilight," the NRSV reflects a technique similar to that of the 𝔊 and translates the first two occurrences "at twilight" (12:6; 16:12) and the remaining occurrences as "in the evening" (29:39, 41; 30:8). In the notes on these verses in *The HarperCollins Study Bible*, however, Greenstein indicates that he believes that this phrase should have been translated in an identical manner throughout Exodus. See Wayne A. Meeks, ed., *The HarperCollins Study Bible: New Revised Standard Version with the Apocryphal/Deuterocanonical Books* (New York: HarperCollins Publishers, 1993).

106. See the discussion in chapter two of the "irrelevant" changes of gender in 𝔐 27:5.

107. The first occurrence of רֶשֶׁת used to describe the workmanship of the grating, is translated by δικτυωτός. This same lexical equivalent for רֶשֶׁת is found also in the second account, which has one rather than two occurrences of רֶשֶׁת.

108. This was discussed in section two and involved the fact that the rings are made on the רֶשֶׁת in 27:4, but are poured out on the four edges of the מִכְבָּר in 38:5.

Identifying Interpretations of the Translators

The choice of lexical equivalents is one factor that identifies the translator's understanding of the text. These interpretations may be as simple as the fact that the translator envisioned the same prominent color scheme being continued with the outer leather covering of the tabernacle. This understanding is seen in both tabernacle accounts in the choice of ὑακίνθινος to translate תַּחַשׁ, which is understood by modern exegetes to be the skin of some unidentified animal.[109] Thus, the inner tent was linen, which was covered with a goat-hair outer tent and with both a red and a blue covering of leather. This is similar to the list of materials used for many of the tabernacle items—blue, purple, crimson, and fine linen. This interpretation does not negate anything in the 𝔐. Instead, it uses a meaningful lexical equivalent that fits the color scheme of the tabernacle rather than using the name of an animal that would possibly be unknown to some of the readers.

A slightly different process of interpretation is seen in the translation of צוה by two different lexical equivalents—ἐντέλλομαι and συντάσσω. Wevers would have us believe that these are synonyms that could possibly be used to support a two-translator theory of the production of the tabernacle accounts.[110] These terms in Exodus, however, were used in the same distinct way as was later seen in the NT, i.e., ἐντέλλομαι meant "to give definite orders, implying authority or official sanction," whereas συντάσσω meant "to give detailed instructions as to what must be done."[111]

As Wevers observed, in the second tabernacle account συντάσσω was the most frequent translation of צוה with ἐντέλλομαι only occurring in 40:16. He attributed this exception in 40:16 to the influence from the first part of Exodus where ἐντέλλομαι was more frequently used. This is a possible explanation especially in light of the usage of lexical equivalents from the first account to maintain lexical cohesion between the two accounts. The singular occurrence at the end of the account, however, raises doubts about this analysis. An examination of the contexts shows that all occurrences of συντάσσω in the second tabernacle account were concerned with fulfilling directions that God gave Moses about the construction of the tabernacle and other related items. Exodus 40:16, however, comes at the end of the passage in which Moses was commanded to set up and anoint the tabernacle and also to anoint Aaron and his sons for a priesthood that

---

109. See the discussion of possible interpretations in Haran, *Temples and Temple-Service*, 162-63.

110. Wevers concludes that the "two are synonyms," but then in a later discussion of the tabernacle accounts he seems to indicate that the first account tended to use one term and the second account used the other term. See WeversNotes, 183, 646.

111. Louw and Nida, *Semantic Domains*, s.v. 33.325, 329. The fact that the words had different meanings in the NT does not mean that the same difference can always be found in the 𝔊. If there is a difference in meaning in the 𝔊, however, it is probable that the same difference, possibly in a modified form, will be seen in the NT.

would continue for eternity. This verse indicates Moses' compliance with all these commands. The translator indicated the "authority or official sanction" behind this set of commands (which included the priesthood) by his choice of ἐντέλλομαι. In the mind of the translator, instructions for sanctifying the tabernacle and establishing the priesthood were not the same as instructions for the building of the tabernacle, though from our Western perspective they both appear to be the same type of detailed, tedious instructions.

This contrast of "detailed instructions" versus "authority or official sanction" can also be seen in the first tabernacle account.[112] Wevers' conclusion that the two words were synonyms would, however, appear to be vindicated by the usage of συντάσσω (31:6) and ἐντέλλομαι (31:11) in almost identical phrases, but a careful analysis of these verses shows that the Greek terms are used with distinct meanings.[113] Other examples in the remainder of Exodus confirm the distinction between these two terms.[114]

---

112. The word συντάσσω is used when Moses was told to "give detailed instructions" to the Israelites about bringing the oil for the lamps (27:20). In contrast, the word ἐντέλλομαι is used when God gave commands with "authority or official sanction" from between the cherubim (25:22). The issue of "authority" is also the reason ἐντέλλομαι is used for the commands given concerning the ordination of the priests (29:35).

113. The Hebrew phrases אֲשֶׁר צִוִּיתִךָ (31:6) and וְעָשׂוּ אֵת כָּל־אֲשֶׁר יַעֲשׂוּ כְּכֹל אֲשֶׁר־צִוִּיתִךָ (31:11) are chiastic clauses that form an inclusio around the list of items that the craftsmen were directed to construct. Assuming that the choice of different terms for "command" was purposeful, the reason for the choice may have been the presence of the preposition כְּ in 31:11. In 31:6, the Greek translation indicates that the craftsmen will do/make all the tabernacle-related items about which God has given Moses detailed instructions. In contrast, the translation of 31:11 states that they will do/make "according to," i.e., within the parameters of, all that God authoritatively commanded Moses, a usage that is similar to that in 𝔐 40:16. This implies that there were additional authoritative commands that were for Moses and had nothing to do with the instructions that the craftsmen would so faithfully complete.

114. In the Hebrew text of Exodus, Pharaoh is twice said to "command" (1:22, 5:6), but in the 𝔊 he only gives "detailed instructions" that are either secretly subverted (as with the throwing of the babies into the Nile) or openly questioned (when straw is no longer given for the making of bricks). God, in contrast, commands "authoritatively" when he speaks to Moses or to Moses and Aaron about what they should say and do (4:28, 7:2, 6, 10). The only exception in 1-13 is when God gives "detailed instructions" to Moses and Aaron concerning Pharaoh and the bringing out of the Israelites from Egypt (6:13), a verse that functions as the conclusion to that particular section. By using the term συντάσσω, the translator may have been implying that God did more that just give a few authoritative commands to Moses and Aaron about the signs. God also gave other detailed instructions that were not explicitly stated in the text. The remaining examples of the translation of צוה in Exodus can be understood in a similar way, but the context of each must be closely examined to see things from the translator's perspective.

Directions for the collection of manna are communicated by either God or Moses using συντάσσω, the term for "detailed instructions" (16:16, 24, 32, 34). The directions about the preparation of the two stone tablets (34:4) are also given with the same term. When Moses first went up on Mt. Sinai, the words of God that are reported are general instructions about the relationship of God to his people. These are referred to by the translator as the giving of "detailed instructions" because there are no

Thus, for the translator(s) of Exodus, the terms ἐντέλλομαι and συντάσσω were used with their natural Greek meaning, but the translator had to decide which term was appropriate for each context. The fact that the translator viewed the "commands" about the building of the tabernacle and its related items as "detailed instructions" that did not merit the same level of authority as God's commands about the priesthood or the commands that God would give from between the cherubim, is an added layer of interpretation that was not present in the Hebrew text. This interpretation would most likely reflect the values of the translator's culture, which possibly placed a higher emphasis on the priesthood and communication from God by contrast to the construction of a tabernacle that no longer existed.

V. Conclusions

Lexical consistency in relatively free translations such as 𝕲 Exodus cannot be easily measured and used as a standard for determining the number of translators that produced a given translation. Relatively free translations are best understood through an examination of the contextual factors that affected the choices of lexical equivalents. Within the tabernacle accounts of 𝕲 Exodus, this type of examination has shown that the same factors affected lexical choices in each section to the same relative degree. On the surface level, the main differences were due to the size of the section examined. Larger sections usually contained a larger variety of contexts and thus allowed for the possible use of a greater variety of lexical equivalents for each Hebrew term. This was especially the case with verbs, as was expected in a relatively free translation.

When three different sets of texts were compared from the tabernacle accounts and the control sample, it was found that the percentage of identical, partially shared, and contrastive lexical equivalents in each set was approximately the same. The relatively small percentage of contrastive lexical equivalents has often been overemphasized in past studies of the tabernacle accounts. Granted, some of the contrasts are striking, but in light of the high percentage of identical and partially shared lexical equivalents, there seems to be little reason for putting such an emphasis on the contrasting lexical equivalents.

---

commands explicitly mentioned and because it is envisioned as overall directions that set the tone for the future of the people (19:7). In contrast, the term ἐντέλλομαι is used for authoritative commands in reference to the Passover (23:15; 34:18), the breaking of God's command by the making of the golden calf (32:8), warnings to obey the covenant that God commanded (34:11), Moses' authoritative commanding of the people to obey all that God spoke on Mt. Sinai (34:32), and God's authoritative commands that were given when Moses spoke with God in the tent outside the camp (34:34). In addition, the word צוה is either contextually interpreted or the translator's text had a different Hebrew word in three verses where צוה is translated by the following verbs: κατισχύω (18:23), εἶπον (35:1), and προστάσσω (36:6).

Rather than contrasting lexical equivalents, the shift in usage of lexical equivalents is the more pervasive characteristic of the translation that must be explained in any discussion of the tabernacle accounts. In the first account, the most characteristic pattern was the usage of distinct lexical equivalents for each contrastive context. This led to a multiplicity of "extra" lexical equivalents that are found only in the first tabernacle account. In the second tabernacle account, in contrast, the characteristic pattern involved a delicate balancing act between three key factors. First, the translator of the second account attempted to maintain lexical cohesion between the two accounts through the repetition of at least one of the lexical equivalents from the first account. Second, the translator of the second account often used a specific term from the first account as a generic term that was substituted for the diversity of lexical equivalents used in the first account. Finally, the translator of the second account strove to resolve ambiguities in the Hebrew text and prevent the creation of any contradictions between accounts through the careful choice of lexical equivalents. The result of maintaining this delicate balance is that despite the problems in the first account, the 𝔊 tabernacle accounts appear to be a unified whole in which the choice of lexical equivalents is context-sensitive and reflects both the natural Greek meaning and the translator's interpretation of the text.

CHAPTER FOUR

Grammatical Consistency

This study of the translation of grammatical structures will show that the control sample and both tabernacle accounts of 𝔊 Exodus were translated using a context-sensitive approach in which a variety of translation equivalents was used to express clearly the wide range of meanings that can be communicated by Hebrew grammatical structures. The general consistency of this approach in both tabernacle accounts could be used as evidence to prove that either one translator produced both tabernacle accounts or that the tabernacle accounts were translated by a multiplicity of translators that shared the same approach to the translation of grammatical structures. Even though both tabernacle accounts use a similar approach, the choice of translation equivalents for grammatical structures is not always identical in parallel verses from both accounts. Minute differences in the choice of translation equivalents are the main evidence from this chapter than can be used to support the theory that the tabernacle accounts were produced by different translators using a similar approach to the translation of grammatical structures.

In this chapter I will first survey past studies of grammatical consistency and then briefly discuss the approach to analyzing grammatical consistency that will be used in this chapter. Second, I will present a detailed analysis of the translation equivalents of the preposition בְּ, simple construct chains, and relative clauses with אֲשֶׁר in the control sample and tabernacle accounts of 𝔊 Exodus. In the third section, I will give a few examples of translation equivalents of grammatical structures that point to contrasting interpretations of identical grammatical structures. In addition, the effect of grammatical context on the choice of translation equivalents will be further demonstrated. Ultimately, the variations in the translation of grammatical structures provide little evidence for proving whether or not the translation was produced by one or more translators, but it does point to the fact that the same type of context-sensitive approach was used throughout the control sample and tabernacle accounts.

I. Defining and Measuring Grammatical Consistency

Past studies of grammatical consistency have primarily focused on identifying Hebraic features of the translation and measuring the degree to which these features occur in the books of the 𝕭 Scriptures. Statistical studies of these grammatical features were used earlier than statistical studies of lexical consistency because of their perceived value in attempting to identify NT books that were translations of Semitic originals. Despite claims about the value of these types of studies, they do not appear to have been widely accepted, despite being periodically resurrected during this last century. Grammatical studies that appear to be gaining in acceptance are those from the Finnish school that emphasize an examination of grammatical features within their contexts. In this section I will first survey the variety of grammatical studies that have been used in the study of the 𝕭 and then I will describe the methodology that I will be using in the analysis of three grammatical structures in section two of this chapter.

Survey of Past Methodologies

Early studies of the grammar of the 𝕭 revolved around the issue of identifying Hebraisms and grouping the putative component translations of the 𝕭 according to the degree to which the grammar reflected "natural" Greek versus "Hebraic" Greek. In Thackeray's discussion of the Semitic elements in the 𝕭, he mentions contrasting translations of the following grammatical structures: infinitive absolutes used with finite verbs; prepositional phrases used for the object of transitive verbs instead of the more "natural" accusative case; and the translation of terms and phrases that function either on the discourse level, such as וַיְהִי, or as modals, such as יֹסֵף. In each case, Thackeray highlights the wide range of options that have been used in the 𝕭 and then emphasizes the tendency to use a more literal translation technique in the books that were translated later. Speaking about this tendency he says, " . . . the reason for the change is to be sought, it appears, rather in a growing reverence for the letter of the Hebrew than in ignorance of Greek."[1]

In contrast to these brief observations, Thackeray presents a detailed analysis of changes in orthography and accidence. This focus is primarily due to the fact that Thackeray and others of his time were trying to "be of service to the textual critic in the reconstruction of the original text of the LXX."[2] Thackeray's focus is also a reflection of the focus of most grammatical studies of that time period, i.e., most studies emphasized phonology, word formation, and lower level grammatical elements.[3] These studies are valuable for the dating of manuscript traditions

---

1. Henry St. John Thackeray, *A Grammar of the Old Testament in Greek According to the Septuagint*, vol. 1, *Introduction, Orthography and Accidence* (Cambridge: Cambridge University Press, 1909), 30. The grammatical features mentioned above are discussed on pp. 46-53.

2. Ibid., x.

3. The current focus in many linguistic fields has shifted to the discourse level and sociolinguistic factors that affect the text. Studies in Biblical Greek and Hebrew have only begun to make this shift and many, like Wallace, are unwilling to move in that direction due to the less concrete nature of discourse studies. See Daniel B. Wallace, *Greek Grammar Beyond the Basics: An Exegetical Syntax of the New Testament* (Grand Rapids, Mich.: Zondervan, 1996), xv. This gradual shift in focus has been

and other foundational studies, but are less valuable for studies such as this in which the consistency of translation technique within one book is the focus.

With the discovery of more papyri, many of the features previously identified as "Hebraic" were found to occur in natural texts. Because of this, Thackeray said,

> The Hebraic character of these books consists in the *accumulation* of a number of just tolerable Greek phrases, which nearly correspond to what is normal and idiomatic in Hebrew. If we take these phrases individually, we can discover isolated parallels to them in the papyri, but in no document outside the Bible or writings directly dependent upon it do we find them in such profusion.[4]

Observations such as this one by Thackeray led to an emphasis on statistical analyses of the frequency of words and other grammatical structures as a basis for discerning translated versus non-translated Greek texts.

In the first part of the twentieth century this interest in the statistical analysis of words and grammatical structures developed into a methodology for identifying translation Greek versus original Greek. This methodology countered the typical approach of detecting translation Greek by the use of the "literal rendering of individual foreign words and idioms, i.e. for traces of, or lapses into systematic representation."[5] Instead of focusing on the translation of individual words, Rife examined word order as a basis for identifying translation Greek. Unlike some more recent studies, however, Rife noted some of the difficulties of statistical approaches due to the changing nature of Greek. Concerning this he said, "the nature of the subject matter is continually upsetting the validity of statistical comparisons, ..."[6] Rife was aware of the fact that syntactical features in various parts of a discourse or in various types of discourses could differ from the norm and thus upset any statistical analysis of the syntax. Nevertheless, Rife concluded that the vast difference in the frequency with which the VSO word ordering was used in the 𝕲 Scriptures in contrast to original Greek texts was a significant indicator that they were translated from a Semitic source. Rife concludes his brief article by stating, "it still appears unlikely that the facts of word-order will offer much support to the theory that any NT books are translation Greek, but they clearly indi-

---

made possible by those like Thackeray, who laid solid foundations on which later generations could build.

4. Thackeray, *Grammar of the Old Testament in Greek*, 29.

5. J. Merle Rife, "The Mechanics of Translation Greek," *Journal of Biblical Literature* 52 (1933): 246.

6. Rife's list of Semitic word-order that does not match the Greek word-order includes the following: "No word comes between the article and its noun. An adjective always immediately follows its substantive. No postpositive conjunctions. A genitive always immediately follows its construct. A direct, personal, pronominal object always follows its governing verb. A demonstrative pronoun always follows its substantive." Ibid., 247.

cate, *per se*, that Judith, I Maccabees, and other LXX books, are from Semitic originals."[7]

Later in the twentieth century, Martin brought syntactical studies of grammatical structures again into focus. In his early article, Martin focused on the differences in the frequency of a variety of prepositions and their usage with various cases. As a result of this study, Martin established percentages of relative frequencies that served as the boundary between translation Greek and original Greek documents.[8] The characteristics that could be measured statistically were then expanded to include a list of seventeen criteria that Jobes accepted and used in her studies of various Greek translations including the Old Greek and Theodotionic recension of Daniel.[9] According to Jobes, her "study validates the usefulness of comparative syntactic analysis as a tool in Septuagint studies" because the "results ... are consistent with current theories about the Greek versions of Daniel reached by other means. . . ." Specifically, she claims, "A similar contour of the profiles corroborates the theory of genetic relationship; dissimilar profiles suggests [*sic*] the texts are not genetically related to each other, at least not in their recent past."[10]

---

7. Ibid., 252.

8. R. A. Martin, "Some Syntactical Criteria of Translation Greek," *Vetus Testamentum* 10 (1960): 295-310. The percentages in his early study were generally revised downward in his more complete study. In R. A. Martin, *Syntactical Evidence of Semitic Sources in Greek Documents*, Septuagint and Cognate Studies, no. 3 (Cambridge, Mass.: Scholars Press, 1974), 9, the following percentages were suggested for the relative frequencies of various prepositions in relationship to the preposition ἐν: διά with all cases .18 - .01; κατά with all cases .19 - .01; περί with all cases .27 - .01; εἰς .49 - .01. According to Martin, texts whose relative percentages fall within these ranges are translated texts, whereas those outside of these ranges are natural Greek texts. When this technique of analyzing the syntax is applied to the four sections of Exodus used in this study, which is a part of a text that everyone claims is almost totally a translation of some type of Hebrew *Vorlage*, the results are not quite as expected. While the percentages for διά (.063) and περί (.028) are well within the "norm" for translated texts, the percentages for κατά (.359) and εἰς (.746) fall outside of that range according to his revised percentages. Granted, I have not used all of Martin's criteria in my computer-produced statistics for these four sections of Exodus, but this sampling alone was enough to raise further questions about the usefulness of these types of purely statistical studies.

9. The rationale for the seventeen criteria used by Jobes may be found in Martin, *Syntactical Evidence of Semitic Sources*. Martin's seventeen criteria, as summarized by Jobes, are, "Criteria #1-8. The relative frequency of occurrence of eight prepositions with respect to the preposition ἐν: 1. διά with the genitive 2. διά in all occurrences 3. εἰς 4. κατά with the accusative 5. κατά in all occurrences 6. περί in all occurrences 7. πρός with the dative 8. ὑπό with the genitive #9. the frequency of occurrence of the coordinating καί relative to δέ #10. the percentage of articles separated from their substantives #11. the relative frequency of dependent genitives following the word on which they depend #12. the relative frequency of occurrence of dependent genitive personal pronouns #13. the relative frequency of genitive personal pronouns dependent on anarthrous substantives #14. the relative frequency of attributive adjectives preceding the word they qualify #15. the relative infrequency of attributive adjectives #16. the relative frequency of adverbial participles #17. the relative frequency of the dative case without the preposition ἐν." See Karen H. Jobes, "A Comparative Syntactic Analysis of the Greek Versions of Daniel: A Test Case for New Methodology," *Bulletin of the International Organization for Septuagint and Cognate Studies* 28 (1995): 20-21.

10. Ibid., 36-37.

McLay, however, has shown the pitfalls of her approach. He especially noted her use of the lack of shared readings to prove genetic linkage, her dependence on criteria that are illustrated by only a few examples in the text, and the lack of an examination of the data in context. McLay concludes, "Without a comparison of where syntactical criteria actually occur in the texts under investigation, Jobes' analysis has determined nothing more than the fact that both are 'translations' according to Martin's criteria." No matter how "enticing" a methodology may appear, the genetic connection of a recension to the 𝕲 cannot be proven on the basis of these kinds of statistical studies in which the grammatical features are divorced from their contexts.[11]

Another approach to evaluating translation techniques with respect to grammatical consistency focuses on identifying the use of natural Greek expressions versus literal translations of Hebrew grammatical structures.[12] These studies from the Finnish school begin with a complete examination of the data in context and then statistics are compiled and presented "either a) as a ration, i.e. as the ratio of actual occurrences to potential occurrences or of actual occurrences to occurrences of a near-synonymous feature, or b) as a percentage, i.e. they are given as the percentage of the number of total possible occurrences."[13] McGregor has questioned the value of these kinds of statistics because of the problems of "the 'significance' of a figure and the need for a representative section."[14] After compiling the statistics, the frequency of the grammatical structure in the Septuagint is often compared with its frequency in non-translated Greek texts from a similar time period to discern how "natural" the translation is in its use of grammatical structures. Within this school of Septuagintal studies, monographs have appeared on such grammatical structures as infinitives, semiprepositions, parataxis, repetition of possessive pronouns, as well as many articles on a variety of grammatical topics.[15] The statistical difficulties of this approach have been

---

11. Tim McLay, "Syntactic Profiles and the Characteristics of Revision: A Response to Karen Jobes," *Bulletin of the International Organization for Septuagint and Cognate Studies* 29 (1996): 17, 20.

12. See Staffan Olofsson, *The LXX Version: A Guide to the Translation Techniques of the Septuagint* (Stockholm: Almqvist & Wiksell International, 1990), 65-66 for a brief discussion of the approach used by the Finnish school and bibliographic references. For a recent example of this approach, see Raija Sollamo, *Repetition of the Possessive Pronouns in the Septuagint*, Septuagint and Cognate Studies, ed. Bernard A. Taylor, no. 40 (Atlanta, Ga.: Scholars Press, 1995). See also Leonard Greenspoon, "'It's All Greek to Me': Septuagint Studies Since 1968," *Currents in Research* 5 (1997): 149-50.

13. Leslie John McGregor, *The Greek Text of Ezekiel: An Examination of Its Homogeneity*, Septuagint and Cognate Studies, ed. Claude E. Cox, no. 18 (Atlanta, Ga.: Scholars Press, 1985), 51.

14. Ibid., 53.

15. See Ilmari Soisalon-Soininen, *Die Infinitive in der Septuaginta* (Helsinki: Suomalainen Tiedeakatemia, 1965); Raija Sollamo, *Rendering of Hebrew Semiprepositions in the Septuagint* (Helsinki: Suomalainen Tiedeakatemia, 1979); Anneli Aejmelaeus, *Parataxis in the Septuagint: A Study of the Renderings of the Hebrew Coordinate Clauses in the Greek Pentateuch*, Annales Academiae Scientiarum Fennicae: Dissertationes Humanarum Litterarum, no. 31 (Helsinki: Suomalainen Tiedeakatemia, 1982); Sollamo, *Repetition of the Possessive Pronouns*; Anneli Aejmelaeus, *On the Trail*

pointed out by McGregor, but the strength of this approach is its careful examination of the data in context, a feature that is often missing in other studies.

The use of the computer has also been advocated for some aspects of the grammatical study of the Septuagint, as discussed by Tov and Wright.[16] After this initial study, Wright used this approach with a larger set of criteria.[17] The features that can most easily be studied with the computer are factors such as changes in word order, the systematic representation of all parts of grammatical words, the representation of specific prepositions and conjunctions, such as בְּ by ἐν and כִּי by ὅτι or διότι, and "the frequency of Greek post-positive particles."[18] These statistical studies are interesting and generally support Thackeray's analysis of the books, but as has been noted with other computer-based approaches, the context is not adequately taken into account.[19]

A broader survey of publications about translation techniques of the Septuagint may be found in Tov's article on the topic.[20] In this work, Tov traces the beginning of the study of translation techniques to the mid-nineteenth century. Tov especially notes the impressionistic nature of the works and the lack of thorough, comparative analyses of the translations of grammatical structures throughout the 𝔊 Scriptures. The work of Tov, Kraft, and others on the aligned text project has made it possible to produce broader studies of translation techniques that interest Tov, but these studies will never replace the detailed analyses of grammatical structures in their contexts, which were noted above. Computer-assisted studies that include context will have to wait for the next generation of computer software and tagged texts. Until then, those who are interested in the context, must struggle with the data and find means other than computer-produced statistics to help the reader grasp the nature of the translation techniques used for grammatical structures in the 𝔊 Scriptures.

Grammatical consistency or the lack thereof is rarely a major piece of evi-

---

of the Septuagint Translators: Collected Essays (Kampen, Netherlands: Kok Pharos, 1993); and Anneli Aejmelaeus and Raija Sollamo, eds., Studien zur Septuaginta-Syntax (Helsinki: Suomalainen Tiedeakatemia, 1987).

16. Emanuel Tov and Benjamin G. Wright, "Computer-Assisted Study of the Criteria for Assessing the Literalness of Translation Units in the LXX," Textus 12 (1985): 149-87.

17. Benjamin G. Wright, No Small Difference: Sirach's Relationship to Its Hebrew Parent Text, Septuagint and Cognate Studies, ed. Claude E. Cox, no. 26 (Atlanta, Ga.: Scholars Press, 1989).

18. Tov and Wright, "Computer-Assisted Study of the Criteria," 158.

19. For a discussion of the methodological issue of how syntax should be studied, including the use of computer-based analyses versus detailed examinations of the text, see Ilmari Soisalon-Soininen, "Methodologische Fragen der Erforschung der Septuaginta-Syntax," in VI Congress of the International Organization for Septuagint and Cognate Studies, Jerusalem, 1986, ed. Claude E. Cox, Septuagint and Cognate Studies, no. 23 (Atlanta, Ga.: Scholars Press, 1987), 425-44.

20. Emanuel Tov, "The Nature and Study of the Translation Technique of the LXX in the Past and Present," in VI Congress of the International Organization for Septuagint and Cognate Studies, Jerusalem, 1986, ed. Claude E. Cox, Septuagint and Cognate Studies, no. 23 (Atlanta, Ga.: Scholars Press, 1987), 337-59.

dence used in the scholarly discussions about the number of translators who produced the tabernacle accounts of 𝕲 Exodus. A few studies, however, have noted small differences that have occasionally been attributed to the work of two translators. For instance, Wevers claims that differences in the translators' styles can be seen in the rendering of the "articulated adjectival phrase" and in the "patterning of compound numbers."[21] Because of the lack of free renderings of conjunctions that is typically found in Exodus, Aejmelaeus has suggested that the final chapters of Exodus (35-40) may be connected with Leviticus rather than having been produced by the translator of the first part of Exodus.[22] Sollamo, on the basis of her study of the repetition of possessive pronouns, however, raises a note of caution showing that in some ways 1-34, rather than 35-40, is more like Leviticus. Sollamo concludes by saying, "But as I have stated before, my material is too sparse to allow reliable conclusions concerning the possible dichotomy between chapters 1-34 and 35-40 of Exod."[23] This cautionary note should be remembered with reference to all grammatical studies based on a limited number of examples or the study of a limited aspect of the grammar. The major problem with these types of grammatical studies is that their broad conclusions are often based on a limited number of "exceptions" or counter-examples that may in reality be caused by other difficulties in the translation or *Vorlage*. Limited data from one aspect of the translation technique, such as these grammatical studies, can at best lend supporting evidence to theories based on other data. Their larger benefit, however, is that they help the reader to understand the general nature of the translation and the extent of the translator's repertoire of translation equivalents for grammatical structures.

---

21. "In Greek two patterns are equally normal; either 'article + noun + article + adjectival modifier' or 'article + adjectival modifier + noun' can occur. In Exod A [first tabernacle account in 𝕲] the former with few exceptions is the pattern found. It should be said that excluded from consideration are all instances in which the modifier is a cardinal or ordinal number, for which both patterns recur throughout Exod." Wevers also notes a few other exceptions and only one example of the "article + adjectival modifier + noun" pattern in the first account, τὸ ἕτερον κλίτος (26:28), whereas in the second account he notes four examples, as follows: τὰ ἅγια καθήκοντα (36:1); τῶν ἐπεσκεμμένων ἀνδρῶν (38.25 [𝕲 39:2]); Τὸ ... λοιπὸν χρυσίον (𝕲 39:11); τὴν καταλειφθεῖσαν ὑάκινθον (𝕲 39:12). Concerning numbers, Wevers says, "... the patterning of compound numbers is also different in Exod B [second tabernacle account of 𝕲]. The pattern in Exod [𝕲] is that of descending grades, i.e. myriads, thousands, hundreds, tens and single units. In ch. 6 these are unconnected with καί but in ch. 39 they are all thus connected except for the final tens and single units." See WeversText, 144. These are interesting differences that Wevers notes, but the scarcity of the examples would raise questions as to their validity for making any major claims. In addition, the examples that he gives of articulated adjectival phrases in the tabernacle accounts all involve pluses in the 𝕲 or texts that have been reinterpreted. When the translator is not following a Hebrew *Vorlage*, it would be expected that a more natural Greek form would be used. I have not chosen to pursue these categories any further due to the relative infrequency of the structures, but a brief computer search of Exodus did produce further examples of the latter pattern of articulated adjectival phrases outside of the tabernacle accounts.

22. Aejmelaeus, *Parataxis in the Septuagint*, 175.

23. Sollamo, *Repetition of the Possessive Pronouns*, 83-84.

Methodology Used in This Study

In this chapter I will examine three grammatical structures that occur with sufficient frequency so that some generalizations can be made about the translation techniques of each of the four sections of Exodus used in this study.[24] The three grammatical structures that will be analyzed in this chapter are the preposition בְּ, simple construct chains, and relative clauses with אֲשֶׁר. In my analysis of each Hebrew grammatical structure, I will describe both the Greek structures that are used as translation equivalents and their semantic functions. As part of this description, the distribution of the various translation equivalents will be noted.

II. Grammatical Consistency within the Tabernacle Accounts

Within the control sample and tabernacle accounts of 𝔊 Exodus, a wide variety of translation equivalents is used to translate grammatical structures. The systematic nature of the variation of translation equivalents points to the fact that the translator(s) interpreted each structure according to its semantic and grammatical context. The translator's choice of translation equivalents for grammatical structures was also affected by the choice of lexical equivalents for the nouns in each grammatical structure. In this section I will analyze the translation equivalents for the preposition בְּ, simple construct chains, and relative clauses with אֲשֶׁר. The similarity of approach seen in these translation equivalents will show that the control sample and tabernacle accounts all used a contextual approach to the translation of grammatical structures.

Preposition בְּ

Tov and Wright refer to the rendering of the Hebrew preposition בְּ by the Greek preposition ἐν as "one of the best criteria for investigating the literalness of translation units." According to Tov and Wright, the frequency with which ἐν is used to translate בְּ is directly proportionate to the literalness of the translation. In general, their findings confirm intuitive analyses of the differences in translation techniques in the books of the 𝔊 Scriptures.[25]

---

24. The rationale for the choice of these four sections was described in detail in previous chapters. The four sections are as follows: control sample (11-13), first tabernacle account (25-31), core of second tabernacle account (36:8-38:20), and the remainder of second tabernacle account (35:1-36:7; 38:21-40:38).

25. For instance, according to Tov and Wright's statistical study, Qoheleth was the most literal (92.4%) and Job was the least literal (27.7%). Exodus was not included in their study, but Numbers, which is generally considered to be a little more literal than Exodus, had a percentage of 47.1%. See Tov and Wright, "Computer-Assisted Study of the Criteria," 159-63.

Table 9. Translation of בְּ by ἐν

	Control sample	First tabernacle account	Core of second tabernacle account	Remainder of second tabernacle account	Combined second tabernacle account
Number of בְּ	85	114	29	68	97
Number of בְּ translated by ἐν	42	35	2	16	18
Percentage of בְּ translated by ἐν	49.4%	30.7%	6.9%	23.5%	18.6%
Percentage adjusted for minuses	50.6%	32.1%	15.4%	27.6%	25.4%

Table 9 presents the percentages of the occurrences of the preposition בְּ that were translated by ἐν in the four sections of Exodus used in this study. Although the control sample and first tabernacle account are generally considered to have been produced by the same translator, the percentages in table 9 would raise doubts about that conclusion, if the percentages are in fact a valid way of assessing translation technique. In addition, if this statistical approach was valid, then the first and the remainder of the second tabernacle accounts would seem to use the same approach in translating בְּ, especially when the percentages are adjusted to account for the minuses. The inordinately low percentage seen in the core of the second tabernacle account, then, would point to its uniqueness, even when adjusted for the minuses. This low percentage found in the core of the second account, however, is probably another example that illustrates the problem of the statistical analyses of small sections of text, which I have discussed elsewhere.[26] Rather than an indicator of differences in translation technique, these statistics indicate the frequency of reference to the semantic functions of means, location (place), and time, which are often translated by ἐν.[27] The control sample is the section that is

---

26. Martha L. Wade, "Evaluating Lexical Consistency in the Old Greek Bible," *Bulletin of the International Organization for Septuagint and Cognate Studies* 33 (2000): 53-75.

27. According to van der Merwe, Naudé, and Kroeze, "Approximately 60% of the cases where this preposition [בְּ] is used in the Hebrew Bible have a locative connotation while 15% have a temporal connotation." They also note "that בְּ in BH [Biblical Hebrew] has a more general meaning than '*in*' or '*within*.' It is a preposition that is not very specialized semantically." For a description of the semantic functions of בְּ see Christo H. J. van der Merwe, Jackie A. Naudé, and Jan H. Kroeze, *A Biblical Hebrew Reference Grammar* (Sheffield: Sheffield Academic Press, 1999), 279-82. Because of the frequency with which בְּ is used in a locative sense, a natural translation equivalent is ἐν, which is often used to indicate a locative function. This is also a natural translation equivalent because like בְּ the

most like a narrative, which naturally includes more references to time and location. The first account contains a large section (29) that is more like a narrative than other sections of the tabernacle accounts, which are more like lists. The core of the second account, in contrast, is primarily a list. The remainder of the second account contains a narrative-like framework at the beginning and the end that increases the percentages for ἐν, but does not totally compensate for the minuses, which mainly indicate location and means (material used in the manufacture of clothing). Thus, rather than indicating differences in translation technique, the percentages in table 9 primarily indicate that each section differed in its semantic content and that some contained more narrative material that included references to location, time, and means.[28]

The variety of translation equivalents used for the 296 occurrences of בְּ in four sections of Exodus indicates that none of the sections uses a woodenly literal translation technique. Rather, each section uses a variety of translation equivalents that are conditioned by the semantic and grammatical contexts of both the Greek and Hebrew. Table 10 lists the translation equivalents used for the preposition בְּ in each of the four sections. Most of these translation equivalents occur in both tabernacle accounts. Of those translation equivalents found in only one section, most of them occur in the control sample.[29] The greater number of transla-

---

preposition ἐν, which in the NT is considered to be the "workhorse of prepositions," is found to occur "more frequently and in more varied situations than any other." See Wallace, *Greek Grammar Beyond the Basics*, 372.

28. This is not to say that the translator did not have choices in the translation of בְּ when it indicates location, time, and means. These functions may also be translated by a variety of other translation equivalents that will be discussed below.

29. Of nine translation equivalents that are only found in one section, six are in the control sample, one in the first account, and two in the remainder of the second account. Translation equivalents that only occur in one of the sections generally translate unique semantic functions of בְּ, unique phrases with בְּ, or indicate the possibility of a different *Vorlage*. For instance, ἀπό is used as the translation equivalent for the starting point of a range of physical items (13:2) or the starting point of a time period (12:15, 18). In addition, it is most frequently found as the translation of בְּ when it is used in a partitive sense to refer to a part of the Passover lamb (12:43, 44, 45, 46, 48). This partitive usage could be due to a difference in *Vorlage* (מִן instead of בְּ), but the repeated use of this phrase and the fact that it is translated with the same preposition in an identical Hebrew phrase in Lev 22:13 would probably indicate the originality of בְּ. This is especially true since the rest of the clause in Lev 22:13 is translated using different verb forms and a different number of pronoun despite the identical nature of the probable Hebrew *Vorlage*. In contrast, it is possible that the usage of ἀπό in 12:22 may indicate that the *Vorlage* used by the translator contained the preposition מִן, rather than בְּ. Elsewhere in the Pentateuch, the preposition בְּ used in combination with the verb טבל is translated using translation equivalents such as εἰς (Lev 4:6), ἐν (Deut 33:24), and the dative case (Gen 37:31), but the use of the dative is probably due to the choice of μολύνω rather than βάπτω for the lexical equivalent of טבל. Because of the lack of further examples of this combination in Exodus, however, no definitive conclusion can be reached about whether ἀπό was a contextual translation unique to Exodus or whether it was based on a different *Vorlage*. The possibility of a different *Vorlage* cannot be quickly dismissed for this one instance of ἀπό. The difference in meaning between בְּ and מִן would, however, be slight, i.e., dipping

Table 10. Translation equivalents of בְּ

Translation equivalents of בְּ	Control sample	First tabernacle account	Core of second tabernacle account	Remainder of second tabernacle account	Totals
Accusative	0	8	1	5	14
Dative	7	16	1	12	36
Genitive	2	13	3	5	23
Nominative	2	1	1	0	4
ἀνά + accusative	0	2	0	1	3
ἀπό + genitive	9	0	0	0	9
διά + genitive (phrase)	0	0	0	2	2
εἰς + accusative	2	4	0	2	8
ἐκ + genitive	0	8	3	3	14
ἐν + dative	42	35	2	16	95
ἐναντίον + genitive (phrase)	4	0	0	0	4
ἐπί + genitive	0	5	2	1	8
ἕως + genitive	2	0	0	0	2
ἡνίκα (with infinitive construct)	1	0	0	1	2
κατά + accusative	2	8	0	3	13
μετά + genitive	2	0	0	0	2
ὅταν (with infinitive construct)	1	7	0	1	9
παρά + accusative	3	0	0	0	3
πρός	0	2	0	0	2
σύν + dative	0	0	0	4	4
ὡς (with infinitive construct)	2	0	0	0	2
Idiomatic translation of phrases	2	0	0	2	4
Minuses	2	5	16	10	33
Totals	85	114	29	68	296

---

the branch into the blood versus dipping some of the blood out of the basin. In either case, the result is the same, i.e., a branch that is covered with enough blood to mark the door posts and lintel.

tion equivalents in the control sample is probably due to the wider range of semantic functions that בְּ signals in this narrative-like section of the text.

   Translation equivalents that are only found in one section include two phrases with בְּ, i.e., בְּעֵינֵי, which is translated by ἐναντίον, when it refers to the location in front of humans (11:3 [3x]; 12:36), and בְּיַד, which is translated by διά, when it indicates human agency (35:29; 38:21 [𝔊 37:19]). Elsewhere in Exodus these phrases are translated by means of a variety of translation equivalents, most of which are controlled by the context. For instance, בְּיַד is translated more "literally," i.e., using the word χείρ and the preposition ἐν, when it refers to a physical hand as the location of an item, ἐν ταῖς χερσὶν (12:11), or with a simple dative when the hands are the instrument or means of doing an activity, ταῖς χερσὶν (35:25). When בְּיַד is used to refer to God's hand as a symbol of his power, it is also translated in a "literal" manner, ἐν ... χειρὶ κραταιᾷ (13:9). These are the only occurrences of בְּיַד in the sections of Exodus used in this study, but in the remainder of Exodus a wide array of translation equivalents are used, both more literal and very idiomatic. The phrase בְּעֵינֵי, in contrast, is never translated literally in Exodus. Elsewhere in Exodus it is either translated ἐναντίον (3:21; 5:21 [2x]; 15:26; 33:13 [2x]), ἐνώπιον (33:17; 34:9), παρά (33:12, 16), or as a dative case due to a change from a nonverbal clause in Hebrew to a verbal clause in Greek (21:8). The difference between these equivalents has not been investigated because בְּעֵינֵי only occurs in the control sample.
   The translation equivalent σύν only occurs in the second tabernacle account. Three of the occurrences are in conjunction with the verb συνυφαίνω (39:3 [𝔊 36:10] [3x]). Thus, the choice of the lexical equivalent συνυφαίνω for the verb עָשָׂה probably determines the translation of the preposition בְּ by σύν. As a result, the gold threads are pictured as being interwoven with the colored yarn, rather than using a generic term as in the 𝔐. There is no parallel of this verse in the first account, but it is likely that if a different lexical equivalent had been used for the verb, the prepositions would have also been translated in a different manner. The fourth occurrence of this translation equivalent, σύν, is part of a clause that is either a reinterpretation of the Hebrew or reflects a different Hebrew *Vorlage*. Again, as with the above example, it is the choice of a lexical equivalent, this time the noun, that determines the translation of the preposition. The 𝔐 contains the noun מַסְעֵיהֶם, but in the 𝔊 τῇ ἀπαρτίᾳ αὐτῶν is found (40:36). As a result, σύν is used because ἀπαρτία refers to the things that were taken with them on their journeys, rather than referring to the actual journeying, as in the 𝔐.
   In 26:4, the preposition בְּ is translated by πρός with the dative case. The preposition πρός is normally used with the accusative case. The only other occurrence with the dative in Exodus is a temporal usage with an articular infinitive, πρὸς τῷ τίκτειν (1:16), which is a free translation of a difficult phrase in Hebrew, עַל־הָאָבְנָיִם. Because of the lack of comparable evidence, it is difficult to determine the exact meaning in 26:4, but it is likely that the choice of lexical equivalents for מַחְבֶּרֶת (as a reference to a joint, συμβολῇ, rather than to a "set") affected the choice of prepositions. The only other translated occurrence of the phrase בַּמַּחְבֶּרֶת is found in a relative clause that will be discussed below. This occurrence has also been reinterpreted rather than translated literally. Thus, the use of πρός with the dative reflects the difference in interpretation of the entire phrase rather than just being an odd translation equivalent for בְּ. The use of πρός with the accusative as a translation equivalent for בְּ is found in 29:5. Like πρός with the dative, this translation equivalent reflects either a reinterpretation (clarification) of the entire clause, אָפַדְתָּ לוֹ בְּחֵשֶׁב הָאֵפֹד, or a distinctly different *Vorlage*. In either case, positing a *Vorlage* that includes אֶל, the more frequent *Vorlage* of πρός, would not resolve all the problems in either 26:4 or 29:5.
   When בְּ is used to refer to the ending point of a period of time or a range of items, it is translated by ἕως (12:18; 13:2), a translation equivalent only found in the control sample. The phrase ἀπὸ ἀνθρώπου ἕως κτήνους (13:2) is found elsewhere in Exodus as the translation of a Hebrew text that contains the prepositions מִן and עַד (9:25; 11:7; 12:12). This, of course, raises questions about the *Vorlage* of 13:2, especially since the phrase בָּאָדָם וּבַבְּהֵמָה is elsewhere translated literally in Exodus with the preposition ἐν (8:13, 14; 9:10). The phrases that are translated literally, however, differ from

Because of the minuses in the second account of the 𝕲 and the usage of בְּ in the more narrative-like sections that do not have parallels in the other tabernacle account, there are fewer parallel passages containing the preposition בְּ than one might expect. In the following discussion, the translation of parallel passages and similar phrases will be highlighted when they contrast, but the main emphasis in this section will be on describing the semantic functions and related issues for each of the twelve remaining translation equivalents of בְּ.

Two of these translation equivalents, ἡνίκα and ὅταν, only occur as translations of בְּ with infinitive constructs. The grammatical form alone, however, is not sufficient for determining whether ἡνίκα and ὅταν should be used. This choice is either controlled by the translator's understanding of the context, an understanding that is not always available to us today, or it represents a stage in the development of the language when one conjunction was starting to be used less frequently and the other was gaining in usage.[30] Within these four sections of

---

13:2 in their semantic function. In the verses where the phrase is translated literally, the "men and cattle" are the location of the item being discussed (gnats and boils). In 13:2, however, the "men and cattle" are part of the description of the firstborn males that belong to God. In Numbers, this same phrase with the preposition בְּ is also translated "non-literally," but again rather than being a location, the phrase modifies the firstborn males who belong to God (Num 8:17; 18:15) or it modifies the plunder that functions as direct object of the clause (Num 31:11). Thus, the semantic function of the object of the preposition in relationship to the larger context is the controlling factor for the translation of the preposition and as a result, it is probable that the *Vorlage* contained בְּ.

When בְּ is used to indicate the attendant circumstances of an activity, μετά with the genitive is the preferred translation (11:8; 12:11). This semantic function is one of the few in which μετά and בְּ overlap. The preposition μετά is elsewhere used for a very wide range of semantic functions that translate a variety of Hebrew words.

The translation equivalent, παρά with the accusative, is used when one item is located in proximity to another item (12:22 [2x]; 13:20). In 13:20, παρά is actually the translation of a phrase בְּקָצֵה, and thus the object of the preposition in effect has determined the choice of lexical equivalents for the preposition. In 12:22, the choice of translation equivalents is again determined by the interpretation of the noun that is the object of the preposition. If סַף had been interpreted as a basin instead of as (a part of) the door, then it is more likely that ἐν would have been used to translate the preposition בְּ. Thus, in all cases in which בְּ is translated by παρά, the determining factor is the object of the preposition.

The translation equivalent ὡς occurs twice with infinitive constructs in the control sample (13:8, 17). In each case, the clause is a temporal clause that refers to the time frame in which the main clause occurs. English translations, like the 𝕲, generally translate both of these occurrences as "when" even though in 13:17 it is actually the translation of a phrase, בְּ יְהִי, that gives more prominence to the subordinate clause. The difference between ὡς and two other translation equivalents, ἡνίκα and ὅταν, which will be discussed below, is not known. Wevers, however, felt strongly enough about the translation technique of 𝕲 Exodus that in the critical text ὅταν rather than ὡς ἄν is used in 28:43 (28:39 in Wevers' text). (See WeversText, 267-68.) At this point, the most that can be said is that the use of ὡς may be an example of dissimilation.

30. Within the tabernacle accounts, ἡνίκα is used to indicate subordinate temporal clauses that are either contingent ("whenever") (40:36) or are viewed as happening in the past (12:27). The conjunction ὅταν is likewise used for subordinate temporal clauses that are either contingent ("whenever") (28:30, 43 [2x]; 30:7, 8, 20 [2x]; 40:32 [𝕲 38:27]) or are viewed as happening in the future

Exodus, the word ὅταν is definitely the more frequently used term. The term ἡνίκα, in contrast, is only found twice, once in the second account and once in the control sample. The most that can be said at this time is that these two represent a case of dissimilation that will only be understood when grammarians are better able to distinguish clearly between the almost overlapping meanings of these two Greek translation equivalents.

Several of the translation equivalents of בְּ could represent a difference in the *Vorlage*, but are best analyzed as contextual translations. This is especially true of the translation equivalents ἀνά and ἐπί. The preposition ἀνά is only found in a phrase, ἀνὰ μέσον, as the translation of the semipreposition בְּתוֹךְ. Similar usages of ἀνά are seen in parallel passages in the tabernacle account, which would indicate that the same basic approach was being used in the translation of prepositions in each account.[31] The translation equivalent ἐπί is also found in both accounts, but due to various difficulties in the second account, it seems likely that two of the occurrences of ἐπί were based on the first account rather than being independent decisions by the translator of the second account.[32]

(12:13). The nature of the temporal clauses, however, is controlled more by the content and context, i.e., the form of the verb and the view of the activity in the context, than by the choice of conjunctions. The difference between these two conjunctions may be due to shifting language usage in that ἡνίκα is used less frequently in the NT than in the LXX. As has been emphasized throughout this study, however, statistical differences in frequency of words may signal nothing more than a difference in the semantic functions of the information being discussed. Nevertheless, it is interesting to note that there is a steady decline in the use of ἡνίκα. In the Pentateuch, which most scholars agree was translated first, ἡνίκα occurs 53 times and ὅταν occurs 55 times. In the remainder of the 𝔊 Scriptures, ἡνίκα occurs 49 times and ὅταν occurs 147 times. In the NT, ἡνίκα only occurs 2 times and ὅταν occurs 123 times. If this change is not connected with semantics, then it indicates a clear shift in language usage.

31. Three occurrences of בְּ are found in the phrase בְּתוֹךְ and are translated by the Greek phrase ἀνὰ μέσον (26:28; 28:33=39:25 [𝔊 36:32]). The majority of the other occurrences of ἀνὰ μέσον in Exodus are translations of בֵּין, which normally occurs in a pair with another בֵּין phrase, though a single occurrence can be used when the two items are identical (25:22). While these forms are similar on the surface level, the underlying meaning is different. When ἀνὰ μέσον is a translation of בֵּין, it is used to communicate the location of one item between two other distinct items, e.g., 30:18. In contrast, a single occurrence of ἀνὰ μέσον as a translation of בְּתוֹךְ is used to communicate the location of one item among or in the middle of many items, e.g., 26:28.

The other two occurrences of the translation equivalent ἀνά are in parallel passages that are similar, but not identical in each language due to the fact that the pomegranates are referred to by a pronominal suffix (Hebrew) or a demonstrative pronoun (Greek) in 28:33, whereas in the parallel passage (39:25 [𝔊 36:32]), the pomegranates are referred to by a noun in both Hebrew and Greek.

32. As discussed in chapter three, the phrase ἑκατὸν ἐφ' ἑκατόν is probably based on a misreading of מֵאָה בָאַמָּה (or it reflects a different *Vorlage*) that was then translated to make it parallel the following phrase, חֲמִשִּׁים בַּחֲמִשִּׁים (27:18). This second phrase is not found in the 𝔐 of the second account and as a result there would have been no parallel phrase to encourage the change to ἑκατὸν ἐφ' ἑκατόν. This assumes, however, that the text of the first account would have been like the 𝔐 rather than the 𝔚, which has "corrected" the second phrase to חמשים באמה. The Hebrew preposition בְּ is probably being used in a distributive sense in this phrase, i.e., fifty to each side. The distributive usage, however, is not a common one for the Greek preposition ἐπί. Wevers offers several ways of under-

The remaining translation equivalents used for בְּ include both prepositions and the use of cases without any prepositions. The nominative, accusative, and genitive cases that appear as translation equivalents for בְּ are frequently the result of the restructuring of the text.[33] The prepositions εἰς and ἐκ are most frequently

---

standing the phrase, but reaches no firm conclusion. See WeversNotes, 440, 613. The exact meaning of the Greek translation ἑκατὸν ἐφ᾽ ἑκατόν may be disputed, but it is found in both accounts (27:18 [2x]; 38:9, 11 [𝔊 37:7, 9]) and it is likely that the translation in the second account is based on the first account. In addition to this unusual meaning, the preposition ἐπί is also used with the typical locative meaning, but in each passage the meaning of the probable Hebrew *Vorlage* has been slightly reinterpreted. As will be discussed in chapter five, in 40:38 the fire is reinterpreted as being "on" the tent rather than "in" the cloud. In 29:3, the lexical equivalent, ἐπιτίθημι, for the first verb, נָתַן, in combination with the first Hebrew preposition used with the basket, עַל, basically "set the course" for the next reference to the basket in which the bread continued to be "on" the basket in Greek, rather than "in" the basket, as in Hebrew. The shift in meaning is slight, but the difference is largely due to the choice of verbs and the choice of using a consistent reference to the relationship of the bread to the basket. Likewise, in 28:29, the use of ἐπί as a translation equivalent represents either a slight shift in meaning or a clarification of the relationship of the names to the breastpiece. The final example (26:4), however, may involve the use of a different *Vorlage* than the current 𝔐 בִּשְׂפַת. Either the text that the 𝔊 translator was using had עַל, the preposition used in the preceding clause with שְׂפַת הַיְרִיעָה, or the translator chose to increase the consistency of the translation by using the same preposition in both clauses. The verbs and the objects of the preposition are identical in the probable Hebrew *Vorlage* of both clauses in 26:4. The greater problem in 26:4 is explaining why the 𝔐 has בְּ and what difference in meaning that might indicate. As all of the above cases show, the preposition ἐπί is not a "normal" lexical equivalent for בְּ. Rather, ἐπί is used when there has been a reinterpretation of the text. With the exception of 26:4, suggesting that the *Vorlage* was עַל instead of בְּ would not resolve all the other changes in the text that are related to the translator's understanding of the text and thus would not in the end be a simpler solution.

33. The nominative case is used when a temporal phrase is shifted from being the object of a preposition to being the topic of either a verbal or nonverbal clause (12:16 [2x]). This results in a shift in focus from the meeting to the day itself as being the important item in 12:16. The last two occurrences of the nominative case (27:19, 38.18 [𝔊 37:16]) occur when complex noun phrases (a noun modified by a prepositional phrase with בְּ) are reinterpreted as coordinated nouns. It is interesting to note that similar restructuring processes are seen in these noun phrases that are in different tabernacle accounts, but are not in parallel verses.

The accusative case also is generally found in verses that have been restructured. For instance, in parallel verses (31:4=35:32) the three metals in Hebrew are referred to as the medium in which the designing is done using a preposition with each of the metals, לַעֲשׂוֹת בַּזָּהָב וּבַכֶּסֶף וּבַנְּחֹשֶׁת. In the 𝔊, however, the three metals are the direct objects that are affected by the designing, ἐργάζεσθαι (ποιεῖν in 35:32) τὸ χρυσίον καὶ τὸ ἀργύριον καὶ τὸν χαλκόν. In later translations this same phrase is translated more literally as τοῦ ποιῆσαι ἐν τῷ χρυσίῳ καὶ ἐν τῷ ἀργυρίῳ καὶ ἐν τῷ χαλκῷ (2 Chr 2:6). Thus, some instances of the translation of בְּ by ἐν are probably good indicators of differences in translation technique. In Exodus, however, both tabernacle accounts have followed the same non-literal approach. A similar type of restructuring may also result in the use of the accusative in 31:5. The restructuring in 37:5 (𝔊 38:4) has been discussed elsewhere and involves a variety of changes among which the use of an accusative instead of a preposition is a rather minor change. In 30:24, however, the phrase σίκλους τοῦ ἁγίου could be considered evidence of a different *Vorlage*. Other phrases of this nature in Hebrew include the term "shekel" with the number and then modify it with the phrase בְּשֶׁקֶל הַקֹּדֶשׁ (e.g., 30:13), in which בְּ is translated in the 𝔊 by κατά. Thus, part of the problem in 30:24

used to translate בְּ in idiomatic phrases and in phrases that contain a distinct directional component.³⁴ The preposition κατά is used with an accusative of ref-

---

is that the verse does not follow the typical Hebrew pattern and as a result the translation has likewise been adjusted. No conclusion can be reached as to the ultimate source of this difference due to lack of comparable data. The remaining usages of the accusative are strictly linguistic in nature in that the Greek temporal word used as the lexical equivalent for בַּבֹּקֶר normally is found in the accusative, (τὸ) πρωὶ (29:39; 30:7 [2x]; 36:3 [2x]).

The genitive case is frequently used as a translation equivalent for בְּ when a Greek genitive construction can effectively communicate the appropriate semantic functions, as may be seen in the following types of genitive found in the control sample and tabernacle accounts: genitive of measure—(number) πήχεων (26:2 [2x], 8 [2x], 27:9; 36:9 [𝔊 37:2] [2x]; 38:12 [𝔊 37:10]); genitive of time—(ἅπαξ) τοῦ ἐνιαυτοῦ (30:10 [2x]); partitive genitive—(πρωτότοκον ἀνθρώπου) τῶν υἱῶν σου (13:13); objective genitive—(πᾶς ὁ ἁπτόμενος) τοῦ θυσιαστηρίου (29:37); (ὁ ἁπτόμενος) αὐτῶν (30:29); genitive of apposition—(πνεῦμα θεῖον) σοφίας καὶ συνέσεως καὶ ἐπιστήμης (31:3 [3x]=35:31 [3x]); genitive of reference—πάντων (35:31); and a genitive of place (28:43). This last example is a regular genitive of place, θυσιαστήριον τοῦ ἁγίου, in Greek, but the verse in which it occurs has been restructured to put the reference to the Holy Place as a defining feature of the altar rather than as a location in the next clause, as will be discussed in chapter five. In the final usage of the genitive case, genitive participial phrases are used as the translation equivalents for בְּ when it is used with freely translated temporal noun phrases (12:29) or with an infinitive construct (40:32 [𝔊 38:27]). In the parallel of this last reference, the first account translates both occurrences of בְּ with the infinitive by means of the translation equivalent ὅταν (30:20), in contrast to the use of the genitive absolute for the first occurrence and ὅταν for the second (40:32 [𝔊 38:27]). This difference, however, may be due to the grammatical structure. In 30:20, both clauses with ὅταν precede the clauses with the independent verb νίψονται to which they are subordinated. In 𝔊 38:27 the ὅταν clause precedes the clause with ἐνίπτοντο to which it is subordinated, but the clause translated by a genitive absolute follows the clause with νίπτωνται to which it is subordinated. Thus, the position of the clause in the 𝔊 in relationship to its main clause may have influenced the choice of the genitive absolute rather than a more frequently used translation equivalent. According to Turner, temporal clauses with ὅταν "precede much more often than they follow" the main clause, a fact that sets them apart from some dependent clause types. Because of this the genitive absolute may have been used when the dependent clause followed the main clause. Due to the fluidity of Greek grammatical structures, no definitive conclusion can be reached on this translation equivalent. See Nigel Turner, *A Grammar of New Testament Greek*, vol. 3, *Syntax* (Edinburgh: T. & T. Clark, 1963), 344. The above examples illustrate that the usage of the genitive in these sections of 𝔊 Exodus falls well within the normal range of Greek usage and generally communicates the same information as the Hebrew prepositional phrase, though some of the translations present a slightly different interpretation than the Hebrew text.

34. The directional component is most clearly seen in relationship to the rings, i.e., when the poles are moved, εἰσάγω, into the rings on the ark or bronze altar the preposition בְּ is translated εἰς (25:14; 27:7). Another occurrence of εἰς as a translation of בְּ involves God's movement, εἰσπορεύομαι, into the middle, בְּתוֹךְ, of Egypt (11:4). The choice of εἰς in all the above cases is partially determined by the choice of verbal lexical equivalents that include the preposition εἰς. In the other occurrences, however, εἰς is either the normal idiomatic usage, such as speaking εἰς τὰ ὦτα (11:2), an idiom that occurs several times in the Pentateuch (e.g., Gen 23:16; Num 14:28; Deut 31:30); an indicator that the translator interpreted the phrase as a purpose (or dative of reference) (26:4; 31:5); or it may indicate a difference in *Vorlage* (40:22, 24). The usage of εἰς in 26:4 is interpreted by Wevers to be a purpose phrase, "for the joining," with the same approximate meaning as πρὸς τῇ συμβολῇ τῇ δευτέρᾳ at the end of the verse. (WeversNotes, 413-14.) Even though Wevers' interpretation clarifies a difficult passage, I believe that this fails to distinguish between the two prepositions. In any case, the

erence and an accusative of measure that identifies the extent of a location that is referred to by the object of the preposition κατά.³⁵ The final two translation equivalents of בְּ are the dative case and the preposition ἐν used in conjunction with the dative case, which are the two most frequently occurring options. Both of these are used to indicate a similar wide range of semantic functions.³⁶ Nothing

---

usage of two different prepositions combined with the choice of lexical equivalents for הֵבֵרָה indicates that the translator was interpreting the passage in a way that differed from that of modern exegetes. The occurrences of εἰς in the placement of the table and lampstand (40:22, 24), when compared with the placement of the ark (40:21) and gold altar (40:26), means that the probable *Vorlage* of each of these verses could have been אֶל (as in 40:21) rather than בְּ (which is translated literally as ἐν in 40:26). In the 𝔐, however, אֶל is the appropriate choice in 40:21 due to the frequent usage of בוֹא with אֶל, and thus cannot be viewed as a very strong piece of supporting evidence for a difference in *Vorlage* in either 40:22 or 40:24.

The preposition ἐκ is used in both accounts to translate an idiomatic phrase, קְרָאתִי בְשֵׁם (31:2) and קְרָא בְּשֵׁם יְהוָה (35:30). This usage of ἐκ could be analyzed as a dative of means. In addition, ἐκ is used to communicate other semantic functions that are normal for ἐκ, as follows: means (26:11; 30:26; 38:8 [𝔊 38:26]; 38:30 [𝔊 39:7]; 39:21 [𝔊 36:28]); separation (?) (26:5; 37:19 [𝔊 38:15] [2x]); partitive (?) (26:13 [2x], 23; 28:32). Some of these semantic functions in the 𝔊 are not identical to those in the 𝔐. For instance, בַּיִרְכָתַיִם in 26:23 is probably a location in the 𝔐, but in the Greek it is translated as a partitive relationship. The differences in interpretation are, however, generally minor unless there have been other changes in the translation.

35. The preposition κατά can be used with the accusative of measure that indicates the extent of a location, rather than referring to a location as a point (11:6; 26:5, 10). Several of these illustrate reinterpretations of the text, as have been discussed elsewhere. More frequently this translation equivalent is used for the more nebulous accusative of reference that relates two items in a more general manner (12:4; 25:40; 28:20; 30:13, 32, 37; 31:5; 38:24 [𝔊 39:1] [2x], 26 [𝔊 39:3]).

36. The dative case alone is most frequently used to signal time (12:3, 8, 18; 13:6; 31:15 [2x], 17; 35:2, 3; 40:2, 17 [2x]). In addition, it may signal means, which in some grammatical systems includes both material (35:35 [2x]; 38:23 [𝔊 37:21] [2x]) and instrument (13:13; 25:20; 26:6; 29:12, 14, 34; 31:18; 35:25; 37:9 [𝔊 38:8]; 40:12). Occasionally, it is also used for other functions such as a dative of reference (30:34) and an indirect object (31:6), though this latter may represent a slight reinterpretation of the text. Alternately it could be read as a locative. When the text has been restructured due to choices of lexical equivalents for the verb, the dative case alone may be used to signal the agent of a passive verb (29:46). Examples of the dative case alone signaling location are rare and in this set of texts only one example is found. In 26:5, Moses is instructed to make the loops τῇ αὐλαίᾳ τῇ μιᾷ. This could be interpreted as a dative of advantage, i.e., "for the one curtain," but the following phrase, which is similar, uses prepositions that more specifically refer to a location and thus the locative usage of the dative is more likely in the context. In addition, the dative case alone sometimes occurs when there has been ellipsis of the preposition in coordinated phrases, such as the ellipsis of ἐν before αὐτόχθοσιν (12:19) and σύν before τῇ πορφύρᾳ (39:3 [𝔊 36:10]). Another grammatical context in which the dative case alone may be used is the infinitive construct with בְּ. If the infinitive construct only adds details to the main clause, then a participial clause in the dative may be used as a temporal participle (13:17; 28:29; 28:35 [2x]). In contrast, the preposition ἐν plus an infinitive is used to translate בְּ plus the infinitive construct when the infinitive construct is interpreted as referring to a purpose (27:7; 29:36).

The preposition ἐν is most frequently used in these texts to translate בְּ when it is used with a locative meaning (11:5, 9; 12:1, 7, 11 [2x], 12 [2x], 13, 19 [2x], 20, 27, 29 [2x], 30, 40, 46, 49; 13:2, 7, 15, 20; 25:8, 15, 33, 34, 40; 26:30, 34; 27:8, 21; 28:17; 29:29 [?], 30, 31, 32, 45; 30:36; 31:18; 35:3, 10, 36:6;

conclusive about the difference between the two forms can be stated from the small quantity of data used in this study, but it is interesting to note that while many of the semantic functions can be signaled by either form, the locative meaning is almost always signaled with the preposition ἐν.[37]

In summary, the preposition בְּ can be translated by a wide variety of translation equivalents. The uses of many of these translation equivalents in the control sample and tabernacle accounts, however, are controlled by the choice of lexical equivalent for the verb or the noun with which they occur, such as παρά, πρός, and σύν. The three conjunctions, ἡνίκα, ὅταν, and ὡς, only occur as a translation equivalent of בְּ with the infinitive construct, but the differences among these three have not yet been determined. Other translation equivalents, ἀνά, διά, and ἐναντίον, are only used to translate semiprepositions that contain בְּ. The translation equivalent ἐπί, the nominative case, and the accusative case often occur when the meaning of the *Vorlage* has been restructured. The translation equivalents ἀπό, εἰς, ἐκ, ἕως, κατά, and μετά are used with a few examples that fall within a narrow range of semantic functions. The translation equivalents of the genitive case, the dative case, and ἐν, in contrast, occur more frequently and with a much wider range of semantic functions. As noted above, the preposition ἐν is the default translation and most frequently indicates a location.

39:10 [𝕲 36:17]; 39:23 [𝕲 36:30]; 40:9, 26). Like the dative case alone, however, the preposition ἐν can also be used for time (12:12, 16, 17, 51; 13:4, 5, 8; 31:14; 35:2; 40:2, 17) and means, which most frequently is an instrument (12:9, 10, 34; 13:3, 9, 14, 16, 21 [2x]; 25:14, 28, 29; 29:2 [2x], 4, 33, 40, 43; 30:4, 38; 37:16 [𝕲 38:12]). In addition, the preposition ἐν, like the dative case alone, may be used to indicate a dative of reference (12:12, 13; 13:9 [?]; 26:12 [?]; 30:12 [2x]; 31:3; 35:33, 34; 36:2, 8; 40:38), manner (35:26), and possibly an indirect object (36:1). Some of these latter examples could be analyzed as other functions such as a locative, if, for instance, the judgment and plague are viewed as happening "among" the stated participants rather than "with reference" to them (12:12, 13). Some of the other examples of the locative usage could also be interpreted in different ways, such as 25:8 in which ἐν ὑμῖν could indicate the agent of the passive verb and in 35:10 ἐν ὑμῖν could be interpreted as a partitive ("every wise person who is part of your group") rather than as a locative ("among you"), but the important thing to notice is that while the dative case and the preposition ἐν overlap in the semantic functions that they signal, they still show distinct tendencies, i.e., the preposition ἐν is most likely to be used in a locative sense, while the dative case used without a preposition is most likely to indicate time or means. Soisalon-Soininen notes the variety of translation equivalents that are used to translate some of the semantic functions of בְּ and concludes for at least the instrumental usages that the evidence cannot be used to identifying clear differences between translators in the Pentateuch, though Deuteronomy does appear to be more literal than some of the others. See Ilmari Soisalon-Soininen, "Die Wiedergabe des בְּ *Instrumenti* im griechischen Pentateuch," in *Studien zur Septuaginta-Syntax*, ed. Anneli Aejmelaeus and Raija Sollamo (Helsinki: Suomalainen Tiedeakatemia, 1987), 129. For a further discussion of the translations of the temporal functions of בְּ see Ilmari Soisalon-Soininen, "Die Wiedergabe einiger Hebräischer, mit der Präposition Bᵉ ausgedrückter Zeitangaben in der Septuaginta," *Annual of the Swedish Theological Institute* 11 (1978): 138-46.

37. By the NT times, "the simple dative is phasing out in Koine Greek, being replaced largely by prepositions, especially ἐν + the dative." See Wallace, *Greek Grammar Beyond the Basics*, 138.

Simple Construct Chains

In this section I will discuss the grammatical structures used in the 𝕲 to translate over five hundred examples of simple construct chains.[38] The majority (slightly over 55%) of the simple construct chains are translated by means of a genitive construction, a structure that conveys a broad range of semantic functions similar to that of construct chains in Hebrew.[39] In addition, however, simple construct chains may be translated by a variety of other structures that are found in all sections of the tabernacle accounts as well as the control sample, as may be seen in table 11. Each of these structures will be discussed below along with the semantic functions that they convey.

Construct chains are most frequently translated by genitive constructions, as noted above. The genitives in these translation equivalents are most frequently either a partitive genitive, a genitive of reference, or a genitive of relationship.[40]

---

38. For the purpose of this study, simple construct chains are defined as a construct form followed by an absolute form that may consist of a noun, noun phrase, or coordinated noun phrases. Complex construct chains, in contrast, involve the use of two or more construct forms followed by an absolute form. In addition, simple construct chains with a number or the word כֹּל have been excluded from this study. In most cases these forms are translated by simple noun phrases in the 𝕲, rather than by genitive constructions. Examples in which there are probable minuses that result in a loss of referential meaning in the 𝕲 with respect to the 𝔐 have likewise been eliminated from this study. Due to the nature of the construct chain and current forms of tagged computer files of the 𝔐, no claims are made about the completeness of this data, though an attempt was made to be exhaustive. Nevertheless, the over 500 identified examples used for this section should provide a sufficient database for initial observations about the translation of the simple construct chain in the tabernacle accounts of 𝕲 Exodus.

39. Soisalon-Soininen estimates that 90-95% of the construct chains in the Pentateuch are translated by genitives. His estimate, though, was not based on any statistical study of the text. If construct chains with numbers and with כֹּל had been included in my data, the percentage of simple construct chains translated by genitive constructions would have been slightly lower than the 55% noted above. See Ilmari Soisalon-Soininen, "Verschiedene Wiedergaben der hebräischen Status-Constructus-Verbindung im griechischen Pentateuch," in *Studien zur Septuaginta-Syntax*, ed. Anneli Aejmelaeus and Raija Sollamo (Helsinki: Suomalainen Tiedeakatemia, 1987), 6J.

40. Examples of these three semantic functions may be found in the control sample and the tabernacle accounts, as follows: partitive—τὴν θύραν τοῦ οἴκου αὐτοῦ (12:22); τὴν κεφαλὴν τοῦ κριοῦ (29:19); ἰστία τῆς αὐλῆς (38:9 [𝕲 37:7]); τὸ κλίτος τῆς σκηνῆς (40:24); reference—ὁ νόμος τοῦ πασχα (12:43); τὴν κιβωτὸν τοῦ μαρτυρίου (30:26); τὸ ἔλαιον τῆς χρίσεως τὸ ἅγιον (37:29 [𝕲 38:25]); τὴν σκηνὴν τοῦ μαρτυρίου (40:22); relationship—πρωτοτόκου τῆς αἰχμαλωτίδος (12:29); υἱοὺς Ααρων (28:1); ὁ τοῦ Αχισαμακ (38:23 [𝕲 37:21]). In this study, the genitive of reference is used in an expansive way. Specifically, it is used as the classification for μαρτυρίου, which comprises the majority of examples of this type of genitive. This usage could be analyzed as several other types of genitive. For example, it could be interpreted as a genitive of apposition, i.e., the tent, that is, the testimony (to God's presence). Other examples of genitives of reference could also be analyzed in alternate ways depending on one's understanding of the text. In a similar way, the genitive of relationship has been expanded to include all interpersonal relationships rather than including these relationships under the category of "possession," as is done in many grammars. This change has been made because of the fact that cross-linguistically interpersonal relationships are often expressed by a different range

Table 11. Translation equivalents of simple construct chains

Translation equivalents of simple construct chains	Control sample	First tabernacle account	Core of second tabernacle account	Remainder of second tabernacle account	Totals
Adjective only	4	3	0	0	7
Adjective + noun	2	1	0	0	3
Genitive construction	39	154	8	90	291
Noun only	2	2	0	3	7
Noun + adjective	8	58	7	24	97
Noun + dative noun	2	1	0	4	7
Noun + noun in apposition	11	5	0	3	19
Noun + participle	0	9	5	8	22
Noun + prepositional phrase	1	8	2	4	15
Participle + noun	1	0	0	1	2
Preposition + noun	1	9	2	1	13
Semipreposition translated by phrase	4	15	0	6	25
Read as an infinitive or participle	0	0	0	3	3
Restructured or reinterpreted	1	3	1	6	11
Totals	76	268	25	153	522

These three types of semantic functions combined account for about 65% of the genitive constructions that translate simple construct chains in this study. The remainder of the genitives indicate at least four other semantic functions.[41] Most of these are usages commonly found in the New Testament, but the genitive construction ἅγιον τοῦ ἁγίου, which is used to translate the Hebrew superlative

---

of grammatical structures than ownership, which is the main category left under the classification of "possession."

41. Other semantic functions indicated by the genitive as a part of the translation equivalent for the construct chain are as follows: attributive genitive—ὀσμὴν εὐωδίας (29:18); ἔργον ἐμπλοκίου (39:15 [𝔊 36:22]); genitive of apposition (generic-specific)—λίθους σαρδίου (25:7); τὸ θυμίαμα τῆς συνθέσεως (39:38 [𝔊 39:15]); possession—τὰς στολὰς τῶν υἱῶν αὐτοῦ (29:21; 31:10; 39:41 [𝔊 39:18]); τῶν κατόπτρων τῶν νηστευσασῶν (38:8 [𝔊 38:26]); subjective genitive—ἔργον ποικιλτοῦ (28:39; 39:29 [𝔊 36:36]); ἔργον μυρεψοῦ (37:29 [𝔊 38:25]).

קֹדֶשׁ קָדָשִׁים (29:37), is a clear example of a literal translation of a grammatical structure, i.e., a Hebraism.[42] While other Hebraic usages certainly appear in the translation of 𝔊 Exodus, the genitive construction generally appears to reflect the Koine Greek of the Ptolemaic times. According to Soisalon-Soininen, the genitive of material is less frequently used in the Pentateuch, which reflects a similar shift in usage seen in the Ptolemaic Papyri.[43] In the control sample and tabernacle accounts, the construct chain that indicates the material from which an item is made is translated most frequently by a noun (or other substantive) followed by an adjective and only infrequently by a genitive construction. In addition, this type of construct chain is occasionally translated by a noun followed by a prepositional phrase with ἐκ or by a nonverbal clause.[44]

The second most frequently used grammatical structure that functions as a translation equivalent for the construct chain is a simple noun phrase composed of a noun followed by an adjective. As with the genitive construction, this structure can also be used to communicate a variety of semantic functions, but most fall within the classification of attributes or material from which an item is constructed.[45] The semantic relationships between the parts of the construct chain in

---

42. The Hebrew superlative is used both as a title for the innermost section of the tabernacle and as a phrase that describes an attribute of an item in the tabernacle accounts of 𝔊 Exodus. When it refers to the innermost section of the tabernacle, the Hebrew form is definite, קֹדֶשׁ הַקֳּדָשִׁים, and the Greek form likewise has an article before the first term and uses a plural for the second term (τοῦ ἁγίου τῶν ἁγίων [26:33] and τῷ ἁγίῳ τῶν ἁγίων [26:34]). When it is used as a descriptive phrase in the tabernacle accounts, the form is indefinite in the Hebrew, קֹדֶשׁ קָדָשִׁים, and it also lacks an article before the first word in the Greek. The genitive in this phrase is found in either a singular form, ἅγιον τοῦ ἁγίου (29:37), or a plural form, i.e., ἅγιον τῶν ἁγίων (30:10, 36; 40:10) or ἅγια τῶν ἁγίων (30:29).

43. Soisalon-Soininen, "Verschiedene Wiedergaben der hebräischen Status-Constructus-Verbindung," 63.

44. Wallace notes that the genitive of material "is quite rare in the NT (the notion of material is somewhat more frequently stated with ἐκ + gen.)." (Wallace, Greek Grammar Beyond the Basics, 91.) Of approximately forty identified examples of construct chains that involve the material from which an item was constructed, there are only two clear examples of the genitive of material in the tabernacle accounts, כַּפֹּרֶת זָהָב טָהוֹר—ἱλαστήριον ἐπίθεμα χρυσίου καθαροῦ (25:17) and פַּחֵי הַזָּהָב—τὰ πέταλα τοῦ χρυσίου (39:3 [𝔊 36:10]). In both cases, there has been either a plus or a significant restructuring that results in appositional phrases either within the phrase (25:17) or with the following noun (𝔊 36:10). In the control sample, there are four other examples of possible genitives of material that refer to the pillar of cloud (13:21, 22) and the pillar of fire (13:21, 22), though some might analyze this as a different type of semantic function, such as a genitive of apposition. Most (approximately thirty) of the construct chains that refer to the material from which an item is constructed are translated by a noun followed by an adjective, e.g., δέρρεις τριχίνας (26:7); κίδαριν βυσσίνην (28:39); (τέσσαρας) δακτυλίους χρυσοῦς (37:3 [𝔊 38:3]); τὸ θυσιαστήριον τὸ χρυσοῦν (40:5). The remaining few examples are either translated by a noun plus a prepositional phrase with ἐκ, e.g., λυχνίαν ἐκ χρυσίου καθαροῦ (25:31) or the information has been restructured as part of a nonverbal clause, e.g., אַדְנֵי־כֶסֶף is restructured as part of the nonverbal clause αἱ βάσεις αὐτῶν τέσσαρες ἀργυραῖ (36:36 [𝔊 37:4]).

45. In the control sample and tabernacle accounts, approximately sixty examples of this gram-

Hebrew, however, are not always identical with the semantic relationships communicated in Greek due to the choice of lexical equivalents.[46] A similar translation equivalent is the use of a noun (or other substantive) followed by a participle. This translation equivalent, while referring ultimately to an event, is functionally an attributive usage similar to that of a noun followed by an adjective.[47]

Two less frequently used translation equivalents are two nouns in apposition and a noun followed by a noun in the dative. Both of these are used to express a limited set of semantic functions.[48] The choice of translation equivalents is partially due to translation technique, but in the 𝔊 Exodus it is largely controlled by the semantic relationship between the two nouns in the construct chain. This can be most clearly seen in the difference between the translation of תְּרוּמַת כֶּסֶף וּנְחֹשֶׁת by appositional nouns, ἀφαίρεμα ἀργύριον καὶ χαλκὸν, to express a generic-specific relationship and the translation of תְּרוּמַת יהוה by a noun followed by a dative noun, τὰ ἀφαιρέματα κυρίῳ, that expresses a dative of advantage, both of which are found in 35.24.[49]

---

matical construction are used to communicate an attribute, e.g., ἐγκρυφίας ἀζύμους (12:39); στολὰς ἁγίας (28:4); ἔργον δικτυωτόν (38:4 [𝔊 38:24]); ἔργον ὑφαντόν (39:3 [𝔊 36:10]). The remaining examples of this translation equivalent generally refer to the material from which an item is constructed, as noted in the examples cited above.

46. The two most obvious examples of this are the change from a generic-specific relationship, עֲצֵי שִׁטִּים, to an attributive relationship, ξύλα ἄσηπτα (25:5); and the change from a part-whole relationship, עֹרֹת תְּחָשִׁים, to the use of an attributive relationship, δέρματα ὑακίνθινα (25:5).

47. All of these examples with participles are found in the tabernacle accounts and generally occur as a part of the translation of תוֹלַעַת שָׁנִי. Participles used in this way include a variety of semantically related terms, as follows: κεκλωσμένου (26:31); διανενησμένου (28:8); νενησμένου (38:18 [𝔊 37:16]). In addition, participles are used in a variety of free translations of construct chains, e.g., פְּתִיל תְּכֵלֶת—ὑακίνθου κεκλωσμένης (28:37) and שַׁרְשְׁרֹת הָעֲבֹתֹת—τὰ κροσσωτὰ τὰ πεπλεγμένα (28:14).

48. When two nouns in apposition are used to translate a Hebrew construct chain, the second term generally defines or identifies the first term. Often this translation equivalent is used for the identifying or naming of geographic locations, such as γῆ Αἰγύπτῳ (11:5) and τῷ ὄρει τῷ Σινα (31:18). In addition, the appositional translation equivalent can be used for a generic-specific relationship, such as Θυσία τὸ πασχα (12:27), or an attributive usage, such as σάββατα ἀνάπαυσις (35:2), though this example has been restructured slightly.

49. The phrase תְּרוּמַת יהוה is consistently translated by a noun followed by κυρίῳ throughout Exodus. While the translation equivalent for this grammatical structure remains consistent throughout Exodus, the choice of lexical equivalents for תְּרוּמָה varies, which results in translations such as εἰσφορὰν κυρίῳ (30:15), ἀπαρχὰς κυρίῳ (35:5), and ἀφαίρεμα κυρίῳ (35:21), as was mentioned in chapter three. In Numbers, however, the translation uses a dative of advantage as well as a genitive of possession to translate יהוה. The difference in translation equivalents in Numbers may be related to whether the offering being discussed is in the process of being offered for God's benefit (dative of advantage) (Num 18:26, 28b), as is the case in all the examples in Exodus, or if it is viewed as a possession belonging to God (genitive) that is entrusted to others (Num 18:28a; 31:29, 41). Wevers, in contrast, says, "The translation of יהוה (תרומת) by a dative, presumably one of possession, is rhetorically unfortunate, since it is followed by another dative indicating indirect object, ..." See John William Wevers, *Notes on the Greek Text of Numbers*, Septuagint and Cognate Studies, ed. Bernard A. Taylor,

Several translation equivalents of construct chains involve prepositions. Often these involve idiomatic translations of the so-called semiprepositions, such as, בְּעֵינֵי, לִפְנֵי, and בְּיַד.[50] A similar translation equivalent, i.e., preposition plus noun, is also found as the translation of other phrases that are not generally considered to be semiprepositions.[51] In addition, phrases such as לִפְאַת נֶגֶב־תֵּימָנָה (27:9) and others are generally translated by a noun modified by a prepositional phrase used to refer to a direction, e.g., εἰς τὸ κλίτος τὸ πρὸς λίβα.[52]

Simple construct chains are also occasionally translated by either a noun or an adjective alone when the Hebrew construct chain is an idiom or when there has been an ellipsis in the Greek due to the presence of a coordinated phrase.[53] Another translation equivalent of the construct chain that occurs infrequently is

---

no. 46 (Atlanta, Ga.: Scholars Press, 1998), 308. The use of the dative versus the genitive might be considered a simple case of dissimilation, but since both translation equivalents are used in Num 18:26, the difference deserves a closer examination to determine if it is a difference that is due to a difference in the meaning, a different *Vorlage*, or the translation technique of dissimilation. As has often been found in Exodus, there are other minute differences in the 𝔊 Numbers that may indicate that the translator's interpretation of the text is the probable source of the differences in translation equivalents.

50. In construct chains, semiprepositions, such as, לִפְנֵי, בְּעֵינֵי, and בְּיַד, are often translated idiomatically, e.g., בְּעֵינֵי מִצְרַיִם—ἐναντίον τῶν Αἰγυπτίων (12:36); לִפְנֵי יְהוָה—ἔναντι κυρίου (28:12); and בְּיַד־מֹשֶׁה—διὰ Μωυσῆ (35:29), as discussed above. For a complete analysis of semiprepositions in the Pentateuch, see Sollamo, *Rendering of Hebrew Semiprepositions*.

51. For example, a preposition followed by a noun is used as the free translation of prepositional phrases that contain construct chains, e.g., בִּקְצֵה הַמִּדְבָּר—παρὰ τὴν ἔρημον (13:20); עַל אֲחֹרֵי הַמִּשְׁכָּן—ὀπίσω τῆς σκηνῆς (26:12); לְעֻמַּת מֶחְבַּרְתּוֹ—κατὰ τὴν συμβολὴν (39:20 [𝔊 36:27]). Almost all examples of this nature involve the location of an item.

52. Most of these occur in the descriptions of the tabernacle (26:18, 20) and the courtyard (27:11, 12, 13; 38:11, 12 [𝔊 37:9, 10]). In addition, a prepositional phrase used attributively as a modifier of a noun can be used to identify an object by means of its location, e.g., דֶּרֶךְ הַמִּדְבָּר—ὁδὸν τὴν εἰς τὴν ἔρημον (13:18). A prepositional phrase used in the translation of a Hebrew construct chain may also occur as a modifier on the clausal level rather than being related attributively to the noun, e.g., מְנֹרַת זָהָב טָהוֹר, which is translated by λυχνίαν ἐκ χρυσίου καθαροῦ (25:31).

53. Construct chains that are translated by a single noun or adjective include the following: חֲרִי־אַף—θυμοῦ (11:8); בֶּן־שָׁנָה—ἐνιαύσιον (12:5); בֵּית הַבּוֹר—τῷ λάκκῳ (12:29); מִקְנַת־כָּסֶף—ἀργυρώνητον (12:44); פִּי־רֹאשׁוֹ—περιστόμιον (28:32); בְּנֵי־שָׁנָה—ἐνιαυσίους (29:38); בֶּן עֶשְׂרִים שָׁנָה—εἰκοσαετοῦς (30:14); חֲרֹשֶׁת אֶבֶן—τὰ λιθουργικὰ (31:5). Some of these phrases, such as חֲרִי־אַף (11:8), could be described as a doublet in the 𝔐 and others, such as τῷ λάκκῳ (12:29), could be described as a minus in the 𝔊, but even when all the dubious examples are eliminated, some examples remain that can only be explained by the fact that in a freer translation idiomatic phrases in Hebrew are sometimes translated by single words, either nouns or adjectives, in Greek.

Construct chains are also occasionally translated by single words when there has been an ellipsis due to the occurrence of the chain in a coordinated structure, as follows: כְּלֵי זָהָב—χρυσᾶ (11:2; 12:35); תּוֹךְ הָאַרְגָּמָן—τῇ πορφύρᾳ (39:3 [𝔊 36:10]). (The ellipsis in the latter example involves the translation of the semipreposition בְּתוֹךְ.) These are technically minuses, but due to the grammatical nature of these ellipses I have chosen to include them here. Minuses in which referential meaning has been lost or which do not occur in coordinated phrases have not been listed here. For a complete description of minuses see the appropriate section in chapter five.

an adjective followed by a noun or a participle followed by a noun.⁵⁴ The remaining identified examples involve either a different reading of the consonantal text or significant restructuring and thus cannot be easily classified.⁵⁵

In summary, simple construct chains can be translated by a variety of translation equivalents. The most frequent or default translation is the genitive construction, which is used with the full range of semantic functions that is found in natural Greek. When the construct chain communicates an attributive function or the material from which an item is made, then the translation equivalent of a noun followed by an adjective may be used. Nouns in apposition, nouns followed by dative nouns, and nouns followed by participles are found in more limited contexts and express a narrower range of semantic functions. The remaining equivalents are found only in the translation of idiomatic phrases and phrases in which there have been ellipses.⁵⁶ In addition, there are a few examples with semiprepositions that have been translated by phrases and a few other examples that have been misread or purposely restructured.

---

54. The only clear examples are phrases that appear to be idiomatic in nature and/or do not occur elsewhere, i.e., μέσας νύκτας (11:4) and ἐρυθρὰν θάλασσαν (13:18). The only other example is found in 28:34, where זָהָב וְרִמּוֹן פַּעֲמֹן is translated by παρὰ ῥοίσκον χρυσοῦν κώδωνα. If the translator's interpretation followed the 𝔐 then the term χρυσοῦν should modify the bells, but if, as discussed elsewhere, the translator was following a different interpretation of the text, then the adjective χρυσοῦν actually modifies the preceding noun and would not be counted in this category.

There are only two examples of simple construct chains being translated by a participle followed by a noun, i.e., μεσούσης τῆς νυκτὸς (12:29) and ἐγγεγλυμμέναι σφραγῖδες (39:14 [𝔊 36:21]). Because of the limited number of examples, no conclusions can be drawn about the reason for this construction being used, but it is interesting to compare the translation of similar phrases. In 11:4 the phrase חֲצֹת הַלַּיְלָה is the object of a preposition in both the 𝔊, περί, and the 𝔐, כְּ. As a result of the context, a forewarning of what the Lord would do, it is translated as an adjective followed by a noun, μέσας νύκτας. This prepositional phrase thus states the approximate time for one particular event. In 12:29, the phrase חֲצִי הַלַּיְלָה is also the object of a preposition, but this preposition is part of a phrase, וַיְהִי בְּ, that "signals that a new scene or episode is subsequent to a previously mentioned scene, and that this scene is part of the mainstream of a larger episode or narrative." (van der Merwe, Naudé, and Kroeze, Biblical Hebrew Reference Grammar, 332.) As a result of this context, the genitive absolute, μεσούσης τῆς νυκτὸς, has been used with Ἐγενήθη to provide a temporal frame of reference for the next clause of the sentence. The discourse structure, therefore, appears to be the main reason for the difference in the translation of similar phrases in 11:4 and 12:29. The difference between the translation of the phrase פִּתּוּחֵי חֹתָם in 𝔊 36:13, by a genitive construction, ἐκκόλαμμα σφραγῖδος, and in 𝔊 36:21, by a nominative absolute participial phrase, ἐγγεγλυμμέναι σφραγῖδες, may be partially due to the choices of lexical equivalents. More importantly, however, the phrase in 39:6 (𝔊 36:13) follows a cognate participle in both Greek and Hebrew, whereas the phrase in 39:14 (𝔊 36:21) is in a verse with appositional phrases that describe the twelve stones. Thus, the grammatical context appears to have influenced the choice of translation equivalents for the construct chain.

55. For instance, several examples appear to involve the reading of a noun as an infinitive, e.g., וּבַחֲרֹשֶׁת עֵץ—καὶ κατεργάζεσθαι τὰ ξύλα (35:33) or a participle, e.g., מִשְׁבְּצֹת זָהָב—περισεσια-λωμένους χρυσίῳ (39:6 [𝔊 36:13]). Examples of restructuring may be due to translation technique or the use of a different Vorlage and often include pluses, e.g., עֲבֹדַת הַלְוִיִּם—τὴν λειτουργίαν εἶναι τῶν Λευιτῶν (38:21 [𝔊 37:19]), and minuses, e.g., לְחָקַּת עוֹלָם—εἰς τὸν αἰῶνα (29:9).

56. These include the adjective only, adjective followed by a noun, noun only, noun followed by a prepositional phrase, a participle followed by a noun, and a preposition followed by a noun.

Relative Clauses with אֲשֶׁר

In this section I will discuss the semantic functions of the relative pronoun and the grammatical structures used in Greek to translate the 122 relative clauses with אֲשֶׁר that are found in the control sample and tabernacle accounts. As is the case with other words, the translation equivalents used for אֲשֶׁר are affected by both the semantic and grammatical contexts. As a result, nine forms are used to translate אֲשֶׁר and an additional five forms are used to translate the phrase כַּאֲשֶׁר. Tables 12 and 13 present the forms and distribution of these translation equivalents. Following the charts, I will discuss both the grammatical structures and semantic functions of the translation equivalents of אֲשֶׁר in relative clauses. The translation of resumptive pronouns in relative clauses has often been identified as an indicator of the degree of literalness of a translation, but due to the limited number of examples of this feature in the probable *Vorlage* of the tabernacle accounts, it cannot serve as a decisive factor in this analysis.[57]

As can be seen in table 13, the occurrences of the phrase כַּאֲשֶׁר are not evenly distributed throughout the ₥. As a result, a statistical comparison of the actual number of occurrences would be irrelevant. The relative pronoun אֲשֶׁר, in contrast, is more evenly distributed (table 12), but like the phrase כַּאֲשֶׁר, more can be learned by examining the translation equivalents and semantic functions than by a purely statistical analysis. The important fact to notice is that the relative pronoun is translated by a variety of semantically and grammatically controlled translation equivalents in each of the four sections.

When אֲשֶׁר refers to an item that is described by the relative clause as being in a certain location, it is consistently translated by an article, ὁ. In all of these cases, the Hebrew and Greek relative clauses are simple prepositional phrases.[58] As is to be expected, in this attributive usage the article that is the translation equivalent of אֲשֶׁר agrees in number and case with the article of the noun that it modifies in

---

57. According to Soisalon-Soininen, the pleonastic pronoun in the entire book of Exodus is omitted sixteen times and retained twenty-eight times. As expected, Exodus is more nearly similar to Genesis than to the remainder of the Pentateuch, which tends to retain more of the pronouns. According to Soisalon-Soininen, "The ratio of omissions of the pleonastic pronoun to retentions of it is as follows: Gen 18 omissions, 22 retentions, . . . , Lev 16 : 49, Num 5 : 34 and Dtn 14 : 61." See Ilmari Soisalon-Soininen, "The Rendering of the Hebrew Relative Clause in the Greek Pentateuch," in *Studien zur Septuaginta-Syntax*, ed. Anneli Aejmelaeus and Raija Sollamo (Helsinki: Suomalainen Tiedeakatemia, 1987), 61. In a more recent article by Sollamo, slightly different statistics are presented, but the same basic conclusion is reached, i.e., that Genesis and Exodus are freer translations than the rest of the Pentateuch. Sollamo summarizes by saying about Genesis and Exodus, "It is characteristic for these good translators, too, that they are not consistent in rendering grammatical structures. In cases of the resumptive element in relative clauses they render freely 44-46% of cases, but literally 51-54% of cases." See Raija Sollamo, "The Pleonastic Use of the Pronoun in Connection with the Relative Pronoun in the Greek Pentateuch," in *VII Congress of the International Organization for Septuagint and Cognate Studies, Leuven, 1989*, ed. Claude E. Cox, Septuagint and Cognate Studies, no. 31 (Atlanta, Ga.: Scholars Press, 1991), 83-84.

58. In the following examples, the relative clauses in both Hebrew and Greek are prepositional phrases: 11:5; 12:22a, 29; 27:21; 29:13, 21, 22, 32; 31:7; 40:9.

Table 12. Translation equivalents of אֲשֶׁר in four sections of Exodus

Translation equivalents of אֲשֶׁר	Control sample	First tabernacle account	Core of second tabernacle account	Remainder of second tabernacle account	Totals
καθά	0	0	0	2	2
κατά	0	1	0	1	2
ὅς	10	18	2	11	41
ὅς ἐστιν	1	3	0	1	5
ὅθεν	0	1	0	0	1
ὅσος	3	6	0	8	17
ὅστις	1	0	0	0	1
ὁ	3	6	0	1	10
ὁ + participle	0	6	0	1	7
Genitive	0	3	1	1	5
Minuses	1	3	2	3	9
Totals	19	47	5	29	100

the main clause. There are, however, several articles that are genitive and do not agree in case with the nouns that are the antecedents of the relative clauses. Rather than indicating the location of an item, the relative clauses in which the relative pronouns are translated by articles in the genitive case communicate either a part-whole relationship or a more generic relationship.[59] The relative clauses that are

---

[59]. In 25:26, the relative clause אֲשֶׁר לְאַרְבַּע רַגְלָיו is translated by the genitive phrase τῶν ποδῶν αὐτῆς, which indicates the "whole" to which the parts, τὰ τέσσαρα μέρη, are related. In 39:19 (𝔊 36:26), the relative clause אֲשֶׁר אֶל־עֵבֶר הָאֵפֹד is likewise translated by a genitive τοῦ ὀπισθίου τῆς ἐπωμίδος and indicates that the corners that were being discussed were the ones that "belonged to" the back part of the ephod, i.e., a partitive genitive. The relationship signaled by the translation of אֲשֶׁר עַל־הַשֻּׁלְחָן (37:16 [𝔊 38:12]) as a genitive phrase τῆς τραπέζης is a bit more nebulous, but there has been a clear reinterpretation of the items as being related to the table instead of being located on the table, as will be discussed further in chapter five.

The offerings from the ram of dedication that was offered up for Aaron and his sons are referred to by the coordinated phrases, מֵאֲשֶׁר לְאַהֲרֹן וּמֵאֲשֶׁר לְבָנָיו (29:27). In the 𝔊 the preposition "from" is retained in the translation, but the relative clauses themselves are translated by genitive phrases within coordinated prepositional phrases, ἀπὸ τοῦ Ααρων καὶ ἀπὸ τῶν υἱῶν αὐτοῦ. These genitive phrases could be a substantival usage that indicates possession, i.e., from (the piece [?] of the ram) belonging to Aaron and from (the piece [?] of the ram) belonging to his sons. Alternately, this could be a reinterpretation of the Hebrew that simply indicates source, i.e., (the ram) from Aaron and his sons. These are the interpretive possibilities seen in the 𝔊, but in some English translations the לְ of the 𝔐 is read as an indicator of the beneficiary or recipient, i.e., "since it is for Aaron and for his sons" (RSV). For a fuller discussion of the interpretation and translation of this phrase see Noel D. Osborn and Howard A. Hatton, *A Handbook on Exodus* (New York: United Bible Societies, 1999), 697-99.

Table 13. Translation equivalents of כַּאֲשֶׁר in four sections of Exodus

Translation equivalents of כַּאֲשֶׁר	Control sample	First tabernacle account	Core of second tabernacle account	Remainder of second tabernacle account	Totals
καθά	2	0	0	7	9
καθάπερ	0	0	0	2	2
καθότι	1	0	0	0	1
κατά + ὁ + participle	0	1	0	0	1
ὃν τρόπον	1	0	0	7	8
Minus	0	0	0	1	1
Totals	4	1	0	17	22

translated by genitive phrases are found in all three of the main sections of the tabernacle accounts, which indicates the similarity of approach to the text throughout both tabernacle accounts.[60]

When Hebrew relative clauses with prepositional phrases occur in more complex constructions, a participle of the verb εἰμί can occur as a plus in the 𝔊.[61] These pluses clarify the grammatical structure by segmenting the clause into meaningful units. In 29:23, the plus προτεθειμένων serves the same function of clarification in the translation of the relative clause, but it also adds an interpretive layer of meaning to the translation. A few relative clauses that contain verbal clauses are also translated using an article as the translation equivalent of אֲשֶׁר and a participle as the form used for the verb of the relative clause. In all of these clauses, the relative pronoun in the Hebrew is the grammatical subject (but not always the agent) of the relative clause.[62]

---

[60]. For a detailed survey of nominal relative clauses, which have been discussed above, see Soisalon-Soininen, "Rendering of the Hebrew Relative Clause," 55–61. In this article, Soisalon-Soininen illustrates the wide variety of Hebrew forms in the Pentateuch and their translations in the 𝔊. Concerning the use of the article to translate אֲשֶׁר he says, "wherever it does occur, the reader of the Greek text gets the impression that the translator is using good Greek. The good stylistic quality of this translation is not due here to any freedom on the part of the translator. This is shown especially by the fact mentioned above that the unusually literal translator of Judges has considered this the normal translation." He concludes his discussion of nominal relative clauses by saying, "Considered statistically, none of the groups of expressions examined indicates significant differences between the various books of the Pentateuch. For example, the relative frequencies of the addition of the copula and of changing the clause into an attribute or a substantive are so similar as to have no bearing upon the quality of the translation. Single exceptions cannot generally be given any decisive significance." Ibid., 57, 59.

[61]. Participial forms of εἰμί occur as pluses in the translation of relative clauses in 25:22a and 30:6a.

[62]. In 25:40 and 26:30, a hophal is translated by a perfect passive. Thus, the subject of the participial clauses (the pattern) is actually the patient of the verb rather than the agent. In 29:46, the

The most frequent translation of אֲשֶׁר is ὅς. The majority of these relative clauses contain verbal clauses in both their Hebrew and Greek forms.[63] The relative pronouns in this group can fill a variety of semantic functions within the relative clause, but most frequently they function as the patient, location of an event, or means (instrument).[64] Only rarely does the relative pronoun ὅς function as the agent of the relative clause.[65] Besides being used to translate relative clauses with

---

article plus a participial clause is used to translate a relative clause in which the grammatical subject functions as "causer." In 36:2b the free translation of a Hebrew idiom results in two parallel participial clauses functioning as one of the coordinated objects of the main clause, πάντας τοὺς ἔχοντας τὴν σοφίαν, . . . , καὶ πάντας τοὺς ἑκουσίως βουλομένους. These objects both function as subjects of their respective participial clauses, the second of which translates a relative clause with אֲשֶׁר. The difference in meaning between this translation equivalent, i.e., the article followed by a participle, and ὅς is not known at this time.

63. The two exceptions are relative clauses that contain either an idiomatic phrase אֲשֶׁר־בְּרַגְלֶיךָ (11:8) or a negative stative clause אֲשֶׁר אֵין־שָׁם מֵת (12:30), both of which are translated by verbal clauses in the 𝔊.

64. Examples of the semantic function of the relative pronoun within the relative clause are as follows: patient (11:8; 12:25a, 39, 40; 13:5; 25:3, 16, 21; 28:3, 4; 29:1, 27 [2x - passive], 38; 35:1, 4 [?], 21a, 29a; 36:3, 4); location (12:7, 13, 30); time (13:3); recipient (36:1a, 2a); means (including instrument) (25:29; 29:33, 42; 30:6; 37:16 [𝔊 38:12]); source (35:23, 24). In 29:42, the relative pronoun is separated from its antecedent and the translator chooses to use οἷς, which "is an indefinite reference to all the foregoing matters, ..." (WeversNotes, 486.) This is also seen in 30:6, which is similar to 29:42, but contrasts with 30:36 where the relative pronoun is translated by ὅθεν and is preceded by a clear antecedent.

65. Some relative pronouns that function as subjects in relative clauses are widely separated from their antecedents. For instance, in 𝔐 29:30, the antecedent of the relative pronoun is probably הַכֹּהֵן, which is separated from the relative clause by other modifying phrases. (This is one of the few uses of "the priest" that refers to someone other than Aaron.) In the 𝔊 the relative pronoun is in apposition to or modifies ὁ ἱερεὺς in the main clause and is also the subject of the relative clause. In 38:8 (𝔊 38:26) the relative clause modifies a substantival participle in the main clause and the relative pronoun is the subject of the same verb in the relative clause, ἐκ τῶν κατόπτρων τῶν νηστευσασῶν, αἳ ἐνήστευσαν. In other cases, the relative clauses in which relative pronouns are subjects are used substantivally (30:33 [2x], 38). In addition, Wevers' text contains ὅς, which immediately follows its antecedent and is the subject of the relative clause, instead of the majority text reading ὡς in 12:27. Wevers justifies his decision by saying, ". . . but Hebrew has אשר, so that the relative pronoun must be original, and the variant arose through homophony." (WeversNotes, 182.) While Wevers is probably correct, it must be noted that this usage of ὅς is not frequently found in the small sampling of data used in this study.

In addition there are two examples of relative pronouns for which the semantic function is ambiguous and the use of ὅς instead of ὅσος is an exception to the description of the usage of ὅσος that is noted below. Both of these are in free translations of idiomatic phrases (25:2; 35:26). The fact that these are free translations with the verb δοκέω probably contributes to the use of the dative forms of the relative pronouns (οἷς and αἷς). In 25:2, the dative plural relative pronoun may be a substantival usage in apposition to υἱοῖς. This interpretation would result in parallel constructions both in the addressees and in the verbal clauses (καὶ λάβετέ . . . καὶ λήμψεσθε), rather than the heavily embedded form of the Hebrew. If this interpretation is correct then the relative clause in the 𝔊 was viewed as being in apposition to τοῖς υἱοῖς Ισραηλ, rather than referring to a subclass of willing people who were from the sons of Israel. This reinterpretation of the Hebrew would also explain why the Greek

verbs, the relative pronoun ὅς in combination with a plus, ἐστιν, is used to translate nonverbal clauses that refer to the possession or location of an item.⁶⁶ A related translation equivalent, ὅστις, only occurs one time in the control sample and refers to a more indefinite item, as would be expected.⁶⁷

Within the control sample and tabernacle accounts, the relative pronoun ὅσος is used mainly to refer to the patient (direct object of an active verb or subject of a passive verb) within the relative clause, although a few other semantic functions are also found.⁶⁸ Frequently it is found in contexts where either the 𝔐 or the 𝔊 has the equivalent of the word "all." This focus on quantity is the factor that generally distinguishes ὅσος from ὅς in the translation of relative clauses with אֲשֶׁר.⁶⁹ The relative pronoun ὅσος occurs occasionally without the equivalent of

---

does not use ὅσος, which is the normal translation equivalent for אֲשֶׁר after the word "all." Wevers, in contrast, explains the dative plural form by saying that it is "plural because of πάντων and dative because of δόξῃ." (WeversNotes, 391.) His explanation is definitely possible and in light of a similar phrase in 35:26, which has a less complex grammatical structure, Wevers' interpretation becomes more likely, but his explanation does not account for the choice of ὅς instead of ὅσος. In 35:26, the resumptive possessive pronoun has been translated, αὐτῶν, whereas this feature is a minus in 25:2. As a result, the meaning is less ambiguous in 35:26. These two verses, however, are not identical in the 𝔐, which may indicate that the *Vorlage* of the 𝔊 was also not identical. Because of this, the comparison of these verses should not be overemphasized. It should be noted, however, that both verses use the most frequent translation equivalent, ὅς, which serves as the default translation that is sometimes used when a passage is unclear to the translator.

66. The use of appropriate forms of ὅς ἐστιν for nonverbal clauses that refer to the possession of an item is due to the fact that Greek has no exact equivalent for the prepositional phrase לְאַהֲרֹן in a relative clause (29:26, 29; 39:1 [𝔊 36:8]). The use of the dative, Ααρων τῷ ἱερεῖ (𝔊 36:8), however, may indicate that the 𝔊 was interpreting Aaron to be the beneficiary, an interpretation reflected in most English translations, i.e., "for Aaron." The other two examples, however, are ambiguous in the 𝔊 due to the fact that Ααρων is indeclinable. In addition, forms of ὅς ἐστιν are used for the location of an item when the relative clause is in a more complex clause (12:22b; 28:8). The referential meaning is probably identical to the use of the article in the translation of similar relative clauses, but the choice of translation equivalents serves to clarify the grammatical structures. These two translation choices may be compared in the translation of identical relative clauses, אֲשֶׁר־בַּסַּף, by τοῦ παρὰ τὴν θύραν and ὅ ἐστιν παρὰ τὴν θύραν in 12:22. The controlling factor in the choice of translation equivalents is probably the complexity of the clause within which each relative clause is located.

67. The indefinite relative pronoun ὅστις is used only to refer to a general event, the wailing of the Egyptians, κραυγὴ μεγάλη, which is predicted in 11:6 and described as being unlike anything before or after it. Because it only occurs in the control sample, the main value of noting this translation equivalent is that it affirms the wide range of translation equivalents that are used in an attempt to communicate accurately the meaning of the text.

68. The relative pronoun ὅσος has the following semantic functions within the relative clause: patient (11:7 [?]; 12:16; 25:9, 22b; 28:38; 29:35; 31:6, 11; 35:10, 21b, 29b; 36:1b, 5; 39:42 [𝔊 39:22]; 40:16); agent (13:12; 35:22).

69. Within Exodus, the combination of a plural form of πᾶς followed by a form of ὅσος, almost always occurs as the translation of כֹּל אֲשֶׁר in the probable Hebrew *Vorlage* (7:2; 18:1, 8, 14, 19:8; 23:13, 22; 24:7; 25:9, 22; 29:35; 31:6, 11; 34:32; 35:10, 22 [𝔐 only]; 36:1; 40:16). The only exception is 34:11 where an unusual phrase, אֵת אֲשֶׁר אָנֹכִי מְצַוְּךָ, was translated as if it were similar to more standard phrases (or its *Vorlage* possibly contained a more standard phrase), such as

the word "all," but in most of these cases the relative clause is being used substantivally, i.e., with no antecedent. This type of substantive usage often contains a thin layer of interpretive meaning that the translator has added to his text.[70]

In two verses, the relative clauses have been reinterpreted and translated as simple prepositional phrases with κατά rather than as dependent clauses. In both cases the relative clause in Hebrew consists of a prepositional phrase that gives further details about the location of the item.[71] This translation choice is found in each tabernacle account, but not in parallel verses. Along with these verses in which the relative clauses are restructured, there are a number of verses in which the relative clause is a minus due to the abbreviated nature of the 𝔊.[72]

The final two translation equivalents for אֲשֶׁר are more adverbial in nature. In 30:36, the translation equivalent is the adverb, ὅθεν, which is used to refer to the location where God will reveal himself.[73] In addition, the translation equiva-

---

אֵת כָּל־אֲשֶׁר צִוִּיתִךָ in 31:6. The word πᾶς is also used with the relative pronoun ὅς, but this combination is not generally used as the translation of a relative clause with אֲשֶׁר. Instead, it is used mainly in the singular (five of seven times) and mostly as a translation of "all" plus a participle (12:15, 19; 31:14, 15) or adjective (35:22). In addition, this type of structure with a plural form of πᾶς occurs once as a plus in the 𝔊 (10:23) and once in an ambiguous structure (25:2) that was discussed above.

70. For instance, in 11:7 the relative clause is used substantivally as the direct object of the verb εἰδῇς. The choice of ὅσος in this verse emphasizes the quantity of ways in which God differentiated between the Egyptians and the Israelites. Likewise, in 12:16 the exception to the "no-work" command is stated in terms of quantity and uses the relative pronoun ὅσος in a substantival relative clause. In 13:12, the relative pronoun may, like the Hebrew relative pronoun, refer back to the equivalent of the word "all," but in light of the reinterpretation of the complex noun phrase in the 𝔊, it is likely that the relative pronoun refers to the herds of animals, rather than the firstborn animals. Thus, the use of ὅσος is focusing on the quantity of animals that will later belong to the Israelites. In 28:38, the focus is on the quantity of holy offerings that will be offered by the Israelites. If the relative pronoun ὅς had been used, then the translation would have been a simple statement of fact, but the use of ὅσος emphasizes the indefinite number of those sin-offerings. Likewise, when the people brought an overabundance of gifts for the construction of the tabernacle, the word ὅσος is used despite the fact that there is no equivalent of the word "all" in the probable Hebrew Vorlage (36:5). In 39:42 (𝔊 39:22), the word כֹּל is present in the probable Hebrew Vorlage, but is not translated in the Greek. Instead, ὅσος is used substantivally and emphasizes the quantity of the things that were commanded by God.

71. In 26:5 the Hebrew text, אֲשֶׁר בַּמַּחְבֶּרֶת הַשֵּׁנִית, further defines the curtain as being one that is in the second set of curtains. The 𝔊, however, interprets the noun differently and as a result has the translation, κατὰ τὴν συμβολὴν τῆς δευτέρας. This translation identifies the position of the part of the curtain, which is at or along the joint, instead of further defining the curtain as in the 𝔐, i.e., the curtain in the second set. In 39:5 (𝔊 36:12), the relative clause אֲשֶׁר עָלָיו is translated καθ' ἑαυτό. This choice is probably affected by the explanatory plus, εἰς ἄλληλα συμπεπλεγμένον, that occurs just before this phrase. This plus gives details about the means by which the decorative band is connected to the ephod.

72. The following occurrences of אֲשֶׁר are either minuses or part of a synonymous variant in the 𝔊: 12:32; 28:26; 30:6b, 37; 35:16; 36:12; 37:13 (𝔊 38:10); 38:30 (𝔊 39:7); 39:39. These minuses will be discussed with other minuses in chapter five.

73. As noted above, this is parallel to the translations in 29:42 and 30:6, but the translation equivalent in this verse is unique. In 30:36 ὅθεν is used instead of ἐν οἷς. This choice may clarify that it

lent καθά is used in two verses that are similar in content to the relative clauses that occur with כַּאֲשֶׁר.[74] Both of these relative clauses have been interpreted by the translator(s) as modifiers of the entire clause, rather than as modifying one element in the clause. In this way, they are functionally equivalent to relative clauses that begin with the phrase כַּאֲשֶׁר. In addition, the reordering of the text may have affected the choice of translation equivalents in 38:22 (𝔊 37:20).[75]

Relative clauses with כַּאֲשֶׁר are generally interpreted as adverbial modifiers of the main clause, though this is not always the case as can be seen in 27:8.[76] Most of these relative clauses are translated as comparatives, but the type or emphasis on the comparison is not always uniform, as can be seen by the variety of translation equivalents used for relative clauses with כַּאֲשֶׁר. In 12:25b, the 𝔊 uses καθότι, which is used with a causal component elsewhere in Exodus and is often used with subjunctive clauses.[77] Another infrequently used translation choice for כַּאֲשֶׁר

---

is the general location that is the focal point for the self-revelation of God and not "all the foregoing matters," as noted above.

74. In 38:21 (𝔊 37:19), the idiomatic Hebrew relative clause, אֲשֶׁר פֻּקַּד עַל־פִּי מֹשֶׁה, is translated into more natural Greek, καθὰ συνετάγη Μωυσῇ. In 38:22 (𝔊 37:20), the Greek translation of the relative clause אֵת כָּל־אֲשֶׁר־צִוָּה יְהוָה אֶת־מֹשֶׁה is identical with other phrases used throughout the second account, καθὰ συνέταξεν κύριος τῷ Μωυσῇ, e.g., 39:5, 7 (𝔊 36:12, 14). This raises the possibility that the translator's *Vorlage* was more like that of the similar phrases or that the translator was increasing the consistency of the translation by using the same phrase as in other passages.

75. In 38:22 (𝔊 37:20), the use of καθά reflects a slight shift in meaning from the Hebrew text. In the 𝔐, the focus is on the fact that Bezalel completed all the tasks that God commanded Moses to do, עָשָׂה אֵת כָּל־אֲשֶׁר־צִוָּה יְהוָה אֶת־מֹשֶׁה. In the 𝔊, in contrast, the focus is on the manner, i.e., Bezalel did just as the Lord commanded Moses, ἐποίησεν καθὰ συνέταξεν κύριος τῷ Μωυσῇ. This shift results in a more appropriate beginning for the list of items that Bezalel constructs in 𝔊 38 in that the introductory summary statement does not emphasize the completion of everything. This shift may also indicate that the larger reordering of the material in the second tabernacle account had already taken place. While the Hebrew phrase is appropriate for its location **after** the making of the furniture for the tabernacle, the Greek phrase is more appropriate for its location **before** the making of the furniture. Thus, if the *Vorlage* was similar to the 𝔐, the choice of this translation equivalent was affected not only by its function in the clause, but also by its position in the entire text. Alternately, this translation equivalent could, of course, be the reflection of a different *Vorlage*.

76. In 27:8, the 𝔊 has interpreted the relative clause with כַּאֲשֶׁר as if it were a preposition followed by a relative clause used substantivally, κατὰ τὸ παραδειχθέν σοι ἐν τῷ ὄρει. This relative clause is similar to the relative clauses in 25:40 and 26:30 in both form and content. The major difference is that there is no antecedent for the relative clause in either Greek or Hebrew and so the participial clause is used substantivally. The choice of lexical equivalents is also unique, i.e., παραδείκνυμι instead of δείκνυμι, which is used in the two similar phrases. Thus, the choice of translation equivalents for this occurrence of כַּאֲשֶׁר was probably influenced by the desire to make it more like the similar passages in the preceding chapters (or it may have had a different *Vorlage*), but the resulting translation was still not identical with that of preceding phrases.

77. According to the standard lexicons, καθότι can be used both causally as well as comparatively. The causal interpretation of the text is probably one factor in the choice of translation equivalents in some verses (e.g., 1:12). Even in the comparative usages, however, the focus may be more on the causative force or reason in the relative clause rather than on a comparison of the manner. This

clauses is καθάπερ, which according to Louw and Nida is a more emphatic form than καθά.⁷⁸ In the tabernacle accounts, καθάπερ is only used in conjunction with two cultic activities, the ritual washing of the priests and the burning of incense for the first time.⁷⁹

The remaining occurrences of כַּאֲשֶׁר are translated by either καθά or ὃν τρόπον, translation equivalents that seem to largely overlap in meaning within the

---

can possibly be seen in 34:4 in which one wonders if Moses went back up the mountain with the new set of stone tables as (comparatively) or because (causally) God commanded him to go. In any case, whether being used comparatively or causally, καθότι is often used when there is a negative element in the context or when it is a hypothetical situation (1:17; 10:10; 21:22). The use of the subjunctive in 12:25, therefore, may have been a factor that contributed to the choice of καθότι. While καθότι does not occur in the tabernacle accounts, it illustrates one more choice that the translator had in his repertoire as a translation equivalent for כַּאֲשֶׁר.

78. The word καθάπερ is one of the "emphatic markers of comparison between events and states," and is said to be more emphatic than καθά in Johannes P. Louw and Eugene A. Nida, eds., *Greek-English Lexicon of the New Testament: Based on Semantic Domains*, 2d ed. (New York: United Bible Societies, 1989), s.v. 64.15.

79. These two occurrences in the Hebrew text are found at the conclusion of the book when worship is instituted for the first time. This might have contributed to the choice of a more emphatic form, but due to the reordering of the text, these two occurrences are widely separated in the 𝔊 (40:27 and 40:32 [𝔊 38:27]). In addition, the other event that might have been expected to use the same emphatic form, the offering up of the first burnt offering (40:29), is a minus in the 𝔊. Thus, the order of these two cultic activities in the Hebrew *Vorlage* of the 𝔊 (if it was like the 𝔐) might have encouraged an emphatic reading, which the translation may reflect, but despite this emphasis the translator or his *Vorlage* did not feel bound to maintain that same order due to other exegetical considerations.

In the remainder of Exodus, καθάπερ is mainly used in situations where an emphatic comparison would not be inappropriate, and often it occurs throughout a passage, though not without an occasional occurrence of a less emphatic form. For instance, the similarity of the quantity of brick in comparison to previous days is emphasized (5:7, 13, 14) and throughout the first part of the account of the ten miracles it is repeatedly emphasized that things are occurring just as predicted or commanded (7:6, 10, 13, 20, 22; 8:9, 11, 15, 23, 27; 9:35). (The occurrence of καθά in 9:12 is unusual. It is also the first occurrence of this form in Exodus, but due to other minute changes in the larger text, the reason for this choice could probably only be understood through a complete analysis of the text, which is beyond the scope of this book.) The emphatic nature of the comparisons in this first part of Exodus, however, eventually disappears and by the time the translator reaches the instructions for the Passover he is simply stating that things are done in accordance with the commands, καθά (12:28, 31, 35, 50). The five remaining occurrences of the emphatic form, καθάπερ, are found in connection with the manna being kept overnight as commanded (16:24); Joshua conquering the Amalekites because he did as commanded (17:10); God's first person command about the feast of unleavened bread (23:15; 34:18 [כַּאֲשֶׁר in the 𝔐]); and the fact that the second set of stone tablets were identical to the first set (34:4). In retrospect it is easy to see that these were important events, but it must be acknowledged that the difference between καθάπερ and καθά is not overwhelming. In addition, while καθάπερ is generally used as a translation of כַּאֲשֶׁר, a few of the examples are emphatic translations of כְּ. This translation of כְּ occurs when the object of this preposition is interpreted as referring either to an activity that is inferred from the context (5:7, 14; 34:4) or the nominal form was read as an infinitive construct (8:9, 27). Likewise, while καθά is generally a translation of כַּאֲשֶׁר, it also can be used as a translation of כְּ, when the object of the preposition is interpreted as referring to an event (or possibly when the unpointed text was read as an infinitive construct rather than as a noun, as in 12:31, 35; 32:28), or as a translation of אֲשֶׁר (38:21, 22 [𝔊 37:19, 20]), as discussed above.

tabernacle accounts. Within Exodus, however, καθά is always used with speech forms, i.e., in conformity with a command, whereas ὃν τρόπον, in addition to being used with speech, is also used in comparisons of other types of events.[80] Modern studies of the tabernacle accounts often emphasize the two seven-fold repetitions of the phrase כַּאֲשֶׁר צִוָּה יְהוָה אֶת־מֹשֶׁה or a similar phrase, which are found in 39 and 40.[81] This "important" seven-fold pattern, however, was either not noticed, purposely obliterated by the translation technique of dissimilation, or else the translator translated contextually focusing on a different type of meaning than what is identified by modern scholars.[82] In any case, the result is that in the 𝔊 neither chapter has a seven-fold repetition.[83]

---

80. In Exodus, καθά is used to translate a variety of Hebrew forms, as noted above, but in all instances it is used to emphasize the compliance of the participants to verbal instructions by stating that an activity was done according to the verbal instructions or commands that are given for that activity (9:12; 12:28, 35, 50; 32:28; 38:21, 22 [𝔊 37:19, 20]; 39:1, 5, 7, 21, 26 [𝔊 36:8, 12, 14, 28, 33], 32 [כאשר in 𝔐] [𝔊 39:10]; 40:19). The phrase ὃν τρόπον can also be used for this type of affirmation that the activity was done according to a previous verbal statement (13:11; 16:34; 39:29, 31 [𝔊 36:36, 38]; 39:43 [𝔊 39:23]; 40:21, 23, 25). In addition, however, ὃν τρόπον can be used to compare two events, such as the similarity in the manner of killing (2:14) and the similarity in the manner of anointing (40:15). The use of ὃν τρόπον in the translation of a complex construction, כִּי אֲשֶׁר רְאִיתֶם אֶת־מִצְרַיִם הַיּוֹם, in 14:13 may indicate that the translator was focusing on the manner in which the Egyptians were seen by the Israelites, i.e., as a conquering armed force that was rapidly approaching (14:10). Modern translations, in contrast, interpret this use of אֲשֶׁר as a substantival relative clause and translate it as a reference to the specific Egyptians seen that day (NIV, NRSV). Interestingly enough, Gesenius identified this as one of the few occurrences where אֲשֶׁר "occurs in the same sense" as כַּאֲשֶׁר. See E. Kautzsch, ed., *Gesenius' Hebrew Grammar*, Second English ed. (Oxford: Clarendon Press, 1910), § 161b. If his understanding of the grammar is correct, then the 𝔊 translation of this verse as a comparison is affirmed and should at least be considered by modern translations. In any case, for the 𝔊 translator the focus was not on the fact that those particular Egyptians would never be seen again, but that the Israelites would never again be in a situation where they would be on the verge of being totally destroyed by a well armed Egyptian army. This translation may, however, simply be a reflection of a *Vorlage* that was similar to that of the 𝔐, כאשר. See Cornelis Houtman, *Exodus*, vol. 2, *Chapters 7:14-19:25*, Historical Commentary on the Old Testament, trans. Sierd Woudstra (Kampen, Netherlands: Kok Publishing House, 1996), 265, who refers to Philo and others who seem to have shared this understanding of the text. These last three examples may affirm that even though ὃν τρόπον and καθά can be used interchangeable in the tabernacle accounts, the focus of ὃν τρόπον is more on the manner in which the activity is done versus the more generic comparison that is signaled by καθά. From a Western perspective, however, there seems to be little difference between these forms in the tabernacle accounts.

81. The following occurrences are generally counted in the two seven-fold repetitions of the clause: 39:1, 5, 7, 21, 26, 29, 31; 40:19, 21, 23, 25, 27, 29, 32. See John I. Durham, *Exodus*, vol. 3, Word Biblical Commentary (Waco, Tex.: Word Books, 1987), 494, 500, though there appears to be a typographic error on p. 494. See also A. H. McNeile, *The Book of Exodus* (London: Methuen and Company, 1908), 155-56, who further expands upon the seven-fold arrangements in the tabernacle accounts. In addition, the same clause is found in the summary statement in 39:43.

82. One might argue that the translator was using a different *Vorlage*, an argument that might be more effective for chapter 40 than for chapter 39, where the only difference in most cases is the choice of ὃν τρόπον versus καθά.

83. In the first seven-fold set, the 𝔊 uses καθά for the first five occurrences (𝔊 36:8, 12, 14, 28,

In summary, relative clauses with אֲשֶׁר and כַּאֲשֶׁר are translated by a slightly smaller variety of translation equivalents than seen in the two previous sections. The default translation of אֲשֶׁר is ὅς, which also can occur with a plus, ὅς ἐστιν, in the translation of nonverbal clauses. The more frequently used form with nonverbal clauses that indicate location is ὁ, which can also occur with the plus of a participle that interprets or clarifies more complex grammatical structures. When the relative pronoun refers to a quantity of items, especially when it occurs with כֹּל, the translation equivalent ὅσος is used. In addition, five other translation equivalents are used for a limited number of semantic functions or interpretations.[84] The default translation of כַּאֲשֶׁר cannot be established on the basis of the tabernacle accounts because it is translated by both καθά and ὃν τρόπον in almost equal amounts. Further study is needed to better understand the difference between these translation equivalents in 𝔊 Exodus. The three remaining translation equivalents are used in limited contexts where they add slight layers of interpretation to the text.[85]

---

33) and ὃν τρόπον for the last two occurrences (𝔊 36:36, 38) and also for the summary (𝔊 39:23), which is, however, located in a different chapter in the 𝔊. In the second set, in contrast, one phrase is a minus in the 𝔊 (40:29); καθά is used for the first occurrence (40:19); ὃν τρόπον is use for the next three occurrences (40:21, 23, 25); and the final two occurrences are translated by καθάπερ (40:27, 32 [𝔊 38:27]).

If the manner or some other focus was the reason for the translator's use of ὃν τρόπον in some places, then the translator was possibly interpreting the dependent clause on a sentence level rather than on a discourse level. If this is the case, the activity for which the manner was being emphasized would be the activity in the immediately preceding clause. If so, the translator was distinguishing the manner in which the following activities were accomplished: the manner in which the sashes were embroidered, the manner of attaching the rosette to the miter, the manner of shielding the ark with the curtain, the manner of placing the bread on the table, and the manner in which the lamps were placed before (facing?) the Lord. In contrast, generic comparisons that simply stated that it was done according to the instructions of the Lord were used for the following activities: the making of the robes for the priest, the workmanship of the band of the ephod, the placement of the stones on the shoulders, the use of the blue cord to keep the breastpiece from swinging away from the ephod, the intermingling of the bells and pomegranates on the hem of the robe, and the stretching out of the outer layers of the tent. These two lists do not appear to be distinctly different in the eyes of the modern reader. The use of these two translation equivalents does, however, raise the important question about whether the translator was reading this phrase, כַּאֲשֶׁר צִוָּה יְהוָה אֶת־מֹשֶׁה, as a discourse level phenomenon (i.e., a phrase used to segment the text in 39 and 40) or whether the translator was simply reading it as a part of the sentence to which it was grammatically connected. This type of variation in translation equivalents could be an important indicator of the level on which the translator was reading his text. Alternately, the variation between καθά and ὃν τρόπον could simply indicate that modern exegetes attach a higher degree of importance to the seven-fold repetition of this phrase than did the translator of 𝔊 Exodus.

84. These include the following translation equivalents: καθά, κατά, ὅθεν, ὅστις, and the genitive case.

85. These three equivalents are καθάπερ, καθότι, and κατά followed by an article and a participle, which involves a reinterpretation of the text.

Summary

In this section I have examined translation equivalents for three grammatical structures—the preposition בְּ, simple construct chains, and relative clauses with אֲשֶׁר. By means of this detailed study, it has been shown that each construction was translated by a multitude of translation equivalents that were chosen according to the semantic and grammatical context in which the structure was found. The preposition בְּ was translated by twenty-one distinct translation equivalents in addition to idiomatic translations of phrases. Of these, eleven were found to occur in both tabernacle accounts. Of the remaining translation equivalents, the control sample was found to contain the largest quantity (six) of translation equivalents that were unique to one section. This is due to the fact that the control sample was also the section in which בְּ was used with the highest relative frequency and with the largest diversity of semantic functions. Thus, the variety in the choice of translation equivalents for בְּ was largely controlled by semantic and grammatical factors in the text, rather than by any difference in translators.

The simple construct chain was likewise translated by a diversity of translation equivalents in addition to examples that were restructured or reinterpreted in the translation. Of the twelve translation equivalents used for construct chains, nine were found in both tabernacle accounts. The remaining three occurred in limited contexts that were found in one of the tabernacle accounts in addition to the control sample. As with the translation equivalents for בְּ, the control sample contained at least one example of almost every translation equivalent despite its relatively small size. This diversity again points to the fact that the variety of semantic and grammatical contexts was the controlling factor in the choice of translation equivalents in the control sample.

The final grammatical structure analyzed, the relative clause with אֲשֶׁר, was translated by fifteen different translation equivalents. Of these, seven occur in both tabernacle accounts. Unlike the two previous grammatical constructions, the control sample did not contain the widest diversity of translation equivalents for the relative clause. This is probably due to the fact that relative clauses tend to be used more in descriptive and procedural material and thus the greatest diversity of contexts occurred in the second tabernacle account, which used eleven different translation equivalents. The difference in distribution is also due to the fact that the relative pronoun occurs much less frequently (122 times) than the preposition בְּ (296 times) or the simple construct chain (over 500 times). This more limited number of examples resulted in a more limited distribution of the translation equivalents. Again, as with the other two grammatical structures, the semantic and grammatical (including discourse-level) contexts were shown to have had an effect on the choice of translation equivalents for the relative clause.

All four sections of Exodus show a similar approach to the translation of grammatical structures. Because of this similar approach to the translation of grammatical structures, the only evidences that may point to a difference in translators are the differences in the interpretations of parallel verses and similar phrases. In the next section, a few of these differences in interpretation will be noted.

IV. Other Observations Gained from Studying the Translation of Grammatical Structures

In a translation that is not woodenly literal, the choice of translation equivalents for grammatical structures, whether consciously or unconsciously made, indicates the translator's interpretation of ambiguous structures. Because of this, differences in the translation equivalents for these structures, in combination with choice of lexical equivalents, may indicate the presence of two interpretations. This choice will not, however, indicate whether the two interpretations derive from one or two translators. At the same time, however, some of these differences in translation equivalents are determined by the grammatical contexts rather than by a difference in interpretation. Distinguishing between differences in translation equivalents caused by differences in interpretation and those caused by differences in grammatical context, both of which will be illustrated below, is one of the major difficulties in any study of the 𝔊.

Clarifying or Reinterpreting Ambiguous Structures

The 𝔊 translation tends to clarify ambiguous grammatical structures such as construct chains, but differences in the manner of clarification may be seen between the two tabernacle accounts. The second tabernacle account's translation of מְעִיל הָאֵפֹד clarifies the relationship between the two items, as can be seen in the translation τὸν ὑποδύτην ὑπὸ τὴν ἐπωμίδα (39:22 [𝔊 36:29]). If the reader had not seen the garments of the high priest or did not know what each term referred to, the construct chain מְעִיל הָאֵפֹד might be interpreted incorrectly as a part-whole construction similar to כְּתֹפֹת הָאֵפֹד (39:7 [𝔊 36:14]). In the first account, in contrast, the identical phrase in the 𝔐 is translated by ὑποδύτην ποδήρη (28:31), a translation that identifies the robe by an attribute rather than by its relationship to the ephod, as in the Hebrew text. The 𝔊 translation of this same phrase in 29:5 probably is a reflection of a unique *Vorlage* that is identical to neither the 𝔐 nor the 𝔚.[86] In any case, the 𝔊 continues to refer to a floor-length garment that is

---

86. In the 𝔐 the phrase וְאֶת־הָאֵפֹד וְאֶת הָאֵפֹד וְאֵת מְעִיל is part of a list of four items with which Moses is told to clothe Aaron. In the 𝔚, in contrast, the list is subdivided by means of additional verbs that are pluses with respect to the 𝔐. As a result, את המעיל is the only direct object in a clause and את האפוד ואת החשן are the direct objects in the next clause.

Grammatical Consistency 143

separate from the ephod, τὸν χιτῶνα τὸν ποδήρη καὶ τὴν ἐπωμίδα. Thus, the phrase מְעִיל הָאֵפֹד is distinctly interpreted in each tabernacle account, but the second account's translation is a more accurate representation of the probable Hebrew *Vorlage* in that both the robe and the ephod are retained and the relationship between the two is clarified.

Some ambiguous construct chains are clarified in an identical manner in both tabernacle accounts. This may be due to the fact that unlike the above "clarification" in the first account, which may not have accurately interpreted the chain, the first account's clarification of אַבְנֵי מִלֻּאִים by λίθους εἰς τὴν γλυφὴν was acceptable enough to be maintained in verses that were otherwise identical (25:7=35:9). In a later, nonparallel verse (35:27), however, a different lexical equivalent, πληρώσεως, was used for מִלֻּאִים, as well as a genitive construction rather than a noun followed by a prepositional phrase. This clarification avoids the combination of two similar prepositional phrases in a row, εἰς τὴν γλυφὴν εἰς τὴν ἐπωμίδα, which is a less frequently used Greek construction.[87] The use of a genitive construction also reflects a change in the interpretation of the construct chain. Rather than being stones that were identified by their location in the settings, the stones were identified with reference to the activity of filling (placing?) them into the ephod and the breastpiece.[88] Thus, while the second account shares the translation found in a verse that is identical to a verse in the first account, the translator of the second account felt free to reinterpret the phrase or use a more neutral translation in a slightly different context.

These two examples of clarification of ambiguous structures illustrate an approach similar to that seen in the choice of lexical equivalents discussed in chapter three. In parallel verses where the first account was fairly accurate, the second account used the same translation equivalent. When, however, the first account was inaccurate, the second account chose a more accurate translation equivalent. If a phrase from the first account was used in a new context in the second account, the translator of the second account felt free to use a translation equivalent that was more appropriate for the context. Thus, a few of the translation equivalents of grammatical structures can be used to support the hypothesis

---

87. A quick computer search produced only five examples in the NT and ten in the 𝔊 that had this exact grammatical form, although a more complex search would certainly produce a few more examples of a similar nature.

88. Alternately, this could be a reference to the dedication, but this is the only occurrence of πλήρωσις in Exodus and so I can only speculate about the exact meaning. On the surface level, this translation appears to be an etymologically based interpretation, a technique that may indicate that the translator did not fully understand the meaning and thus used the default translation of the grammatical structure, a genitive construction, and an etymologically based lexical equivalent. See Emanuel Tov, "Did the Septuagint Translators Always Understand Their Hebrew Text?," in *De Septuaginta: Studies in Honour of John William Wevers on His Sixty-fifth Birthday*, ed. Albert Pietersma and Claude E. Cox (Mississauga, Ontario, Canada: Benden Publications, 1984), 67-68, for a discussion of etymological translation as a technique used when translators did not understand the text.

that a second translator likely produced the second tabernacle account of the 𝕲 Exodus using the translation of the first tabernacle account as a point of reference.[89]

Grammatically Influenced Choices

Most translation equivalents are primarily affected by the semantic context. In light of these semantic contexts, the translator chooses translation equivalents that clarify or reinterpret the meaning of ambiguous phrases. A few choices of translation equivalents for grammatical structures, however, are more strongly affected by the grammatical context than by the semantic context. These grammatical contexts influence the choice between similar translation equivalents that in other contexts clearly distinguish differences in meaning. Thus, the difference in meaning between two translation equivalents is effectively neutralized in some grammatical contexts. As a result, two different translation equivalents will sometimes communicate the same basic meaning.

The translation of קֹדֶשׁ in the *nomen rectum* of a construct chain provides a good illustration of the neutralization of differences in meaning between two otherwise contrastive translation equivalents. The noun קֹדֶשׁ, when it is used independently in the tabernacle accounts, refers to a part of the tabernacle, i.e., the Holy Place.[90] When the singular form of this noun is used in the *nomen rectum* of a construct chain, however, it can be translated by one of two translation equivalents, i.e., an adjective that agrees with the preceding noun or a genitive form used substantivally that modifies the preceding noun. The adjective is used to convey an attribute of an item, i.e., a holy item, but the genitive form refers to the fact that the substantive in the *nomen regens* is in some type of relationship to the part of the tabernacle that is called the Holy Place. Most items that are in a construct chain with קֹדֶשׁ are consistently translated by means of one or the other of the translation equivalents so that the item is either considered holy or is related to

---

89. Another example of contrasting choice of translation equivalents for a prepositional phrase is the translation of לְמַטֵּה יְהוּדָה by τῆς φυλῆς Ιουδα in the first account (31:2) and by ἐκ φυλῆς Ιουδα in the second account (35:30; 38:22 [𝕲 37:20]). Contrasting translations are also seen for the phrase קֹדֶשׁ לַיהוָה, which is translated Ἁγίασμα κυρίου in the first account (28:36) and Ἁγίασμα κυρίῳ in the parallel verse of the second account (39:30 [𝕲 36:37]). In a different context in the first account the same phrase is also translated ἁγία τῷ κυρίῳ (31:15), when it is used as a description of the Sabbath rather than as the inscription on the rosette. Other differences in the translation of grammatical structures are noted in appendix B.

90. When the independent noun קֹדֶשׁ refers to the Holy Place, it is almost always an articulated singular noun in both Greek and Hebrew (26:33; 28:29, 35, 43), though the 𝕲 has been slightly restructured in 28:43, as discussed elsewhere. In 29:30, however, the plural, τοῖς ἁγίοις, is used. Wevers sees this as a reference to both the Holy Place and Holy of Holies due to the translator's understanding of this verse as referring to the high priest, who goes into both parts of the tabernacle. See WeversNotes, 480.

the Holy Place.⁹¹ Unfortunately, some of these items are only referred to in one section of the text and this limited context may have contributed to the uniform choice of translation equivalents. The translations of שֶׁקֶל הַקֹּדֶשׁ and בִּגְדֵי־קֹדֶשׁ, however, illustrate the use of both translation equivalents to refer seemingly to the same items. For these two phrases the conditioning factor for the choice of translation equivalents is either the translation technique or the grammatical context.⁹² Thus, because of grammatical context and/or translation technique, the

---

91. For instance, when קֹדֶשׁ is used with a noun that refers to work, the genitive form is always used. This probably indicates that the work itself was not viewed as holy. Instead, קֹדֶשׁ was interpreted as referring to the Holy Place and the work was work done with reference to the Holy Place, as can be seen in the following examples: מְלֶאכֶת עֲבֹדַת הַקֹּדֶשׁ—τὰ ἔργα τοῦ ἁγίου (36:3); מְלֶאכֶת הַקֹּדֶשׁ—τὰ ἔργα τοῦ ἁγίου (36:4). As with the use of the plural to refer to the Holy Place and the Holy of Holies, as noted above, a similar choice of the plural may be seen in 38:24 (𝔊 39:1) where the work is referring to the gold that was used not only in the Holy Place, but also in the Holy of Holies, if the use of the plural is indeed purposeful in the 𝔊. The translation and restructuring of מְלֶאכֶת עֲבֹדַת הַקֹּדֶשׁ in 36:1 by τὰ ἔργα κατὰ τὰ ἅγια καθήκοντα may be due to literary restructuring involving the use of lexical equivalents that link this section with the first part of Exodus. For a discussion of the choice of lexical equivalents in this verse and the contrasting of the work here and in 5:13, see Detlef Fraenkel, "Übersetzungsnorm und literarische Gestaltung—Spuren individueller Übersetzungstechnik in Exodus 25ff. + 35ff.," in *VIII Congress of the International Organization for Septuagint and Cognate Studies, Paris, 1991*, ed. Leonard Greenspoon and Olivier Munnich, Septuagint and Cognate Studies, no. 41 (Atlanta, Ga.: Scholars Press, 1995), 83-84. Likewise, offerings of various types are considered to be related to the Holy Place rather than being holy in and of themselves, תְּרוּמַת הַקֹּדֶשׁ—τὰς ἀπαρχὰς τοῦ ἁγίου (36:6). In contrast, the oil of anointing is holy and the adjectival form is used as the translation equivalent for the unarticulated form of קֹדֶשׁ, as follows: שֶׁמֶן מִשְׁחַת־קֹדֶשׁ—ἔλαιον χρῖσμα ἅγιον (30:25 [2x]); שֶׁמֶן מִשְׁחַת־קֹדֶשׁ—"Ἔλαιον ἄλειμμα χρίσεως ἅγιον (30:31). In 37:29 (𝔊 38:25), the oil of anointing is described as holy in a clearly attributive usage, שֶׁמֶן הַמִּשְׁחָה קֹדֶשׁ, rather than by means of a construct chain. The translation in Greek, however, uses the same adjectival form (with the addition of articulation) as was also seen in the translation equivalents for the construct chains, τὸ ἔλαιον τῆς χρίσεως τὸ ἅγιον. Soisalon-Soininen also noted the variations in the translation of קֹדֶשׁ in the Pentateuch, but in contrast to the above description he suggested that the word קֹדֶשׁ is translated by an adjective when it cannot refer to the sanctuary. See Soisalon-Soininen, "Verschiedene Wiedergaben der hebräischen Status-Constructus-Verbindung," 65-66.

92. In the first tabernacle account, two different lexical equivalents are used for שֶׁקֶל and two translation equivalents are likewise used for הַקֹּדֶשׁ in the construct chain. When שֶׁקֶל is used for a monetary unit in the first account, the shekel is described as holy, τὸ δίδραχμον τὸ ἅγιον (30:13). Later, when the shekel refers to a unit of measure, however, the first account refers to it as being related to the Holy Place using a genitive, σίκλους τοῦ ἁγίου (30:24). In the second tabernacle account the choice of translation equivalents for the construct chain illustrates a technique similar to that used for the choice of lexical equivalents, as discussed in chapter three. The translator compromised in order to maintain continuity with the first tabernacle account. As a result, the translator used the lexical equivalent of 30:24 and the translation equivalent for the construct chain seen in 30:13, which resulted in the form τὸν σίκλον τὸν ἅγιον (38:24, 26 [𝔊 39:1, 3]).

In contrast to the translation of the holy shekel, the holy garments are not affected by lexical equivalents, but two different translation equivalents for the construct chain are found in both tabernacle accounts. The word קֹדֶשׁ is translated by an adjective when it is followed by a construction indi-

difference between otherwise distinct translation equivalents is effectively neutralized and both translation equivalents with these specific phrases should be interpreted in an identical manner.

Summary

Within a free translation, such as 𝔊 Exodus, the choice of translation equivalents for grammatical structures is one of the indicators of a difference in the translator's interpretation of the text. Thus, small differences between the two tabernacle accounts may be the result of a difference in translators. Each context, however, must be carefully examined for its effect on the choice of translation equivalents. In some grammatical contexts, the difference between two otherwise contrastive translation equivalents may be effectively neutralized so that there is no difference in meaning. The choice of lexical equivalents in these contexts is almost completely controlled by the difference in grammatical context. Examples such as the ones discussed in this section, then, emphasize the importance of context and point to the tension that exists between assigning a discrete meaning difference to every grammatical structure versus acknowledging the semantic similarity of contrasting grammatical structures in some contexts. This kind of tension, however, is common in all languages and is thus another indicator of the naturalness of the 𝔊 translation of Exodus.

IV. Conclusions

Over the last century scholars have attempted to quantify the differences that they intuitively know to be present in the translation of grammatical structures in the putative component parts of the 𝔊 Scriptures. These studies have produced statistics that appear to support conclusions that have been made on a more intuitive

---

cating the person for whom the garments are made or to whom they belong, as follows: בִּגְדֵי־קֹדֶשׁ—στολὰς—בִּגְדֵי־קֹדֶשׁ לְאַהֲרֹן אָחִיךָ וּלְבָנָיו (28:2), στολὴν ἁγίαν Ααρων τῷ ἀδελφῷ σου—לְאַהֲרֹן אָחִיךָ ἁγίας Ααρων καὶ τοῖς υἱοῖς αὐτοῦ (28:4), בִּגְדֵי הַקֹּדֶשׁ לְאַהֲרֹן הַכֹּהֵן—τὰς στολὰς τὰς ἁγίας Ααρων τοῦ ἱερέως (35:19). When קֹדֶשׁ is followed by a relative clause or is in a construct chain used independently, קֹדֶשׁ is generally translated by a genitive, as follows: בִּגְדֵי הַקֹּדֶשׁ אֲשֶׁר לְאַהֲרֹן—ἡ στολὴ τοῦ ἁγίου, ἥ ἐστιν Ααρων (29:29), בִּגְדֵי הַקֹּדֶשׁ אֲשֶׁר—τὰς στολὰς τοῦ ἁγίου (35:21), לְאַהֲרֹן—τὰς στολὰς τῶν ἁγίων, αἵ εἰσιν Ααρων τῷ ἱερεῖ (39:1 [𝔊 36:8—τῷ ἱερεῖ is a plus in the 𝔊]). The only exception is in 40:13, וְהִלְבַּשְׁתָּ אֶת־אַהֲרֹן אֵת בִּגְדֵי הַקֹּדֶשׁ—καὶ ἐνδύσεις Ααρων τὰς στολὰς τὰς ἁγίας. This verse, however, could be confusing due to the presence of Ααρων, which is indeclinable, before the noun phrase τὰς στολὰς τὰς ἁγίας. The similarity of the translation of this phrase to other above mentioned phrases with an adjective, i.e., the fact that the name Aaron is adjacent to the noun phrase, possibly influenced the translator's choice of the adjective form as the translation equivalent for קֹדֶשׁ. This may not have been a conscious choice, but translators often evaluate phrases on the basis of the way they "sound" and intuitively choose the less ambiguous or less complex translation equivalent.

basis, especially in delineating the most literally translated books from the most freely translated books. Studies of smaller sections and portions that are not as distinct in their translation techniques, however, highlight the problems of these types of statistical studies. In addition, several of the grammatical features studied include such a small sampling of data that they cannot be used as major pieces of evidence for any theory about the number of translators that produced the tabernacle accounts of 𝕲 Exodus. Because of these types of difficulties, I chose to study three frequently occurring Hebrew structures and focused on identifying the grammatical structures that were used to translate these three structures. Within the four sections of Exodus used in this book, each of these Hebrew structures was translated by a wide array of translation equivalents, each of which was generally connected with a small cluster of semantic functions. Some of the grammatical structures were found to share a few semantic functions, but in general each Greek structure was used to translate a defined range of semantic functions. In addition, one of the translation equivalents for each structure served as the "catch-all" or default translation that was probably used for any questionable Hebrew structures. For the preposition בְּ, the default translation was ἐν; for the simple construct chain, the default translation was the Greek genitive construction; and for the relative clause with אֲשֶׁר, the default translation was ὅς. Each of these default translation equivalents was a very generic term that was used for a wide range of meanings in natural Greek. This natural fit between Greek and Hebrew grammatical structures, however, did not stop the translator from using a full range of more specific Greek translation equivalents that were controlled by the semantic and grammatical contexts.

    The translation equivalents used for these grammatical structures were not evenly distributed among all four sections. The tabernacle accounts seemed to share half or more of the translation equivalents that were available for each grammatical structure. The shared translation equivalents were due in most cases to shared semantic functions that were translated in similar ways, some of which were in parallel verses. This high degree of shared equivalents seemed to point to a similar approach to the choice of translation equivalents. The translation equivalents that were not shared were primarily due to the lack of shared semantic functions, rather than the translator(s) having chosen to translate grammatical structures in conflicting ways. There were, however, a few examples of choices of translation equivalents that clearly illustrated different interpretations of the text. As with the choices of lexical equivalents, however, the translator of the second account only diverged from the first account when the translation in the first account was questionable or when there was no exact parallel of a context in the first account. It is only with a few examples of this nature that the two-translator theory of the production of the tabernacle accounts might be supported. Aside from that, both tabernacle accounts seem to use the same context-sensitive approach to the translation of grammatical structures.

The primary value of this study of the translation of grammatical structures is that it has shown that all parts of the tabernacle accounts of the 𝔊 Exodus are carefully crafted pieces of translation, whether done intuitively or consciously. Claims by Gooding and Fin that the translation was sloppy and inconsistent have already been shown to be invalid in the area of lexical equivalents and in this chapter have been shown to be invalid in the area of translation equivalents of grammatical structures. There are, admittedly, cases where the semantic difference between two contrasting translation equivalents is effectively neutralized due to the grammatical context, but this type of neutralization of contrast can be found cross-linguistically in many areas of linguistic studies. These types of conditioning factors rather than pointing to a sloppy translation, show that 𝔊 Exodus is a translation in natural Greek by a translator or translators who interpreted the text and then translated it in a manner that was appropriate for the semantic and grammatical context.

CHAPTER FIVE

Accuracy

Within the tabernacle accounts of ⅏ Exodus, pluses, minuses, synonymous variants, and differences in order affect the meaning of the text in similar ways, but not in similar proportions. The most significant difference between the two accounts is found in the minuses. The majority of the minuses in the first account are largely those one would expect in any translation. In contrast, the minuses in the second account produce an abbreviated text that is evidence of either a different approach to the text (i.e., a different translator or the work of an editor) or a different *Vorlage*. Even though the second account is highly abbreviated, the same approach to lexical equivalents is seen throughout the second account, including the major pluses. This indicates that the pluses were probably produced by the same translator that produced the remainder of the second account, rather than by Gooding's inept editor. This translator also produced "improved" versions of sections of the first account that were especially ambiguous. Because of our lack of knowledge about translation techniques and definitions of accuracy in antiquity, however, no definitive conclusion can be reached about the question of whether the abbreviation of the text was due to the work of the translator or due to the nature of the *Vorlage* that he used. Rather, the most that can be accomplished at this time is to produce a careful description of the effect of textual variants on the meaning communicated in both tabernacle accounts. Within that description, a variety of differences will be identified that can be used as evidence to support the hypothesis that a second translator likely produced the second tabernacle account of the Old Greek Exodus using the translation of the first tabernacle account as a point of reference.

In this chapter, after briefly defining accuracy I will review the methodology used in two recent text critical analyses of Exodus. This review will provide a basis of comparison for my methodology, which is an adaptation of current theory used by some modern Bible translators. Next, I will define and illustrate the six categories that will be used in the analysis of the differences in meaning that result from textual variants in the tabernacle accounts. In the second section, I will present an analysis of the pluses, minuses, synonymous variants, and differences in order in the control sample and tabernacle accounts in light of the impact of these variants on the meaning. Because of the large quantity of variants (over nine hundred), the analysis will at times consist of categorized lists in the notes, but all interesting variants will be briefly discussed. In section three, the accuracy of the tabernacle accounts will be compared and illustrated by a detailed examination of two passages in the first account that are more ambiguous than their parallel passages in the second account. In addition, I will discuss the pluses that Gooding believed were the key to the proper analysis of the second tabernacle account. In the fourth section, the unanswerable questions about translation techniques and accuracy in antiquity will be briefly discussed.

I. Defining and Measuring Accuracy

An accurate translation is one that conveys "what the original author intended to communicate to his readers/hearers."[1] In the process of conveying this meaning that the author intended, translators make numerous adjustments in at least the following areas: participant referencing (the use of nouns, pronouns, proper names, pronominal suffixes and verbal affixes to indicate to whom or to what the author is referring), definiteness, and verbal systems.[2] These kinds of adjustments may not change the underlying meaning of the text, but they usually result in differences in the surface form of the text. Adjustments of this nature are regularly found in the 𝔊 in addition to changes that reflect a difference in meaning. As a result of these adjustments, the 𝔊 contains many pluses, minuses, synonymous variants, and differences in order with respect to the 𝔐. All of these variants must be evaluated as possible evidence of a different *Vorlage*, but many of the variants are due to the adjustments that are required by the process of translation. Since the *Vorlage* of the 𝔊 is unknown, accuracy, as used in this chapter, will refer to the degree to which the 𝔐 and 𝔊 communicate the same meaning. Differences in meaning, therefore, may represent differences in the *Vorlage*, differences due to translation techniques, or differences that arose in the process of the transmission of the text.

Survey of Past Methodologies

The methodology that will be used in this chapter combines standard categories used in previous text critical studies with an evaluation of the differences in

---

1. Ernst R. Wendland, *Language, Society, and Bible Translation: With Special Reference to the Style and Structure of Segments of Direct Speech in the Scriptures* (Roggebaai, Cape Town, South Africa: Bible Society of South Africa, 1985), 216-17.

2. See John William Wevers, "The Use of Versions for Text Criticism: The Septuagint," in *La Septuaginta en la investigacion contemporanea: V Congreso de la IOSCS*, ed. Natalio Fernandez Marcos, Textos y Estudios «Cardenal Cisneros» de la Biblia Poliglota Matritense, no. 34 (Madrid: Instituto «Arias Montano» C.S.I.C., 1985), 18, who says about the addition of pronouns, "Such plusses have no textual basis; they simply represent the translator's attempt to render the intent of the source language unambiguously."

meaning between the 𝔐 and 𝔊 using categories from modern translation theory. Traditional text critical studies, however, are not identical in nature. Each study is uniquely influenced by the author's presuppositions and the goal of the study. This can be seen in the following survey of the text critical aspects of two recent studies that discuss some of the pluses, minuses, synonymous variants, and differences in order that are also discussed in this chapter.

In Sanderson's analysis of variants in 4QpaleoExod^m, 𝔐, 𝔚, and 𝔊, she focuses on classifying variants as either preferable, secondary, or synonymous variants. These classifications are acknowledged as subjective, but are based on careful argumentation that differentiates between a variant that is an error, which would be the work of a scribe, versus a "less smooth reading," which would be the work of a "composer or editor."[3] While emphasizing the art of textual criticism as opposed to the use of standard rules, she notes that her studies of Exodus have affirmed the validity of the general rule that shorter readings are to be preferred.[4] Having critically evaluated each variant, Sanderson then groups the variants within each category "first by their attestation, and second by their type." These variants are then described using labels such as "shorter, longer, less familiar word," and many other descriptive phrases that "give indication of the nature of that text or group."[5] Because the main goal of Sanderson's work is to establish the textual affinity and character of 4QpaleoExod^m with respect to the three other main witnesses to the text (𝔐, 𝔚, and 𝔊), a large part of her work concentrates on calculating the number and types of shared and independent readings. In combination with the statistical evaluation of the witnesses, however, Sanderson also describes the character of each witness and the types of changes that have been made in these witnesses. On the basis of her study of a limited number of variants (less than two hundred), she concludes that 4QpaleoExod^m is most closely related to the 𝔚 tradition and notes concerning the 𝔊 "that while it deserves its reputation of being expansionist, it nevertheless preserves some preferable shorter readings as well."[6] These are just a few of the observations found in Sanderson's detailed examination of a wide variety of variants.

---

3. In Sanderson's discussion of the rule about "the more difficult reading," she notes, "It has seemed more helpful to me to distinguish actual errors, which have produced readings that are grammatically or syntactically wrong (to the best of our knowledge from this distance), from readings which appear to be possible but not quite smooth. In the case of errors, one normally attributes the correct reading to the composer or editor and the error to scribes. But in the case of readings that have made a text read more smoothly, one normally attributes the less smooth reading to the composer or editor and the more smooth, more flowing, more consistent reading to a scribe." Judith E. Sanderson, *An Exodus Scroll from Qumran: 4QpaleoExod^m and the Samaritan Tradition* (Atlanta, Ga.: Scholars Press, 1986), 46.

4. Ibid., 47. Her studies, however, were limited to the parts of Exodus extant in the 4QpaleoExod^m scroll and therefore did not include much of the second tabernacle account.

5. Ibid., 50.

6. Ibid., 311.

Nelson's study of Exodus, in contrast to Sanderson's traditional text critical approach, focuses on the development of the texts of the tabernacle accounts. Nelson emphasizes the use of the vocabulary of the 𝔊 as evidence of the priority of the *Vorlage* of 𝔊 37-38. Because of his presupposition that the 𝔊 is a generally accurate representation of a shorter Hebrew *Vorlage* in the second account, Nelson rarely refers to minuses in the 𝔊. Rather, the text is viewed as continually expanding with further pluses, substitutions, and order changes as the Hebrew text developed and was anchored into its current setting by narrative additions. In his notes, he points to the pluses that occur in both accounts of the 𝔊 and 𝔐 and describes them in terms of "explicating glosses, additions from the same or nearby verse; additions from similar, but more distant, verse; ... conflations of variant readings; and readings which suggest a different Vorlage than MT I."[7] Nelson does, however, note that "small changes have occurred through normal copyist's errors, such as dittographies, haplographies, and the like."[8] His primary focus, however, is on identifying textual variants that point to an intentional revision of the text, rather than minor differences due to the work of scribes.

The contrast between these two approaches is obvious, even though both discuss textual variants. As a result of their contrasting approaches, their analyses of the evidence from variants in the 𝔊 are also contrasting. Nelson gives priority to the 𝔊 and finds evidence of the "original" text in the unrevised "core" section of the second account (𝔊 37-38). Sanderson, in contrast, strives not to be biased and as a result concludes that many differences are synonymous variants of equal status that reflect the variety of text forms that were in existence before the text was canonized. Sanderson finds very few preferable readings among the variants that are unique to the 𝔊. Ultimately, the difference between Nelson's and Sanderson's approaches to the text involves their presuppositions about the existence and development of an *Urtext*, a topic that is beyond the scope of this book.

This study will use some of the categories seen in more traditional text critical studies, such as Sanderson's. In contrast to the traditional emphasis on the size of the variant, however, this factor will be largely ignored in my analysis due to the fact that the size of the variant in a translation does not always reflect the impact of the variant, as can be seen in a comparison of the impact of a "large" plus in 29:20 and a "minor" synonymous variant in 38:3 (𝔊 38:23).[9] In addition, rather

---

7. Nelson, 295.
8. Ibid., 259.
9. In 29:20, the plus τοῦ δεξιοῦ καὶ ἐπὶ τὸ ἄκρον τῆς χειρὸς τῆς δεξιᾶς καὶ ἐπὶ τὸ ἄκρον τοῦ ποδὸς τοῦ δεξιοῦ may slightly affect the focus or emphasis of the passage, but primarily this plus "fills in" information that is implicitly present in the elliptical statement in the 𝔐. The source of the plus in the 𝔊 could be ascribed to a scribal expansion in the 𝔊 or in its Hebrew *Vorlage* or a minus in the 𝔐 with respect to the original text. This type of investigation of the development of the text, however, is beyond the scope of this study. The important point for this study is that the 𝔊 and 𝔐 are equivalent in meaning, with the only difference being that the meaning has been explicitly stated in the 𝔊 in contrast to the 𝔐, which has left the meaning implicit.

than analyzing the variants in the hopes of finding the preferable reading, as was done by Sanderson, the textual variants will be examined to identify the similarities and differences of the meaning in the 𝔊 and 𝔐, i.e., how "accurate" the 𝔊 is with respect to the 𝔐. To accomplish this comparison, the text will be examined using the tools of modern translation methodology in combination with categories similar to those of Sanderson, as will be discussed below.

Methodology Used in This Study

In this study I will evaluate the accuracy of the translation of the 𝔊 tabernacle accounts by comparing the types of meaning differences that are seen in the pluses, minuses, synonymous variants, and differences in order of the 𝔊 with respect to the 𝔐. Pluses and minuses will be identified based on the increase or decrease in the number of words in the text.[10] Synonymous variants will include the substitution of a Greek word or group of words for its Hebrew counterpart as well as the substitution of grammatical forms, such as differences in the person and/or number of a verb. Differences in order, both within the clause and on a larger textual level, will be discussed after examining the other variants. Variants that involve only conjunctions, articles, and prepositions will not generally be included due to the limited nature of this study.[11]

This large plus contrasts with a "minor" synonymous variant in which a singular is used instead of a plural in 38:3 (𝔊 38:23). Most differences of this nature in the 𝔊 do not represent a difference in meaning. More often they represent language differences in which one language uses a singular collective and the other uses a plural. As a result, this type of "minor" difference in the 𝔊 is usually ignored in text critical studies, but in 38:3 (𝔊 38:23) the minor synonymous variant indicates a small, but significant difference in meaning. Rather than using a plural to refer to the censers used with the altar in the 𝔐, the 𝔊 uses the singular πυρεῖον, which is also used in 𝔊 38:24 to refer to an integral part of the bronze altar. Thus, a minor synonymous variant (the use of a singular) probably indicates a difference in meaning in the 𝔊, whereas the large plus in 29:20 did not change the meaning.

10. For this study, Hebrew conjunctions, object suffixes, and similar grammatical units will be treated as "words" in the sense that they function independently of the other "words" to which they are attached. More importantly, they are treated as "words" because a literal translation in the Greek language would use an independent word to represent them.

11. As was discussed in chapter two, conjunctions and articles are often used to clarify ambiguous passages and thus, the variants that involve these items are important in text critical studies of different Hebrew texts. Because of the differences in the usage of these words in Hebrew and Greek, however, it is difficult to determine if the variant is due to an underlying difference in the Hebrew *Vorlage* of the 𝔊 or if the variant is due to standard usage in Greek. Conjunctions probably provide the clearest examples of the importance of examining all the variants in the text. In the 𝔐, several appositional items have been reinterpreted in the 𝔊 as separate items in lists. One example of this is seen in 36:2, in which the appositional phrase, כֹּל אֲשֶׁר נְשָׂאוֹ לִבּוֹ לְקָרְבָה אֶל־הַמְּלָאכָה, has been reinterpreted in the 𝔊 as a separate group of people, as can be seen by the "addition" of the conjunction, καὶ πάντας τοὺς ἑκουσίως βουλομένους προσπορεύεσθαι πρὸς τὰ ἔργα. It is possible that this is an explicative usage of the conjunction, but this would not be the natural reading. English translations do not follow the interpretation in the 𝔊. Instead, they are divided between interpreting this clause as a true apposition (NRSV, NJPS) versus a coordinated restrictive relative clause (NIV, TEV). For a brief

Rather than evaluating the size or grammatical structure of these variants in the 𝔊, I will instead focus on the differences in the types of meaning communicated in the 𝔊 and the 𝔐. Each of the four sections of Exodus (the control sample, first tabernacle account, core of second tabernacle account, and remainder of the second tabernacle account) will be compared both with respect to the quantity of pluses, minuses, synonymous variants, and differences in order, as well as the differences in the types of meaning within each of these groups. In this section on methodology, I will define and give examples that illustrate the six categories that will be used in the presentation of the data from the control sample and tabernacle accounts of 𝔊 Exodus.

According to Larson, every text contains three types of meaning—referential, organizational, and situational. Referential meaning is the "information content" of the text. This information is then formed into a coherent text that contains organizational meaning, which is signaled by "deictics, repetition, groupings, and by many other features in the grammatical structure of a text." In addition to referential and organizational meaning, each text includes situational meaning that derives from the culture(s) in which the text was written and from the culture of the addressee(s).[12] This last category will be modified slightly for this study in that it will also include the culture of the translator(s), e.g., his presuppositions and hermeneutical principles.

---

discussion of interpretive options see Noel D. Osborn and Howard A. Hatton, *A Handbook on Exodus* (New York: United Bible Societies, 1999), 840. Another example of a reinterpreted appositional phrase may be see in 12:38, in which the appositional phrase מִקְנֶה כָּבֵד מְאֹד has been interpreted as a third item καὶ κτήνη πολλὰ σφόδρα.

In addition to lists, conjunctions can also be important for understanding the differences between clausal relationships in the 𝔐 and the 𝔊. For instance, the plus οὗτος at the beginning of every verse in 𝔊 38:18-26 has often been discussed, but the focus has generally been on the reportedly unusual usage of οὗτος. The absence of conjunctions in the Greek has scarcely been mentioned. The lack of a translation of the Hebrew conjunctions, however, is an important factor in showing that this section has been clearly shifted from a event-oriented, sequential "narrative" to a descriptive list. Similar descriptive clauses may be seen as integrated parts of lists in Genesis (Gen 2:11, 13, 14; 4:20-21; 10:8-9), but in these cases both the 𝔐 and 𝔊 are descriptive in nature and both lack conjunctions. These clauses in Genesis are not identical with the clauses in Exodus, but they illustrate both the use of the demonstrative οὗτος and the lack of conjunctions in descriptive lists. Thus, conjunctions may be difficult to assess in the 𝔊, but these types of variants should never be ignored.

Most prepositions that are pluses make explicit the meaning of grammatical structures, such as construct chains, e.g., in 25:7 אַבְנֵי מִלֻּאִים is translated λίθους εἰς τὴν γλυφήν. Due to the limited nature of this study, prepositions are not normally counted as independent pluses. Rather, they are treated as part of the translation of grammatical structures, but prepositions are nevertheless important. For instance, the preposition ἐπί in 36:36 (𝔊 37:4), expresses more clearly the meaning of the 𝔊 verb ἐπέθηκαν. In addition, this plus is further evidence of the difference in meaning between the 𝔐 and the 𝔊 form of this verse, which has been adjusted to be more like that of the first account (26:32). Thus, prepositions are important, but due to limitations of space they will not generally be included in this study.

12. Mildred L. Larson, *Meaning-Based Translation: A Guide to Cross-Language Equivalence*, 2d ed. (Lanham, Md.: University Press of America, 1998), 41-43.

Each of these three types of information may be communicated either explicitly or implicitly.

> **Explicit** information . . . is the information which is overtly stated by lexical items and grammatical forms. It is part of the surface structure form. The **implicit** information is that for which there is no form but the information is part of the total communication intended or assumed by the writer.[13]

Many of the pluses and minuses in the 𝕲 do not involve a difference in meaning, but rather reflect a difference in the status of the information, i.e., whether the information is implicit or explicit. Pluses often reflect information that is implicit in the Hebrew text, but has been made explicit in the Greek. Likewise, minuses often reflect information that is explicit in the Hebrew text, but left implicit in the Greek. In addition to information that changes in status from either implicit to explicit or vice versa, there are also true differences in the quantity of information, i.e., information that is absent in the Hebrew text is present in the Greek and vice versa. These differences in the quantity of information may involve differences in either referential, organizational, or situational meaning. Synonymous variants, by contrast, involve a substitution of one referential, organizational, or situational meaning for another. The use of these categories, however, says nothing about the source(s) of the differences. These differences may be due either to the translator, his *Vorlage*, or differences that arose in the transmission of the text.

The combination of these three types of meaning in conjunction with changes in either the quantity or status (implicit or explicit) of the meaning will provide the six categories that will be used throughout this chapter. (See table 14.) Each of these categories will be explained and illustrated below. As could be expected, many of the differences in the 𝕲 with respect to the 𝔐 could be categorized in several different ways. In fact, most changes in organizational and situational meaning also affect referential meaning. In each case, however, I have made a subjective decision and assigned the variant to a single category.

The quantity of referential meaning in the 𝕲 may be either greater (plus), lesser (minus), or simply different (synonymous variant) from that in the 𝔐. For instance, the plus ἄνωθεν τῆς κιβωτοῦ in 37:6 (𝕲 38:5) is a quantitative increase of referential meaning that explains the exact location of the mercy seat. The phrase is not found elsewhere in the text though the same information is contained in 25:21, ἐπὶ τὴν κιβωτὸν ἄνωθεν, which is a nonparallel verse in the first tabernacle account.

The quantity of referential meaning is also affected by situational meaning. Specifically, in the 𝕲 the quantity of referential meaning is often different because of the scribe's or translator's desire that the text be internally consistent as well as consistent with the rest of the Pentateuch. For instance, the plus ἐκ τῶν πυρείων τῶν χαλκῶν, ἃ ἦν τοῖς ἀνδράσιν τοῖς καταστασιάσασι μετὰ τῆς Κορε συν-

---

13. Ibid., 44.

Table 14. Categories of meaning

	Referential meaning	Situational meaning	Organizational meaning
Quantity	Quantity of referential meaning	Quantity of situational meaning	Quantity of organizational meaning
Status (implicit or explicit)	Status of referential meaning	Status of situational meaning	Status of organizational meaning

ἀγωγῆς in 38:1 (𝔊 38:22) attempts to resolve a potential contradiction between Exodus and Numbers concerning the etiology of the bronze used to make the altar of burnt offering, as will be discussed further below. The important fact is that the 𝔊 (or its *Vorlage*) contains more referential meaning than the 𝔐 and that this plus is probably due to a desire to make the text more consistent. This desire for consistency is probably a reflection of the fact that the situation (culture) in which the text(s) were produced placed an emphasis on the consistency of God's Word.[14] This type of difference is classified as a difference in the quantity of situational meaning.

The quantity of organizational meaning is the most difficult to define in terms of pluses, minuses, and synonymous variants. Variants that affect the quantity of organizational meaning often involve some type of emphasis. For instance, the minus לְךָ (30:23) is a reflexive usage of a prepositional phrase with a pronominal suffix that has "an additional emphatic nuance" in Hebrew.[15] Literal translations of words with this type of emphatic function rarely communicate the same organizational meaning (emphasis) as the original language. As a result, they are often minuses in translations that focus more on the meaning than on the form.[16]

---

14. This decision is based partially on the known characteristic of the 𝔐 that led to increased consistency and harmonization of the text, as was discussed in chapter two. Although the 𝔊 of Exodus does not show the same degree of concern about grammatical minutiae, there are still many examples that point to a similar concern being present in the 𝔊.

15. Bruce K. Waltke and M. O'Connor, *An Introduction to Biblical Hebrew Syntax* (Winona Lake, Ind.: Eisenbrauns, 1990), 305. Waltke and O'Connor would, however, classify this as an ethical dative in contrast to van der Merwe, Naudé, and Kroeze, who classify the "so-called ethical dative" as a reflexive. In any case, whether classified as a reflexive or an ethical dative, this form affects the organizational meaning by a change of emphasis rather than producing a change of referential meaning. See Christo H. J. van der Merwe, Jackie A. Naudé, and Jan H. Kroeze, *A Biblical Hebrew Reference Grammar* (Sheffield: Sheffield Academic Press, 1999), 287.

16. This reflexive pronoun is not translated literally in most English translations. In the NIV and NRSV, the simple imperative is used, which is probably a sufficient functional equivalent. No

The status of referential meaning can be changed through pluses, minuses, and synonymous variants that make the implicit referential meaning of the Hebrew explicit in the Greek or that allow explicit meaning in the Hebrew to be left implicit in the Greek. A clear example of this is seen in the minus טַבָּעֹת in 37:3 (𝔊 38:3). The 𝔐 explicitly states that there were two rings that were placed on one side, שְׁתֵּי טַבָּעֹת עַל־צַלְעוֹ הָאֶחָת, whereas the 𝔊 leaves the rings implicit, δύο ἐπὶ τὸ κλίτος τὸ ἕν. Due to the context, there is no loss of referential meaning. Rather, the fact that the rings are implicit in the 𝔊 increases the coherence of the passage, i.e., the passage must be read in context to be understood.

The status of situational meaning is probably the least frequently used in this study of the 𝔊 because of our lack of knowledge of the *Vorlage* and of the culture of the translator. In the tabernacle accounts, one example of situational meaning is the designation of Aaron as "the priest." For those who shared the translator's knowledge of the Scriptures, this designation would have been unnecessary because Aaron was a well known person in the Scriptures. For people who were less aware of Aaron's identity, however, there would be the possibility that Aaron the priest might be confused with some other Aaron.[17] Thus, it is not surprising that the term priest is found as both a plus and a minus in the 𝔊. In each instance, this might reflect either a different *Vorlage* or the translator's decision to make explicit or leave implicit Aaron's role in the text.[18] If these variants are the result of the translator's decision, then context is probably the controlling factor. In either case, whether in the Hebrew *Vorlage* or in the Old Greek, the presence or absence of the term priest does not affect the referential meaning of the text.[19] Rather, it affects the status of the situational meaning, i.e., the known cultural information about Aaron's role as priest.

---

translation is able to fully communicate all of the meaning in the original. Organizational meaning, especially emphasis, is the most frequently "lost" meaning.

17. In the Scriptures, both the 𝔊 and 𝔐, however, the name Aaron is limited to references to Moses' brother and to the descendants of Moses' brother, i.e., "sons of Aaron." This latter phrase is used as a generic reference for priests.

18. Aaron's designation as a priest can be found as a minus הַכֹּהֵן (31:10; 39:41 [𝔊 39:18]) and as a plus τῷ ἱερεῖ (39:1 [𝔊 36:8]). The plus in 𝔊 36:8 is perhaps "necessary" because of the displaced nature of the text in the 𝔊. In the 𝔐, it is preceded by a description of other garments that are specifically for service לְשָׁרֵת בַּקֹּדֶשׁ (39:1), but in the 𝔊 those garments for service, λειτουργεῖν ἐν αὐταῖς ἐν τῷ ἁγίῳ, are referred to in a later section of the text (𝔊 39:12), and the garments in 𝔊 36:8 are simply described as τὰς στολὰς τῶν ἁγίων. This change may have contributed to the presence of the plus, though the possibility of a different *Vorlage* cannot be eliminated. The minuses could be explained by a reversal of this same argument because they both occur in contexts in which the garments are described as being לְכַהֵן, which is translated as ἱερατεύειν μοι (31:10) and εἰς τὴν ἱερατείαν (𝔊 39:18). Because of the presence of a reference to priestly service, the designation of Aaron as הַכֹּהֵן may have been less necessary in the 𝔊.

19. See E. J. Revell, *The Designation of the Individual: Expressive Usage in Biblical Narrative* (Kampen, Netherlands: Kok Pharos, 1996), 162. Revell's work refers specifically to narratives, but the function of titles that he discusses is relevant in all texts even though it may be expressed by slightly different means in a non-narrative text.

The status of organizational meaning is frequently affected by pluses, minuses, and synonymous variants. These types of variants most frequently reflect the differences in participant referencing between Hebrew and Greek, i.e., each language has a distinct way of using nouns, pronouns, and verbal suffixes to refer to participants in the text. As a result of these different strategies, participants that are referred to in Hebrew by a pronoun are not referred to in the 𝔊 or vice versa. For instance, the term טַבַּעַת occurs in a possessed form, טַבְּעֹתֵיהֶם, in 26:29, but in the 𝔊 the text simply reads τοὺς δακτυλίους. The reference to the posts (3p pronoun) is left implicit in the 𝔊 because the relationship of the rings and the posts can be understood from the context. This example reflects the general tendency to use more possessed forms in Hebrew, whereas in Greek the context and use of definite and indefinite noun phrases accomplish the same purpose of keeping track of the participants in the text.

Summary

Recent text critical studies of the tabernacle accounts have used more traditional approaches and focused on either the development of the text (Nelson) or the assessing of textual affinities and preferable readings (Sanderson). This study, in contrast, will focus on evaluating the accuracy of the 𝔊, i.e., the similarities and differences in the meaning communicated by the 𝔊 and 𝔐. To accomplish this task, I will evaluate the status and quantity of the referential, situational, and organizational meaning in the pluses, minuses, synonymous variants, and differences in order of the 𝔊 with respect to the 𝔐.

II. Accuracy in the Tabernacle Accounts

A detailed examination of the control sample and tabernacle accounts produces a list of over nine hundred variants, of which almost eight hundred are found in the tabernacle accounts. Minuses were found to be the most frequently occurring type of variant in the tabernacle accounts and differences in order were the least frequently occurring type of variant in all sections. The quantity of variants, however, does not indicate the quantity of difference in meaning between the two texts. Approximately half of the variants in the pluses, minuses, and synonymous variants resulted in a difference in the status (implicit or explicit) of the meaning, rather than a difference in the meaning. While a few of the variants resulted in a meaning that differed greatly from the 𝔐, most of the variants that affected the quantity of meaning resulted in a text in which ambiguities had been clarified, locations had been more clearly explained, and discrepancies between parts of the text had been removed by means of a hermeneutical approach that assumes that the text should be consistent and contain no internal contradictions.

In the following sections, the pluses, minuses, synonymous variants, and differences in order that have been identified in the control sample and tabernacle accounts will be categorized and briefly discussed in the notes. In each section, the variants that agree with the 𝔐 will be discussed first due to the high probability that these agreements may indicate that the *Vorlage* followed by the 𝔊 was similar to that of the 𝔐. After discussing the variants that agree with the 𝔐, the remaining variants will be discussed using the six categories listed above. These categories will be grouped according to whether the variants affect the status of the meaning or the quantity of the meaning.

Pluses

The majority of pluses in the control sample and tabernacle accounts either make explicit the status of organizational meaning or result in a quantitative increase in the referential meaning of the text. In both the core and the remainder of the second tabernacle account, the majority of pluses are evenly distributed between those that affect the status of the meaning and those that affect the quantity of the meaning. In the control sample and first tabernacle account, however, there are more than twice as many pluses in the category of status of organizational meaning as there are in the category of quantitative increases in referential meaning. This means that even though there is a similar number of pluses in both tabernacle accounts, the effect of those pluses on the meaning is different. The pluses in the second account are more likely to "add" meaning to the text, while the pluses in the control sample and first account are more likely to make explicit the meaning that was already present in the probable Vorlage. In the following sections, I will first discuss the pluses in which the 𝔊 and 𝔐 agree. Following that I will discuss pluses that affect the status of meaning and then pluses that affect the quantity of meaning. The source of these pluses can be debated, but the fact that pluses affect the meaning of the 𝔊 text in different ways is the focus of this section.

That Reflect a Vorlage Similar to the 𝔐. Within the control sample and tabernacle accounts there are over thirty pluses in which the 𝔊 and 𝔐 agree. These pluses are almost evenly divided between the two major categories, i.e., differences in the quantity of meaning and differences in the status (implicit or explicit) of the meaning. Pluses in each of these categories will be discussed below.

Implicit meaning that is made explicit in both the 𝔐 and 𝔊 is divided among all three categories—referential, organizational, and situational. Referential meaning that is made explicit include pluses such as πήχεων (אמה in the 𝔐), which explicitly states the unit of measurement for a number that is present in all three major texts.[20] Some pluses found in both the 𝔊 and 𝔐 reflect situational

---

20. This plus (cubit) is found in both the 𝔐 and the 𝔊 (27:11, 15). Another example of implicit referential meaning being stated explicitly can be found in 39:26 (𝔊 36:33). In this verse, the bells on the high priest's garment are explicitly said to be χρυσοῦς in the 𝔊 (and the 𝔐), whereas this meaning is implicit in the 𝔐 form of this verse. The fact that the bells were golden, however, can be found explicitly stated in the previous verse of all three texts. A final example of implicit referential meaning

Table 15. Types of meaning in the pluses of 𝕲 Exodus

	Control sample	First tabernacle account	Core of second tabernacle account	Remainder of second tabernacle account	Totals
Quantity of organizational meaning	1	0	5	0	6
Quantity of referential meaning	11	26	5	30	72
Quantity of situational meaning	6	17	6	12	41
Status of organizational meaning	30	53	9	23	115
Status of referential meaning	3	18	0	6	27
Status of situational meaning	11	2	0	4	17
Totals	62	116	25	75	278

(cultural) meaning that is made explicit, such as the fact that יהוה is an אלהים.[21] Most, however, are differences in the status of the organizational meaning. These

---

that is made explicit in both the 𝔐 and the 𝕲 is τὰς θύρας in 𝕲 29:10. This meaning is explicitly stated in all three texts in 29:11. Because of this, it would be hard to argue that this is a true addition of referential meaning to the larger text. The text that the translator of the 𝕲 used was, however, probably not identical to the 𝔐, as can be seen by an examination of the three major texts of 29:10. In this verse, Moses is instructed to bring the bull before the tent of meeting in the 𝔐, but in the 𝔚 this is more carefully specified using a phrase that is identical to that which is found in all texts (𝔐, 𝔚, and 𝕲) in 29:11, לִפְנֵי יְהוָה פֶּתַח אֹהֶל מוֹעֵד. The 𝕲, however, has a copy of this fuller phrase as a plus at the end of 29:10, since the placing of the hands on the bull is part of the ceremony done "before the Lord." At the beginning of the verse, however, the 𝕲 specifies that the bull is brought to the doors of the tent of meeting, but the 𝕲 does not follow the 𝔚 in saying that the bull was brought into the presence of the Lord. Thus, the 𝕲 either had a text that differed from that of the 𝔚 or the translator felt free to present the information in a manner that agreed with his understanding of the passage.

21. Within Exodus, most of the occurrences (about thirty of over forty occurrences) of κύριος ὁ θεός are based on a Hebrew *Vorlage* like the 𝔐 that contains some form of יהוה אלהים. There are at least eight occurrences, however, where the 𝔐 has only יהוה (10:9, 24; 12:31; 13:5, 8, 11; 19:22; 23:17

pluses include differences in participant referencing and the "filling in" of elliptical statements with a copy of a word or phrase left implicit in the 𝔐.[22] One of the

---

[?]), but the 𝔊 has a longer phrase. Two of these have יהוה אלהים in the 𝔐 (13:5, 11). The remaining examples of κύριος ὁ θεός could be either explanatory pluses added by the translator of the 𝔊 or reflections of a *Vorlage* with a fuller text. Wevers' conclusion, based on a fuller range of data, seems to be that these differences are either exegetical in nature or glosses, since there are no clear patterns that would point to a difference in *Vorlage*. See WeversText, 240-41. This type of plus is, however, only found in the control sample and thus is outside of the main focus of this book. In any case, there is no difference in the referential meaning of text. Instead, these pluses only make cultural knowledge explicit, i.e., that the "Lord" referred to in the 𝔊 text is God.

Another plus that could be classified as the making explicit of implicit situational (cultural) knowledge is the plus υἱῶν, which is found three times in the control sample, two of which are also in the 𝔐. The original audience of the Hebrew *Vorlage* would presumably have known that Israel was not only the name of a person, but also the name of a people group, i.e., the "sons" of Israel. The presence of υἱῶν in phrases with the name Israel in the 𝔊, therefore, makes explicit cultural knowledge about the name, i.e., that the name is being used to refer to the descendants of Israel and not the person himself. In addition to making cultural knowledge explicit, these pluses also make the phrase more nearly parallel to the translation of the frequently occurring phrase, עֲדַת בְּנֵי־יִשְׂרָאֵל (16:1, 2, 9, 10; 17:1; 35:1, 4, 20). In 12, however, the 𝔐 contains four cases of עֲדַת־יִשְׂרָאֵל (12:3, 6, 19, 47). Of these, two are found in the fuller form in both the 𝔐, עדת בני ישראל, and 𝔊, συναγωγὴ υἱῶν Ισραηλ (12:3, 6). One is found in the fuller form only in the 𝔊 (12:47), and one is found in the shorter form in all three texts. Interestingly, in all the verses where one or more of the texts contain the fuller form of the phrase, the people of Israel are viewed as acting as a unit. In 12:19, however, the instructions are given for the "cutting off" of a disobedient member, whether that person was a sojourner (i.e., not a "son") or a native-born person. This contextual difference may have been a contributing factor to the difference in the text. In 12:3, 6, 47, the *Vorlage* used by the 𝔊 translator probably contained the fuller phrase, עֲדַת בְּנֵי־יִשְׂרָאֵל, but even if it did not contain the fuller form, the plus would have only made explicit information that would have been known to the original audience.

The final example of a plus that makes situational (cultural) knowledge explicit is γῆ, which occurs as a plus before the word Αἴγυπτος. In Greek, this plus would have resulted in information being marked twice, i.e., in the word γῆ and also in the lexical equivalent Αἴγυπτος, which is used for the land in contrast to Αἰγύπτιος, which is used for the people. The choice of lexical equivalents in Greek is influenced by the presence of אֶרֶץ in its *Vorlage*. Two of these pluses in the 𝔊 are reflections of the plus אֶרֶץ in the 𝔐 (12:40; 13:3). Wevers, however, has failed to note this plus in the 𝔐. This failure in combination with his understanding of the translation techniques used in Exodus results in his rejection of γῆς in the critical text of 13:3. (See WeversText, 238-39.) In addition to the pluses that are shared with the 𝔐, γῆ is also found two times in the 𝔊 only, both of which may be a reflection of a *Vorlage* that differed from the 𝔐 (12:30; 13:14). In any case, whether or not the plus in the 𝔊 reflects a different *Vorlage*, there is no change in the referential meaning of the text since this information is cultural knowledge that would have been known whether or not it was explicitly stated, i.e., that Egypt refers to a geographical region.

22. Pluses in the 𝔊 that parallel pluses in the 𝔐 frequently reflect a difference in participant referencing, as follows: verbal suffix only (3ms) in 𝔐 → verbal suffix plus a proper noun in 𝔊—Ιωσηφ (13:19); zero reference in 𝔐 → pronoun or pronoun in a prepositional phrase in 𝔊—σου (13:5, 11); ἐν αὐτοῖς (37:5 [𝔊 38:4]). The pluses σου (13:5, 11) are both part of larger pluses, ὁ θεός σου, but unlike the implicit cultural knowledge that יהוה is God, the pronoun σου is organizational information that is specific to the context in which Moses is addressing the people of Israel. In another context, a different pronoun would be used to signal the relationship between God and the people of Israel.

Several words that are missing in the 𝔐 due to ellipses have been "filled in" in the 𝔊 (and the 𝔐), as follows: ἔσονται (26:3); ποιήσεις (26:10); τὸν ἕνα (26:16).

pluses in this last category highlights the ambiguity of implicit organizational meaning in the 𝔐. In most English translations, אַבְנֵי זִכָּרֹן לִבְנֵי יִשְׂרָאֵל is interpreted as an explanatory appositional phrase, i.e., "as stones of remembrance for the sons of Israel (NRSV 28:12)." In the 𝔐 and 𝔊, however, it was interpreted as an independent equative clause that provides explanatory information. The 𝔐 technically allows both readings because the organizational meaning has been left implicit, but the 𝔐 and 𝔊 have made their reading of the organizational meaning explicit through a plus.[23] As a result, the function of the stones is more prominent in the structure of the 𝔐 and 𝔊 because it is presented in a main clause, rather than being in a structure that is normally read as an appositional aside.

Some shared pluses in the 𝔐 and 𝔊 also reflect differences in the quantity of either referential or situational meaning. In the sections of Exodus examined for this book, the most frequently shared plus that reflects a true, if small, increase in the meaning is the word "all."[24] Other pluses that increase the quantity of referential meaning are explanatory phrases based on a general knowledge of the text.[25] In addition to general quantitative increases in the referential meaning, some pluses reflect the harmonizing hermeneutic that has been identified in both the 𝔐 and 𝔊.[26] These differences in the referential meaning are due to the influence of

---

23. In the 𝔐 the plus is in the form of a pronoun, הִנֵּה, which functions as a copula, whereas in the 𝔊 the plus is an equative verb, εἰσίν.

24. The word πᾶς is a plus that is probably based on a text similar to the 𝔐 in 30:27; 31:8; 35:14; 40:33. In addition, πᾶς is also found in the following verses in the 𝔊 where the 𝔐, like the 𝔐, has a shorter text: 11:3; 12:30; 13:22; 35:21 (2x), 32; 36:3. Some of these are parts of larger pluses in the text (35:32). In light of the 𝔐, it is possible that many of these pluses reflect a different *Vorlage*.

Another plus that may reflect an increase in the quantity of referential information is καὶ ἐμπλόκια (35:22). The 𝔐 contains the word עָגִיל that is translated with the same term in 𝔊 Num 31:50. There are, however, differences in the lists. Because of these differences and the difficulty of envisioning a theological or textual need to harmonize these two lists of jewelry, this plus has been included in the more general category of a simple quantitative increase in referential meaning.

25. In the second account, a larger plus in the 𝔊, which is similar to the 𝔐, is ἐκπορευομένων αὐτῶν ἐξ Αἰγύπτου (40:17). This plus makes the text like similar phrases in the Pentateuch (e.g., Num 1:1; 9:1), but more importantly it explains the meaning of the "second year," a phrase that is ambiguous when taken out of the larger context of the book. It is also similar to the plus עֹלַת תָּמִיד, which is discussed below, in that the two occurrences in Exodus (16:1; 40:17) are translated contextually and not identically.

A similar phrase that seems to provide explanatory information about the place where Moses was shown the pattern of the tabernacle is seen in the plus, ἐν τῷ ὄρει (25:9), which is also found in the 𝔐. This could be viewed as another example of the promise/fulfillment motif that will be discussed below, but the fact that it is a common phrase used throughout Exodus makes this less likely.

26. One example of this is found in 28:20. The 𝔐 contains the phrase מוּסַבֹּת מִשְׁבְּצוֹת זָהָב, which is the same as the second account of both the 𝔐 and 𝔐, מוּסַבֹּת מִשְׁבְּצֹת זָהָב (39:13), whereas in 28:20 the 𝔐 simply reads מְשֻׁבָּצִים זָהָב. The 𝔊 of the first account, like the 𝔐, uses a phrase with two participles and in addition contains a repetition of the word gold, περικεκαλυμμένα χρυσίῳ, συνδεδεμένα ἐν χρυσίῳ. The second account in the 𝔊 has modified the grammar slightly and made one "improvement" in choice of lexical equivalents similar to those discussed in chapter three, περι-

situational (cultural) meaning that affirms the unity and consistency of the text and hence feels free to "add" referential meaning that emphasizes the exact fulfillment of promises in the text and also bring the texts into agreement with texts in other parts of the Pentateuch.[27] The fact that the *Vorlage* of the 𝔊 (a text similar to the 𝔐) tended to harmonize the text, though, does not necessarily mean that the translator of the 𝔊 was always following the same principle, as may be seen in the different translations of עלת תמיד in the 𝔊.[28]

That Reflect a Difference in the Status of Meaning. The majority of pluses in the 𝔊 reflect a difference in the status of the referential, organizational, or situational meaning in the text. Most pluses fall into the category of differences in the status of organizational meaning, which includes participant referencing, i.e.,

---

κεκυκλωμένα χρυσίῳ καὶ συνδεδεμένα χρυσίῳ (𝔊 36:20). Another example of the harmonization of the two accounts is seen in similar pluses in the 𝔐 and 𝔊 in the parallel passages 28:33=39:24 (𝔊 36:31). The 𝔊 contains the respective pluses, καὶ βύσσου κεκλωσμένης and καὶ βύσσου, which result in the last phrases in each account being identical with similar phrases throughout the book.

27. For example, the promise in 𝔐 11:2 is lacking the clothing found in 12:35, but the 𝔐 has the same items in each place. The 𝔊 also contains a plus, καὶ ἱματισμόν, with respect to the 𝔐. In addition, the 𝔐 form of 11:3 contains an extended plus that includes a promise concerning the death of the first-borns. The 𝔊 does not follow this extended plus, but it does contain a plus, καὶ ἔχρησαν αὐτοῖς, which is probably the translation of a *Vorlage* similar to that of the 𝔐, וישאילום. This same verb in the qal form is found in the parallel text in 12:35 of both 𝔐 and 𝔐. The source of this difference in 𝔊 11:3 could theoretically be either a minus in the 𝔐 or a plus in the tradition represented in the 𝔐 and 𝔊, but this decision ultimately rests on the overall character of the texts.

A different type of harmonization is seen in the 𝔊 plus καὶ ἐν γῇ Χανααν (12:40), which is similar to that of the 𝔐, but occurs in a different order. According to Wevers, this is an attempt to resolve the issue of the problematic 430 years and related matters. See WeversNotes, 190. See also David W. Gooding, "On the Use of the LXX for Dating Midrashic Elements in the Targums," *Journal of Theological Studies* 25 (1974): 4, who cites early (late third century B.C.) witnesses that refer to a similar interpretation of the 430 years. The two pluses in 13:5, καὶ Γεργεσαίων and καὶ Φερεζαίων, result in a fuller list of nations similar to that in the 𝔐 form of this verse as well as in other parts of the Pentateuch. (For a discussion of some of the problems with this list, see WeversText, 157 58.) All of these pluses, however, are in the control sample and are outside of the main focus of this book. They do, however, illustrate the harmonizing tendency of the 𝔐, which appears to have been similar to the *Vorlage* of the 𝔊.

28. In 29:38, the 𝔐 contains the plus עלת תמיד, which is an exact copy of the phrase that occurs at the beginning of 29:42. This phrase is also used in the description of the same offering in Num 28:3-6. This plus in the 𝔐 may be due to a desire to identify clearly the first reference to this important burnt offering in the Pentateuch. The 𝔊 translations of these two occurrences of עלת תמיד (𝔐 29:38, 42), however, are not identical. In 29:38 the phrase is translated κάρπωμα ἐνδελεχισμοῦ, while in 29:42 it is translated θυσίαν ἐνδελεχισμοῦ. Thus, while the translator's *Vorlage*, if it was similar to the 𝔐, tended towards increased harmonization and consistency, the context sensitive approach of the 𝔊 took precedence over this type of harmonization. In both the 𝔐 and 𝔊 there is a clear difference in the quantity of meaning when compared with the 𝔐. In the 𝔐 this plus is clearly motivated by the desire to harmonize the text and make it consistent, but the plus in the 𝔊 may be simply a contextual translation of the *Vorlage* that lay before the translator.

how a participant is referred to in the text.²⁹ Pluses also include the "filling in" of ellipses and other adjustments due to grammatical differences in the languages. These types of pluses all indicate differences in the status of the organizational meaning.³⁰ The placement of pluses in relationship to other grammatical struc-

---

29. Examples of pluses that result in more explicit participant referencing may be found in the control sample and both tabernacle accounts, as follows: verbal affix (3ms verb) in 𝔐 → verbal affix plus a proper noun or noun phrase in 𝔊—Μωυσῆς (11:8); Φαραω (12:31); οἱ υἱοὶ Ισραηλ (13:20); verbal affix in 𝔐 → verbal affix plus of a pronoun in 𝔊—τις (12:48); ἐγώ (31:11); zero reference in 𝔐 → proper noun in 𝔊—Ααρων (39:1 [𝔊 39:12 (?)]); τῷ Μωυσῇ (39:43 [𝔊 39:23]); zero reference in 𝔐 → pronoun, pronoun combined with a reflexive pronoun, or pronoun in a prepositional phrase in 𝔊—ὑμᾶς (11:1b); αὐτοῦ (11:3; 12:36; 29:22); σου (11:8b; 13:12; 29:5); αὐτοῖς (12:27, 31, 35); ὑμῶν (12:31); πρὸς αὐτούς (12:50); ἐν αὐτοῖς (25:27); αὐταῖς (26:4); αὐτῶν (26:32; 28:42; 36:36 [𝔊 37:4]; 39:29 [𝔊 36:36]); περὶ αὐτῶν (28:12); πρὸς ἑαυτούς (28:43); αὐτούς (29:1, 29); αὐτὸ (29:7); ἐμοὶ (29:9); ὑμῖν ἑαυτοῖς (30:32); μοι (31:10); αὐτῆς (35:12; 40:25); ἐν αὐταῖς (35:19; 37:14 [𝔊 38:10]; 39:1 [𝔊 39:12]); αὐτὰ (35:29; 39:43 [𝔊 39:23]); αὐτῷ (38:5 [𝔊 38:24]); ἐξ αὐτοῦ (40:32 [𝔊 38:27]); pronominal suffix in 𝔐 → pronoun plus a reflexive pronoun in 𝔊—ἑαυτοῖς (12:21; 30:37); αὐτῶν (35:5). Some of these pluses are due to or at least connected with other changes in the surrounding environment (e.g., the lexical choices and interpretation of grammatical structures in 𝔐 38:5 is part of the reason for the plus αὐτῷ [𝔊 38:24]).

30. The "filling in" of ellipses or restructured translations that would have resulted in elliptical statements are frequent sources of pluses in the 𝔊. Examples of this type of plus may be found in the control sample and both tabernacle accounts, as follows: μήτραν (13:12, 13); ποιήσεις (26:16); τῆς σκηνῆς (26:35); τοῦ ἱλαστηρίου (37:8 [𝔊 38:7]); χρυσοῦς and χρυσᾶς (modified for gender and number) (37:23 [𝔊 38:17]); and χρυσίῳ (28:20; 39:13 [𝔊 36:20], which was discussed above).

In the first account, one plus (𝔊 25:9—καὶ ποιήσεις μοι) is an exact copy of material in the preceding verse (25:8). This plus in the 𝔊 does not add meaning, but simply interprets the elliptical phrase in the 𝔐 and makes information explicit according to the translator's understanding of the verse. In addition, the first clause has been joined to the preceding verses with a conjunction and the remainder of the first clause has been restructured and combined with the second clause so that it is composed of a fronted topic in a juxtaposed clause that further explains the first clause. Thus, the *waw* conjunction has been translated, not by an explicit word, but by the structure, i.e., the juxtaposing of two clauses. English translations have taken two approaches to this verse, both of which collapse the verse into one convoluted clause rather than using the elliptical reading that the 𝔊 illustrates. In the first approach (followed by NRSV and NJPS), the structure of the 𝔐 is followed, which results in a fronted, very complex topic in English, and וְכֵן is translated as an anaphoric reference ("so") to the fronted topic. These translations keep the focus on the objects, but the English sentence structure is problematic. In the second approach (followed by NIV and CEV), the verse is restructured so that the verb is fronted and translated as an imperative rather than a future with imperatival force. In addition, there appears to be no translation of וְכֵן either by a word or by a syntactic structure. This results in a much more readable English sentence, but it also results in a shift of focus from the objects to the activity. A plus that is similar to the plus in 25:9 is also found in 36:8 (𝔊 37:1), Καὶ ἐποίησαν. This plus is related to the differences in order of material between the 𝔐 and the 𝔊 and may be analyzed as a duplicate translation of the 𝔐 verb so that the clause in its new context has a verb rather than being an elliptical clause. (The translation of most of 36:8 can be found in either 𝔊 36:8a or 𝔊 37:1.)

Another language difference that sometimes results in pluses is seen in the coordination of phrases and clauses. In the 𝔐, prepositional phrases may be coordinated either as separate phrases (each phrase preceded by the same preposition) or as one phrase with coordinated objects of one preposition. While the 𝔊 generally follows the 𝔐 in conveying this type of organizational meaning,

tures is a strong indicator of the probable lack of a Hebrew *Vorlage* for at least a

occasionally a preposition occurs as a plus in the 𝔊 so that the coordinated items each have a preposition, e.g., ἕως (12:29). More frequently, however, a preposition in coordinated phrases of the 𝔐 is a minus in the 𝔊 and the 𝔊 has a related plus, τε, that signals the coordination. For example, τε is used to join the objects of a preposition (12:19), or direct objects that are marked in Hebrew with אֵת (28:1; 37:16 [𝔊 38:12]), or indirect objects (35:34). (This usage of τε could be viewed as a synonymous variant of the prepositions that are minuses in the 𝔊 of these verses, but because τε has a wider range of functions, I have chosen to treat it as a separate plus.)

Pluses may also be seen in the coordination of negated clauses. In 12:9, the 𝔊 contains an "extra" negative term due to language differences in the scope of negation, i.e., the amount of material "negated" by one negative term. In Hebrew, the scope of negation extends from אַל, at the beginning of the verse, until כִּי אִם with the result that two clauses are negated. In Greek, however, each of these clauses is independently negated with its own negative word and thus the 𝔊 contains a "plus" that occurs with the conjunction, οὐδὲ. Another example occurs in 28:43 in combination with the reinterpretation of the second clause. In the 𝔐, the second clause is a coordinate clause that is negated together with the first clause, but in the 𝔊 it has been restructured as a subordinate purpose clause and is negated separately. Thus, the 𝔊 contains the "plus" μὴ in addition to the negative οὐκ, which occurs in the first clause.

In the 𝔐, descriptive statements (e.g., ownership, attribution, identification, and location) are often communicated by means of either a noun phrase or a non-verbal clause, but in the 𝔊 these phrases and non-verbal clauses are often transformed into stative verbal clauses by means of a plus, as follows: ἐστε (12:13); εἶναι (12:42); ὄντων (25:22); ἔσται (26:2 [2x], 8 [2x]; 28:17; 30:2); ἔστιν (28:8; 29:1, 22, 26, 29, 33; 30:13; 31:14); εἰμι (29:46); εἶναι (29:46; 38:21 [𝔊 37:19]); ὄντος (30:6); ἔχοντας (36:2); εἰσιν (39:1 [𝔊 36:8]); ἔχον (39:23 [𝔊 36:30]); ἦν (40:38). These pluses may be due to translation technique or to a difference in *Vorlage*. For instance, in the first account ἔχον has a known *Vorlage* יִהְיֶה (28:32), but in the parallel passage ἔχον is a plus with reference to the 𝔐. This plus could be the result of either an independently made translation decision, a *Vorlage* that was more like that of the first account, or an attempt to make the second account more like the first. The number of other differences in this verse, however, make it obvious that if it was copied, the "copying" was not done by a scribe mindlessly following the first account. In any case, none of these pluses change the referential meaning of the text. Rather, they make explicit the organizational meaning in the text using structures that are suitable for the Greek language. Pluses of this nature are sometimes found in combination with a relative clause marker and are used to make the organizational meaning explicit rather than using juxtaposed structures as in the 𝔐. Often these pluses are found in conjunction with other changes in the text. The following pluses of relative pronouns with or without a stative verb are found in the tabernacle accounts: ὅ ἐστιν (30:13); ᾧ (35:22); ὅς (38:23 [𝔊 37:21]); αἵ εἰσιν (39:41 [𝔊 39:18]).

In the 𝔊, quotations are often introduced with the word λέγων or ὅτι. These most frequently represent the translation of לֵאמֹר, but three times these are found as pluses with respect to the 𝔐, as follows: λέγων (12:43); ὅτι (12:33; 13:14). These types of pluses are difficult to evaluate because of the naturalness of the phrase in 𝔊. They could represent either a plus that was added by the translator or a different Hebrew *Vorlage*. These pluses do not, however, change the referential meaning. Rather, they explicitly indicate the beginning of a quotation instead of allowing it to be determined by the reader.

Logical relationships between clauses are made explicit by the following pluses: ὥστε (12:42b); γάρ (13:4; 29:14); ἵνα (28:32). In addition, the highlighted nature of the fronted infinitive in 35:34 is made explicit in Greek with the plus γε. Fronted infinitives are more frequently used in Greek than in Hebrew and as a result the translator made explicit the organizational emphasis of the Hebrew by adding γε.

Deixis involves organizational meaning because the deictic reference is only relevant within the context of a specific text. Deictic reference to preceding phrases and clauses is signaled by the plus

few of the pluses.³¹ In addition to differences in the status of the organizational meaning, there are a number of pluses that involve differences in the status (implicit versus explicit) of the referential meaning.³² Finally, some of the pluses involve meaning that would have been generally known from the cultural setting, i.e., implicit situational meaning that is made more explicit in the 𝔊.³³

οὕτως (25:35). In the 𝔐, deixis was often implicit in the structure, but in the 𝔊 this has been made explicit through the deictic usage of the number one and other similar pluses, as follows: τοῦ ἑνός (26:4); ἑνὸς and ἕτερον (26:28); τῷ ἑνί (27:14). In addition, the plus ἑνὶ in 26:26 probably fits in this category. According to Wevers, the singular pillar in the 𝔊 is a collective usage and thus ἑνὶ makes explicit the fact that five bars were made for each set of pillars. See WeversNotes, 425-26.

31. For example, in 37:8b (𝔊 38:7b), the phrase מִקְצָה מִזֶּה מִן־הַכַּפֹּרֶת is translated by τὸ ἄκρον τὸ δεύτερον τοῦ ἱλαστηρίου, which follows the general order of the 𝔐 of both accounts (25:19=37:8). The copy of τοῦ ἱλαστηρίου that is a plus in 37:8a (𝔊 38:7a), however, is placed more centrally in the noun phrase τὸ ἄκρον τοῦ ἱλαστηρίου τὸ ἕν. This placement of τοῦ ἱλαστηρίου points to its probable lack of dependence on a Hebrew *Vorlage* because this would be a less natural word order in Hebrew, even though it is acceptable in Greek.

32. Pluses of this nature include the following: τοῦ πρώτου (12:18); τὰ ἀρσενικά (13:12); ἁγιάσεις (13:12); δύο (25:19); τῶν δέρρεων (26:13); ἑνὸς (26:16); ἱστία (27:13); τὴν ἁγίαν (28:3); εἰς τὸ ἅγιον (28:30); ἔναντι κυρίου παρὰ τὰς θύρας τῆς σκηνῆς τοῦ μαρτυρίου (29:10); ὕδατι (29:17; 30:19); τοῦ δεξιοῦ καὶ ἐπὶ τὸ ἄκρον τῆς χειρὸς τῆς δεξιᾶς καὶ ἐπὶ τὸ ἄκρον τοῦ ποδὸς τοῦ δεξιοῦ (29:20); τοῦ κριοῦ (29:20 [𝔊 29:21]); προτεθειμένων (29:23); ἐπὶ τὸ θυσιαστήριον (29:38); σίκλους (30:23); ἔργον (30:35); τοῦ ἁγίου (35:35); μία (38:26 [𝔊 39:3]); σίκλους (38:28 [𝔊 39:5]); τοὺς χρυσοῦς (39:16 [𝔊 36:23]); τὸ χρυσοῦν (39:30 [𝔊 36:37]). On the surface level, ποιήσει (25:38) would also appear to be a plus, but if it is a plus, then it is combined with an identical minus in the next verse. Rather, it might best be viewed as a reshuffling of the basic meaning with the verbal event being made explicit a clause earlier than it is stated in the 𝔐. In light of this, it will be listed with differences in order. Some of the above pluses were made necessary by other translation decisions, e.g., the verbal translation of בָּרָאשׁ in 12:18. Pluses like ἁγιάσεις (13:12) could be viewed as a change in the quantity of referential meaning, i.e., an exegetical gloss, but I have chosen to analyze this as the making explicit of meaning that was implicit in the 𝔐 phrase הַזְּכָרִים לַיהוָה. Other pluses, such as the long one in 29:20, could possibly be categorized as an ellipsis and thus a member of a different category, i.e., organizational meaning. While the categorizations of some of these pluses can be disputed, it cannot, however, be disputed that many of the pluses in the 𝔊 simply make explicit a type of meaning that is implicit in the 𝔐.

33. For instance, the fact that Aaron was a priest and also the brother of Moses is information that the original readers would have known, as discussed above. Pluses of this nature, therefore, are implicit cultural information that is made explicit in the 𝔊, as follows: τὸν ἀδελφόν (29:5); τῷ ἱερεῖ (39:1 [𝔊 36:8]). Additional implicit cultural information is seen in the plus ἀνδρῶν (38:25 [𝔊 39:2]), which makes explicit the fact that the "sons" of Israel who were to take part in the census in 30:11-16 were in fact only the men.

If the word τρίχας (25:4; 35:6, 26) is considered to be a plus, then it would fall into this category of situational meaning. This plus is based on the cultural knowledge that goat hair and not goats were used to make the curtains. This "plus," however, is part of a phrase that is used as a lexical equivalent for עֵז when it occurs as an independent noun. When עֵז occurs in the *nomen rectum* of a construct chain with יְרִיעָה, it is translated by the adjective τρίχινος (26:7). Positing a *Vorlage* that contained a phrase with a one-to-one equivalent for τρίχας αἰγείας would be non-productive because the usual Hebrew term, שֵׂעָר, that is translated by the lexical equivalent θρίξ does not co-occur with עֵז in the 𝔐.

While all of these pluses only reflect differences in the status of the meaning and not in the quantity of the meaning, they do at times appear to follow a different exegetical tack than that of modern translators, who sometimes allow ambiguities to remain in the translated text. This contrasting approach is seen in 39:29 (𝔊 36:36). The 𝔐 refers to a belt (singular), but the 𝔊 uses the plural noun for belt and as a result the pronoun used (a plus in the 𝔊) is also plural, αὐτῶν. This plus makes it explicit that the sons of Aaron, like their father, wore belts, as was also seen in the first account (28:40). This collective/distributive usage of the singular form of אַבְנֵט was also seen in 𝔐 29:9, where it was likewise translated by a plural in the 𝔊, though this was likely based on a *Vorlage* similar to the 𝔚, אבניטים. Modern English translations, in contrast, leave the reader with the possible misunderstanding (in 39:29, but not in 29:9) that only one belt was made, whereas it was actually one belt per person that was made. For some this is an exegetical decision, but for others it is probably just a matter of following the number of the Hebrew noun and choosing to leave it ambiguous.[34]

That Reflect a Difference in the Quantity of Meaning. Pluses may quantitatively increase the referential, organizational, or situational meaning in the text. In the control sample and tabernacle accounts, only a few pluses could be said to change the quantity of organizational meaning.[35] Referential and situational

---

34. In 39:29, the plural is used in a few translations (NJPS, CEV), but most follow the singular translation (NIV, NRSV, TEV). Osborn and Hatton advocate the singular translation saying, "since it is singular it must refer only to Aaron's 'sash.'" (Osborn and Hatton, *Handbook on Exodus*, 889.) It is interesting, though, that neither a recent Jewish translation (NJPS) nor the ancient Jewish translation (𝔊) follow that interpretation of the verse. See also Cornelis Houtman, *Exodus*, vol. 3, *Chapters 20-40*, Historical Commentary on the Old Testament, trans. Sierd Woudstra (Leuven: Peeters, 2000), 521-22 for a discussion of the belt.

35. In the control sample, a difference in organizational meaning is seen with the plus ταύτην after ἐντολήν in 12:17. The translation of this noun is based on a text like the 𝔚 הַמִּצְוָה. If the term had been left unmodified, however, a reader in a later time period may have misunderstood it as a reference to the entire Law of Moses rather than to the particular command that was referred to in that passage, though this is definitely a less frequent usage of ἐντολή. Because of this, the plus becomes almost a necessity to ensure that the verse is properly interpreted.

In the second account, a change in organizational meaning is signaled by the plus οὗτος (37:29 [𝔊 38:25]; 38:1, 3, 4, 8 [𝔊 38:22, 23, 24, 26]). This plus, in addition to the corresponding minuses of the conjunction in each of these verses, signals the change in structure from the sequential, event-oriented text of the 𝔐 to the descriptive text of the 𝔊 that focuses on the materials used in the construction, as was discussed above. This plus causes no change in the referential meaning. The source of this plus is, of course, widely debated. Aejmelaeus argues strongly for a difference in *Vorlage*, but even she notes, "This style is highly exceptional, but perhaps still not absolutely impossible in Hebrew." See Anneli Aejmelaeus, "Septuagintal Translation Techniques—A Solution to the Problem of the Tabernacle Account," in *Septuagint, Scrolls and Cognate Writings: Papers Presented to the International Symposium on the Septuagint and Its Relations to the Dead Sea Scrolls and Other Writings, Manchester, 1990*, ed. George J. Brooke and Barnabas Lindars, Septuagint and Cognate Studies, no. 33 (Atlanta, Ga.: Scholars Press, 1992), 394.

meanings, however, are often affected by pluses in the text. In this section, pluses that are assigned to the category of situational meaning are those that illustrate either an obvious attempt to harmonize the two tabernacle accounts or a significant difference in the referential meaning such that the meaning cannot be derived from the immediate context. This decision is based on the assumption that major differences in the text are most likely to be products of the cultural situation in which either the *Vorlage* or the translation was produced, rather than simply being products of the translation technique or accidents of textual transmission, though one cannot deny that accidents have occurred in the transmission of texts. Other pluses, including those that appear to be errors rather than intentional changes, will be discussed under the category of referential meaning.

Pluses that reflect a quantitative difference in referential meaning are generally explanatory in nature. Often these pluses add a thin layer of interpretive meaning to the text, such as the plus κρυφῇ (11:2) that modifies God's command to the people in a contextually appropriate manner, even though it is unlikely to have been a part of the *Vorlage*.[36] Explanatory pluses may involve the use of more specific words, the clarification of an ambiguous phrase, specification of a location, or other types of explanations.[37] Some of these explanatory pluses are

---

36. For instance, in 11:10 the 𝔐 and 𝔚 say that Pharaoh לֹא־שִׁלַּח the children of Israel out of his land, but the 𝔊 says that Pharaoh οὐκ ἠθέλησεν ἐξαποστεῖλαι the children of Israel. The 𝔊 contains all the referential meaning found in the Hebrew text of this phrase, but it also contains an additional piece of information, i.e., the fact that Pharaoh in addition to not sending them away, did not even want to send them away. This plus comes in the form of a modal verb in the 𝔊 and its probable source is the translator. This same plus is also found in parallel phrases in 8:28 and 10:4. This plus could be placed in other categories, e.g., implicit referential meaning that is made explicit, if one assumes that the 𝔐 contained this meaning implicitly. Alternately, it could be viewed as a change in the quantity of situational meaning that is reflected in a difference in referential meaning, if it reflected a larger cultural or exegetical issue. At this time, however, no larger cultural or exegetical issue has been found that would have motivated this change. Thus, it is considered to be a plus of referential meaning.

Another interpretative plus can be seen in 11:3. The 𝔐 simply states that Moses was very great (a non-verbal clause in Hebrew), but in the 𝔊, rather than using a simple "be" verb, the translator chooses a form of γίνομαι, which indicates that Moses' state of being "great" is a new state that represents a change. In the context of the verse, the plus, ἐγενήθη, would imply that this greatness is a result of God's activity rather than something that comes from Moses' inherent personality traits. This is a minor change, but it does represent the translator's understanding of the passage, an understanding that can be drawn from the Hebrew, but definitely is not explicit in the 𝔐.

The plus ποιεῖν (35:29) is a bit more complex, though it ultimately is derivable from the text. The preceding verses state that some of the people were actually helping to do the work (the spinning) and were not simply bringing the material for the work. Thus, the translator added a plus that made this passage harmonize in a minor way with the context. Another plus that may be in the text for similar reason is συνιέναι (35:35).

37. An example of the use of a more specific term is seen in the plus ἐπ᾿ ἄκρου. This plus could almost be classified as a doublet of ἐπὶ τὰ δύο πτερύγια, which is used to translate עַל־שְׁנֵי קְצוֹת (39:19 [𝔊 36:26]). By the use of this piling up of specific terms, the translator was attempting to clarify a passage that was not accurately translated in the first account. (See the discussion of the construction of the breastpiece in the next section of this chapter.)

In 𝔊 30:7 the plus λεπτόν is a copy of a specific term that is part of the description of the making of the incense for the offering in 30:36. This plus ties together two sections of instructions about

Accuracy 169

identical with longer phrases in the Hebrew *Vorlage* and thus raise the issue of whether they are pluses derived from the translation technique or reflections of a different *Vorlage*.³⁸ A few explanatory pluses are generally considered to be

---

the incense, which is especially important in light of the lack of the phrase קְטֹרֶת סַמִּים in 30:36, a phrase that more fully identifies this special kind of incense, in contrast to "strange" incense. In addition, the use of this plus, λεπτόν, helps define the boundaries of a section that begins and ends with a mention of God making himself known at the place where this incense is offered. These boundaries unite a section of the text that might otherwise appear to be a jumbled set of unrelated instructions. The translator, however, saw the unity and encouraged the reading of the text in this way by the use of lexical cohesion created by a plus in the text or possibly by a plus in the *Vorlage* that he used. Normally, this plus is considered to be a gloss, but whether a later gloss or the work of the translator, the placement of this term encourages the reading of the text as the first part of an inclusio and cannot be considered to be a random gloss that happened to be inserted into the text at this point.

In the second account, the bronze grating of the bronze altar in 𝔐 38:5 is referred to as מִכְבַּר הַנְּחֹשֶׁת, but in the 𝔊 the grating is referred to as τοῦ παραθέματος τοῦ θυσιαστηρίου χαλκοῦς (𝔊 38:24). One way of analyzing this 'plus' is that the translator interpreted הַנְּחֹשֶׁת as a substantive referring to the altar, i.e., the bronze thing, and then stated this explicitly in the translation. All other occurrences of the articulated form, הַנְּחֹשֶׁת, however, are part of the minuses in the tabernacle accounts. This lack of comparative evidence means that no firm conclusion can be reached as to the source of this plus, but in any case the information in the plus could have been derived from the 𝔐.

In the first account, the plus τῆς θυσίας (29:34) clarifies an ambiguous phrase that indicates the relationship between the meat and the ordination of the priests. This fact is probably implicit in the general context of the 𝔐 and yet the phrase that is created by the plus in the 𝔊, τῆς θυσίας τῆς τελειώσεως, is not found elsewhere in this exact form in the 𝔊 Scriptures. (The closest parallel to this phrase is found in 2 Macc 2:9.) Another example of clarification of ambiguities in the text is seen in 𝔐 29:12, where it says that "all" the blood was poured out at the base of the altar. This usage of "all," however, is relative since the text just stated that some of the blood had been put on the horns of the altar. To clarify this potential contradiction, the 𝔊 has τὸ ... λοιπὸν πᾶν, i.e., the blood was put on the horns of the altar and then the remainder was poured out at the base of the altar. This is a sensible translation and several major English translations follow this same approach (NIV "the rest," NRSV "all the rest"). In addition to these pluses, other pluses that clarify and prevent misinterpretation include the following: ἐξ ἀλλήλων (26:3); εἰς ἀμφότερα τὰ μέρη αὐτοῦ (26:21 [2x], 25); κατὰ τὸ μέρος (26:22); ἑτέρα τὴν ἑτέραν (28:7); ἐξισούμενοι ἀλλήλοις (37:18 [𝔊 38:15]); ἀμφοτέρων (37:18 [𝔊 38:14]); ἀφαίρεμα (38:25 [𝔊 39:2]); εἰς ἄλληλα συμπεπλεγμένον (39:5 [𝔊 36:12]); ἀμφοτέρους (39:6 [𝔊 36:13]); ἀμφοτέρων (39;17 [𝔊 36:24]); τῆς σκηνῆς (40:22), λειτουργεῖν (40:32 [𝔊 38:27]).

Explanatory pluses that specify the location are as follows: ἐν γῇ Αἰγύπτῳ (11:10); εἰς τὴν ὁδόν (12:39); κατὰ τὰς παρωμίδας αὐτῶν ἐκ τῶν ἐμπροσθίων (28:14); ἄνωθεν τῆς κιβωτοῦ (37:6 [𝔊 38:5]).

In the second account two pluses are found as summary statements at the end of lists or parts of lists, as follows: καὶ πάντα τὰ σκεύη αὐτοῦ (39:38 [𝔊 39:15]); καὶ πάντα τὰ ἐργαλεῖα τὰ εἰς τὰ ἔργα τῆς σκηνῆς τοῦ μαρτυρίου (39:40 [𝔊 39:21]).

38. In both the first and second account, the first reference to the ark in the 𝔐 is אָרֹן, but in the 𝔊 it is found in an expanded form—κιβωτὸν μαρτυρίου (25:10) and κιβωτὸν τοῦ μαρτυρίου (35:12). An examination of the 𝔐 shows that the phrase אֲרֹון הָעֵדֻת is not used until after directions are given for the putting of the stone tablets in the ark. After that event (end of 25:21), all following references to the ark in the first account of the 𝔐 are with the phrase אֲרֹון הָעֵדֻת, which is generally translated by a form of κιβωτὸς τοῦ μαρτυρίου, except in 31:7, where הָאָרֹן לָעֵדֻת is translated κιβωτὸν τῆς διαθήκης. (The choice of διαθήκη in this verse was discussed in chapter three.) Thus, positing a *Vorlage* that contained הָעֵדֻת in 𝔐 25:10 would not "fit" with the usage throughout the remainder of the first account. In the 𝔐 of the second account, the ark is likewise referred to simply by אָרֹן until after the completion of the construction. After that it is generally referred to by אֲרֹון הָעֵדֻת, except when it

doublets.[39] The use of a doublet is, however, sometimes necessitated by the fact that the Hebrew word can refer to two aspects of a process for which there is no

---

is the second occurrence of the term in a verse (40:3) or when the testimony (tablets) is placed in the ark (40:20). In these latter cases it is simply referred to by אָרֹן. In chapter three it was argued that the use of expanded translation equivalents for both כַּפֹּרֶת (25:17) and שֶׁמֶן (30:31) was an appropriate technique in the translation of the initial occurrences of words in some types of discourse. With these latter two terms, the evidence was insufficient for proving the source of the pluses (ἐπίθεμα [25:17]; ἄλειμμα [30:31]), i.e., whether they were glosses in the 𝔊 or whether the pluses were part of the translation technique. For the pluses of μαρτυρίου (25:10) and τοῦ μαρτυρίου (35:12), however, the evidence points to translation technique as the source due to the fact that while it is a common way of referring to the ark, it is inappropriate to posit a fuller form in the Hebrew *Vorlage* due to the larger context of the 𝔐. In addition, the use of a pronoun instead of a noun phrase in 37:5 (𝔊 38:4) points to the willingness of the translator of the second account to use translation techniques other than one-to-one, formal translation equivalents. The fact that these two expanded forms of the term are in parallel verses means that the choice was probably made in one account and simply accepted and used in the other account.

A similar plus is seen in the first occurrence of שֵׁשׁ in both tabernacle accounts (25:4=35:6). In the 𝔐 both accounts have the unmodified form שֵׁשׁ, but in the 𝔊 both have βύσσον κεκλωσμένην, which is the normal translation of שֵׁשׁ מָשְׁזָר. This plus possibly produces a slight shift in meaning in that the emphasis is placed on the material being in a particular form, i.e., spun, but this is hard to prove from the examples in the text. The fact that both pluses occur in parallel verses probably indicates the interdependence of the verses, i.e., because of translation technique or *Vorlage*, one account had the fuller form and this was copied to the other account. The only other plus with this term occurs in 39:3 (𝔊 36:10). This plus, however, is more likely to be due to translation technique. In 39:2 (𝔊 36:9) the linen is referred to by the fuller phrase שֵׁשׁ מָשְׁזָר, but in the next verse that refers back to the same item (39:3 [𝔊 36:10]), the Hebrew text used the shorter form and simply said שֵׁשׁ. The 𝔊, however, chose to maintain the same longer form, τῇ βύσσῳ τῇ κεκλωσμένῃ, when referring to the same item. This difference may also be due to the fact that Hebrew uses a construct chain תוֹךְ הַשֵּׁשׁ, which would have become more complicated with the longer form, whereas the prepositional phrase in 𝔊 allows the use of the longer phrase without any difficulty.

In the control sample, 11:3 contains the plus καὶ ἐναντίον Φαραω, which makes it more like other phrases that refer to Pharaoh and his servants in the 𝔊 (e.g., 5:21; 7:9, 10, 20; 9:8). Some of these phrases, however, also reflect a plus with reference to the 𝔐. For instance, in 7:9 and 9:8, only Pharaoh is mentioned in the 𝔐, but in the 𝔊 the servants are also present, which fits with the probable cultural understanding that Pharaoh would always be accompanied by his servants, especially when meeting with foreigners.

In 27:12 it is explicitly stated that the western side of the courtyard has ten pillars and ten bases. In the next verse (27:13), which refers to the parallel side, the overall length is stated, but in the 𝔐 the pillars are enumerated according to the three sections of that side (27:14-16). In the 𝔊 text, however, the identical nature of the two sides is emphasized by means of a plus, στῦλοι αὐτῶν δέκα, καὶ αἱ βάσεις αὐτῶν δέκα, in 27:13. This plus could have been in the *Vorlage* and it definitely does not contradict any referential meaning in the text. The effect of the plus is to emphasize the uniformity of the opposing sides of the courtyard by means of a doublet-like construction in which the same information is stated twice.

The plus κατὰ πάντα τὰ ἔργα (35:32) may be related to the minus at the end of the previous verse that was discussed in chapter three. Other pluses that may reflect a different *Vorlage*, though some are less likely, include the following: τὰ σημεῖα καὶ (11:9, 10); τοῦ μαρτυρίου (36:37 [𝔊 37:5]; 40:5, 22); ἔργον (39:5 [𝔊 36:12]). The last example, however, may simply be an attempt to harmonize 𝔊 36:12 with 39:3 (𝔊 36:10) where ἔργον ὑφαντόν occurs as a translation of מַעֲשֵׂה חֹשֵׁב.

39. For instance, in the second account the 𝔐 text has one participle, but the 𝔊 uses two par-

one-word equivalent in the Greek. A theologically important example of this is seen in the translation of כְּפֻרִים and כֹּפֶר in 30:10.⁴⁰

Pluses in the quantity of situational meaning include a variety of small pluses that indicate that the translator or his *Vorlage* understood the text in a way that differed from that seen in the 𝔐.⁴¹ Some of these statements that appear to

---

ticiples, which may be part of the translation technique, i.e., using a term similar to a term in the first account, γεγλυμμένους καὶ, and also using a second term, ἐκκεκολαμμένους, that matches the 𝔐 pattern of a participle followed by a cognate noun (39:6 [𝔊 36:13]). The plus τὸ κάλυμμα τοῦ καταπετάσματος is often considered to be a doublet (40:5). Both of these terms are used in the first account, but κάλυμμα is used as the lexical equivalent of מָסָךְ when it refers to the curtain at the gate of the courtyard in the first account (27:16). Since the translator of the second account had envisioned the curtain of the tent as being of the same type of material as the inner curtain, as was discussed in chapter three, the translator chose to combine the formal lexical equivalent for מָסָךְ with the term used more frequently for the curtain at the door of the tent, καταπέτασμα. By doing this, the translator has connected the accounts through lexical cohesion and at the same time has emphasized for the reader that this is the same type of curtain that was previously discussed and that functions to cover the opening at the door of the tent. The genitive construction is thus an appositional genitive in which the second term more clearly identifies the first.

Other examples of pluses that are possible doublets are as follows: ἀντιπίπτουσαι (26:5); καθαρὸν (27:20); ποικιλτοῦ (28:6); κατάπαυσις (35:2); καὶ συνέσεως (35:35). Other doublet-like forms that are probably due to translation technique, i.e., the use of a phrase to translate one term, are as follows: στρεπτὰ κυμάτια (25:24); στρεπτὸν κυμάτιον (25:25); στρεπτὴν στεφάνην (30:4); τὰ ἔργα τὰ τεκτονικὰ (31:5).

40. The two forms of כפר in 30:10 are translated by distinct, one-word equivalents, ἐξιλάσεται and καθαριεῖ, which capture the fact that the word כפר refers to an activity that affects both God and the altar, but in different ways. This difference is signaled both by the choice of verbs and also by the semantic function of the altar. In the first occurrence of the verb, the translator has stated that atonement is done on the horns of the altar, i.e., the altar is the location of the act that is focused toward God. In the second occurrence of the verb כפר, however, the altar is the direct object of καθαρίζω and is thus the item affected by the atoning process. Given the duel aspects of the Hebrew term כפר, the translator brought both aspects of the meaning of the term into the translation of the phrase הַכִּפֻּרִים by using a doublet, i.e., two translations of הַכִּפֻּרִים—τοῦ αἵματος τοῦ καθαρισμοῦ τῶν ἁμαρτιῶν τοῦ ἐξιλασμοῦ. Technically, τοῦ καθαρισμοῦ is a plus that could be a later gloss. This plus, however, is best explained as the intentional creation of the translator who used nominal forms of both the verbs used to translate כפר, rather than being an accident of textual transmission.

41. In the second account, the inner and outer curtain of the tent were identical in design as can be seen in the plus χερουβιμ (36:37 [𝔊 37:5]). This differs from the first account, but this difference between the two accounts is probably minimized by the use of an unusual translation equivalent, ἐπίσπαστρον, for the outer curtain in the first account, as well as a minus, לְפֶתַח הָאֹהֶל, that makes the referent ambiguous in the 𝔊 of the first account (26:36). In a similar way, the woven material of the breastpiece was also considered to be embroidered in the second account as can be seen in the plus ποικιλίᾳ (39:8 [𝔊 36:15]).

In 39:40 (𝔊 39:19), the 𝔊 contains a plus, τῆς θύρας τῆς σκηνῆς καὶ, that expands the meaning of the 𝔐 by the inclusion of the curtain at the door of the tent, which appears to be either missing in the list or incorporated into one of the generic terms. This same combination of the door of the tent and the gate of the courtyard is also part of a large plus (𝔊 38:20), which may indicate that the pluses came from the same source.

In 28:33, the 𝔊 contains a plus, κάτωθεν ὡσεὶ ἐξανθούσης ῥόας, which clarifies the text by

contradict the 𝔐 may have been found in the *Vorlage* or may have been due to an error, but the result is a plus in the text that cannot be derived from the 𝔐 itself.⁴²

---

describing the form and clarifying the position of the pomegranates in relationship to the hem of the garment. This plus, however, must be analyzed in conjunction with other changes both in the same verse and also in 28:34. At the end of 28:33 the 𝔊 contains the plus τὸ αὐτὸ . . . εἶδος ῥοΐσκους, in which the pomegranates rather than the bells are described as χρυσοῦς in the 𝔊. This same "reassignment" of the modifier "golden" to the pomegranates instead of the bells is also seen in 28:34, although the phrase, παρὰ ῥοΐσκον χρυσοῦν κώδωνα, is ambiguous. In addition, 𝔊 28:34 contains the plus, καὶ ἄνθινον, which emphasizes the floral nature of the one kind of pomegranate. As a result of these pluses, it is apparent that while the 𝔐 has only one kind of pomegranate, the 𝔊 has two kinds of pomegranates, one made of multicolored yarns and one made of gold, that were intermingled with the bells along the hem of the garment. (See WeversNotes, 459-60, for a detailed discussion of the text.) These pluses in the text may reflect an early understanding of a standard motif in both the tabernacle and the temple. While this motif with two kinds of pomegranates is not found elsewhere in the 𝔐, it is found in 𝔊 2 Chr 4:13, which describes the capitals of the columns as being covered with golden bells (an apparent contradiction since the capitals were made of bronze) and two kinds of pomegranates (δύο γένη ῥοΐσκων), rather than two rows of pomegranates. Since the capitals were made of bronze, these pomegranates were by no means identical with the pomegranates on the garment, but these references may indicate that in the Hellenistic times, motifs with bells and pomegranates included two kinds of pomegranates, flowering and non-flowering, which may be part of the justification for this "plus" in 28:33. Flowers were also a plus in the gold chains that were part of the design of the breastpiece, as can be seen in the plus ἐν ἄνθεσιν (28:14). Meyers notes that pomegranates were combined with flowers on "the stone menorah from Ḥammath Tiberias." See Carol L. Meyers, *The Tabernacle Menorah: A Synthetic Study of a Symbol from the Biblical Cult*, American Schools of Oriental Research Dissertation Series, ed. David Noel Freedman (Missoula, Mont.: Scholars Press, 1976), 54 n. 124 and L. H. Vincent, "Les fouilles juives d'el-Ḥammam, à Tibériade," *Revue Biblique* 31 (1922): 119.

A similar, but slightly modified (ὡς instead of ὡσει) plus, κάτωθεν ὡς ἐξανθούσης ῥόας, is also found in 39:24 (𝔊 36:31). Other changes in the surrounding text point towards the interdependence of the two accounts rather than one account being the exact copy of the other. The direction of that interdependence cannot, however, be decided on the basis of the information in this verse. In the second account, however, the text is more like the 𝔐 in that there are no golden pomegranates. The phrase that is ambiguous in 𝔊 28:34 is no longer a problem in the translation of the nearly identical first part of 39:26 (𝔊 36:33), because the second account follows a text similar to the 𝔐, which clearly identified the bells as being golden.

42. Wevers suggests several possible ways of understanding the plus καὶ αἱ βάσεις περιηργυρωμέναι in 27:11, but concludes that this information is not based on the 𝔐. (See WeversNotes, 437.) Gooding likewise sees it as a misstatement, but in addition he sees it as a part of the translator's attempt to "vary the expression." See Gooding, 27. Given the other problems in this section of the first account, it is likely that this is an error.

The plus of τὸ ὕψος (27:14, 15, 16) is a mistake according to Gooding. (Ibid., 25-26.) Wevers, however, tries to explain it in a reasonable manner and says, "The term probably comes from the weaving trade and designates the position on the loom, the indefinite length being the upright weave. That ὕψος means length of the hangings is clear from fifteen plus twenty plus fifteen constituting the breadth (hardly height) of the south end of the court." (WeversNotes, 439.) Nelson includes these pluses in his list of "explicating glosses." (Nelson, 295 n. 31.) One possible source for these pluses is found in the second account. The 𝔐 of the parallel account contains the phrase אֹרֶךְ וְקוֹמָה בְרֹחַב, which is part of two clauses and has been translated in the 𝔊 as τὸ μῆκος, καὶ τὸ ὕψος καὶ τὸ εὖρος (38:18 [𝔊 37:16]). Modern translators and exegetes continue to struggle with this phrase as can been seen in the variety of translations. Some have simply "deleted" the translation of בְרֹחַב (NIV). See also

Some pluses, rather than creating contradictions, lead to an overall increase of the consistency and coherence within both the immediate text and the Pentateuch as a whole.[43] Included in this type of plus are the pluses that obviously result in

---

John I. Durham, *Exodus*, vol. 3, Word Biblical Commentary (Waco, Tex.: Word Books, 1987), 485. Others, in contrast, have in one way or another equated the two terms for height and width—"along the width of it, five cubits high" (NRSV) and "height—or width —" (NJPS). While this is not quite the same problem as that found in the first account, it does illustrate the difficulty involved in describing two-dimensional items that can be viewed from several different perspectives.

In the second account, confusion seems to be the result of the addition of τῶν λοιπῶν (39:34 [𝔊 39:20]) and τὰς στολὰς (39:33 [𝔊 39:13]), though Wevers sees the latter plus as a reference back to the immediately preceding verses, which are a "major" plus. If so, this small plus functions to tie the "major" plus in with the rest of the text. Concerning the other plus, Wevers has speculated that τῶν λοιπῶν τὰ ἐπικαλύμματα, "is a cover term for all other coverings not specifically included...." See WeversNotes, 639, 642.

43. In the control sample, the one large plus is a command in 𝔊 12:10 (καὶ ὀστοῦν οὐ συντρίψετε ἀπ' αὐτοῦ) that makes the first set of commands more nearly parallel to the Passover commands in 12:46. This illustrates the same general harmonizing tendency seen in the 𝔐, as was discussed in chapter two.

In the first account, the clause τὸ πλεονάζον τῶν δέρρεων τῆς σκηνῆς ὑποκαλύψεις (26:12), which is a slightly modified version of the previous clause, is a plus that indicates several differences in the way the translator understood the text. This understanding was probably the source of other differences in the text, including what could be called a synonymous variant, i.e., instead of the fronted topic in the 𝔐, the 𝔊 has an independent clause and instead of reading הָעֹדֵף as a 3fs verb, as is done by most modern translators, the 𝔊 read the text as a 2ms verb, a reading that fits well with the surrounding context. See U. Cassuto, *A Commentary on the Book of Exodus* (Jerusalem: Magnes Press, 1967), 353, who also read it as a 2ms verb. In addition to these synonymous variants, the 𝔊 contains the plus mentioned above, which Wevers understands as an attempt by the translator to eliminate a possible contradiction. In 26:9, some of the excess was to be put over the front of the tent, whereas in 𝔐 26:12 all the excess appears to be put at the back of the tent. (WeversNotes, 418.) Nelson, in contrast, labels this plus as being caused by dittography, but this fails to account for the change from ἐν ταῖς δέρρεσιν to τῶν δέρρεων in the plus. (See Nelson, 297.) This difference may indicate a slight change in meaning or it may point to the fact that the first occurrence is a more literal translation of the Hebrew text whereas the second is a more natural usage that was possible since there was no Hebrew *Vorlage*. In either case, simple dittography will not explain this plus nor the other changes in the text. Rather, this reflects the translator's general practice of bringing increased consistency to the text through eliminating minor discrepancies, a tendency that was also seen in the 𝔐.

The plus ἀμώμους (29:38) makes explicit the fact that the lamb was without defect. The rams for the dedication of the priests have been described in this way in 29:1, so the term is known to the reader, but it is a difference in the quantity of referential meaning about the lamb. This difference is probably motivated by a desire to harmonize this verse with Num 28:3, where the lambs for this sacrifice are explicitly said to be without defect, as was discussed above in connection with the plus עֹלַת תָּמִיד in both the 𝔐 and 𝔊.

On a larger scale, the first account in the 𝔊 is brought into closer agreement with the 𝔐 version of the second account through a plus, καὶ τὴν ὑάκινθον καὶ τὴν πορφύραν καὶ τὸ κόκκινον τὸ νηστὸν καὶ τὴν βύσσον τὴν κεκλωσμένην, in 31:4. This plus makes explicit God's promise that he would fill the men with the needed skill to work in fabrics, as well as in metal and stone. The fulfillment of this promise is seen in 𝔐 35:35, but the 𝔊 form of this verse only contains an abbreviated list. This plus in the first account, therefore, may indicate that the translator had access to the second

bringing the two tabernacle accounts into greater agreement whether due to a

---

account in a form similar to the 𝔐, but did not have (or at least did not use) the Greek translation of the second account, at least not one like the current version.

In the second account, the common phrase, ἐγὼ κύριος, occurs as a plus in 35:3, which is copied from a similar (but not identical) verse in the first account (31:13). Just as the second account begins where the first account ended, i.e., with commands concerning the Sabbath, in a similar way, but on a smaller scale, the plus ἐγὼ κύριος in 𝔊 35:3 means that the commands about the Sabbath end in the second account where the first account began, i.e., the first reason stated for the Sabbath in the first account is that the people will know that ἐγὼ κύριος and in the second account of the 𝔊 this is the last stated reason that substantiates the Sabbath laws. Thus, the plus in the 𝔊 adds to the coherence of the two accounts and results in an inclusio-like bracketing of the Sabbath laws. Within the larger context of the Pentateuch, these two parallel versions of the Sabbath laws differ also in that the first account looks back to the creation while the second account looks forward, as signaled by the seemingly misplaced command about not kindling a fire on the Sabbath. This command is important because it clearly lays the ground work for the stoning of the man that was gathering firewood (presumably for the kindling of a fire) on the Sabbath in Num 15:32-36. The prohibition about kindling a fire on the Sabbath is apparently not found elsewhere, but the effect of this command on both daily living and on the construction of the tabernacle is obvious.

The plus καὶ τοὺς λίθους τῆς σμαράγδου (35:12a) brings coherence to the text by stating that the material later used in the making of the ephod and breastpiece has been brought as part of the offering. (Compare with 28:9 in the first account.) In 35:9, the λίθους σαρδίου were brought, which is parallel to the first account (25:7). Unfortunately, the first account used several terms to translate שֹׁהַם, as was discussed in chapter three. To compensate for this usage of multiple translation equivalents in the first account, the second account has both types of stones explicitly stated as being brought for use in making the tabernacle related items, which results in a plus in the second account.

In 37:10 (𝔊 38:9) the table is carefully identified by the phrase τὴν προκειμένην, which is a plus. This exact wording is not found elsewhere in Exodus, but it is the translation used for the phrase, שֻׁלְחַן הַפָּנִים, in Num 4:7. The fact that these translations are interdependent is obvious, but the direction of interdependency cannot be proven due to lack of data. This may have been the common terminology in use among the religious communities to which the translator(s) belonged, as can be seen by the fact that the bread is described with a similar phrase, τοὺς ἄρτους τοὺς προκειμένους (39:36 [𝔊 39:17]). This was not, however, the only terminology being used for the table, as can be seen by the fact that the table is referred to with a different plus, τῆς προθέσεως, in the same verse with the bread.

Likewise, in 37:17 (𝔊 38:13) the lampstand is more fully described with the plus, ἣ φωτίζει, which is similar to the description in Num 4:9, τὴν λυχνίαν τὴν φωτίζουσαν. In Num 4:9 this is the translation of a phrase, מְנֹרַת הַמָּאוֹר, which is translated τὴν λυχνίαν τοῦ φωτὸς in 35:14. Thus, the source of the plus cannot be explained, but the effect is that the lampstand, like the table, is reintroduced into the text by means of a new descriptive label.

The major plus in 38:8 (𝔊 38:26), ἐν ᾗ ἡμέρᾳ ἔπηξεν αὐτήν, clarifies the potential ambiguity about the identity of the tent of meeting and also the potential temporal contradiction concerning the time when the women "served/fasted." The major plus in 38:1 (𝔊 38:22), ἐκ τῶν πυρείων τῶν χαλκῶν, ἃ ἦν τοῖς ἀνδράσιν τοῖς καταστασιάσασι μετὰ τῆς Κορε συναγωγῆς, likewise attempts to resolve a potential contradiction between Exodus and Numbers concerning the etiology of the bronze used to make the altar of burnt offering. This plus creates a potential temporal contradiction for Western readers, but for the translator it involved a minor telescoping of two events, both of which could be placed at Sinai. The account of Korah's rebellion in Numbers 16-17 is surrounded by laws, which at a later time were all assumed to have been delivered at Sinai, as can be seen in Ezra's recital of the history of Israel (Neh 9:13-14). This indirect connection of Korah's rebellion with the giving of laws at Sinai, in combination with the lack of firm chronological connections to the surrounding narratives in

purposeful choice or because the *Vorlage* was more internally consistent.⁴⁴ These pluses do not, however, always set forth the same viewpoint throughout the tabernacle accounts, as can be seen in the difference in approach towards "pure" gold.⁴⁵

Numbers, may have contributed to the fact that the translator viewed the connecting of Korah's rebellion and the construction of the tabernacle as a minor telescoping of the time-line. By combining these two events, the translator was able to eliminate the apparent contradiction that was of greater concern to him, i.e., the source of the bronze for the altar. For a contrary interpretation of these two pluses, see David W. Gooding, "Two Possible Examples of Midrashic Interpretation in the Septuagint Exodus," in *Wort, Lied und Gottesspruch: Festschrift für Joseph Ziegler*, ed. Josef Schreiner (Echter Verlag: Katholisches Bibelwerk, 1972), 39-48. For a fuller discussion of both of these pluses and a critique of Gooding's approach see Martha L. Wade, "Translation as Interpretation in the Old Greek Exodus" (paper presented at the Fellowship of Professors, Johnson Bible College, 1999).

44. A clear example of a smaller plus of this nature is ὕφασμα κατάλιθον (39:10 [𝔊 36:17]). The 𝔐 of the first account (28:17) contains an additional phrase with respect to the parallel verse in the second account, but due to the plus in the second account of the 𝔊 the verses are identical except for the choice of verbs, which was discussed in chapter three, and the difference between the active and passive structures of the clauses.

Another example of this is the plus at the end of 35:19, καὶ τὸ ἔλαιον τοῦ χρίσματος καὶ τὸ θυμίαμα τῆς συνθέσεως, which is a slightly modified version of 31:11 (𝔊 31:11 uses χρίσις instead of χρῖσμα and also modifies the incense with the phrase τοῦ ἁγίου, a phrase that is also present in the probable *Vorlage*.) As with the reordering and plus in 𝔊 38:27, which will be discussed below, this plus (𝔊 35:19) brings the list at the beginning of the second account into closer agreement with the end of the first account. (In the first account, 31:10 refers to the priestly garments and is followed by the oil and incense. The list at beginning of the second account in the 𝔐 ends with the priestly garments in 35:19.) Thus, the two accounts are in accord both in the related minuses (25:6=35:8) as well as in the plus that makes the second account more like the conclusion of the first account. Since the oil and incense are manufactured items rather than raw materials, they have been removed from the initial list in the first account (25:6), which was largely "copied" in the second account. The confusing part in the second account is that the oil appears in two different positions in the list (𝔊 35:12a, 19). The plus in 35:19 brings the second account into agreement with the conclusion of the first account, which is immediately followed by the note that everything was done as commanded. The apparent plus in 𝔊 35:12a is actually a translation of part of 35:15 that has been reordered. Though there is repetition due to the pluses, in many ways this is similar to the translation techniques discussed in previous chapters in which the translator of the second account is trying to be faithful to his Hebrew *Vorlage* as well as trying to bring the two accounts into greater harmony.

45. In the first account, καθαρός occurs three times as a plus with gold in the 𝔊 (25:28; 28:13; 30:4). In the second account, however, the term טָהוֹר is often a minus in the 𝔊 (37:16, 17, 23 [𝔊 38:12, 13, 17]; 39:25 [𝔊 36:32]). If 𝔊 38:16 is considered to contain the translation of 𝔐 37:22, then καθαρός is also a minus in this verse. In addition, it is a minus due to the fact that it is a part of verses that are minuses in the 𝔊 (37:11, 24, 26). This appears to be a clearly contrastive emphasis in the two tabernacle accounts. The first account in the 𝔊 appears to be more concerned with the issue of the quality or type of gold than the second account in the 𝔊. Nelson sees this as evidence of the early nature of the *Vorlage* of the text in the second account. As a result he sees καθαρός as one of the "explicating glosses" added as the text developed. (Nelson, 295-96.) Wevers fails to note the difference between the two accounts and thus he tries to explain away the differences when there is no textual support for the longer phrase in the 𝔊. This also affects his reading of 𝔊 38:5, about which he says, "That Exod [𝔊] should have rendered זָהָב טָהוֹר by ἐκ χρυσίου would be strange indeed." Instead, he explains the absence of καθαροῦ in some manuscripts by saying, "Its omission was originally probably due to

In either case, the result of these pluses in the text is that the meaning of the 𝔊 differs with that of the 𝔐. These pluses, however, often co-occur with other differences in the text and hence it is the overall impact of the pluses, minuses, and synonymous variants that result in a difference of meaning in the text rather than the impact of the plus in isolation, as can be seen in the combination of different types of variants in 37:4 and 37:15 (𝔊 38:11).[46]

Minuses

The minuses in the second tabernacle account of the 𝔊 are the most frequently commented upon difference between the 𝔐 and the 𝔊. An examination of all minuses affirms the fact that there are quantitatively more minuses in the second tabernacle account and that those minuses are generally larger sections of text. A comparison of the distribution of minuses, however, shows that the same basic types of minuses can be found in the control sample and all sections of the tabernacle accounts. (See table 16.) The main difference is that in the control sample and first tabernacle account there are over three times as many minuses that reflect a difference in the status of organizational meaning as there are minuses that reflect a difference in the quantity of referential meaning. In both parts of the second tabernacle account, by contrast, most of the differences are in the quantity of referential meaning. This affirms what has been intuitively noticed in most

---

homoioteleuton." Because of this he has incorporated καθαροῦ into his critical text of 𝔊 38:5, despite the textual evidence. (WeversText, 257.) Contra Wevers, the better explanation is that טָהוֹר was often a minus in the second account and that this was part of the overall pattern of simplification that is seen throughout the second account. The word καθαρός is, however, retained as a modifier of χρυσίον with a limited number of items, as follows: chains connecting ephod and breastpiece (39:15 [𝔊 36:22]); rosette on high priest's turban (39:30 [𝔊 36:37]); material used for the ark (37:2 [𝔊 38:2]); material used for the table (37:11 [𝔊 38:9]).

46. For instance, the plus τῆς κιβωτοῦ καὶ τῆς τραπέζης (37:15 [𝔊 38:11]) at first appears to be a combination of implicit information made explicit (the 𝔐 is referring to the poles of the table in this verse) and additional information that seems out of place (the poles of the ark). When, however, one recognizes that this plus is needed because of a minus in the 𝔊 with respect to the 𝔐 (𝔐 37:4 is missing in the 𝔊.), then the information no longer seems inappropriate. The making of both sets of poles is present in both texts, but the information has been reordered. In addition, it is obvious that the plus and minus are also related to the change in vocabulary, the use of εὑρεῖς, that was discussed in chapter three. Thus, the plus in this text is related to other differences in the text and cannot be analyzed in isolation.

Another example is seen in 𝔊 28:29a, which may be viewed as a plus that consists of an entire verse, but some of the contents of this plus are very similar to the corresponding minus (𝔐 28:23-28) and thus this is best analyzed as a synonymous variant in which two different versions of the information are presented. This text and its parallel passage in the second account will be discussed later in this chapter. Another large plus that must be evaluated in light of the entire text is 𝔊 38:18-21, which shares some features with 𝔐 36:34, but is largely an independent plus. Likewise, the large plus in 𝔊 39:11-12a is based on an earlier piece of information, but is basically a plus in relationship to the 𝔐. Both of these pluses will be discussed in a later section of this chapter.

Table 16. Types of meaning in the minuses of 𝔊 Exodus

	Control sample	First tabernacle account	Core of second tabernacle account	Remainder of second tabernacle account	Totals
Quantity of organizational meaning	8	6	1	7	22
Quantity of referential meaning	5	27	32	77	141
Quantity of situational meaning	1	1	4	4	10
Status of organizational meaning	20	87	6	34	147
Status of referential meaning	2	13	14	10	39
Status of situational meaning	0	2	0	1	3
Totals	36	136	57	133	362

analyses. Most minuses in the first account do not change the referential meaning, while those in the second account result in a significant difference in referential meaning. Aside from the absence of most of the construction of the tabernacle itself, the meaning in the remainder of the minuses of the second account could be classified as explanatory details.[47] There are, however, several recurrent minuses of significant items that will be discussed below.

In the following sections, I will discuss the types of minuses found in the control sample and the tabernacle accounts using the six categories that were discussed above. These will be broadly grouped into those that reflect a difference in the status of the meaning and those that reflect a difference in the quantity of the meaning in the texts. The few minuses in which the 𝔐 and 𝔊 agree will be discussed separately before proceeding to the minuses that are found in the 𝔊 alone.

---

47. These details include items such as the material, measurements, and workmanship of the furniture; the peripheral items attached to the main pieces of furniture; and phrases that specify the placement of peripheral items and of the furniture pieces themselves. All of these minuses are listed below.

That Reflect a Vorlage Similar to the 𝕞. Minuses in which there are agreements between the 𝕞 and 𝕲 are less frequent than pluses. Of the twelve minuses identified, half reflect a decrease in the quantity of referential meaning and the other half reflect a difference in the status (implicit versus explicit) of the meaning. Differences in the status of meaning can be found in both referential and organizational meanings.

Referential meaning that is left implicit in both the 𝕞 and the 𝕲 generally involves phrases that have been repeated in the 𝔐, though other small minuses may also fit this category.[48] Other minuses are pronominal suffixes and grammatical markers that make the organizational meaning explicit in the 𝔐. In the 𝕲 and 𝕞, however, this meaning has been left implicit.[49] At times it is difficult to decide whether the organizational meaning has been left implicit or if there has been a true decrease in the organizational meaning, e.g., a loss of emphasis that was signaled in the 𝔐 through the repetition of a word or a phrase.[50]

Referential meaning that is absent in both the 𝕞 and 𝕲 is generally rather minor items or modifiers that more clearly identify an item in the 𝔐.[51] Some of

---

48. For instance, the phrase בְּשֶׁקֶל הַקֹּדֶשׁ is found in the 𝔐 in both 38:24 (𝕲 39:1) and 38:25 (𝕲 39:2), but the second occurrence is a minus in both the 𝕞 and 𝕲. The result of this minus is that the meaning is left implicit and the reader would naturally read 38:25 (𝕲 39:2) in light of the description of the type of shekel that has been given in the preceding verse. In 35:22 the word אִישׁ is a minus in both the 𝕞 and 𝕲. This minus results in a minor piece of referential meaning being left implicit. This type of minus, however, is part of the translation technique used with relative clauses throughout Exodus.

49. For instance, two pronominal suffixes on infinitive constructs are absent in the 𝕞 (28:1, 4). The 𝕲 also has no lexical equivalents for these suffixes. The organizational meaning, however, is still implicitly present in the texts due to the grammatical structure. A similar minus is also seen in 35:5 where the 3fs suffix in the 𝔐 refers to the offerings, but is absent in the 𝕞 and 𝕲. All of these may, however, be functioning in the 𝔐 to signal emphasis, another aspect of organizational meaning. If so, then these minuses reflect a loss of emphasis that was present in the 𝔐, but not in the 𝕞 and 𝕲.

In 29:41 the grammatical marker לְ that signals the grammatical and semantic function of רֵיחַ is a minus in the 𝕞 and 𝕲. This minus results in a less explicitly marked construction that is in reality probably easier to understand due to the simplification of the grammatical structure. A similar example is seen in 29:13 where the 𝔐 has הַיֹּתֶרֶת עַל־הַכָּבֵד, whereas the 𝕲 has τὸν λοβὸν τοῦ ἥπατος, which reflects the 𝕞 יותרת הכבד'. The difference in meaning between these two forms of the text is slight, though one could say that in the 𝔐 the "appendage" is seen more as an independent unit than in the 𝕲 and 𝕞. The difference is probably more organizational (emphasis) than referential. This could, however, be the result of the translation technique rather than the use of a *Vorlage* similar to that of the 𝕞.

50. For instance, in 39:25 (𝕲 36:32) the phrase בְּתוֹךְ הָרִמֹּנִים is repeated in the 𝔐, but the first occurrence of this phrase in the 𝔐 is a minus in the 𝕲 and 𝕞. The lack of this phrase does not change the referential meaning conveyed in the verse, but it possibly results in a lack of emphasis on the position of the bells in relationship to the pomegranates. Some modern translations contain a similar minus (NIV), whereas others have kept the repetition (NRSV, NJPS).

51. For instance, one of the decreases in referential meaning is due to the absence of the second item וַחֲשׁוּקֵיהֶם (38:17 [𝕲 37:15]) in a word pair that frequently co-occurs. This meaning may simply have been left implicit, but it is probably absent. Another minor item that is a minus in both the 𝕞 and 𝕲 is כֹּל (39:32 [𝕲 39:10]). (See discussion of כֹּל under pluses.) In 29:5 the word הָאֵפֹד in the 𝔐 serves to more specifically identify the מְעִיל that is mentioned in the text. This word is a minus in both the 𝕲 and 𝕞, but the affect of its absence is different in each text, as was discussed in chapter four.

these shared minuses in the 𝔊 and 𝔐 may point to a text that was shorter due to parablepsis.⁵² The fact that the 𝔊 and 𝔐 share some minuses does not, however, necessarily mean that they share every minus.⁵³

That Reflect a Difference in the Status of Meaning. A limited number of minuses in the 𝔊 reflect a difference in the status of referential, organizational, and situational meaning. Minuses that reflect a difference in the status of the situational meaning are the least frequent. Of these few examples, the source of the differences between the 𝔐 and the 𝔊 is open to debate.⁵⁴ In any case, neither these examples nor any of the other differences in the status of the meaning results in a difference in referential meaning between the 𝔐 and 𝔊.⁵⁵

Referential meaning that is left implicit in the 𝔊 often involves differences in the ways languages express things idiomatically.⁵⁶ These differences, while most frequently semantic in nature, sometimes are connected with specific grammatical structures.⁵⁷ In addition, minuses often involve referential meaning that has

---

52. Parablepsis could easily have been the source of the minus לִפְנֵי הַכַּפֹּרֶת אֲשֶׁר עַל־הָעֵדֻת (30:6).

53. In 35:14, both the 𝔐 and the 𝔊 share the minus וְאֶת־נֵרֹתֶיהָ, but the 𝔊 is also lacking a translation of the following phrase in the 𝔐.

54. For instance, the minus אָחִיו (28:4), which results in the culturally known information about Moses and Aaron's relationship being implicit rather than explicit, may in reality be a plus in the 𝔐. The source of this plus in the 𝔐 would have been derived from a desire to make this kinship relationship explicit in as many occurrences as possible. In addition to situational meaning, this minus involves organizational meaning (a 2ms suffix) that is left implicit. Another example is the minus הַכֹּהֵן (31:10; 39:41 [𝔊 39:18]), which was discussed above.

55. Some differences are more apparent than real in that they are almost required by language differences. One language difference that results in a minus (technically) in the text is the use of one word to translate a Hebrew number phrase, i.e., שְׁנֵי עָשָׂר → δώδεκα (28:21). Some of these number phrases, however, can be translated by two words, as can be seen by a comparison of Rahlfs' choice of δέκα δύο and Wevers' choice of δώδεκα in 28:21. Because of this, the effect of translation technique on numbers cannot be totally dismissed. See Wevers' comments on the differences between numbers in the first and second accounts in WeversText, 144.

56. In 12:6 the 𝔐 explicitly states that the number fourteen refers to the fourteenth day, יוֹם, of the month. In the 𝔊, however, it was sufficient to just say τῆς τεσσαρεσκαιδεκάτης τοῦ μηνὸς for the original audience to understand that the number fourteen was referring to the day of the month. Thus, the information is still present in 𝔊, but it is implicit, which represents a change in the status of the meaning. Other examples of a similar nature are as follows: כִּכַּר (29:23); לֵב (36:2, 8a); בַּיִת (40:38). In addition, doublet-like phrases in the 𝔐 are sometimes expressed by a single term in the 𝔊, as can be seen in the following examples: נֶגְבָּה תֵּימָנָה → νότον (26:18 [𝔊 26:20]); נֶגֶב־תֵּימָנָה → λίβα (27:9; 38:9 [𝔊 37:7]); קֵדְמָה מִזְרָחָה → νότον (27:13); קֵדְמָה מִזְרָחָה → ἀνατολὰς (38:13 [𝔊 37:11]). While these technically involve minuses, the use of one word instead of two is not the source of any difference in the referential meaning.

57. For instance, relative clauses in Hebrew often explicitly state that a human, אִישׁ, is involved, whereas in the 𝔊 this information was frequently left implicit, which is reflected in the minus אִישׁ (25:2; 30:33, 38; 35:23; 36:1, 2). In 37:22 (𝔊 38:16) the minus אַחַת is probably connected with the change in grammatical structure from a non-verbal clause to a noun phrase, στερεὸν ὅλον χρυσοῦν.

been stated elsewhere in the general context, though not in an identical construction, i.e., these are not ellipses.[58]

Organizational meaning that is left implicit in the 𝔊 has generally been stated explicitly elsewhere in the immediate context.[59] One type of minus in which organizational meaning is left implicit is due to the language specific differences in ellipses. As noted in the discussion of pluses, the 𝔊 "fills in" some elliptical statements in the 𝔐, but the reverse process can also be seen in 𝔊.[60] In addition,

---

As a result, the "oneness" of the hammered work of the parts of the lamp is left implicit rather than adding further complexity to an already complex noun phrase. In addition, this minus may provide further support for Brooke's suggestion about the amount of gold used in the construction of the lampstand, as will be discussed below.

58. In the 𝔐, Pharaoh's address to Moses contains two similar phrases, כְּדַבֶּרְכֶם (12:31) and כַּאֲשֶׁר דִּבַּרְתֶּם (12:32), that refer back to previous speeches. In the 𝔊, however, the second phrase is a minus. Because the two verses are closely linked, however, it is highly likely that this information would have been implicit in the 𝔊 rather than actually representing a "loss" of referential meaning.

Slightly different examples of this can be seen in the two minuses שְׁתֵּי in 39:17 (𝔊 36:24). In the previous verse it was clearly stated that there were two rings, which means that this information would have been implicit in 39:17 (𝔊 36:24), especially since the plural form of rings is used. In addition, however, there were two chains, as indicated by the use of the plural form, τὰ ἐμπλόκια. Possibly this could be a real "loss" of meaning, in that more chains could be implied, but the most natural reading would be to assume that there were two chains, one for each ring. Further, this is explicitly stated in the next verse. Thus, these minuses could represent a different Vorlage, but ultimately there is no difference in the quantity of the referential meaning. Only the status of the information is changed since it is implicit in the 𝔊.

Some of the following examples involve organizational meaning to a limited degree, but they are classified here as referential meaning if they involve nouns or verbs that do not occur in parallel constructions. Examples of this type of minus that results in referential meaning being left implicit in the 𝔊 are as follows: אַרְבַּע (25:26); הַלֻּלָאֹת (26:5); הָאַמָּה (26:16); הַמִּשְׁכָּן (26:20); בְּאֹרֶךְ (27:11); בְּלֹב (31:6); הַיְרִיעֹת (36:9 [𝔊 37:2]); עָשָׂה אֹתָהּ (36:35 [𝔊 37:3]); טַבָּעֹת (37:3 [𝔊 38:3] [2x]); יַעַשׂ (37:7 [𝔊 38:6]); אֶת־הַשֻּׁלְחָן (37:14 [𝔊 38:10]); עָשָׂה אֶת־הַמְּנֹרָה (37:17 [𝔊 38:13]); יַעַשׂ (37:23 [𝔊 38:17]); כָּל־כֵּלָיו עָשָׂה (38:3 [𝔊 38:23]); נְחֹשֶׁת (38:4 [𝔊 38:24]); וַיַּעֲשׂוּ (39:1 [𝔊 36:8]). Minuses that involve only pronouns or participants that are marked on the verbs will be discussed under the category of organizational meaning.

59. For instance, in 11:1 מִזֶּה is a minus in the 𝔊, but this same phrase occurs earlier in the verse with a different verb to refer to the same event and location. Thus, this minus leads to no "loss" of organizational meaning, but the meaning is implicit in the 𝔊 rather than explicit, as in the 𝔐. Other minuses that would fit in this category are as follows: יְהוָה (13:15; 36:1); שָׁם (29:42); מִמֶּנָּה (30:36).

60. In the 𝔐, the term כְּלִי is repeated, i.e., vessels of gold and vessels of silver (11:2, 12:35), but in the 𝔊 the second כְּלִי is a minus due to ellipsis in a coordinated noun phrase. Other common elliptical statements in the 𝔊 involve prepositional phrases. In the 𝔐, the grammatical structure involves two coordinated prepositional phrases, but the 𝔊 has coordinated objects of one preposition. As a result several prepositions are minuses in the 𝔊 with respect to the 𝔐, as follows: בֵּין (11:7); אֶל (12:1); מִן (12:5); בְּ (12:19); לְ (25:7; 28:2, 40). This type of ellipsis, however, is rare and many similar examples can be found in which the technique of ellipsis was not used. In any case, there is no difference in referential or organizational meaning, but only a change in the status of the organizational meaning. The Vorlage of the 𝔊 in these cases could be lacking the second preposition, which would suggest that the 𝔐 form contains the more frequently occurring pattern of repeated prepositions, but this cannot be proven. These examples are, however, interesting in that most are closely related pairs of items,

languages often communicate distributive meaning and emphasis by means of repetition, but Greek and Hebrew differ in this feature and this is reflected in several minuses in the text.⁶¹ Participant referencing is another area where languages

---

which would have made it more likely in both Hebrew and Greek to emphasize their relatedness by omitting a preposition.

In addition to elliptical statements, the 𝔊 sometimes combines appositional noun phrases into one noun phrase. For instance, in 26:25, the 𝔐 uses two noun phrases, וְאַדְנֵיהֶם כֶּסֶף שִׁשָּׁה עָשָׂר אֲדָנִים, to communicate the material and the quantity of bases. The 𝔊, in contrast, uses one clause with both concepts, καὶ αἱ βάσεις αὐτῶν ἀργυραῖ δέκα ἕξ. This results in a minus, אֲדָנִים. Another possible example of this type of minus is בַּדֵּי (27:6), though the difference in order seen in the textual variants also affects the analysis of this text. In 38:21 the 𝔐 has two construct chains that are in apposition, פְקוּדֵי הַמִּשְׁכָּן מִשְׁכַּן הָעֵדֻת (𝔊 37:19). These phrases include the repetition of the term מִשְׁכָּן, which creates a type of organizational meaning (emphasis). In the 𝔊, however, this repetition is gone and the appositional phrases are collapsed into one phrase, σύνταξις τῆς σκηνῆς τοῦ μαρτυρίου. There has been no loss in referential meaning, but there may have been a loss of organizational meaning (emphasis).

61. For instance, in 25:33, the 𝔐 contains a repetition of the first clause, וּשְׁלֹשָׁה גְבִעִים מְשֻׁקָּדִים בַּקָּנֶה הָאֶחָד כַּפְתֹּר וָפֶרַח, and then concludes with a statement about the extent of the distribution of these constructions, i.e., to all six "reeds." In the 𝔊, however, this repetition of the descriptive phrase is a minus. Thus the 𝔊 communicates the distributive concept by stating the item once and then stating the extent of the distribution. There is no "loss" of meaning, but rather the 𝔐 communicates this organizational meaning more explicitly, i.e., by repeating it, whereas the 𝔊 communicates the same organizational meaning implicitly, i.e., without repeating it.

The minus וְכַפְתֹּר תַּחַת־שְׁנֵי הַקָּנִים מִמֶּנָּה in 25:35 appears at first to be similar to 25:33, i.e., the last repetition is a minus. This minus, however, is combined with a synonymous variant in the preceding phrase, i.e., 𝔐 refers to two reeds whereas 𝔊 refers to four. The result is a text that is more ambiguous than that of the 𝔐. This in turn may have contributed to the fact that the translation of this passage in the parallel second tabernacle account reflects a new approach to the text rather than a copying of the translation of the first account, as will be discussed in the next section.

A slightly different form of this kind of minus is seen in 28:34. While the 𝔐 has two occurrences of the phrase פַּעֲמֹן זָהָב וְרִמּוֹן to indicate the distribution of the bells and pomegranates, the 𝔊 has one phrase παρὰ ῥοΐσκον χρυσοῦν κώδωνα. A similar minus, פַּעֲמֹן וְרִמּוֹן, is seen in the parallel passage (39:26 [𝔊 36:33]), though the translation is slightly different, κώδων χρυσοῦς καὶ ῥοΐσκος.

Likewise, the minus עָשִׂיתָ לָהֶם (28:40) does not result in a loss of referential meaning since a similar phrase occurs two more times in the verse. What this may affect, however, is the emphasis on the belts, i.e., they are "demoted" from an item of equal importance with the tunic and turban to a subordinate item that accompanies the tunic. A similar type of minus is found in 30:12, בִּפְקֹד אֹתָם. As with the previous minus, it is the middle "repetition" that is a minus and even though the repetitions in the 𝔐 are not identical, the translation of the remaining repetitions are the same in the 𝔊. The effect of the minus in 30:12 is that referential meaning is left implicit rather than being explicitly stated. The main shift, however, is probably organizational. In combination with the choice of verb forms, the minus results in the two main clauses being more clearly connected together in contrast to the subordinate ἐάν clause at the beginning of the sentence. Many English translations give prominence to the final negative clause, but the 𝔊 would probably not have been read in that manner.

The phrase אֲנִי יְהוָה is a minus in its second occurrence in 29:46. In the 𝔊 the end of this verse has been significantly restructured, which probably contributes to the minus in 𝔊. There is no actual loss of referential meaning, since this phrase is an exact repetition of an earlier phrase. The 𝔊 does, however, lack the symmetry of the 𝔐, which has the same statement at the beginning and end. Thus, the 𝔊 is probably lacking the same type of emphasis that is seen in the 𝔐.

often differ and this is reflected in pronominal references that are minuses in the 𝔊 due to the fact that the organizational meaning is left implicit.[62] A final type of organizational meaning is logical relationships, which may also be left implicit in Greek and communicated simply through the juxtapositioning of two clauses.[63] As with other differences, organizational meaning that is left implicit is often found in conjunction with other variants in the text.[64]

---

62. In 25:26, the 𝔐 says that the rings are made לוֹ, i.e., for the table. In the 𝔊 this is a minus, but the same information is communicated in the remainder of the clause since the rings are put on the "feet" of the table. Thus, even though technically לוֹ is a minus in the 𝔊, the meaning of that minus has not been lost, but rather is implicit in the text. Other minuses of pronominal forms that reflect this same change in the status of organizational meaning are as follows: אֹתוֹ (28:1; 38:23 [𝔊 37:21]); לָהּ (29:41); אֹתָהּ (36:5, 7). In addition, pronominal suffixes are often left implicit. In the 𝔐, their main function is keeping track of referents (participant referencing) and uniting parts of sentences. Examples of this type of minus in the 𝔊 are as follows: 3ms (11:5; 12:8, 9 [3x], 29, 34; 25:10 [3x], 19, 23 [3x], 25, 29 [3x]; 26:24; 27:2 [3x], 4; 28:3, 8 [2x], 16 [2x], 29 [2x], 35 [2x]; 29:14 [2x], 16, 17 [5x], 31; 30:2 [2x]; 35:5, 11 [5x]; 36:2; 37:3 [𝔊 38:3] [2x]; 37:16 [𝔊 38:12] [3x]; 39:4 [𝔊 36:11], 9 [𝔊 36:16] [2x]; 18 [𝔊 36:25], 19 [𝔊 36:26], 20 [𝔊 36:27], 23 [𝔊 36:30] [2x], 33 [𝔊 39:13] [2x]; 40:18 [3x]; 3fs (25:17 [2x], 31 [4x], 32 [2x], 34, 36; 26:3 [2x], 5, 6, 17; 35:25; 37:22 [𝔊 38:16]; 39:40 [𝔊 39:19], 40 [𝔊 39:21]); 3mp (12:34; 25:36 [2x]; 26:24, 29; 27:10; 29:28 [2x]; 30:19 [2x], 21 [2x]; 39:18 [𝔊 36:25], 20 [𝔊 36:27]; 40:15, 31 [𝔊 38:27]); 2mp (12:11 [2x]). Some of these minuses are due to differences in the ways languages handle the repetition of possessive pronouns in lists, e.g., in 𝔊 25:29 the first of four items in the list has a possessive pronoun, but the last three possessive pronouns in the 𝔐 are a minus in the 𝔊. For a complete analysis of this phenomenon in the Pentateuch, see Raija Sollamo, *Repetition of the Possessive Pronouns in the Septuagint*, Septuagint and Cognate Studies, ed. Bernard A. Taylor, no. 40 (Atlanta, Ga.: Scholars Press, 1995).

A slightly different change in the status of the organizational meaning is seen in 28:10, where the 𝔐 has שִׁשָּׁה מִשְּׁמֹתָם, but the 𝔊 has ἓξ ὀνόματα. In the 𝔊, organizational meaning has been left implicit and the reader must understand from context that these six names are half of the ones referred to in the previous verse. In the 𝔐, in contrast, this organizational meaning is made explicit by the use of the possessive pronoun and the partitive preposition. There is no difference in organizational meaning in the 𝔐 and 𝔊, but in the 𝔊 the organizational meaning is implicit rather than being stated explicitly.

63. The conjunction כִּי is a minus three times in the 𝔊 (12:15, 19; 31:14). With reference to the minuses in 12:15 and 12:19, Wevers claims that this demonstrates a change in meaning, "MT continues with a כִּי clause as though the reason for getting rid of leaven was the threat of excommunication from the community. Exod [𝔊] removes such fear as the basis for obedience by leaving out the כִּי, making the simple statement: everyone who eats leaven, that person shall be destroyed from Israel." (WeversNotes, 176.) Wevers' analysis is probably based on the assumption that juxtapositioning of clauses does not communicate a semantic relationship, but this can be easily disproved by a cross-linguistic study of juxtapositioning. See Larson, *Meaning-Based Translation*, 341-46 for a brief discussion of some semantic functions that are realized by the juxtapositioning of clauses in other languages. Rather, this minus in the 𝔊 represents a shift in the status of organizational meaning from explicit in the 𝔐 to implicit in the 𝔊.

64. For instance, in 38:26 (𝔊 39:3), the 𝔐 contains an explanatory phrase, לְכֹל הָעֹבֵר עַל־הַפְּקֻדִים מִבֶּן עֶשְׂרִים שָׁנָה וָמַעְלָה, that is in apposition to לַגֻּלְגֹּלֶת. In the 𝔊, however, the explanatory phrase is in the nominative and is the subject of the next clause. This represents a minus of a preposition, לְ, and organizational meaning is left implicit in the 𝔊 in that the reader must understand that "head" and "all" refer to the same group. By making this organizational information implicit, the

That Reflect a Difference in the Quantity of Meaning. Most minuses in the 𝔊 reflect a decrease in the quantity of the organizational or referential meaning. While minuses are present in both tabernacle accounts, the difference in the quantity of minuses between the two accounts is striking, as can be seen above in table 16.

Most quantitative decreases in organizational meaning in the 𝔊 involve pronouns and other particles that are used to communicate emphasis in the 𝔐.[65] Likewise, when the verb היה is a minus, the grammatical structure is reorganized and there is probably a loss of some emphasis.[66] All quantitative decreases of organizational meaning must, however, be closely examined because some of them may also reflect a slight change in referential meaning.[67]

---

translator was able to divide a complex non-verbal clause in the 𝔐 into two less complex non-verbal clauses in the 𝔊, with the presumed result that the text was more readable.

65. In 12:3 the phrase לָהֶם is a minus in the 𝔊. In the 𝔐, this phrase functions as a reflexive pronoun that emphasizes the fact that these are instructions for each Israelite household. While there is no translation of the phrase לָהֶם in the 𝔊, this "loss" is partially compensated for by the choice of the lexical equivalent ἕκαστος for the term אִישׁ. In addition to this example, the following pronouns, prepositions with pronominal suffixes, and other particles that signal some type of emphasis are also minuses in the 𝔊: עֶצֶם (12:17, 51); הוּא (12:30; 29:18); אֹתָם (28:14; 35:29); בָּם (29:29); לְךָ (30:23); הִנֵּה (31:6); אֹתוֹ (35:21); אֹתָהּ (35:26). In addition, the phrase לָכֶם (12:26) is a minus that involves the loss of both referential and organizational meaning.

66. For instance, the minus הָיָה changes the structure from a verbal clause in the 𝔐 to a fronted topic in the 𝔊 (39:9 [𝔊 36:16]). Comparing emphasis cross-linguistically is difficult. Ultimately, there may have been only a minor decrease of emphasis in the 𝔊 in comparison to the 𝔐. Other minuses of a similar nature are as follows: הָיָה (12:25; 13:14); יְהִי (13:15, 17); יִהְיֶה (28:32).

67. For instance, אַהֲרֹן וּבָנָיו, which is in apposition to אֹתָם, is a minus in 𝔊 29:9. At first glance this minus appears to be an appropriate adjustment in that the same participants (apparently) have just been referred to with אֹתָם and the minus is an emphatic identification of the 3p referents. Thus, at the most this minus would represent a loss of organizational meaning, i.e., emphasis. Without this phrase, however, the text can be read in a slightly different manner, i.e., 29:5-7 only refers to Aaron and 29:8-9a only refers to the sons. This may even be viewed as a correction in that Aaron, as high priest, wears the μίτρα (29:6), but not the κίδαρις (29:9). See Osborn and Hatton, *Handbook on Exodus*, 683-84 for a discussion of this variant and of HOTTP's B rating of the 𝔐 text, אַהֲרֹן וּבָנָיו. See Dominique Barthélemy and others, *Preliminary and Interim Report on the Hebrew Old Testament Text Project*, vol. 1, *Pentateuch* (New York: United Bible Societies, 1973), 137.

In 40:16, the minus כְּ reflects a relatively small, but significant change of meaning that emphasizes the completeness of Moses fulfillment of God's authoritative commands. Moses did not just complete things within the parameters of what was commanded (as in the 𝔐). Instead, he actually did all that God authoritatively commanded. See chapters three and four for a more comprehensive discussion of this phrase.

The minus יִהְיֶה לָכֶם (35:2) makes the 𝔊 text more like the parallel 𝔊 text (31:15), but the verses are still not identical. Phrases identical to this are regularly translated literally in the 𝔊 (12:5, 16; 30:32). This minus, therefore, raises the possibility that the translator either had a different *Vorlage* or intentionally tried to make the accounts more nearly similar, as was seen with the plus ἐγὼ κύριος (35:3), which was discussed above. In either case, this minus is a loss of organizational meaning and not of any substantial referential meaning.

Most minuses that affect referential meaning are also small and have a relatively slight impact on the whole text.⁶⁸ A few of these minuses, however, are related to other differences in the text and therefore must be evaluated in context before determining their impact on referential meaning.⁶⁹ When contexts are

---

68. The minus כָּל is often connected with other changes in relative clauses. This word was discussed above in connection with pluses, but minuses involving כָּל have been listed here for the sake of completeness. Minuses that involve a relatively small decrease in referential meaning are as follows: כָּל (12:50; 27:19; 31:7; 35:21 [2x], 23, 24; 36:4, 7; 38:22 [𝔊 37:20]; 38:31 [𝔊 39:8] [2x]; 39:33 [𝔊 39:13]; 40:36); שִׁטִּים (26:37); הַשֵּׁנִי (28:5; 35:25, 35; 38:23 [𝔊 37:21]; 39:1 [𝔊 39:12]); תָּמִיד (28:29); וְחַלֹּת מַצֹּת (29:2); חֻקַּת (29:9); וְהָאֵלְיָה (29:22—See chapter two for a discussion of variants in the 𝔐 and related problems.); אַיִל (29:22); אַחַת . . . חַלַּת לֶחֶם (29:23); מְקֻטַּר (30:1); עֲבֹדַת (36:1, 3); הָעֲבֹדָה (36:5); סָבִיב (38:16 [𝔊 37:14]); הַבַּד (39:28 [𝔊 36:35]); מְשֻׁזָּר (39:29 [𝔊 36] [See also the above discussion of pluses in the translation of שֵׁשׁ.]); תְּכֵלֶת (39:32 [𝔊 39:9]); כְּכֹל (39:42 [𝔊 39:22]); שָׁם (40:3); הָעֶרֶת (40:5). A few of these minuses involve terms that have sometimes been considered doublets and thus may result in relatively little loss of referential meaning.

69. The minus זָהָב (25:25) may fall in the category of a decrease in the quantity of referential meaning, if one accepts Wevers' analysis. (WeversNotes, 403.) This minus, however, might be better classified as a change in the status of the referential meaning. The items before and after this minus in the text are specifically said to be golden or made of gold. Because of this it seems likely that the original readers would have assumed that the molding was likewise gold. Thus, the minus may represent simply a change in status from explicit to implicit information. A closer examination of the text indicates that the meaning may have been reorganized, but not left implicit. In 25:24, the 𝔐 uses the singular word זֵר, but the 𝔊 uses a plural phrase στρεπτὰ κυμάτια. Since this is the same term used for the item whose construction material is disputed in the next verse, it seems likely that the plural word in the 𝔊 (𝔊 25:24) refers to both of the זֵר in the 𝔐 (25:24, 25). If this is the correct understanding of the plural in the 𝔊, then in the 𝔊 as well as in the 𝔐, both of these items are golden and there has been no real change in the quantity of the referential meaning of the text. In 25:11, however, the singular זֵר has also been translated by a plural, κυμάτια στρεπτά, in contrast to the זֵר on the incense altar, which was translated by a singular, στρεπτὴν στεφάνην (30:3). The use of the plural form with the ark may point to the fact that the translator envisioned a similarity in construction between the ark and the table, i.e., that both of them had two moldings. This would be similar to the grouping of the golden altar and bronze altar that will be discussed below. This would also affirm the grouping of the ark and table seen in the second account when the poles of the table and ark are combined in 𝔊 38:11. The singular molding of the ark in the 𝔐 was, however, more accurately translated in the second account, which according to the critical text reads κυμάτιον χρυσοῦν (37:2 [𝔊 38:2]). This phrase is missing in some of the older Greek manuscripts, but Wevers dismisses this as a simple case of parablepsis in WeversText, 257. For a further discussion of זֵר, see Houtman, *Exodus*, 376-77 and 394-95.

In 11:3, the phrase וּבְעֵינֵי הָעָם is a minus in the 𝔊. Strictly speaking this minus represents a quantitative decrease of referential meaning in the 𝔊, but because of other changes in the text, i.e., the translation of בְּאֶרֶץ מִצְרַיִם by ἐναντίον τῶν Αἰγυπτίων, the referent, i.e., the (Egyptian) people, is still explicitly stated in the 𝔊. As a result of these changes, the information that is lacking an equivalent in the 𝔊 is בְּאֶרֶץ מִצְרַיִם, if that phrase does actually refer to the geographical territory rather than to the inhabitants of that geographical territory. See, however, Osborn and Hatton, who say, "**In the land of Egypt** may be omitted (see TEV), since this is understood by the reference to **the Egyptians**." (Osborn and Hatton, *Handbook on Exodus*, 260.)

In 25:24, the phrase וְצִפִּיתָ אֹתוֹ זָהָב טָהוֹר, which describes the construction of the golden table, is a minus in the 𝔊. This minus, however, is related to a synonymous variant in the preceding verse and will be discussed below. The minus מִסְבְּצֹת זָהָב תַּעֲשֶׂה אֹתָם (28:11) is connected with differences in the following text about the construction of the breastpiece, which will be dis-

examined carefully, a few differences in referential meaning are found to be more apparent than real.[70] Minuses of referential meaning sometimes also involve the

---

cussed in the next section. The minus לָשֵׂאת אֶת־הַשֻּׁלְחָן (37:15 [𝔊 38:11]) is "required" due to the fact that this verse in the 𝔊 refers to both the poles of the table and the poles of the ark. Translating this part of the verse literally would have created a problem in the text. The minus הַזָּהָב (39:38 [𝔊 39:15]) in conjunction with the absence of the following verse (39:39), has raised many questions about which altar is being discussed in the 𝔊 and at what stage the incense altar was known in the cult. Wevers in WeversNotes, 640, argues that this text refers to the bronze altar because of its combination with the phrase "and its vessels," which is connected with the bronze altar in the next verse, as well as the lack of references elsewhere to the golden altar. See, however, my discussion of this issue later in this chapter.

The minus לְפֶתַח הָאֹהֶל (26:36) is one of many differences in the 𝔊 with respect to the 𝔐 that has resulted in confusion about the curtains of the tent and the related issue of the placement of the incense altar in Heb 9:4. This particular minus results in a quantitative decrease in referential meaning. Other related minuses are as follows: הַמָּסָךְ (35:12); אֶת־מָסַךְ הַפֶּתַח לְפֶתַח הַמִּשְׁכָּן (35:15); וְאֵת מָסַךְ פֶּתַח הָאֹהֶל (39:38 [𝔊 39:15]); וַיָּשֶׂם אֶת־מָסַךְ הַפֶּתַח לַמִּשְׁכָּן (40:28—This minus is an entire verse.). In addition, there are several minuses related to the courtyard curtain that are mentioned below. For a fuller discussion of the problems created by these minuses and the choice of lexical equivalents for the curtain at the gate of the courtyard and the two curtains of the tent, see Wade, "Translation as Interpretation."

A minus of a slightly different nature, עֹמְדִים (26:15), may be connected with the choice of lexical equivalents in the 𝔊. Since הַקְּרָשִׁים is translated using the term στύλους, it may no longer have been necessary to specify that they were עֹמְדִים. This also applies to the minus אֹרֶךְ (26:16), which could have created a collocational clash, as discussed in chapter three. Likewise, the minus שְׁתֵּי (27:7) is technically a "loss" of referential meaning, but because of the choice of lexical equivalents and the use of the plural, τὰ πλευρά, the reader would almost certainly have assumed that there were two sides.

The clause וַיָּשֶׂם אֶת־קְרָשָׁיו (40:18) may technically be a minus, but due to assimilation the same lexical equivalent is used for both קֶרֶשׁ and עַמּוּד, both of which occur in this verse. As is the practice with other such occurrences and with other examples of assimilation, one of the terms is "dropped." Since the pillars are stood up at the end of the verse in the 𝔐, it may be that this "minus" is due to the choice of lexical equivalents, i.e., the pillars could not be both "put" and "stood up" in the 𝔊.

In the 𝔊, 𝔐 37:4, which describes the making of the poles for the ark, is a minus, but these poles "reappear" in a plus in 37:15 (𝔊 38:11) that describes their construction along with the construction of the poles of the table. The reason for the minus (37:4) is unknown, but it is interdependent on the synonymous variant in 37:5 (𝔊 38:4). In the 𝔐, the poles are moved into the rings along the side of the ark, but in the 𝔊, the rings are simply described as being wide enough for the poles. This lexical equivalent is used because of the fact that the poles had not yet been made in the 𝔊. See the discussion of this issue in chapter three.

Other minuses that might fit in this category are as follows: הַמִּשְׁכָּן (27:19); הַדָּבָר (29:1); מְלָאכָה (35:31); יְהוָה (40:38).

70. For instance, in 39:3 (𝔊 36:10) וַיְרַקְּעוּ and וְקִצֵּץ are translated by καὶ ἐτμήθη. The first activity, רקע, is technically a minus, but the fact that it is thin sheets of gold that are cut shows that the first activity in the 𝔐 is presumed to have happened in the 𝔊. The focus has been shifted from the agents in the 𝔐 to the objects in the 𝔊, as shown by the use of the passive. This shift in focus may partially account for the first activity being a minus in the 𝔊.

A similar example occurs in 39:33 (𝔊 39:13) where הַמִּשְׁכָּן is apparently a minus. The referent of הַמִּשְׁכָּן is, however, referred to by the translation of אֶת־הָאֹהֶל and thus this minus does not ultimately result in the loss of referential meaning due to assimilation of lexical equivalents. Combined

"loss" of organizational meaning (emphasis) that was present in the 𝔐.[71] Longer phrases that are minuses, however, sometimes result in a significant loss of meaning, although often the meaning lost is not essential for understanding the main point of the text. Some of this loss of referential meaning may be purposeful in that it corrects problems that could arise in interpreting the text.[72]

---

with this minus, however, is the plus τὰς στολὰς, which has been much discussed in the literature. See Gooding, 89-91, who views this as some of the "floating debris in the Greek text." According to Gooding, "it is the Greek and not the Hebrew order that has suffered change." Gooding's discussion also includes a summary of Popper's view. Wevers, in contrast, describes τὰς στολὰς as a substitution for הַמִּשְׁכָּן and says that τὰς στολὰς ties this verse to the preceding section and combined with "'tent' serves as a kind of superscription for the materials that follow, . . ." See WeversNotes, 639.

In addition, the phrase מִשְׁכַּן אֹהֶל מוֹעֵד, which is translated τὴν σκηνὴν τοῦ μαρτυρίου, could be described as containing a minus, מִשְׁכַּן (40:2). This difference, however, is probably due to the translation technique that has been discussed in previous chapters. Other examples of this phrase are as follows: 39:32 (𝔊 39:9b); 40:6, 29.

71. In 12:41, the clause וַיְהִי בְּעֶצֶם הַיּוֹם הַזֶּה is a minus in the 𝔊. The main function of this clause, however, is to emphasize the time frame for the exodus from Egypt, which has just been stated. Thus, there is a decrease of emphasis in the 𝔊. Smaller minuses of the same nature, עֶצֶם, were discussed above.

72. For instance, 30:37 identifies the incense using a relative clause, אֲשֶׁר תַּעֲשֶׂה בְּמַתְכֻּנְתָּהּ, but then immediately says that you will not make it. In the 𝔊, אֲשֶׁר תַּעֲשֶׂה is a minus and thus the apparent contradiction of making and not making is eliminated, while at the same time the incense is still carefully enough identified so that there would be no loss in overall referential meaning.

One minus that results in a more significant loss of referential meaning in the control sample is לְהָאִיר לָהֶם לָלֶכֶת יוֹמָם וָלָיְלָה (13:21). In addition, there are a few minuses in the first account that result in a loss of referential meaning, as follows: וְאֶת־בִּגְדֵי (31:9); וְאֶת־כָּל־כֵּלָיו (27:19); וְכָל־יְתֵדֹתָיו (31:10).

In the second tabernacle account the nature of these "more significant" minuses that are only partial verses is best understood when they are grouped according to the items that are being described. Minuses that fit into this category are related to the following items:

minuses related to materials collected and workmen—
    תְּכֵלֶת וְאַרְגָּמָן וְתוֹלַעַת שָׁנִי and וְעִזִּים (35:23);
    לְמַלֹּאת (35:33);
    וְאָרַג (35:35);
    בַּתְּכֵלֶת וּבָאַרְגָּמָן (35:35);
    בֶּן־חוּר (38:22 [𝔊 37:20]);
    בַּתְּכֵלֶת וּבָאַרְגָּמָן (38:23 [𝔊 37:21]);
minuses related to the tabernacle—
    וְאֶת־קְרָשָׁיו (35:11);
    וְאֶת־אֲדָנָיו (35:11);
    שֵׁשׁ מָשְׁזָר וּתְכֵלֶת וְאַרְגָּמָן וְתוֹלַעַת שָׁנִי כְּרֻבִים מַעֲשֵׂה חֹשֵׁב עָשָׂה אֹתָם (36:8 [𝔊 37:1]);
    לַמִּשְׁכָּן וְ (38:20 [𝔊 37:18]);
    קְרָסָיו קְרָשָׁיו (39:33 [𝔊 39:13]);
minuses related to the ark—
    עֲצֵי שִׁטִּים אַמָּתַיִם וָחֵצִי אָרְכּוֹ וְאַמָּה וָחֵצִי רָחְבּוֹ וְאַמָּה וָחֵצִי קֹמָתוֹ (37:1 [𝔊 38:1]);
    עַל אַרְבַּע פַּעֲמֹתָיו (37:3 [𝔊 38:3]);
    אַמָּתַיִם וָחֵצִי אָרְכָּהּ וְאַמָּה וָחֵצִי רָחְבָּהּ (37:6 [𝔊 38:5]);
    מִקְשָׁה עָשָׂה אֹתָם מִשְּׁנֵי קְצוֹת הַכַּפֹּרֶת (37:7 [𝔊 38:6]);
    עָשָׂה אֶת־הַכְּרֻבִים מִשְּׁנֵי קְצוֹתָיו (37:8 [𝔊 38:7]);

Small quantitative decreases in referential meaning should not be ignored because these decreases occasionally appear to be purposeful corrections of the

וַיִּהְיוּ הַכְּרֻבִים פֹּרְשֵׂי כְנָפַיִם לְמַעְלָה (37:9 [𝕲 38:8]);
וּפְנֵיהֶם אִישׁ אֶל־אָחִיו אֶל־הַכַּפֹּרֶת הָיוּ פְּנֵי הַכְּרֻבִים (37:9 [𝕲 38:8]);
וְאֶת־הַכַּפֹּרֶת (39:35 [𝕲 39:14]);
וַיִּתֵּן אֶת־הַכַּפֹּרֶת עַל־הָאָרֹן מִלְמָעְלָה (40:20);
minuses related to the lampstand—
וְאֵת שֶׁמֶן הַמָּאוֹר (35:14);
וְאֶת־הַשֶּׁמֶן לַמָּאוֹר (35:28);
וְאֶת־כָּל־כֵּלֶיהָ (39:37 [𝕲 39:16]);
נֹכַח הַשֻּׁלְחָן (40:24);
minuses related to the table—
וְאֶת־בַּדָּיו (35:13);
וְאֵת לֶחֶם הַפָּנִים (35:13);
עֲצֵי שִׁטִּים אַמָּתַיִם אָרְכּוֹ וְאַמָּה רָחְבּוֹ וְאַמָּה וָחֵצִי קֹמָתוֹ (37:10 [𝕲 38:9]);
וַיְצַפֵּהוּ (37:11 [𝕲 38:9]);
וַיַּעַשׂ לוֹ זֵר זָהָב סָבִיב (37:11 [𝕲 38:9]);
הָיוּ הַטַּבָּעֹת לְעֻמַּת הַמִּסְגֶּרֶת (37:14 [𝕲 38:10]);
עֲצֵי שִׁטִּים (37:15 [𝕲 38:11]);
minuses related to the incense altar—
וְאֶת־מִזְבַּח הַקְּטֹרֶת וְאֶת־בַּדָּיו (35:15 [𝕲 35:12a]);
הַזָּהָב (39:38 [𝕲 39:15]);
minuses related to the altar of burnt offering—
הָעֹלָה וְאֶת־מִכְבַּר הַנְּחֹשֶׁת אֲשֶׁר־לוֹ אֶת־בַּדָּיו (35:16);
עֲצֵי שִׁטִּים חָמֵשׁ אַמּוֹת אָרְכּוֹ וְחָמֵשׁ־אַמּוֹת רָחְבּוֹ רָבוּעַ וְשָׁלֹשׁ אַמּוֹת קֹמָתוֹ (38:1 [𝕲 38:22]);
וְאֶת־הַיָּעִים (38:3 [𝕲 38:23]);
וַיָּבֵא אֶת־הַבַּדִּים בַּטַּבָּעֹת עַל צַלְעֹת הַמִּזְבֵּחַ (38:7 [𝕲 38:24]);
נְבוּב לֻחֹת עָשָׂה אֹתוֹ (38:7 [𝕲 38:24]);
minuses related to the laver—
אֶת־הַכִּיֹּר וְאֶת־כַּנּוֹ (35:16);
בֵּין־אֹהֶל מוֹעֵד וּבֵין הַמִּזְבֵּחַ וַיִּתֵּן שָׁמָּה מַיִם לְרָחְצָה (40:30 [𝕲 38:27]);
minuses related to the courtyard—
וְאֶת־אֲדָנֶיהָ וְאֵת מָסַךְ שַׁעַר הֶחָצֵר (35:17 [𝕲 35:12a]);
נְחֹשֶׁת וָוֵי הָעַמֻּדִים וַחֲשֻׁקֵיהֶם כָּסֶף (38:10 [𝕲 37:8]);
נְחֹשֶׁת וָוֵי הָעַמֻּדִים וַחֲשֻׁקֵיהֶם כָּסֶף (38:11 [𝕲 37:9]);
וָוֵי הָעַמּוּדִים וַחֲשׁוּקֵיהֶם כָּסֶף (38:12 [𝕲 37:10]);
אֶת־מֵיתָרָיו (39:40 [𝕲 39:19]);
וְנָתַתָּ אֶת־מָסַךְ שַׁעַר הֶחָצֵר (40:8);
וַיִּתֵּן אֶת־מָסַךְ שַׁעַר הֶחָצֵר (40:33);
minuses related to the garments—
הַשְּׂרָד (35:19);
בַּקֹּדֶשׁ (35:19);
אֲפֻדָּתוֹ אֲשֶׁר (39:5 [𝕲 36:12]);
בְּמִלֻּאֹתָם (39:13 [𝕲 36:20]);
פַּאֲרֵי (39:28 [𝕲 36:35]);
אֶת־בִּגְדֵי הַשְּׂרָד לְשָׁרֵת בַּקֹּדֶשׁ (39:41 [𝕲 39:18]).

In addition to these minuses, there are verses and entire sections that are also minuses, as will be listed below.

text due to the situational meaning.⁷³ These kinds of decreases in referential meaning are often related to other variants in the text that reflect situational meaning, e.g., the translator's hermeneutical approach that results in the absence of the bronze altar from the list in 38:30 (𝔊 39:9).⁷⁴ In addition to minuses that are parts of verses, there are in both accounts, but especially the second account, entire verses and large sections that are minuses in the 𝔊.⁷⁵ Accounting for these is one of the major problems in the tabernacle accounts that will be discussed below.

---

73. In 13:11, the 𝔊 contains a small minus, לְךָ, that may be a correction of the referential meaning. The 𝔐 says that God made an oath to "you" and your fathers. Since there is no record of God making this oath directly to the people being addressed by Moses, this minus may be a correction by the translator. (See WeversNotes, 199.) Assuming that this was not an accidental minus, this would be classified as a quantitative decrease in referential meaning due to the translator's culture (situational meaning), which required that the text be consistent from the perspective of the reader. This minus also makes the text more like similar phrases in Deuteronomy, e.g., Deut 6:10, in which the promise is just to "your fathers," rather than to "you," even though the "you" is affected by the promise.

⁷⁴In 38:1 (𝔊 38:22) the 𝔊 contains a large plus that harmonizes Numbers 16-17 with the construction of the bronze altar in Exodus. In that plus, the material for the altar itself is said to be the firepans of Korah's congregation. Because of this plus, there is a corresponding minus, וְאֵת מִזְבַּח הַנְּחֹשֶׁת (38:30 [𝔊 39:9]), which eliminates the bronze altar (but not the grating and other items) from the list of items that are constructed from the bronze that was given by the people. This minor minus, then, is an important part of the harmonizing hermeneutic of the translator (or of his *Vorlage*) and cannot be treated in isolation as a minor minus of referential meaning. This minus also leads to a synonymous variant (change in participant referencing) that is found in the next phrase, i.e., because the noun (bronze altar) is a minus, the following pronominal suffix that refers to the altar in the 𝔐 phrase, אֲשֶׁר־לוֹ, had to be translated by a noun, τοῦ θυσιαστηρίου, rather than by a pronoun (38:30 [𝔊 39:9]).

In 36:36 (𝔊 37:4), the minus יִצֹק לָהֶם, which results in a quantitative decrease of referential meaning, is just one of many adjustments that makes this verse more nearly similar to the parallel verse in the first account (26:32) and shifts the focus from the constructing to the assembling of the pillars and curtain, as discussed in chapter three.

The minus וְזָהָב תְּכֵלֶת וְאַרְגָּמָן תּוֹלַעַת שָׁנִי (28:6) reflects an exegetical approach similar to that which was seen in the 𝕸, though not reflecting the exact text of the 𝕸. This exegetical difference may be due to the translator's or his *Vorlage*'s desire to harmonize the instructions and the fulfillment of those commands, as was discussed in chapter two.

In 40:29 the minus וַיַּעַל עָלָיו אֶת־הָעֹלָה וְאֶת־הַמִּנְחָה כַּאֲשֶׁר צִוָּה יְהוָה אֶת־מֹשֶׁה was "necessary" because offerings were not offered until after the ordination of the priest, which is described in Leviticus. Because of the translator's (or his *Vorlage*'s) harmonizing hermeneutic, this part of the verse is a minus.

The differences between the translation of טָהוֹר in the first and second accounts have been discussed above. While this does not represent a major difference in meaning, the consistency of the difference points to a purposeful choice either by the translator or in his *Vorlage*. The word טָהוֹר is a minus in 37:16, 17, 22, 23 (𝔊 38:12, 13, 16, 17); 39:25 (𝔊 36:32).

75. In the first account, only 25:6 is a minus. (In addition, 28:23-28 is missing, but this has been treated as a synonymous variant with respect to the plus 𝔊 28:29a and will be discussed in the next section.) In the second account, the following verses, which have been grouped according to content, are minuses: oil and spices (35:8); items related to tabernacle and courtyard (35:18; 36:10-33); items related to the table (37:12); items related to material of the lampstand (37:24); items related to

Synonymous Variants

Synonymous variants in this chapter are defined as differences between the 𝔐 and 𝔊 that cannot be easily explained on the basis of pluses, minuses, or choices of lex-

---

the incense altar (37:25-28); items related to the bronze altar (38:2, 6; 39:39a); items related to the laver (39:39b; 40:7, 11). In addition, 36:34 is probably a minus, though most of the elements of the verse are seen in 𝔊 38:18. Many of these minuses are due to the effect of situational meaning in the form of the translator's or editor's intent. Most of these minuses have been discussed elsewhere in this chapter and a few more will be discussed below.

Exodus 39:39, which refers to the bronze altar, laver, and related items, is a minus in the 𝔊 that cannot be easily explained. Some argue that the altar in 39:38 (𝔊 39:15) refers to the bronze altar since the gold altar is never described as being accompanied by vessels. Numbers 4:12, however, appears to refer to vessels that are in some way connected with the gold altar and are distinct from the vessels of the bronze altar, which are described in Num 4:14. Thus, this plus, καὶ πάντα τὰ σκεύη αὐτοῦ (39:38 [𝔊 39:15]), may harmonize this detail that might appear to be a difference between the two accounts. It is possible that the bronze altar and the laver are absent from the list in 39:39 due to the unusual sources of their material, a fact that is only mentioned in the second account and is not a part of God's instructions in the first account. Whether the minus was intentional, a result of the *Vorlage*, or simply an accident of textual transmission, the result fits well with the harmonizing tendencies that have been noted in the translation. The absence of the bronze altar, laver, and related items from the list of items brought to Moses means that a possible contradiction is avoided in that the translation does not state that these items were made according to God's instructions to Moses. This, however, is only speculation and thus this minus remains one of the minuses that is more difficult to explain. More important, perhaps, is the fact that the laver and associated items are treated as a unit with the bronze altar in this verse.

The bronze laver is also a separate minus in several verses, but like the bronze altar, each context must be examined individually to determine the reason for the minus. For instance, in 35:16 the bronze laver and its stand is a minus, but it is not the only minus. The grating and poles are also minuses. In the abbreviated form of the 𝔊, only the essential, unmodified item and a generic summary of the accompanying items are mentioned, καὶ τὸ θυσιαστήριον καὶ πάντα τὰ σκεύη αὐτοῦ. As with 39:38, however, this phrase is ambiguous because only one altar is mentioned in the 𝔊 translation of 35:15-16. The verses containing the instructions for the placement of the laver and the anointing of the laver (40:7, 11) are also minuses in the 𝔊, but these minuses are best seen in light of 35:16. Just as the laver was subsumed under the generic term, καὶ πάντα τὰ σκεύη αὐτοῦ, in 35:16, so also it is included in a similar phrase in 40:10 and is not listed separately in the instructions in order to maintain the consistency of the passages. In the 𝔊, the laver is not attributed a high status. Rather, it is relegated to simply one of the pieces of equipment associated with the bronze altar.

Brooke suggested that the absence of 37:24 in the 𝔊 may be due to an exegetical issue in the 𝔐, i.e., "whether the lampstand, and all its lamps and connected utensils were made from one talent of gold, or whether the lampstand alone was made from one talent, another talent being used for everything else." In 𝔊 25:39 this problem is resolved in favor of the use of two talents, as can be seen in the translation πάντα τὰ σκεύη ταῦτα. Brooke says that this solution is similar to the dual form, ככרים, found in the Temple Scroll that refers to the amount of gold for the lampstand, i.e., two talents of gold total being used. Thus, the absence of 37:24 in the second account of the 𝔊 seems to confirm that interpretation. Brooke says, "Perhaps the LXX omits any mention of the amount of pure gold because for Exodus 25 the decision has already been made to interpret the Hebrew to mean that two talents of gold were required. To this extent 11QT^α and LXX seem to agree in their exegetical handling of the tradition, if not in their wording of the text." See George J. Brooke, "The Temple Scroll and LXX Exodus 35-40," in *Septuagint, Scrolls and Cognate Writings: Papers Presented to the International Sym-*

ical equivalents. Most differences in this category are small, reflecting linguistic differences between Hebrew and Greek. Other synonymous variants, however, involve large sections in the 𝔊 that communicate information about the same topic, but not in the same way. These large synonymous variants can best be explained by looking at the parallel passages in both tabernacle accounts, as will be done in a later section.⁷⁶ In this section, I will first discuss synonymous variants that reflect a *Vorlage* similar to the 𝔐. Next, I will discuss other synonymous variants that are unique to the 𝔊. These synonymous variants include variants that reflect a difference in the status of the meaning of the text and variants that reflect a difference in the actual meaning of the text.

Table 17 summarizes the distribution of the types of meaning that are found in the synonymous variants of the control sample and tabernacle accounts. When these are compared, it is found that the two largest sections of the tabernacle accounts contain about the same proportionate number of variants, though the totals are distributed in slightly different ways. Thus, despite the differences in the texts, many of the same types of synonymous variants were used with the same approximate frequency in both tabernacle accounts.

That Reflect a Vorlage Similar to the 𝔐. Over forty synonymous variants in the 𝔊 reflect a *Vorlage* similar to the 𝔐. Of these, approximately half involve a difference in the actual meaning with respect to the 𝔐. These synonymous variants generally result in a text that is less ambiguous and more consistent. Many of these

---

posium on the Septuagint and Its Relations to the Dead Sea Scrolls and Other Writings, Manchester, 1990, ed. George J. Brooke and Barnabas Lindars, Septuagint and Cognate Studies, no. 33 (Atlanta, Ga.: Scholars Press, 1990), 93-94. If Brooke's understanding of the passage is correct, then the minus of the entire verse (37:4) and also the minus אֹתָהּ (25:39) would be due to the effect of situational meaning, i.e., the translator's interpretation of the text.

The minus 37:25-28 has generally been attributed to the supposedly late addition of the incense altar to the cultic setting. This is also reportedly the reason for the placement of the incense altar in 30:1-10 rather than with all the other tabernacle furniture. As was discussed in chapter two, however, the placement of the incense altar in the first account of the 𝔐 reflects instead its unique function in worship as a place where different realms of sanctity meet. In contrast, the structure of the 𝔐 in the second tabernacle account has placed the incense altar in a position in the list of constructed items that reflects the order in which the items were placed in the completed tabernacle. In the 𝔊, however, the order reflects more that of the first account, in which the incense altar appears to be "out of place." This displaced order in combination with other similar changes in the text, may reflect the translator's or his *Vorlage*'s intent to make the first and second accounts more nearly similar at least in the order of the essential aspects of the tabernacle, as will be discussed below. In either case, whether due to the "late" introduction of the incense altar to the cult or the translator's desire to make the second account more like the first with respect to order, the quantitative change in referential meaning is due to the situational meaning, i.e., the culture and the intent of the translator or editor.

76. The synonymous variants in the descriptions of the breastpiece in the first account (28:23-28 [𝔊 28:29a]) and the lampstand in the second account (37:17-22 [𝔊 38:13-16]) together with their parallel accounts will be discussed in a later section.

Table 17. Types of meaning in the synonymous variants of 𝔊 Exodus

	Control sample	First tabernacle account	Core of second tabernacle account	Remainder of second tabernacle account	Totals
Difference in organizational meaning	1	24	1	9	35
Difference in referential meaning	2	13	10	9	34
Difference in situational meaning	1	1	0	0	2
Status of organizational meaning	11	24	6	13	54
Status of referential meaning	12	43	0	30	85
Status of situational meaning	0	0	0	0	0
Totals	27	105	17	61	210

differences were probably the result of the scribe's hermeneutical approach to the text and thus can be classified as differences influenced by the situational meaning.[77] Other synonymous variants in the 𝔊 may reflect scribal errors and other modifications of a *Vorlage* similar in form to that of the 𝔐.[78] Linguistic differ-

---

77. The use of the number six rather than seven in 𝔊 13:6 reflects a *Vorlage* similar to the 𝔐, which tends to harmonize apparent discrepancies in the Pentateuch. This variant brings 𝔐 13:6 into closer agreement with Deut 16:8, which uses the number six in both the 𝔐 and 𝔐. The translations of these two verses in the 𝔊, however, are hardly identical. This points to the probability that the difference was found in the *Vorlage* rather than being "created" in the translation. In addition, in 26:24 the 𝔊 reflects a *Vorlage* similar to that of the 𝔐 in that it uses the same lexical equivalent ἴσος for both of the occurrences of תְּאֹמִים in the 𝔐, whereas the 𝔐 has two different terms, תֹּאֲמִים and תַּמִּים.

78. For instance, the 𝔊 reflects a *Vorlage* similar to the hiphil in the 𝔐 (35:21, 22). This difference between hiphil in the 𝔐 and qal in the 𝔐 could have been due to either a scribal slip of the pen or to the scribe's desire to make the text more consistent. In either case, the 𝔊 reflects a form more like that of the 𝔐, as discussed in chapter two.

In 12:17, the 𝔐 has הַמִּצְוָה instead of הַמַּצּוֹת as the object of שׁמר, which is reflected in the 𝔊 τὴν ἐντολὴν. The reading in the 𝔐 and 𝔊 is a more frequently occurring phrase in the Pentateuch than

ences in the use of singular and plural nouns often affect the status of the referential meaning, e.g., the plural nature of the items referred to by a singular collective is made explicit through the use of a plural and vice versa. This may occasionally be a matter of interpretation, but it is largely a matter of linguistic preferences, which may change even within one language over a period of time.[79] All of these variants reflect a difference in referential meaning.

---

the phrase used in the 𝔐. Because of this, the 𝔊 could be either an independently derived variant or a reflection of a *Vorlage* similar to the 𝔐.

A slightly different type of agreement between the 𝔐 and 𝔊 is also seen in another synonymous variant in 12:17. In the 𝔊 a more generic term, ποιήσετε, is used instead of the more specific term in the 𝔐, שְׁמַרְתֶּם. This could be described simply as another lexical equivalent for שמר instead of the more common lexical equivalent φυλάσσω, which was used at the beginning of the verse. The 𝔐, however, may provide the key to understanding this choice in that it contains a "doublet," שמרתם ועשיתם. These three synonymous variants of the text (𝔐, 𝔐, and 𝔊) could have been derived in a number of ways, but for the purpose of this study it is sufficient to classify ποιήσετε as a synonymous variant that was probably based on a *Vorlage* that was similar to the 𝔐.

The difference between 𝔐 שׁ הַקֶּרֶשׁ תַּחַת and 𝔐 לקרש is difficult to categorize, but a *Vorlage* similar to that of the 𝔐 may have resulted in the use of the dative case alone in the 𝔊, i.e., τῷ στύλῳ (26:25). This difference results in a slight change in meaning in that the focus is on a more generic relationship of the bases to the frames (pillars) rather than their physical location in relationship to the frames (pillars). A similar emphasis on relationship rather than location is seen in all three texts in 26:27, which discusses the bars.

79. One linguistic difference between the Hebrew of the 𝔐 and the 𝔐 is seen in the difference in the use of קֶרֶשׁ versus קרשים with the number twenty. This same difference is reflected in the 𝔊, which agrees with the 𝔐 in the use of the plural (26:18, 19, 20). The source of these particular agreements may be a *Vorlage* similar to the 𝔐, but these may also be accidental agreements. A similar linguistic adjustment is seen in the use of the plural τάλαντα with the number one hundred, but with this word both the 𝔐 and the 𝔐 use the singular כִּכָּר (38:27 [𝔊 39:4]) instead of the plural. This change in the 𝔊 makes explicit the agreement within a noun phrase, which is a type of organizational meaning.

In addition to making explicit agreement within noun phrases, plural synonymous variants also make explicit referential meaning, i.e., the fact that the item referred to by a singular in the 𝔐 is actually referring to a plurality of items. This results in greater consistency in the text. For instance, in 12:11, the 𝔐 uses the plural terms for feet and sandals, but the terms for hand and staff are singular. In the 𝔐 these are all consistently plural, as is also found in the 𝔊, βακτηρίαι and χερσὶν (12:11). Other shared agreements that probably fit in this category, though adjustments in number may have been made for other reasons, are as follows: singular in 𝔐 and plural in 𝔊 (and 𝔐)—καλαμίσκοι (25:31); ζώναις (29:9); συνθέσεις (35:28).

Some shared agreements of differences in number, however, could be based on a different exegetical understanding of the text, such as the use of the singular in the 𝔊, πυρεῖον, (and the probable singular form in the 𝔐, מחתיתו) versus the plural in 𝔐 מַחְתֹּתָיו (27:3). The plural would have been the expected form in order to agree with the other plural objects, but it may be singular because it refers to a part of the bronze altar rather than to individual censers. This same term is used in the second tabernacle account to translate כַּרְכֹּב. If this is the reason for the difference, then the singular in the 𝔊 (and possibly the 𝔐) contains a different referential meaning than that in the 𝔐. This same singular form is maintained in the parallel account of the 𝔊 (38:3 [𝔊 38:23]) even though the 𝔐 and 𝔐 both contain the plural. Thus, the synonymous variant that could have been based on the 𝔐 in the first account was adopted by the second account without a similar known Hebrew *Vorlage*, though one could have existed. Moreover, read within the context, the natural interpretation in the second

Other differences, however, primarily involve organizational meaning, though there may also be a slight shift in referential meaning.[80] One type of organizational meaning reflected in synonymous variants is participant referencing, e.g., use of a pronoun instead of a noun.[81] In addition to this type of synonymous variant, verbal and pronominal suffixes often differ in number. These differences reflect not so much a difference in referential meaning as a difference in the perspective of the author, translator, or scribe with reference to whether a group is referred to as individuals within a group or collectively as a group.[82] Occasionally, there are differences in person and/or number that are due to the shift from a passive to an active structure.[83] This type of synonymous variant affects only the organizational meaning (focus) and not the referential meaning.[84] Other synony-

---

account would be that the word πυρεῖον in 𝔊 38:23 and πυρεῖου in 𝔊 38:24 refer to the same item, even though they do not translate the same Hebrew terms. Thus, the "odd" singular form in the first tabernacle account becomes a completely integrated part of the second tabernacle account, despite the differences in the known Hebrew texts.

80. For instance, in the 𝔐 25:36 the number one, אַחַת, is feminine and modifies מִקְשָׁה. In the 𝔚, however, the number one, אחד, is masculine. The 𝔊 translation of this word by a prepositional phrase ἐξ ἑνὸς reflects this same separation of the number from the noun מִקְשָׁה. This synonymous variant reflects a change in the organizational meaning and possibly a slight change in the referential meaning. Thus, in the 𝔊 it is a hammered piece from one (talent ?) of pure gold, rather than being "one hammered piece" as in the 𝔐. This synonymous variant possibly provides another piece of evidence that supports Brooke's claim about the interpretation of the amount of gold used in the making of the lamp and its equipment, as was discussed above.

81. Cross-linguistically, nouns are considered to be a more prominent or specific form of referencing than pronouns. The 𝔚 and 𝔊 twice agree in the use of a pronoun (𝔊 αὐτῶν) rather than the noun that is used in the 𝔐, הָעַמֻּדִים (27:10; 38:17 [𝔊 37:15]). This results is a less specific form of participant referencing than was used in the 𝔐.

82. The 𝔚 and 𝔊 agree on the following changes in number of the subjects of verbs: 2mp 𝔐 → 2s 𝔊 (11:7; 25:9, 10, 19); 2ms 𝔐 → 2p 𝔊 (12:46); infinitive absolute functioning as 2s imperative 𝔐 → 2p 𝔊 (13:3); 3ms 𝔐 → 3p 𝔊 (25:37; 30:4, 14; 35:10 [2x]; 39:8, 22 [𝔊 36:15, 29]). This same difference is also seen in pronouns, as follows: 2s 𝔐 → 2p 𝔊 (12:48; 30:37). Most of these changes result in increased consistency within the text.

83. For instance, in 12:39 the 𝔐 contains a clause with a verb in the pual, גֹּרְשׁוּ מִמִּצְרַיִם, but in the 𝔚 this has been seemingly transformed to an active, גרשום מצרים, though it is likely that the change may have been prompted by a scribal error in the division of words. In any case, the 𝔊 reflects a similar active structure with an explicit subject and object, ἐξέβαλον γὰρ αὐτοὺς οἱ Αἰγύπτιοι. Referentially these two clauses are very similar, but the 𝔊 makes explicit that the agents were the Egyptians. Though this variant may have been derived from a *Vorlage* similar to the 𝔚, it is also possible that it is based on an independent reading of the consonantal text of the 𝔐. Another example of this type of change in organizational meaning is seen in 27:7 where the 𝔐 has וְהוּבָא, but the 𝔊 has καὶ εἰσάξεις, which agrees with the 𝔚 variant והבאת.

84. In 25:37, the 𝔊 ἐπιθήσεις reflects a reading similar to the 𝔚 העלית. The 𝔐, in contrast, contains a 3ms hiphil form, הֶעֱלָה. This difference in organizational meaning allows the text to remain focused on the agent ("you") rather than switching to a 3ms subject. Along with these changes, the 𝔚 uses האירו in the final clause rather than the 𝔐 הֵאִיר. This form in the 𝔚 is likewise reflected in the 𝔊 φανοῦσιν and resolves the ambiguity in the 𝔐, which has a plural noun that is apparently the subject of the 3ms verb in the final clause. In the final analysis, the 𝔚 and the 𝔊 are much more grammatically

mous variants that involve differences of person and number result in a text that is more internally consistent than that of the 𝔐.[85]

That Reflect a Difference in the Status of Meaning. Most of the synonymous variants in the 𝔊 do not reflect a difference in the referential meaning of the text. Rather, they reflect differences in the status of the referential and organizational meaning. Most frequently these involve differences in the use of singulars and plurals that result in a text with either more explicit or more implicit referential and organizational meaning.

Differences in the status of the referential meaning most frequently reflect language specific use of singular terms as collectives. Differences of this nature can be found in both languages, i.e., the implicit meaning in a singular collective of the 𝔐 may be explicit in the 𝔊 plural or the explicit meaning in a 𝔐 plural can be left implicit in the singular collective of the 𝔊.[86] Often these changes are found in

---

consistent texts than that of 𝔐 25:37. If increased consistency is the result of the work of scribes and translators, then these readings would all be considered secondary with respect to the less consistent 𝔐. For a discussion of the possible meanings of the hiphil and its translation in related passages see E. Talstra, "Reconstructing the Menorah on Disk: Some Syntactic Remarks," in *Studies in the Book of Exodus: Redaction-Reception-Interpretation,* ed. Marc Vervenne (Leuven: Leuven University Press, 1996), 332-33.

85. This is probably the case in 13:16 where the 𝔐 uses the first person plural suffix and the 𝔚 and 𝔊 use the second person singular for the direct object. Throughout this section of the text the addressee (2s) has been consistently referred to without the inclusion of the speaker. Because of this, the sudden inclusion of the speaker by means of the first person plural reference in the 𝔐 results in inconsistency. This difficulty, however, is resolved in the 𝔚 and 𝔊 by the use of the 2s form for the direct object. The change from the 3mp pronoun in the 𝔐 to the 2p pronoun in the 𝔚 and the 𝔊 forms of 25:8 is likewise due to a difference in perspective within the quotation. Examples similar to these include the following: 3ms pronoun 𝔐 → 3p pronoun 𝔊 (27:11); 3mp pronoun 𝔐 → 2p pronoun 𝔊 (27:21).

86. Singular collectives (both nouns and participles used substantivally) of the 𝔐 are translated by the following plurals in the 𝔊: κρέα (12:8; 29:14, 31, 32); ἐνδοσθίοις (12:9); καταλειπόμενα (12:10); γιώραις and αὐτόχθοσιν (12:19); ἀπαρχὰς (25:2 [2x]); κεφαλῶν (26:24); κρίσεις (28:30); ἁμαρτήματα (28:38); ἄρτους (29:2, 32); χεῖρας (29:9 [2x], 29, 35); ἐνδόσθια (29:17); ὤτων, ἄκρα τῶν χειρῶν, and ἄκρα τῶν ποδῶν (29:20); ἁγίοις (29:30); ἅγια (29:33); κρεῶν, ἄρτων, and λοιπὰ (29:34); ἔργα (31:5, 15; 35:2, 21, 24; 36:1, 2, 3, 4, 5, 7; 38:24 [𝔊 39:1]; 39:43 [𝔊 39:23]; 40:33); τὰ ἔργα τὰ τεκτονικὰ (31:5); ξύλων (31:5); σάββατα (31:14, 15, 16); σαββάτων (35:2, 3); ἀφαιρέματα (35:22, 24; 36:3); τὰ ἅγια καθήκοντα (36:1); τὰ προσφερόμενα (36:3); ἀπαρχὰς (36:6); ἁγίων (38:24 [𝔊 39:1]); ἁγία (40:9); καρπωμάτων (40:10, 29); ἁγίας (40:13). Some of these synonymous variants, however, signal exegetical differences. For instance, when the word הָעֵדֻת refers to the tablets that are to be put in the ark (25:16, 21; 40:20) or in front of which incense can be placed (30:36), rather than referring to the covenant itself (an abstract noun), the plural noun μαρτύρια is used in the 𝔊. Context does not require the same interpretation in 30:6, but this difference in reference (tablets versus the covenant itself) is a possible explanation for the use of μαρτυρίων. Likewise, the use of the plural στρεπτὰ κυμάτια for the singular זֵר (25:24) reflects a difference in reference, as was discussed in connection with a minus in 25:25. Other possible exegetical differences were mentioned in chapter four.

In addition to these examples, there are over one hundred occurrences of כֹּל, which are translated as either plurals or singulars that agree in number with the nouns that they modify or with the

conjunction with lexical equivalents that are more generic, more specific, or based on a different *Vorlage* than the 𝔐.[87] This difference in the use of singular versus plural nouns also affects the status of organizational meaning in the text since pronominal references will agree with the nouns to which they refer.[88] Differences in organizational meaning that are similar to those found in the agreements of the 𝔊 and 𝔐 are also found in the 𝔊 alone.[89]

---

relative clauses that modify the substantival use of "all." These examples have not been examined in detail, but most of the usages of the plural could probably be classified as the making explicit of implicit referential meaning, i.e., the plurality of the referents. In addition, these variants in the 𝔊 reflect the grammatical agreement that is the norm within Greek noun phrases, which is a type of organizational meaning that is being made explicit in the 𝔊.

Duals and plurals of the 𝔐 are translated by the following singular collectives in the 𝔊: μύλον (11:5); ἐκδίκησιν (12:12); κατοικητηρίῳ (12:20); γερουσίαν (12:21); ἱματισμόν (12:35); στύλῳ (26:26, 27 [2x] [See discussion of 26:26-27 above under pluses and below in the section on 𝔊 38:18-21.]); ἐκτύπωμα (28:36); καθαρισμοῦ (29:36); εἰσφορᾶς (30:16); κατοικία (35:3); σύνταξις (38:21 [𝔊 37:19]); συνθέσεως (40:27). Some of these, however, could represent exegetical differences. For instance, in 28:2 and 28:3, the 𝔐 commands the making of the בִגְדֵי for Aaron and uses this term to refer to all the different parts of Aaron's attire. In the 𝔊, however, the singular, στολὴν, is used and it is possible that the translator meant for this to represent the main garment for Aaron, of which there would be only one. If this were the case, there would be an actual change in referential meaning in the 𝔊. In 28:4, however, the plural is used in both languages with the parts of the attire listed. This seems to indicate that the phrase στολὴν ἁγίαν (28:2, 3 [articulated]) is a collective term used to refer to the entire attire of Aaron. Thus, there is no change in referential meaning. The usage of ἡ στολὴ αὐτοῦ in 29:21, however, is a little more ambiguous and could be interpreted either way. In 29:29, if the singular refers to one item, an apparent contradiction would be created in the translation by the retention of the plural pronoun, αὐτὰ, that refers to the garment(s) (29:30). The phrase ἡ στολὴ τοῦ ἁγίου should, therefore, probably be interpreted as a collective term rather than as a reference to a single garment.

87. For instance, in 30:16 the 𝔐 uses the plural term הַכִּפֻּרִים, whereas 𝔊 uses the collective singular term, εἰσφορᾶς, a more generic term than that of the 𝔐. Differences in number are also found in conjunction with possible variants in the *Vorlage*, such as the plural הַסִּירֹת, which is translated by the singular τὴν βάσιν (38:3 [𝔊 38:23]). Wevers, however, considers הַסִּירֹת to be a minus in 38:3 (𝔊 38:23) because it is not translated by a term that Wevers considers to be an appropriate equivalent. See WeversNotes, 629.

88. For instance, in the 𝔐 the term הַשַּׁבָּת is used twice in the same clause (31:16). In the 𝔊, however, the first reference is translated by a plural noun and the next reference is translated by a plural pronoun. The use of a pronoun instead of a noun could be expected, but the choice of a plural pronoun is dependent on the use of a plural noun in the 𝔊 that makes explicit the status of the referential meaning, i.e., that the noun in the 𝔐 is a collective singular. Similar examples can be seen in the use of αὐτὰ in 36:2, 3; 39:43 (𝔊 39:23). This same usage of plurals can be seen with deictics such as ταῦτα (29:1, 38). Other changes in pronouns also make explicit organizational meaning and do not change the referential meaning, such as, 3ms pronominal suffix in 𝔐 → 3p pronoun in 𝔊 (12:7, 9; 35:21 [2x]) and 3mp pronominal suffix in 𝔐 → 3s pronoun in 𝔊 (30:21).

89. In 35:19 the 𝔐 uses a 3ms pronominal suffix to refer to Aaron, but the 𝔊 uses his proper name. The result of this synonymous variant is that the organizational meaning is more explicit in the 𝔊 than in the 𝔐. The reason for this difference may be due to the differences in order that are found prior to this variant in the 𝔊. In 39:40 (𝔊 39:19), a similar variant is found, but this time the 𝔐 has the more specific form, the phrase לְאֹהֶל מוֹעֵד, whereas the 𝔊 has the pronoun, αὐτῆς. In the 𝔊, the tent

Synonymous variants that involve differences in number often make explicit the organizational meaning, i.e., the unity of the text. If the Hebrew text had been translated literally, the inconsistencies in number probably would have resulted in a disjointed text in the 𝔊. As a result, the translator made explicit the organizational unity of the text by using the types of verbal agreements that were normal for Greek.[90]

---

has just been mentioned and as a result only the pronoun is used rather than a noun phrase, as in the 𝔐. Other examples of the use of a noun phrase or proper noun instead of the pronominal suffix of the 𝔐 are as follows: 3mp suffix 𝔐 → τῶν υἱῶν Ισραηλ (28:12); 3ms suffix 𝔐 → τοῦ ὑποδύτου (28:33 [2x]); 3ms suffix 𝔐 → Ααρων (28:38).

90. For instance, in 11:2, the 𝔐 uses a 3mp subject to refer to the people, who are asking the Egyptians for gold and silver vessels, but the same referents are referred to by 3ms and 3fs pronominal suffixes later in the clause. The 𝔊, in contrast, uses a 3s subject of the verb and definite, non-possessed forms for the neighbors and thus avoids the inconsistency of the 𝔐. Another example of this desire for consistency affecting the person of the verb may be seen in the use of a 3s form in the critical text of the 𝔊 instead of the 2mp verb in 𝔐 30:32. This 3s form in the 𝔊 brings the verse into agreement with the following verse, which uses a 3ms verb. In addition to the desire for increased consistency, another factor that sometimes results in a change to a singular form of the verb is the fact that neuter plural subjects use the singular form of the verb in Greek, as can be seen in 25:31. Examples of these and other variants in the number of the subject of the verb are as follows: 3ms 𝔐 → 3p 𝔊 (35:22; 36:35, 36, 37, 38 [𝔊 37:3, 4, 5, 6]; 38:28 [𝔊 39:5]; 3mp 𝔐 → 3s 𝔊 (12:27; 13:17; 29:29; 30:29; 35:20; 36:8; 38:24 [𝔊 39:1]; 39:30 [𝔊 36:37]); 3fp 𝔐 → 3s 𝔊 (27:2); 3mp pronominal suffix on infinitive in 𝔐 → singular participle in 𝔊 (13:17); 2mp 𝔐 → 2s 𝔊 (25:8).

After surveying the translations of indefinite singular and plural subjects in ancient translations, Rabin concludes, "We may thus with some confidence advance the view that the determining factor in the choice of construction in the various Versions is the style of the target language, and that the actual textual picture is the result of an interplay between this factor and the tendency to adhere to the construction found in the source language. It results from this that deviations from the Hebrew construction have no text-critical value. There may indeed have been a different *Vorlage*, but the deviation in the Version does not prove it." See Chaim Rabin, "The Ancient Versions and the Indefinite Subject," *Textus* 2 (1962): 76. While Rabin's conclusion is generally valid for indefinite subjects, this conclusion cannot be expanded and used to dismiss all differences in singular and plural subjects. Occasionally, differences in number reflect a difference in the referent or at least a changed perspective on the referent. For instance, in 28:30, the 𝔐 uses a plural verb to refer to the fact that the Urim and Thummim are on Aaron's chest, but the 𝔊 uses a singular, which refers to the breastpiece being on Aaron's chest. This is a referential difference, but the change may have been influenced by the fact that the Urim and Thummim were translated in an etymological fashion with abstract nouns, τὴν δήλωσιν καὶ τὴν ἀλήθειαν, which would have made it more difficult to envision them as being placed on Aaron's chest. Ultimately, the change in referential meaning is slight since the 𝔊 refers to the breastpiece as a whole and the 𝔐 refers to items that are an integral part of the breastpiece.

Likewise, the difference in the translation of indefinite subjects in 38:28 (𝔊 39:5) may be interpretive in nature when read in light of the larger context. While the 𝔐 has 3ms subject (Bezalel?) for all three verbs, the 𝔊 indicates that a larger group (3p) made the silver objects and one individual (Bezalel?) covered their "heads" with gold and decorated them. This difference could be viewed as a change in referential meaning or the making explicit of the meaning in the 𝔐, which has kept the focus on Bezalel despite the fact that he probably did not personally make each item. This contrasts with the translation of a similar phrase in 36:38 (𝔊 37:6), in which צִפָּה is translated by the 3p κατεχρύσωσαν. This translation, however, occurs in the section before Bezalel is reintroduced (𝔊 37:21) and becomes the center of focus in 𝔊 38:1. Thus, Bezalel was not "on stage" and is not individually highlighted in the

On the surface, many of these synonymous variants that do not change the referential meaning of the text may appear to be "automatic" due to the requirements of Greek. A close examination of the text, however, shows that the translator had to make decisions even about the use of singular and plural forms. For instance, even though most translations of מְלָאכָה and תְּרוּמָה are interpreted as collectives and translated by plurals, they can also be translated by singular forms when one person (especially a 3s referent) is the subject of the verb in the 𝕲. This type of careful, contextual translation of singular and plural forms of identical singular Hebrew nouns can be found together in the same verses (35:2, 24; 36:4).

That Reflect a Difference in the Meaning. Some synonymous variants reflect a difference in the meaning. Most frequently this is a difference in the referential meaning, but it may also be a difference in the organizational or situational meaning. Differences in meaning vary greatly in the impact they have on the overall meaning of the text, but most do not greatly change the referential meaning.[91]

Differences in referential meaning are often combined with changes in grammatical structures, such as the grammatical and semantic shift that causes Moses to "disappear" from 36:3.[92] A few of these synonymous variants have been

---

translation. Modern English translations likewise differ in their interpretation of the indefinite subject in this passage (38:28-31) with most following the 3s subject of the 𝔐 (NRSV, NJPS, TEV), the NIV using a 3p subject throughout, and the CEV neatly avoiding the issue by using a passive and keeping the focus on the material being used.

91. Some of the "larger" synonymous variants are seen in the instructions concerning the breastpiece and the construction of the lampstand, which will be discussed in the next section. In addition, the construction of the table has been a widely discussed issue that could be considered a complex synonymous variant or a synonymous variant with a related minus, as has been done in this study. In the first account, the 𝔐 describes the table as being constructed of acacia wood and covered with gold (25.23-24). The 𝕲, in contrast, simply says ποιήσεις τράπεζαν χρυσίου καθαροῦ. Aejmelaeus and others claim that this points to the use of a different *Vorlage* in which the table was made of solid gold in contrast to the gold covered table of the 𝔐. (See Aejmelaeus, "Septuagintal Translation Techniques," 392 and Nelson, 231-32.) Wevers, however, assigns this difference to the translator saying, "It is clear that Exod [𝕲] intentionally increases the value of the table by making it of pure gold just as its moldings, rings and vessels, leaving only the poles to be made of gilded wood." (WeversText, 121.) In the second account, the table is likewise described in the 𝕲 as being made ἐκ χρυσίου καθαροῦ (37:10-11 [𝕲 38:9]), instead of being made from wood and covered with gold as in the 𝔐. The table, in contrast with other larger items, is described in such a way as to make it similar to smaller items that were made of solid gold. The source of this difference cannot be proven. The interrelatedness of the two 𝕲 accounts is obvious. The only question is the direction of the dependency and the original source of the synonymous variant, i.e., the translator or a different *Vorlage*.

92. The following examples of synonymous variants involve slight differences in referential meaning in combination with the use of different grammatical structures than were used in the 𝔐. Most of these types of restructuring occur in the second account, though a few similar examples can be found in the first account. In 35:34, the 𝔐 describes God as putting the desire to teach בְּלִבּוֹ, but in the 𝕲 a more idiomatic means of expression is used in the synonymous variant αὐτῷ ἐν τῇ διανοίᾳ, so that the person rather than the mind/heart is viewed as the recipient. This is a slight shift in meaning due to the language.

referred to as stylistic improvements, in that they are more like a natural Greek phrase than a literal translation of the Hebrew.[93] These differences generally result

---

In 36:3, the 𝔐 describes the event using an active form in which the people bringing the gifts are focused upon as seen by the fact that they are referred to by an independent pronoun, הֵם, and are also the subject of the verb הֵבִיאוּ. In the 𝔊, however, this focus has been changed to those who are receiving the gifts, as can be seen by the choice of lexical equivalents for the verb, προσεδέχοντο. This shift in focus is also seen in the fact that the independent pronoun in the 𝔊, αὐτοί, refers to those who are receiving the gifts rather than those giving the gifts and the plus, παρὰ τῶν φερόντων, refers to the people who were the subject of the sentence in the 𝔐. This synonymous variant results in a shift of focus that highlights the ones who were helping Moses to receive the gifts. As a result of the shift in focus, there is greater continuity between the clauses in the verse in that they share the same subject, but Moses has completely receded into the background and is absent in the 𝔊 clause.

Exodus 39:40 (𝔊 39:19) concludes with a complex noun phrase that summarizes all the vessels, וְאֵת כָּל־כְּלֵי עֲבֹדַת הַמִּשְׁכָּן לְאֹהֶל מוֹעֵד. The 𝔊, however, has a synonymous variant with two noun phrases that give equal emphasis to both the vessels and the work. This variant also includes several changes that could be analyzed as pluses. The result of this synonymous variant, however, is to simplify the grammatical structure and increase the emphasis placed on the work, an emphasis that is also seen in the plus in 𝔊 39:21 that refers to the work of the tent of meeting.

In 38:19 (𝔊 37:18) the 𝔐 has חֲשֻׁקֵיהֶם, but the 𝔊 has αὐτοὶ περιηργυρωμένοι. This synonymous variant is largely due to the choice of a verbal form to translate חֲשֻׁקֵיהֶם. Having made that choice, the organizational meaning was maintained through the use of a nominative pronoun rather than the expected possessive pronoun that would have been used with a noun.

In 39:23 (𝔊 36:30) the 𝔐 uses a clause, לֹא יִקָּרֵעַ, whereas the 𝔊 uses a word, ἀδιάλυτον, to communicate the same information. A similar variant is found in 25:15 where the 𝔐 has a clause, לֹא יָסֻרוּ מִמֶּנּוּ, but the 𝔊 has one word, ἀκίνητοι.

In 39:5 (𝔊 36:12) the 𝔐 has הוּא as the subject of a nonverbal clause followed by an appositional statement, but in 𝔊 this has been transformed to a verbal clause that has ἐποίησαν instead of the 3ms pronoun of the 𝔐. Likewise, the fronted topic of the clause in 𝔐 26:12 appears in the 𝔊 as an independent verbal clause, in which the synonymous variant ὑποθήσεις τὸ πλεονάζον has replaced סֶרַח הָעֹדֵף.

The synonymous variant in 39:23 (𝔊 36:30) illustrates the difference between the use of a comparison in the 𝔐, כְּפִי תַחְרָא, and a functionally equivalent expression of the meaning of the comparison, διυφασμένον συμπλεκτόν, which is the form that appears in the 𝔊. A similar structure was used in the parallel passage (28:32), but the choice of lexical equivalents was unique, τὴν συμβολὴν συνυφασμένην. This type of translation of the meaning rather than the form of a simile is a frequently used translation technique in modern functional equivalent translations.

93. Wevers refers to the use of μετ᾽ αὐτόν as a stylistic improvement in 30:21. He considers this to be a translation of the phrase לְדֹרֹתָם, which is the last phrase in the 𝔐, but I believe it is more likely that it represents לְזַרְעוֹ, because of the consistency with which זוּר is translated in this type of phrase. This does, however, mean that there is an inversion of the order of phrases in the translation, a problem that makes Wevers' interpretation the simpler solution. (See WeversNotes, 498.) In either case, the meaning has changed slightly, but the greatest difference is the switch to a more natural Greek phrase. The change from a noun phrase in Hebrew to an adjective in Greek may also be a "stylistic" difference that has little affect on the referential meaning, as follows: אַרְבָּעָה טוּרִים → τετράστιχον (28:17); אַרְבָּעָה טוּרִי → τετράστιχον (39:10 [𝔊 36:17]).

Instead of literally translating the phrase אִישׁ אֶל־אָחִיו in 25:20, the 𝔊 uses a synonymous variant that could be viewed as a more natural Greek equivalent, εἰς ἄλληλα. The Hebrew term יַחְדָּו is translated by the phrase κατὰ τὸ αὐτό (26:24), an equivalent that can probably be attributed to translation technique. The parallel text is a minus in the second account and the only other occurrence of

in the meaning being more explicit and more consistent within the larger context. This, however, is not always the case as may be seen in the synonymous variant in 25:35.⁹⁴

---

the term in Exodus is translated contextual as ὁμοθυμαδὸν (19:8), which is appropriate since it refers to an animate rather than an inanimate subject, as in the tabernacle account.

94. As discussed above, the use of τέσσαρας instead of the expected translation of שְׁנֵי, in combination with a minus in 25:35, results in confusion in the first account's description of the lampstand. This will be discussed in more detail in a later section of this chapter. Other synonymous variants discussed below, however, do result in a more consistent text.

In 26:24, the 𝔐 uses the verb יִהְיֶה in a clause that envisions the future state, but the 𝔊 uses the verb ποιήσεις, which has been used throughout the instructions for the building of the tabernacle. This synonymous variant in the 𝔊 makes it explicit that the "envisioned future state" will be accomplished through an activity that Moses (and others) are instructed to do. This synonymous variant involves both the choice of a more specific lexical equivalent as well as the use of a 2s verb that results in a shift of focus.

In the "large" synonymous variant in 37:13-14 (𝔊 38:10), the 𝔊 presents a simpler and clearer explanation of the placement of the rings on the table than the description seen in the 𝔐. The more generic terminology used in the 𝔊 is almost identical with the placement of the four rings on the ark in 37:3 (𝔊 38:3). Thus, rather than following the translation of the parallel passage in the first account, the translation in the second account was modeled on a similar construction in the preceding section of the second account. While the wording is similar to that of 37:3 (𝔊 38:3), it is not an exact copy. Instead of using an accusative case with the preposition ἐπί as was done in 37:3 (𝔊 38:3) and its parallel text in 25:12, the genitive case was used. The reason for this is not known, but it may be that the freer translation in 𝔊 38:10, which was not based on a parallel text, allowed the translator to use a more "natural" choice of case. According to Mayser, the genitive is the case that most frequently occurs with ἐπί in the Ptolemaic papyri. Because of the lack of semantic contexts, this statistic alone is not a decisive factor. Three cases are used with ἐπί and no grammarian is definitive about the reason for this variety. The translator's technique would, however, undeniably have influenced the choice of case. See Edwin Mayser, *Grammatik der griechischen Papyri aus der Ptolemäerzeit*, Bd. 2, Nr. 2 (Berlin: Walter de Gruyter & Co., 1934), 462 and Nigel Turner, *A Grammar of New Testament Greek*, vol. 3, *Syntax* (Edinburgh: T. & T. Clark, 1963), 271-72.

Another interesting, but minor, synonymous variant clarifies the meaning of the 𝔐. In 37:16 (𝔊 38:12), the 𝔐 uses the phrase אֲשֶׁר עַל־הַשֻּׁלְחָן, which could be misunderstood as meaning that these vessels are physically placed on the table. The meaning of the text as expressed by the 𝔊, τῆς τραπέζης, however, is that the vessels are related to the table in some significant way. They "belong" to the table and the various rituals performed on the table. The opposite change can be seen in 37:23 (𝔊 38:17), where the 𝔐 reads נֵרֹתֶיהָ, but the 𝔊 has λύχνους ἐπ' αὐτῆς. In this case the lights were physically placed upon the lampstand in contrast to the accompanying tools that "belong" to the lamp. These tools, in contrast to the lamps, are modified with possessive pronouns in the 𝔊 and pronominal suffixes in 𝔐, e.g., λαβίδας αὐτῆς—מַלְקָחֶיהָ. The issue of whether the lamps were an integral part of the lampstand or removable is often discussed, though modern scholars generally agree that they were removable. See Nahum M. Sarna, *Exodus: The Traditional Hebrew Text with the New JPS Translation*, The JPS Torah Commentary (Philadelphia: The Jewish Publication Society, 1991), 166, who refers to an earlier debate of the issue. As can be seen in this translation, for the translator of the second account the answer was clearly that the lamps were removable.

The synonymous variants in 38:9, 11 (𝔊 37:7, 9) result in a text form in the 𝔊 that is more like that of the first account (27:18). The 𝔐 has מֵאָה בָאַמָּה, but the 𝔊 reads ἑκατὸν ἐφ' ἑκατόν in both verses. See the discussion in chapter three, which identified the first account as the probable source of this variant in the second account.

200   *Consistency of Translation Techniques*

  The trend toward consistency is especially seen in the synonymous variants that involve pronouns and other indicators of organizational meaning.[95] Some of these synonymous variants result in a text that is more internally consistent and parallel to other phrases in the immediate and larger context.[96] While most of these changes result in greater consistency, some reflect a different exegetical understanding of the text.[97] Other differences in organizational meaning may

---

  95. Some synonymous variants initially appear to be differences between the use of the singular collective versus plural, as was discussed above, but a closer examination shows that there may be an exegetical difference behind the change in pronouns. For instance, in 27:2 the 𝔐 uses a 3ms pronoun to refer to the item covered (the entire bronze altar), whereas in the 𝔊 a 3p pronoun is used that refers back to the horns on the altar as the items being covered. This exegetical difference also coincides with a difference in the choice of lexical equivalents for צפה that was discussed in chapter three. It is possible that the translator of the 𝔊 had a different *Vorlage* or that he wrongly interpreted the 𝔐 3ms pronoun as a collective. In any case, the result is that the referential meaning of the 𝔊 is slightly different from that of the 𝔐. A similar change is also seen in the instructions for the construction of the golden incense altar in 30:3. In the 𝔐, the 3ms object pronoun is clearly referring to the altar as a whole, followed by an appositional phrase that describes the parts of that altar, i.e., אֶת־גַּגּוֹ וְאֶת־קִירֹתָיו סָבִיב וְאֶת־קַרְנֹתָיו. The 𝔊, however, uses a 3p pronoun, αὐτά, to refer to that same appositional phrase, i.e., the parts of the altar. Thus, in 30:3 the difference in usage is more clearly seen as a difference in perspective, i.e., focusing on the whole versus focusing on the parts. This difference in referential meaning is very slight, but it is indicative of the types of differences found in the tabernacle accounts. A similar difference was also seen in the number of the subject of the verb in 28:30, as discussed above.

  Differences in the person/number of verbs, which indicates a type of organizational meaning, also result in an increase of the internal consistency of the text. For instance, in the 𝔐 Moses is seemingly instructed to make the incense in 30:35, as can be seen by the use of the 2ms verb, עָשִׂיתָ. In 31:11, however, the text says that the craftsmen will make the incense, יַעֲשׂוּ. The 𝔊 uses ποιήσουσιν in both verses and thus remedies the apparent contradiction and acknowledges the fact that while the commands were given to Moses, they were carried out by other people, as is explicitly stated in 𝔐 31:11.

  96. For instance, in 40:38, the 𝔐 reports that the fire is in the cloud, בּוֹ, whereas the 𝔊 envisions the fire being upon the tent, ἐπ᾽ αὐτῆς, just as the cloud was upon the tent. Thus, the synonymous variant in the 𝔊 places the fire in the same relationship to the tent as that affirmed for the cloud. Ultimately, little is changed in the overall meaning, but the 𝔊 is probably more consistent with earlier passages, which refer to the pillar of cloud and the pillar of fire, rather than a pillar of cloud with fire in it. The fact that it is more consistent with the earlier texts, however, reflects more on the impact of situational meaning (desire for consistency) than the probable *Vorlage*. Another example of increased consistency in the synonymous variants of the 𝔊 is seen in the use of a 2p pronoun instead of a 1s pronoun in 𝔐 30:31. This change in organizational meaning makes the verse more consistent with similar phrases in following verses (30:32, 36).

  97. For instance, in 27:5 the 𝔐, 𝔖𝔪, and 𝔊 reflect three separate interpretive traditions about the construction of the altar. The 𝔐 uses אֹתָהּ to refer to the רֶשֶׁת as the item being placed under the ledge, the 𝔖𝔪 uses אֹתוֹ to refer to the מִכְבָּר, and the 𝔊 uses αὐτούς to refer to the δακτυλίους, as was discussed in chapters two and three. Each of these conveys a distinctly different referential meaning, though admittedly it does not change the overall meaning of the larger text.

  A similar difference is seen in 27:10 where the 𝔐 and 𝔖𝔪 contain a 3ms suffix on the pillars, עַמֻּדָיו, that refers back to the courtyard, but the 𝔊 has a 3p pronoun, αὐτῶν, that probably refers to the curtains. This is a minor difference in that the curtains are part of the courtyard, but it illustrates the use of a more specific referent, i.e., a part (curtains) of the whole (courtyard). The curtains may also be

reflect a difference in the *Vorlage* or a different reading of the consonantal text.⁹⁸ A few synonymous variants, such as changes from active to passive verbs, result in a change of focus, which is also a type of organizational meaning.⁹⁹

---

a more appropriate referent in that they are directly connected to the pillars. The overall meaning has not changed, but the organizational meaning has changed and that change reflects a slightly different interpretation of the passage. Other differences in subject of verbs that probably reflect a slight change in the meaning are as follows: 3mp 𝔐 → 3s 𝔊 (39:21 [𝔊 36:28], 39:30 [𝔊 36:37]). Both of these changes involve activities that would probably have been limited to one person by the nature of the activity, i.e., tying the breastpiece to the ephod with a cord and writing on the rosette. Thus, the 𝔊 states that it was one of the "they" that performed these two particular activities.

In 29:43, the change from a 3ms niphal in the 𝔐 to a 1s future passive in the 𝔊 represents a difference in meaning in that the object that is sanctified has changed from the place to God himself, but the main change is probably one of focus. This clause is surrounded by clauses in which God (1s) is the subject of the verb. In the 𝔊, this focus is kept consistent by the use of the 1s form, but the focus of the 𝔐 is shifted briefly by the use of the 3ms niphal נִקְדַּשׁ. The source of this synonymous variant is open to speculation. The effect, however, is that the 𝔊 maintains a consistent focus at the cost of a slightly different referential meaning. The referential meaning that is "lost," however, is conveyed in the following verses, so there is ultimately no loss of meaning within the larger context.

98. In 30:8 and 30:10, the 𝔐 uses a 2mp pronominal suffix, but the 𝔊 uses a 3p possessive pronoun. Both forms of the phrase are found in the 𝔐 in verses where the 𝔐 and 𝔊 agree (לְדֹרֹתָם [12:42; 31:16; 40:15] and לְדֹרֹתֵיכֶם [12:14, 17; 29:42; 30:31; 31:13]). In 27:21, the 𝔐 and 𝔊 agree on the use of the 2p in contrast to the 3p in the 𝔐. In 30:21, the 𝔊 alone uses a 3s pronoun instead of a 3p, but the analysis of this verse is complicated by the use of a synonymous variant for לְזַרְעוֹ, which was discussed above. In light of these differences, it is possible that these synonymous variants (30:8, 10) were present in the *Vorlage*. In any case, the difference in meaning is organizational and not referential, as the same general referents are being referred to with either form of the phrase.

In 26:12, the 𝔐 תִּסְרַח can be read as a 3fs form or a 2ms form, but the 𝔊 read the text as a 2ms form and translated it accordingly as ὑποκαλύψεις. The other differences in the 𝔊 may be related to this difference. Whether because of a different *Vorlage* or a different reading of the text, the result is that the 𝔊 retains its focus on the 2s agent in this verse rather than shifting focus to the curtains, as is probably the meaning of the 𝔐. These two interpretations are also seen in modern commentaries and translations. Most interpret it as a 3fs form (NJPS, NIV, NRSV), but a few interpret it as a 2ms form (TEV and Cassuto, *Commentary on the Book of Exodus*, 353.).

In 31:15, the 𝔐 contains the verb יֵעָשֶׂה and in the parallel text, 35:2, the 𝔐 has the form תֵּעָשֶׂה. Both of these are translated by ποιήσεις in the 𝔊. The interdependence of the 𝔊 forms is probable, but the source of this difference is debatable. In the second account (35:2) it is possible that a consonantal text similar to the 𝔐 was read as a 2ms qal imperfect rather than as a 3fs niphal imperfect. Given that the 𝔊 often appears to follow a *Vorlage* similar to the 𝔐, however, this possible explanation would be eliminated because the 𝔐 uses the same form, יעשה, in both verses. A more likely explanation is that the 𝔊 followed its normal pattern of increasing the consistency of the text through a shift from the focus on work in the 𝔐 to the focus on the person doing the work in the 𝔊. This shift probably originated in the first account and then was accepted by the translator of the second account along with other adjustments that made the second account more like that of the first account. The reverse argument could also be made for the derivation of these synonymous variants, but the decision must ultimately be made on the basis of the preponderance of evidence for the source of differences in the 𝔊 translation.

99. In 39:10 (𝔊 36:17) the 𝔐 uses an active form with a 3mp subject. The 𝔊, in contrast, uses a 3s passive verb and includes the plus, ὕφασμα κατάλιθον, which is the translation of a phrase found only in the parallel account (28:17). Another example of a change from passive to active is seen in

Differences in situational meaning are much more difficult to identify clearly among the synonymous variants. The clearest example of this type occurs in 27:3, in which the phrase סִירֹתָיו לְדַשְּׁנוֹ וְיָעָיו of the 𝔐 is translated by στεφάνην τῷ θυσιαστηρίῳ καὶ τὸν καλυπτῆρα αὐτοῦ in the 𝔊. This synonymous variant could, of course, be due to a different *Vorlage*, but whether the changes occurred before or during the translation process, they can only be understood in light of a literalistic interpretation that seeks to harmonize this passage with other Pentateuchal passages.[100] This reflects a type of situational meaning.

25:29 where the 𝔐 uses a 3ms hophal imperfect and the 𝔊 uses a 2s future active verb. In addition to shifts of focus due to changes from the passive to the active, some shifts of focus occur with the choice of singular versus plural for verbs used with coordinated subjects, a strategy that both Greek and Hebrew uses to highlight the first member of a coordinated pair. This difference in focus may be seen in the following verses: 3ms 𝔐 ⟶ 3p 𝔊 (29:10, 32).

A slightly different type of focus is seen in 31:6. In the 𝔐, Oholiab is simply the person who accompanies Bezalel, אִתּוֹ. In the 𝔊, however, the status of Oholiab is raised as both Bezalel and Oholiab are coordinated objects of the verb through the use of the synonymous variant αὐτὸν καὶ. For a discussion of the reportedly different perceptions of the roles of Bezalel and Oholiab as presented in the 𝔐, 𝔊, and Old Latin, see P. M. Bogaert, "L'importance de la Septante et du «Monacensis» de la Vetus Latina pour l'exégèse du livre de l'Exode (chap. 35-40)," in *Studies in the Book of Exodus: Redaction-Reception-Interpretation*, ed. Marc Vervenne (Leuven: Leuven University Press, 1996), 399-428.

100. In Gooding's analysis of 27:3, he points to the unity of the view presented in the 𝔊 and in some of the rabbinical discussions and concludes that the 𝔊 represents "a traditional view... the idea that the altar needed a καλυπτήρ only arises when one chooses to interpret another biblical passage in a literalistic way... if you interpret Lev. 6:6 (13) in a literalistic fashion to mean that the fire had to be kept burning not only when the altar was stationary but even when it was being transported, then you cannot spread a cloth on the altar during the journey unless you first cover the glowing embers with a substantial covering." This covering in some of the rabbinical discussions was one of the large pots, which is a possible explanation for the replacement of the pots with a cover in the 𝔊, since both had the same function. Thus, this synonymous variant represents an alternate tradition that Gooding suggests is secondary and derived from a literalistic approach to interpreting the Scriptures, a factor that has been seen elsewhere in the 𝔊 tabernacle accounts. See Gooding, "Use of the LXX for Dating Midrashic Elements," 6-11.

One part of this same synonymous variant, στεφάνην τῷ θυσιαστηρίῳ, is also an indicator that in the first account either the translator's *Vorlage* or the translator himself envisioned the golden altar and the bronze altar as being constructed in a similar fashion, i.e., both had a type of molding or rim. In the 𝔐 the terms זֵר and מִסְגֶּרֶת are distinct terms that refer to a molding and a rim respectively. As is typical in the first tabernacle account, however, both terms have been translated contextually. This has resulted in the molding of the table and altar being translated by the term κυμάτιον, which is modified by the term στρεπτός (25:11, 25, 27). The molding of the golden altar, in contrast, is translated by the term στεφάνη, which is likewise modified by the term στρεπτός (30:3). The rim, מִסְגֶּרֶת, which is only found in the 𝔐 on the table, is translated by στεφάνη, but as the text itself says, the molding was made "for the rim," and so these two parts of the table (molding and rim) become practically speaking one item that was defined more by the item it was attached to than by the Hebrew term that was being translated. Because of the harmonization of Scripture discussed above, the bronze altar, which in the 𝔐 has neither rim nor molding, was envisioned as having some sort of rim/molding that would have kept the pot or covering in position. Because the bronze altar was envisioned as being similar in form to the gold altar, the term στεφάνη was used, though in an unmodified form, i.e., without the term στρεπτός (𝔊 27:3). This similarity of construction style is also supported by the fact that in

Synonymous variants are often interdependent on other pluses and minuses in the context.¹⁰¹ As a result, the 𝔊 translation of identical Hebrew phrases may diverge and yet continue to communicate the same basic meaning. This can be clearly seen in the divergent translations of the phrase חָרָשׁ וְחֹשֵׁב וְרֹקֵם, which is found in two different contexts in the second tabernacle account (35:35; 38:23 [𝔊 37:21]).¹⁰²

---

the 𝔊 the golden altar, as well as the bronze altar, had an ἐσχάραν (30:3). In the 𝔐, in contrast, the golden altar had a נֵּז, a more solid platform for the burning of the incense. Thus, through the choice of a lexical equivalent for נֵּז as well as through the synonymous variant στεφάνην, the bronze altar and the golden altar became more identical in form in the first account of the 𝔊. In the second account, the details of the altar are largely absent so the images of the altars are not clear, but a modification of a similar type was seen in the description of the curtain at the door of the tent in the second account, as was discussed above.

101. See the discussion of 37:5 (𝔊 38:4) both above and in chapter three.

102. In both of these verses in the 𝔊, the phrase חָרָשׁ וְחֹשֵׁב וְרֹקֵם is interpreted as referring to the product of the craftsmen and not to the craftsmen themselves, as in the 𝔐. These two verses share some lexical equivalents, but aside from that they differ because of their contexts, i.e., their functions in their respective clauses. In 𝔐 35:35 this phrase defines the work, but in the 𝔊, instead of defining the type of work, this phrase is translated as an activity and the products that will be made once they have the knowledge, i.e., καὶ τὰ ὑφαντὰ καὶ τὰ ποικιλτὰ ὑφᾶναι. The 𝔊 contains references to the two main types of products that are made, i.e., woven things and embroidered things (וְחֹשֵׁב וְרֹקֵם), but these are viewed as a hendiadys or at least as some natural grouping of items, as can be seen by the use of a single article in Rahlfs' text. Wevers' critical text, however, includes the article with both terms because, "The translator would hardly have articulated the first one and not the second." (Wevers-Text, 160.) Wevers' text critical decision, however, rests more on his evaluation of what the translator would/should have done, rather than on the evidence of the manuscripts. In 38:23 (𝔊 37:21) the same phrase is translated as τὰ ὑφαντὰ καὶ τὰ ῥαφιδευτὰ καὶ τὰ ποικιλτικὰ ὑφᾶναι, using three terms to describe the workmanship. Articulation of these three words is also disputed. Rahlfs' text articulates the first two of the three, but Wevers articulates all and comments about the last two, which are disputed, "It would be stylistically quite inept to leave one of them without an article as Ra [Rahlfs] does. Admittedly, the support is not overly widespread, but one might note that the two articles in question share a number of witnesses, ... , and if one were to adopt one as original text one would have to adopt both." If one were to adopt as original the form with only one article both here and in 35:35, then both would only refer to one general grouping of materials that are characterized as woven material with needle-works and embroidery. See Daniel B. Wallace, *Greek Grammar Beyond the Basics: An Exegetical Syntax of the New Testament* (Grand Rapids, Mich.: Zondervan, 1996), 277-83, for a discussion of the variety of semantic relationships that can exist between coordinated terms that share one article. The use of the doublet-like ῥαφιδευτὰ καὶ ποικιλτικὰ would then be just another example of the translator's technique of using vocabulary similar to that of the first account (27:16) to unite the two tabernacle accounts. In both verses חָרָשׁ is translated ὑφᾶναι, which is a specific translation of a generic verb that can refer to all types of designing and constructing. In addition, in 38:23 (𝔊 37:21) the synonymous variant in the 𝔊 contains an additional verb that connects the materials to the context in which they are used to identify Oholiab, i.e., ἠρχιτεκτόνησεν. The 𝔐 form of 38:23 is a rather complex series of appositional phrases. The 𝔊, in contrast, has simplified the grammar by placing the translation of the last appositional phrase in a relative clause, ὃς ἠρχιτεκτόνησεν τὰ ὑφαντὰ καὶ τὰ ῥαφιδευτὰ καὶ τὰ ποικιλτικὰ ὑφᾶναι τῷ κοκκίνῳ καὶ τῇ βύσσῳ. This analysis does not resolve all the difficulties of these translations of identical phrases, but it does identify the fact that the translation in the 𝔊 was moving toward a simplified grammar that was adjusted to fit the context and that employed vocabulary from the first account in order to unite the two accounts.

Differences in Order

The 𝔊 tends to follow the 𝔐 fairly literally with respect to word order and general sentence structure. As with the other differences between the 𝔊 and 𝔐, the differences in order derive from a variety of sources including the use of a different *Vorlage*, grammatical differences between Greek and Hebrew, and the hermeneutical approach or intent of the translator or editor. The effects of these differences in order are also varied, though the majority of them result in a difference in organizational meaning (e.g., emphasis). (See table 18.)

That Reflect a Vorlage Similar to the 𝔚. Only four differences in order in the 𝔚 are reflected in the 𝔊. All are relatively minor differences that at most reflect a slight difference in organizational meaning (emphasis).[103] The major difference of order in the 𝔚, the placement of 30:1-10 after 26:35, was discussed in chapter two and is not followed by the 𝔊. Nelson attempts to use the difference in order in 𝔊 26:8 to support his conclusion concerning the revised nature of the first tabernacle account in the 𝔐, but his failure to recognize the presence of this same difference in order in the 𝔚 raises doubts about the use of this piece of evidence.[104]

---

103. In 11:5, the 𝔊 πρωτοτόκου παντὸς κτήνους, reflects the order of the 𝔚 instead of the order of the 𝔐, כָּל בְּכוֹר בְּהֵמָה. This difference in order results in a slightly different emphasis from that of the 𝔐. In the 𝔐 the emphasis is on the totality of the firstborns, but in the 𝔊 the emphasis is on the totality of the "cattle."

In 26:10 the 𝔐 contains the phrase חֲמִשִּׁים לֻלָאֹת, which is inverted in the 𝔚 and 𝔊. This inversion, as with many other differences in order, does not change the referential meaning, but it does make the text more like that of the parallel in the second account (36:17). This increases the overall consistency of the 𝔚, but the parallel text is missing in the 𝔊. Thus, the source of this difference in order was probably a *Vorlage* similar to the 𝔚. The final difference in order involves the inversion of two words in 40:38: The 𝔐 contains the order לַיְלָה בּוֹ, but the 𝔚 and the 𝔊 reverse this order, which might involve a slight shift in emphasis, a type of organizational meaning.

104. In 26:8, the 𝔐 has the order רֹחַב אַרְבַּע בָּאַמָּה הַיְרִיעָה הָאֶחָת, the 𝔚 has ארבע אמות רחב היריעה האחת, and the 𝔊 has τεσσάρων πήχεων τὸ εὖρος τῆς δέρρεως τῆς μιᾶς. According to Nelson, "While Gk I [first account in the 𝔊] in (26:8) preserves an original order, MT I [first account in 𝔐] has changed this order to agree with the order of the first part of the verse." (Nelson, 197.) Nelson's conclusion is based on his presuppositions about the development of the text and the fact that the same order is preserved in the second tabernacle account of the 𝔐 (36:15). Nelson, however, fails to recognize that the 𝔊 is based on a *Vorlage* similar to the 𝔚 and that the difference in order in the 𝔚 is part of a pervasive revision that makes the first account more like the second account, as discussed in chapter two. If this had been an isolated difference in order, then Nelson's suggestion would be worth further consideration, but in light of the 𝔚, other explanations for the difference must be sought. In 26:8, the difference in order in the 𝔚, which is reflected in the 𝔊, results in a chiastic-like structure in the 𝔊 in contrast to a parallel structure in the 𝔐. There is no change in referential meaning as a result of this literacy technique. The most one can say is that the order in the 𝔐 and 𝔊 represent synonymous variants in organizational meaning, i.e., two different ways of structuring a passage to indicate its unity. On a larger scale, this change in order reflects the scribal attempt in the probable *Vorlage* of the 𝔊 to make the first and second tabernacle accounts more consistent, as was seen in the 𝔚.

Table 18. Types of meaning in the differences in order of 𝕲 Exodus

	Control sample	First tabernacle account	Core of second tabernacle account	Remainder of second tabernacle account	Totals
Difference in organizational meaning	12	22	8	20	62
Difference in referential meaning	0	1	1	2	4
Difference in situational meaning	0	4	2	4	10
Status of organizational meaning	1	5	0	5	11
Status of referential meaning	1	3	0	0	4
Status of situational meaning	0	0	0	0	0
Totals	14	35	11	31	91

That Reflect a Difference in the Status of Meaning. Some of the differences in order in the control sample and tabernacle accounts are "required" by the Greek grammar, e.g., the placement of δὲ after the first element of the clause.[105] Simi-

---

105. The fact that the translator chose to use δὲ or γάρ is important, but the difference in order that these create is less important because it does not involve a choice. A few of these occurrences are actually pluses in the text, but due to the limited nature of this study they have not been counted with the other pluses. The occurrences of δὲ and γάρ from the control sample and tabernacle accounts are simply listed here, but are not used in any of the statistical analyses: δὲ (11:1 [2x], 3, 7, 8, 9, 10 [2x]; 12:1, 4, 10, 11, 15, 20, 21, 22 [2x], 25, 27, 29, 32, 34, 35, 37, 40, 43, 48; 13:1, 3, 6, 13, 14, 15, 17, 18, 20, 21 [2x]; 25:13, 32; 26:3; 27:5, 12, 18; 28:33; 29:12, 14, 20 [𝕲 29:21], 34; 30:13; 31:15; 35:2; 39:23 [𝕲 36:30]; 𝕲 39:11 [The verse is a plus in the 𝕲.]; 40:36, 37); γάρ (12:17, 30, 33, 39 [2x], 13:3, 4, 9, 16, 17, 19; 29:14, 22, 28, 33, 34; 40:38).

Other differences in order that are probably related to grammatical features of the languages include the difference between אַתָּה מָרְאֶה and τὸν δεδειγμένον σοι (25:40). This difference is probably due to the fact that in the 𝔐 the "causee/indirect object" with a hophal participle is the subject and

larly, numbers above ten are generally presented in different orders in Hebrew and Greek. This is one type of grammatical difference that results in a difference in order, but not a difference in meaning.[106]

When differences in order occur in conjunction with other changes, the difference in order may assist in properly interpreting the phrase. Though this kind of difference may involve a shift in emphasis (organizational meaning), the primary function of these types of differences in order is to make explicit the referential meaning of the text.[107]

---

tends to come before the verb, whereas the 2s pronoun in the 𝔊 is a dative and tends to come after the participle.

106. Examples of numbers in the 𝔊 that occur in inverted order from that of the 𝔐 are as follows: ἔτη τετρακόσια τριάκοντα (12:40); δέκα ἕξ (26:25); διακοσίους πεντήκοντα (30:23 [2x]); ἑβδομήκοντα πέντε (38:25, 28 [𝔊 39:2, 5]). In addition to these clear examples of inversion of numbers, the number שֵׁשׁ־מֵאוֹת אֶלֶף is handled in contrasting ways. In the control sample the Hebrew approach is basically used, ἑξακοσίας χιλιάδας (12:37). In the second account, however, this same phrase is translated ἑξήκοντα μυριάδας (38:26 [𝔊 39:3]). This difference is primarily due to the choice of lexical equivalents, but the regrouping of the numerical concepts in the second account is rather unique. The fact that this phrase is part of a larger number may have influenced the choice of lexical equivalents. This example has not, however, been counted in any of the statistics.

107. For instance, in 𝔊 11:9 the possessive pronoun is fronted rather than placing the pronoun in the normal order after the noun in imitation of the Hebrew pronominal suffix. This placement of the possessive pronoun before the plus τὰ σημεῖα καὶ indicates that the phrase μου τὰ σημεῖα καὶ τὰ τέρατα is meant to be read as a hendiadys. Thus, the difference in order brings clarity to the text. A similar example is seen in the placement of the number at the end of the phrase in the 𝔊 form of 29:1, μοσχάριον ἐκ βοῶν ἕν. This placement makes explicit the explanatory nature of the appositional phrase in the 𝔐, פַּר אֶחָד בֶּן־בָּקָר.

Likewise, the difference in order seen in 26:26 involves the clarification of a complex construct chain in the 𝔐, לְקַרְשֵׁי צֶלַע־הַמִּשְׁכָּן הָאֶחָד. In Hebrew, the number one could technically modify either הַמִּשְׁכָּן or צֶלַע, but the 𝔊 translation clarifies the issue and translates it as τοῦ ἑνὸς μέρους τῆς σκηνῆς, a translation that is also followed in most English translations. Thus, this difference in order simply reflects an appropriate exegetical choice.

A more complex example is seen in 28:43. By means of the difference in order, the referential meaning of the text is clarified, i.e., that the altar mentioned in the text is the altar in the Holy Place. In the 𝔐, the altar and the location are placed in separate clauses, בְּגִשְׁתָּם אֶל־הַמִּזְבֵּחַ לְשָׁרֵת בַּקֹּדֶשׁ, but in the 𝔊 the information has been reorganized so that the identification of the altar is clear, ὅταν προσπορεύωνται λειτουργεῖν πρὸς τὸ θυσιαστήριον τοῦ ἁγίου. A similar reordering is seen in 40:20. In the 𝔐, the direct object follows the two verbs, וַיִּקַּח וַיִּתֵּן אֶת־הָעֵדֻת. In the 𝔊, however, the direct object is located immediately following the first verb in the clause, λαβὼν τὰ μαρτύρια ἐνέβαλεν.

The final clause in 29:20 in the 𝔐 is located at the end of 𝔊 29:21. The result of this difference in order is that the logical order (a progression from the most to the least important) and the temporal order are made explicit, i.e., placing blood on the body parts of Aaron and his sons, sprinkling Aaron and his sons with blood and oil, and then pouring out the blood around the altar.

In 29:33 the 3p pronominal reference that refers to the food has been shifted from the subordinate explanatory clause in the 𝔐 to the main clause in the 𝔊. This shift makes explicit that the holy items being discussed in the 𝔊 are the food items. Another example that may fit in this category is the movement of "all" to a position before the infinitives in 35:35 so that the 𝔊 reads πάντα συνιέναι ποιῆσαι τὰ ἔργα instead of 𝔐 לַעֲשׂוֹת כָּל־מְלָאכֶת. This difference in order, however, does not as clearly affect the meaning.

That Reflect a Difference in the Meaning. Most differences in order between the 𝔊 and the 𝔐 are minor inversions of elements within a phrase or clause. These differences in order do not change the referential meaning, but they may at times change the organizational meaning by shifting emphasis to the fronted item.[108]

The difference in order in 40:2 is difficult to assess, but it ultimately seems to result in a clearer text in the 𝔊, though it is still probably more redundant than a natural Greek temporal phrase. The 𝔐 reads בְּיוֹם־הַחֹדֶשׁ הָרִאשׁוֹן בְּאֶחָד, whereas 𝔊 reads Ἐν ἡμέρᾳ μιᾷ τοῦ μηνὸς τοῦ πρώτου.

108. In 13:3, the 𝔐 has the construct chain יָד חֹזֶק, which is translated in the 𝔊 with a change in the order of elements, χειρὶ κραταιᾷ. This may result in a slight change in emphasis, but there is definitely no change in referential meaning. This same difference in order is seen in identical phrases in 13:14, 16.

The similarity of some differences in order suggests that one initial difference, whether in the *Vorlage* or in the translation, led to other differences in order. Compare for example these two differences in order: יְהוָה אֶתְכֶם →ὑμᾶς κύριος (13:3) and אֱלֹהִים אֶתְכֶם → ὑμᾶς κύριος (13:19).

The placement of the possessive pronoun before the noun it possesses is often cited as a sign of a more natural Greek expression and a freer translation style. Examples of this type of reordering are as follows: עַצְמֹתַי → μου τὰ ὀστᾶ (13:19); יָדָם → αὐτῶν τὰς χεῖρας (29:35); כֵּלָיו → αὐτοῦ τὰ σκεύη (30:28; 40:10); כֵּלָיו → αὐτῆς τὰ σκεύη (39:36 [𝔊 39:17]); שְׁמוֹ → ἑαυτοῦ ὀνόματος (39:14 [𝔊 36:21]).

Other differences in order are seen in the following inverted phrases and clauses, some of which may be due to nominal forms being read as verbal forms: לַיהוָה שֹׁמְרִים → προφυλακὴ κυρίῳ (12:42); לַגֵּר הַגָּר → τῷ προσελθόντι προσηλύτῳ (12:49); וְהָאֱמֹרִי וְהַחִוִּי → Εὐαίων ... καὶ Ἀμορραίων (13:4); חֲמִשִּׁים קְרָסֵי → κρίκους πεντήκοντα (26:6); אַרְבָּעָה אַדְנֵי־כָסֶף → αἱ βάσεις αὐτῶν τέσσαρες ἀργυραῖ (26:32=36:36 [𝔊 37:4]); מֵאָה בָאַמָּה אֹרֶךְ → μῆκος ἑκατὸν πηχῶν (27:9); אֶבֶן טוּר → στίχος λίθων (28:17); לְפִיו סָבִיב → κύκλῳ τοῦ περιστομίου (28:32); פְּתִיל תְּכֵלֶת → ὑακίνθου κεκλωσμένης (28:37); בְּשַׂר עֶרְוָה → ἀσχημοσύνην χρωτός (28:42); כָּל־הָאַיִל → τὸν κριὸν ὅλον (29:18); צִוִּיתִךָ → σοι συνέταξα (31:6); בוֹ מְלָאכָה → ἔργον ἐν αὐτῇ (35:2); וְאֵת שֶׁמֶן הַמִּשְׁחָה וְאֶת קְטֹרֶת הַסַּמִּים → καὶ τὸ ἔλαιον τοῦ χρίσματος (35:15 [𝔊 35:12a]); קְטֹרֶת הַסַּמִּים → θυμίαμα σύνθεσιν τοῦ θυμιάματος (35:28; 37:29 [𝔊 38:25]); דַּיָּם → αὐτοῖς ἱκανά (36:7); לַבַּדִּים לָשֵׂאת → αἴρειν τοῖς διωστῆρσιν (37:14 [𝔊 38:10]); צִפּוּי רָאשֵׁיהֶם → αἱ κεφαλίδες αὐτῶν περιηργυρωμέναι (38:17, 19 [𝔊 37:15, 17]); מִלְמַטָּה מִמּוּל פָּנָיו → κάτωθεν αὐτοῦ κατὰ πρόσωπον (39:20 [𝔊 36:27]); וְאֵת הַמִּצְנֶפֶת שֵׁשׁ וְאֶת־פַּאֲרֵי הַמִּגְבָּעֹת שֵׁשׁ לְפִיו סָבִיב →κύκλῳ τὸ περιστόμιον (39:23 [𝔊 36:30]); τὰς κιδάρεις ἐκ βύσσου καὶ τὴν μίτραν ἐκ βύσσου (39:28 [𝔊 36:35]); יְהוָה אֹתוֹ → αὐτῷ κύριος (40:16); עֶרֶךְ לֶחֶם → ἄρτους τῆς προθέσεως (40:23).

Differences in order often involve numbers that are moved to a position before the noun or at the end of a noun phrase. This type of difference in order is often considered to be a sign of a freer translation, as can be seen in the following examples: נֶגַע אֶחָד → μίαν πληγήν (11:1); קָנֶה הָאֶחָד → τῷ ἑνὶ καλαμίσκῳ (25:33); לַפֵּאָה הָאֶחָת → τῷ ἑνὶ κλίτει (27:9); אֶת־שְׁמוֹת הַשִּׁשָּׁה → τὰ ἓξ ὀνόματα (28:10); אֵילִם שְׁנַיִם תְּמִימִם → κριοὺς ἀμώμους δύο (29:1); בַּשָּׁנָה הַשֵּׁנִית → τῷ δευτέρῳ ἔτει (40:17).

A more complex difference in order is seen in 25:11 in which the 𝔊 has the order ἔξωθεν καὶ ἔσωθεν in contrast to the order seen in the 𝔐 מִבַּיִת וּמִחוּץ, an order that is followed in the 𝔊 of the second account (37:2 [𝔊 38:2]). This difference in order may have affected the choice of lexical equivalents for צפה, as was discussed in chapter three.

Another complex set of differences in order is seen in 36:9 (𝔊 37:2). Rather than following the order in the 𝔐 and in the parallel verse in 26:2, the 𝔊 inverts the dimension and the measurement that goes with that dimension for both the length and width, i.e., the 𝔐 reads רֹחַב אַרְבַּע בָּאַמָּה הַיְרִיעָה הָאֶחָת, but the 𝔊 reads τεσσάρων πηχῶν τὸ εὖρος τῆς αὐλαίας τῆς μιᾶς. This difference in order, however, makes it like other statements about length (38:18 [𝔊 37:16]; 39:9 [𝔊 36:16]) and width (39:9 [𝔊 36:16]) in both the 𝔊 and 𝔐 of the second account. In addition to these differences in

Occasionally the difference in order in the 𝕲 brings the clause back to a more standard order (verb first) rather than maintaining the fronted element of the 𝔐.[109] Most of these probably do not reflect the use of a different *Vorlage*. For a few examples, however, the possibility of a different *Vorlage* cannot be discounted.[110]

Differences in referential meaning that occur because of differences in order are occasionally balanced by an equal and opposite difference in order that ensures that the overall referential meaning remains unchanged.[111] Other differ-

---

order within two of the main clauses, the last clause of the 𝔐 form of the verse occurs as the middle clause in the 𝕲. All other similar clauses in the 𝕲 occur at the end so there is no obvious reason for this difference in order, but the result is only a difference in organizational meaning (emphasis) and not in referential meaning.

109. A clear example of this may be seen in 28:14. In the 𝔐 the verb תַּעֲשֶׂה occurs after the fronted direct object. In the 𝕲, however, the verb ποιήσεις is placed first in the clause after the conjunction. This difference in order means that the 𝕲 is in the more frequently used order and the focus in the clause is kept on the activity rather than on the object. In contrast, the difference in order in 25:39 is difficult to assess because the verb, ποιήσεις, could be either a part of the clause in 25:39 or of the clause in 25:38, as in the printed text. If this verb is part of 25:39, then the difference in order reflects a shift in focus in that the 𝔐 focuses on the amount of gold (the fronted element in the clause), whereas the Greek maintains the focus on the activity by placing the verb first. If ποιήσεις is part of the preceding clause, then the difference in order would place the items being discussed in the first position, a much more common order. In either case, the difference in order alone does not affect the referential meaning. A similar example is seen in 39:4 (𝕲 36:11) in which כְּתֵפֹת is fronted in the 𝔐, but in the 𝕲, ἐποίησαν αὐτὸ is fronted. In the critical text of the 𝕲, however, ἐποίησαν αὐτὸ has been interpreted as belonging to the previous clause, which would affect one's assessment of pluses and minuses. Because of the similarity of the reordering pattern, I have chosen to keep the words with 𝕲 36:11, despite the difficulty of the double accusative.

The reason for the difference in order in 29:15 is more problematic. While the 𝕲 does retain the ram as a fronted topic, it also retains the number in the appropriate place for the direct object so that there is no confusion about the direct object, τὸν κριὸν λήμψῃ τὸν ἕνα. This unusual approach to fronted topics in the 𝔐 has not been found elsewhere in the 𝕲 of the tabernacle accounts.

The opposite difference in order is also found in the 𝕲 and often occurs when there is a plus in the text. For instance, 37:15 (𝕲 38:11) contains the plus τῆς κιβωτοῦ καὶ and the resulting noun phrase that functions as the direct object has been fronted in contrast to the location of the verb at the beginning of the clause in the 𝔐. Another example in which the direct object has been fronted can be seen in 40:6. In the 𝔐 the verb is first, but in the 𝕲 the direct object, which is the altar of burnt offering, has been fronted to give it prominence or possibly as the reflection of a *Vorlage* in which it was fronted.

110. For instance, in 12:29, the same difference in order, πρωτοτόκου παντὸς κτήνους, is found that was seen in 11:5, a difference that was based on a *Vorlage* similar to the 𝔚. This difference in order in 12:29 could have originated either at the hand of a translator that was trying to increase the consistency of the translation, or the *Vorlage* he was using could have contained the same order as was found in 11:5.

In 35:23, the 𝔐 gives the order of red skins and then fine leather (blue skins), but in the 𝕲 these two are reversed. This is the only place in the tabernacle accounts where these items are reversed. This could have been due to a difference in the *Vorlage* or a scribal reversal at some point in the transmission of the text.

111. One clear example of this is the inversion of north and south that occurs in 26:18 and 26:20. This difference was discussed in chapter three in conjunction with Fraenkel's suggestion that this inversion is a literary device.

ences in order, however, occur in combination with pluses, minuses, and synonymous variants that result in a meaning that is different from that of the 𝔐.[112]

Some differences in order result in the material of the second account being in an order that resembles that of the first account.[113] This type of difference in

---

112. In 28:33 the 𝔐 clearly describes the bells as being golden, וּפַעֲמֹנֵי זָהָב, but in the 𝔊 a difference in order has placed the adjective χρυσοῦς with the pomegranates. Likewise in 28:34 a difference in order has placed χρυσοῦν in an ambiguous position before the bells and as a result the meaning of the text is possibly different. These verses have been discussed above.

Another example is found in 35:19 in which the referential meaning of the verse is slightly transformed. In the 𝔐, this verse consists of one generic phrase, אֶת־בִּגְדֵי הַשְּׂרָד לְשָׁרֵת בַּקֹּדֶשׁ, that is further defined by a list of two types of garments that belong to this generic classification, אֶת־בִּגְדֵי הַקֹּדֶשׁ לְאַהֲרֹן הַכֹּהֵן וְאֶת־בִּגְדֵי בָנָיו לְכַהֵן. In the 𝔊, however, the generic term is transformed by several minuses and placed second in the list. As a result, the 𝔊 lists three types of garments—Aaron's set of holy garments, general outer garments in which to serve, and tunics of the priesthood for the sons. Thus, the difference in order is an integral part of the change in meaning that highlights Aaron's set of garments by placing it at the front of a list of three items. This difference may, however, reflect the reading of the 𝔐, though the difference in order is not present in the 𝔐. Instead, the 𝔐 has a plus of a conjunction before the second item of the list and thus the 𝔐 like the 𝔊 refers to three items in a list rather than a generic term that is defined by the two following terms, as in the 𝔐. A similar three-category reading is also seen in the 𝔐 and 𝔐 of the parallel verse (31:10), but the 𝔊 in that verse is abbreviated and contains only two sets of garments. Thus the 𝔊 of the second account reflects the most common understanding of these terms (i.e., three distinct sets of garments) as seen in four out of six forms of this list. More importantly, the 𝔊 does not follow the abbreviated first account, but rather follows a *Vorlage* that had three categories of garments.

In 36:5, the 𝔐 uses a modal verb to emphasize the repetitious nature of the activity of bringing, מַרְבִּים הָעָם לְהָבִיא. In the 𝔊, as also in most English translations, the emphasis on the activity has been shifted to an emphasis on the quantity of the objects brought, Πλῆθος φέρει ὁ λαὸς, along with adjustments in word order.

In the 𝔐 form of 36:38 (𝔊 37:6), the activity of covering items with gold appears to apply just to רָאשֵׁיהֶם וַחֲשֻׁקֵיהֶם, but in the 𝔊, the verb is located at the end of the clause which means that four categories of items are covered with gold, καὶ τοὺς στύλους αὐτῶν πέντε καὶ τοὺς κρίκους αὐτῶν, καὶ τὰς κεφαλίδας αὐτῶν καὶ τὰς ψαλίδας αὐτῶν. (See WeversNotes, 612.) This change in order results in the meaning of the text, but not the form, being more nearly similar to its parallel verse in 26:37.

113. This can happen on both the clausal level, as well as with larger sections of the text. In 39:14 (𝔊 36:21), the 𝔐 3fp pronoun, הֵנָּה, is translated by ἦσαν and placed in a position after the subject. At first this appears to be a simple difference in order combined with the choice of lexical equivalents. A comparison of this and the first account (28:21), however, shows that as a result of these differences the second account is more like the first account, except for the difference in tense. The remainder of the verse, however, is not identical so these changes are not a matter of simply copying from one account to another. The *Vorlage* of the second account could possibly have been more like the first account, but there is no other textual evidence to support this conclusion.

The second account in the 𝔊 contains a verse (35:12a) that on the surface appears to be a "plus," but a closer examination of the contents shows that some of the material includes reordered elements of 35:15 (incense and oil) and 35:17 (curtains of courtyard and its pillars). The reason for these differences in order that occur in conjunction with other pluses and minuses is not known. It is interesting to note, however, that the list in 31 contains a nebulous phrase, וְאֵת כָּל־כְּלֵי הָאֹהֶל, in the same position in the list, i.e., after the ark (31:7). In the first account this is translated by διασκευὴν τῆς σκηνῆς, a phrase that uses a rare term that only occurs elsewhere in the 𝔊 Scriptures in 1 Macc 11:10. Wevers speculates that this phrase would refer to items such as, "the curtains, pillars, veils, bars

order along with differences of order in lists may reflect the influence of situational meaning, i.e., the intent of the editor, scribe, or translator to transform the text so that it complies with another standard.[114] The general reordering of the

---

and screens, not otherwise in the inventory list." (WeversNotes, 510.) If Wevers is correct, then the elements from 35:17, καὶ τὰ ἱστία τῆς αὐλῆς καὶ τοὺς στύλους αὐτῆς, which have been reordered to a parallel position in the list of the second account, would make the two lists more nearly similar. The other reordered elements and the plus in 𝔊 35:12a, however, do not as easily fit into this category of כְּלֵי הָאֹהֶל. All that can be noted about them is that these elements (stones for the Urim and Thummim, incense, and oil) are all connected with the worship in the Holy of Holies and the ark, which is the last major item in the preceding verse (35:12). These items might, therefore, be classified as the "vessels" of that part of the tent.

In addition, 𝔊 38:27 is another verse that on the surface appears to be a "plus," but on a closer examination is seen to be a modification of 40:30-32. In the 𝔐, 38:8 (𝔊 38:26), which describes the making of the laver, is immediately followed by the construction of the courtyard. In the 𝔊, however, this verse is followed by a "plus," 𝔊 38:27, that makes the passage more nearly parallel to the first account (30:18-21). In the first account the construction of the laver is followed by a description of its placement and purpose, i.e., for ceremonial washing. The physical placement of the laver between the tent and the altar and the filling of the laver with water that is found in the first account and also in the 𝔐 version of the second account is missing in the 𝔊 version of the second account, but the purpose of the laver is stated. In this purpose, the "plus" resembles more the second account because Moses, as well as Aaron and his sons are mentioned as the ones who will do the washing, whereas in the first account the directions just pertain to Aaron and his sons. It is more like the first account, however, in that it includes a stated purpose for approaching the altar, i.e., λειτουργεῖν. In the first account a fuller more explicit purpose is given, than in the second account of the 𝔐. Thus, while the text of 𝔊 38:27 is primarily that of 40:30-32, there is one minor "plus" in addition to the reordering of the material that results in the final form of the text being more nearly parallel to the first account. In addition, this difference in order in the 𝔊 resolves the minor difficulty of the *waw* consecutive plus perfect and the imperfect in 40:31-32. The grammatical structure is interpreted in the 𝔊 as being habitual in nature and as a result is placed with the description of the making of the laver, which is a more appropriate place than its placement in the setting up of the tabernacle, as in the 𝔐.

114. In the two lists of items at the end of the first tabernacle account, there are differences in order that result in the table always being placed after the altars. In 𝔐 30:27, the table occurs before the lampstand, a position found throughout the 𝔐 in the instructions for the construction and also the actual construction and placement of the table in the tabernacle. In the 𝔊, however, the table occurs after the two altars in 30:28: In 𝔊 31:8 the table also occurs after both altars. This time, however, the difference in order occurs in the placement of the altars, which occur in the 𝔐 in 31:8b and 31:9a, but in the 𝔊 in 31:8a. This difference maintains the order of altars followed by table, but this time the unit occurs before the lampstand rather than after as in 30:28: In 35, in contrast, there are no differences between the ordering of this part of the list in the 𝔊 and the 𝔐, though there are minuses. Nelson tries to account for this difference in the first account by saying, "The Gk I [first account in 𝔊] arrangement (placing the altars after the ark) may have been influenced by the general order of MT I [first account in 𝔐], where the altar of burnt sacrifice follows the tabernacle section. Combining the references to the altars may have allowed the arrangement of placing the altar of incense after the ark and its mercy seat, which were also placed inside the tabernacle." Nelson sees this as an attempt "to revise the lists according to the MT I general order." (Nelson, 337.) While this does point to a source outside of the text as the influencing factor for the change, i.e., the editor's or translator's desire to arrange the material more systematically, I do not believe that the "MT I general order" provides the needed solution to the problem because the order in the first account of the 𝔐 is still that of 𝔐 30 and 𝔐 31, i.e., ark, table,

second tabernacle account has been described in detail in almost every major (and minor) work on the tabernacle accounts and will not be the focus of this study.[115] The reason for the two major differences in order noted by Gooding is a source of much speculation, but they are probably intentional differences. One can only speculate whether the change occurred in the *Vorlage* or through the work of a translator or as the result of the work of a later editor of the translation.[116]

---

lampstand. If the ordering in the 𝔊 and 𝔐 reflect in any sense the degree of importance of the item, then the difference in the 𝔊 would point to the increased importance of the altars in the time of the translator with respect to the table or with respect to both the lampstand and table. At no time, however, do the altars take priority over the ark. Supporting evidence of a cultural change in the value placed on the altar in relationship to the table can possibly be seen in the order of the list of items taken from the temple in 1 Macc 1:21-22, which contains the order of golden altar, lampstand, and table along with assorted vessels connected with the lampstand and table. This cannot, however, be taken as conclusive proof of the reason for the differences in order, but it at least raises the question of whether the difference was purposeful or not.

The list of items in 𝔐 39:33-41 (𝔊 39:13-21) has likewise been reordered either in the process of translation or in the *Vorlage*. The 𝔐 order proceeds from the tabernacle to the furniture (ark, table, lampstand, golden altar, bronze altar) and then to the courtyard with the priestly garments being the last items brought to Moses. The 𝔊 likewise begins with the inner tent of the tabernacle (after the plus [or synonymous variant] στολὰς) and the furniture, but the order of the furniture is different (ark, altar, lampstand, table). This order combines aspects of the order in 𝔊 30 and 𝔊 31 as seen in the placement of an altar (but singular rather than plural) after the ark, which like the ark in 31:7 is called τὴν κιβωτὸν τῆς διαθήκης, rather than τὴν κιβωτὸν τοῦ μαρτυρίου. Like 30, the lampstand precedes rather than follows the table. The similarity in order as well as the unique lexical equivalent, διαθήκης, points to the probable interdependence of these lists. The furniture is then followed by the priestly garments (as also in 31) with the last items being the courtyard and the outer tent, which differs from the 𝔐. The mixed evidence of all the lists is thoroughly discussed by Nelson, 332-59, though his conclusions are contrary those discussed above.

As discussed above, the τὸ πυρεῖον in 38:3 (𝔊 38:23) may refer to one of the integral parts of the altar. Because of this, the translator may have placed it more towards the top of the list (closer to the altar) than its placement in the 𝔐. If this is the case, then Wevers' placement of τὸ πυρεῖον in the second position, despite strong manuscript evidence, should be reconsidered and Rahlfs' text order accepted as the preferred text. See discussion in WeversText, 181.

The difference in order of the items in 38:30-31 is probably due to the minus וְאֵת מִזְבַּח הַנְּחֹשֶׁת (38:30 [𝔊 39:9]). Because of the absence of the altar, it was "logical" to place the bases of the courtyard and the tent pegs after the bases of the entranceway of the tent and then after that to proceed to the vessels connected with the bronze altar. This reordering involves the placing of the translation of 38:31 between the first and last parts of 38:30.

The difference in order of the bases in 39:33 (𝔊 39:13), however, is harder to explain and so it will simply be noted here. Both the 𝔐 and the 𝔊 normally have the term for bases after the term for pillars, but in this abbreviated list, the bases are after the vessels in the 𝔊 whereas in the 𝔐 they are after the pillars.

115. Henry Barclay Swete, *An Introduction to the Old Testament in Greek* (Peabody, Mass.: Hendrickson Publishers, 1989), 235, contains one of the clearest charts of the differences in order in the second tabernacle account.

116. Gooding identifies these two major differences as "first, the position of the furniture. The

212   *Consistency of Translation Techniques*

Summary

In this section I have listed and briefly discussed the effects of over nine hundred textual variants on the meaning in the control sample and tabernacle accounts of 𝔊 Exodus. Of these variants, fewer than one hundred reflect agreements of the 𝔐 and 𝔊, most of which were pluses or synonymous variants. In the categories of pluses and minuses, the totals were evenly divided between those that affected the status (implicit versus explicit) of the meaning and those that affected the quantity of the meaning. Synonymous variants and changes of order, however, did not follow this pattern. Synonymous variants were almost twice as likely to affect the status of the meaning (implicit versus explicit) than the quantity of the meaning, i.e., the actual meaning of the passage was less likely to be affected by synonymous variants than by pluses and minuses. Most changes in order, by contrast, affected the quantity of meaning, but this almost always involved organizational meaning (e.g., emphasis) rather than referential meaning. Throughout this section, however, it was repeatedly shown that textual variants cannot be evaluated in isolation. Rather, it is the total impact of a variety of textual variants in context that has produced the differences in the status and quantity of meaning seen in the 𝔊.

III. Evaluating the Tabernacle Accounts in Light of Accuracy

The large quantity of variants (over nine hundred) analyzed in the previous section would, on the surface, raise serious questions about the accuracy of both tabernacle accounts. The majority of these variants, however, involve the standard types of adjustments seen in all translations, i.e., shifts in emphasis (organizational meaning) and differences in the status (implicit or explicit) of organizational and referential meaning. In this section I will first give a brief comparison of the differences between the accuracy of the two tabernacle accounts. Next, I will present a detailed analysis of the parallel passages that describe the instructions for and construction of the breastpiece and the lampstand. These two sets of par-

---

M.T. puts the court hangings, gate and pillars *after* the furniture; the Greek puts them *before* the furniture immediately after the tabernacle curtains, veils and pillars; second, the position of the vestments. The M.T. puts them in ch. 39, the Greek in ch. 36." (Gooding, 78.) Gooding attributes this difference to a later editor using evidence from the pluses that will be discussed in the next section. Nelson sees this as the reflection of a different *Vorlage*. Wevers sees this as the work of the translator, who arranged the material according to a different logical arrangement, i.e., by materials. According to Wevers, the translator purposefully reported the constructing of the tabernacle before the items that would be permanently placed in it. Given the fact that reordering was a technique used to clarify the meaning within smaller sections of the text, the unresolved issue is whether or not the same technique would have been used on a larger scale. For details about the conclusions of these three authors see Gooding, 99-101; Nelson, 368-70; and WeversText, 143-45.

allel passages clearly illustrate the differences of approach that are regularly seen throughout the tabernacle accounts. Finally, I will discuss two pluses that Gooding viewed as the key evidence of an inept editor's work. Gooding assigned much of 𝔊 38 and the general reordering of the second account to this later editor on the basis of apparent contradictions. In the final part of this section I will show that these pluses use the same approach to lexical equivalents that has been seen throughout the second tabernacle account. Because of this, the pluses are best attributed to the translator of the second account, rather than to an inept editor.

Comparison of the Two Accounts

The above detailed examination of pluses, minuses, synonymous variants, and differences in order illustrates that there are differences between the two accounts, but the differences are not in the types of textual variants, most of which are seen in each account. Rather, the pluses and minuses in the tabernacle accounts differ in their impact on the meaning. In the second account, the majority of pluses and minuses result in a difference in the referential meaning. In the first account, by contrast, the majority of pluses and minuses result in the meaning of the text being stated explicitly rather than being left implicit as in the 𝔐. In addition, even though the size of the variants was ignored in the assembling of the statistics, a brief glance at the data shows that most of the minuses in the second account are significantly larger in size, i.e., ranging from a word to over 20 verses. In contrast, the majority of the minuses in the first account were pronominal suffixes with a small percentage of words and larger units. Thus, there has been a greater loss of referential meaning in the second account. Except for the details of the construction of the tabernacle, however, most of the meaning of the second account of the 𝔐 can be found in some abbreviated form in the 𝔊.[117] Thus, despite the "loss" of referential meaning most of the key information is still present in the 𝔊. This is due to the fact that most of the minuses involve "non-essential" information, as can be seen in the classification of minuses in appendix A.[118] Since the second

---

117. I can only speculate about the reason for the absence of the tabernacle details in the second account. First, the tabernacle itself was not the focus of worship and hence was not as important as the actual furniture that was housed in and around the tabernacle. Second, and more importantly, the tabernacle section in the first account was translated in a fairly accurate manner with no serious problems that needed correction. This contrasted greatly with the courtyard section, which had been (incorrectly?) reoriented in the first account and was then corrected in the second account. Thus, the "missing" section in the second account is one of the few that could have been left out without a loss of meaning in the larger text and without a loss of focus on the furniture and other items that were important for maintaining the focus on worship.

118. All of the minuses classified in appendix A have been discussed above. Besides the minuses that include the construction of the tabernacle (36:10-33), the most difficult to explain are the many minuses involving the curtains at the entranceways. These are admittedly "peripheral" items of the tabernacle and courtyard, but these minuses contributed to the ambiguity of the text, which has been mentioned above. The absence of the gold altar, bronze altar, and laver is more frequently the

tabernacle account is the second part of a unit in the present form of all three major texts, this "loss" of meaning (almost all of which can be found in the first account) may be a reflection of the "shared information" that according to Larson is part of all communication.[119]

In addition, however, it must be noted that while there are significant differences between the two accounts in the 𝔊, there are also phrases that are more nearly similar in the 𝔊 than they are in the 𝔐.[120] There are also sporadic identical translations that could have been produced either by the same translator or by one translator copying the work of the other. In general, however, each account tends to follow its respective probable Hebrew *Vorlage* using the contextual approach to the translation of words and grammatical structures that has been discussed in preceding chapters. The minute differences between the two accounts, however, are the more perplexing problem. Appendix B contains a list of the identical verses and identical minuses, as well as other minute similarities and differences that have been found in the parallel accounts. These are differences that cannot be explained on the basis of any obvious contextual factors.

Some of these differences could be due to changes in the Greek that arose in the process of the transmission of the text, but one would normally expect scribes to "correct" these types of grammatical differences rather than increasing the

---

focus of discussions. Most of these minuses, however, relate to the adjustments in order that make the second account more like the first account and other adjustments that harmonize the making of the bronze altar and laver with their appropriate sources of material, rather than being included in the lists of items made from the metal given as gifts. Most of these differences have been discussed above. The final items that are difficult to explain are the absence of various materials in the list in 35. Some of these minuses make the list more like the first account, but their absence there also needs explanation. The oil and incense may be minuses because they did not have to be "constructed" and were not used in the construction of the furniture. Rather, both the oil and incense are used in worship after the construction is completed and hence could be left out of the list of materials. A suggestion similar to this is made by A. H. Finn, "The Tabernacle Chapters," *Journal of Theological Studies* 16 (1915): 463-64. This, however, is pure speculation and there is no other supporting evidence. The remainder of the minuses that were not discussed in detail above include peripheral items; materials, measurements, and construction methods; location and placement of items; and summary statements. While these involve a loss of meaning, the result is similar to a *"Reader's Digest"* version of the account rather than an account that has undergone sporadic, inconsistent minuses. Alternately, the second account in the 𝔐 could be viewed as the "amplified" version of a *Vorlage* similar to the 𝔊, as suggested by Nelson, but there are innumerable problems with his approach as have been noted throughout this study.

119. See Larson, *Meaning-Based Translation*, 43. The amount of information left implicit is defined both by the culture and the discourse type. Some studies of the tabernacle account have disparaged the repetitious nature of the instructions in the first account followed by a very similar repetition of the text in the fulfillment of those instructions in the second tabernacle account. Culturally similar forms, however, have been found in Ugaritic and other extra-Biblical texts that describe the construction of buildings in repetitious ways. See Cassuto, *Commentary on the Book of Exodus*, 452-53 and Victor Avigdor Hurowitz, "The Priestly Account of Building the Tabernacle," *Vetus Testamentum, Supplements* 29 (1978): 25-30.

120. Compare 26:32 and 36:36 (𝔊 37:4).

number of differences. The list in the appendix is not complete, but the fact that these similarities and differences are found scattered throughout the parallel sections raises the question of whether they can be attributed to one source, i.e., a second translator who was "improving" the translation at the same time as making the two accounts internally consistent. As discussed in chapters three and four, the choices of lexical equivalents and choices of grammatical structures in the parallel accounts often reflect an attempt to improve upon the first account, rather than just copying the first account. The changes in appendix B, then, may be another reflection of the same attempt to improve on the text through synonymous variants such as differences in case, additions of prepositions to clarify grammatical relationships, and other minor "improvements." At the least, these differences indicate that the accounts were to some degree interdependent, but were not identical copies even when they were very similar.

Sections That Are More Ambiguous in First Account

The attempt by the translator of the second account to improve on the first account can be clearly seen in two parallel sections that have been treated as synonymous variants. The first section involves the construction of the breastpiece (28:15-29=39:8-21 [𝔊 36:15-28]), which was probably translated in an abbreviated form in the first account due to problems in the Hebrew text. The second section involves the construction of the lampstand (25:31-39=37:17-24 [𝔊 38:13-17]). In this section, the translation of the first account is fairly complete, but due to problems in the translation, especially in lexical equivalents, the second account has studiously avoided problematic terminology and created a fairly clear, but abbreviated translation. Both of these sections will be discussed in detail in order to demonstrate the differences in translation techniques seen in the two accounts.

Construction of the Breastpiece. The construction of the breastpiece is one of the few sections of the tabernacle account in which the first account is significantly shorter than the second account. The source of this difference is variously attributed to a shorter (earlier) *Vorlage* (Nelson), omission by the translator due to a defective translation (Finn), or abbreviation of a difficult text (Wevers).[121] The abbreviated nature of the translation of 28:22-29, however, can only be understood by comparing the parallel passages that give the instructions and the fulfillment of those instructions in both the 𝔐 and the 𝔊, as can be seen in appendix C.

---

121. See Finn, "The Tabernacle Chapters," 459; WeversText, 120, 125; and Nelson, 257. This passage in the first account creates difficulties for Nelson as can be seen in his comment, "While this type of expansion is common for MT I and MT II, it is unusual that Gk I preserves an earlier text and Gk II renders a later expansion."

The main element that creates a difficulty in comparing the 𝔊 and 𝔐 accounts of these parallel passages is the making of the two gold filigree settings. In the 𝔐, 𝔚, and 𝔊 of the first account, the instructions for the two gold filigree settings are found before the construction of the actual breastpiece (28:13). In the 𝔐 and 𝔊 of the second account, however, the gold filigree settings are reported as being constructed after the construction of the breastpiece (39:16 [𝔊 36:23]). The solution to this apparent discrepancy, however, is found in the 𝔚 28:23, which contains the plus שתי משבצות זהב. Thus, in the first account of the 𝔚 the instructions for the construction of the gold filigree settings are repeated along with the repetition of the instructions for the two gold chains (28:14, 22). Most commentators seem to think that the gold chains in 28:22 are the same chains as those mentioned in 28:14, but there are some doubts about this interpretation.[122] The 𝔊, in contrast, viewed the chains in 28:14 and 28:22 as separate items, as can be seen by the distinct choices of lexical equivalents.[123] These choices may reflect the difference between the 𝔐 שַׁרְשְׁרֹת (28:14) and שַׁרְשֹׁת (28:22), but this difference is not present in the 𝔚, which has שרשרות in both places. In any case, the difference in terminology in combination with the explanatory plus, κατὰ τὰς παρωμίδας αὐτῶν ἐκ τῶν ἐμπροσθίων, which specifies more exactly the location of the floral chains in 𝔊 28:14, points towards the fact that for the translator of the first account there were two separate sets of gold chains. In the second account, however, there was only one set of chains, which in both the 𝔐 and the 𝔊 were constructed after the making of the breastpiece. In contrast to the first account's term for chains that was connected with warfare, the translator of the second account chose to use ἐμπλοκίον, a term found elsewhere in lists of jewelry (35:22; Num 31:50). Thus, while keeping the verse (𝔊 36:22) almost identical with the first account (28:22), the translator of the second account avoided the warfare imagery.

The other major problem with this section is that 28:23-28 is a minus in the 𝔊. This section describes in a complex way the making of various gold rings and the attaching of chains and a blue thread to complete the assembly of the breast-

---

122. According to this view, the chains in 28:14 are more fully described in 28:22-28. See Cassuto, *Commentary on the Book of Exodus*, 377 and Sarna, *Exodus*, 180. For a contrasting view, or at least discussions that allow for the other interpretation, see Durham, *Exodus*, 387 and Osborn and Hatton, *Handbook on Exodus*, 662-63.

123. In the 𝔊 the chains are referred to by κροσσωτὰ (28:14) and by κροσσοὺς (28:22). More interesting is the difference in terminology of some of the accompanying phrases and the plus ἐν ἄνθεσιν in 28:14. In 28:14 the lexical equivalents seem to be drawn from terminology for decorations in which the overall workmanship is described as πλοκῆς, a term often connected with the braiding of hair. In addition, this braided work is intermingled with a floral motif that is not present in the 𝔐. In 28:22, in contrast, the chains are described as being the workmanship of ἁλυσιδωτὸν, which elsewhere is used in the description of armor (1 Sam 17:5; 1 Macc 6:35). Rather than being intermingled with flowers, these chains, κροσσοὺς, are simply συμπεπλεγμένους, a more generic term used for fastening things together.

piece and related items. One can only speculate as to whether this was lacking in the *Vorlage* or if its absence was due to the translator's confusion about the gold rings, but the second set of chains was not left unattached in the first account. In the plus in 𝔊 28:29a, instructions are given for the placement of the chains on the sides of the breastpiece (presumably to attach the lower part of the breastpiece to the ephod) and the placement of the gold filigree settings (with their floral braids already attached below or along the shoulder straps) on the shoulders towards the front. This abbreviated translation clearly specifies where each set of chains is to be placed, whereas the 𝔐 is ambiguous due to the ambiguity concerning the number of sets of chains. The major information that is lost is the specific means of attaching the chains (i.e., the gold rings) and the information about the use of the blue thread to keep the breastpiece from swinging away from the ephod.

The construction of the breastpiece in the second account, in contrast, follows the 𝔐 very closely, including all the details of the means of attaching the chains. Unlike the first account, which was translating an ambiguous source text, the known Hebrew texts of the second account unambiguously refer to the making of one pair of gold filigree settings and one pair of chains.[124] Where the first account in the 𝔊 is present, the translation in the second account is very similar to that of the first account, but the translator chose terminology for the chains that was more like the chains of 28:14 than those of 28:22. He also used more accurate terminology for the translation of other words, as has been discussed in chapter three.[125]

Construction of the Lampstand. The first and second tabernacle accounts in the 𝔊 also differ in their descriptions of the lampstand. Unlike the sections that describe the breastpiece, however, the 𝔊 of the first account, which gives the instructions for the lampstand, closely follows the order of a known Hebrew

---

124. In the first account, the 𝔐 does not specify that there were only two gold filigree settings. This is implicit in 28:13 due to the fact that the gold filigree settings are for the Urim and Thummim. In the 𝔐 this information is made explicit in 28:23. In the second account, in contrast, the 𝔐 explicitly states that there were two gold filigree settings (39:16 [𝔊 36:23]). Thus, the translator of the second account had an easier text to translate and was very faithful to that text, which must have been very similar to the 𝔐.

Filigree-like settings for the twelve other stones are also referred to in the 𝔐. In the 𝔊 of both accounts, however, these twelve settings were described using verbal forms, i.e., they were not viewed as being identical to the gold filigree settings for the Urim and Thummim. As a result of these changes, the 𝔊 was a distinctly less ambiguous text than the 𝔐. In addition, a similar phrase used in reference to the Urim and Thummim, מְסַבֹּת מִשְׁבְּצוֹת זָהָב תַּעֲשֶׂה אֹתָם, is also a minus in the 𝔊 (28:11). As a result of this minus, the making of the gold filigree settings for the Urim and Thummim is only referred to once in the first account of the 𝔊.

125. The second account, however, does not follow the pluses of the first account in 28:13-14. Only the first tabernacle account contains the plus καθαροῦ (28:13); the floral plus, ἐν ἄνθεσιν (28:14); and the explanatory plus about the location of the chains, κατὰ τὰς παρωμίδας αὐτῶν ἐκ τῶν ἐμπροσθίων (28:14).

Vorlage with only minor grammatical variants due to language specific differences in the presentation of organizational meaning.[126] The two main minuses in the first tabernacle account of this section are in distributive lists. If these two minuses were isolated phenomena, the standard analysis, i.e., that they are due to scribal errors, would be the best choice. This type of minus, however, is a regular part of the translation technique that is used in several different grammatical structures, as was discussed above. Thus, the text communicates the same meaning without the extra repetitions seen in the 𝔐. Rather than minuses, the major difficulties in the translation of the first account are those caused by choices of lexical equivalents and the confusion connected with the relationship of the branches and main stem to the cups, calyxes, and petals. These difficulties can be most clearly identified when seen in relationship to the 𝔊 of the second account.

Both tabernacle accounts share lexical equivalents for the entire lampstand, λυχνία; main stem, καυλός; branches, καλαμίσκος; and lamps, λύχνος. These are the undisputed parts that are clearly understood in both accounts. The lexical equivalents for the smaller, more decorative aspects of the lampstand and its accompanying equipment, however, are unique in each account, though some of the choices are related. For instance, both accounts share the understanding that one of the items on the lampstand was similar in form to an almond and that one of the pieces of equipment connected with the lampstand was an oil-pouring vessel of some type.[127]

When the choices of lexical equivalents for the decorative aspects of the lamp in the two accounts are compared with the remainder of the 𝔊 Scriptures, the inadequacy of the choices in the first account becomes obvious. While the first account uses the term κρατήρ, a term that can be used for a wide variety of bowls including drinking bowls, to translate גְּבִיעַ, the second account uses λαμπάδιον, a term used for the bowl upon which lamps are placed both here and in several other 𝔊 passages.[128] Further, in the 𝔊 of the second account these λαμπάδια are

---

126. One of the most obvious differences between the 𝔊 and 𝔐 is the lack of the repetition of possessive pronouns, as follows: 25:31 (4x), 32 (2x), 34.

127. The bowls in Hebrew are described as מְשֻׁקָּדִים, which is translated by a participial phrase in the first account, ἐκτετυπωμένοι καρυίσκους (25:33), and by an adjective in the second account, καρυωτὰ (37:19 ? [𝔊 38:16]). Both of these communicate similar referential meaning, but the grammatical forms used in each are unique.

In the first tabernacle account of the 𝔊, the oil-pouring vessel is referred to by the term ἐπαρυστῆρα (25:38), whereas in the second tabernacle account the term ἐπαρυστρίδας is used, but occurs in an inverted order from that of the first account (37:23 [𝔊 38:17]). This difference in order, as well as the use of a singular in the first account of the 𝔊, raises some doubts about whether or not the translator of the first account was using a *Vorlage* similar to the 𝔐. The 𝔐 text contains two plural items, וּמַלְקָחֶיהָ וּמַחְתֹּתֶיהָ, neither of which are oil-pouring vessels. In other texts about lamps, however, oil-pouring vessels are often present in the 𝔊 (Num 4:9; 1 Kgs 7:35; Zech 4:2, 12), so this choice of equipment to accompany the lampstand is a natural choice.

128. The term λαμπάδιον is used with λύχνους and ἐπαρυστρίδας in 1 Kgs 7:49 (𝔊 1 Kgs 7:35) and Zech 4:2, where the λύχνοι are upon the λαμπάδιον that is on the λυχνία. The term λαμπάδιον,

clearly described as having ἐνθέμια, upon which the lamps are placed. The phrase with ἐνθέμια clarifies the placement of the lamps, but has no equivalent in the 𝔐.[129]

For the phrase כַּפְתֹּר וָפֶרַח, which is translated as "calyx and petals" in the NRSV (25:33), the 𝔊 of the second account has βλαστός (37:19 [𝔊 38:15]), a more generic term for blossom that includes both of the items in the 𝔐.[130] This use of a generic term avoids some of the less-than-ideal lexical equivalents used in the first account of the 𝔊. The term σφαιρωτήρ, used in the first account to translate כַּפְתֹּר, is not found elsewhere in the 𝔊 Scriptures with this meaning.[131] The term κρίνον, which is used to translate פֶּרַח in the first account, is a common term that is generally used to refer to a lily or to a lily-shaped decorative item (שׁוֹשָׁן or שׁוּשַׁן), such as those found on the rim of the molten sea (1 Kgs 7:26 [𝔊 1 Kgs 7:12]) and on the pillars (1 Kgs 7:19 [𝔊 1 Kgs 7:8]). Unfortunately, the use of κρίνον creates the image of an almond-shaped cup with lily-like blossoms, when one might assume that the blossoms would also be like those of an almond.[132] This minor potential ambiguity in combination with the difficulty of the other term probably led to the use of the generic term βλαστός in the second account.

In addition to the confusion of lexical items, there is also the difficulty with the quantity and placement of the cups, calyxes, and petals in relationship to the branches and the main stem of the lampstand. In the 𝔐, three cups with their calyxes and petals are located on the top of each of the six branches.[133] In addi-

---

however, is not used as a set lexical equivalent for one Hebrew word, as can be seen by the fact that in each book it translates a separate Hebrew word. Rather, the translator, after mentally picturing the item as described in his Hebrew *Vorlage*, uses natural Greek terms to describe an elaborate version of a common item, a lampstand.

129. While this could be viewed as a separate explanatory plus, I have counted this whole section as a synonymous variant because of the variety of differences between the 𝔐 and the 𝔊. The term ἐνθέμια has been widely discussed and disputed. (See Gooding, 55-57 for a summary of the discussion.) Gooding's conclusions about the vocabulary and translation style of the lampstand section in the second account is worth noting, "The ch. 38 account is a paraphrase, and, because of the general laxity in the use of technical terms, it is impossible to say with certainty what Hebrew words lie behind its description." This conclusion reflects Gooding's presupposition that technical terms should be translated consistently. See also the discussion of ἐνθέμια in Nelson, 249-50.

130. Meyers says that this phrase is a hendiadys, which adds further credibility to the 𝔊 translation of the phrase. See Meyers, *Tabernacle Menorah*, 25.

131. Aside from the occurrences of σφαιρωτήρ in 25, it is only used in Gen 14:23 as a translation of שְׂרוֹךְ, which refers to a part of a sandal.

132. Meyers, however, describes them as being lily-like possibly due to her examination of the 𝔊 of the first account without considering the 𝔊 of the second account. (Ibid., 24-26.) The interpretation of the petals as being lily-like is found in both ancient and modern sources. This may be due to the fact that כַּפְתֹּר is often used as a term for the capital of a column and lilies were a standard part of architectural decorations on columns in ancient times. See Sarna, *Exodus*, 165.

133. Cassuto and others, however, envision only one cup on the end of the branch and two other cups placed along each branch. (Cassuto, *Commentary on the Book of Exodus*, 343.) The text itself only designates that they are בְּ the branch. The difficulty with having the three cups on the top is

tion, there are four cups with their calyxes and petals on the top of the main stem and three calyxes positioned on the main stem at the places where opposing branches come out of the main stem. An alternate interpretation of the calyxes under the pairs of branches is that these three calyxes are three of the four that are described as being on the main stem of the lampstand. If this interpretation is followed, then there would be only one cup with its calyx and petal on top of the main stem of the lampstand.[134]

In the first account of the 𝔊, the translation is confused in at least two points. First, in the process of translating the repetitions in 25:35, the translation ended up with a calyx under four branches, rather than the expected two branches. This error would most certainly have resulted in an ambiguous translation, which is the probable instigating factor for the corrections of this phrase in various manuscripts.[135] In addition, in 25:34 there is a well-attested variant rejected by Wevers that may hint at the traditional understanding of the lampstand as consisting of seven branches.[136] In this variant the ἐν τῷ ἑνὶ καλαμίσκῳ is in apposi-

---

in interpreting the relationship of one lamp to the three cups. The second tabernacle account of the 𝔊 has, however, resolved this problem through the introduction of lampholders, ἐνθέμια.

An additional, though minor, problem is the fact that the translator appears to have followed the use of singular and plural for the calyx and petal that is found in the 𝔐 rather than adjusting the term to a plural in the appropriate places. (If the singular were interpreted literally, this could be interpreted as meaning that there was only one calyx and petal for the three bowls, rather than one for each bowl.) In other 𝔊 translations, it has been noted that the translator falls back on a very literal translation style ("formal equivalency translation") when the passage is not understood. Thus the use of the singular may be one more indication of the confusion in this section of the translation. See John H. Sailhamer, *The Translational Technique of the Greek Septuagint for the Hebrew Verbs and Participles in Psalms 3-41*, Studies in Biblical Greek, ed. D. A. Carson, no. 2 (New York: Peter Lang, 1991), 209. If the 𝔊 of the first account was as confusing to the original reader as it was to Gooding, then the need for a fresh approach to the translation in the second account would have been obvious. See Gooding, 55-57.

134. This interpretation is seemingly dependent on the reading of the *waw* as a *waw*-explicative in 25:35 and is described in Meyers, *Tabernacle Menorah*, 25-26. The problem with this interpretation, however, is that the normal combination of calyx and petal is not present under the opposing branches. Instead, just the calyx is present. Because of this, Meyers' interpretation seems unlikely, but it seems to be the preferred interpretation in commentaries that clarify the issue. See Cassuto, *Commentary on the Book of Exodus*, 343; Durham, *Exodus*, 364; Houtman, *Exodus*, 406; and Osborn and Hatton, *Handbook on Exodus*, 603.

Another exegetical difficulty is the interpretation of וְקַפְתֹּרֵיהֶם (25:36), i.e., whether these refer to the same items as הַקָּנִים (25:35). The difference in form probably means that it refers to different items, as has been argued by Cassuto and as is reflected in the translation of the NJPS "stems" instead of "branches." (See Cassuto, *Commentary on the Book of Exodus*, 343-44.) In the first account of the 𝔊, however, both of these terms were translated by the same lexical equivalent, καλαμίσκος. This same approach is also followed by most modern English translations.

135. See the discussion of textual variants in WeversNotes, 408.

136. See Erwin R. Goodenough, "The Menorah among Jews of the Roman World," *Hebrew Union College Annual* 23 (1950-51): 449-50, who refers to the traditional seven-branched menorah and the rabbinical discussions about the number of branches allowable on menorah used at home.

tion to the phrase ἐν τῇ λυχνίᾳ and thus defines the lampstand (i.e., its main stem) as a branch. If this is the interpretation meant in the original translation, then the use of the number ἑνὶ is that of a deictic, i.e., on that particular branch, a semantic function for the number one that has been seen elsewhere in the tabernacle accounts. Other problems in the first account involve singular and plural forms of the terms used for calyx and petal that result in a general confusion about the number of these items, as noted above.

The second account, possibly as a result of the confusion in the first account, describes the lampstand in a simplified fashion. There is no mention of calyxes under the opposing branches and on the top of the main stem there is only one "cup" and its associated lampholder. The only possible ambiguity in the text is found in 𝕲 38:15. The 𝕲 uses the phrase τρεῖς ἐκ τούτου καὶ τρεῖς ἐκ τούτου, ἐξισούμενοι ἀλλήλοις, which according to Wevers refers to the branches coming out from the main stem.[137] The natural reading, especially in light of the nominative participle, however, is that this refers to the βλαστοὶ, three of which were located on each branch. If this natural reading is the meaning of the 𝕲, then the 𝕲 of the second account has left implicit the fact that there were six branches. This fact is implied by the use of τὸ ἐνθέμιον τὸ ἕβδομον in 𝕲 38:16, but it is not explicitly stated. This would also mean that the translator assumes that his audience knows how many branches there are on the lampstand and that this information does not need to be repeated.

When the translations in the two 𝕲 accounts are compared, it becomes obvious that the first account was deficient due to vocabulary choices, confusion about the number and placement of the calyxes and petals, and probable errors in the process of translating the repetitious phrases of a *Vorlage* similar to the 𝔐. This confused account was used as the starting point for the second account, as can be seen by the shared vocabulary items. Instead of perpetuating the confusion of the first account, however, the translator of the second account chose to use vocabulary items commonly used for the parts of lamps and lampstands. In addition, he avoided the issue of where the calyxes were located on the main stem, a problem that is still discussed in modern scholarly works. The translator also chose to add information about the placement of the lamps on the branches and on the main stem. These pluses, like other clarifying pluses found in the 𝕲, more carefully specify the placement of one item in relationship to another.[138] This results in a clearer, simplified description of the lampstand in the second account in which

---

137. WeversNotes, 624. Wevers' interpretation is not, however, derived as much from the 𝕲 as from the presupposition that the Greek must reflect the Hebrew text accurately and so he points the reader to 25:32 for a proper understanding of this phrase in the 𝕲.

138. For instance, in the 𝔐 the placement of the four cups, calyxes, and petals on the main stem is only stated generically in the 𝔐, בַּמְּנֹרָה (25:34; 37:20). In the first account of the 𝕲 this is translated literally ἐν τῇ λυχνίᾳ (𝕲 25:34), but in the second account, the placement of the seventh lampholder, ἐνθέμιον, is very carefully specified, ἐπ' ἄκρου τοῦ λαμπαδίου ἐπὶ τῆς κορυφῆς ἄνωθεν (𝕲 38:16).

the translator assumes that the readers have some knowledge of seven-branched lampstands. This simplified translation was either based on a simplified *Vorlage* or the translator chose to avoid a difficult issue, just as he avoided the use of ambiguous vocabulary from the first account.

Structurally Significant Pluses

Gooding spends an entire chapter comparing the order of the 𝔐 and the 𝔊 in the second account and demonstrating clearly the probability that the 𝔊 was based on a text that was similar to the 𝔐 in order as well as general content. For Gooding, the key passages that led him to the conclusion that the difference in order was accomplished by a later editor, rather than the translator, are the pluses in 𝔊 38:18-20 and 𝔊 39:10-13. According to Gooding, these verses, especially 𝔊 38:18-20, contain contradictions and appear to be compiled by an editor who "either did not know Hebrew well, or else did not trouble to consult the Hebrew underlying the original before rearranging the Greek."[139] The source of these pluses continues to be debated.[140] When these passages are analyzed in light of the translation techniques discussed throughout this study, however, they are found to be consistent in technique with the rest of the second account, contra Gooding. Choice of lexical equivalents and the influence of the harmonizing hermeneutic of the translator or editor are shown to be the keys to understanding the pluses in 𝔊 38:18-21 and 𝔊 39:11-12a.[141]

𝔊 *38:18-21.* As mentioned in chapter three, 𝔊 38:18-21 contains lexical equivalents from both of the tabernacle accounts that have been juxtaposed in a manner that creates apparent contradictions, if the words are examined without attention to their contexts. This is one of the features that led Gooding to conclude that chapter 38 and the reordering of the second account were the work of a later editor who did not understand the text. Whether the work of an editor or of the translator of the second account, this section functions as a bridge between the description of the making of the gold items of the tent and the bronze items of the courtyard. This bridging effect is accomplished by introducing into the text the gold, silver, and bronze items of the tabernacle and courtyard. The combina-

---

139. Gooding, 101.

140. As to be expected, Nelson argues that these texts translate a Hebrew *Vorlage* that "fits the pattern of the Old Greek throughout the tabernacle and court sections." (Nelson, 223.) Wevers simply says, "That there is something wrong about vv. 18-21 seems obvious." He then proceeds to describe those "obvious" problems. (WeversNotes, 626.) Wevers also says that these verses, "have no particular Hebrew parent text." See WeversText, 135.

141. Gooding specifically mentions 𝔊 38:18-20 and 𝔊 39:10-13, but his discussion and the discussions in other studies led me to slightly modify the range of verses that I would discuss in this study. (See Gooding, 79, 101.) Thus, I have chosen to discuss 𝔊 38:18-21 and 𝔊 39:11-12a, which I believe will cover the most important issues with regard to textual variants.

tion of the minus of the construction of the golden incense altar (37:25-28) and the plus of this bridge section results in a final form that is more nearly parallel to the order in the first account, which proceeds from the lampstand to the tent and then to the bronze altar.[142]

The major problem in these verses is identifying the referents for κεφαλίς, στῦλος, κρίκος, and ἀγκύλη in such a way that it is consistent with the descriptions of parts of the tabernacle and courtyard found in other parts of the text. When the Greek terms are read in context, however, the majority of the problems disappear. This type of close reading of the text illustrates that textual variants should not be too quickly dismissed as "mistakes," because these variants often prove to be the key to understanding the passage.[143] Repeatedly, this section illustrates the importance of context in that identical words are used to refer to different items. For instance, the κεφαλίς of the tent refers to the base of the frames of the tabernacle, which were cast out of silver. The κεφαλίς of the door of the tent and of the gate of the courtyard refers to the heads or capitals of these pillars, which are envisioned in the 𝔊 as being cast out of bronze and covered with silver.[144] This passage also demonstrates repeatedly a knowledge of vocabulary

---

142. The only major discrepancy in order in the second account is the fact that the bridge section contains references to some items connected with the courtyard curtains and gate, which are not described in the first account until after the instructions for the bronze altar.

143. The first two clauses of 𝔊 38:18 appear to be in error about the construction of the pillars, but the key to the problem is provided by the textual variant τῷ στύλῳ, which Wevers dismisses as a "careless mistake" because "the plural is demanded by the sense of the passage." (WeversText, 201.) Most analyses of 𝔊 38:18 assume that the pillars referred to in the first clause are the same as those referred to by the second clause. Because of this, most of their discussions center on the word περιηργύρωσεν, which is viewed either as an error or a generic usage of a specific term because everyone "knows" that the frames of the tabernacle were gold covered, as can be seen in 𝔐 36:34. In the second clause, the rings are said to be made τῷ στύλῳ, a singular term referring to the set of pillars on the side of the tabernacle. This same usage was noted in 26:26-27 and discussed earlier in this chapter. In light of this, the first clause probably refers to the pillars of the courtyard, which were silver, and the second reference (the singular pillar), refers to the set(s) of pillars, i.e., the frames of the sides of the tabernacle. The lack of further description of the frames fits the context of the second tabernacle account in the 𝔊, which assumes their existence, but does not describe their construction. The third reference to pillars specifies that it is the pillars of the τοῦ καταπετάσματος, which are covered with gold. Thus, three different types of pillars are referred to in this verse—the silver pillars of the courtyard, the gold pillars of the (inner ?) curtain, and the set(s) of pillars of the tabernacle for which the gold rings are made.

144. As was noted in chapter three, κεφαλίς was used to refer to the bases of the tent, but not of the door of the tent. Thus in 𝔊 38:20, the first occurrence of κεφαλίς refers to the silver bases of the tabernacle, which everyone agrees were silver and which are referred to again by κεφαλίς in 38:27 (𝔊 39:4). The next occurrence of κεφαλίς, however, refers to the "heads" of the pillars of the gate of the tent and courtyard, rather than the bases, which are referred to by the term βάσις in 38:30 (𝔊 39:7). Many object to this interpretation on the basis of the "fact" that the capitals of the pillars of both gates were silver. Nelson resolves this issue by simply positing a different *Vorlage*. "Either Gk II [second account in the 𝔊] is rendering an older textual tradition where the capitals were silver for the tabernacle and bronze for the door of the tent, or bases were replaced by capitals in the *Vorlage* of Gk II and

usage in both the first and second accounts.¹⁴⁵ In addition to knowledge of both accounts, this section shares a phrase that is only found elsewhere in a plus in the

---

so rendered κεφαλίδας here. Both possibilities have some Gk II support. In either case Gk II was reading ראשים in its Vorlage." (Nelson, 221.) A simpler solution may, however, be found within the texts as they now exist. The tabernacle section of the second account (36:10-33) does not exist in our current version of the 𝕲, but the construction of the pillars of the courtyard are discussed. The heads of both the pillars of the courtyard itself and also of the gates of the courtyard are said to have צִפּוּי ראשֵׁיהֶם, a phrase that is not found in the first account of the 𝔐. The problem is that the text never describes the materials from which the heads themselves are composed. In the 𝔐 it would appear that the heads were simply the top part of the wooden posts that were then covered with metal. These heads appeared to be separate entities due to the banding of the pillars, which was discussed in chapter three, and also the use of a different type of metal for the head. In 𝕲 38:20, however, the heads of the posts are envisioned as capitals that are cast out of metal just as the bases were cast out of metal. For the gates these capitals in the 𝕲 were cast out of bronze and then covered with silver, οὗτος περιηργύρωσεν αὐτάς. This same description of the gate's pillars is seen in 𝕲 37:17, καὶ αἱ κεφαλίδες αὐτῶν περιηργυρωμέναι ἀργυρίῳ. This might also explain the feminine plural pronoun at the end of 𝕲 38:20, though it is still difficult due to the distance between the pronoun and its referent. Wevers dismisses the feminine plural pronoun as inappropriate despite the manuscript evidence and instead uses the masculine form that would refer back to the pillars. (See WeversText, 193-94.) If my interpretation is correct, then the appearance of the heads of the pillars of the gate of the courtyard and of the door of the tabernacle is identical to that in the 𝔐, i.e., silver on the outside. The difference, though, is that information left implicit in the 𝔐, i.e., the exact construction of the heads, has been made explicit in the 𝕲. Most commentators would probably say that the translator supplied incorrect implicit information, but the translator probably based his construction of the heads of the pillars on the technology that was current in his day, i.e., cheaper metal covered by a thin layer of more expensive metal. This technology was known in antiquity and is probably being referred to in Isa 40:19, where metal idols are covered with gold. See *The Anchor Bible Dictionary*, s.v. "Overlay," 5:52.

145. As with κεφαλίς, the term κρίκος is used in 𝕲 38:19 to refer to different items, both usages of which were found in the first tabernacle account. The first usage refers to the golden clasps and the third usage refers to the bronze clasps for the outer coverings of the tent. These two usages are rarely disputed. As with the pillars, however, the middle occurrence of the term κρίκος does not contain a clear designation of the material from which it is made. One would assume bronze from the context, but a comparison of this verse with 27:10 shows that materials of the κρίκος in that verse were also not individually described, but from the context one would assume that they were silver. In addition, rather than being clasps, the middle occurrence would seem to refer to hooks on the pillars of the courtyard, as in 27:10. The usage of κρίκος thus resembles that of στῦλος in the preceding verse with multiple referents and an unspecified middle term. Nelson attributes this middle usage of κρίκος to the development of the text claiming that "... as the court section was expanded the clasps were lost or replaced by hooks of the frame unit. (38:19, 20) would, therefore, be the only place where both the clasps and hooks were retained. The structure of (38:19) obscures the distinction of the clasps of the tabernacle from the clasps of the court by the metals from which they were made." (Nelson, 220.) While Nelson's suggestion is possible, it is not necessary in light of clear usages of κρίκος to refer to the hooks of the courtyard in the first account. Gooding berates this section because of the duplication of information seen in the usage of ἀγκύλη to refer to the hooks (𝕲 38:19-20). This pattern of dissimilation, i.e., the translation of one Hebrew word by several Greek words, however, has been seen repeatedly in the tabernacle accounts. Gooding himself has correctly seen the solution to this "problem," but refuses to accept it because of his presuppositions about languages and translations, as may be seen in the following quote: "It might be argued that *v.* 20 describes the hooks on the gate pillars only and not the hooks on the rest of the court pillars; but the distinction, if intended, is not valid,

second tabernacle account.[146] The final verse of this section contains no new information, but it does provide one more reference to the metal tent pegs, which Bezalel was responsible for making.[147] Thus, contra Gooding, this plus (𝔊 38:18-21) was used by the translator (or editor) to bring greater unity to the tabernacle accounts through three different tactics. First, vocabulary from both accounts was combined in a non-contradictory manner. Second, the second account was brought into closer conformity to the order of the first account through the absence of the incense altar and the presence of the metal tabernacle and courtyard parts. Third, the plus functioned as a bridge from the equipment made of gold to the equipment made of bronze. None of the information in this plus is new information, but it has been placed in a new context in order to encourage the reading of the two tabernacle accounts as a unified whole.

𝔊 *39:11-12a.* The smaller plus, 𝔊 39:11-12a, serves to unite the first and last parts of the second tabernacle account by providing a resolution for information that was introduced, but never resolved in the 𝔐. In 36:7, the text states that the people gave so generously that there was material left-over. These "leftovers" were part of the offerings of the people. With food items from the Passover and from other offerings, clear instructions had been given for the disposal of the excess because of its sacred nature. In the 𝔐 there are no further statements about the "left-over" offerings of materials for the tabernacle. In the 𝔊, however, this problem is resolved by a plus, 𝔊 39:11-12a, which describes the making of gold dishes for service in the tabernacle, and the using of the "left-over" material for extra garments for the priests.[148] The vocabulary of this plus, especially the use of

---

since the Hebrew word is the same for all the hooks, and the seeming difference caused by the varying translations in the Greek is not a real one." (Gooding, 43 n. 1.) Whether the distinction is "real" or not, depends on one's cultural and linguistic perspective. Since we do not have a full knowledge of the culture of the translator(s) of the 𝔊, all we can do is describe what they did rather than prescribe what they should have done. Gooding's failure in correctly analyzing this passage is due not to a lack of analytical insight, but to a failure to accept that other cultures may have different presuppositions about the process of translating.

146. In both 𝔊 38:20 and 39:40 (𝔊 39:19), the 𝔊 contains a plus that unites the door of the tent and the gate of the courtyard in a coordinate phrase. This phrase is not found at any point in a known Hebrew *Vorlage*, which may point to the fact that the source was the editor or translator of the second account, who in the process of summarizing often combined related items. (See also the combining of the poles of the table and the ark, which was discussed above.)

147. The description of the tent pegs in 𝔊 38:21 is almost identical to 38:31 (𝔊 39:8). The major difference is the larger context. In 𝔊 38:21, the items are referred to as being made, whereas 38:31 (𝔊 39:8) occurs as part of a list of items that were made from the bronze. In the first account the tent-pegs of the tent and the courtyard are mentioned together in 27:19 in a summary statement at the end of the construction of the courtyard. Due to either the inaccuracy (?) of the first account, the use of a different *Vorlage*, or the deletion of the items because the location seemed inappropriate, the tent pegs of the tabernacle are missing in 𝔊 27:19. The plus in 𝔊 38:21 remedies this problem of the first account.

148. In 39:1 (𝔊 39:12), the preposition מִן can indicate either a partitive meaning or the actual

ἀφαίρεμα, indicates its connection with the initial part of the second tabernacle account as well as the first part of 𝔊 39.[149]

Summary

A comparison of the tabernacle accounts reveals that there are significant differences between the two tabernacle accounts, especially in the category of minuses. These minuses, however, involve the "non-essential" aspects of the second account. In addition to the minuses, each account uses separate approaches to "problem" passages. The differences between these approaches are best seen in their unique handling of the translation of the passages describing the breastpiece and the lampstand. While the translations of both passages in the first account are ambiguous, those of the second account are clear. The pluses claimed by Gooding to be evidence of the work of a later editor were shown in this section to be consistent with the rest of the second tabernacle account. Therefore, these pluses cannot be used as evidence to prove that it must have been someone other than the translator who rearranged the text. Gooding's attempt to separate the reorganizing of the text from the work of the translator indicates his basic presupposition that a translator in ancient times would have just translated the text and not rearranged the text. This presupposition and other unanswerable questions about translation techniques in antiquity will be the focus of the next section.

---

material being used in the making of the garments. If it is the actual material, the plus, τὴν καταλειφθεῖσαν, would be a further clarification of which material is used for the making of these garments, i.e., the material that was left-over. This also brings a resolution to the question of what was done with the "leftovers" that were mentioned in 36:7 and thus would fit in the category of situational meaning in that it is intentionally added to the text to harmonize the text internally.

Gooding noted the connection of 36:7 and 39:1 (𝔊 39:12) and says, "It could only make sense if the στολαί of ch. 39.13 [𝔊 39.12] were thought of as additional to those mentioned in ch. 36; but this is manifestly not the meaning either of the Greek or of the Hebrew which the Greek 39.13 [𝔊 39.12] is meant to translate." Thus, Gooding has again analyzed the "plus" correctly, but because of his presuppositions about translation (i.e., that a translator would not "add to" or reinterpret the meaning), he rejects that option and uses this plus as evidence that a later editor must have changed the order of the text. See Gooding, 89.

It might appear surprising that there is no plus concerning the left-over bronze and silver. An examination of 𝔊 39:1-9, however, shows that the silver is accounted for exactly and the bronze items contain a rather complete list with a summary statement at the end. The gold, in contrast, is not accounted for exactly. This lack of an exact account in combination with the absence of 37:24, which specifies the amount of gold used on the lampstand and its equipment, leaves the possibility open that there was gold from the offering that was "left-over."

149. The description of the gold as χρυσίον τοῦ ἀφαιρέματος (𝔊 39:11) is a designation found only in the second account due to the translator's choices of lexical equivalents, as discussed in chapter three. (See also ἀφαιρέματα χρυσίου in 35:22.) This designation is also similar to that used for the silver and bronze (𝔊 39:2, 6), but not the gold, earlier in 𝔊 39.

IV. Unanswerable Questions about Translation Techniques

Ultimately, the resolution of the text critical problems of the tabernacle accounts revolves around the issue of the purpose of the translation and the extent to which the translator can "modify" the text without affecting the acceptance of the translation by the community for which it is produced. In the absence of historical evidence that could be used to resolve these issues, the best that can be done in this brief section is to survey past observations that often reach opposite conclusions. First, I will discuss the two basic approaches to translation that were referred to in antiquity and the relationship of Exodus to these two approaches. Second, I will discuss the problem of faithfulness and whether reordering of material is permissible in a text that aims at being faithful.

Two Approaches to Translation in Antiquity

In ancient times there were reportedly two major types of translation that served separate functions. According to Brock, these could be described as literary translations that attempt to communicate the meaning and non-literary translations that are word-for-word translations. Non-literary translations were generally used for legal documents, business affairs, and literature used in a school setting.[150] Thus, the crucial issue is whether the Scriptures were viewed as literature or as legal documents. The standard thought is that the translation effort began with the relatively free, but accurate translation style seen in Genesis and Exodus and then moved steadily toward a more literal word-for-word approach, as the Scriptures came to be viewed as sacred. Fraenkel, however, notes that the sociolinguistic setting was not that simple.[151] Even in antiquity opposite approaches coexisted both in the later translations, as seen in the free translation style of Isaiah as opposed to Qoheleth, and also in the later revisions of the 𝕲, as may be seen in the contrasting approaches of Aquila and Symmachus. Thus, rather than a united approach, translation techniques have from antiquity exhibited the same contrasting approaches that are seen even today.

---

150. Sebastian P. Brock, "Aspects of Translation Technique in Antiquity," in *Syriac Perspectives on Late Antiquity* (London: Variorum Reprints, 1984), 69-87. See also idem, "To Revise or Not to Revise: Attitudes to Jewish Biblical Translation," in *Septuagint, Scrolls and Cognate Writings: Papers Presented to the International Symposium on the Septuagint and Its Relations to the Dead Sea Scrolls and Other Writings, Manchester, 1990*, ed. George J. Brooke and Barnabas Lindars, Septuagint and Cognate Studies, no. 33 (Atlanta, Ga.: Scholars Press, 1992), 301-38.

151. Detlef Fraenkel, "Übersetzungsnorm und literarische Gestaltung—Spuren individueller Übersetzungstechnik in Exodus 25ff. + 35ff.," in *VIII Congress of the International Organization for Septuagint and Cognate Studies, Paris, 1991*, ed. Leonard Greenspoon and Olivier Munnich, Septuagint and Cognate Studies, no. 41 (Atlanta, Ga.: Scholars Press, 1995), 74-76.

Barr claims that translations in antiquity were generally literal and that the key issue was to determine the degree and type of literalness. Specifically, Barr outlines six categories by which the literalness of a translation can be characterized and notes that translations may be more literal in one aspect of the translation than in another.[152] While Exodus has been described as a relatively free translation throughout this study, Barr's comments are in a sense applicable even to Exodus. When the 𝔐 and 𝔊 forms of Exodus are seen in an aligned text file, the 𝔊 appears to fairly consistently follow the 𝔐 in the areas of general structure of the verses, word order in clauses, and in providing a translation for each word or phrase. The freedom of the translation, however, is seen in the semantically and grammatically controlled choices of lexical equivalents and in the variety of structures used in translating Hebrew grammatical structures. Thus, the tabernacle accounts, like other ancient translations, combine more literal and less literal aspects of translation into a unified whole. For the second tabernacle account, however, the key question is whether or not a translator, who is generally faithful to a *Vorlage* similar to the 𝔐, would rearrange the text as a part of the translation process.

Faithfulness and Reordering

The source of the differences in order in the second tabernacle account has generally been attributed to either a different translator, a later editor, or a different *Vorlage*. Presuppositions about what a translator would and would not do appear to be the major problem. Aejmelaeus' position can be clearly seen in her statement, "Since this kind of editing and abridging would be most unusual in the Greek Pentateuch and not easily ascribed to the translators, various theories have been developed to explain it."[153] This presupposition is not, however, shared by all. Similar editing and rearranging of the text have been identified in Proverbs and used by Cook as a basis for suggesting that 𝔊 38 can be understood in a similar light, i.e., as the work of the translator.[154] While many share Aejmelaeus' presup-

---

152. Barr lists the following "modes of difference between a more literal and a less literal rendering of a Hebrew text: 1. The division into elements or segments, and the sequence in which these elements are represented. 2. The quantitative addition or subtraction of elements. 3. Consistency or non-consistency in the rendering, i.e. the degree to which a particular versional term is used for all (or most) cases of a particular term of the original. 4. Accuracy and level of semantic information, especially in cases of metaphor and idiom. 5. Coded "etymological" indication of formal/semantic relationships obtaining in the vocabulary of the original languages. 6. Level of text and level of analysis." See James Barr, *The Typology of Literalism in Ancient Biblical Translations*, Mitteilungen des Septuaginta-Unternehmens, no. 15 (Göttingen: Vandenhoeck & Ruprecht, 1979), 294.

153. Aejmelaeus, "Septuagintal Translation Techniques," 385-86.

154. Johann Cook, "Exodus 38 and Proverbs 31: A Case of Different Order of Verses and Chapters in the Septuagint," in *Studies in the Book of Exodus: Redaction-Reception-Interpretation*, ed. Marc Vervenne (Leuven: Leuven University Press, 1996), 545-49.

position about translators, evidence from the literature of the Intertestamental period clearly indicates that this type of reorganizing of information in Hebrew was not unusual. For instance, Brooke points to the rearrangement of information in the Temple Scroll that is similar to the information in the tabernacle accounts and uses this as his basis for positing a different *Vorlage* for the 𝔊 tabernacle accounts.[155] Given that rearrangements of texts are known to exist in Hebrew from the general time period of the 𝔊 translation of the tabernacle accounts, would the translator of the second account have assumed that that type of rearranging and abbreviating would be acceptable if it improved the literary effect? Or, would the translator have felt bound to translate the text as a legal document in a very literal manner? The crucial and unanswerable question is the definition of faithfulness or accuracy used by the translator of Exodus. Could a faithful/accurate translation include the rearrangement of material according to a different logical system? Sanderson notes about ancient editorial and scribal processes,

> It seems, then, that the <u>words</u> of revelation were treated with more care than the <u>form</u> and <u>structure</u> of revelation. <u>Words</u> from Deuteronomy could be brought into Exodus even if they were thus out of their revealed <u>position</u>. Apparently the scribes attributed greater revelatory significance to exactness of wording than to the structure of a pericope or of a scroll. This freedom extended even to a certain disregard for time and place in narratives. If Yahweh had ever at any time in Moses' life promised a prophet to come (or commanded the building of an altar on Gerizim!), then those words could be placed during the theophany at Sinai.[156]

If this attitude was prevalent in the culture at the time when the 𝔐 and 4QpaleoExod^m were developing, it is hard to imagine that translators of the tabernacle accounts were somehow aloof to that influence despite the fact that minute exegetical similarities between the 𝔐 and 𝔊 have been noted throughout this study. Modern translators definitely use this technique, though there is always a continuing debate about the extent to which it should be used.[157] Ultimately, the

---

155. Brooke, "Temple Scroll and LXX Exodus 35-40," 81-106.
156. Sanderson, *Exodus Scroll from Qumran*, 271.
157. Modern translation organizations often use an abbreviated Old Testament that eliminates many of the tedious, detailed sections and adds summaries to connect the passages. The Papua New Guinea Branch of the Summer Institute of Linguistics has prepared a suggested "short" Old Testament with summaries that includes approximately 27% of the material in the Old Testament. See International Translation Department, *Old Testament Selections*, Translator's Workplace Version 2.0 [CD-ROM] (Summer Institute of Linguistics et al., 1995). Their choice of material from the tabernacle account illustrates a modern approach to the redundancy. From the first account, selected verses interspersed with summaries of the longer, more detailed passages are used to communicate the information. The second account, however, begins with a very brief summary that states that Moses followed God's command, asked the people for offerings and then Bezalel, Oholiab, and the skilled

limits of acceptability are set by the community for which the translation is being produced. This is the information that we are lacking for the tabernacle accounts of 𝔊 Exodus and hence the question remains unresolved. The danger in all speculations of this sort is that we as modern readers will either assume that the translators in antiquity shared the same presuppositions about translation that we hold or that we will limit translators due to our perception of the "unenlightened" techniques of the past.

V. Conclusions

Accuracy, as defined in this chapter, centers around the issue of whether or not the same meaning is communicated in the 𝔊 as is present in the 𝔐. Modern translation theory recognizes that each text contains three types of meaning—referential, organizational, and situational. All three of these types of meaning can either be communicated explicitly or implicitly in the text without changing the meaning of the text. A detailed examination and categorization of over nine hundred identified variants in the control sample and tabernacle accounts revealed that approximately half of the pluses, minuses, synonymous variants, and differences in order resulted in a change in the status of the meaning from explicit to implicit or vice versa, rather than resulting in a difference in the meaning. The other half of the variants, however, were real, though often minute, differences in the meaning. Many of the more "significant" differences could be traced to an exegetical interest in harmonizing the text both internally and with respect to other Pentateuchal passages, a tendency that was also seen in the 𝔐. Other differences added a slight layer of meaning to the text that probably reflected the translator's interpretation or the interpretation that was current in his community. Whatever the source of these differences, the important fact is that they were distributed throughout both tabernacle accounts with similar types of changes being made in both accounts.

The most significant difference between the two accounts was found in the minuses. The second tabernacle account had a significantly higher number of minuses. These minuses were also significantly larger and resulted in a greater loss of referential meaning than those seen in the first account. Most of the meaning that was lost, however, was of a secondary nature, such as materials, measurements, and peripheral items. Accounting for these differences has led to much speculation about the source of the differences, i.e., the use of a shorter *Vorlage*, the work of the translator, or the work of a later editor.

---

workers made everything according to the way God had shown Moses. The only translated sections are 39:32-40; 40:1-2, 16-38. As abbreviated as this "short" Old Testament might appear, it is still a much greater amount of material than two other forms of "short" Old Testaments in which the tabernacle accounts are basically eliminated.

Along with the minuses, however, there was a pervasive layer of minute changes in grammatical forms (included in appendix B) that highlighted the fact that the two tabernacle accounts were related, but were not identical copies, i.e., the parallel passages in the 𝕾 were not generally copied from one account to the other. The interdependence of the two accounts was seen in the similarities between the accounts despite these minute differences.[158] The direction of dependency, however, could not be proven from that evidence. It was only in a detailed comparison of the parallel sections about the breastpiece and the lampstand that the translation in the second account was shown to be a distinct improvement on the ambiguous and less accurate translation that was found in the first account. Thus, the second account, when compared to the first account, was shown to be a careful translation that used the first translation as its point of reference and left much information implicit with the assumption that the reader would have already read and basically understood the first account. Interestingly, the largest section missing in the second account was the building of the tabernacle, a section that was translated with a much greater degree of accuracy than other parallel sections in the first account. In contrast, the courtyard and the instructions for the breastpiece, both of which were less accurately translated in the first account, appear in very complete forms in the second tabernacle account.

The reason for the reordering of the material in the second account has been the source of much speculation, but the variants in 𝕾 38 point to the fact that the translation emphasizes the material used in the construction of the items rather than using the sequential, event-oriented form of the 𝔐. This reordering was not discussed in this chapter, but most studies agree that both the 𝕾 and 𝔐 systems have a certain logic about them, i.e., the arrangement appears purposeful rather than just being an accident that occurred in the process of transmitting the text.[159] Gooding sought to assign the rearranging of the text to the editor, who also added several pluses, two of which were discussed above. A careful study of the pluses,

---

158. The fact that these differences in parallel passages were not harmonized could be viewed as additional evidence against the hypothesis that the minuses and reordering were the work of an editor, if editors are presupposed to "correct" these kinds of grammatical differences.

159. Swete says, "It is clear from this comparison that both 𝕾 and 𝔐 follow a system, i.e. that the difference of sequence is due to a deliberate rearrangement of the groups. Either the Alexandrian translator has purposely changed their relative order, giving precedence to the ornaments of the priesthood ... or he had before him ... another Hebrew text in which the present Greek order was observed." (Swete, *Introduction to the Old Testament in Greek*, 235.) Wevers attributes the reordering to the translator and notes, "The answer to this cannot, of course, be an absolute one, and it must also be methodologically conditioned by the principle that different parent texts should only be postulated if reasonable attempts to understand Exod [𝕾] on the basis of a text more or less like 𝔐 have been made." (WeversText, 144-45.) Finn likewise attributes the reordering to the translator, but says, "Unskilful [sic] condensation and rearrangement of a fuller original would account for all these peculiarities. *Where the order differs, the Hebrew is consistent and natural, the Greek confused and contradictory.*" See Finn, "The Tabernacle Chapters," 466.

however, shows that the vocabulary in those pluses is being used in the same way as other words in the second tabernacle account. Thus, the pluses are probably the work of the translator of the second account. With no other textual evidence that necessitates a hypothetical editor, we are forced to face the issue that is at the core of all analyses of the tabernacle accounts—our presuppositions about translators. If translators are envisioned as being bound by a literal mind-set in which Scriptures must be handled carefully, then the only options are to either posit a shorter *Vorlage* or an editor who was somehow not bound by the same scruples as the translator. If, however, translators are envisioned as being products of their cultural time period in which multiple forms of Hebrew Scriptures were present and in which scriptural texts were rearranged, interspersed with commentary, and harmonized with other scriptural passages, then it is hard to image how translators could have escaped that influence and approached the text as a legal document that had to be rendered very literally. Even Philo, who held the Greek translation in high esteem, regularly modified the passages he quoted and added his own interpretation.[160]

This question about the translator's approach to the text will never be resolved due to our lack of a clear knowledge of the translator's culture. Rather than continuing the debate that hinges on presuppositions about what translators would and would not have done in antiquity, this chapter has simply described in detail the differences between the 𝔊 and the 𝔐. By accumulating similar detailed descriptions of the differences between the 𝔊 and the 𝔐, we may eventually arrive at a clearer picture of the nature of the 𝔊 translations and their translators. This type of accumulated evidence, instead of our presuppositions, would provide a better basis for deciding whether or not the differences are due to the translator or are the evidence of a different *Vorlage*.

---

160. Speaking about Philo, Swete said, "Nevertheless he did not scruple to quote his text freely, changing words at pleasure, and sometimes mingling interpretation with citation. This method of dealing with a source, however high its authority, was probably not peculiar to Philo, but a literary habit which he shared with other Jewish writers of his age." See Swete, *Introduction to the Old Testament in Greek*, 376.

CHAPTER SIX

Conclusion

The tabernacle accounts of 𝔊 Exodus represent one of the most difficult text critical problems in the Pentateuch. This problem was recognized at the beginning of text critical work and in modern times a variety of solutions have been proposed that involve differing views of the development of the text and differing views of the number of translators involved in the production of the 𝔊 translation. In this book a multifaceted approach was used to establish a clearer picture of the nature of the translation. Because of our lack of knowledge of the translator's culture, no definitive conclusion can be reached about this text critical problem. The cumulative effect of minute differences between the two tabernacle accounts, however, points to the likelihood that the second tabernacle account was produced by a second translator using the translation of the first tabernacle account as a point of reference.

In this chapter I will first summarize the findings of the four main chapters of this book. Next, I will briefly evaluate the major theories about the production of the tabernacle accounts in light of the findings of this study with respect to the unity of the core and the remainder of the second tabernacle account, the unity of the first and second tabernacle accounts, and the nature of the translation. Finally, I will conclude by describing a hypothetical sociological setting that would support the view of the production of the tabernacle accounts suggested by the findings of this study.

I. Summary of Four Main Chapters

The four main chapters (chapters two through five) of this book each dealt with a distinct aspect of the text of the tabernacle accounts. Chapter two examined Hebrew textual variants in order to identify variants that may have affected the 𝔊 translation. In the next three chapters, the control sample (11-13) provided a point of comparison for the analysis of the three sections of the tabernacle accounts: first tabernacle account (25-31), core of second tabernacle account (36:8-38:20), and the remainder of the second tabernacle account (35:1-36:7; 38:21-40:38). Chapter three compared the lexical consistency of the translation of nouns and verbs. In chapter four, the grammatical consistency of the translation of three grammatical structures was compared. Chapter five compared the accuracy with which the 𝔊 conveyed the meaning of the 𝔐. In this section I will summarize the findings of each of these chapters.

In chapter two, textual variants in the 𝔚 and 𝔔 manuscripts were discussed in relationship to the 𝔐 in order to identify variants that could have affected the 𝔊 translation. While the 𝔔 manuscripts yielded a few unique variants, the majority of the Hebrew textual variants were found in the 𝔚. Many textual variants that are normally ignored as irrelevant to the analysis of the 𝔊, as well as the textual variants that are normally considered "important," were found either to provide key insights for the interpretation seen in the 𝔊 or to identify a difficulty in the text that the 𝔚 resolved in one manner and the 𝔊 resolved in another. In any case, the "irrelevant" variants often proved to be far from irrelevant in the understanding of the 𝔊. Of the "important" textual variants, it was found that while the 𝔊 did not share some of the major differences in the 𝔚, the 𝔊 and 𝔚 often did share the same exegetical understanding of the text. In addition, it was found that on certain small grammatical differences found throughout the text, the 𝔊 was more likely to follow the reading of the 𝔚 than that of the 𝔐. In conjunction with minute changes it was also shown that at the time of the production of the 𝔚, the complete text in a form similar to the 𝔐 was available, as shown by over one hundred minute changes that resulted in the two tabernacle accounts being more consistent in the 𝔚. Most of these changes resulted either in the first account being conformed to the second account or in both accounts being conformed to a new standard. This indicates that at the time that the 𝔚 recension was produced both accounts were essentially complete.

In chapter three, past studies of lexical consistency were surveyed in order to place in perspective the approach used in this book. In contrast to past studies, which assumed that the 𝔊 was a literal translation that used terms in a stereotypical manner, this study showed that in all four sections of Exodus both nouns and verbs were translated in a context-sensitive manner. Because of the difference in the nature of nouns and verbs, however, this meant that nouns, which tend to refer more often to the same items, were translated with a greater degree of "consistency" than were the verbs. This study also showed that the greater the number of occurrences of a noun or verb, the more likely it was that a wider variety of lexical equivalents would be used due to the wider variety of contexts. While all four sections showed a similar approach to the choice of lexical equivalents, the two accounts did contrast in the choice of a few lexical equivalents, but hardly enough to support a two-translator theory of the production of the tabernacle accounts. Rather, the major difference between the two tabernacle accounts could best be seen in shifts in the usage of lexical equivalents. In the first account, distinct lexical equivalents were generally used for each new context, which led to a multiplicity of lexical equivalents. In the second account, however, the translator used a variety of techniques including the use of lexical equivalents from the first account to create lexical cohesion between the two accounts. While striving to maintain lexical cohesion between the two accounts, the translator of the second account at the same time tried to resolve ambiguities in the Hebrew text and prevent any contradictions between the two accounts. As a result of his careful work, the tabernacle accounts appear to be a unified whole in which the choices of lexical equivalents are context-sensitive and reflect both the natural Greek meaning and the translator's interpretation of the text.

In chapter four, the survey of past grammatical studies illustrated the repeated attempts by scholars to devise statistical means of objectively measuring the grammatical consistency of translations in the 𝔊 Scriptures. These objective methodologies, however, failed to identify the semantic and grammatical bases for differences in the translation of grammatical structures, such as those that were identified by the analysis of three grammatical structures in this chapter (the preposition בְּ, the simple construct chain, the relative clause with אֲשֶׁר). Each structure did, however, have a "default" translation that was the one that occurred most frequently and was probably the translation choice most likely to be used when the translator was unsure of the interpretation of a structure. Despite the use of a context-sensitive approach in all sections, there were minute differences in interpretation reflected in the translation of a few structures that could be used as supporting evidence for the two-translator theory of the production of the 𝔊 tabernacle accounts. The most significant insight from this chapter, however, was that the tabernacle accounts were shown to be consistently context-sensitive in their translation of grammatical structures in contrast to Gooding's picture of a consistently inconsistent translator.

In chapter five, a review of two text-critical studies of Exodus pointed to the effect of presuppositions on the interpretation of textual variants. Rather than attempting to identify the preferred readings, as has been the case in many text-critical studies, this study of the accuracy of the tabernacle accounts was done from the perspective of modern translation theory in which the meaning of the 𝔊 was compared with that of the 𝔐 to identify the differences in meaning. These differences were then categorized according to whether they were quantitative differences or differences in status (implicit versus explicit) with respect to the referential, organizational (participant referencing and other grammatical factors), or situational (cultural) meaning. This categorization of over nine hundred textual variants in the four sections of Exodus showed that the same types of variants were found in all sections. The major difference between the two accounts that was quantified by this study (but was already intuitively identified in all past studies) was the fact that the second tabernacle account differed significantly in the quantity of minuses that affected referential meaning. An examination of these minuses, however, showed that the information that was "missing" was not the main facts, but was primarily the explanatory details. With the exception of the minuses, this categorization of textual variants showed that the types of adjustments made throughout the tabernacle accounts were those that are common to all translations, both ancient and modern. Despite the similarities, however, differences in approach seen in parallel passages showed that sections that were translated in an ambiguous or inaccurate manner in the first account had been used by the translator of the second account to produce a more accurate, though sometimes abbreviated, translation. In addition, it was shown in chapter five that the two large pluses most often identified as containing contradictions with respect to the remainder of the text, were in fact shown to be consistent as long as the terms were read in context, rather than as abstract terms used in a stereotypical manner. Despite the clarity of the differences between translation techniques used in these parallel passages, the problem of the number of translators and the source of the differences between the two tabernacle accounts proved to be ultimately unsolvable because all conclusions rest on our presuppositions about what a translator in antiquity would or would not have done in the process of producing a translation. Specifically, we have no historical evidence that would prove that abbreviation of a text would have been accepted in the ancient community for which the 𝔊 translation was produced.

II. Comparison with Previous Hypotheses

Previous hypotheses about the production of the tabernacle accounts of 𝔊 Exodus have divided over three major issues, each of which will be addressed in this section. First, the unity or lack of unity of the second account has been a major factor in almost every theory due to the disordered nature of the center section of the second account in 𝔊. Second, several theories have concentrated on proving or disproving the consistency of translation techniques used in the first and second tabernacle accounts. Finally, underlying differences are seen in the scholarly presuppositions about the nature of translations in antiquity.

Unity of the Core and Remainder of Second Account

In past scholarly analyses, the second account has been divided in two distinct ways. Popper and Nelson separated out the core of the second tabernacle account (36:8-38:20), which contains the majority of the minuses, large pluses, reordering, and "contradictory" lexical equivalents. Popper assigned this core of the second tabernacle account to one of the later strata in the development of the Hebrew text and claimed that the difference in ordering in the 𝔊 was due to a *Vorlage* that differed from the 𝔐, which had not yet been completed.[1] Nelson shared Popper's

---

1. Julius Popper, *Der biblische Bericht über die Stiftshütte: Ein Beitrag zur Geschichte der Composition und Diaskeue des Pentateuch.* (Leipzig: Heinrich Hunger, 1862). A summary of Popper's conclusions is found in Gooding, 5-6. For a more detailed description of Popper's argumentation see Nelson, 3-8.

view of the distinctiveness of this core section and likewise assigned these differences primarily to a difference in *Vorlage*. Unlike Popper, however, Nelson concluded that the *Vorlage* of this core section in the 𝔊 was the original part of the tabernacle account that was then used as the basis for the development of the first account and a fuller, revised form of the second account. One of the main pieces of evidence used to support this view was the supposed early nature of the vocabulary used in the 𝔊 of the core of the second account.² Thus, Popper and Nelson saw the difference in 36:8-38:20 as one of the *Vorlage*, primarily because of the difference in ordering, content, and vocabulary. A difference in *Vorlage* for both of these theories also meant a difference in translators because of the view that the text developed over a long period of time. Gooding, in contrast, thought that the *Vorlage* of 𝔊 Exodus was similar to the 𝔐 and he also assigned most of the differences in vocabulary and the minuses to the translator's consistently inconsistent translation technique. In contrast to Popper and Nelson, Gooding thought that 𝔊 38 was the only section that was different in nature from the remainder of the second account.³ Gooding assigned this difference to an editor because of internal contradictions in 𝔊 38. He also assigned the reordering of the center part of the second tabernacle account to the same editor because he did not believe that the reordering would have been done by the primary translator.

In this study, which focused on translation technique rather than on the development of the text, the core of the second tabernacle account was compared with the remainder of the second tabernacle account with respect to the lexical consistency, grammatical consistency, and accuracy. In all areas, the core and the remainder of the second tabernacle account were found to use the same approach to the translation of the text. Statistical differences between the core and the remainder of the second tabernacle account were primarily due to the size of the core section, rather than the nature of the translation. All of the statistical studies used in this book highlighted problems that related to statistical analyses of small texts. When the actual choices of equivalents for words and grammatical structures were examined, however, no significant differences were found. Moreover, the supposed internal contradictions of the lexical equivalents in the larger pluses were found to be consistent with the translation techniques of the second tabernacle account. The difficulty with Gooding's analysis proved to be his presuppositions about the nature of a translation and the resulting rejection of his own analytical observations, rather than a problem in the translation itself, as discussed in chapter five. Nelson's attempt to prove the antiquity of the vocabulary of the core of the second account was also shown to be invalid or at least questionable in all of the examples examined in chapter three. While I did not discuss all of the over 140 words examined by Nelson, the examples chosen were some of the

---

2. Ibid., 364-67.
3. Gooding, 47, 59, 100-101.

key ones that supposedly proved the validity of his analysis. On the basis of my analysis of the lexical and grammatical consistency of the core and remainder of the second tabernacle account, any theory based on the lack of consistency in the translation of words and grammatical structures within the second tabernacle account is unlikely to be valid.

This study was not, however, able to seriously address the issue of the differences of order within the second account and the source(s) of the minuses and pluses, though suggestions have been made throughout the study. With respect to the minuses, it was shown that most of the minuses in the second account of 𝔊 Exodus were generally information that was secondary to the major points of the text. While these could be due to the use of a shorter *Vorlage*, it was noted that the effect of the minuses, i.e., information left implicit in the second account, was to increase the cohesion between the two accounts because a "correct" understanding of the second tabernacle account in the 𝔊 could only be obtained by reading it in tandem with the first account. The larger pluses, in contrast, were generally viewed by scholars as additions by an editor or a revisor rather than as the translation of a different *Vorlage*.[4] Several of these larger pluses in the second account served as bridges to connect sections within the text in a more consistent manner. Other larger pluses demonstrated a distinct hermeneutical approach to the text that was based on the presupposition that the text was a unified, non-contradictory whole. This same hermeneutical approach was seen in the 𝔐, though it was often manifested in distinct ways in the 𝔊. Thus, while the pluses could have derived from a later editor, the nature of the pluses suited the general hermeneutical approach that was characteristic of the general time period of the translator.

Differences in order in the second account have proven to be the most difficult to assign to a probable source. While an editor could have produced the reordering in the text, the more likely source would have been either the translator himself or the use of a *Vorlage* that contained a different order. This was especially true since the supposed internal inconsistencies that necessitated Gooding's positing of an editor were shown to be actually consistent with the general approach in the second account. Ultimately, however, the decision about the differences in order, pluses, and minuses in the second account depended on the scholar's perception of the nature of translation in antiquity, which will be discussed below.

Unity of the First and Second Tabernacle Accounts

Most scholarly discussions of the unity or lack of unity between the first and second accounts have hinged on the reported differences in choices of lexical equiva-

---

4. See Nelson, 365 and David W. Gooding, "Two Possible Examples of Midrashic Interpretation in the Septuagint Exodus," in *Wort, Lied und Gottesspruch: Festschrift für Joseph Ziegler*, ed. Josef Schreiner (Echter Verlag: Katholisches Bibelwerk, 1972), 44-48, who emphasizes the midrashic nature of some of these pluses.

lents. McNeile pointed to the contrasting choices of lexical equivalents and noted that the first and second accounts used different terms and therefore must have been produced by different translators.[5] Finn and Gooding, however, were easily able to show the fallacies of McNeile's data and his approach to the problem. Instead of two distinct translators, Finn and Gooding showed that the same translator produced most of both tabernacle accounts using the same consistently inconsistent approach.[6] While Nelson argued against the unity of the second tabernacle account, he contended that the first and last sections of the second tabernacle account were part of the same Palestinian revision that was seen in the first tabernacle account.[7] In contrast to these general arguments for the unity of the first account with at least parts of the second account, there has been a steadily growing undercurrent that has noted differences between the accounts that have not been accounted for by those who argue for the complete or partial unity of the two accounts. Initially, this came in a small article by Bogaert on the differences in the orientation of the courtyard in the two accounts, an analysis that was accepted by Wevers.[8] In addition to this difference in vocabulary, Wevers noted a few grammatical differences between the two accounts and other small differences in vocabulary items. Rather than arguing for a second translator as the source of the differences in order and the abbreviation of the text, however, Wevers assumed that these differences could have been produced by a translator using a text similar to the 𝔐 and that the approach in the second account was different enough from the first account that it must have been the product of a second translator. Wevers' main interest, however, was in the nature of the translation, rather than in trying to prove a particular theory.[9]

As with the core and remainder of the second account, this study has shown that both the first and second accounts used a context-sensitive approach to the choice of lexical equivalents and the translation of grammatical structures. The actual contrasting lexical equivalents in the two accounts, in contrast to the shared

---

5. A. H. McNeile, *The Book of Exodus* (London: Methuen and Company, 1908), 226.

6. A. H. Finn, "The Tabernacle Chapters," *Journal of Theological Studies* 16 (1915): 449-53 and Gooding, 32-37.

7. Nelson, 130.

8. P. M. Bogaert, "L'orientation du parvis du sanctuaire dans la version grecque de l'Exode (*Ex.*, 27, 9-13 LXX)," *L'Antiquité classique* 50 (1981): 79-85 and WeversText, 123.

9. This is most clearly seen in the introduction to his comparison of the two tabernacle accounts where he says, "I propose to approach the problem from a somewhat different vantage point. I should not want to give priority to the question How well or how accurately did Exod [𝔊] reproduce 𝔐, or better said, its parent text, but rather How did the translator(s) make sense out of his parent text? In other words, Does Exod make sense, not Does Exod accurately equal the Hebrew? In fact, I would without prejudice start with a basic assumption which I would abandon only if the investigation led me to do so, viz. that Exod must have made sense to its creator(s). I find it difficult to conceive of the Alexandrian community accepting a translation as a canonical text that was illogical, confused and inconsistent." Ibid., 119.

and partially overlapping choices of lexical equivalents, were so minimal that any theory built on these differences alone is likely to collapse under the weight of the similarities. This is true to an even greater extent in the consistency of the approach used in the translation of grammatical structures. Both tabernacle accounts used a similar wide range of translation equivalents to express the same types of semantic functions in each account. Likewise, the pluses, minuses, synonymous variants, and differences in order had similar effects on the referential, organizational, and situational meaning in both tabernacle accounts. The differences between the two accounts were seen in the proportion of changes in the second account rather than in the types of changes. Thus, on the surface level, arguments based on grammatical and lexical consistency would support the claim that the two accounts should be viewed as a unit. This "proof" of the unity of the two tabernacle accounts, however, begins to unravel when one examines the lexical equivalents in detail. Each account was shown to use a distinct approach. In the first account this led to a multiplicity of lexical equivalents in which different terms were used for each context. In the second account, in contrast, the translator was able to assess the lexical equivalents used in the first account and use enough of them to create lexical cohesion between the two accounts while at the same time correcting ambiguities and other problems in the first account. This resulted in a second account that appeared to be a unit with the first account and yet on the whole is a more accurate translation. This same type of minute differences was seen in the translation of grammatical structures, though the differences in grammatical consistency were mainly seen in the interpretation, as evidenced in the choice of translation equivalents, rather than by a difference in the types of translation equivalents used in each account. Ultimately, the problem of the minuses and the differences in order became the key contrasts between the two accounts. While the first account is not lacking in some of these same types of differences, the sheer quantity of the differences raises questions that either result in the hypothesis that the second tabernacle account was based on a *Vorlage* that was different from the 𝔐 or that a different approach to the translation was used, which in all likelihood would mean that the account was produced by a different translator. Again, however, the key question was whether or not a translator in antiquity would have felt free to abbreviate and reorder his text.

Nature of the Translation

The attributed source of the differences in the second tabernacle, whether the *Vorlage* or the translator, ultimately is determined by the scholar's presuppositions about the nature of translation in antiquity. Aejmelaeus argued that differences in the tabernacle accounts should not be a case of either differences in *Vorlage* or differences due to translation technique, but rather a case of both differences due to *Vorlage* and differences due to translation technique. At the same time, however, she rejected the notion that the major differences could be due to the translator because translators in antiquity supposedly would not have departed that drastically from their text.[10] While Aejmelaeus is correct in that some changes are due to a difference in *Vorlage* and some are due to translation technique, she has effectively drawn the line at how much she is willing to assign to the translator. It is this presupposition that has effectively determined her conclusions about the tabernacle account. Coincidentally, her analysis also happened to fit well with her historico-critical approach to the development of the text in which she followed Kuenen and Noth.[11] A different approach to the argument about the order in the second account was seen in Brooke, who pointed to similar differences in order in the Temple Scroll and argued that the ⅏ could have been based on a *Vorlage* that already was abbreviated and contained the differences in order.[12] As can be seen in his article and other studies of texts from Qumran, there was a multiplicity of forms of texts at Qumran and this highlights the fact that texts were handled in a slightly different manner in antiquity than in modern times. Unfortunately, no ℚ manuscripts have yet been found to support directly the existence of a different order of the text in the second tabernacle account of Exodus. If such a scroll had been found, then there would have been little need for this study because the text critical problem of the tabernacle accounts of ⅏ Exodus would have been solved.

On the other side of the argument, however, are those such as Cook, who argued that the reordering in 38 was similar to that of Proverbs 31 and thus was the product of the translator rather than due to a difference in *Vorlage*.[13] Wevers took a different tack and generally strove to show the reasonableness of the ⅏ translation. Wevers emphasized the fact that the translator perceived his task as

---

10. Anneli Aejmelaeus, "Septuagintal Translation Techniques—A Solution to the Problem of the Tabernacle Account," in *Septuagint, Scrolls and Cognate Writings: Papers Presented to the International Symposium on the Septuagint and Its Relations to the Dead Sea Scrolls and Other Writings, Manchester, 1990*, ed. George J. Brooke and Barnabas Lindars, Septuagint and Cognate Studies, no. 33 (Atlanta, Ga.: Scholars Press, 1992), 385-86.

11. Ibid., 396, 399. Bogaert in "L'importance de la Septante et du «Monacensis» de la Vetus Latina pour l'exégèse du livre de l'Exode (chap. 35-40)," in *Studies in the Book of Exodus: Redaction-Reception-Interpretation*, ed. Marc Vervenne (Leuven: Leuven University Press, 1996), 399-428, likewise argues for differences in the *Vorlage*, but his argument in a sense boils down to an advocacy of the value of studying the Old Latin as another witness to an early stage in the development of the text. Due to the narrow scope of this study, I was unable to evaluate critically Bogaert's claims concerning this particular text. In theory, though, I would agree that examining more early translations would ultimately improve the quality of a text critic's work.

12. George J. Brooke, "The Temple Scroll and LXX Exodus 35-40," in *Septuagint, Scrolls and Cognate Writings: Papers Presented to the International Symposium on the Septuagint and Its Relations to the Dead Sea Scrolls and Other Writings, Manchester, 1990*, ed. George J. Brooke and Barnabas Lindars, Septuagint and Cognate Studies, no. 33 (Atlanta, Ga.: Scholars Press, 1990), 81-106.

13. Johann Cook, "Exodus 38 and Proverbs 31: A Case of Different Order of Verses and Chapters in the Septuagint," in *Studies in the Book of Exodus: Redaction-Reception-Interpretation*, ed. Marc Vervenne (Leuven: Leuven University Press, 1996), 537-49.

that of communicating the message of a *Vorlage*, which was probably similar to that of the 𝔐. Because of the high esteem with which Wevers viewed the 𝔊 translation, however, he sometimes made text critical decisions based on what the translator should have done and also interpreted the ambiguities of the 𝔊 in light of the 𝔐, as discussed in chapter five. Thus, the major difference in perspective seems to be between those who presuppose that a translator can make major adjustments or reinterpretations in the text and those who presuppose that the ancient translator would not have been free to do such a thing.

Concerning a similar text-critical problem in Jeremiah, Tov comments as follows:

> In text-critical studies, cases of a short versus a long text are normally evaluated individually on the basis of internal evidence. However, unlike other books of the LXX, the »omissions« of Jer do not occur occasionally; rather, they characterize the LXX of this book as a whole. For this reason they should be explained collectively.... Either we adopt the solution suggested above that the Hebrew text of the translator was shorter than MT or we assume that the translator deliberately shortened the Hebrew Vorlage. In any event, the attempt should be made to explain individual »omissions« as much as possible according to one of the two possible hypotheses.... It would be methodologically unsound to invoke one principle in one passage and another one elsewhere. For since the same types of omissions recur throughout the book, they should be approached with the same method.[14]

While there are differences between 35-40 and Jeremiah, the similarity of the problem is such that Tov's suggestion about trying to explain all of the changes by means of one hypothesis, rather than going back and forth between the two, is definitely valid. In this book I have not tried to specifically argue for one position versus another, but the cumulative weight of the minute differences between the accounts and the similar nature of the minuses could all be explained by the theory that the second tabernacle account was produced by a second translator who used the translation of the first tabernacle account as his point of reference. This, however, would only be acceptable if one were willing to allow ancient translators the same freedom that is often ascribed to ancient editors and that resulted in the

---

14. Tov did, however, allow that there would be "exceptions from the general theory." Among these he noted the omission of particles due to translation technique and omissions due to scribal errors and other errors that occurred in the transmission of the text, but he emphasized that these "should be reduced to an absolute minimum, in order that as many details as possible might be ascribed to the overall theory." See Emanuel Tov, "Exegetical Notes on the Hebrew Vorlage of the LXX of Jeremiah 27 (34)," *Zeitschrift für die alttestamentliche Wissenschaft* 91 (1979): 76. Janzen quotes Tov as part of his critique of Soderlund's "mediating" position that goes back and forth between alternate approaches to explaining the differences in Jeremiah. See J. Gerald Janzen, "A Critique of Sven Soderlund's *The Greek Text of Jeremiah: A Revised Hypothesis*," *Bulletin of the International Organization for Septuagint and Cognate Studies* 22 (1989): 16-47.

variety of text forms that are found at Qumran.¹⁵ In any case, whether or not the abbreviation and reordering were the work of the translator of the second account, it is unlikely that the translator of the first account would have produced the second tabernacle account using an abbreviated *Vorlage*. An abbreviated *Vorlage* in and of itself would not have resulted in the shift in lexical equivalents and the retranslation of sections that were ambiguous in the first account, both of which are most easily explained by the hypothesis of a second translator rather than a sudden improvement in the translation technique of the first translator.

III. One View of the Production of the Tabernacle Accounts

Given the likelihood that the second tabernacle account was produced by a second translator using the translation of the first tabernacle account as a point of reference, several remaining tensions need to be explained. Specifically, any hypothesis concerning the production of the 𝔊 tabernacle accounts needs to account for the similarity in the general translation technique while at the same time explaining why the first account was not revised to correspond more closing to the second account, if indeed the second account was translated at a later time. While this can only be a matter of speculation, it may provide some explanation for Wevers' "tentative conclusion that Exod B was created later (not necessarily much later), and by another translator seems to be a not unreasonable one."¹⁶ The unity of the tabernacle accounts as seen in the general style and the context-sensitive approach points to translators who were schooled in the same approach to the text. This similarity in training, whether formal or informal, would account for the similarity of the lexical and grammatical consistency seen throughout all sections of the text. Some scholars have suggested that the presence of a second translator points of necessity to the fact that the second account was not present when the first translator did his work. Based on my experience with modern translators, however, I would suggest that while that is one possible explanation, it is not the only explanation for the translator not continuing on through the second tabernacle account.¹⁷ For whatever reason, a fairly convincing argument can be made that

---

15. Because of my background as a modern missionary Bible translator, I am predisposed to envisioning the translators of antiquity in light of modern translators, who vary greatly in both ability and approach to the text. My predisposition has been reinforced through working with 𝔊 Exodus and learning to appreciate the care with which most translation decisions were made and the creativity used in solving translation problems, though the translation is by no means perfect.

16. WeversText, 146.

17. While working with national translators in Papua New Guinea, I have noticed two opposite reactions when translators are assigned a section very similar to one they have just completed. For some, it is a sigh of relief in that they have solved the problems once and the second time through is

another translator completed the task by translating the second tabernacle account. Given the improved quality of the second account, despite its abbreviated nature, one might wonder why that translator did not go back and revise the first account. If, however, the second translator was a contemporary of the first and especially if the first translator was the teacher or at least the more experienced translator, then cultural restrictions may have made revision work next to impossible.[18] If the second translator had lived in a distinctly different time period from that in which the translator of the first account lived, then it would have been more likely that a revision of the first account would have been possible, as indeed both accounts were later revised in similar ways.[19] Thus, a working hypothesis would be that 1-34 was completed by an elderly translator, who was possibly the teacher of the second translator. The second translator, for whatever reason, was allowed to complete the task begun by his master and while his own distinct translation style shone through the translation, the student was skilled enough to make the work sound like that of his teacher, while not repeating the errors found in his teacher's work. Out of respect for his teacher he left the first account unrevised, but at the same time he did everything he could to make sure that there were no contradictions between the two accounts, just as he also made sure that the tabernacle accounts did not contradict the larger text, i.e., the Pentateuch.[20] Again, this is sheer speculation, but it does set a stage that would provide a basis for the similarities and differences seen in the tabernacle accounts of 𝔊 Exodus.

This study ultimately makes no claims about proving or disproving any particular theory of the number of translators that produced the tabernacle accounts

---

viewed as being easier. Others, however, whether due to boredom or frustration, basically refuse to do a similar passage and insist that someone else be given the "opportunity" to translate the material.

18. This is based on two presuppositions. First, in cultures where elders are respected, their decision is correct even if it is actually wrong. Respect of elders is seen throughout Scriptures and it is still a major factor in many modern cultures. Because of this, my presupposition is that if the translator who produced 1-34 had been an older translator or a teacher, then his work would have been inherently respected, though this would not have eliminated improvements in a separate work based on the elder's work. My second presupposition is a presupposition about human pride. Modern translators of all nationalities become very involved with their work to the point that criticism of the work is viewed as criticism of the translator. If ancient translators suffered from the same problem of pride, then it would have been very hard for a second translator to revise the first account without offending someone, especially if the first translator was still living or if the memory of the first translator was still alive.

19. In the Hexaplaric recension, sections from both tabernacle accounts (e.g., 28:23-28 and 37:24-28) that were minuses in the 𝔊 have been translated from a text similar to the 𝔐 and "added" to the translation. These Hexaplaric additions are included in all critical editions of the text. This revisionary work, however, was probably accomplished at least a century after the original translation, assuming the latest possible date for the 𝔊 and the earliest possible date for the revisionary work.

20. This hermeneutical approach was discussed in chapter five with reference to the plus about Korah's rebellion in 𝔊 38:22.

of the 𝔊 Exodus. Rather than proving a particular theory, the exhaustive analysis of lexical consistency, grammatical consistency, and accuracy of the four sections of Exodus emphasizes the fact that the translator(s) of these sections generally understood the text and tried to communicate that meaning in natural Greek using a full range of translation techniques similar to those used by modern Bible translators. Past claims that have disparaged the nature of the translation failed to view the translation through a translator's eyes and also failed to recognize that these translations, as a form of interpretation, sometimes differed from the original texts that they were translating, or rather they differed from our modern interpretation of the Hebrew texts that we now use. While no claims can be made about proving or disproving a particular theory, this detailed, multifaceted examination of the tabernacle accounts identified consistent, minute differences between the approaches in the two accounts, especially in the translation of the parallel accounts that were ambiguous in the first account. On the basis of this accumulation of minutiae, it seems likely that the second tabernacle account was produced by a second translator who used the translation of the first tabernacle account as a point of reference.

APPENDIX A

CLASSIFICATION OF MINUSES IN THE SECOND ACCOUNT

Type of information in minus	Number of occurrences
Lexical choices—assimilation and words left implicit due to context	31
Location and placement of items	17
Materials, measurements, and construction method	17
Minuses that are either related to exegesis or missing in *Vorlage*	16
Modifiers of noun phrases and other phrases that clarify or emphasize	34
Parallels first account	3
Participant referencing	39
Peripheral items	17
Result of other changes	2
Summary statements	7
Vorlage—Missing in ܡ	7
Total	190

APPENDIX B

COMPARISON OF SOME PARALLEL PASSAGES

First account	Second account in 𝔐	Second account in 𝔊	Adjustment	Comparison
25:4	35:6		identical pluses of modifier	Identical plus
25:5	35:7		identical verses	Identical
25:6	35:8		identical minuses of a verse in both accounts	Identical minus
25:7	35:9		identical verses in both	Identical
25:10	35:12		both contain similar pluses	Similar plus
25:12	37:3	38:3	first account is self-contradictory and second omits problem clause	Second improves on first
25:17	37:6	38:5	both contain explanatory pluses, but pluses are unique in each	Similar plus
25:17	37:6	38:5	second account contains preposition ἐκ as a plus before material	Distinct
25:19	37:8	38:7	second account contains preposition ἐπί, which is based on parallel first account	Second based on first
25:20	37:9	38:8	two accounts use different cases with same preposition	Distinct
25:23	37:10	38:9	second account contains preposition ἐκ as a plus before material	Distinct
25:23-24	37:10-11	38:9	wood and covering it (with gold) are missing in both accounts	Similar minus
25:29	37:16	38:12	opposite order of same items in list	Distinct
26:2	36:9	37:2	opposite order of phrases and clauses	Distinct
26:32	36:36	37:4	second account follows first account, but has added a preposition ἐν and changed the case with ἐπί	Second is a modification of first

First account	Second account in 𝔐	Second account in 𝔊	Adjustment	Comparison
26:36	36:37	37:5	minus in first account not followed in second account —lexical equivalent may have affected this	Distinct
26:37	36:38	37:6	second account reordered to communicate same material as in first	Second based on first
27:3	38:3	38:23	items in list reordered in second account	Distinct
27:9	38:9	37:7	plus in first account not followed in second	Distinct
27:11	38:11	37:9	two accounts use different cases with same Hebrew construction, though may be affected by context	Distinct
27:15	38:15	37:13	two accounts use different vocabulary and grammatical structures for same Hebrew construction	Distinct
27:19	38:20	37:18	tent pegs of tabernacle missing in both but found in plus in 𝔊 38:21	Similar minus
28:11	39:6	36:13	minus in first account not followed in second	Distinct
28:12	39:7	36:14	two accounts use different cases with same preposition	Distinct
28:17	39:10	36:17	plus in second makes like first	Second based on first
28:18	39:11	36:18	identical verses	Identical
28:19	39:12	36:19	identical verses	Identical
28:20	39:13	36:20	first account contains the plus of a preposition ἐν and the second account contains a minus of the last phrase	Distinct
28:32	39:23	36:30	plus of verb makes second like first, but case of noun changed	Second based on first

Appendix B

First account	Second account in 𝔐	Second account in 𝔊	Adjustment	Comparison
28:32	39:23	36:30	meaning rather than form of simile translated in both	Similar change
28:33	39:24	36:31	similar plus in both accounts, but unique particles used	Similar plus
28:33	39:24	36:31	case changed with ἐπί	Distinct
28:34	39:26	36:33	similar minus of repeated phrases in both	Similar minus
28:36	39:30	36:37	case of noun changed	Distinct
28:37	39:31	36:38	case changed with ἐπί (2x), but context may affect these	Distinct
31:2	35:30		second account contains plus of preposition ἐκ	Distinct
31:3	35:31		identical except translation of last phrase	Similar
31:4	35:35		plus makes first account like second of 𝔐, but not 𝔊	First conforms to Hebrew second
31:11	35:19		plus in second account is similar to first account	Second based on first
31:13	35:3		plus in second account makes it more like first account	Second based on first
31:15	35:2		shared change of person/number of verb	Identical
31:15	35:2		minus in second account makes it more like first account	Second based on first

APPENDIX C

CONSTRUCTION AND ASSEMBLY OF THE BREASTPIECE

	First account in 𝔐	First acccount in 𝔊	Second account in 𝔐	Second acccount in 𝔊
make gold filigree settings	28:13	28:13	Missing	Missing
make two chains of pure gold	28:14a שַׁרְשְׁרֹת	28:14a (plus—with flowers)	Missing	Missing
put two rope chains on gold filigree settings	28:14b	28:14b (plus—toward the front)	Missing	Missing
make breastpiece and first 3 rows of stones	28:15-19	28:15-19	39:8-12	36:15-19
row 4—slight improvements in second account	28:20	28:20 (follows 𝔐 and second account of 𝔐)	39:13	36:20
12 names carved on stones	28:21	28:21	39:14	36:21
make two chains upon the breastpiece	28:22 שַׁרְשֹׁת	28:22	39:15 שַׁרְשְׁרֹת	36:22
make two gold filigree settings	(𝔐 28:23)	Missing	39:16a	36:23a
make and attach rings and other items	28:23-27	Missing	39:16b-20	36:23b-27
bind breastpiece to ephod with thread through rings	28:28 (𝔐 28:28b make Urim and Thummim)	Missing	39:21	36:28
Aaron's role in wearing the breastpiece	28:29	28:29	Missing	Missing
put two chains and settings on breastpiece	Missing	28:29a	Missing	Missing

Bibliography

Accordance 3.0. OakTree Software Specialists, Altamonte Springs, Fla., Altamonte Springs, Fla.

Aejmelaeus, Anneli. *Parataxis in the Septuagint: A Study of the Renderings of the Hebrew Coordinate Clauses in the Greek Pentateuch*. Annales Academiae Scientiarum Fennicae: Dissertationes Humanarum Litterarum, no. 31. Helsinki: Suomalainen Tiedeakatemia, 1982.

———. "What Can We Know about the Hebrew *Vorlage* of the Septuagint." *Zeitschrift für die alttestamentliche Wissenschaft* 99 (1987): 58-89.

———. "Septuagintal Translation Techniques—A Solution to the Problem of the Tabernacle Account." In *Septuagint, Scrolls and Cognate Writings: Papers Presented to the International Symposium on the Septuagint and Its Relations to the Dead Sea Scrolls and Other Writings, Manchester, 1990*, ed. George J. Brooke and Barnabas Lindars, Septuagint and Cognate Studies, no. 33, 381-402. Atlanta, Ga.: Scholars Press, 1992.

———. *On the Trail of the Septuagint Translators: Collected Essays*. Kampen, Netherlands: Kok Pharos, 1993.

Aejmelaeus, Anneli, and Raija Sollamo, eds. *Studien zur Septuaginta-Syntax*. Helsinki: Suomalainen Tiedeakatemia, 1987.

The Anchor Bible Dictionary. Edited by David Noel Freedman. 6 vols., New York: Doubleday, 1992.

S.v. "Overlay," by Carol Meyers. 5:52.

S.v. "Samaritan Pentateuch," by Bruce K. Waltke. 5:932-40.

Baab, Otto J. "A Theory of Two Translators for the Greek Genesis." *Journal of Biblical Literature* 52 (1933): 239-43.

Baillet, M., J. T. Milik, and R. de Vaux. *Les 'Petites Grottes' de Qumrân: Exploration de la falaise, Les grottes 2Q, 3Q, 5Q, 6Q, 7Q à 10Q, Le rouleau de cuivre*. Vol. 3, pt. 1. Discoveries in the Judaean Desert of Jordan. Oxford: Clarendon Press, 1962.

Barnwell, Katherine, Paul Dancy, and Anthony G. Pope. *Key Biblical Terms in the New Testament: An Aid for Bible Translators*. Dallas, Tex.: Summer Institute of Linguistics, forthcoming.

Barr, James. *The Typology of Literalism in Ancient Biblical Translations*. Mitteilungen des Septuaginta-Unternehmens, no. 15. Göttingen: Vandenhoeck & Ruprecht, 1979.

———. *The Variable Spellings of the Hebrew Bible: The Schweich Lectures of the British Academy 1986*. Oxford: Oxford University Press, 1989.

Barthélemy, Dominique, A. R. Hulst, Norbert Lohfink, W. D. McHardy, H. P. Rüger, and James A. Sanders. *Preliminary and Interim Report on the Hebrew Old Testament Text Project*. Vol. 1, *Pentateuch*. New York: United Bible Societies, 1973.

Bogaert, P. M. "L'orientation du parvis du sanctuaire dans la version grecque de l'Exode (*Ex.*, 27, 9-13 LXX)." *L'Antiquité classique* 50 (1981): 79-85.

———. "L'importance de la Septante et du «Monacensis» de la Vetus Latina pour l'exégèse du livre de l'Exode (chap. 35-40)." In *Studies in the Book of Exodus: Redaction-Reception-Interpretation*, ed. Marc Vervenne, 399-428. Leuven: Leuven University Press, 1996.

Brock, Sebastian P. "Aspects of Translation Technique in Antiquity." In *Syriac Perspectives on Late Antiquity*, 69-87. London: Variorum Reprints, 1984.

———. "To Revise or Not to Revise: Attitudes to Jewish Biblical Translation." In *Septuagint, Scrolls and Cognate Writings: Papers Presented to the International Symposium on the Septuagint and Its Relations to the Dead Sea Scrolls and Other Writings, Manchester, 1990*, ed. George J. Brooke and Barnabas Lindars, Septuagint and Cognate Studies, no. 33, 301-38. Atlanta, Ga.: Scholars Press, 1992.

Brooke, George J. "The Temple Scroll and LXX Exodus 35-40." In *Septuagint, Scrolls and Cognate Writings: Papers Presented to the International Symposium on the Septuagint and Its Relations to the Dead Sea Scrolls and Other Writings, Manchester, 1990*, ed. George J. Brooke and Barnabas Lindars, Septuagint and Cognate Studies, no. 33, 81-106. Atlanta, Ga.: Scholars Press, 1990.

Brooks, James A., and Carlton L. Winbery. *Syntax of New Testament Greek*. Lanham, Md.: University Press of America, 1979.

Brown, William P. *Structure, Role, and Ideology in the Hebrew and Greek Text of Genesis 1:1-2:3*. SBL Dissertation Series, no. 132. Atlanta, Ga.: Scholars Press, 1993.

Callow, Kathleen. *Discourse Considerations in Translating the Word of God*. Grand Rapids, Mich.: Zondervan, 1974.

Cassuto, U. *A Commentary on the Book of Exodus*. Jerusalem: Magnes Press, 1967.

Cook, Johann. "Exodus 38 and Proverbs 31: A Case of Different Order of Verses and Chapters in the Septuagint." In *Studies in the Book of Exodus: Redaction-Reception-Interpretation*, ed. Marc Vervenne, 537-49. Leuven: Leuven University Press, 1996.

Cross, Frank Moore. "The History of the Biblical Text in the Light of Discoveries in the Judaean Desert." In *Qumran and the History of the Biblical Text*, ed.

Frank Moore Cross and Shemaryahu Talmon, 177-95. Cambridge, Mass.: Harvard University Press, 1975.

Davila, James R. "Text-Type and Terminology: Genesis and Exodus as Test Cases." *Revue de Qumran* 16 (1993): 3-37.

De Vries, Simon J. "The Hexateuchal Criticism of Abraham Kuenen." *Journal of Biblical Literature* 82 (1963): 31-57.

Driver, S. R. *The Book of Exodus*. The Cambridge Bible for Schools and Colleges, ed. A. F. Kirkpatrick. Cambridge: Cambridge University Press, 1918.

Durham, John I. *Exodus*. Vol. 3. Word Biblical Commentary. Waco, Tex.: Word Books, 1987.

Elliger, K., and W. Rudolph, eds. *Biblia Hebraica Stuttgartensia*. Stuttgart: Deutsche Bibelgesellschaft, 1977.

Finn, A. H. "The Tabernacle Chapters." *Journal of Theological Studies* 16 (1915): 449-82.

Flint, Peter W. "Methods for Determining Relationships between Manuscripts, with Special Reference to the Psalms Scrolls." In *Methods of Investigation of the Dead Sea Scrolls and the Khirbet Qumran Site: Present Realities and Future Prospects*, ed. Michael O. Wise, Norman Golb, John J. Collins, and Dennis G. Pardee, Vol. 722, Annals of the New York Academy of Science, 197-209. New York: The New York Academy of Sciences, 1994.

Fraenkel, Detlef. "Die Quellen der asterisierten Zusätze im zweiten Tabernakelbericht Exod 35-40." In *Studien zur Septuaginta—Robert Hanhart zu Ehren: Aus Anlass seines 65. Geburtstages*, ed. Detlef Fraenkel, Udo Quast, and John William Wevers, Mitteilungen des Septuaginta-Unternehmens, no. 20, 140-86. Göttingen: Vandenhoeck & Ruprecht, 1990.

———. "Übersetzungsnorm und literarische Gestaltung—Spuren individueller Übersetzungstechnik in Exodus 25ff. + 35ff." In *VIII Congress of the International Organization for Septuagint and Cognate Studies, Paris, 1991*, ed. Leonard Greenspoon and Olivier Munnich, Septuagint and Cognate Studies, no. 41, 73-87. Atlanta, Ga.: Scholars Press, 1995.

Frankel, Z. *Ueber den Einfluss der palästinischen Exegese auf die alexandrinische Hermeneutik*. Leipzig: Joh. Ambr. Barth, 1851.

Freedman, David Noel. "The Massoretic Text and the Qumran Scrolls: A Study in Orthography." In *Qumran and the History of the Biblical Text*, ed. Frank Moore Cross and Shemaryahu Talmon, 196-211. Cambridge, Mass.: Harvard University Press, 1975.

Fritsch, Charles T. *The Anti-anthropomorphisms of the Greek Pentateuch*. Princeton: Princeton University Press, 1943.

Glanzman, George S. Review of *The Account of the Tabernacle: Translation and Textual Problems of the Greek Exodus*, by David W. Gooding. *Theological Studies* 23 (1962): 106-8.

Goodenough, Erwin R. "The Menorah among Jews of the Roman World." *Hebrew Union College Annual* 23 (1950-51): 449-92.

Gooding, David W. *The Account of the Tabernacle: Translation and Textual Problems of the Greek Exodus*. Texts and Studies: Contributions to Biblical and Patristic Literature, ed. C. H. Dodd, no. 6. Cambridge: Cambridge University Press, 1959.

———. "Two Possible Examples of Midrashic Interpretation in the Septuagint Exodus." In *Wort, Lied und Gottesspruch: Festschrift für Joseph Ziegler*, ed. Josef Schreiner, 39-48. Echter Verlag: Katholisches Bibelwerk, 1972.

———. "On the Use of the LXX for Dating Midrashic Elements in the Targums." *Journal of Theological Studies* 25 (1974): 1-11.

Greenspoon, Leonard. "'It's All Greek to Me': Septuagint Studies Since 1968." *Currents in Research* 5 (1997): 147-74.

Haran, Menahem. *Temples and Temple-Service in Ancient Israel: An Inquiry into Biblical Cult Phenomena and the Historical Setting of the Priestly School*. Winona Lake, Ind.: Eisenbrauns, 1985.

Harl, Marguerite, Gilles Dorival, and Olivier Munnich. *La Bible grecque des Septante: Du judaïsme hellénistique au christianisme ancien*. Initiations au christianisme ancien. Paris: Cerf, 1988.

Houtman, Cornelis. *Exodus*. Vol. 2, *Chapters 7:14-19:25*. Historical Commentary on the Old Testament. Translated by Sierd Woudstra. Kampen, Netherlands: Kok Publishing House, 1996.

———. *Exodus*. Vol. 3, *Chapters 20-40*. Historical Commentary on the Old Testament. Translated by Sierd Woudstra. Leuven: Peeters, 2000.

Hurowitz, Victor Avigdor. "The Priestly Account of Building the Tabernacle." *Vetus Testamentum, Supplements* 29 (1978): 21-30.

International Translation Department. *Old Testament Selections*. Translator's Workplace Version 2.0. Summer Institute of Linguistics et al., 1995. CD-ROM.

Janzen, J. Gerald. *Studies in the Text of Jeremiah*. Harvard Semitic Monographs, no. 6. Cambridge, Mass.: Harvard University Press, 1973.

———. "A Critique of Sven Soderlund's *The Greek Text of Jeremiah: A Revised Hypothesis*." *Bulletin of the International Organization for Septuagint and Cognate Studies* 22 (1989): 16-47.

Jobes, Karen H. "A Comparative Syntactic Analysis of the Greek Versions of Daniel: A Test Case for New Methodology." *Bulletin of the International Organization for Septuagint and Cognate Studies* 28 (1995): 19-41.

Kautzsch, E., ed. *Gesenius' Hebrew Grammar*. Second English ed. Oxford: Clarendon Press, 1910.

Koch, Klaus. "Some Considerations on the Translation of kapporet in the Septuagint." In *Pomegranates and Golden Bells: Studies in Biblical, Jewish, and Near Eastern Ritual, Law, and Literature in Honor of Jacob Milgrom*, ed. David P. Wright, David Noel Freedman, and Avi Hurvitz, 65-75. Winona Lake, Ind.: Eisenbrauns, 1995.

Kuenen, Abraham. *An Historico-critical Inquiry into the Origin and Composition of the Hexateuch (Pentateuch and Book of Joshua)*. Translated by Philip H. Wiksteed. London: Macmillan and Co., 1886.

Larson, Mildred L. *Meaning-Based Translation: A Guide to Cross-Language Equivalence*. 2d ed. Lanham, Md.: University Press of America, 1998.

Le Boulluec, Alain, and Pierre Sandevoir. *L'Exode*. Vol. 2. La Bible D'Alexandrie, ed. Marguerite Harl. Paris: Cerf, 1989.

Lee, J. A. L. *A Lexical Study of the Septuagint Version of the Pentateuch*. Septuagint and Cognate Studies, no. 14. Chico, Calif.: Scholars Press, 1983.

Leitier, Nechama. "Assimilation and Dissimilation Techniques in the LXX of the Book of Balaam." *Textus* 12 (1985): 79-95.

Liddell, Henry George, and Robert Scott. *A Greek-English Lexicon*. 9th rev. and augmented with Revised Supplement ed. Oxford: Oxford University Press, 1996.

Longacre, Robert E. "Building for the Worship of God: Exodus 25:1-30:10." In *Discourse Analysis of Biblical Literature: What It Is and What It Offers*, ed. Walter R. Bodine, 21-49. Atlanta, Ga.: Scholars Press, 1995.

Louw, Johannes P., and Eugene A. Nida, eds. *Greek-English Lexicon of the New Testament: Based on Semantic Domains*. 2d ed. New York: United Bible Societies, 1989.

Lowy, S. *The Principles of Samaritan Bible Exegesis*. Leiden: E. J. Brill, 1977.

Martin, R. A. "Some Syntactical Criteria of Translation Greek." *Vetus Testamentum* 10 (1960): 295-310.

———. *Syntactical Evidence of Semitic Sources in Greek Documents*. Septuagint and Cognate Studies, no. 3. Cambridge, Mass.: Scholars Press, 1974.

Mayser, Edwin. *Grammatik der griechischen Papyri aus der Ptolemäerzeit*. Bd. 2, Nr. 2. Berlin: Walter de Gruyter & Co., 1934.

McGregor, Leslie John. *The Greek Text of Ezekiel: An Examination of Its Homogeneity*. Septuagint and Cognate Studies, ed. Claude E. Cox, no. 18. Atlanta, Ga.: Scholars Press, 1985.

McLay, Tim. "Syntactic Profiles and the Characteristics of Revision: A Response to Karen Jobes." *Bulletin of the International Organization for Septuagint and Cognate Studies* 29 (1996): 15-21.

McNeile, A. H. *The Book of Exodus*. London: Methuen and Company, 1908.

Meeks, Wayne A., ed. *The HarperCollins Study Bible: New Revised Standard Version with the Apocryphal/Deuterocanonical Books*. New York: HarperCollins Publishers, 1993.

Meyers, Carol L. *The Tabernacle Menorah: A Synthetic Study of a Symbol from the Biblical Cult*. American Schools of Oriental Research Dissertation Series, ed. David Noel Freedman. Missoula, Mont.: Scholars Press, 1976.

———. "Realms of Sanctity: The Case of the "Misplaced" Incense Altar in the Tabernacle Texts of Exodus." In *Texts, Temples and Traditions: A Tribute to*

Menahem Haran, ed. Michael V. Fox, Victor Avigdor Hurowitz, Avi Hurvitz, Michael L. Klein, Baruch J. Schwartz, and Nili Shupak, 33-46. Winona Lake, Ind.: Eisenbrauns, 1996.

Miller, Cynthia L. *The Representation of Speech in Biblical Hebrew Narrative: A Linguistic Analysis*. Harvard Semitic Monographs, ed. Peter Machinist. Atlanta, Ga.: Scholars Press, 1996.

Moulton, James Hope, and George Milligan. *The Vocabulary of the Greek Testament: Illustrated from the Papyri and Other Non-Literary Sources*. London: Hodder and Stoughton, 1952.

Muraoka, Takamitsu. *Emphatic Words and Structures in Biblical Hebrew*. Leiden: E. J. Brill, 1985.

Myers-Scotton, Carol. *Duelling Languages: Grammatical Structure in Code-switching*. Oxford: Clarendon Press, 1993.

Nelson, Russell David. *Studies in the Development of the Text of the Tabernacle Account*. Ph.D. diss., Harvard University, 1986.

O'Connell, Kevin G., S. J. *The Theodotionic Revision of the Book of Exodus: A Contribution to the Study of the Early History of the Transmission of the Old Testament in Greek*. Cambridge, Mass.: Harvard University Press, 1972.

O'Connor, M. *Hebrew Verse Structure*. Winona Lake, Ind.: Eisenbrauns, 1980.

Olofsson, Staffan. *The LXX Version: A Guide to the Translation Techniques of the Septuagint*. Stockholm: Almqvist & Wiksell International, 1990.

———. "Consistency as a Translation Technique." *Scandinavian Journal of the Old Testament* 6 (1992): 14-30.

Omanson, Roger G. "Translation as Communication." *The Bible Translator* 47 (1996): 407-13.

Osborn, Noel D., and Howard A. Hatton. *A Handbook on Exodus*. New York: United Bible Societies, 1999.

Popper, Julius. *Der biblische Bericht über die Stiftshütte: Ein Beitrag zur Geschichte der Composition und Diaskeue des Pentateuch*. Leipzig: Heinrich Hunger, 1862.

Rabin, Chaim. "The Ancient Versions and the Indefinite Subject." *Textus* 2 (1962): 60-76.

Rahlfs, Alfred, ed. *Septuaginta*. Stuttgart: Deutsche Bibelgesellschaft, 1935.

Revell, E. J. *The Designation of the Individual: Expressive Usage in Biblical Narrative*. Kampen, Netherlands: Kok Pharos, 1996.

Rife, J. Merle. "The Mechanics of Translation Greek." *Journal of Biblical Literature* 52 (1933): 244-52.

Sailhamer, John H. *The Translational Technique of the Greek Septuagint for the Hebrew Verbs and Participles in Psalms 3-41*. Studies in Biblical Greek, ed. D. A. Carson, no. 2. New York: Peter Lang, 1991.

Sanderson, Judith E. *An Exodus Scroll from Qumran: 4QpaleoExod^m and the Samaritan Tradition*. Atlanta, Ga.: Scholars Press, 1986.

Sarna, Nahum M. *Exodus: The Traditional Hebrew Text with the New JPS Translation*. The JPS Torah Commentary. Philadelphia: The Jewish Publication Society, 1991.
Seow, Choon-Leong. *Ecclesiastes: A New Translation with Introduction and Commentary*. Vol. 18C. The Anchor Bible. New York: Doubleday, 1997.
Skehan, Patrick W. "The Qumran Manuscripts and Textual Criticism." In *Qumran and the History of the Biblical Text*, ed. Frank Moore Cross and Shemaryahu Talmon, 212-25. Cambridge, Mass.: Harvard University Press, 1975.
Skehan, Patrick W., Eugene Ulrich, Judith E. Sanderson, and P. J. Parson. *Qumran Cave 4.IV Palaeo-Hebrew and Greek Biblical Manuscripts*. Vol. 9. Discoveries in the Judaean Desert. Oxford: Clarendon Press, 1992.
Smith, W. Robertson. *The Old Testament in the Jewish Church: A Course of Lectures on Biblical Criticism*. 2d ed. London: Adam and Charles Black, 1892.
Soisalon-Soininen, Ilmari. *Die Infinitive in der Septuaginta*. Helsinki: Suomalainen Tiedeakatemia, 1965.
———. "Die Wiedergabe einiger Hebräischer, mit der Präposition B^e ausgedrückter Zeitangaben in der Septuaginta." *Annual of the Swedish Theological Institute* 11 (1978): 138-46.
———. "Die Wiedergabe des ב *Instrumenti* im griechischen Pentateuch." In *Studien zur Septuaginta-Syntax*, ed. Anneli Aejmelaeus and Raija Sollamo, 116-30. Helsinki: Suomalainen Tiedeakatemia, 1987.
———. "Methodologische Fragen der Erforschung der Septuaginta-Syntax." In *VI Congress of the International Organization for Septuagint and Cognate Studies, Jerusalem, 1986*, ed. Claude E. Cox, Septuagint and Cognate Studies, no. 23, 425-44. Atlanta, Ga.: Scholars Press, 1987.
———. "The Rendering of the Hebrew Relative Clause in the Greek Pentateuch." In *Studien zur Septuaginta-Syntax*, ed. Anneli Aejmelaeus and Raija Sollamo, 55-61. Helsinki: Suomalainen Tiedeakatemia, 1987.
———. "Verschiedene Wiedergaben der hebräischen Status-Constructus-Verbindung im griechischen Pentateuch." In *Studien zur Septuaginta-Syntax*, ed. Anneli Aejmelaeus and Raija Sollamo, 62-70. Helsinki: Suomalainen Tiedeakatemia, 1987.
Sollamo, Raija. *Rendering of Hebrew Semiprepositions in the Septuagint*. Helsinki: Suomalainen Tiedeakatemia, 1979.
———. "The LXX Renderings of the Infinitive Absolute Used with a Paranymous Finite Verb in the Pentateuch." In *La Septuaginta en la Investigacion Contemporanea: V Congreso de la IOSCS*, ed. Natalio Fernandez Marcos, Textos Y Estudios «Cardenal Cisneros» de la Biblia Poliglota Matritense, no. 34, 101-13. Madrid: Instituto «Arias Montano» C.S.I.C., 1985.
———. "The Pleonastic Use of the Pronoun in Connection with the Relative Pronoun in the Greek Pentateuch." In *VII Congress of the International Organization for Septuagint and Cognate Studies, Leuven, 1989*, ed. Claude E. Cox,

Septuagint and Cognate Studies, no. 31, 75-85. Atlanta, Ga.: Scholars Press, 1991.

———. *Repetition of the Possessive Pronouns in the Septuagint.* Septuagint and Cognate Studies, ed. Bernard A. Taylor, no. 40. Atlanta, Ga.: Scholars Press, 1995.

Steinmann, Andrew E. "Jacob's Family Goes to Egypt: Varying Portraits of Unity and Disunity in the Textual Traditions of Exodus 1:1-5." *TC: A Journal of Biblical Textual Criticism [http://purl.org/TC]* 2 (1997).

Swete, Henry Barclay. *An Introduction to the Old Testament in Greek.* Peabody, Mass.: Hendrickson Publishers, 1989.

Tal, Abraham. *The Samaritan Pentateuch: Edited According to MS 6 (C) of the Shekhem Synagogue.* Tel Aviv: Tel Aviv University, 1994.

Talstra, E. "Reconstructing the Menorah on Disk: Some Syntactic Remarks." In *Studies in the Book of Exodus: Redaction-Reception-Interpretation,* ed. Marc Vervenne, 523-33. Leuven: Leuven University Press, 1996.

Thackeray, Henry St. John. "The Greek Translators of Jeremiah." *Journal of Theological Studies* 4 (1902-3): 245-66.

———. "The Bisection of Books in Primitive Septuagint MSS." *Journal of Theological Studies* 9 (1907): 88-98.

———. *A Grammar of the Old Testament in Greek According to the Septuagint.* Vol. 1, *Introduction, Orthography and Accidence.* Cambridge: Cambridge University Press, 1909.

Theological Dictionary of the New Testament. Edited by Gerhard Kittel and Gerhard Friedrich. 10 vols., Grand Rapids, Mich.: Eerdmans, 1964-76. S.v. "καρδία," by Johannes Behm. 3:605-14.

Thornhill, Raymond. Review of *The Account of the Tabernacle: Translation and Textual Problems of the Greek Exodus,* by David W. Gooding. *Journal of Theological Studies,* n.s. 11 (1960): 124-27.

Tigay, Jeffrey H., ed. *Empirical Models for Biblical Criticism.* Philadelphia: University of Pennsylvania Press, 1985.

Tov, Emanuel. *The Septuagint Translation of Jeremiah and Baruch: A Discussion of an Early Revision of the LXX of Jeremiah 29-52 and Baruch 1:1-3:8.* Harvard Semitic Monographs, no. 8. Missoula, Mont.: Scholars Press, 1976.

———. "Exegetical Notes on the Hebrew Vorlage of the LXX of Jeremiah 27 (34)." *Zeitschrift für die alttestamentliche Wissenschaft* 91 (1979): 73-93.

———. "The Representation of the Causative Aspects of the *Hiph'il* in the LXX: A Study in Translation Technique." *Biblica* 63 (1982): 417-24.

———. "Did the Septuagint Translators Always Understand Their Hebrew Text?" In *De Septuaginta: Studies in Honour of John William Wevers on His Sixty-fifth Birthday,* ed. Albert Pietersma and Claude E. Cox, 55-70. Mississauga, Ontario, Canada: Benden Publications, 1984.

———. "The Nature and Study of the Translation Technique of the LXX in the Past and Present." In *VI Congress of the International Organization for Septuagint and Cognate Studies, Jerusalem, 1986*, ed. Claude E. Cox, Septuagint and Cognate Studies, no. 23, 337-59. Atlanta, Ga.: Scholars Press, 1987.

———. "Renderings of Combinations of the Infinitive Absolute and Finite Verbs in the LXX—Their Nature and Distribution." In *Studien zur Septuaginta—Robert Hanhart zu Ehren: Aus Anlass seines 65. Geburtstages*, ed. Detlef Fraenkel, Udo Quast, and John William Wevers, Mitteilungen des Septuaginta-Unternehmens, no. 20, 64-73. Göttingen: Vandenhoeck & Ruprecht, 1990.

———. *Textual Criticism of the Hebrew Bible*. Minneapolis, Minn.: Fortress Press, 1992.

———. *The Text-Critical Use of the Septuagint in Biblical Research: Second Edition, Revised and Enlarged*. Jerusalem: Simor, 1997.

Tov, Emanuel, and Benjamin G. Wright. "Computer-Assisted Study of the Criteria for Assessing the Literalness of Translation Units in the LXX." *Textus* 12 (1985): 149-87.

Turner, Nigel. *A Grammar of New Testament Greek*. Vol. 3, *Syntax*. Edinburgh: T. & T. Clark, 1963.

Ulrich, Eugene, Frank Moore Cross, James R. Davila, Nathan Jastram, Judith E. Sanderson, Emanuel Tov, and John Strugnell. *Qumran Cave 4.VII: Genesis to Numbers*. Vol. 12. Discoveries in the Judaean Desert. Oxford: Clarendon Press, 1994.

van der Merwe, Christo H. J., Jackie A. Naudé, and Jan H. Kroeze. *A Biblical Hebrew Reference Grammar*. Sheffield: Sheffield Academic Press, 1999.

Vincent, L. H. "Les fouilles juives d'el-Ḥammam, à Tibériade." *Revue Biblique* 31 (1922): 115-25.

von Gall, August Freiherrn. *Der hebräische Pentateuch der Samaritaner*. Berlin: Alfred Töpelmann Verlag, 1966.

Wade, Martha L. "Translation as Interpretation in the Old Greek Exodus." A paper delivered at the Fellowship of Professors, Johnson Bible College, 1999.

———. "Evaluating Lexical Consistency in the Old Greek Bible." *Bulletin of the International Organization for Septuagint and Cognate Studies* 33 (2000): 53-75.

Wallace, Daniel B. *Greek Grammar Beyond the Basics: An Exegetical Syntax of the New Testament*. Grand Rapids, Mich.: Zondervan, 1996.

Waltke, Bruce K. "The Samaritan Pentateuch and the Text of the Old Testament." In *New Perspectives on the Old Testament*, ed. J. B. Payne, 212-39. Waco, Tex.: Word Books, 1970.

Waltke, Bruce K., and M. O'Connor. *An Introduction to Biblical Hebrew Syntax*. Winona Lake, Ind.: Eisenbrauns, 1990.

Wendland, Ernst R. *Language, Society, and Bible Translation: With Special Reference to the Style and Structure of Segments of Direct Speech in the Scriptures.* Roggebaai, Cape Town, South Africa: Bible Society of South Africa, 1985.

Wevers, John William. "The Use of Versions for Text Criticism: The Septuagint." In *La Septuaginta en la investigacion contemporanea: V Congreso de la IOSCS*, ed. Natalio Fernandez Marcos, Textos y Estudios «Cardenal Cisneros» de la Biblia Poliglota Matritense, no. 34, 15-24. Madrid: Instituto «Arias Montano» C.S.I.C., 1985.

———. *Notes on the Greek Text of Exodus.* Septuagint and Cognate Studies, ed. Claude E. Cox, no. 30. Atlanta, Ga.: Scholars Press, 1990.

———. "PreOrigen Recensional Activity in the Greek Exodus." In *Studien zur Septuaginta—Robert Hanhart zu Ehren: Aus Anlass seines 65. Geburtstages*, ed. Detlef Fraenkel, Udo Quast, and John William Wevers, Mitteilungen des Septuaginta-Unternehmens, no. 20, 121-39. Göttingen: Vandenhoeck & Ruprecht, 1990.

———. "The Göttingen Pentateuch: Some Post-partem Reflections." In *VII Congress of the International Organization for Septuagint and Cognate Studies, Leuven, 1989*, ed. Claude E. Cox, Septuagint and Cognate Studies, no. 31, 51-60. Atlanta, Ga.: Scholars Press, 1991.

———. *Text History of the Greek Exodus.* Mitteilungen des Septuaginta-Unternehmens, no. 21. Göttingen: Vandenhoeck & Ruprecht, 1992.

———. "The Building of the Tabernacle." *Journal of Northwest Semitic Languages* 19 (1993): 123-31.

———. *Notes on the Greek Text of Numbers.* Septuagint and Cognate Studies, ed. Bernard A. Taylor, no. 46. Atlanta, Ga.: Scholars Press, 1998.

———, ed. *Exodus.* Vol. 2, Septuaginta. Vetus Testamentum Graecum Auctoritate Academiae Scientiarum Gottingensis editum. Göttingen: Vandenhoeck & Ruprecht, 1991.

Wright, Benjamin G. *No Small Difference: Sirach's Relationship to Its Hebrew Parent Text.* Septuagint and Cognate Studies, ed. Claude E. Cox, no. 26. Atlanta, Ga.: Scholars Press, 1989.

———. "Δοῦλος and Παῖς as Translations of עבד: Lexical Equivalences and Conceptual Transformations." In *IX Congress of the International Organization for Septuagint and Cognate Studies, Cambridge, 1995*, ed. Dirk Büchner and Bernard A. Taylor, Septuagint and Cognate Studies, no. 45, 261-77. Atlanta, Ga.: Scholars Press, 1997.

Indexes

Passages

Old Testament

Genesis
1:7	77
1:20	77
2:11	154
2:13	154
2:14	154
4:20-21	154
8:2	36
10:8-9	154
13:14	99
14:23	219
23:16	122
28:14	99
37:31	116
38	65

Exodus
1:1-23:19	68
1:2-4	22
1:8	87
1:12	137
1:16	118
1:17	138
1:22	104
1-13	104
1-34	113, 244
2:14	139
2:17	87
2:24	76
3:21	118
4:28	104
5:6	104
5:7	138
5:13	138, 145
5:14	138
5:21	118, 170
6	113
6:4	76, 87
6:13	104
7:2	104, 135
7:6	104, 138
7:9	170
7:10	104, 138, 170
7:13	138
7:20	138, 170
7:22	138
8:9	138
8:11	138
8:13	118
8:14	118
8:15	138
8:23	138
8:27	138
8:28	168
9:8	170
9:10	118
9:12	138, 139
9:25	118
9:35	138
10.4	168
10:9	160
10:10	138
10:23	87, 136
10:24	160
11:1	63, 164, 180, 205, 207
11:2	122, 129, 163, 168, 180, 196
11:3	59, 118, 162, 163, 164, 168, 170, 184, 205
11:4	63, 122, 130
11:5	123, 128, 131, 182, 195, 204, 208
11:6	123, 135

11:7	118, 135, 136, 180, 193, 205	12:36	118, 129, 164
		12:37	205, 206
11:8	59, 63, 119, 129, 134, 164, 205	12:38	63, 154
		12:39	63, 128, 134, 169, 193, 205
11:9	123, 170, 205, 206		
11:10	168, 169, 170, 205	12:40	123, 134, 161, 163, 205, 206
11-13	10, 62, 63, 67, 68, 114, 233		
		12:41	186
12	161	12:42	165, 201, 207
12:1	123, 180, 205	12:43	116, 125, 165, 205
12:3	123, 161, 183	12:44	116, 129
12:4	123, 205	12:45	116
12:5	129, 180, 183	12:46	63, 66, 116, 123, 173, 193
12:6	101, 102, 161, 179	12:47	161
12:7	123, 134, 195	12:48	63, 116, 164, 193, 205
12:8	66, 123, 182, 194	12:49	123, 207
12:9	124, 165, 182, 194, 195	12:50	138, 139, 164, 184
12:10	124, 173, 194, 205	12:51	124, 183
12:11	118, 119, 123, 182, 192, 205	13:1	205
		13:2	116, 118, 119, 123
12:12	118, 123, 124, 195	13:3	124, 134, 161, 193, 205, 207
12:13	63, 120, 123, 124, 134, 165		
		13:4	63, 124, 165, 205, 207
12:14	26, 201	13:5	124, 134, 160, 161, 163
12:15	116, 136, 182, 205	13:6	123, 191, 205
12:16	121, 124, 135, 136, 183	13:7	123
12:17	26, 124, 167, 183, 191, 192, 201, 205	13:8	119, 124, 160
		13:9	118, 124, 205
12:18	116, 118, 123, 166	13:11	139, 160, 161, 188
12:19	123, 136, 161, 165, 180, 182, 194	13:12	135, 136, 164, 166
		13:13	122, 123, 164, 205
12:20	123, 195, 205	13:14	124, 161, 165, 183, 205, 207
12:21	164, 195, 205		
12:22	116, 119, 125, 131, 135, 205	13:15	123, 180, 183, 205
		13:16	124, 194, 205, 207
12:25	134, 137, 138, 183, 205	13:17	119, 123, 183, 196, 205
12:26	183	13:18	63, 129, 130, 205
12:27	119, 123, 128, 134, 164, 196, 205	13:19	63, 161, 205, 207
		13:20	119, 123, 129, 164, 205
12:28	138, 139	13:21	124, 127, 186, 205
12:29	122, 123, 125, 129, 130, 131, 165, 182, 205, 208	13:22	127, 162
		14:10	139
12:30	87, 123, 134, 161, 162, 183, 205	14:13	139
		15:26	118
12:31	87, 138, 160, 164, 180	16:1	161, 162
12:32	136, 180, 205	16:2	161
12:33	165, 205	16:9	161
12:34	124, 182, 205	16:10	161
12:35	129, 138, 139, 163, 164, 180, 195, 205	16:12	101, 102
		16:16	104

16:24	104, 138	25:18-19	84
16:32	104	25:19	27, 75, 166, 182, 193, 247
16:34	104, 139	25:19 (ш 25:18)	22
17:1	161	25:20	38, 39, 50, 51, 75, 78, 87, 123, 198, 247
17:10	138		
18:1	135	25:21	42, 52, 76, 134, 155, 169, 194
18:8	135		
18:14	135	25:22	19, 20, 75, 76, 104, 120, 133, 135, 165
18:23	105		
19:5	76	25:23	182, 247
19:7	105	25:23-24	197, 247
19:8	135, 199	25:24	34, 66, 171, 184, 194
19:22	160	25:25	34, 171, 182, 184, 194, 202
21:8	118		
21:19	87	25:26	42, 52, 53, 65, 71, 132, 180, 182
21:22	138		
23:13	135	25:27	40, 43, 48, 53, 90, 164, 202
23:15	105, 138		
23:17	160	25:28	27, 38, 84, 90, 124, 175
23:22	135	25:29	16, 17, 20, 27, 30, 48, 50, 51, 75, 78, 124, 134, 182, 202, 247
23:20-40:38	68		
24:7	135		
24:13	87	25:30	52
25	189, 219	25:31	18, 21, 22, 48, 50, 66, 86, 127, 129, 182, 192, 196, 218
25:1	37		
25:1-28:19	52		
25:2	19, 78, 80, 81, 134, 135, 136, 179, 194	25:31-39	86, 215
		25:31-40	33
		25:31-27:8	33
25:3	22, 50, 80, 134	25:32	86, 87, 182, 205, 218, 221
25:4	22, 50, 166, 170, 247	25:33	45, 48, 50, 87, 123, 181, 207, 218, 219
25:5	128, 247		
25:6	22, 48, 175, 188, 247	25:34	123, 182, 218, 220, 221
25:7	22, 48, 126, 143, 154, 174, 180, 247	25:35	87, 166, 181, 199, 220
		25:36	17, 50, 86, 182, 193, 220
25:8	64, 123, 124, 164, 194, 196	25:37	27, 34, 35, 193, 194
		25:38	85, 166, 208, 218
25:9	27, 43, 63, 135, 162, 164, 193	25:39	22, 48, 189, 190, 208
		25:39 (ᴏ 25:38)	27
25:10	27, 169, 170, 182, 193, 247	25:40	43, 123, 133, 137, 205
		25-27	32
25:11	34, 41, 48, 84, 85, 184, 202, 207	25-28	27
		25-29	6, 49
25:12	52, 53, 71, 199, 247	25-31	2, 5, 10, 52, 67, 68, 114, 233
25:13	66, 84, 90, 205		
25:14	51, 53, 63, 90, 122, 124	26	98
25:15	53, 90, 123, 198	26:1	22, 50, 70, 75, 82, 91
25:16	52, 76, 134, 194	26:1-35	33
25:17	16, 50, 65, 78, 79, 127, 170, 182, 247	26:2	91, 122, 165, 207, 247
		26:3	22, 23, 36, 39, 45, 48, 50, 52, 91, 161, 169, 182, 205
25:18	18, 75, 86		

26:4	34, 36, 50, 91, 118, 121, 122, 164, 166	26:37	44, 66, 85, 94, 95, 96, 184, 209, 248
26:5	36, 39, 48, 52, 91, 123, 136, 171, 180, 182	27	98
		27:1	21
26:6	39, 48, 52, 91, 96, 123, 182, 207	27:1-8	33
		27:2	85, 182, 196, 200
26:7	66, 91, 127, 166	27:3	75, 192, 202, 248
26:8	23, 24, 30, 40, 48, 50, 91, 122, 165, 204	27:4	17, 53, 71, 82, 102, 182
		27:4-5	102
26:9	84, 91, 173	27:5	17, 52, 102, 200, 205
26:10	30, 36, 45, 48, 91, 123, 161, 204	27:6	38, 85, 90, 181
		27:7	24, 27, 29, 40, 48, 53, 90, 122, 123, 185, 193
26:11	66, 91, 96, 123		
26:12	34, 91, 124, 129, 173, 198, 201	27:8	22, 43, 63, 123, 137
		27:9	19, 20, 50, 84, 91, 98, 100, 122, 129, 179, 207, 248
26:13	34, 35, 86, 91, 123, 166		
26:15	185		
26:16	22, 44, 50, 93, 161, 164, 166, 180, 185	27:9-13	98, 99, 100
		27:10	22, 26, 51, 94, 96, 182, 193, 200, 224
26:17	38, 39, 48, 182		
26:18 (ᴏ 26:20)	18, 48, 51, 98, 99, 100, 129, 179, 192, 208	27:11	19, 20, 22, 26, 27, 35, 48, 50, 77, 84, 92, 93, 94, 96, 98, 129, 159, 172, 180, 194, 248
26:18-22	98, 99		
26:19	18, 35, 38, 48, 50, 94, 192	27:12	19, 26, 40, 42, 44, 50, 51, 92, 94, 98, 99, 129, 170, 205
26:20 (ᴏ 26:18)	18, 19, 45, 48, 50, 98, 99, 129, 180, 192, 208		
26:21	38, 94, 169	27:13	92, 98, 100, 129, 166, 170, 179
26:22	98, 99, 169		
26:23	123	27:14	22, 26, 42, 44, 84, 91, 92, 94, 166, 172
26:24	19, 22, 34, 36, 48, 50, 95, 182, 191, 194, 198, 199		
		27:14-16	170
26:25	34, 35, 38, 48, 94, 169, 181, 192, 206	27:15	26, 35, 42, 44, 48, 84, 92, 94, 159, 172, 248
26:26	35, 38, 48, 166, 195, 206	27:16	26, 42, 44, 70, 82, 92, 94, 171, 172, 203
26:26-27	195, 223		
26:27	35, 51, 192, 195	27:17	94, 95, 96
26:28	113, 120, 166	27:18	35, 75, 94, 120, 121, 199, 205
26:29	53, 66, 84, 158, 182		
26:30	39, 43, 87, 123, 133, 137	27:19	21, 22, 34, 43, 45, 46, 121, 184, 185, 186, 225, 248
26:31	27, 51, 75, 128		
26:32	52, 69, 85, 94, 95, 96, 154, 164, 188, 207, 214, 247	27:20	19, 79, 104, 171
		27:21	19, 26, 29, 76, 123, 131, 194, 201
26:33	19, 20, 52, 63, 76, 127, 144	28:1	40, 63, 125, 165, 178, 182
26:34	52, 76, 123, 127	28:2	146, 180, 195
26:35	15, 19, 20, 31, 35, 37, 98, 164, 204	28:3	18, 40, 81, 85, 134, 166, 182, 195
26:36	70, 171, 185, 248	28:4	22, 40, 46, 128, 134, 146, 178, 179, 195
26:36-37	33		

28:5	23, 46, 184	28:33-40	52
28:6	46, 47, 171, 188	28:34	51, 130, 172, 181, 209, 249
28:7	18, 22, 34, 35, 48, 84, 169		
28:8	82, 128, 135, 165, 182	28:35	123, 144, 182
28:9	21, 174	28:36	65, 144, 195, 249
28:10	182, 207	28:37	128, 207, 249
28:11	29, 184, 217, 248	28:38	135, 136, 194, 196
28:12	44, 84, 129, 162, 164, 196, 248	28:39	126, 127
		28:40	167, 180, 181
28:13	175, 216, 217, 250	28:41	29, 85
28:13-14	217	28:42	66, 164, 207
28:13-29	86	28:43	119, 122, 144, 164, 165, 206
28:14	36, 52, 128, 169, 172, 183, 208, 216, 217, 250	29	116
28:15	50, 82	29:1	40, 52, 134, 164, 165, 173, 185, 195, 206, 207
28:15-19	250		
28:15-29	215	29:2	42, 79, 124, 184, 194
28:16	84, 182	29:3	52, 63, 121
28:17	41, 85, 123, 165, 175, 198, 201, 207, 248	29:4	64, 124
		29:5	41, 45, 48, 118, 142, 164, 166, 178
28:17-20	74		
28:18	248	29:5-7	183
28:19	248	29:6	52, 183
28:20	17, 22, 45, 48, 123, 162, 164, 248, 250	29:7	75, 79, 164
		29:8-9	183
28:20-32	52	29:9	18, 85, 130, 164, 167, 183, 184, 192, 194
28:21	78, 179, 209, 250		
28:22	36, 216, 217, 250	29:10	29, 44, 160, 166, 202
28:22-28	216	29:11	160
28:22-29	215	29:12	52, 94, 123, 169, 205
28:23	250	29:13	40, 64, 131, 178
28:23 (⅁ 28:29)	41, 44, 48, 52, 53, 84, 188, 216, 217	29:14	17, 66, 123, 165, 182, 194, 205
28:23-27	250	29:15	28, 29, 208
28:23-28 (⅁ 28:29)	53, 176, 188, 190, 216, 244	29:16	182
		29:17	52, 63, 166, 182, 194
28:24	34, 48, 51, 52, 53	29:18	30, 41, 48, 64, 84, 126, 183, 207
28:25	23, 50, 52		
28:26	34, 35, 50, 53, 136	29:19	29, 125
28:27	52, 53	29:20	52, 152, 153, 166, 194
28:28	19, 53, 250	29:20 (⅁ 29:21)	166, 205, 206
28:29	81, 121, 123, 144, 182, 184, 250	29:21	21, 25, 28, 30, 31, 48, 75, 79, 126, 131, 195
28:30	34, 45, 50, 52, 63, 81, 119, 166, 194, 196, 200	29:22	21, 22, 24, 40, 131, 164, 165, 184, 205
28:31	142	29:23	79, 133, 166, 179, 184
28:32	85, 123, 129, 165, 183, 198, 207, 248, 249	29:24	78, 86
		29:25	41, 42, 44, 64, 84
28:33	44, 48, 50, 120, 163, 171, 172, 196, 205, 209, 249	29:26	43, 86, 135, 165
		29:27	80, 86, 132, 134

29:27-28	31	30:14	28, 80, 129, 193
29:28	31, 80, 182, 205	30:15	80, 81, 128
29:29	85, 123, 135, 146, 164, 165, 183, 194, 195, 196	30:16	35, 51, 52, 195
		30:17	37
29:30	63, 123, 134, 144, 194, 195	30:18	19, 52, 64, 94, 120
		30:18-21	210
29:31	66, 123, 182, 194	30:19	28, 29, 30, 31, 64, 166, 182
29:32	29, 51, 66, 123, 131, 194, 202		
		30:20	64, 119, 122
29:33	18, 22, 43, 85, 124, 134, 165, 194, 205, 206	30:21	17, 18, 22, 43, 64, 182, 195, 198, 201
29:34	66, 123, 169, 194, 205	30:22	37
29:35	85, 104, 135, 194, 207	30:23	156, 166, 183, 206
29:36	123, 195	30:24	79, 81, 121, 145
29:37	122, 127	30:25	43, 75, 79, 82, 145
29:38	32, 44, 129, 134, 163, 166, 173, 195	30:26	76, 123, 125
		30:27	44, 162, 210
29:38-46	32	30:28	22, 84, 94, 207, 210
29:39	51, 101, 102, 122	30:29	122, 127, 196
29:40	17, 79, 124	30:30	40
29:41	17, 41, 66, 101, 102, 178, 182	30:31	43, 75, 79, 145, 170, 200, 201
29:42	20, 26, 84, 134, 136, 163, 180, 201	30:32	19, 22, 66, 123, 164, 183, 196, 200
		30:33	78, 134, 179
29:43	20, 36, 124, 201	30:34	17, 37, 45, 123
29:44	40	30:34-38	37
29:45	64, 123	30:35	17, 51, 166, 200
29:46	63, 64, 123, 133, 165, 181	30:36	17, 20, 52, 76, 123, 127, 134, 136, 168, 169, 180, 194, 200
29-31	28		
30	210, 211		
30:1	35, 184	30:37	26, 123, 136, 164, 186, 193
30:1-5	33		
30:1-10	15, 31, 32, 33, 190, 204	30:38	78, 124, 134, 179
30:2	165, 182	30-31	7
30:3	34, 84, 184, 200, 202, 203	31	209, 210, 211
30:4	28, 53, 65, 86, 90, 124, 171, 175, 193	31:1	37
		31:2	35, 123, 144, 249
30:5	84, 90	31:3	66, 78, 82, 83, 85, 122, 124, 249
30:6	20, 42, 52, 76, 133, 134, 136, 165, 179, 194		
		31:4	36, 83, 121, 173, 249
30:6-10	33	31:5	82, 83, 121, 122, 123, 129, 171, 194
30:7	17, 64, 119, 122, 168		
30:8	63, 64, 101, 102, 119, 201	31:6	81, 104, 123, 135, 136, 180, 183, 202, 207
30:9	63, 84		
30:10	122, 127, 171, 201	31:7	22, 76, 131, 169, 184, 209, 211
30:11	37		
30:11-16	166	31:8	22, 44, 162, 210
30:12	78, 124, 181	31:9	22, 94, 186, 210
30:13	30, 41, 44, 51, 80, 81, 121, 123, 145, 165, 205	31:10	22, 40, 126, 157, 164, 175, 179, 186, 209

Passages

31:11	22, 75, 79, 104, 135, 164, 175, 200, 249	35:13	26, 187
31:12	37	35:14	22, 26, 41, 42, 44, 162, 174, 179, 187
31:12-17	37	35:15 (ⓢ 35:12)	75, 79, 175, 185, 187, 207, 209
31:13	17, 174, 201, 249		
31:13-14	42	35:15-16	189
31:14	17, 63, 82, 124, 136, 165, 182, 194	35:16	22, 26, 136, 187, 189
		35:17 (ⓢ 35:12)	22, 92, 94, 187, 209, 210
31:15	51, 82, 123, 136, 144, 183, 194, 201, 205, 249	35:18	4, 22, 188
		35:19	22, 40, 79, 146, 164, 175, 187, 195, 209, 249
31:16	76, 194, 195, 201		
31:17	17, 123	35:20	161, 196
31:18	18, 66, 76, 86, 123, 128	35:21	29, 44, 78, 80, 81, 83, 128, 134, 135, 146, 162, 183, 184, 191, 194, 195
32:1	87		
32:6	87		
32:8	105	35:21-29	81
32:25	87	35:22	22, 27, 28, 29, 41, 44, 78, 80, 86, 135, 136, 162, 165, 178, 191, 194, 196, 216, 226
32:28	138, 139		
33:8	87		
33:10	87		
33:12	118	35:23	78, 134, 179, 184, 186, 208
33:13	118		
33:16	118	35:24	22, 41, 80, 83, 128, 134, 184, 194, 197
33:17	118		
34:4	104, 138	35:25	18, 22, 23, 27, 28, 118, 123, 182, 184
34:9	118		
34:11	105, 135	35:26	124, 134, 135, 166, 183
34:18	105, 138	35:27	143
34:32	105, 135	35:28	18, 41, 75, 79, 187, 192, 207
34:34	105		
35	81, 210, 214	35:29	22, 30, 31, 78, 80, 83, 118, 129, 134, 135, 164, 168, 183
35:1	105, 134, 161		
35:1-36:7	67, 68, 80, 114, 233		
35:2	17, 28, 50, 51, 83, 123, 124, 128, 171, 183, 194, 197, 201, 205, 207, 249	35:30	34, 35, 123, 144, 249
		35:31	22, 78, 83, 85, 122, 185, 249
35:3	19, 123, 174, 183, 194, 195, 249	35:32	121, 162, 170
35:4	134, 161	35:33	83, 124, 130, 186
35:5	22, 50, 80, 81, 128, 164, 178, 182	35:34	124, 165, 197
		35:35	22, 28, 83, 85, 123, 166, 168, 171, 173, 184, 186, 203, 206, 249
35:6	22, 50, 166, 170, 247		
35:7	247		
35:8	4, 48, 175, 188, 247	35-39	49
35:9	48, 143, 174, 247	35-40	1, 2, 5, 6, 8, 9, 10, 27, 28, 52, 113, 242
35:10	19, 27, 28, 81, 83, 123, 124, 135, 193	36	98
		36:1	30, 31, 78, 81, 83, 113, 124, 134, 135, 145, 179, 180, 184, 194
35:11	22, 66, 93, 94, 182, 186		
35:12	90, 164, 169, 170, 174, 185, 210, 247		

36:2	63, 77, 78, 81, 83, 124, 134, 153, 165, 179, 182, 194, 195	36:36 (𝔊 37:4)	69, 84, 94, 95, 96, 127, 154, 164, 188, 196, 207, 214, 247
36:3	63, 80, 83, 122, 134, 145, 162, 184, 194, 195, 197, 198	36:37 (𝔊 37:5)	69, 70, 82, 170, 171, 196, 248
36:4	29, 78, 83, 134, 145, 184, 194, 197	36:38 (𝔊 37:6)	22, 84, 94, 96, 196, 209, 248
36:5	37, 83, 135, 136, 182, 184, 194, 209	36-38	5
		37 (𝔊 38)	90, 137, 213, 219, 222, 228, 231, 237, 241
36:6	27, 28, 36, 78, 80, 83, 105, 123, 145, 194	37:1 (𝔊 38:1)	186, 196
		37:1-38:8	
36:7	28, 83, 182, 184, 194, 207, 225, 226	(𝔊 38:1-26)	3, 4, 7, 9
		37:2 (𝔊 38:2)	34, 48, 65, 84, 85, 176, 184, 207
36:8	18, 53, 67, 69, 83, 124, 164, 179, 196	37:3 (𝔊 38:3)	53, 65, 71, 127, 157, 180, 182, 186, 199, 247
36:8 (𝔊 37:1)	18, 22, 45, 50, 91, 164, 186	37:4	176, 185, 190
36:8-38:20		37:5 (𝔊 38:4)	43, 51, 53, 90, 121, 161, 170, 185, 203
(𝔊 37-38)	5, 6, 7, 51, 67, 68, 114, 152, 233, 236, 237	37:6 (𝔊 38:5)	16, 50, 79, 155, 169, 175, 176, 186, 247
36:8-39:31	3		
36:9 (𝔊 37:2)	91, 122, 180, 207, 247	37:7 (𝔊 38:6)	65, 75, 180, 186
36:10	23, 48, 50, 52	37:8 (𝔊 38:7)	75, 84, 164, 166, 186, 247
36:10-33	4, 188, 213, 224	37:9 (𝔊 38:8)	19, 39, 50, 51, 78, 87, 123, 187, 247
36:11	22, 34, 50		
36:12	48, 52, 136	37:10 (𝔊 38:9)	174, 187, 247
36:13	48, 52	37:10-11 (𝔊 38:9)	197, 247
36:15	23, 30, 40, 48, 50, 204	37:11 (𝔊 38:9)	34, 175, 176, 187
36:17	30, 44, 48, 204	37:12	4, 34, 188
36:21	22, 44, 50	37:13 (𝔊 38:10)	34, 42, 53, 71, 136, 199
36:22	48	37:13-14 (𝔊 38:10)	199
36:23	19, 20, 48, 49, 51, 100	37:14 (𝔊 38:10)	40, 48, 53, 90, 164, 180, 187, 207
36:24	35, 38, 48, 50, 94		
36:25	19, 48, 50	37:15 (𝔊 38:11)	66, 84, 90, 176, 184, 185, 187, 208
36:26	94		
36:29	19, 22, 36, 48, 50	37:16 (𝔊 38:12)	16, 30, 48, 50, 75, 78, 124, 132, 134, 165, 175, 182, 188, 199, 247
36:30	38, 48, 94		
36:31	28, 38, 48		
36:32	44, 51	37:17 (𝔊 38:13)	18, 22, 48, 50, 66, 86, 174, 175, 180, 188
36:34 (𝔊 38:18)	53, 85, 93, 189, 223		
36:34 (𝔊 38:18-20)	93, 222	37:17-22	
36:34 (𝔊 38:18-21)	176, 195, 222, 225	(𝔊 38:13-16)	190
𝔊 only (𝔊 38:18-26)	154	37:17-24	
𝔊 only (𝔊 38:19)	224	(𝔊 38:13-17)	33, 86, 215
𝔊 only (𝔊 38:19-20)	224	37:17-38:7	
𝔊 only (𝔊 38:20)	94, 171, 223, 224, 225	(𝔊 38:13-24)	33
𝔊 only (𝔊 38:21)	225, 248	37:18 (𝔊 38:14)	86, 169
36:35 (𝔊 37:3)	21, 51, 69, 70, 75, 82, 180, 196	37:18 (𝔊 38:15)	169
		37:19 (𝔊 38:15)	48, 50, 87, 123, 219, 221

Passages

37:19 (𝔊 38:16)	218	38:19 (𝔊 37:17)	26, 77, 94, 97, 207, 224
37:20 (𝔊 38:16)	221	38:19 (𝔊 37:17-18)	97
37:21 (𝔊 38:16)	221	38:19 (𝔊 37:18)	198
37:22 (𝔊 38:16)	17, 50, 175, 179, 182, 188	38:20 (𝔊 37:18)	186, 248
37:23 (𝔊 38:17)	85, 164, 175, 180, 188, 199, 218	38:21 (𝔊 37:19)	76, 118, 130, 137, 138, 139, 165, 181, 195
37:24	48, 175, 188, 189, 226	38:21-40:38	67, 68, 114, 233
37:24-28	4, 244	38:22 (𝔊 37:20)	35, 137, 138, 139, 144, 184, 186
37:25-28	33, 189, 190, 223		
37:26	34, 175	38:23 (𝔊 37:21)	123, 125, 165, 182, 184, 186, 196, 203
37:27	53		
37:29 (𝔊 38:25)	33, 75, 79, 82, 125, 126, 145, 167, 207	38:24 (𝔊 39:1)	17, 42, 80, 83, 123, 145, 178, 194, 196
38	97	38:24-31 (𝔊 39:1-9)	93, 226
38 (𝔊 37)	98	38:25 (𝔊 39:2)	22, 42, 51, 80, 113, 166, 169, 178, 206, 226
38 (𝔊 39)	93, 113, 226		
38:1 (𝔊 38:22)	40, 83, 84, 156, 167, 174, 187, 188, 244	38:26 (𝔊 39:3)	42, 81, 123, 145, 166, 182, 206
38:1-7 (𝔊 38:22-24)	33	38:27 (𝔊 39:4)	23, 83, 94, 192, 223
38:2	4, 189	38:28 (𝔊 39:5)	22, 84, 97, 166, 196, 206
38:3 (𝔊 38:23)	75, 94, 152, 153, 167, 180, 187, 192, 193, 195, 211, 248	38:28-31 (𝔊 39:5-9)	197
		38:29 (𝔊 39:6)	80, 226
		38:30 (𝔊 39:7)	25, 94, 123, 136, 211, 223
38:4 (𝔊 38:24)	82, 128, 153, 167, 180, 193	38:30 (𝔊 39:9)	188, 211
		38:30-31 (𝔊 39:7-9)	211
38:5 (𝔊 38:24)	42, 53, 71, 90, 102, 164, 169	38:31 (𝔊 39:8)	94, 184, 211, 225
38:6	4, 189	39	5, 139, 140
38:7 (𝔊 38:24)	48, 53, 187	39 (𝔊 36)	28, 52, 53, 212
38:8 (𝔊 38:26)	64, 65, 94, 123, 126, 134, 167, 174, 210	39:1 (𝔊 36:8)	45, 46, 135, 139, 146, 157, 165, 166, 180
38:9 (𝔊 37:7)	19, 50, 75, 91, 98, 100, 121, 125, 179, 199, 248	39:1 (𝔊 39:12)	157, 164, 184, 225, 226
		39:1-31 (𝔊 36:8-38)	3
38:9-13 (𝔊 37:7-11)	100	39:2 (𝔊 36:9)	28, 170
38:9-20 (𝔊 37:7-18)	3	39:3 (𝔊 36:10)	23, 28, 82, 85, 118, 123, 127, 128, 129, 170, 185
38:10 (𝔊 37:8)	22, 42, 51, 94, 187	39:4 (𝔊 36:11)	28, 34, 48, 84, 182, 208
38:11 (𝔊 37:9)	19, 35, 48, 50, 75, 94, 98, 121, 129, 187, 199, 248	39:5 (𝔊 36:12)	82, 136, 137, 139, 169, 170, 187, 198
38:12 (𝔊 37:10)	19, 40, 50, 51, 92, 94, 98, 122, 129, 187	39:6 (𝔊 36:13)	130, 169, 171, 248
		39:7 (𝔊 36:14)	17, 28, 84, 137, 139, 142, 248
38:13 (𝔊 37:11)	98, 179	39:8 (𝔊 36:15)	28, 50, 171, 193
38:14 (𝔊 37:12)	84, 91, 94	39:8-12 (𝔊 36:15-19)	250
38:15 (𝔊 37:13)	48, 84, 92, 94, 248		
38:16 (𝔊 37:14)	92, 184	39:8-21 (𝔊 36:15-28)	86, 215
38:17 (𝔊 37:15)	26, 41, 43, 77, 94, 97, 178, 193, 207	39:9 (𝔊 36:16)	28, 41, 84, 182, 183, 207
38:18 (𝔊 37:16)	26, 70, 82, 92, 121, 128, 172, 207	39:10 (𝔊 36:17)	41, 85, 124, 175, 198, 201, 248

39:10-13		39:35 (𝔊 39:14)	76, 90, 187
(𝔊 36:17-20)	74	39:36 (𝔊 39:17)	22, 174, 207
39:11 (𝔊 36:18)	248	39:37 (𝔊 39:16)	22, 33, 79, 187
39:12 (𝔊 36:19)	248	39:38 (𝔊 39:15)	33, 75, 79, 126, 169, 185,
39:13 (𝔊 36:20)	45, 48, 162, 163, 164,		187, 189
	187, 248, 250	39:38-39 (𝔊 39:15)	33
39:14 (𝔊 36:21)	78, 130, 207, 209, 250	39:39	4, 22, 33, 136, 185, 189
39:15 (𝔊 36:22)	36, 65, 126, 176, 216, 250	39:40 (𝔊 39:19)	17, 92, 171, 182, 187,
39:16 (𝔊 36:23)	41, 44, 48, 53, 66, 84,		195, 198, 225
	166, 216, 217, 250	39:40 (𝔊 39:21)	22, 94, 169, 182, 198
39:16-20		39:41 (𝔊 39:18)	22, 40, 126, 157, 165,
(𝔊 36:23-27)	250		179, 187
39:16-21		39:42 (𝔊 39:22)	42, 135, 136, 184
(𝔊 36:23-28)	53	39:43 (𝔊 39:23)	44, 83, 139, 140, 164,
39:17 (𝔊 36:24)	21, 24, 34, 48, 51, 52, 53,		194, 195
	169, 180	40	5, 139, 140
39:18 (𝔊 36:25)	23, 50, 52, 84, 182	40:1-2	230
39:19 (𝔊 36:26)	34, 35, 50, 53, 71, 84,	40:2	24, 66, 87, 123, 124, 186,
	132, 168, 182		207
39:20 (𝔊 36:27)	36, 52, 53, 71, 84, 129,	40:3	35, 76, 87, 170, 184
	182, 207	40:4	33, 63
39:21 (𝔊 36:28)	18, 45, 50, 53, 123, 139,	40:4-6	33
	201, 250	40:5	33, 52, 127, 170, 171, 184
39:22 (𝔊 36:29)	28, 41, 142, 193	40:6	24, 33, 52, 66, 84, 186,
39:23 (𝔊 36:30)	41, 124, 165, 182, 198,		208
	205, 207, 248, 249	40:7	4, 52, 189
39:24 (𝔊 36:31)	44, 48, 50, 163, 172, 249	40:8	52, 187
39:25 (𝔊 36:32)	42, 120, 175, 178, 188	40:9	26, 75, 79, 124, 131, 194
39:26 (𝔊 36:33)	44, 50, 51, 139, 140, 159,	40:10	29, 84, 127, 189, 194, 207
	172, 181, 249	40:11	4, 189
39:28 (𝔊 36:35)	184, 187, 207	40:12	29, 30, 64, 123
39:29 (𝔊 36:36)	22, 126, 139, 140, 164,	40:13	146, 194
	167, 184	40:14	21, 24
39:30 (𝔊 36:37)	144, 166, 176, 196, 201,	40:15	139, 182, 201
	249	40:16	27, 103, 104, 135, 183,
39:31 (𝔊 36:38)	139, 140, 249		207
39:32 (𝔊 39:9)	24, 66, 184, 186	40:16-38	230
39:32 (𝔊 39:10)	42, 86, 139, 178	40:17	21, 43, 87, 123, 124, 162,
𝔊 only (𝔊 39:11)	80, 113, 205, 226		207
𝔊 only (𝔊 39:11-12)	176, 222, 225	40:18	42, 83, 87, 93, 94, 182,
𝔊 only (𝔊 39:12)	113, 226		185
39:32-33		40:19	36, 66, 91, 139, 140
(𝔊 39:10-13)	222	40:20	34, 41, 76, 90, 170, 187,
39:32-40			194, 206
(𝔊 39:10-21)	230	40:21	24, 76, 87, 123, 139, 140
39:33 (𝔊 39:13)	26, 83, 93, 94, 173, 182,	40:22	20, 34, 35, 37, 66, 98,
	184, 185, 186, 211		122, 123, 125, 169, 170
39:33-41		40:23	139, 140, 207
(𝔊 39:13-21)	211	40:24	35, 66, 98, 100, 122, 123,
39:34 (𝔊 39:20)	173		125, 187

Passages

40:25	139, 140, 164	28:3-6	163
40:26	65, 123, 124	31:11	119
40:27	43, 64, 138, 139, 140, 195	31:29	128
40:28	4, 185	31:41	128
40:29	24, 43, 66, 84, 138, 139, 140, 186, 188, 194	31:50	44, 162, 216
		35:5	99
40:30 (𝔊 38:27)	19, 23, 175, 187		
40:30-32 (𝔊 38:27)	210	Deuteronomy	
40:31 (𝔊 38:27)	22, 23, 27, 28, 29, 31, 64, 182	3:27	99
		6:10	188
40:31-32 (𝔊 38:27)	23, 210	12:11	64
40:32 (𝔊 38:27)	64, 119, 122, 138, 139, 140, 164, 169, 210	14:23	64
		16:2	64
40:33	23, 44, 83, 86, 87, 162, 187, 194	16:6	64
		16:8	191
40:34	85	16:11	64
40:35	64, 85	26:2	64
40:36	118, 119, 184, 205	31:30	122
40:37	205	33:24	116
40:38	30, 31, 121, 124, 165, 179, 185, 200, 204, 205		
		Joshua	
Leviticus		3:6	76
3:15	40	17:10	99
4:6	116		
6:6	202	1 Samuel	
8	5	2:22	65
8:7	45, 48	17:5	216
8:16	40		
8:21	31, 48	1 Kings	
8:22-30	31	7:19 (𝔊 7:8)	219
8:29	31	7:26 (𝔊 7:12)	219
8:30	31, 48	7:46	71
22:13	116	7:49 (𝔊 7:35)	218
Numbers		1 Chronicles	
1:1	43, 162	28:18	87
4:7	30, 174		
4:9	174, 218	2 Chronicles	
4:12	189	2:6	121
4:14	189	4:13	172
4:23	65		
8:17	119	Nehemiah	
9:1	43, 162	9:13-14	174
14:28	122		
15:32-36	174	Proverbs	
16-17	174, 188	31	9, 241
18:15	119		
18:26	128	Isaiah	
18:28	128	40:19	224
28:3	44, 173		

Ezekiel
40:41 84
40:44 84
46:19 84
47:20 99

Zechariah
4:2   218
4:12 218

Apocrypha
Judith
10:21 85
14:14 92

1 Maccabees
1:21-22 211
6:35   216
11:10   209

2 Maccabees
2:9   169
14:41 92

New Testament
Galatians
5:12   65

Hebrews
9:4   97, 185

Greek Words

Ἀαρών, 125, 132, 135, 146, 164, 196
ἁγιάζω, 166
ἁγίασμα, 83, 144
ἅγιος, 83, 113, 121, 122, 125, 126, 127, 128, 144, 145, 146, 157, 166, 175, 194, 195, 206
ἀγκύλη, 95, 96, 97, 223, 224
ἄγω, 63
ἀδελφός, 146, 166
ἀδιάλυτος, 198
ἄζυμος, 128
αἴγειος, 166
Αἰγύπτιος, 129, 161, 184, 193
Αἴγυπτος, 128, 161, 162, 169
αἷμα, 171
αἴρω, 207
αἰχμαλωτίς, 125
αἰών, 130
ἀκίνητος, 198
ἄκρος, 84, 152, 166, 168, 194, 221
ἄλειμμα, 79, 145, 170
ἀλήθεια, 196
ἀλλήλων, 136, 169, 198, 221
ἁλυσιδωτός, 216
ἁμάρτημα, 194
ἁμαρτία, 171
Ἀμορραῖος, 207
ἀμφότερος, 169

ἄμωμος, 173, 207
ἄν, 67, 68, 119
ἀνά, 117, 120, 124
ἀναβαίνω, 63
ἀνάπαυσις, 128
ἀνατολή, 98, 99, 100, 179
ἀναφέρω, 63, 64
ἀναφορεύς, 89, 90
ἀνήρ, 78, 113, 155, 166, 174
ἄνθινος, 172
ἄνθος, 172, 216, 217
ἄνθρωπος, 118, 122
ἀνίστημι, 87
ἀντιπίπτω, 171
ἄνωθεν, 155, 169, 221
ἅπαξ, 122
ἀπαρτία, 118
ἀπαρχή, 80, 81, 128, 145, 194
ἀπηλιώτης, 98, 99
ἀπό, 43, 116, 117, 118, 124, 132, 173
ἅπτω, 122
ἀργύριον, 77, 121, 128, 224
ἄργυρος, 77
ἀργυροῦς, 127, 181, 207
ἀργυρώνητος, 129
ἀρσενικός, 166
ἄρτος, 174, 194, 207
ἀρχή, 84
ἀρχιτεκτονέω, 203
ἄσηπτος, 128

ἀσχημοσύνη, 207
αὐλαία, 66, 90, 91, 92, 123, 207
αὐλή, 98, 125, 210
αὐτός, 26, 118, 122, 125, 126, 127, 132, 135, 146, 157, 161, 162, 163, 164, 167, 169, 170, 172, 173, 174, 181, 189, 193, 195, 197, 198, 199, 200, 202, 207, 208, 209, 210, 216, 217, 224
αὐτόχθων, 123, 194
ἀφαίρεμα, 80, 81, 128, 169, 194, 226
ἀφαιρέω, 74
ἀφορίζω, 86
Αχισαμακ, 125

βακτηρία, 192
βάπτω, 116
βάσις, 26, 93, 94, 127, 170, 172, 181, 195, 207, 223
βλαστός, 219, 221
βορρᾶς, 98, 99, 100
βούλομαι, 134, 153
βοῦς, 206
βύσσινος, 127
βύσσος, 46, 163, 170, 173, 203, 207

Greek Words

γάρ, 165, 193, 205
γε, 165
γενεά, 74
γένος, 172
Γεργεσαῖος, 163
γερουσία, 195
γῆ, 128, 161, 163, 169
γίνομαι, 130, 168
γινώσκω, 20
γιώρας, 194
γλυφή, 143, 154
γλύφω, 171
γράφω, 74

δακτύλιος, 127, 158, 200
δέ, 110, 205
δείκνυμι, 63, 137, 205
δειλινός, 101
δέκα, 170, 179, 181, 206
δεξιός, 152, 166
δέρμα, 128
δέρρις, 66, 90, 91, 127, 166, 173, 204
δεύτερος, 122, 136, 166, 207
δήλωσις, 196
διά, 110, 117, 118, 124, 129
διαθήκη, 75, 76, 169, 211
διακόσιοι, 206
διανήθω, 128
διάνοια, 81, 82, 92, 97, 197
διασκευή, 209
δίδραχμον, 81, 145
δίδωμι, 35
δικτυωτός, 102, 128
διότι, 112
διπλοῦς, 84
διυφαίνω, 198
διωστήρ, 89, 90, 207
δοκέω, 78, 134, 135
δοῦλος, 58
δραχμή, 81
δύο, 157, 166, 168, 172, 179, 207
δύσις, 99
δυσμή, 99
δώδεκα, 179

ἐάν, 67, 68, 181
ἑαυτοῦ, 136, 164, 207
ἑβδομήκοντα, 206

ἕβδομος, 221
ἐγγλύφω, 130
ἐγκρυφίας, 128
ἐγώ, 157, 164, 174, 183, 206, 207
εἶδος, 172
εἰκοσαετής, 129
εἰμί, 44, 130, 132, 133, 135, 140, 146, 155, 161, 162, 165, 174, 209
εἶπον, 37, 105
εἷς, 123, 157, 161, 166, 193, 204, 206, 207, 208, 220, 221
εἰς, 35, 41, 110, 116, 117, 121, 122, 123, 124, 129, 130, 136, 143, 154, 157, 166, 169, 198
εἰσάγω, 29, 63, 122, 193
εἰσέρχομαι, 63
εἰσπορεύομαι, 63, 122
εἰσφέρω, 63
εἰσφορά, 80, 128, 195
ἐκ, 46, 117, 121, 123, 124, 127, 129, 134, 144, 155, 162, 164, 169, 174, 175, 193, 197, 206, 207, 216, 217, 221, 247, 249
ἕκαστος, 78, 183
ἑκατόν, 75, 120, 121, 199, 207
ἐκβάλλω, 193
ἐκβολή, 63
ἐκδίκησις, 195
ἐκεῖ, 20
ἐκεῖθεν, 20
ἐκκολάπτω, 130, 171
ἑκουσίως, 134, 153
ἐκπορεύομαι, 63, 87, 162
ἐκτείνω, 87
ἐκτυπόω, 218
ἐκτύπωμα, 195
ἐκφέρω, 63
ἔλαιον, 79, 125, 145, 175, 207
ἐμβάλλω, 206
ἐμπίπλημι, 85
ἐμπλόκιον, 126, 162, 180, 216

ἐμπρόσθιος, 169, 216, 217
ἐν, 69, 83, 110, 112, 114, 115, 116, 117, 118, 119, 121, 123, 124, 136, 137, 147, 157, 161, 162, 163, 164, 169, 172, 173, 174, 197, 207, 216, 217, 220, 221, 247, 248
ἔναντι, 68, 129, 166
ἐναντίον, 67, 117, 118, 124, 129, 170, 184
ἐνδελεχισμός, 163
ἐνδόσθια, 194
ἐνδύω, 146
ἐνθέμιον, 219, 220, 221
ἐνιαύσιος, 129
ἐνιαυτός, 122
ἐντέλλομαι, 103, 104, 105
ἐντολή, 167, 191
ἐνώπιον, 118
ἔξ, 181, 182, 206, 207
ἐξάγω, 63
ἑξακόσιοι, 206
ἐξανθέω, 171, 172
ἐξανίστημι, 87
ἐξαποστέλλω, 168
ἐξάπτω, 63
ἐξέρχομαι, 63
ἐξέχω, 87
ἑξήκοντα, 206
ἐξιλάσκομαι, 171
ἐξιλασμός, 171
ἐξισόω, 169, 221
ἔξωθεν, 207
ἐπαρυστήρ, 85, 218
ἐπαρυστρίς, 218
ἐπί, 35, 40, 75, 117, 120, 121, 124, 152, 154, 155, 157, 166, 168, 199, 200, 221, 247, 249
ἐπιδιπλόω, 84
ἐπίθεμα, 78, 79, 127, 170
ἐπικαλέω, 64
ἐπικάλυμμα, 173
ἐπισκέπτω, 113
ἐπισκιάζω, 64
ἐπισκοπή, 63
ἐπίσπαστρον, 171
ἐπιστήμη, 122

ἐπιτίθημι, 35, 63, 64, 69, 71,
    121, 154, 193
ἐπωμίς, 84, 132, 142, 143
ἐργάζομαι, 69, 83, 121
ἐργαλεῖον, 169
ἐργασία, 82, 83
ἔργον, 82, 83, 126, 128, 145,
    153, 166, 169, 170,
    171, 194, 206, 207
ἔρημος, 129
ἐρυθροδανόω, 74
ἐρυθρός, 130
ἔρχομαι, 63
ἑσπέρα, 101
ἐσχάρα, 102, 203
ἔσωθεν, 207
ἕτερος, 113, 166, 169
ἔτος, 206, 207
Εὐαῖος, 207
εὖρος, 172, 204, 207
εὐρύς, 90, 176
εὐωδία, 126
ἔχω, 36, 134, 165
ἕως, 117, 118, 124, 165

ζώνη, 192

ἥδυσμα, 17
ἡμέρα, 174, 207
ἡνίκα, 67, 117, 119, 120, 124
ἧπαρ, 41, 178

θάλασσα, 74, 98, 99, 100,
    130
θάνατος, 63
θεῖος, 66, 122
θέλω, 168
θεός, 66, 77, 160, 161
θεράπων, 58, 59
θρίξ, 166
θυΐσκη, 78
θυμίαμα, 126, 175, 207
θυμιάω, 64
θυμός, 129
θύρα, 125, 135, 160, 166, 171
θυσία, 84, 128, 163, 169
θυσιαστήριον, 84, 122, 127,
    166, 169, 188, 189,
    202, 206

ἱερατεία, 157
ἱερατεύω, 157
ἱερεύς, 74, 134, 135, 146,
    157, 166
ἱκανός, 207
ἱλαστήριον, 78, 79, 127, 164,
    166
ἱματισμός, 163, 195
ἵνα, 165
Ἰούδα, 144
ἴσος, 36, 191
Ἰσραήλ, 134, 161, 164, 196
ἵστημι, 87
ἱστίον, 90, 91, 92, 125, 166,
    210
Ἰωσήφ, 161

καθά, 132, 133, 137, 138,
    139, 140
καθάπερ, 133, 138, 140
καθαρίζω, 171
καθαρισμός, 171, 195
καθαρός, 127, 129, 171, 175,
    176, 197, 217
καθήκω, 113, 145, 194
καθότι, 133, 137, 138, 140
καθυφαίνω, 85
καί, 110, 113
καλαμίσκος, 192, 207, 218,
    220
κάλυμμα, 171
καλυπτήρ, 202
καλύπτω, 85
καρδία, 81, 82, 97
κάρπωμα, 84, 163, 194
καρυΐσκος, 218
καρυωτός, 218
κατά, 83, 99, 110, 117, 121,
    122, 123, 124, 129,
    132, 133, 136, 137,
    140, 145, 169, 170,
    198, 207, 216, 217
καταλείπω, 113, 194, 226
κατάλιθος, 175, 201
κατάπαυσις, 171
καταπαύω, 86
καταπέτασμα, 171, 223
κατασκευή, 83
καταστασιάζω, 155, 174
καταχρυσόω, 69, 84, 85, 196

κατεργάζομαι, 130
κατισχύω, 105
κατοικητήριον, 195
κατοικία, 195
κάτοπτρον, 126, 134
κάτωθεν, 171, 172, 207
καυλός, 66, 218
κεφαλή, 125, 194
κεφαλίς, 93, 94, 95, 96, 97,
    207, 209, 223, 224
κιβωτός, 125, 155, 169, 176,
    208, 211
κίδαρις, 127, 183, 207
κλίτος, 66, 84, 86, 113, 125,
    129, 157, 207
κλώθω, 46, 128, 163, 170,
    173, 207
κόκκινος, 173, 203
Κόρε, 155, 174
κορυφή, 221
κραταιός, 118, 207
κρατήρ, 218
κραυγή, 135
κρεάγρα, 75
κρέας, 66, 194
κρίκος, 95, 96, 97, 207, 209,
    223, 224
κρίνον, 219
κριός, 74, 125, 166, 207, 208
κρίσις, 194
κροσσός, 36, 216
κροσσωτός, 36, 128, 216
κρυφῇ, 168
κτῆνος, 118, 154, 204, 208
κύαθος, 75
κύκλος, 207
κυμάτιον, 171, 184, 194, 202
κύριος, 128, 129, 137, 144,
    160, 161, 166, 174,
    183, 207
κώδων, 130, 172, 181

λαβίς, 85, 199
λάκκος, 129
λαλέω, 37
λαμβάνω, 74, 134, 206, 208
λαμπάδιον, 218, 221
λαός, 74, 209
λέγω, 165
λειτουργέω, 65, 74, 157, 169,
    206, 210

Greek Words

λειτουργία, 130
λεπτός, 168, 169
Λευίτης, 130
λίθος, 126, 143, 154, 174, 207
λιθουργικός, 129
λίψ, 98, 99, 100, 129, 179
λοβός, 41, 178
λοιπός, 113, 169, 173, 194
λούω, 63, 64
λυχνία, 127, 129, 174, 218, 221
λύχνος, 199, 218

μαρτύριον, 24, 66, 75, 76, 125, 166, 169, 170, 181, 186, 194, 206, 211
μέγας, 135
μέρος, 84, 86, 132, 169, 206
μέσος, 120, 130
μεσόω, 130
μετά, 117, 119, 124, 155, 174, 198
μή, 165
μῆκος, 93, 172, 207
μήν, 179, 207
μηρός, 66
μήτρα, 164
μίτρα, 183, 207
μολύνω, 116
μοσχάριον, 206
μοχλός, 89, 90
μύλος, 195
μυρεψός, 126
μυριάς, 206
Μωϋσῆς, 129, 137, 164

νήθω, 128
νηστεύω, 65, 126, 134
νηστός, 173
νίπτω, 63, 122
νόμος, 125
νότος, 98, 99, 100, 179
νύξ, 130
νῶτον, 84

ξύλον, 128, 130, 194

ὁ, 131, 132, 133, 140
ὁδός, 129, 169

ὅθεν, 132, 134, 136, 140
οἶδα, 136
οἰκέτης, 58
οἶκος, 125
ὁλοκαύτωμα, 84
ὁλοκαύτωσις, 84
ὅλος, 179, 207
ὁμοθυμαδόν, 199
ὄνομα, 74, 182, 207
ὀπίσθιος, 132
ὀπίσω, 129
ὁράω, 63, 64
ὅρκος, 63
ὅρος, 128, 137, 162
ὅς, 67, 132, 133, 134, 135, 136, 138, 139, 140, 146, 147, 155, 165, 174, 203
ὀσμή, 126
ὅσος, 67, 132, 134, 135, 136, 140
ὅστις, 67, 132, 135, 140
ὀστοῦν, 173, 207
ὅταν, 117, 119, 120, 122, 124, 206
ὅτι, 112, 165
οὐ, 165, 168, 173
οὐδέ, 165
οὖς, 122, 194
οὗτος, 154, 167, 189, 195, 221, 224
οὕτως, 166
ὀψέ, 101

παῖς, 58, 59
παρά, 117, 118, 119, 124, 129, 130, 135, 166, 172, 181, 198
παραγίνομαι, 29
παραδείκνυμι, 63, 137
παράθεμα, 169
παράρρυμα, 66
παρεμβολή, 74
παρωμίς, 169, 216, 217
πᾶς, 81, 83, 122, 134, 135, 136, 153, 162, 169, 170, 189, 204, 206, 208
πάσχα, 125, 128
πέντε, 206, 209

πεντήκοντα, 206, 207
περί, 110, 130, 164
περιαργυρόω, 41, 85, 172, 198, 207, 223, 224
περικαλύπτω, 162
περικυκλόω, 163
περισιαλόω, 130
περιστόμιον, 129, 207
περιχαλκόω, 85
πέταλον, 127
πήγνυμι, 174
πῆχυς, 122, 159, 204, 207
πίμπλημι, 85
πλάγιος, 86
πλέκω, 128
πλεονάζω, 173, 198
πλευρόν, 86, 185
πληγή, 207
πλῆθος, 209
πλήρωσις, 143
πλοκή, 216
πλύνω, 63
πνεῦμα, 78, 122
ποδήρης, 142, 143
ποιέω, 28, 69, 93, 121, 137, 161, 164, 166, 168, 192, 197, 198, 199, 200, 201, 206, 208
ποίησις, 82
ποικιλία, 82, 171
ποικιλτής, 70, 126, 171
ποικιλτικός, 203
ποικιλτός, 203
πολύς, 154
πορφύρα, 123, 129, 173
πούς, 74, 132, 152, 166, 194
πρόθεσις, 174, 207
πρόκειμαι, 174
πρός, 99, 100, 101, 110, 117, 118, 122, 124, 129, 153, 164, 206
προσάγω, 63
προσδέχομαι, 198
προσέρχομαι, 63, 207
προσήλυτος, 207
προσπορεύομαι, 63, 153, 206
προστάσσω, 105
προσφέρω, 63, 194
πρόσωπον, 207
προτίθημι, 133, 166

προφυλακή, 207
πρωί, 66, 101, 122
πρωινός, 66, 101
πρῶτος, 166, 207
πρωτότοκος, 122, 125, 204, 208
πτερύγιον, 84, 168
πτέρυξ, 74
πῦρ, 74
πυρεῖον, 102, 153, 155, 174, 192, 193, 211

ῥαφιδευτός, 203
ῥόα, 171, 172
ῥοΐσκος, 130, 172, 181
ῥυθμός, 82

σάββατον, 128, 194
σάρδιον, 74, 126, 174
σάρξ, 66
σημεῖον, 170, 206
σίκλος, 81, 121, 145, 166
Σινά, 128
σκεπάζω, 87
σκέπη, 66
σκεῦος, 169, 189, 207
σκηνή, 24, 66, 83, 93, 98, 125, 129, 164, 166, 169, 171, 173, 181, 186, 206, 209
σκιάζω, 87
σκυτάλη, 89, 90
σμάραγδος, 74, 174
σοφία, 122, 134
σοφός, 81
σπένδω, 74
σπονδεῖον, 75
στερεός, 86, 179
στεφάνη, 171, 184, 202, 203
στῆθος, 81
στίχος, 207
στολή, 126, 128, 146, 157, 173, 186, 195, 211, 226
στρεπτός, 171, 184, 194, 202
στῦλος, 93, 170, 185, 192, 195, 209, 210, 223, 224
σύ, 122, 124, 137, 146, 161, 164, 205, 207

συμβολή, 36, 84, 118, 122, 129, 136, 198
συμπλεκτός, 198
συμπλέκω, 136, 169, 216
σύν, 16, 117, 118, 123, 124
συναγωγή, 156, 161, 174
συναναβαίνω, 63
συναναφέρω, 63
συνάπτω, 36
συνδέω, 162, 163
σύνειμι, 206
σύνεσις, 122, 171
συνέχω, 36
σύνθεσις, 126, 175, 192, 195, 207
συνίημι, 168
σύνταξις, 181, 195
συντάσσω, 103, 104, 105, 137, 207
συντελέω, 86
συντρίβω, 173
συνυφαίνω, 85, 118, 198
συσκιάζω, 87
σφαιρωτήρ, 219
σφόδρα, 154
σφραγίς, 130

τάλαντον, 192
τε, 165
τεκτονικός, 171, 194
τελειόω, 85
τελείωσις, 169
τέμνω, 185
τέρας, 206
τέσσαρες, 127, 132, 199, 204, 207
τεσσαρεσκαιδέκατος, 179
τετράγωνος, 74
τετρακόσιοι, 206
τετράστιχος, 198
τέχνη, 82
τίθημι, 37
τίκτω, 118
τις, 164
τορευτός, 86
τράπεζα, 16, 74, 132, 176, 197, 199
τρεῖς, 221
τριάκοντα, 206
τρίχινος, 127, 166

τρόπος, 133, 138, 139, 140
τρυβλίον, 75

ὑακίνθινος, 103, 128
ὑάκινθος, 113, 128, 173, 207
ὕδωρ, 74, 166
υἱός, 74, 122, 125, 126, 132, 134, 146, 161, 164, 196
ὑπεναντίος, 87
ὑπό, 110, 142
ὑποδύτης, 142, 196
ὑποκαλύπτω, 173, 201
ὑποτίθημι, 198
ὑφαίνω, 203
ὑφαντός, 70, 128, 170, 203
ὕφασμα, 175, 201
ὕψος, 92, 172

φαίνω, 193
Φαραώ, 164, 170
Φερεζαῖος, 163
φέρω, 29, 63, 86, 198, 209
φιάλη, 75
φορεύς, 89, 90
φυλάσσω, 192
φυλή, 144
φῶς, 174
φωτίζω, 174

χαλκός, 121, 128
χαλκοῦς, 84, 155, 169, 174
Χανάαν, 163
χείρ, 77, 118, 152, 166, 192, 194, 207
χερουβ, 75
χερουβιμ, 75, 171
χιλιάς, 206
χιτών, 143
χράω, 163
χρῖσις, 75, 125, 145, 175
χρῖσμα, 75, 145, 175, 207
χρυσίον, 65, 113, 121, 127, 129, 130, 162, 163, 164, 175, 176, 197, 226
χρυσοῦς, 65, 127, 129, 130, 159, 164, 166, 172, 179, 181, 184, 209
χρυσόω, 69, 85

Hebrew Words

χρώς, 66, 207
χωνεύω, 71

ψαλίς, 96, 97, 209

ψυχή, 78

ὦμος, 84
ὡς, 117, 119, 124, 134, 172

ὡσεί, 171, 172
ὥστε, 165

Hebrew Words

אָבֵן, 41, 66, 77, 118, 129, 143, 154, 162, 207
אַבְנֵט, 45, 167
אָדָם, 118
אָדֹם, 74
אֹדֶם, 74
אֹהֶל, 26, 38, 83, 93, 94, 95, 127, 181, 186, 187, 207
אֹהֶל, 24, 51, 66, 83, 91, 93, 160, 171, 185, 186, 187, 195, 198, 209, 210
אַהֲרֹן, 51, 132, 135, 146, 183, 209
אוֹר, 186, 193
אוּרִי, 35
אָח, 38, 39, 146, 179, 187, 198
אֶחָד, 38, 39, 44, 52, 157, 179, 181, 184, 193, 204, 206, 207
אָחוֹר, 129
אָחוֹת, 38, 52
אַיִל, 74, 184, 207
אֵין, 134
אִישׁ, 38, 39, 41, 44, 78, 178, 179, 183, 187, 198
אַל, 165
אֵל, 34, 35, 38, 39, 42, 47, 118, 123, 132, 153, 180, 187, 198, 206
אֱלֹהִים, 66, 77, 160, 161, 207
אֵלִיָּה, 184
אֶלֶף, 206
אִם, 165
אַמָּה, 35, 44, 75, 120, 159, 180, 186, 187, 199, 204, 207
אָמַר, 37, 45, 165
אֱמֹרִי, 207
אֲנִי, 181
אָנֹכִי, 135
אַף, 129

אֵפֹד, 118
אֲפֻדָּה, 187
אֵפוֹד, 41, 84, 118, 132, 142, 143, 178
אַרְבַּע, 132, 180, 186, 198, 204, 207
אָרַג, 186
אַרְגָּמָן, 129, 186, 188
אָרוֹן, 76, 169, 170, 187
אֹרֶךְ, 35, 93, 172, 180, 185, 186, 187, 207
אֶרֶץ, 161, 184
אֵשׁ, 74
אִשָּׁה, 38, 78
אֲשֶׁר, 12, 41, 42, 43, 104, 107, 114, 131, 132, 133, 134, 135, 136, 137, 138, 139, 140, 141, 146, 147, 153, 179, 180, 186, 187, 188, 199, 235
אֵת, 16, 20, 27, 42, 44, 45, 104, 135, 136, 137, 139, 140, 142, 146, 165, 179, 180, 181, 182, 183, 184, 185, 186, 187, 188, 190, 198, 200, 202, 207, 209, 211, 217
אַתָּה, 205

בְּ, 12, 16, 35, 36, 40, 42, 43, 51, 69, 71, 75, 83, 107, 112, 114, 115, 116, 117, 118, 119, 120, 121, 122, 123, 124, 129, 130, 134, 135, 136, 141, 147, 157, 166, 172, 178, 180, 181, 183, 184, 186, 187, 197, 199, 200, 204, 206, 207, 209, 219, 221, 235

בֶּגֶד, 145, 146, 186, 187, 195, 209
בַּד, 40, 89, 90, 181, 184, 187, 207
בְּהֵמָה, 118, 204
בּוֹא, 29, 63, 123, 187, 193, 198, 209
בּוֹר, 129
בֵּין, 101, 120, 180, 187
בַּיִת, 129, 179, 207
בְּכוֹר, 204
בֵּן, 74, 129, 132, 146, 161, 162, 182, 183, 186, 206, 209
בָּעַר, 19
בָּקַע, 81
בָּקָר, 206
בֹּקֶר, 51, 66, 77, 122
בְּרִיחַ, 90
בְּרִית, 76
בָּרֶקֶת, 74
בָּשָׂר, 66, 207

גָּבִיעַ, 181, 218
גַּג, 200, 203
גּוּר, 207
גֻּלְגֹּלֶת, 182
גֵּר, 207
גָּרַשׁ, 193

דָּבַר, 37, 180
דָּבָר, 185
דּוֹר, 43, 74, 198, 201
דַּי, 207
דָּם, 171
דַּעַת, 83
דֶּרֶךְ, 129
דָּרַשׁ, 36
דָּשֵׁן, 202

הוּא, 17, 25, 183, 198
הָיָה, 45, 85, 108, 119, 130, 165, 183, 186, 187, 199

הָלַךְ, 186
הֵם, 46, 162, 198, 209
הִנֵּה, 183
הַר, 43

וְ, 25, 27, 95, 96, 97, 187

זֶה, 166, 180, 186
זָהָב, 44, 50, 65, 66, 75, 121,
    127, 129, 130, 162,
    175, 181, 184, 185,
    187, 188, 209, 216,
    217
זָכַר, 166
זִכָּרוֹן, 162
זֵר, 184, 187, 194, 202
זֶרַע, 198, 201

חָבֵר, 35, 36
חֹבֶרֶת, 36, 123
חָגַר, 45
חֹדֶשׁ, 207
חִוִּי, 207
חוּץ, 207
חוּר, 186
חוּרִי, 35
חָזַק, 207
חַטָּאת, 171
חָכְמָה, 83
חֵלֶב, 21
חַלָּה, 184
חֹמֶשׁ, 187
חֲמִשִּׁים, 35, 75, 120, 204, 207
חָצוֹת, 130
חֲצִי, 130, 186, 187
חָצֵר, 187
חֻקָּה, 130, 184
חֲרִי, 129
חָרָשׁ, 203
חֲרֹשֶׁת, 129, 130
חָשַׁב, 70, 170, 186, 203
חֶשֶׁב, 118
חָשׁוּק, 41, 96, 97, 178, 187,
    198, 209
חֹשֶׁן, 142
חָשַׁק, 41
חוֹתָם, 130

טָבַל, 116
טַבַּעַת, 53, 157, 158, 180, 187

טָהוֹר, 44, 65, 127, 129, 175,
    176, 184, 188
טוּר, 198, 207

יָד, 35, 118, 129, 207
יְהוּדָה, 144
יהוה, 42, 43, 44, 77, 123, 128,
    129, 137, 139, 140,
    144, 160, 161, 166,
    180, 181, 185, 188,
    207
יוֹם, 139, 179, 186, 207
יוֹמָם, 186
יַחַד, 198
יָם, 19, 74, 98, 99
יְסוֹד, 94
יָסַף, 108
יֵעַ, 187, 202
יָעַד, 19, 20, 36
יָצָא, 43, 63, 87
יָצַק, 70, 71, 188
יְרִיעָה, 90, 91, 121, 166, 180,
    204, 207
יָרֵךְ, 35, 66
יַרְכָה, 123
יִשְׂרָאֵל, 161, 162
יַחַד, 35, 186
יֹתֶרֶת, 40, 178

כְּ, 39, 42, 104, 130, 131, 133,
    137, 138, 139, 140,
    180, 183, 184, 188,
    198
כָּבֵד, 40, 154, 178
כֹּהֵן, 40, 157, 209
כֹּהֵן, 74, 134, 146, 157, 179,
    209
כִּי, 112, 139, 165, 182
כִּיּוֹר, 187
כִּכָּר, 179, 189, 192
כֹּל, 41, 42, 44, 47, 83, 104,
    125, 135, 136, 137,
    140, 153, 178, 180,
    182, 184, 186, 187,
    194, 198, 204, 206,
    207, 209
כָּלָא, 36
כָּלָה, 36, 86, 184
כְּלִי, 44, 129, 180, 186, 187,
    198, 207, 209, 210

כֵּן, 94, 164, 187
כָּנָף, 74, 187
כֶּסֶף, 66, 77, 121, 127, 128,
    129, 181, 187, 207
כַּף, 77
כָּפַל, 41, 84
כֹּפֶר, 79, 171
כִּפֻּרִים, 171, 195
כַּפֹּרֶת, 35, 42, 78, 79, 127,
    166, 170, 179, 186,
    187
כַּפְתּוֹר, 181, 219
כְּרוּב, 75, 186, 187
כַּרְכֹּב, 102, 192
כָּתַב, 74
כָּתֵף, 35, 84, 142, 208

לְ, 34, 37, 40, 41, 42, 43, 45,
    118, 121, 129, 130,
    132, 135, 144, 146,
    153, 156, 157, 160,
    162, 165, 166, 169,
    171, 178, 179, 180,
    181, 182, 183, 185,
    186, 187, 188, 192,
    195, 198, 201, 202,
    206, 207, 209
לֹא, 168, 198
לֵב, 81, 82, 92, 97, 153, 179,
    180, 197
לְבֵנָה, 17
לָבַשׁ, 45, 146
לוּחַ, 187
לֵוִי, 130
לֶחֶם, 184, 187, 207
לַיְלָה, 130, 186, 204
לְלָאוֹת, 97, 180, 204
לָקַח, 74, 206

מְאֹד, 154
מֵאָה, 35, 75, 120, 199, 206,
    207
מָאוֹר, 174, 187
מִגְבָּעָה, 207
מִדְבָּר, 129
מוּל, 207
מוֹעֵד, 24, 66, 160, 186, 187,
    195, 198
מוּת, 134
מִזְבֵּחַ, 187, 188, 206, 211

Hebrew Words

מָזְלֵג, 75
מִזְרָח, 98, 179
מִזְרָק, 75
מַחְבֶּרֶת, 36, 118, 129, 136
מַחֲנֶה, 74
מַחֲצִית, 41
מַחְתָּה, 192, 218
מַטֶּה, 144
מַטֶּה, 207
מַיִם, 74, 187
מֵיתָר, 187
מִכְבָּר, 17, 71, 84, 102, 169, 187, 200
מָלֵא, 85, 186
מְלָאכָה, 44, 69, 82, 83, 145, 153, 185, 197, 206, 207
מִלּוּאִים, 143, 154, 187
מֶלְקָחַיִם, 85, 86, 199, 218
מִן, 41, 43, 116, 118, 132, 166, 180, 181, 182, 186, 193, 198, 207, 225
מְנוֹרָה, 129, 174, 180, 221
מִנְחָה, 188
מְנַקִּיּוֹת, 30, 75
מִסְגֶּרֶת, 187, 202
מָסָךְ, 171, 185, 187
מַסַּע, 118
מְעִיל, 142, 143, 178
מַעַל, 41, 182, 187
מַעֲשֶׂה, 17, 82, 170, 186
מַצָּה, 184, 191
מִצְוָה, 167, 191
מִצְנֶפֶת, 207
מִצְרַיִם, 43, 129, 139, 184, 193
מִקְטָר, 35, 184
מִקְנֶה, 129
מִקְנֶה, 154
מִקְשָׁה, 86, 186, 193
מִשְׁבְּצוֹת, 44, 45, 130, 162, 184, 216, 217
מֹשֶׁה, 42, 129, 137, 139, 140, 188
מָשַׁח, 42
מִשְׁחָה, 75, 145, 207
מִשְׁכָּן, 24, 35, 42, 66, 83, 93, 94, 129, 180, 181, 185, 186, 198, 206
מִשְׁפָּט, 39
מַתְכֹּנֶת, 186

נָבָב, 187
נֶגֶב, 19, 98, 100, 129, 179
נָגַע, 207
נָגַשׁ, 206
נְדָבָה, 80
נוֹף, 86
נְחֹשֶׁת, 42, 44, 66, 75, 121, 128, 169, 180, 187, 188, 211
נֹכַח, 187
נֶסֶךְ, 74
נֶפֶשׁ, 78
נֵר, 42, 179, 199
נָשָׂא, 153, 185, 207
נָתַן, 34, 35, 36, 37, 42, 52, 121, 187, 206

סָבַב, 45, 162, 184, 217
סָבִיב, 41, 184, 187, 200, 207
סוּךְ, 19
סוּר, 198
סִיר, 94, 195, 202
סָכַךְ, 87
סַם, 169, 207
סַף, 119, 135
סָרַח, 173, 201
סֶרַח, 198

עֲבֹדָה, 130, 145, 184, 198
עָבַר, 182
עֵבֶר, 35, 132
עָבֹת, 128
עָגִיל, 44, 162
עַד, 118
עֵדָה, 161
עֵדוּת, 42, 75, 76, 169, 179, 181, 184, 194, 206
עֹדֶף, 198
עוֹלָם, 77, 130
עוֹר, 128
עֵז, 66, 77, 166, 186
עַיִן, 118, 129, 184
עַל, 34, 35, 40, 42, 47, 118, 121, 129, 132, 136, 137, 157, 168, 178, 179, 182, 186, 187, 188, 199
עֹלָה, 63, 188, 193
עָלָה, 44, 83, 84, 162, 163, 173, 187, 188

עַם, 74, 184, 209
עָמַד, 93, 185
עָמָּה, 129, 187
עַמּוּד, 25, 27, 93, 94, 185, 187, 193, 200
עֵץ, 128, 130, 186, 187
עֶצֶם, 183, 186, 207
עֶרֶב, 101
עֶרְוָה, 207
עָרַךְ, 19
עֵרֶךְ, 207
עָשָׂה, 21, 28, 38, 44, 45, 65, 66, 69, 83, 85, 95, 104, 118, 121, 137, 180, 181, 184, 186, 187, 192, 200, 201, 206, 208, 217
עֶשֶׂר, 179, 181
עֶשְׂרִים, 18, 129, 182

פֵּאָה, 35, 129, 207
פְּאֵר, 187, 207
פֶּה, 129, 137, 198, 207
פַּח, 127
פָּנָה, 42, 43, 129, 160, 174, 179, 187, 207
פַּעַם, 186
פַּעֲמֹן, 130, 181, 209
פָּקַד, 137, 181
פְּקוּדִים, 51, 181, 182
פַּר, 206
פֶּרַח, 181, 219
פָּרֹכֶת, 35, 94
פָּרָשׁ, 36, 87, 187
פִּתּוּחַ, 130
פֶּתַח, 44, 160, 171, 185
פָּתִיל, 128, 207

צָבָא, 64, 65
צַד, 86
צָוָה, 42, 103, 104, 105, 135, 136, 137, 139, 140, 188, 207
צוּם, 64
צֶלַע, 35, 44, 157, 187, 206
צִפָּה, 65, 66, 84, 85, 95, 184, 187, 196, 200, 207
צִפּוּי, 207, 224
צָפוֹן, 19, 98

קֶדֶם, 98, 179

קָדַשׁ, 201
קֹדֶשׁ, 42, 44, 51, 83, 94, 121,
127, 144, 145, 146,
157, 178, 186, 187,
206, 209
קוּם, 87
קוֹמָה, 172, 186, 187
קָטַר, 35, 63, 64
קְטֹרֶת, 17, 169, 187, 207
קִיר, 200
קֶלַע, 90, 91, 92, 94
קָנֶה, 181, 207, 220
קְעָרָה, 75
קָצָה, 84, 166, 168, 186
קִצָּה, 119, 129
קָצָץ, 185
קָרָא, 123
קָרַב, 63, 153
קֶרֶן, 200
קֶרֶס, 96, 97, 186, 207
קָרַע, 198
קֶרֶשׁ, 18, 38, 93, 94, 185, 186,
192, 206
קַשְׂוָה, 30, 51, 75

רָאָה, 63, 139, 205
רֹאשׁ, 95, 96, 97, 129, 207,
209, 224
רִאשׁוֹן, 166, 207
רְבָה, 209
רֶבַע, 74, 187
רֶגֶל, 74, 132, 134
רוּחַ, 78

רוּם, 74
רֹחַב, 172, 186, 187, 204, 207
רָחַץ, 22, 63, 187
רֵיחַ, 178
רִמּוֹן, 42, 130, 178, 181
רָקַח, 51
רָקַם, 70, 203
רָקַע, 185
רֶשֶׁת, 71, 102, 200

שִׂים, 37, 185
שֵׂעָר, 166
שָׂפָה, 121
שָׂרָד, 187, 209
שָׂרוֹךְ, 219

שָׁאַל, 163
שֶׁבֶץ, 45, 162
שַׁבָּת, 195
שָׁחַם, 74, 75, 174
שׁוּשָׁן, 219
שׁוֹר, 44, 46, 170, 184, 186
שִׁטָּה, 128, 184, 186, 187
שָׁכַן, 64
שָׁלַח, 168
שֻׁלְחָן, 16, 74, 132, 174, 180,
185, 187, 199
שָׁלֵשׁ, 181, 187
שָׁם, 19, 20, 134, 180, 184, 187
שֵׁם, 74, 123, 182, 207
שֶׁמֶן, 42, 79, 145, 170, 187,
207
שָׁמַר, 191, 192

שִׁמֻּרִים, 207
שָׁנָה, 129, 182, 207
שָׁנִי, 23, 128, 184, 186, 188
שֵׁנִי, 136, 207
שְׁנַיִם, 18, 38, 41, 44, 157, 168,
179, 180, 181, 185,
186, 199, 207, 216
שַׁעַר, 187
שָׁקַד, 181, 218
שֶׁקֶל, 42, 81, 121, 145, 178
שָׁרְשָׁה, 36, 216, 250
שַׁרְשְׁרָה, 36, 128, 216, 250
שָׁרַת, 74, 157, 187, 206, 209
שֵׁשׁ, 44, 46, 66, 75, 170, 181,
182, 184, 186, 206,
207

תְּאַם, 36, 191
תְּבוּנָה, 83
תּוֹךְ, 42, 120, 122, 129, 170,
178
תּוֹלָעָה, 23, 128, 186, 188
תַּחְרָא, 198
תַּחַשׁ, 103, 128
תַּחַת, 38, 181, 192
תֵּימָן, 98, 129, 179
תְּכֵלֶת, 65, 75, 128, 186, 188,
207
תֹּם, 36, 191, 207
תָּמִיד, 44, 162, 163, 173, 184
תְּנוּפָה, 80
תְּרוּמָה, 80, 82, 92, 128, 145,
197

Other Titles in the Septuagint and Cognate Studies Series

ROBERT A. KRAFT (editor)
Septuagintal Lexicography (1975)
Code: 06 04 01

ROBERT A. KRAFT (editor)
1972 Proceedings: Septuagint and Pseudepigrapha Seminars (1973)
Code: 06 04 02

RAYMOND A. MARTIN
Syntactical Evidence of Semitic Studies in Greek Documents (1974)
Code: 06 04 03

GEORGE W. E. NICKLESBURG, JR. (editor)
Studies on the Testament of Moses (1973)
Code: 06 04 04

GEORGE W. E. NICKLESBURG, JR. (editor)
Studies on the Testament of Joseph (1975)
Code: 06 04 05

GEORGE W. E. NICKLESBURG, JR. (editor)
Studies on the Testament of Abraham (1976)
Code: 06 04 06

JAMES H. CHARLESWORTH
Pseudepigrapha and Modern Research (1976)
Code: 06 04 07

JAMES H. CHARLESWORTH
Pseudepigrapha and Modern Research with a Supplement (1981)
Code: 06 04 07 S

JOHN W. OLLEY
"Righteousness" in the Septuagint of Isaiah: A Contextual Study (1979)
Code: 06 04 08

MELVIN K. H. PETERS
An Analysis of the Textual Character of the Bohairic of Deuteronomy (1980)
Code: 06 04 09

DAVID G. BURKE
The Poetry of Baruch (1982)
Code: 06 04 10

JOSEPH L. TRAFTON
Syriac Version of the Psalms of Solomon (1985)
Code: 06 04 11

JOHN COLLINS, GEORGE W. E. NICKLESBURG
Ideal Figures in Ancient Judaism: Profiles and Paradigms (1980)
Code: 06 04 12

ROBERT HANN
The Manuscript History of the Psalms of Solomon (1982)
Code: 06 04 13

J. A. L. LEE
A Lexical Study of the Septuagint Version of the Pentateuch (1983)
Code: 06 04 14

MELVIN K. H. PETERS
A Critical Edition of the Coptic (Bohairic) Pentateuch Vol. 5: Deuteronomy (1983)
Code: 06 04 15

T. MURAOKA
A Greek-Hebrew/Aramaic Index to I Esdras (1984)
Code: 06 04 16

JOHN RUSSIANO MILES
Retroversion and Text Criticism: The Predictability of Syntax in An Ancient Translation from Greek to Ethiopic (1985)
Code: 06 04 17

LESLIE J. MCGREGOR
The Greek Text of Ezekiel (1985)
Code: 06 04 18

MELVIN K. H. PETERS
A Critical Edition of the Coptic (Bohairic) Pentateuch,
Vol. 1: *Genesis* (1985)
Code: 06 04 19

Robert A. Kraft and Emanuel Tov (project directors)
Computer Assisted Tools for Septuagint Studies
Vol 1: *Ruth* (1986)
Code: 06 04 20

Claude E. Cox
Hexaplaric Materials Preserved in the Armenian Version (1986)
Code: 06 04 21

Melvin K. H. Peters
A Critical Edition of the Coptic (Bohairic) Pentateuch
Vol. 2: *Exodus* (1986)
Code: 06 04 22

Claude E. Cox (editor)
VI Congress of the International Organization for Septuagint and Cognate Studies: Jerusalem 1986
Code: 06 04 23

John Kampen
The Hasideans and the Origin of Pharisaism: A Study of 1 and 2 Maccabees
Code: 06 04 24

Theodore Bergren
Fifth Ezra: The Text, Origin, and Early History
Code: 06 04 25

Benjamin Wright
No Small Difference: Sirach's Relationship to Its Hebrew Parent Text
Code: 06 04 26

Robert J. V. Hiebert
The "Syrohexaplaric" Psalter
Code: 06 04 27
Takamitsu Muraoka (editor)
Melbourne Symposium on Septuagint Lexicography
Code: 06 04 28

John Jarick
Gregory Thaumaturgos' Paraphrase of Ecclesiastes
Code: 06 04 29

JOHN WILLIAM WEVERS
Notes on the Greek Text of Exodus
Code: 06 04 30

CLAUDE E. COX (editor)
VII Congress of the International Organization for Septuagint and Cognate Studies
Code: 06 04 31

J. J. S. WEITENBERG AND A. DE LEEUW VAN WEENEN
Lemmatized Index of the Armenian Version of Deuteronomy
Code: 06 04 32

GEORGE J. BROOKE AND BARNABAS LINDARS, S. S. F. (editors)
Septuagint, Scrolls and Cognate Writings: Papers Presented to the International Symposium on the Septuagint and Its Relations to the Dead Sea Scrolls and Other Writings
Code: 06 04 33

MICHAEL E. STONE
A Textual Commentary on the Armenian Version of IV Ezra
Code: 06 04 34

JOHN WILLIAM WEVERS
Notes on the Greek Text of Genesis
Code: 06 04 35

JOHN JARICK
A Comprehensive Bilingual Concordance of the Hebrew and Greek Texts of Ecclesiastes
Code: 06 04 36

DAVID S. NEW
Old Testament Quotations in the Synoptic Gospels, and the Two-Document Hypothesis
Code: 06 04 37

PETER JOHN GENTRY
The Asterisked Materials in the Greek Job
Code: 06 04 38

JOHN WILLIAM WEVERS
Notes on the Greek Text of Deuteronomy
Code: 06 04 39

RAIJA SOLLAMO
Repetition of the Possessive Pronouns in the Septuagint
Code: 06 04 40

LEONARD GREENSPOON AND OLIVIER MUNNICH (editors)
VIII Congress of the International Organization for Septuagint and Cognate Studies
Code: 06 04 41

CLAUDE E. COX
Aquila, Symmachus and Theodotion in Armenia
Code: 06 04 42

TIM MCLAY
The OG and Th Versions of Daniel
Code: 06 04 43

JOHN WILLIAM WEVERS
Notes on the Greek Text of Leviticus
Code: 06 04 44

BERNARD A. TAYLOR, editor
IX Congress of the International Organization for Septuagint and Cognate Studies
Code: 06 04 45

JOHN WILLIAM WEVERS
Notes on the Greek Text of Numbers
Code: 06 04 46

ZIPORA TALSHIR
I Esdras. From Origin to Translation
Code: 06 04 47

KRISTIN DE TROYER
The End of the Alpha Text of Esther
Code: 06 04 48

MARTHA LYNN WADE
Consistency of Translation Techniques in the Tabernacle Accounts of Exodus in the Old Greek
Code: 06 04 49

ZIPORA TALSHIR
I Esdras: A Text Critical Commentary
Code: 06 04 50

BERNARD A. TAYLOR
X Congress of the International Organization for Septuagint and Cognate Studies, Oslo, 1998
Code: 06 04 51

Ingram Content Group UK Ltd.
Milton Keynes UK
UKHW011259260723
425816UK00001B/107